Fundamentals of Forensic Science

To everyone who thinks impartial forensic science is necessary for justice. —MMH

To Tommy and Ben – you are our legacy and our future and a source of great joy. —JAS

Fundamentals of Forensic Science

Third Edition

Max M. Houck, PhD, FRSC
Vice President, Forensic and Intelligence Services, LLC

Jay A. Siegel, PhD
Professor Emeritus of Forensic Science
Michigan State University
East Lansing, MI, USA

AMSTERDAM • BOSTON • HEIDELBERG • LONDON
NEW YORK • OXFORD • PARIS • SAN DIEGO
SAN FRANCISCO • SINGAPORE • SYDNEY • TOKYO

Academic Press is an imprint of Elsevier

Academic Press is an imprint of Elsevier
The Boulevard, Langford Lane, Kidlington, Oxford, OX5 1GB
525 B Street, Suite 1800, San Diego, CA 92101-4495, USA

ISBN: 978-0-12-800037-3

Published 2016
Reprinted 2016

British Library Cataloguing in Publication Data
A catalogue record for this book is available from the British Library

Library of Congress Cataloging-in-Publication Data
A catalog record for this book is available from the Library of Congress

For information on all Academic Press publications
visit our website at http://store.elsevier.com/

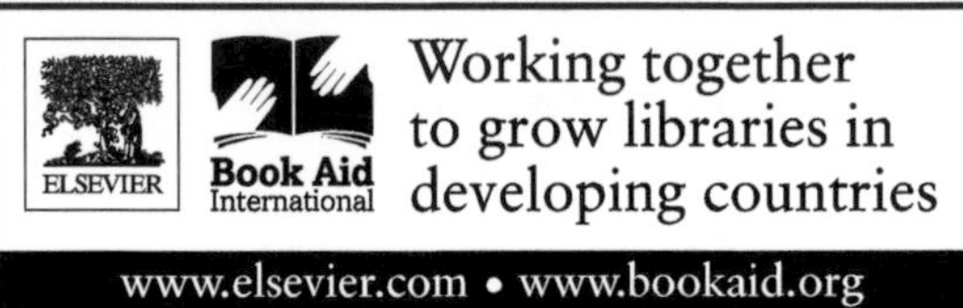

Publisher: Nikki Levy
Acquisition Editor: Elizabeth Brown
Editorial Project Manager: Joslyn Chaiprasert-Paguio
Production Project Manager: Lisa Jones
Designer: Matthew Limbert

Typeset by TNQ Books and Journals
www.tnq.co.in

Printed and bound in the United Kingdom

Contents

PART 2 ANALYTICAL TOOLS

See: http://booksite.elsevier.com/9780128000373/ for supplementary materials.

Editor: Biographies

MAX M. HOUCK

Dr Max M. Houck is an internationally recognized forensic expert who has worked in federal and local laboratories, the private sector, and academia. His casework includes the Branch Davidian Investigation, the September 11 attacks on the Pentagon, the D.B. Cooper case, and the West Memphis Three case, among hundreds of others. He serves on a variety of committees, including for Interpol. Dr Houck has published widely and is a founding Editor of the journal Forensic Science Policy and Management and has also co-authored numerous books. Dr Houck is a Fellow of the Royal Society of Chemistry.

JAY A. SIEGEL

Jay Siegel, PhD is retired director of the Forensic and Investigative Sciences Program and chair of the Department of Chemistry and Chemical Biology at Indiana University Purdue University Indianapolis. He was director of the Forensic Science Program at Michigan State University for 25 years from 1980 to 2004 until his retirement as Professor Emeritus. Dr Siegel is a Distinguished Member of the American Academy of Forensic Sciences and was named as Distinguished Alumni Scholar by his alma mater, George Washington University in 2011. He is co-editor of Forensic Science Policy and Management: An International Journal. He was a member of the National Academy of Sciences Forensic Science Committee from 2006 to 2009.

Foreword

Forensic science is at a transformational moment. The implications of the 2009 report from the National Academy of Sciences (NAS), *Strengthening Forensic Science in the United States: A Path Forward*, is finally being addressed, in part, by the formation of a National Commission on Forensic Science (NCFS) and the creation of Organization Scientific Area Committees (OSAC) overseen by the National Institute of Standards and Technology (NIST). The fundamental scientific basis that underlies many forensic disciplines is under review, and the role of "human factors"—issues of cognitive bias and laboratory organization—is now recognized to be of vital importance. However, what is not being addressed by either the Commission or the OSAC is the underlying validity (or lack thereof) of many impression, pattern, and trace evidence disciplines. Although NIST has agreed to validate and set measurement standards for a select subset of disciplines, it needs to do so for *all* the forensic disciplines it supervises in the OSAC structure. This gap is unfortunate since the absence of validation was an overarching concern of the 2009 NAS report. It makes little sense to assess the validity of some but not all, as *each* of the forensic disciplines is utilized in criminal investigations and adjudications affecting life and liberty.

The coauthors of this treatise, Max Houck and Jay Siegel, have been the central players in efforts to improve forensic science. They are not only thoughtful scholars in the academy but draw upon experience as bench scientists, laboratory managers, and, on occasion, expert witnesses. They wrote this extremely useful treatise to appeal to beginning forensic science students in college and high school (who have had some basic chemistry and biology) as well as a reference for science faculty and researchers as well as attorneys and judges.

Not only are the common forensic science topics (biology, chemistry, pattern evidence, law) covered but also the "ologies"—anthropology, entomology, and pathology. There are chapters on basic forensic science tools, spectroscopy, chromatography, and microscopy. There are also two new chapters in rapidly emerging fields: ethics for forensic service providers and computer forensics. In short, this is one stop shopping for those who are trying to get an introduction to the fundamentals of forensic science and its broad reach.

Most importantly, this book discusses some of the implications of the 2009 NAS report (Jay Siegel served on the NAS panel that wrote it and Max Houck testified twice before the Committee) throughout the text, especially in the controversial pattern evidence areas. There is also a new, extensive discussion of cognitive bias issues and its implications for forensic science. This includes an analysis of conformational bias in the famous Madrid Bombing case involving an erroneous fingerprint association led to the false arrest of Oregon lawyer Brandon Mayfield. Our only wish is that the authors would more directly take on all the too frequently exaggerated claims by forensic practitioners about the probative value of various forms of forensic evidence.

The book is both up to date and accessible to beginners. Each chapter begins with a real case as an illustration of the discipline at issue and revisits the case again at the end of the chapter. While acknowledging the continued popularity of forensic science in media (books, TV, and movies), this book will teach readers how forensic science is really practiced and what its real status is in court—no sugar coating or pandering to popular culture.

In his Foreword to the 2nd edition (Dwight Adams, retired FBI Laboratory Director) concluded by stating "This book, as its predecessor, will become a standard reference for those beginning their education in forensic science." We concur that the tradition continues!

Barry Scheck and Peter Neufeld
Cofounders and Codirectors of the Innocence Project

Preface to the Third Edition

We have written the 3rd edition of *Fundamentals of Forensic Science* because forensic science is once again at a crossroads with much at stake. Ever since commentators such as Saks and Kohler questioned the paradigm of individualization of scientific evidence, the pace of change and challenge has sped up. This was hastened by the landmark 2009 National Academy of Sciences report on forensic science, which acknowledged the strengths but demonstrated many weaknesses of the profession and the science. Since the NAS report came out, little has been accomplished until recently. The Departments of Justice and Commerce formed a National Commission on Forensic Science to help drive a national agenda on improving forensic science. The Commission, in turn, created an Organization of Scientific Advisory Committees, whose task is to develop consensus standards for the treatment of forensic evidence. Much hope is riding on these efforts to finally push for reform and garner resources to address the shortcomings of forensic science.

But that's not the most interesting part. The NAS report called for greatly increased research into the validity of forensic science methods of analysis. Research efforts have begun to accelerate in response. For example, preliminary research data show that fingerprint analysis, which has been undergoing increased scrutiny ever since the Madrid bombing case, has a false positive rate of 0.1% and a false negative rate of 7.5%. If letting a guilty person go free is better than convicting an innocent person that is good news indeed. Several studies in firearms, another discipline that has been increasingly challenged, have demonstrated overall error rates as low as 0.1% and only as high as 1.0% for false positives. Meanwhile, DNA analysis, the discipline that the NAS report called "the gold standard," is showing a mismatch between detection and interpretation. Numerous workshops held by the National Institute of Standards and Technology (NIST) have shown that forensic biologists using the same method for interpreting samples with more than one contributor (mixtures) get different answers—which are all potentially valid estimates of probability. No scientific or national standards exist for these methods. Forensic DNA is now in a position to detect more than it may be able to reliably interpret, which is troubling. Coupled with that is the next big shift in forensic DNA analysis, called next generation sequencing. That method is a few years off but it is coming and will utterly transform many aspects of the forensic profession, from technology to interpretation to privacy issues. When pattern evidence is proven reliable and DNA is beginning to be questioned, it is time to buckle up for a bumpy ride.

Other issues in the profession are looming. Lapses in integrity and the lack of an enforceable national code of ethics result in too many "forensic failure" headlines these days. And it is not only a few "bad apples," sometimes the entire crop is to blame. To stretch the metaphor, this brings the accountability and responsibility of the farmer (the manager or director) into question. Just about all cases of forensic science laboratory malfeasance demonstrate the importance of laboratory management and leadership. For example, Annie Dookhan, the drug analyst who lied about her credentials and falsified evidence in hundreds of drug cases, has cost the state of Massachusetts $8.5 million in case reviews thus far and the state has budgeted another $8.6 million to complete the process. Dookhan is now serving 3–5 years in prison. It is easy to blame Dookhan for her crimes but what about laboratory management? Fellow employees complained about Dookhan's productivity, five times the normal average, even though they rarely saw her working at an instrument. Laboratory management praised Dookhan's work ethic and kept her on the bench. The search for solutions has to move beyond "blaming and shaming" individuals and toward a review of processes and systems and management.

Great gains often come with great pains and forensic science is no stranger to either. We have updated this edition to better reflect the changes that have occurred in forensic science since the 2nd edition and to anticipate some of the new trends on the horizon. Expanded discussion about policy, new methods, and new disciplines, such as digital evidence, demonstrate that forensic science is a dynamic field with great potential for progress and many issues to resolve. We hope you enjoy the 3rd edition of *Fundamentals of Forensic Science* and it helps you to understand this fascinating and engaging field of science.

MMH
JAS

Preface to the Second Edition

Much has happened in forensic science in the 3 years since the first edition of *Fundamentals of Forensic Science* was first published. The media are paying increasing attention to the accomplishments and problems in the field. The Madrid Bombing case highlighted the limitations of fingerprint science and the role of contextual bias in forensic science. Pattern evidence is increasingly being questioned in the courts. Forensic laboratories are working with public interest groups to test for DNA exonerations. The National Academy of Sciences released a long awaited report on the needs of forensic science that made 13 recommendations to improve the practice and development of forensic science. The number of forensic science degree programs in the United States continues to increase at both the BS and MS levels. The Forensic Science Education Program Accreditation Commission (FEPAC) is in full swing and has accredited over 26 forensic science degree programs. Science continues to progress in the areas of materials science, microfluidics, nanotechnology, and fundamental discoveries. We indicated in the preface to the first edition of *Fundamentals* that forensic science education was entering an exciting era. We reiterate that now but with greater emphasis. The field faces great challenges, not the least of which is a seemingly insurmountable backlog of cases, caused in part by an insufficient number of forensic scientists. Joseph Peterson, in his 2005 *Census of Public Crime Laboratories*, estimated that it would take more than 1900 new forensic scientists to get the nationwide case turnaround time to 30 days. This means that forensic science education programs must be able to produce quality science students. The other side of this yet-to-be-balanced equation is that the laboratories must be able to hire, train, and manage all these new scientists.

We wrote *Fundamentals of Forensic Science* to provide a realistic view of the field of forensic science from the viewpoint of the forensic scientist—both of us have been and continue to be active as practitioners in the field. As current academics, we know this book must convey how forensic science is done in the field, in the laboratory, and in the courtroom, otherwise it has little legitimacy. Our philosophy hasn't changed and the second edition of *Fundamentals* reflects that. We have kept the same chapter structure in the same order: Forensic science is presented from crime scene to courtroom. We offer foundational material in the beginning; crime scene, evidence, and the tools of the laboratory; microscopy, separation science, and spectroscopy. We then present many of the most common and not so common types of forensic evidence collected by the types of science that are employed in their analysis; physical, chemical, and biological. The "-ologies": pathology, entomology, odontology, and anthropology are still there. The book is designed to be used in a one-semester or two-semester format and is suitable for any student who has a basic science background. To us, this reflects where forensic science must, as a discipline, stand shoulder-to-shoulder with its peer sciences.

Fundamentals is also “new and improved.” Most of the chapters begin with a discussion of real cases in that area and they are referred to throughout the chapter. Other real cases are also discussed throughout the chapters, albeit in encapsulated form. In place of the key words at the beginning of each chapter, terms are now defined as they come up within the chapter, reinforcing the concept while you are still reading. All of the materials have been updated; some new materials were added where they were needed and we upgraded figures and added some new ones. The bottom line: we have taken a good thing and made it better. We hope that you will agree.

MMH
JAS

Preface to the First Edition

Fundamentals of Forensic Science represents a different, albeit more realistic, view of the field of forensic science than is found in other textbooks. This view includes areas that are central to criminal investigations but fall outside the typical definition of "criminalistics." From the beginning, we decided to make *Fundamentals of Forensic Science* reflect how professional forensic scientists work and not how forensic science academicians teach. This enabled us to include the "-ologies" (pathology, entomology, anthropology, etc.) that many instructors don't traditionally teach—but that's probably because the chapters don't exist in other books. We felt that many instructors would like to teach these topics but don't have the fundamental resource materials to do so; additionally, students may want to read about a discipline that interests them but isn't covered in the course. The instructor may have local experts lecture on these specialties but, without these chapters, the students don't have any foundation to appreciate what the expert presents. If the instructor uses a video of a case, in the absence of a local expert, the students can be even more lost—the application of the methods in the case are key and the background information may be glossed over. In this regard, *Fundamentals of Forensic Science* provides the basis for the integration of these critical topics into the overall course. Our hope is that *Fundamentals of Forensic Science* fills this need.

We also offer a new perspective on the nature of forensic evidence. In his *Science* article, "Criminalistics" from 1963, Kirk opines that the principles that bind the various disciplines into the whole of forensic science "center on identification and individualization of persons and of physical objects." But this is only part of the larger nature of the discipline: The binding principles relate to relationships between people, places, and things as demonstrated by transferred evidence. It doesn't matter so much that this ceramic shard came from a particular lamp—it *does* matter, however, that the shard was found in the dead person's head and the suspect's fingerprints are found on the lamp. It is not merely the identification or individualization of the objects but it is the *context* of those people, places, and things and their relationship or interrelatedness within that context that provides its value in the justice system. A crime scene is a set of spatial relationships and/or properties; all evidence is spatial in that sense. Even an item of evidence discarded a distance from the scene by the perpetrator has meaning. A crime scene can also be viewed as a piece of recent history. It has a story to tell and the various pieces of evidence carry the facts of the story within them. In that sense, forensic scientists are auditors and storytellers.

In *Fundamentals of Forensic Science*, we stress these associations and how they relate the evidence to the facts of the crime. We also emphasize that *all* evidence is *transfer* evidence (à la Locard), even evidence that may not have been characterized as such, like DNA (semen transferred by sexual contact in a sexual assault), pathology (the pattern of a weapon transferred and recorded in the wound of a victim), or entomology (the number and kinds of maggots that have accumulated—transferred from the environment—on a decomposing body). Locard's Exchange Principle, then, is *the* binding principle in forensic science because it focuses on reconstructing relationships in the commission of a crime through the analysis of transferred information.

Forensic science education is entering an exciting era, ushered in largely by the work of the Technical Working Group on Education and Training in Forensic Science (TWGED). This group, sponsored by the National Institute of Justice (NIJ) and West Virginia University, generated guidelines for building careers in forensic science, curricula for undergraduates and graduates, and continuing education for professional forensic scientists. These guidelines led the American Academy of Forensic Sciences (AAFS) to form the Forensic Education Program Accrediting Commission (FEPAC), an accrediting body for forensic science educational programs. New forensic science educational programs appear weekly, it seems, and, because the quality of education goes to the heart of any profession, standards are a necessary component to assure that they prepare students properly for careers in our field.

The teaching of forensic science has spread from graduate and 4-year programs to community colleges and high schools. While writing a book targeted for one end of that spectrum most likely makes it unsuitable for the other end, we see *Fundamentals of Forensic Science* as being appropriate across that spectrum. Educators teaching a forensic science course for the first time will find the supplemental course materials helpful in getting started. Experienced educators will find these resources helpful as well but will also appreciate the breadth and depth of the chapters of this text. Despite its broad applicability, our intent in writing *Fundamentals of Forensic Science* was for students who have already taken basic science courses.

Fundamentals of Forensic Science is organized roughly along the timeline of a real case. It begins with an introduction and history of forensic science as background to the discipline and the structure of a modern forensic science laboratory. Chapter 2 covers the processing of crime scenes and Chapter 3 covers the nature of forensic evidence. In Chapters 4 (Microscopy), 5 (Spectroscopy), and 6 (Chromatography), we cover the basic methods of analysis used in most, if not all, forensic science examinations. The biological sciences are then presented: Pathology (Chapter 7), anthropology, and odontology (Chapter 8), entomology (Chapter 9), serology and blood pattern analysis (Chapter 10), DNA (Chapter 11), and finally hairs (Chapter 12). The next chapters address the chemical sciences, drugs (Chapter 13), toxicology (Chapter 14), fibers (Chapter 15), paints (Chapter 16), soils and glass (Chapter 17), and arson/explosives (Chapter 18). The third section covers physical evidence, including friction ridges (Chapter 19), questioned documents (Chapter 20), firearms and toolmarks (Chapter 21), shoeprints, tire treads, and other impression evidence (Chapter 22). The final chapter in the book looks at the intersection of forensic science and the law (Chapter 23).

Feature boxes throughout the book emphasize resources on the World Wide Web ("On the Web"), historical events in forensic science ("History"), practical issues in laboratory analysis ("In the Lab") and topics for further reading or interest ("In More Detail"). Each chapter ends with two types of questions to help with chapter review and discussion: "Test Your Knowledge" questions target key terms and information from the chapters while the questions under "Consider This..." offer topics and issues that should challenge the students knowledge and understanding of the chapter contents.

With a project like writing a textbook (we submit that *no* project is like writing a textbook!), compromises must invariably take place. Our aim was to yield only where necessary and to dig in when we felt our vision of the book was in jeopardy. We feel that the decisions we made have resulted in a better product and hope that you do as well.

MMH
JAS

Acknowledgments

The authors would like to thank everyone who offered suggestions, comments, criticism, and ideas for this textbook: Without you, it would not be the quality text that it is.

PART

Criminal Justice and Forensic Science

1

CHAPTER

Introduction

1

CHAPTER OUTLINE

KEY TERMS

- American Society for Testing and Materials, International (ASTM)
- American Society of Crime Laboratory Directors (ASCLD)
- ASCLD Laboratory Accreditation Board (ASCLD-LAB)
- Behavioral sciences
- Chain of custody
- Criminalistics
- Criminalists
- Forensic anthropology

- Forensic engineering
- Forensic odontology
- Forensic pathology
- Forensic science
- Forensic Science Education Programs Accreditation Commission (FEPAC)
- International Organization for Standardization (ISO)
- Questioned documents
- Technical Working Group on Education and Training in Forensic Science (TWGED)
- Toxicology

WHAT IS FORENSIC SCIENCE?

The *Oxford English Dictionary* lists one of the first uses of the phrase "forensic science" to describe "a mixed science" (*Oxford English Dictionary*, 2005). The early days of forensic science could certainly be called mixed, when science served justice by its application to questions before the court. Forensic science has grown as a profession and into a science in its own right. Given the public's interest in using science to solve crimes, it looks as if forensic science has an active, if hectic, future.

Forensic science describes the science of associating people, places, and things involved in criminal activities; these scientific disciplines assist in investigating and adjudicating criminal and civil cases. The discipline divides neatly into halves, like the words that describes it. "Science" is the collection of systematic methodologies used to increasingly understand the physical world. The word "forensic" is derived from the Latin *forum* for "public" (*Oxford English Dictionary*, 2005). In ancient Rome, the Senate met in the Forum, a public place where the political and policy issues of the day were discussed and debated; even today, high school or university teams that compete in debates or public speaking are called "forensics teams." More technically, "forensic" means "as applied to public or legal concerns." Together, "forensic science" is an apt term for the profession of scientists whose work answers questions for the courts through reports and testimony.

IN MORE DETAIL: CRIMINALISTICS AND TRACE EVIDENCE

The term **criminalistics** is sometimes used synonymously with forensic science. "Criminalistics" is a word imported into English from the German *kriminalistik*. The word was coined to capture the various aspects of applying scientific and technological methods to the investigation and resolution of legal matters. In some forensic science laboratories, forensic scientists may be called **criminalists**. Criminalistics is generally thought of as the branch of forensic science that involves the collection and analysis of physical evidence generated by criminal activity. It includes areas such as drugs, firearms and toolmarks, fingerprints, blood and body fluids, footwear, and trace evidence. "Trace evidence" is a term of art that means different things to different people. It might include fire and explosive residues, glass, soils, hairs, fibers, paints, plastics and other polymers, wood, metals, and chemicals. These items are generally analyzed by forensic science or forensic science laboratories. To avoid confusion, unnecessary terminology and regionalism, the phrases "forensic sciences" and "forensic scientists" instead of "criminalistics" and "criminalist" will be used.

AREAS OF FORENSIC SCIENCE

The areas of forensic science covered in this textbook are listed in the table of contents by chapter. They can be broadly characterized into chemical, biological, and physical sciences. Some areas may overlap (aren't fingerprints, tool marks and shoe prints all impression evidence?) but this text focuses on their original source or production method to organize the topics to make the most sense.

Many kinds of scientists may be called upon to play a role in a forensic investigation. This does not mean, however, that this is their full-time job: their area of expertise may need to be called upon only rarely or only in particular cases. Artists, biologists, chemists, and other specialists may be needed to answer questions in investigations as diverse as mass disasters, aeroplane crashes, missing persons, and art forgeries (see "In More Detail: Birds of a Forensic Feather").

IN MORE DETAIL: BIRDS OF A FORENSIC FEATHER

When US Airways Flight 1549 made its amazing crash landing in the Hudson River in 2009, probably the last thing on anyone's mind was the word "snarge." The word may sound funny, but "snarge" is the technical term for the pulverized bird guts resulting from the collision of an aeroplane and a bird. Dr Carla Dove, at the Smithsonian Institution's Museum of Natural History in Washington, DC, is the Director of the Feather Identification Laboratory, where thousands of bird samples are sent each year for identification, most of them involving bird strikes with aeroplanes. Forensic feather identification is important not only to determine the cause of a crash but also to potentially help rule out other types of causes, such as mechanical issues or terrorist activities. The feathers or other bird parts are examined and compared with the laboratory's extensive reference collection (over 620,000 samples, some collected by Theodore Roosevelt and possibly Charles Darwin, representing 85% of the world's bird species) to determine the bird's species (see Figure 1.1). If that does not work, the snarge is sent to the DNA laboratory

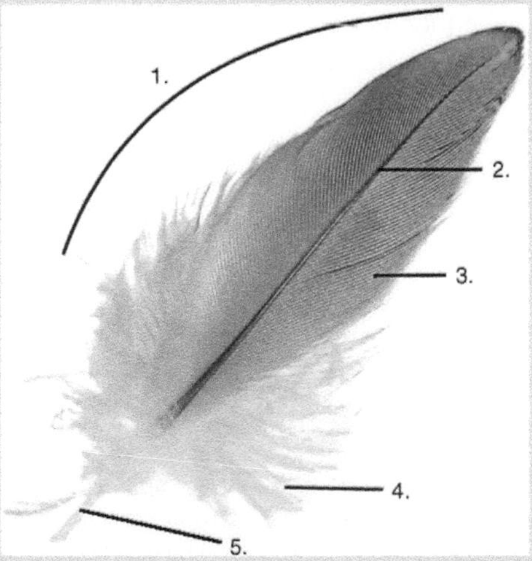

FIGURE 1.1

The anatomy of a feather. (1) Vane; (2) Rachis; (3) Barb; (4) Afterfeather; (5) Hollow shaft, calamus.

Public domain image at www.wikipedia.com.

(Continued)

IN MORE DETAIL: BIRDS OF A FORENSIC FEATHER—cont'd

for genetic analysis. A working knowledge of avian anatomy is still crucial in the age of forensic DNA work. In one case, deer DNA was identified on a plane that had a strike at 1500 ft—clearly not possible. Analysis of a tiny piece of feather identified the bird as a black vulture, which apparently had flesh from a deer carcass in its stomach. The laboratory, which started analyzing bird remains from aeroplane crashes in 1960, does work for military crashes as well as commercial airlines. Forensic feather analysis will become more important as the world's climate changes and birds begin to appear where they are not expected to be, either geographically or seasonally.

Wald, M., January 25, 2009. They Can Say which Bird Hit a Plane, Even When Not Much Bird Is Left. New York Times, p. 27.

A BIT OF FORENSIC SCIENCE HISTORY

Some forms of what we would now call forensic medicine were practiced as far back as the fifth century. During the next thousand years there were many advances in science, but only forensic medicine was practiced to any great extent. The science of toxicology was one of the first "new" forensic sciences to emerge. In an early case, Mr Lefarge died under mysterious circumstances and his wife fell under suspicion. The French scientist Mathieu Orfilia, in 1840, examined Lafarge's remains and determined that he had ingested arsenic. He further showed that the source of the arsenic could only have been poisoning, and his wife was subsequently convicted of the crime (Wilson and Wilson, 2003).

The eighteenth and nineteenth centuries saw considerable advances in the science of personal identification. As police photography had not been developed and fingerprints weren't being used, methods of reliably tracking a person either through the police process or during incarceration were needed. Enter Alphonse Bertillon, a French criminologist, who developed a method of recording physical features of a person in such a way that the record would be unique to that person, referred to as *anthropometry* or *Bertillonage*, after its creator. He developed a set of precise measuring instruments to be used with his method. The Bertillonage system became very popular throughout Europe and the United States. It became widely used in US prisons, which needed a way to track the prisoners. The Bertillon system was plagued by problems of reproducibility and was finally discredited in the United States Penitentiary (USP) Leavenworth in Kansas. In 1903, William West was admitted to the prison to serve a sentence. When he was measured using the Bertillon system, it was found that a man with the name William West with virtually the same set of measurements was already at the prison! This sounded the death knell for Bertillonage and opened the door for the study of fingerprints. Bertillon used fingerprints in his system but didn't have a good way to organize them for mass searches (Wilson and Wilson, 2003). Dr Juan Vucetich, a Croatian who lived in Argentina and worked for the La Plata police force, conceived of a method of fingerprint classification in 1894 that provided for 1,048,576 primary classifications of fingerprints. As history and culture would have it, his work was largely unheard of in Europe until much later. Sir William Herschel, a British officer in India and Henry Faulds, a Scottish medical doctor, both studied fingerprints as a scientific endeavor to see whether they could be used reliably for identification. In 1901, Sir Edward Henry devised a fingerprint classification system still used today to categorize sets of fingerprints and store them for easy retrieval (Thorwald, 1964). Pioneers, such as Alexandre Lacassagne and his protege Edmund Locard, set the practical and philosophical foundations for much of the developing forensic sciences. Located convinced the police department in Lyon, France, to give him two small rooms and two helpers, starting what would be the world's first forensic science laboratory in 1910.

Modern blood and body fluid typing got its start around 1900 when Karl Landsteiner showed that human blood came in different types, and his work led to the ABO blood typing system. This work, in turn, led to the discovery of other blood antigen systems such as Rh, MnSs, and the Lewis systems. White blood cell antigen systems were also discovered. From these discoveries came the forensic typing of blood to help distinguish one individual from another (Nuland, 1988).

After Watson and Crick discovered the structure and functions of DNA in the early 1950s, it wasn't until Sir Alec Jeffries developed the first forensic DNA typing method, which he coined, regrettably, "DNA fingerprinting," in 1984 that forensic DNA technology was born. The work of Kary Mullis in the 1980s led to the discovery of the polymerase chain reaction (PCR), the way our bodies reproduce DNA. This discovery led to Mullis' being awarded the 1993 Nobel Prize in Chemistry (Malmstrom, 1997).

In the early part of the twentieth century, Goddard popularized the comparison microscope, which is two standard microscopes joined by an optical bridge. This revolutionized the comparison of bullets, cartridges, toolmarks, hairs, and fibers. Microscopy is the mainstay of forensic science laboratories and includes newer methods, such as the scanning electron microscope.

Several professional forensic organizations help forensic scientists keep current and membership can convey many benefits, not the least of which is meeting other forensic scientists and developing contacts. Many of these organizations have journals associated with them. Refer to "On the Web: Professional Forensic Organizations" for more information about these groups.

ON THE WEB: PROFESSIONAL FORENSIC ORGANIZATIONS

Some professional forensic organizations have regional groups affiliated with them; check the Web sites for contact information.

American Academy of Forensic Sciences	www.aafs.org
International Association for Identification	www.theiai.org
Association of Firearms and Toolmarks Examiners	www.afte.org
American Society of Questioned Document Examiners	www.asqde.org
Society of Forensic Toxicologists	www.soft-tox.org

FORENSIC SCIENCE LABORATORY ORGANIZATION AND SERVICES

Although it may seem contradictory, there is no single structure for the organization of a forensic science laboratory. Their organization varies by jurisdiction, agency, and history. The variation becomes more pronounced when laboratories in the United States are compared with those in other countries. The examinations and services that a forensic science laboratory offers will also vary, depending on budget, personnel, equipment, and crime statistics. This section will focus on laboratories in the United States and answer two questions: First, how is the laboratory administered and second, what services does the laboratory provide?

FORENSIC SCIENCE LABORATORY ADMINISTRATION

The vast majority of forensic science laboratories in the United States are public; that is, they are financed and operated by a federal, state, or local unit of government. These number something over 470 today. There are also an undetermined number of private forensic science laboratories.

Private Forensic Science Laboratories

Most private laboratories serve a niche by performing only one or two examinations, such as drugs, toxicology, or **questioned documents**—many are "one-person" operations, often a retired forensic scientist providing services in the specialties practiced when employed in a public laboratory. Today, a significant number of the private laboratories are devoted to DNA analysis in either criminal cases or in the civil area, chiefly in paternity testing. Private laboratories serve a necessary function in our criminal justice system in that they are able to provide forensic science services directly to persons accused of crimes. Most public laboratories can provide forensic science services only to police or other law enforcement departments and will not analyze evidence requested by an accused person except under a court order. Some public laboratories, however, will accept evidence from private citizens and the fee is subsidized by the jurisdiction where the laboratory operates.

Public Forensic Science Laboratories

Public forensic science laboratories are administered and financed by a unit of government which varies with the jurisdiction. Different states have different models, and the federal government has its own collection of laboratories. Laboratories administered by the federal government, typical state systems, and local laboratories will be discussed separately.

The Bureau of Justice Statistics conducts occasional censuses on public forensic science laboratories to provide a basis for better understanding the industry. The reports are available free from the National Criminal Justice Reference Service (www.ncjrs.gov), but the most recent census (Durose et al., 2012) revealed some troubling facts:

- Nearly 1.2 million cases were backlogged at the end of 2009 (see Table 1.1).
- Although forensic biology accounted for only one-third of all requests for service, about three-quarters of the total backlog is for these type of requests.
- About one-third of laboratories sent casework to a private laboratory to try to stay current in their work.

The census also showed hope for the quality of the nation's forensic laboratories:

- Over 80% of public forensic laboratories are accredited.
- Over 80% have some sort of laboratory information management system.
- The overall number of forensic scientists rose to over 13,000.

Another approach to understanding the forensic industry is the FORESIGHT Project, originally funded by the National Institute of Justice (NIJ) through West Virginia University's College of Business and Economics. Volunteer laboratories in local, state, and national jurisdictions across North America submit standardized business measures for analysis, and this provides a comparison between laboratories' effectiveness (a process called "benchmarking"). The laboratories, in turn, can now self-evaluate their performance against their peers and allocate their resources to the best result. For example, some descriptive statistics on laboratory operations from

Table 1.1 The Nation's Public Forensic Laboratories' Backlogged Cases (Durose et al., 2012)

	Year End 2008		Year End 2009	
Type of Request	**Number**	**Percent (%)**	**Number**	**Percent (%)**
All requests	1,184,500	100	1,193,800	100
Forensic biology	887,400	75	905,200	76
Convicted offender/ arrestee samples	522,100	44	498,500	42
Casework	365,200	31	406,700	34
Controlled substances	142,100	12	137,700	12
Latent prints	53,100	4	49,500	4
Firearms/toolmarks	46,700	4	48,700	4
Toxicology	30,400	3	28,600	2
Trace evidence	14,700	1	13,200	1
Impressions	5500	–	5700	–
Questioned documents	2100	–	2400	–
Digital evidence	1300	–	1300	–
Other forensic requests	1100	–	1500	–

Durose et al. (2012).

Table 1.2a Average Number of Cases Worked per Full Time Employee for a Variety of Case Types in a Forensic Laboratory

Investigative Area	Mean	Median	Standard Deviation
Blood alcohol	857	831	580
Crime scene investigation	54	22	65
Digital evidence—audio and video	23	18	9
DNA casework	82	82	28
DNA database	2604	2523	493
Document examination	33	26	25
Drugs—controlled substances	545	468	239
Evidence screening and processing	194	162	85
Explosives	32	28	24
Fingerprints	367	310	250
Fire analysis	103	99	68
Firearms and ballistics	136	119	93
Forensic pathology	46	44	7
Gunshot residue (GSR)	85	74	62
Marks and impressions	33	24	27
Serology/biology	167	165	77
Toxicology ante-mortem (excluding BAC)	245	193	147
Toxicology postmortem (excluding BAC)	217	195	135
Trace evidence	46	40	27

the FORESIGHT Project are shown in Table 1.2a and b. Table 1.2a shows the average (mean and median) and standard deviation for what it costs to work a forensic case for various areas of the laboratory. Table 1.2b shows how many cases on average each full-time employee works per year. With these kinds of performance metrics, laboratory managers can more efficiently allocate resources to meet goals. More on the FORESIGHT Project can be found at www.be.wvu.edu/forensic.

FEDERAL GOVERNMENT FORENSIC SCIENCE LABORATORIES

When most people think of federal forensic science laboratories, the only name that usually pops up is the Federal Bureau of Investigation (FBI) Laboratory. While this is certainly the most famous forensic science laboratory in the United States, if not in the world, it is far from being the only one in the federal government. There are a surprising number and types of laboratories administered by several departments of the US government.

The Department of Justice

The FBI is a unit of the Department of Justice. It has one laboratory, in Quantico, Virginia, near its training academy. It also maintains a research laboratory, the Forensic

Table 1.2b Average Cost per Case for a Variety of Cases in a Forensic Laboratory

Investigative Area	Mean ($)	Median ($)	Standard Deviation ($)
Blood alcohol	271	121	360
Crime scene investigation	4433	5409	3441
Digital evidence—audio and video	4527	4824	1011
DNA casework	1902	1746	641
DNA database	71	54	54
Document examination	3965	3899	2071
Drugs—controlled substances	229	187	105
Evidence screening and processing	520	525	121
Explosives	8542	5205	6949
Fingerprints	416	326	348
Fire analysis	2088	956	1957
Firearms and ballistics	1331	820	1402
Forensic pathology	3115	3291	644
Gunshot residue (GSR)	2168	1215	1852
Marks and impressions	4349	3989	3078
Serology/biology	690	591	370
Toxicology ante-mortem (excluding BAC)	694	607	561
Toxicology postmortem (excluding BAC)	715	637	412
Trace evidence	5679	2843	7201

From www.be.wvu.edu/forensic.

Science Research and Training Center in Quantico. The FBI laboratory supports investigative efforts of the FBI and will, upon request, analyze certain types of evidence for state and local law enforcement agencies and forensic science laboratories.

The Drug Enforcement Administration (DEA) is responsible for investigating major illicit drug enterprises and to help interdict shipments of drugs from other countries. In support of this function, the DEA maintains a network of seven drug laboratories throughout the United States. There is also a research and support laboratory, the Special Testing and Research Laboratory. The DEA laboratories not only support the efforts of the DEA investigators but also work with local law enforcement in joint operations.

The Bureau of Alcohol, Tobacco, Firearms and Explosives (ATF) has three regional laboratories; they also maintain a unique fire research laboratory. Although the primary responsibilities of the ATF are embodied in its name—the regulation of alcohol, tobacco, and firearms—the laboratories have particular expertise in fire scene analysis and explosives.

Department of Homeland Security

The Department of Homeland Security (DHS) has several laboratories that it inherited from other agencies when DHS was created in. The first laboratory is the Secret

Service Laboratory in Washington, DC. This laboratory has two major functions. The first is in the area of counterfeiting and fraud; counterfeit currency, fraudulent credit cards, and related documents are handled in this laboratory. One of the world's largest libraries of ink standards is located here, and questioned document analysis is also a major function. The second major component of the Secret Service laboratory supports its function of executive protection. This laboratory engages in research and development of countermeasures and protection of the president and other officials.

The Department of the Interior

The Department of the Interior has a unique laboratory: The US Fish and Wildlife Service operates a forensic science laboratory in Ashland, Oregon. One of the few animal-oriented forensic science laboratories in the world, its mission is to support the efforts of the service's investigators who patrol the national parks. Among other duties, these agents apprehend poachers and people who kill or injure animals on the endangered species list. Thus, the laboratory does many examinations involving animals and has particular expertise in the identification of hooves, hairs, feathers, bone, and other animal tissues. The laboratory also provides consulting services for other countries in their efforts to track people who traffic in animal parts such as bear gall (in certain parts of Asia bear gallbladders are thought to improve sexual potency) and elephant ivory. The laboratory maintains some of the most sophisticated instrumentation and has some of the world's leading experts in animal forensic science.

The US Postal Service

Although the Postal Service is not strictly a federal agency, nor is it managed by one, it is considered to be a quasi-federal agency. The service maintains a laboratory that supports the service's efforts to combat postal fraud. This effort mainly involves questioned document analysis although the laboratory also has fingerprint and trace evidence capabilities.

Additional federal laboratories include the Department of Defense, Customs and Border Patrol (DHS) and Department of the Treasury.

STATE AND LOCAL FORENSIC SCIENCE LABORATORIES

Every state in the United States maintains at least one forensic science laboratory. Historically, there has been no nationwide effort to standardize laboratory organization or function, so each state has developed a system that meets its particular needs. These forensic science laboratories have arisen from two sources. The most prevalent is law enforcement. The majority of forensic science laboratories are administered by a unit of a state or local police or other law enforcement agency. The other source of forensic science laboratories is health departments or other scientific agencies. In Michigan, for example, the modern Michigan State

Police Laboratory system developed from the merger of a smaller MSP laboratory and the state's health department laboratory. The Michigan State Police laboratory had expertise in firearms, questioned documents, and fingerprints, whereas the health department laboratory had expertise in drugs, toxicology, and trace evidence, such as hairs and fibers. The state police in Michigan now operates a network of seven regional laboratories. In all states, there is a statewide laboratory or laboratory system that is operated by the state police, state department of justice, or as an independent state laboratory system, such as in Virginia. In California, for example, the state department of justice operates an extensive network of state-financed laboratories, whereas West Virginia has a single laboratory that serves the whole state.

Besides the statewide laboratory system, most states also have one or more laboratories operated by a local governmental unit. For example, in Maryland some counties have laboratories under the jurisdiction of the county police department separate from the state system. In Texas, some police or sheriffs' departments in major cities operate city laboratories, as in Fort Worth; and in California, Los Angeles has a county and a city laboratory. The District of Columbia has a local laboratory that serves not only the D.C. Metropolitan Police Department but also any of the federal agencies in the district, including the United States Attorney's Office and public defenders' offices. This patchwork of political, geographical, and historical jurisdictions can be confusing but is usually maintained because of perceived societal needs, such as population levels, crime rates, and geography.

FORENSIC SCIENCE LABORATORY SERVICES

Forensic science laboratories offer different levels of service. In a statewide system, for example, at least one laboratory will offer a full range of forensic science services (typically at the headquarters laboratory) while the regional laboratories may offer only limited services (say, fingerprints and drugs) and then send the other evidence to the headquarters laboratory. This section discusses the capabilities of a typical full-service forensic laboratory. Keep in mind that the designation of "full service" may mean different things in different states—a laboratory may not offer gunshot residue analysis in even its best-equipped laboratory but would still describe it as "full service" (see Table 1.3).

STANDARD LABORATORY SERVICES

Evidence Intake

All forensic science laboratories have a system for receiving evidence. The laboratory may have employees assigned to manage this unit full time, depending on the volume of evidence and casework. The evidence intake unit will have a secured area

Table 1.3 Forensic Functions Performed by Laboratories, 2009, by Type of Jurisdiction*

Forensic Function	All Labs	State	County	Municipal	Federal
Controlled substances	82%	86%	85%	75%	59%
Latent prints	60	54	63	78	65
Forensic biology	59	64	66	49	26
Firearms/toolmarks	55	55	63	62	21
Crime scene	52	44	62	71	44
Trace evidence	50	50	55	44	50
Impressions	44	44	53	43	24
Toxicology	42	50	43	35	9
Digital evidence	19	10	21	32	44
Questioned documents	16	13	13	24	29
Other functions	13	10	14	12	24
Number of reporting labs	397	211	88	63	35

**Data may total more than 100% because some laboratories reported more than one function; the total includes federal laboratories, not shown separately (Durose et al., 2012).*

for storing evidence, the size of which depends again on the volume of work: it may be a room or a warehouse. A police officer or investigator will bring evidence to the laboratory and fill out a form that describes the evidence and the types of examinations requested. A unique laboratory number will be assigned to the case, and each item of evidence will be labeled with this number, along with other identifying information, such as the item number. This continues the **chain of custody** of the evidence, which is the documentation of who had what items of evidence and when, from the smallest fiber to an entire car. The chain of custody begins at the crime scene when the evidence is collected. The job of the evidence intake unit is like that of inventory control for a business.

Modern intake systems use computerized systems that generate barcodes that are placed on each item of evidence or its container. The barcode is scanned by each unit of the laboratory that takes possession of that item so the evidence can be easily traced by computer as it makes its way through the laboratory. Paperwork accompanies the evidence, either in hard copy or electronically, as each analyst signs or accepts possession of the evidence.

Analytical Sections

Once the evidence has been received by the laboratory, it will be assigned to one or more forensic units for analysis; each unit, in turn, assigns a scientist to take charge of the evidence and its analysis. Many times, more than one scientist will be asked to analyze an item of evidence, and then arrangements must be made to get the evidence to each scientist in a logical order. For example, a gun may have to be test fired, but also may contain fingerprints and suspected blood. The examinations must be performed in an order that will not disrupt or destroy any of the evidence on the gun. In some laboratories, one forensic scientist may be certified to examine several of these evidence types; in larger laboratories that have the luxury of specialization, a scientist may examine only one or two.

OTHER LABORATORY SERVICES

Some laboratories offer services in addition to those listed in the preceding section, depending on the need for such services and the availability of qualified scientists. Laboratories that have an occasional need for these services may submit the evidence to the FBI laboratory, a private laboratory, or a local specialist. Specialists areas include bloodstain pattern analysis, entomology, odontology, and anthropology.

ADMINISTRATIVE ISSUES WITH FORENSIC SCIENCE LABORATORIES

Forensic science laboratories are faced with ever-increasing demands and workloads. Courts have come to expect more and higher quality expert testimony and speedier turnaround times from forensic laboratories. More scrutiny also has been placed on the forensic science systems around the world by the public, the media, and government officials. This has caused a number of administrative issues to assume greater importance; two of the major ones are accountability and access.

ACCOUNTABILITY

Virtually every hospital and clinic in the United States has to be accredited by a responsible agency. Environmental and pharmaceutical companies, among others, also have accreditation procedures. Thus, it might come as a surprise to many people to find out that there is no mandatory accreditation process for the nation's forensic science laboratories. Considering the impact that forensic science can have on trials, this situation is disturbing.

Arguably, the major reason for this state of affairs is that forensic science laboratories historically have arisen within police agencies whose focus is not science. Movements in the United States and worldwide to accredit forensic science laboratories have had some success: some states make it mandatory for forensic laboratories to be accredited, but many (over 80%) seek accreditation voluntarily. In the United States, the standard for accreditation is ISO 17025

General requirements for the competence of testing and calibration laboratories. The accreditation process is rigorous and involves a self-study process, an extensive checklist of requirements, and an on-site evaluation by trained members of the accrediting board. It should be stressed that accreditation does not directly address the competence of the individual forensic scientists who work at the laboratory. It does mean that the laboratory meets certain minimum criteria for the physical plant (facilities, heating–cooling, etc.), security, training, equipment, quality assurance and control, and other essential features. Reaccreditation is required every 5 years to maintain the laboratory's status. Several accrediting vendors provide this service.

Standard methods play a major role in helping laboratories become accredited. The **American Society for Testing and Materials, International** (**ASTM**), publishes voluntary consensus standards for a wide variety of sciences, including forensic science (Committee E30, Volume 14.02). They are voluntary because individuals and agencies independently choose to adhere to them. The standards are written through a consensus process, meaning that everyone on the subcommittee, committee, and the society has had a chance to read, comment, and vote on the standard.

ACCESS TO LABORATORY SERVICES

The majority of forensic science laboratories in the United States are funded by the public and administered by a unit of federal, state, or local government. These laboratories support the functions of the parent agency or the government. Police officers, detectives, crime scene investigators, and prosecutors generally have open access to the services of the laboratory, including expert testimony by its forensic sciences at no cost to the other agency. Considering that the public pays for these services, it might seem obvious that a citizen accused of a crime should also have access to these services. That, however, is not the case. Very few public forensic science laboratories will permit accused persons access to forensic science services even if that person is willing and able to pay for them.

How then do criminal defendants gain access to forensic science services? The options are limited. Private laboratories serve defendants (and anyone, really), but the cost is generally high and often courts will not authorize enough money for indigent defendants to cover the costs of analysis and testimony. If an accused person has a public defender for an attorney, most public defenders' offices do not have sufficient funds to pay for analyzes of evidence. Even people willing and able to pay may not have a qualified forensic science laboratory available. This results in an imbalance in the resources available to the prosecution and defense in a criminal case. One of the recommendations made by the National Academy of Sciences was that forensic laboratories should be independent, either administratively or financially, from law enforcement (see 'In More Detail: Laboratory Independence').

IN MORE DETAIL: LABORATORY INDEPENDENCE

Forensic service providers inhabit a necessary, if unique, role in the criminal justice system. The forensic sciences have many stakeholders, primarily the public they serve but also governmental ones, including law enforcement, attorneys and the courts. For historical and political reasons, most forensic service providers are administratively a subset of law enforcement agencies. Occupying a subordinate role in a para-military organization sets boundaries on the laboratory's relationships with their parent agency and aligned agencies. For example, the laboratory director may be a sworn officer with no science education or training; this will affect the management of scientific resources depending on the officer. Being in law enforcement also frames the way in which externalities, such as budgets, politics and accreditation, are dealt with for the laboratory to perform adequately or succeed.

Recently, the 'law enforcement' paradigm for forensic laboratories was challenged by the National Academy of Sciences' 2009 report on the forensic sciences that recommended the forensic service providers be administratively or financially independent of law enforcement-based parent agencies. The community response varied and concerns were raised: What about political clout during the budget process, who oversees the operations, how would the laboratory participate in investigations, what would be gained or lost through independence? In the face of these valid questions, some jurisdictions have created independent forensic agencies to meet the challenge of the NAS committee. Washington, D.C.'s Department of Forensic Sciences and the Houston Forensic Science, LGC in Texas are but two examples of forensic laboratories that have been created independent of law enforcement; some have already existed in that environment, such as Virginia's Department of Forensic Sciences and Rhode Island's Forensic Science Laboratory housed in its Department of Public Health.

Their vision was for the laboratory director to have a voice equivalent with or at least proportional to others in the jurisdiction and the justice system on matters involving the laboratory and related agencies. The committee felt that the laboratory should also be able to establish and maintain prioritization of cases, expenditures and other resources while also having budgetary autonomy to set its own financial goals. It was hoped that by establishing forensic laboratories as separate but equal entities, the political and professional pressures related to the different goals, missions and values of scientific laboratories and law enforcement agencies could be mitigated, if not resolved.

Independence is not a panacea, of course – the professional disaster at the Hinton, MA laboratory where Annie Dookhan worked was part of the Department of Health when the problems occurred, for example. And no government agency is *truly* independent; they serve the leaders the people of their jurisdiction elected. Removing forensic service providers from administrative oversight by law enforcement (to include prosecutor's offices) does, however, address the 'fox guarding the hen house' issue; those responsible for acting on the jurisdiction's or defendant's behalf in court are not in charge of the neutral arbiter of facts that support or refute criminal allegations. The implication is not that all law enforcement oversight of laboratory functions is biased but that – purely based on mandated responsibilities – the potential for *that particular brand of bias* is greater than if the laboratories were independent. Other types of bias may occur but, as an independent agency, the laboratory can at least act on them without collateral repercussions and resistance due to professional cultural differences (Harris, 2012). It remains to be seen whether these "independent" laboratories will remain so or if political interference pushes aside the objectivity of science for prosecutorial gains.

The question remains, however, how will the community move forward to evaluate and implement any new or adjusted business models for independent forensic laboratories. The need for strategic leadership in forensic science is critical and the lack of a historical systems-level view has slowed the development of strong strategic leadership. Forensic service providers, traditionally under law enforcement agencies, have had few opportunities to have a collective, distinctive political voice that served them alone. Whether the change is evolutionary or revolutionary remains to be seen; 'the true measure of a successful revolution is the realization there is no going back' (Davis, 2013).

Excerpted from Houck, M., 2014. What Does Independence Mean for a Forensic Laboratory? Evidence Technology Magazine. http://www.evidencemagazine.com/.

THE FORENSIC SCIENTIST

Forensic scientists have two major duties: performing scientific analysis of evidence and offering expert testimony in criminal and civil proceedings. There are sometimes other responsibilities, such as offering training in evidence collection and preservation, doing research, or performing other studies such as validation procedures for new methods, but the major duties take up most of the forensic scientist's time.

EDUCATION AND TRAINING OF FORENSIC SCIENTISTS

Science is the heart of forensic science. Court decisions, such as *Daubert* versus *Merrell Dow* (1993), have reinforced this fact. A forensic scientist must be well versed in the methods and requirements of good science in general and in the specific techniques used in the particular disciplines being practiced. Additionally, the forensic scientist must be familiar with the rules of evidence and court procedures in the relevant jurisdictions. The knowledge, skills, and aptitudes needed in these areas are gained by a combination of formal education, formal training, and experience.

Education

Historically, forensic scientists were recruited from the ranks of chemistry or biology majors in college. Little or no education was provided in the forensic sciences themselves—all of that was learnt on the job. Since the middle of the twentieth century, undergraduate, and then graduate, programs in forensic science have been offered by a handful of colleges and universities in the United States. The early bachelor's degree programs provided a strong chemical, mathematical, biological, and physical science background coupled with applied laboratory experience in the analysis of evidence with classes in law and criminal procedure mixed in. These programs also offered opportunities for a practicum in a functioning forensic science laboratory to see how science was applied in forensic laboratories.

In the past 20 years or so, graduate degrees, particularly at the master's level, have become the norm. They typically require a bachelor's degree in a science and then teach the applications of the science to forensic work, as well as relevant aspects of law, criminal investigation, and criminal justice classes. A research component is also generally required. For more information about forensic science educational accreditation standards, see "In More Detail: FEPAC."

IN MORE DETAIL: FEPAC

The American Academy of Forensic Sciences (AAFS) initiated the **Forensic Science Education Programs Accreditation Commission (FEPAC)** as a standing committee of the academy. The mission of the FEPAC is to maintain and to enhance the quality of forensic science education through a formal evaluation and recognition of 4-year, college-level academic programs. The primary function of the commission is to develop and maintain standards and to administer an accreditation program that recognizes and distinguishes high-quality undergraduate and graduate forensic science

IN MORE DETAIL: FEPAC—cont'd

programs. In 2009, FEPAC began a process for programs offering degrees in digital evidence and computer forensic investigation. The FEPAC Standards are based on a guideline published by the National Institute of Justice, *Education and Training in Forensic Science*, which was the work product of the Technical Working Group on Education and Training in Forensic Science (TWGED). For more information about FEPAC and a listing of accredited forensic science programs, visit www.aafs.org.

Educational programs are not, however, designed to provide training so that graduates can start working cases on their first day in a forensic science laboratory.

Formal Training

Once scientists are employed by a forensic science laboratory, they begin formal training. New scientists are normally hired as specialists; they will learn how to analyze evidence in one or a group of related areas. Thus, someone may be hired as a drug analyst, a DNA analyst, or a firearms examiner. Training requires a period of apprenticeship where the newly hired scientist works closely with an experienced scientist. The length of time for training varies widely with the discipline and the laboratory. For example, a drug chemist may train for 3–6 months before taking cases, while a DNA analyst may train longer, and a questioned document examiner may spend a year or more in apprenticeship. Training usually involves mock casework as well as assisting in real cases. Ideally, it will also include proficiency testing at intervals and mock trials at the end of the training.

On-the-Job Training: Experience

Once a forensic science student graduates, his or her professional learning really has only begun. Laboratories train new employees in the technical and administrative aspects specific to that agency. Each case is a project of sorts and managing time and resources is a new experience for many new employees. The pressures of testifying in court must be managed, the "hurry up and wait" of testifying, the media (possibly) and dealing with harried attorneys are all important skills not taught in college courses. These aspects of the forensic career are difficult to convey to someone who has not experienced them.

ANALYSIS OF EVIDENCE

The reason someone wants to become a forensic scientist is to analyze evidence. The science and method of this process fill much of the rest of this book. But besides the routine analysis of evidence, many important aspects other than science affect how evidence gets analyzed:

- *Chain of custody*: The forensic scientist must be constantly aware of the requirements of the chain of custody. Evidence can be rendered inadmissible if the chain of custody is not properly constructed and maintained.
- *Turn-around time*: There are federal and state "speedy trial" laws that require an accused person be brought to trial within a specified window of time after arrest; this is usually 180 days or fewer but may vary with the jurisdiction.

If the forensic science laboratory cannot analyze and report evidence out in a timely manner, the laboratory's stakeholders can't make use of the information.

- *Preservation and spoilage*: Forensic scientists have a duty to preserve as much of the evidence as is practical in each case and to ensure that the evidence is not spoiled or ruined. In some cases, so little evidence exists that there is only one chance for analysis. In such cases, the prosecutor and defense attorney should be apprised before the analysis takes place.
- *Sampling*: In many cases there is so much evidence that sampling becomes an issue. This often happens with large drug cases in which there may be hundreds or thousands of similar exhibits; it can also be true of bloodstains, fibers, or any type of evidence. The opposite may also be true: insufficient sample for complete or repeat analysis. Finally, in some cases any type of analysis may be destructive, and there is no opportunity for reanalysis.
- *Reports*: Every laboratory has protocols for writing laboratory reports, but a surprising lack of uniformity exists from laboratory to laboratory. Some laboratories mandate complete reports for each case, whereas others have bare-bones reports with a minimum of description and explanation. Reports of forensic science analysis are scientific reports and should be complete like any other scientific report.

EXPERT TESTIMONY

Being a competent analytical scientist is only half the battle in a forensic science laboratory. The forensic scientist must also be able to explain his or her findings to a judge or jury in a court of law. This is one of the key factors that distinguish careers in forensic science from those in other sciences.

There are a number of definitions of an expert. For forensic science purposes, an expert may be thought of as a person who possesses a combination of knowledge, skills, and abilities in a particular area that permit him or her to draw inferences from facts that the average person would not be competent to do. In short, an expert knows more about something than the average person and has the credentials to prove it. An expert does not have to possess a PhD. Many experts have accumulated expertise over many years of experience and may not have much education. For example, suppose that a man is killed while driving his car because the brakes failed and he crashed into a tree. If an average group of people were to inspect the brakes of the car, those people would not be competent to determine why the brakes failed or even if they did. This would require the services of an expert mechanic to examine the brake system and then make conclusions about if, why, and how the brakes failed. A difference exists, however, between an expert and a forensic scientist: A mechanic is not a forensic scientist. That difference is what this book is about.

SUMMARY

Forensic science is a wide-ranging field with a rich, if untapped, history. In many ways, the discipline has suffered from that lack of historical knowledge and our ignorance of it—not knowing the past dooms one to repeat it, and so forth. Forensic science also occupies what may be a unique niche between law enforcement and the courts. The pressures from either side color much of what is accepted as forensic science, and yet practitioners must adhere to the tenets of science. Because forensic science is seen as a growth industry, one would be hard pressed to find another discipline with so much rich material to mine or such promise in the dazzling future of technology.

TEST YOUR KNOWLEDGE

1. What is forensic science?
2. How is forensic science different from other sciences, like biology and physics?
3. What does the word "forensic" mean?
4. Name four disciplines within the forensic sciences.
5. What are the two kinds of forensic science laboratories?
6. What is the main difference between these two types of forensic laboratories?
7. Name three federal agencies that have forensic science laboratories.
8. What is a chain of custody?
9. Who accredits forensic science laboratories?
10. Who was Will West?
11. What is FORESIGHT?
12. What is ASTM?
13. ISO 17025?
14. To whom are forensic laboratories accountable?
15. Who is a forensic anthropologist?
16. Who was Bertillon?
17. What laboratory analyzes wildlife samples in criminal cases?
18. Why would the Department of Defense need forensic laboratories?
19. Who is a forensic toxicologist? How would this differ from a regular toxicologist?
20. Who's an expert?

CONSIDER THIS...

1. Why do you think a mechanic who helps to determine if the brakes failed in one automobile accident is or is not a "forensic scientist?"
2. What are the benefits to forensic laboratory independence? What might be some detriments?
3. Why is formal training necessary once someone is hired by a forensic science laboratory? Why is a forensic science education alone not sufficient?

BIBLIOGRAPHY AND FURTHER READING

Beavan, C., 2001. Fingerprints: The Origins of Crime Detection and the Murder Case that Launched Forensic Science. Hyperion, New York, NY.

Brandi, J., Wilson-Wilde, L., 2013. Standard methods. In: Siegel, J., Saukko, P. (Eds.), Encyclopedia of Forensic Sciences, second ed. Elsevier, Amsterdam, pp. 522–527.

Crispino, F., Houck, M., 2013. Principles of forensic science. In: Siegel, J., Saukko, P. (Eds.), Encyclopedia of Forensic Sciences, second ed. Elsevier, Amsterdam, pp. 278–281.

Davis, W., May 2013. Revolution. Smithsonian Magazine 11–12.

Durose, M., Walsh, K., Burch, A., 2012. Census of Publicly Funded Crime Laboratories, 2009. Bureau of Justice Statistics, Washington, DC.

Harris, D., 2012. Failed Evidence: Why Law Enforcement Resists Science. New York University Press, New York City.

Hebrard, J., Daoust, F., 2013. History of forensic sciences. In: Siegel, J., Saukko, P. (Eds.), Encyclopedia of Forensic Sciences, second ed. Elsevier, Amsterdam, pp. 273–277.

Houck, M., 2013. Effectiveness. In: Siegel, J., Saukko, P. (Eds.), Encyclopedia of Forensic Sciences, second ed. Elsevier, Amsterdam, pp. 532–534.

Houck, M., 2013. Interpretation/the comparative method. In: Siegel, J., Saukko, P. (Eds.), Encyclopedia of Forensic Sciences, second ed. Elsevier, Amsterdam, pp. 314–317.

Houck, M., 2013. Forensic classification of evidence. In: Siegel, J., Saukko, P. (Eds.), Encyclopedia of Forensic Sciences, second ed. Elsevier, Amsterdam, pp. 318–321.

Malmstrom, B.G., (Ed.), 1997. Nobel Lectures, Chemistry 1991–1995, World Scientific Publishing, Co, Singapore.

Nuland, S.B., 1988. Doctors and the Biography of Medicine, Alfred A. Knopf, Inc., New York City.

National Research Council, 2009. Strengthening Forensic Science in the United States: A Path Forward. National Academies Press, Washington, DC.

Oxford English Dictionary, 2005. Oxford English Dictionary. Oxford University Press, Oxford, United Kingdom.

Palmbach,, T., 2013. Education and accreditation in forensic science. In: Siegel, J., Saukko, P. (Eds.), Encyclopedia of Forensic Sciences, second ed. Elsevier, Amsterdam, pp. 171–174.

Rankin, B., Welsh, C., 2013. Accreditation. In: Siegel, J., Saukko, P. (Eds.), Encyclopedia of Forensic Sciences, second ed. Elsevier, Amsterdam, pp. 515–518.

Rule, A., 1980. The Stranger beside Me. W.W. Norton, New York City.

Thorwald, J., 1964. The Century of the Detective Harcourt. Brace & World, New York City.

Vosk, T., 2013. Measurement uncertainty. In: Siegel, J., Saukko, P. (Eds.), Encyclopedia of Forensic Sciences, second ed. Elsevier, Amsterdam, pp. 322–331.

Welsh, C., Aitchison, G., 2013. Training to competence. In: Siegel, J., Saukko, P. (Eds.), Encyclopedia of Forensic Sciences, second ed. Elsevier, Amsterdam, pp. 185–189.

Wilson, C., Wilson, D., 2003. Written in Blood: A History of Forensic Detection. Carroll and Graf Publishers, New York City.

CHAPTER

Crime Scene Investigation

2

CHAPTER OUTLINE

KEY TERMS

- Artifact
- Bloodborne pathogens (BBPs)
- Context
- Crime scene investigator (CSI)
- Datum
- Feature
- Material safety data sheet (MSDS)

- Organic or environmental remains
- Provenance
- Universal precautions

INTRODUCTION

An argument becomes heated, old emotional wounds are reopened, lingering hate resurfaces, there is a struggle, finally a heavy ceramic vase is hefted and crashes down on someone's head—and a crime is committed. Suddenly, normal household items are transformed into evidence, their importance changed forever. Processing a crime scene, collecting these items, the evidence, appears deceptively simple at first. But this perception comes from the investigations we read in novels and see on television and the movies where we *know* what's important (the camera lingers on the crucial evidence), *who* the short list of suspects are (they wouldn't be on the show if they weren't involved), and that it will be wrapped up in an hour (with commercials). We see the murder weapon being collected, bagged, and the next time it appears, it's presented in court to the witness! The reality of crime scene processing is more involved and detailed than what we read or see in the media.

Without a crime scene, nothing would happen in a forensic laboratory. The scene of the crime is the center of the forensic world, where everything starts, and the foundation upon which all subsequent analyzes are based. Normal household items are transformed from the mundane into that special category called "evidence." The importance of a properly processed crime scene cannot be overemphasized—and yet, it is where devastating mistakes occur that affect an entire case. Many agencies have recognized the significance of the crime scene and employ specially and extensively trained personnel to process them. The processing of a crime scene is a method of "careful destruction": It is a one-way street, and one can never go back and undo an action. Standard operating procedures and protocols guide the **crime scene investigator (CSI)**, providing a framework for comprehensive and accurate evidence collection, documentation, and transmittal to the laboratory.

This chapter will focus on the scene itself and the collection of evidence. Because the nature of evidence and how things become evidence can be complex, this subject will be discussed separately and in depth in the next chapter.

OF ARTIFACTS AND EVIDENCE

The goal of an archaeological excavation is to carefully collect and record all the available information about a prehistoric or historic site of human activity. The goal of processing a crime scene is to collect and preserve evidence for later analysis and reporting. What these two processes have in common is that they are *one-way*: Once an action is taken, an artifact moved, a piece of evidence collected, it can't be undone any more than a bell can be "un-rung." Crime scenes and archaeological sites are made up of the physical remains of past human activity and, in a sense, are snapshots of the "leftovers" of a completed process. As mentioned previously, when a scene is processed or a site dug, the procedure is one of "careful destruction": The scene or site will never exist in exactly the same way as it did before the process started. All the information, the relationships, the **context** of the items must be documented as they are destroyed to allow for some level of reconstruction in the laboratory or museum. It is an awesome responsibility to work a scene or excavate a site, and neither should be taken lightly.

Several technical terms that are used in archaeology may be of use in crime scene processing. The first is the idea of a **datum**, a fixed reference point for all three-dimensional measurements. The datum should be something permanent, or nearly so, like a light switch (pick a corner!), a tree, or a post. If no datum easily suggests itself, an artificial one, such as a post, nail, or mark, can be made. Ultimately, all measurements must be able to be referenced to the datum.

Other terms that can be borrowed from archaeology suggest the nature of what is found. An **artifact** is a human-made or modified portable object. A **feature** is a non-portable artifact, such as a fire pit, a house, or a garden. **Organic** or **environmental remains** (non-artifactual) are natural remnants that nonetheless indicate human activity, such as animal bones or plant remains but also soils and sediments. An archaeological site, then, can be thought of as a place where artifacts, features, and organic remains are found together. Their location in relation to each other sets the internal context of the site. To reconstruct this context once the site or scene has been processed, the investigator needs to locate the position of each item within the surrounding material (the **matrix**), be it soil, water, or a living room. Thus, the **provenance** is the origin and derivation of an item in three-dimensional space, in relation to a datum and other items. When an artifact is uncovered at a site, it is measured to the reference points for that excavation unit including its depth. A similar process occurs at a crime scene when evidence is located. As the noted archaeologists, Colin Renfrew and Paul Bahn put it:

> *In order to reconstruct past human activity at a site it is crucially important to understand the context of a find, whether artifact, feature, structure or organic remain. A find's context consists of its immediate matrix (the material surrounding it), its provenience (horizontal and vertical position within the matrix), and its association with other finds (occurrence together with other archaeological remains, usually in the same matrix).*
>
> **(2000, p. 50)**

The similarities between archaeology and crime scene processing are numerous and deep. Serious crime scene students would do well to study archaeological methods to enhance their forensic skills.

Evidence can be defined as information, whether personal testimony, documents, or material objects, that is given in a legal investigation to make a fact or proposition more or less likely. Most of the evidence discussed in this chapter relates to physical evidence—that is, things involved in the commission of the crime under investigation. The nature of evidence will be discussed in more depth in the next chapter.

CRIME SCENE INVESTIGATION

As Paul Kirk, the noted forensic science pioneer, described it, forensic science is interested in the "unlikely and the unusual" (Kirk, 1963, p. 368). This is certainly true of crime scenes: Each one is unique. The crime committed, the location, the items used, the people involved, all vary from scene to scene. Although nearly every police and forensic agency has written protocols about processing a crime scene, these may be trumped by the circumstances of the crime scene. As Barry Fisher, retired Director of the Los Angeles County Sheriff's Department Crime Laboratory notes, "There are few absolute rules in crime scene investigations.... There are always cases where guidelines cannot be followed.... Situations demand that investigators be flexible and creative when necessary" (2004, p. 49). That is, CSIs, must know and follow their agency's protocols but must be ready to improvise, within accepted limits, to protect and/or preserve evidence, as shown in the example in Figure 2.1.

FIRST ON THE SCENE

The success of any crime scene investigation depends in large part on the actions taken in the first few minutes after the First Officer (or FO) or CSI arrives. This sounds odd, to be sure. "How can a few minutes matter to a crime scene that's just been sitting there for hours or days?" one may ask. But crime scenes are a complex mix of static and dynamic information, a scene fixed in time like a photograph but slowly degrading, much like poorly archived historical photographs. The majority of the physical evidence will be generated by the processing of the crime scene, and the relationships between the people, places, and things (the context) will tell the story of what happened. Remember, facts alone are not sufficient; by themselves, they explain nothing. Facts must be interpreted in light of the circumstances or context surrounding the crime. Once an item is moved, it can never be placed back exactly as it was: The context is disturbed, and the subsequent interpretation may be biased and inaccurate.

The primary task of the FO at a crime scene is to *secure the scene and prevent destruction or alteration of the critical and sometimes fragile context of a crime scene*. The assumption is that the perpetrator has left physical evidence at the crime scene. Therefore, the FO's duties are simple in concept but complex in execution:

1. Detain any potential suspects.
2. Render medical assistance to those who need it.
3. Do not destroy, alter, or add any evidence at the scene.
4. Prevent others, even superiors, from doing the same.

FIGURE 2.1

This little fellow, along with three of its littermates, was at the scene of a triple homicide in the northwest United States. Before they could be rounded up, they tracked blood around the crime scene; this photo was taken as a reminder. The cats were adopted by various agency personnel.

Anonymous by submitter's request.

But not all crime scenes are equal. A homicide in a small house's bedroom is certainly easier to seal and guard than a body found in the middle of a wooded park or a busy highway. The FO should not simply rush into a scene but approach it carefully, thoughtfully. Sometimes the best thing to do is just prevent further entry until additional agency staff arrive.

Once the immediate scene is secured, the lead investigator further defines and evaluates the scene. The scene may be large or small, extensive, or discrete, made up of several locations or centered in one area. With the crime scene defined and its borders identified, the initial surveyor begins to develop an overview and devise a plan of action.

PLAN OF ACTION

Preparation

The officers or investigators assigned to the scene should have obtained a search warrant, if necessary, by the time the crime scene processing begins. If there is time, the search should be discussed with involved personnel before arriving at the scene.

A command station for communication and decision-making should be established in an area away from the scene but still within the secured perimeter. If personnel task assignments don't already exist, they should be made before arrival at the scene. Depending on the number of personnel available, each may be assigned multiple responsibilities.

Optimally, the person in charge of the scene is responsible for scene security, evidence or administrative log, the preliminary survey, the narrative description, problem resolution, and final decision-making. The person in charge of photography arranges, takes, and coordinates photography and keeps the photograph log. The person assigned to prepare the sketch does so in coordination with other methods of documentation; for complex scenes, multiple personnel may be assigned to this task for reconstructive purposes (Figure 2.2). An evidence custodian takes charge of items collected as evidence, logs them in, and assures that the packaging is labeled properly and sealed.

Communication between the various agencies' representatives, such as medical examiners, laboratory personnel, emergency medical technicians, and attorneys, is crucial to a smooth and successfully executed crime scene process. Questions that arise during the crime scene search can be resolved more easily (with less administrative backlash later) by involving and engaging the proper individuals.

Think ahead. Fifteen minutes of thought can save hours, and possibly lives, later on. Prepare the paperwork to document the search *before* searching. Agree-upon terminology—if everyone refers to an area as the "living room," then there will be less

FIGURE 2.2

Crimes scenes can be very complex, involving many agencies with sometimes competing goals and directives. The 2014 shootings at the Navy Yard complex in Washington, D.C. involved military, federal, and local agencies all responding to the mass shooting scene with an active shooter.

AP Wire, with permission.

confusion afterward if questions come up ("Did we collect that from the *front* room?" "Do you mean the *living* room?"). Arrange for protective clothing, communication, lighting, shelter, transportation, equipment, food, water, medical assistance, and security for personnel. Processing crime scenes can be tedious, physically demanding work, and people, even professionals, perform poorly when they are tired. In prolonged searches, use multiple shifts or teams. If one doesn't exist, develop a transfer mechanism for paperwork and responsibility from one team to the next.

Secure the Scene, Secure the Item

If the FO hasn't done so, take control of the scene *immediately*. Determine the extent to which the scene has, or has not, been protected. Talk to personnel who have knowledge of the original condition. Keep out unauthorized personnel. Record who enters and leaves, even if they are an agency's superiors. Dick Worthington, a noted forensic instructor, suggests renaming the sign in/sign out form for a crime scene to "subpoena contact form," to signal that entering a crime scene may make an individual eligible to testify about his or her presence. Now and throughout the processing of the scene, it is impossible to take too many notes.

Regarding note taking, it is important to remember the central nature of crime scene notes. These are the documentation of who did what and when, contemporaneous with those activities. The adage from quality assurance, "if it is not written down, it didn't happen," is a good guide on what to record. This means that if a supervisor tells a CSI to "process the front bedroom," the supervisor makes a note of that and the time in his or her notes—as does the employee in *his or her own notes*. Later, the two sets of notes should correspond, and if a question arises (say, in court), then the activities can be corroborated. Taking contemporaneous notes is crucial to a successful crime scene investigation.

Securing the scene is so critically important that we cannot overstate this point. Even the perception of an unsecured scene can show up in court, as it did in the Simpson–Goldman murder trial, where video was used to critique the testimony of a crime scene analyst. Video cameras from television crews, police cruisers, surveillance systems, not to mention photojournalists, police photographers, and the general public (with their cellphone cameras) can collect images that may portray reality or be used to distort it. What is important is that the *photographs*, the *notes*, the *documentation* demonstrate the quality of the work at the scene and that each item was properly collected and secured.

PRELIMINARY SURVEY

The survey is an organizational stage to plan for the search. A few minutes' planning and discussion can be of great value later. Cautiously walk the scene. Crime scenes can be emotional experiences, but professionalism and calm are called for. Take preliminary photographs to establish the scene and delineate the extent of the search area. The initial perimeter may be expanded later if more evidence is found. Make note of special "problem" areas, such as tight spaces, complex evidence arrangements, or environments with transient physical evidence (blood in a running shower, for example). Take extensive notes to document the scene, physical and environmental conditions, and personnel tasks and activities.

Evaluate what physical evidence collection requirements there may be. Make sure enough supplies are available: running out of packaging or gloves halfway through is no good! Focus first on evidence that could be lost or damaged; leave the more robust evidence for last. All personnel should consider the variety of possible evidence, not just evidence within their specialties.

Collection of evidence is more than just "bagging and tagging." The easily accessible areas, of course, are processed first, but then move on to out-of-the-way locations, like in cupboards, under rugs or carpeting, or in drawers. Look for hidden items, secret compartments, and false fronts. Things may not be what they seem, and crime scene personnel must evaluate whether evidence appears to have been moved or altered. Remember, things at a crime scene are just things until they are designated as evidence and then recorded and collected. In that sense, the evidence listing is like a "reverse shopping list," a tally of all the things that might be needed but only after they have been found. Another important reminder is that the scene may not even be *the* scene—the scene may be contrived to look like an accident or some other type of crime.

PHOTOGRAPHY

The photography of the crime scene should begin as soon as possible. The photographic log documents all the photographs taken and a description and location of what's in the photograph. A progression of establishing (overall or perspective views), medium (within 6 ft), and close-up (within 12 in) views of the crime scene should be collected. Multiple views, such as eye level, top, side, and bottom, help to represent what the scene or a piece of evidence looked like in place. Start with the most fragile areas of the crime scene first; move through the scene as evidence is collected and processing continues. Document the process itself, including stages of the crime scene investigation, discoveries, and procedures. Photographs must at least be taken *before* the evidence is recovered.

Photographs should be taken with and without a scale. Photographs that include a scale should also have the photographer's initials and the date. This is easily accomplished by using a disposable plastic ruler and writing the pertinent information (case number, item number, etc.) on it with a permanent marker. Scales allow photographs to be reproduced at defined scales (1:1, 1:2, 1:10, etc.). Photograph the crime scene in an overlapping series using a wide-angle lens, if possible; 50 mm lenses are the standard issue for cameras—use both and lots of film. It's almost impossible to take too many photographs. All these images can help later with reconstruction questions.

When the exterior crime scene is photographed, establish the location of the scene by a series of overall photographs, including one or more landmarks, with 360° of coverage. Photograph entrances and exits. Prior photographs, blueprints, or maps of the scene may be of assistance, and they should be obtained, if available.

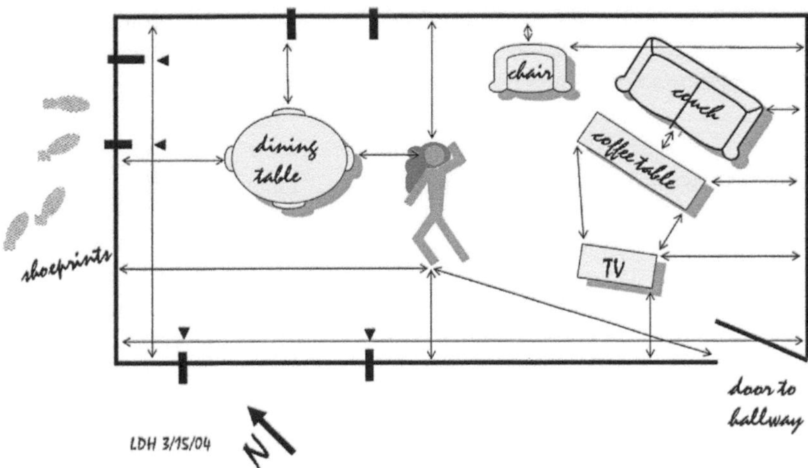

FIGURE 2.3

A typical crime scene sketch; measurements would accompany all the arrows and descriptions when the scene is completed.

SKETCH

Crime scene sketches may look crude at times, but they contain one very important element for reconstruction: numbers. Distances, angles, time, temperature—all these elements make the crime scene sketch, an example of which is shown in Figure 2.3, central to all subsequent work. Sketches complement photographs and vice versa. Items of evidence can be located on the sketch as it is made to help establish locations later. Although sketches are quantitative, they are normally not drawn to scale. However, sketches should have measurements and details for a drawn-to-scale diagram. A sketch should include the following:

- The case identifier
- Date, time, and location
- Weather and lighting conditions
- Identity and assignments of personnel
- Dimensions of rooms, furniture, doors, and windows
- Distances between objects, persons, bodies, entrances, and exits
- An arrow pointing toward magnetic north

CHAIN OF CUSTODY

Arguably, the single most important piece of paper generated at a crime scene is the chain of custody. This form, an example of which is shown in Figure 2.4, documents the movement of evidence from the time it is obtained to the time it is presented in court. The most compelling evidence in the world can be rendered useless if inaccuracies or gaps exist in a chain of custody. Where was the evidence? Who had control

Bakersfield Forensic Laboratory
123 Main Street
Bakersfield, WV 26501

Agency Number 72204

Laboratory number 615243

Chain of Custody

Received From	Delivered to	Date/Time	Items
D. Green (Print Name) David Green (Signature)	B. Putnam (Print Name) Bradford Putnam (Signature)	7/22/04 2:14p	1-26, 28
D. Green (Print Name) David Green (Signature)	B. Schneckster (Print Name) B Schneckster (Signature)	7/22/04 2:45p	27, 29
B. Putnam (Print Name) Bradford Putnam (Signature)	D. Green (Print Name) David Green (Signature)	7/29/04 9:16 am	1-26, 28
Print Name Signature	Print Name Signature		
Print Name Signature	Print Name Signature		
Print Name Signature	Print Name Signature		

Page ___ of _____

FIGURE 2.4

The chain of custody form documents the movement of evidence from the time it is obtained to the time it is presented in court. The most compelling evidence in the world can be rendered useless if inaccuracies or gaps exist in a chain of custody.

of it? When? Who last had this item? Could it have been tampered with during this gap in time? Having to document each exchange of an item from person, to evidence locker, to person, to agency may seem to be a nuisance, but it is the foundation that permits forensic science results to enter into a courtroom.

CRIME SCENE SEARCH AND EVIDENCE COLLECTION

The crime scene search should be methodical and performed in a specific pattern. The choice of pattern may be dictated by the location, size, or conditions of the scene. Typical patterns are spiral, strip or lane, and grid and are shown in Figure 2.5. Adhering to the selected pattern prevents "bagging and tagging" random items with no organization or system. Measurements showing the location of evidence should be taken with each object located by two or more measurements from non-movable items, such as doors or walls. These measurements should be taken from perpendicular angles to each other to allow for triangulation.

Be alert for all evidence: The perpetrator had to enter or exit the scene! Mark evidence locations on the sketch and complete the evidence log with notations for each item of evidence. If possible, having one person serving as evidence custodian makes collection more regular, organized, and orderly. Again, if possible, two persons should observe evidence in place, during recovery, and being marked for identification. Use tags, or if feasible, mark directly on the evidence.

Wear gloves to avoid leaving fingerprints—but be aware that after about 30 min, it is possible to leave fingerprints *through* latex gloves! Evidence should not be handled excessively after recovery. Seal all evidence packages with tamper-evident tape at

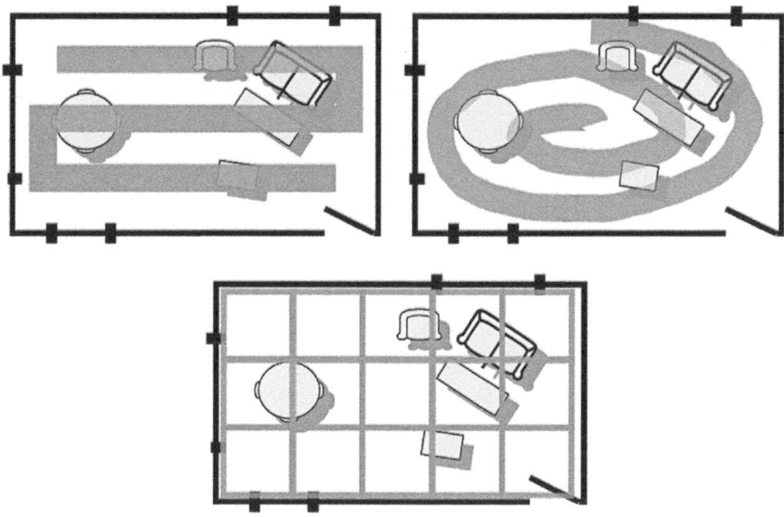

FIGURE 2.5

It is best to have an organized systematic search of a crime scene. The strip (or lane), the spiral, and the grid are three of the most common patterns.

the crime scene. An important activity often overlooked is the collection of known standards from the scene, such as fiber samples from a known carpet or glass from a broken window. Monitor the paperwork, packaging, and other information throughout the process for typographic errors, clarity, and consistency.

Simple geometry can help locate and reconstruct where things were in a sketch. Always take measurements from at least two locations. This will help with checking distances and triangulating "untaken" measurements later. In trigonometry and elementary geometry, triangulation is the process of finding a distance to a point by calculating the length of one side of a triangle, given measurements of angles and sides of the triangle formed by that point and two other reference points. In many ways, measuring a crime scene is surveying, the art and science of accurately determining the position of points and the distances between them; the points are usually on the surface of the earth. Surveying is often used to establish land boundaries for ownership (such as buying a house) or governmental purposes (geographic surveys). Large crime scenes may require standard surveying (and the prepared CSI would do well to learn a bit of surveying), but processing an *indoors* crime scene is much the same except for issues of points (guns, not mountains) and scale (inches, not miles).

FINAL SURVEY

When the crime scene is finished, there is still work to be done! A final survey is recommended to review all aspects of the search. Discuss the search and ask questions of each other. Read over the paperwork for a final check for completeness. Take photographs of the scene showing the final condition. Secure all evidence and retrieve all equipment. A final walk-through with at least two people from different agencies (if possible) as a check on completeness is a must.

The crime scene can be released after the final survey; this event should be documented in the paperwork, including the time and date of release, to whom and by whom it was released. Remember that other specialists, such as a bloodstain pattern analyst or medical examiner, may need access to the scene before it is released. Once the scene has been released, re-entry may require a warrant; therefore, the scene should be released only when all personnel are satisfied that the scene was searched correctly and completely.

SUBMISSION OF EVIDENCE TO THE LABORATORY

The collected evidence may be submitted to the laboratory by that agency's personnel (that is, laboratory personnel) or by CSIs or law enforcement officers. A form is typically filled out or a letter written detailing what is submitted, under what criminal circumstances, who is submitting the items, and what laboratory examinations are requested.

SAFETY

Walking into a crime scene is one of the most hazardous activities a forensic scientist or CSI can do. Chemical and biological threats abound, not to mention knives, firearms, explosives… the list goes on. Worse, coming in at or near the end of the

FBI TEN MOST WANTED FUGITIVE

ERIC ROBERT RUDOLPH

FIGURE 2.6

(Above) Bystanders protect themselves seconds after a second explosion detonated outside the Atlanta Northside Family Planning Services building in Atlanta on Thursday, January 16, 1997. Associated Press file photo. (Below) Eric Rudolph, the longtime fugitive charged in the 1996 Olympic Park bombing in Atlanta and in attacks at an abortion clinic and a gay nightclub, was arrested June 1, 2003, in the mountains of North Carolina by a local sheriff's deputy.

action, crime scene personnel have little or no foreknowledge of what's in store for them. Add in the prospect of intentional manufacture or use of chemical or biological agents or explosives by terrorists, and the issue of safety for crime scene personnel becomes of paramount concern, as shown in Figure 2.6.

The increase in **bloodborne pathogens (BBPs)** (AIDS and hepatitis, for example) and other pathogens that may be encountered at crime scenes (like the Hantavirus) has made law enforcement and CSIs more aware of personal protection when responding to crime scenes. Although the risk of infection to crime scene responders is exceedingly low, precautions are typically mandated by individual agencies' protocols. Additionally, federal laws or regulations from one of several health agencies may be applicable to crime scene personnel (see "On the Web: Safety").

ON THE WEB: SAFETY

Occupational Safety and Health Administration, www.osha.gov

The mission of the Occupational Safety and Health Administration is to save lives, prevent injuries and protect the health of America's workers. To accomplish this, federal and state governments must work in partnership with the more than 100 million working men and women and their six and a half million employers who are covered by the Occupational Safety and Health Act of 1970.

The Centers for Disease Control, www.cdc.gov

The Centers for Disease Control and Prevention (CDC) is recognized as the lead federal agency for protecting the health and safety of people, at home and abroad, providing credible information to enhance health decisions and promoting health through strong partnerships. The CDC serves as the national focus for developing and applying disease prevention and control, environmental health and health promotion and education activities designed to improve the health of the people of the United States.

The *Morbidity and Mortality Weekly Report*, www.cdc.gov/mmwr

The *Morbidity and Mortality Weekly Report* (*MMWR*) series is prepared by the CDC. The data in the weekly *MMWR* are provisional, based on weekly reports to the CDC by state health departments. The reporting week concludes at close of business on Friday; compiled data on a national basis are officially released to the public on the succeeding Friday. An electronic subscription to *MMWR* is free.

National Institute for Occupational Safety and Health, www.cdc.gov/niosh

The National Institute for Occupational Safety and Health (NIOSH) is the federal agency responsible for conducting research and making recommendations for the prevention of work-related disease and injury. The institute is part of the CDC. NIOSH is responsible for conducting research on the full scope of occupational disease and injury ranging from lung disease in miners to carpal tunnel syndrome in computer users. In addition to conducting research, NIOSH investigates potentially hazardous working conditions when requested by employers or employees; makes recommendations; disseminates information on preventing workplace disease, injury and disability and provides training to occupational safety and health professionals. Headquartered in Washington, DC, NIOSH has offices in Atlanta, Georgia, and research divisions in Cincinnati, Ohio; Morgantown, West Virginia; Bruceton, Pennsylvania and Spokane, Washington.

SOURCES AND FORMS OF DANGEROUS MATERIALS

Inhalation

At a crime scene, airborne contaminants can occur as dust, aerosol, smoke, vapor, gas, or fume. Immediate respiratory irritation or trauma might ensue when these contaminants are inhaled; some airborne contaminants can enter the bloodstream through the lungs and cause chronic damage to the liver, kidneys, central nervous system, heart, and other organs. Remember that some of these inhalants may be invisible!

Skin Contact

Because processing a crime scene requires the physical collection of items, skin contact is a frequent route of contaminant entry into the body. Direct effects can result in skin irritation or trauma at the point of contact, such as a rash, redness, swelling, or burning. Systemic effects, such as dizziness, tremors, nausea, blurred vision, liver and kidney damage, shock or collapse, can occur once the substances are absorbed through the skin and circulated throughout the body. The use of appropriate gloves, safety glasses, goggles, face shields, and protective clothing can prevent this contamination.

Ingestion

Ingestion is a less common route of exposure. Ingestion of a corrosive material can cause damage to the mouth, throat, and digestive tract. When swallowed, toxic chemicals can be absorbed by the body through the stomach and intestines. To prevent entry of chemicals or biological contaminants into the mouth, wash hands before eating, drinking, smoking or applying cosmetics. Also, do not bring food, drink or cigarettes into areas where contamination can occur.

Injection

Needlesticks and cuts from contaminated glass, hypodermic syringes or other sharp objects can inject contaminants directly into the bloodstream. Extreme caution should be exercised when handling objects with sharp or jagged edges.

UNIVERSAL PRECAUTIONS

The Occupational Safety and Health Administration issued regulations regarding occupational exposure to BBPs in December 1991. Those occupations at risk for exposure to BBPs include law enforcement, emergency response, and forensic laboratory personnel (Title 29 CFR, 1910.1030).

Fundamental to the BBP Standard is the primary concept for infection control called **Universal Precautions**. These measures require employees to treat all human blood, body fluids, or other potentially infectious materials as if they *are* infected with diseases such as hepatitis B virus (HBV), hepatitis C virus (HCV), and human immunodeficiency virus (HIV). The following protective measures should be taken to avoid direct contact with these potentially infectious materials (Title 29 CFR, 1991):

- Use barrier protection such as disposable gloves, coveralls, and shoe covers when handling potentially infectious materials. Gloves should be worn, especially if there are cuts, scratches, or other breaks in the skin.
- Change gloves when torn, punctured, or when their ability to function as a barrier is compromised.
- Wear appropriate eye and face protection to protect against splashes, sprays, and spatters of infectious materials. Similar precautions should be followed when collecting dried bloodstains.
- Place contaminated sharps in appropriate closable, leak-proof, puncture-resistant containers when transported or discarded. Label the containers with a BIOHAZARD warning label. Do not bend, recap, remove, or otherwise handle contaminated needles or other sharps.

- Prohibit eating, drinking, smoking, or applying cosmetics where human blood, body fluids or other potentially infectious materials are present.
- Wash hands after removing gloves or other personal protective equipment (PPE). Remove gloves and other PPE in a manner that will not result in the contamination of unprotected skin or clothing.
- Decontaminate equipment after use with a solution of household bleach diluted 1:10, 70% isopropyl alcohol, or other disinfectant. Noncorrosive disinfectants are commercially available. Allow sufficient contact time to complete disinfection.

In addition to Universal Precautions, prudent work practices and proper packaging serve to reduce or eliminate exposure to potentially infectious materials. Packaging examples include puncture-resistant containers used for storage and disposal of sharps.

Chemical Safety

A wide variety of health and safety hazards can be encountered at a crime scene. Some of those hazards are listed in Table 2.1. This awareness comes from the information contained in a **Material Safety Data Sheet (MSDS)** (for example, http://www.msdssolutions.com or http://siri.uvm.edu) and appropriate training. The MSDS provides information on the hazards of a particular material so that personnel can work safely and responsibly with hazardous materials; MSDSs are typically available through a vendor's website.

Table 2.1 Numerous Chemical Safety Hazards Can Be Encountered at Crime Scenes

Material	Examples
Flammable or combustible materials	Gasoline, acetone, ether, and similar materials ignite easily when exposed to air and an ignition source, such as a spark or flame.
Explosive materials	Over time, some explosive materials, such as nitroglycerine and nitroglycerine-based dynamite, deteriorate to become chemically unstable. In particular, ether will form peroxides around the mouth of the vessel in which it is stored. All explosive materials are sensitive to heat, shock, and friction, which are employed to initiate explosives.
Pyrophoric materials	Phosphorus, sodium, barium, and similar materials can be liquid or solid and can ignite in air temperatures less than 130 °F (540 °C) without an external ignition source.
Oxidizers	Nitrates, hydrogen peroxide, concentrated sulfuric acid, and similar materials are a class of chemical compounds that readily yield oxygen to promote combustion. Avoid storage with flammable and combustible materials or substances that could rapidly accelerate its decomposition.

Source: National Research Council, 1981.

Remember, when working with chemicals, be aware of hazardous materials, disposal techniques, personal protection, packaging and shipping procedures, and emergency preparedness.

PERSONAL PROTECTIVE EQUIPMENT

Hand Protection

Hand protection should be selected on the basis of the type of material being handled and the hazard or hazards associated with the material. Detailed information can be obtained from the manufacturer. Nitrile gloves provide protection from acids, alkaline solutions, hydraulic fluid, photographic solutions, fuels, aromatics, and some solvents. It is also cut resistant. Neoprene gloves offer protection from acids, solvents, alkalies, bases, and most refrigerants. Polyvinyl chloride is resistant to alkalies, oils, and low concentrations of nitric and chromic acids. Latex or natural rubber gloves resist mild acids, caustic materials, and germicides. Latex will degrade if exposed to gasoline or kerosene and prolonged exposure to excessive heat or direct sunlight. Latex gloves can degrade, losing their integrity. Some people are allergic to latex and can avoid irritation by wearing nitrile or neoprene gloves.

Gloves should be inspected for holes, punctures, and tears before use. Rings, jewellery, or other sharp objects that can cause punctures should be removed. Double gloving may be necessary when working with heavily contaminated materials; double gloving is also helpful if "clean" hands are needed occasionally. If a glove is torn or punctured, replace it. Remove disposable gloves by carefully peeling them off by the cuffs, slowly turning them inside out. Discard disposable gloves in designated containers and, it should go without saying, do not reuse them.

Eye Protection

Safety glasses and goggles should be worn when handling biological, chemical, and radioactive materials. Face shields can offer better protection when there is a potential for splashing or flying debris. Face shields alone are not sufficient eye protection; they must be worn in combination with safety glasses. Contact lens users should wear safety glasses or goggles to protect their eyes. Protective eyewear is available for those with prescription glasses and should be worn over them.

Foot Protection

Shoes that completely cover and protect the foot are essential – *no sandals or sneakers*! Protective footwear should be used at crime scenes when there is a danger of foot injuries due to falling or rolling objects or to objects piercing the sole and when feet are exposed to electrical hazards. In some situations, shoe covers can provide protection to shoes and prevent contamination to the perimeter and areas outside the crime scene.

Other Protection

Certain crime scenes, such as bombings and clandestine drug laboratories, can produce noxious fumes requiring respiratory protection. In certain crime scenes, such as bombings or fires where structural damage can occur, protective helmets should be worn.

TRANSPORTING HAZARDOUS MATERIALS

Title 49 of the Code of Federal Regulations codifies specific requirements that must be observed in preparing hazardous materials for shipment by air, highway, rail, or water. All air transporters follow these regulations, which describe how to package and prepare hazardous materials for air shipment. Title 49 CFR 172.101 (http://hazmat.dot.gov) provides a Hazardous Materials Table that identifies items considered hazardous for the purpose of transportation, special provisions, hazardous materials communications, emergency response information, and training requirements. Training is required to properly package and ship hazardous materials employing any form of commercial transportation.

SUMMARY

The crime scene is the center of the forensic world. The importance of a carefully processed crime scene cannot be overstated. The processing of a crime scene is a one-way street; there is no going back. Standard operating procedures and protocols guide the CSI, but training, experience, and education all play a role in adapting to each unique crime scene.

TEST YOUR KNOWLEDGE

1. What is a chain of custody?
2. What is a crime scene?
3. What should the first officer or CSI at the crime scene do?
4. Name four safety issues for CSIs.
5. Is it okay to only take photographs or only draw sketches? Why not?
6. How many photographs should you take at a crime scene?
7. Name three agencies that regulate worker safety.
8. What is a datum?
9. What is provenance?
10. When is it acceptable to release a crime scene?
11. What is an MSDS?
12. Who should be involved in the final walk-through of a crime scene?
13. What should be included in a crime scene sketch?
14. Should you take photographs with or without a scale?

15. What does "BBP" stand for?
16. Which type of protective gloves should be used when handling bases and oils?
17. What is a "Universal Precaution"?
18. Why is processing a crime scene considered "careful destruction"?
19. What's involved in making a plan for a crime scene?
20. Why is it important to have a plan for a crime scene?

CONSIDER THIS...

1. How would you process an underwater crime scene? A homicide scene on a beach? Outside during a thunderstorm? What protocols would change? How would you process and package evidence? How would you maintain the integrity of the evidence?
2. How would you process a crime scene (use Figure 2.4 as a basis) with two people? Assign tasks and duties. How would you process the same scene with 10 people? What would you do the same or do differently? Would the quality of the scene processing be the same?
3. Take one of the extreme examples in Consider This #1. How would you explain to a jury that you followed your agency's protocols – but also did not?

BIBLIOGRAPHY AND FURTHER READING

American National Standard, 1989. American National Standard Practice for Occupational and Educational Eye and Face Protection 1989. American National Standards Institute, New York, NY (ANSI Z87.1–1989).

Chisum, W.J., Turvey, B., 2007. Crime Reconstruction. Academic Press, San Diego.

Chisum, W., 2013. Crime scene analysis and reconstruction. In: Siegel, J., Saukko, P. (Eds.), Encyclopedia of Forensic Sciences, second ed. Elsevier, Amsterdam, pp. 378–382.

Crispino, F., 2013. Preservation. In: Siegel, J., Saukko, P. (Eds.), Encyclopedia of Forensic Sciences, second ed. Elsevier, Amsterdam, pp. 364–367.

Gorman, C. (Ed.), 1991. Hazardous Waste Handling Pocket Guide 1991. Genium, Schenectady, New York.

Houck, M., Crispino, F., McAdam, T., 2012. The Science of Crime Scenes. Elsevier, Amsterdam.

Horswell, J., 2013a. Major incident scene management. In: Siegel, J., Saukko, P. (Eds.), Encyclopedia of Forensic Sciences, second ed. Elsevier, Amsterdam, pp. 352–354.

Horswell, J., 2013b. Packaging. In: Siegel, J., Saukko, P. (Eds.), Encyclopedia of Forensic Sciences, second ed. Elsevier, Amsterdam, pp. 355–363.

Horswell, J., 2013c. Recording. In: Siegel, J., Saukko, P. (Eds.), Encyclopedia of Forensic Sciences, second ed. Elsevier, Amsterdam, pp. 368–371.

Kirk, P.L., 1963. Criminalistics. Science 140 (3565), 367–370.

National Institute of Justice, 2000a. A Guide for Explosion and Bombing Scene Investigation. National Institute of Justice, Washington, DC.

National Institute of Justice, 2000b. Fire and Arson Scene Evidence: A Guide for Public Safety Personnel. National Institute of Justice, Washington, DC.

National Research Council, 1981. Committee on Hazardous Substances in the Laboratory. Prudent Practices for Handling Hazardous Chemicals in Laboratories. National Academy, Washington, DC.

Osterburg, J., 2000. Criminal Investigation. Anderson Publishing, Cincinnati.

Poole, F., 2013. Collection and chain of evidence. In: Siegel, J., Saukko, P. (Eds.), Encyclopedia of Forensic Sciences, second ed. Elsevier, Amsterdam, pp. 333–336.

Renfrew, C., Bahn, P., 2000. Archaeology: Theories, Methods, and Practice, third ed. Thames and Hudson, New York.

U.S. Department of Labor, 1991a. Title 29 CFR Section 1910.1030. Occupational Exposure Reference for CFR 29 to Bloodborne Pathogens: Final Rule U.S. Department of Labor. Occupational Safety and Health Administration, Washington, DC. Available: p_id=10051”>http://www.osha.gov/pls/oshaweb/owadisp.show_document?p_table=STANDARDS&p_id=10051.

U.S. Department of Labor, 1991b. Title 29 CFR Section 1910.134. Respiratory Protection U.S. Department of Labor. Occupational Safety and Health Administration, Washington, DC.

U.S. Department of Labor, 1991c. Title 29 CFR Section 1910.136. Foot Protection U.S. Department of Labor. Occupational Safety and Health Administration, Washington, DC.

U.S. Department of Transportation, 1991. Title 29 CFR Section 172.101. Purpose and Use of Hazardous Materials Table. U.S. Department of Transportation, Office of Hazardous Materials Safety, Washington, DC.

Upfal, M.J., 1991. In: Stuart, J.R. (Ed.), Pocket Guide to First Aid for Chemical Injuries. Genium, Schenectady, New York.

CHAPTER

The Nature of Evidence

3

CHAPTER OUTLINE

KEY TERMS

- Class
- Coincidental associations
- Common source
- Comparison
- Contamination
- Demonstrative evidence
- Direct transfer
- Evidence
- False negative (Type II error)
- False positive (Type I error)
- Hypotheses

- Identification
- Indirect transfer
- Individualization
- Known evidence
- Locard exchange principle
- Negative control
- Persistence
- Positive control
- Probative value
- Proxy data
- Questioned evidence
- Repeatability
- Scientific method
- Testability
- Trier of fact

INTRODUCTION

John Adams, in his *Argument in Defense of the Soldiers in the Boston Massacre Trials*, in December 1770, said, "Facts are stubborn things; and whatever may be our wishes, our inclinations or the dictates of our passion, they cannot alter the state of facts and evidence" (Zobel, 1996, p. 293). Evidence is critical to a trial; it provides the foundation for the arguments the attorneys plan to offer. It is viewed as the impartial, objective and, yes, stubborn, information that leads a judge or jury to their conclusions. Evidence is a complicated thing and much goes into getting evidence ready before it can go into court.

WHAT IS EVIDENCE?

In a trial, the jury or judge hears the facts or statements of the case to decide the issues; whoever determines guilt or innocence is called the **trier-of-fact**. During the trial, the trier-of-fact must decide whether or not the statements made by witnesses are true. This is done mainly through the presentation of information or evidence. **Evidence** can be defined as information—whether in the form of personal testimony, the language of documents, or the production of material objects—that is given in a legal investigation to make a fact or proposition more or less likely. For example, someone is seen leaving the scene of a homicide with a gun, and it is later shown by scientific examination that bullets removed from the body of the victim were fired from that gun. This could be considered evidence that the accused person committed the homicide. Having the association of the bullets to the gun makes the proposition that the accused is the perpetrator more probable than it would be if the evidence didn't exist. In this chapter, we will explore the nature of evidence, how it is classified and how we decide what value the evidence has in proving or disproving a proposition.

KINDS OF EVIDENCE

Most evidence is real; that is, it is generated as a part of the crime and recovered at the scene or at a place where the suspect or victim had been before or after the crime. Hairs, fingerprints, paint, blood, and shoeprints are all real evidence. Sometimes, however, items of evidence may be created to augment or explain real evidence. For example, diagrams of hair characteristics, a computer simulation of a crime scene, or a demonstration of bloodstain pattern mechanics may be prepared to help the trier-of-fact understand complex testimony. Such **demonstrative evidence** was not generated directly from the incident but is created later. Because it helps explain the significance of real evidence, it does help make a proposition more or less probable and is, therefore, evidence. "In More Detail: Kinds of Evidence" lists other varieties of evidence.

IN MORE DETAIL: KINDS OF EVIDENCE

Circumstantial evidence: Evidence based on inference and not on personal knowledge or observation.
Conclusive evidence: Evidence so strong as to overbear any other evidence to the contrary.
Conflicting evidence: Irreconcilable evidence that comes from different sources.
Corroborating evidence: Evidence that differs from but strengthens or confirms other evidence.
Derivative evidence: Evidence that is discovered as a result of illegally obtained evidence and is therefore inadmissible because of the primary taint.
Exculpatory evidence: Evidence tending to establish a criminal defendant's innocence.
Foundational evidence: Evidence that determines the admissibility of other evidence.
Hearsay: Testimony that is given by a witness who relates not what he or she knows personally, but what others have said, and that is therefore dependent on the credibility of someone other than the witness.
Incriminating evidence: Evidence tending to establish guilt or from which a fact trier can infer guilt.
Presumptive evidence: Evidence deemed true and sufficient unless discredited by other evidence.
Prima facie (**prī**-mə **fay**-shə) *evidence*: Evidence that will establish a fact or sustain a judgment unless contradictory evidence is produced.
Probative evidence: Evidence that tends to prove or disprove a point in issue.
Rebuttal evidence: Evidence offered to disprove or contradict the evidence presented by an opposing party.
Tainted evidence: Evidence that is inadmissible because it was directly or indirectly obtained by illegal means.

Source: *Garner (2000).*

LEVELS OF EVIDENCE

Not all evidence is created equal—some items of evidence have more importance than others. The context of the crime and the type, amount, and quality of the evidence will dictate what can be determined and interpreted. Most of the items in our daily lives are produced or manufactured *en masse*, including biological materials (you have thousands of hairs on your body, for example). This has implications for what can be said about the relationships between people, places, and things surrounding a crime.

FORENSIC SCIENCE IS HISTORY

Forensic science is a historical science: The events in question have already occurred and are in the past. Forensic scientists do not view the crime as it occurs (unless they're witnesses); they assist the investigation through the analysis of the physical remains of the criminal activity. Many sciences, such as geology, astronomy, archaeology, paleontology, and evolutionary biology, work in the same way: No data are seen *as they are created,* but only the remnants, or **proxy data**, of those events are left behind. Archaeologists, for example, analyze cultural artifacts of past civilizations to interpret their activities and practices. Likewise, forensic scientists analyze evidence of past criminal events to interpret the actions of the perpetrator(s) and victim(s); Table 3.1 compares differences between some historical sciences.

Just as archaeologists must sift through layers of soil and debris to find the few items of interest at an archaeological site, forensic scientists must sort through all the items at a crime scene (think of all the things in your home, for example) to find the few items of evidence that will help reconstruct the crime. In this sense, crime scene evidence is like a pronoun, grammatically standing in for a noun; evidence at a crime scene "stands in for" the actual items or are indicative of the actions taken at the scene. The nature and circumstances of the crime will guide the crime scene investigators and the forensic scientists to choose the most relevant evidence and examinations. Many methods may seem "forensic" but the definition may occasionally be stretched; see "In More Detail: But Is It *Forensic* Science?" for a discussion of this issue.

Table 3.1 Forensic Science Is a Historical Science

	Forensic Science	**Archaeology**	**Geology**
Time frame	Hours, days, months	Hundreds to thousands of years	Millions of years
Activity level	Personal, individual	Social, populations	Global
Proxy data	Mass-produced	Hand-made	Natural

IN MORE DETAIL: BUT IS IT *FORENSIC* SCIENCE?

Many people identify forensic science as "science applied to law" but in truth the definition isn't that simple. If a structural engineer is consulted to determine why a bridge failed, writes a report, testifies once, and then never works on a legal case again, is he or she a *forensic* engineer? Most people wouldn't think so, but what if that engineer did it 3, 9, or even 21 times in her career? Many forensic scientists don't work at government forensic laboratories, so the term can't be defined that way. At what point does the *application* of science in the legal arena shift to *forensic* science?

Reconstructing events to assist the justice system happens all the time without being forensic science proper. A good example is the case of a Florida dentist who unwittingly passed on his or her HIV infection to several of his or her patients (Ou et al., 1992). Ou's group reported in 1990 that a young woman with AIDS had probably contracted her HIV infection during an invasive dental procedure. The dentist had been diagnosed with AIDS in 1986 and continued to practice general dentistry for two more years. The dentist went public for the safety of his patients, requesting that they all be tested for HIV infection. Out of 1100 people who were tested, 7 patients were identified as being HIV-positive.

HIV is genetically flexible and changes its genetic make-up during its life cycle, resulting in a variety of related viral family lines or strains (called quasi-species). Investigators used the degree of genetic similarity among the HIV strains in the seven infected patients, along with epidemiologic information, to evaluate whether the infections originated with the dentist or were from other sources. The investigators used genetic distance, constructed "family tree" diagrams, and developed amino acid "signature patterns."

Of the seven patients, five had no identified HIV risk other than visiting the dentist. These five patients were infected with HIV strains that were closely related to those of the dentist's infection; moreover, these strains were different from the strains found in the other 2 HIV-infected patients and 35 other HIV-infected people in the same geographical area. As the authors of the paper note:

> *In the current investigation, the divergence of HIV sequences within the Florida background population was sufficient to identify strain variation…this investigation demonstrates that detailed analysis of HIV genetic variation is a new and powerful tool for understanding the epidemiology of HIV transmission.*
>
> **Ou et al. (1992, p. 1170)**

They call it an "investigation"; they're doing DNA analysis; they're reconstructing the transfer of something from one person to others. But is this *forensic* science?

Don't be confused simply because science is *historical*, because it uses proxy data to represent past events, or because it uses the same techniques or methods as a forensic science. Forensic science is the demonstration of relationships between people, places, and things involved in legal cases through the identification, analysis and, if possible, individualization of evidence. Because nothing legal is at issue in the dentist "case," it isn't forensic. With the increased popularity of forensic science, students and professionals must be cautious about the use of "forensic" as a buzzword in the media and professional publications.

Source: *Ou et al. (1992).*

THE BASIS OF EVIDENCE: TRANSFER AND PERSISTENCE

When two things come into contact, information is exchanged. Seems pretty simple and yet it is the central guiding theory of forensic science. Developed by Edmund Locard, a French forensic microscopist in the early part of the twentieth century, the theory posits that this exchange of information occurs, even if the results are not

Table 3.2 In a Sense, *All Evidence Is Transfer Evidence* in that It Has a Source and Moves or Is Moved from that source to a Target/Location

Item	Transferred *From* (Source)	Transferred *To* (Target/Location)
Drugs	Dealer	Buyer's pocket or car
Bloodstains	Victim's body	Bedroom wall
Alcohol	Glass	Drunk driver's bloodstream
Semen	Assailant	Victim
Ink	Writer's pen	Stolen check
Handwriting	Writer's hand/brain	Falsified document
Fibers	Kidnapper's car	Victim's jacket
Paint chips/smear	Vehicle	Hit-and-run victim
Bullet	Shooter's gun	Victim's body
Striations	Barrel of shooter's gun	Discharged bullet
Imperfections	Barrel cutting tool	Shooter's gun's barrel

Note that there are levels to various types of evidence, from the fundamental (striations on the barrel cutting tool) to the specific (the bullet in the victim's body identified by the striations).

identified or are too small to have been found (Locard, 1930). The results of such a transfer would be proxy data: not the transfer itself, but the remnants of that transaction. Because forensic science demonstrates associations between people, places, and things through the analysis of proxy data, essentially *all evidence is transfer evidence*. Table 3.2 lists some examples in support of this concept.

The conditions that affect transfer amounts include the following:

- The pressure applied during contact;
- The number of contacts (six contacts between two objects should result in more transferred material than one contact);
- How easily the item transfers material (mud transfers more readily than does concrete);
- The form of the evidence (solid/particulate, liquid, or gas/aerosol);
- How much of the item is involved in the contact (a square inch should transfer less than a square yard of the same material).

Evidence that is transferred from a source to a location with no intermediaries is said to have undergone **direct transfer**; it has transferred from A to B. **Indirect transfer** involves one or more intermediate objects—the evidence transfers from A to B to C, as shown in Figure 3.1.

Indirect transfer can become complicated and poses potential limits on interpretation. For example, a person who owns two dogs, pets them each day before going to work. At work, he sits at his desk chair and talks on the phone. This person gets up to get a cup of coffee; when he returns, a colleague is sitting in his chair waiting to tell him some news. The dog owner has experienced a *direct transfer* of their dogs' hairs from the dogs to their pants. The chair, however, has

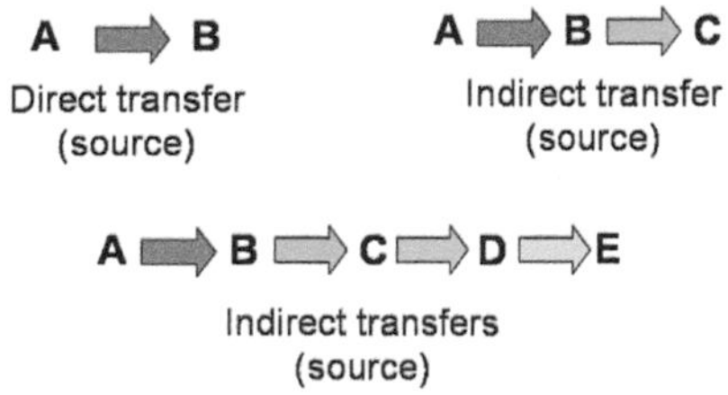

FIGURE 3.1

Direct transfer describes the movement of items from the source to the recipient (A to B), whereas indirect transfer involves an intermediate object that conveys the items to the recipient (A to B to C). Sometimes, direct transfer is referred to as *primary* transfer and indirect transfers are listed as *secondary*, *tertiary*, etc., but this terminology becomes clumsy after several exchanges. It may be more accurate to speak of direct and indirect *sources*.

received an *indirect transfer* of the dogs' hairs—the dogs have never sat in the office chair! The colleague who sat in the dog owner's chair has also experienced an indirect transfer of anything on the chair, except for any fibers originating from the chair's upholstery. How should finding the dog hairs on the colleague's pants be interpreted if there was no knowledge of her sitting in the dog owner's chair? While direct transfer may be straightforward to interpret, indirect transfers can be complicated and potentially misleading. It may be more accurate to speak of direct and indirect *sources*, referring to whether the originating source of the evidence is the transferring item, but the "transfer" terminology has stuck. This leads to unsupportable statements regarding certain types of indirect transfer (secondary, tertiary, etc.); in almost no cases can a forensic scientist tell the difference between secondary (one intermediary) and tertiary (two intermediaries) transfer.

IN MORE DETAIL: THE FIVE-SECOND RULE

If a piece of food is dropped on the floor, how long can it sit there and still be edible? The prevailing popular joke is 5 s, leading to the five-second rule. Some scientists, however, took this principle to heart and decided to test it. Dawson and co-workers found that bacteria (*Salmonella*) survived on wood, tiles, and carpet after 28 days (2007). After exposing the surfaces to the bacteria for 8 h, the researchers found that bread and bologna were contaminated in under 5 s; after a minute, the contamination increased significantly.

What does this test have to do with forensic science? The five-second rule is a popular example of the **Locard Exchange Principle**, which states that information is transferred when two things come into contact. The rule also shows how the underpinnings of forensic science exist throughout other sciences. When critics claim that forensic science is not a "real" science or is only an "applied" science, think of the five-second rule or some of the other examples offered in sidebars in this textbook, such as uniformitarianism and the drift of ocean currents. Forensic science is not just a bundle of techniques or methods from other sciences; it has unique principles and philosophy, as well as applications. Forensic science deserves to sit proudly alongside its sibling sciences.

Sources: *McGee (2007) and Dawson et al. (2007).*

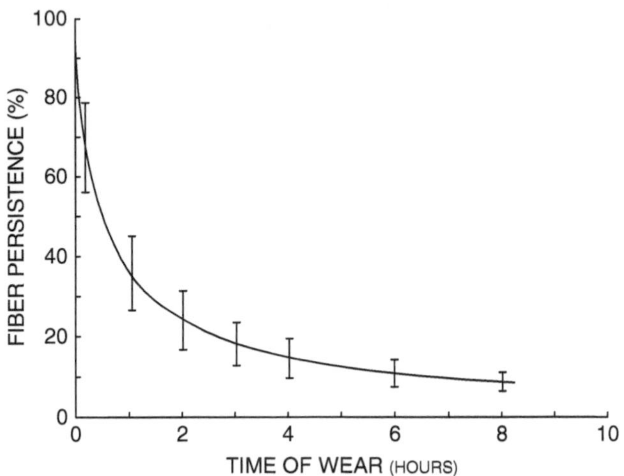

FIGURE 3.2

Trace evidence, such as fibers, tends to be lost at a geometric rate with normal activity. This graph shows a typical fiber loss curve (for acrylic and wool fibers) showing one standard deviation limits.

Pounds and Smalldon (1975, p. 34).

The second part of the transfer process is **persistence**. Once the evidence transfers, it will remain, or persist, in that location until it further transfers (and, potentially, is lost), degrades until it is unusable or unrecognizable, or is collected as evidence. How long evidence persists depends on the following:

- What the evidence is (such as hairs, blood, toolmarks, accelerants);
- The location of the evidence;
- The environment around the evidence;
- Time from transfer to collection;
- "Activity" of or around the evidence location.

For example, numerous fiber transfer studies demonstrate that, from the time of transfer with normal activity, after about 4 h, 80% of the transferred fibers are lost. Transfer and persistence studies with other evidence types have shown similar loss rates, as depicted in Figure 3.2.

CONTAMINATION

Once the activity surrounding the crime has stopped, any transfers that take place may be considered **contamination**, that is, an undesired transfer of information between items of evidence. You would not want to package, for example, a wet bloody shirt from the victim of a homicide with clothes from a suspect; in fact, *every* item of evidence (where practical) should be packaged *separately*. Contamination is itself evidence of a kind; this is why it is so difficult to falsify a case or plant evidence. Based on Locard's Principle, *every* contact produces some level of exchange, including contamination. It is nearly impossible to completely prevent contamination, but it can be severely minimized through properly designed facilities, adequate protective clothing, and quality-centered protocols that specify the handling and packaging of evidence.

IDENTITY, CLASS, AND INDIVIDUALIZATION

All things are considered to be unique in space and time. No two (or more) objects are absolutely identical. Consider, for example, a mass-produced product like a tennis shoe. Thousands of shoes of a particular type may be produced in any one year. The manufacturer's goal, to help sell more shoes, is to make them all look and perform the same—consumers demand consistency. This effort is a help and a hindrance to forensic scientists because it enables them to easily separate one item from another (this red tennis shoe is different from this white one), but these same characteristics make it difficult to separate items with many of the same characteristics (two red tennis shoes). Think about two white tennis shoes that come off the production line one after the next. How would you tell them apart? An observer might say, "this one" and "that one," but if they were mixed up, he or she probably couldn't sort them again. He or she would have to label them somehow, like numbering them "1" and "2."

Now consider if the two shoes are the same except for color: One's white and one's red. Of course, they could be easily distinguished by color but would they be put in the same category? Compared with a brown dress shoe, the two tennis shoes would have more in common with each other than with the dress shoe. All the shoes, however, are more alike than if any of them is compared to, say, a baseball bat. Forensic scientists have developed terminology to clarify the way they communicate about these issues.

Identification is the examination of the chemical and physical properties of an object and using them to categorize the object as a member of a group. What is the object made of? What is its color, mass, and/or volume? The process of examining a white powder, performing one or two analyzes and concluding it is cocaine is identification. Determining that a small colored chip is automotive paint is identification. Looking at debris from a crime scene and deciding it contains hairs from a Black Labrador Retriever is identification (of those hairs). All the characteristics used to identify an object helps to refine that object's identity and its membership in various groups. The debris has fibrous objects in it, and that restricts what they could be—most likely hairs or fibers rather than bullets, to use an absurd example. The microscopic characteristics indicate that some of the fibrous objects are hairs, that they are from a dog and the hairs are most like those from a specific breed of dog. This description places the hairs into a group of objects with similar characteristics, called a **class**. All Black Labrador Retriever hairs would fall into a class; these hairs belong to a larger class of items called *dog hairs*. Further, all dog hairs can be included in the class of *nonhuman hairs* and, ultimately, into a more inclusive class called *hairs*. Going in the other direction, as the process of identification of evidence becomes

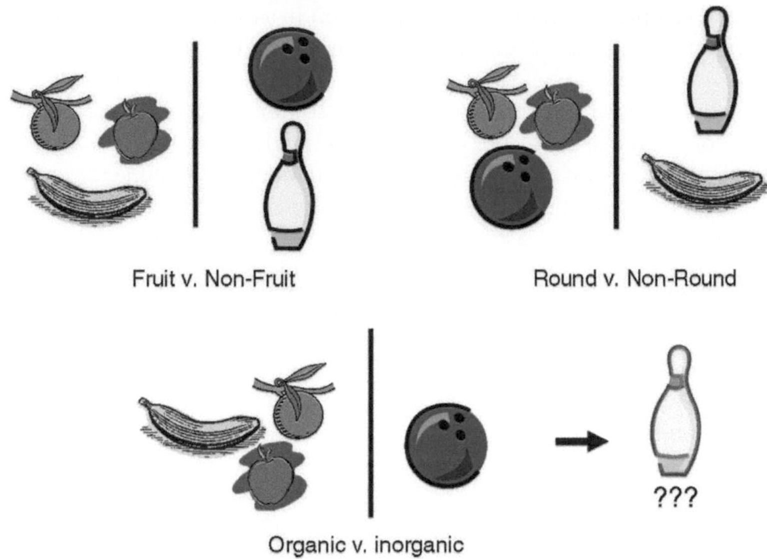

FIGURE 3.3

A class is a group of things with similar characteristics. The size of the class can vary widely depending on the characteristics used for definition, such as the class "all oranges" versus the class "all oranges in your refrigerator."

more specific, the analyst becomes able to classify the evidence into successively smaller classes of objects.

Class is a movable definition; it may not be necessary to classify the evidence beyond *dog hairs* because you are looking for human hairs or textile fibers. Although it is possible to define the dog hairs more completely, you may not need to do so in the case at hand. Multiple items can be classified differently, depending on what questions need to be asked. For example, an orange, an apple, a bowling ball, a bowling pin, and a banana could be classified, as shown in Figure 3.3, by *fruit v non-fruit*, *round things v non-round things*, *sporting goods v edible*, and *organic v inorganic*. Notice that the bowling pin doesn't fit into either of the classes in the last example because it is made of wood (which is organic) but is painted (which has inorganic components).

Stating that two objects share a class identity may indicate they come from a **common source**. What is meant by a "common source" depends on the material in question, the mode of production, and the specificity of the examinations used to classify the object. A couple of examples should demonstrate the potential complexity of what constitutes a common source. Going back to the two white tennis shoes, what is their common source—the factory, the owner, or where they are found? Because shoes come in pairs, finding one at a crime scene and another in the suspect's apartment could be considered useful to the investigation. The forensic examinations would look for characteristics to determine if the two shoes were owned by the same person (the common source). If the question centered on identifying the production source of the shoes, then the factory would be the common source.

Another example is fibers found on a body left in a ditch that are determined to be from an automobile. A suspect is developed, and fibers from his or her car are found to be analytically indistinguishable in all tested traits from the crime scene fibers. Is the suspect's car the common source? For investigative and legal purposes, the car should be considered as such. But certainly it is not the only car with that carpeting. Other models from that car manufacturer or even other car manufacturers may have used that carpeting, and the carpeting may not be the only product with those fibers. But given the context of the case, it may be reasonable to conclude that the most logical source for the fibers is the suspect's car. If the fibers were found on the body but no suspect was developed, part of the investigation may be to determine who made the fibers and track what products those fibers went into in an effort to find someone who owns that product. In that instance, the common source could be the fiber manufacturer, the carpet manufacturer, or the potential suspect's car, depending on what question is being asked.

If an object can be classified into a group with only one member (itself), it is said to have been "individualized." An individualized object has been associated with one, and only one, source: It is unique. The traits that allow for **individualization** depend, in large part but not exclusively, on the raw materials, manufacturing methods, and history of use. Sometimes, sufficiently increasing class traits can lead nearly to individualization; for example, John Thornton's article (1986) on the classification of firearms evidence is an excellent, if overlooked, treatment of this issue.

ON THE WEB

How Products Are Made: www.madehow.com. An excellent source to begin learning about the production and material characteristics of things that appear as evidence.

INDIVIDUALIZATION OF EVIDENCE

A definition for individualization was offered in the preceding section, that is, categorizing an item in a set or class that has one and only one member. To that extent, individualization is the logical extension of classification. The concept of individualization rests on two assumptions:

- All things are unique in space and time; and
- The properties by which a thing is classified are constant over time.

Without these assumptions being in effect, statements such as "Yes, that is a Phillips head screwdriver and it is mine," could not be properly understood. Questions ("What's a screwdriver? What's a 'Phillips head' mean? How do you know it's yours?") would plague even the simplest statements. These two assumptions come with baggage, however.

First, the assumption of uniqueness of space is an inherently non-provable situation. The population size of "all things that might be evidence" is simply too large to account for; think of all the fingerprints on all the surfaces all over the world.

A contributing factor to this is, throughout its history, forensic science has been casework driven, not research driven. Thus, many principles and concepts are derived from years of work-related experience, which is, regrettably, inconclusive from a research standpoint. A jury may reach a decision, a person may confess, and an accomplice may inform, but from a purely scientific perspective, *we do not know what really happened.* In a laboratory experiment, the scientist has control of all the variables of interest except one; any change in that variable leads to a stronger cause-and-effect statement. In forensic science, the scientist has absolutely no control over the circumstances during the crime. Put a bit more simply, casework is not research.

Second, things do not stay the same over time or change at the same rate. The value of some forensic evidence, in fact, is based on it changing over time, like shoeprints. Not knowing the amount and rate of change can hamper the interpretation of evidence and its interpretation. Forensic science is relegated to making interpretive statements based on statistical methods because it deals with so many uncertainties. As Schum clearly explains,

> *Such evidence, if it existed, would make necessary a particular hypothesis or possible conclusion being entertained. In lieu of such perfection we often make use of masses of inconclusive evidence having additional properties: The evidence is incomplete on matters relevant to our conclusions, and it comes to us from sources (including our own observations) that are, for various reasons, not completely credible. Thus, inferences from such evidence can only be probabilistic in nature.*
>
> **Schum (1994, p. 2)**

Schum's point is that if scientists were absolutely certain of their samples or the accuracy of their methods, statistics would not be needed. Forensic science deals with the ultimate uncertainties in the real world of criminal activities with varying physical objects. The gap between the controlled laboratory and the real world is central to forensic science's fundamentals: Uncertainty is everywhere. Even in DNA analysis, where each person's genetic material—except for identical twins—is known to be unique, statistics are used. Statistics are, in fact, what give forensic DNA analysis its power.

Does this mean, then, that individualization is a bankrupt concept? Only if it is considered as a provable scientific statement. Consider two statements:

1. A forensic scientist says, "The questioned item came from the known source to the exclusion of any other similar object that currently exists, has ever existed or will ever exist."
2. A friend says, "This is my friend Howard."

Both are statements of individualization. Statement #2 is provable in a personal sense; that person knows Howard to the exclusion of anyone else he or she might meet. Statement #1, however, is problematic in that one could not possibly check all other similar items currently in the world, let alone all that have ever existed or ever will exist (this is not an extreme statement taken out of context, some forensic examiners still testify this way) to absolutely ascertain that the questioned item came from the known source and only the known source.

Forensic scientists are beginning to recognize the complexity of their evidence and are adjusting their methods. Recent work on fracture matches, where an item has been physically broken into two or more pieces and those pieces are positively associated, promises hope for a statistical treatment of forensic interpretations. The innumerable variables, such as force used to break the object, shape of the object, microstructure and chemical nature of the material, and direction of the blow, all lead to those characteristics that forensic scientists use to compare the fragments. These can lead to exciting research and applications of physics, chemistry, materials science, and nanoscience.

KNOWN AND QUESTIONED ITEMS

Continuing with the hit-and-run example, say a motorist strikes a pedestrian with his or her car and then flees the scene in the vehicle. When the pedestrian's clothing is examined, small flakes and smears of paint are found embedded in the fabric. When the automobile is impounded and examined, fibers are found embedded in an area that clearly has been damaged recently. How can this evidence be classified? The paint on the victim's coat is **questioned evidence** because we don't know the original source of the paint. Likewise, the fibers found on the damaged area of the car are also questioned items. The co-location of the fibers and damaged area and the wounds/damage and paint smears are indicative of recent contact. When we analyze the paint on the clothing, we will compare it to paint from the car; this is **known evidence** because it is known where the sample originated. When we analyze the fibers on the car, we will compare them to fibers taken from the clothing, which makes them known items as well. Thus, the coat *and* the car are sources of *both* kinds of items, which allow for their re-association, but it is their *context* that makes them questioned or known.

Back at the scene where the body is found, there are some pieces of yellow, hard, irregularly shaped material. In the laboratory, the forensic scientist will examine this debris and will determine that it is plastic, rather than glass and further it is polypropylene. This material has now been put in the class of substances that are yellow and made of polypropylene plastic. Further testing may reveal the density, refractive index, hardness, and exact chemical composition of the plastic. This process puts the material into successively smaller classes. It is not just yellow polypropylene plastic but has a certain shape, refractive index, density, hardness, etc. In many cases, this may be all that is possible with such evidence. We have not been able to determine the exact source of the evidence, but only that it could have come from any of a number of places where this material is used—class evidence.

Suppose that the car suspected to be involved in the hit-and-run case has a turn signal lens that is broken and some of the plastic is missing. The pieces are too small and the edges too indefinite for a physical match. Pieces of this plastic can be tested to determine if it has the same physical and chemical characteristics as the plastic found at the crime scene (color, chemical composition, refractive index, etc.). If so, it could be reported that the plastic found at the scene could have come from that broken lens. This is still class evidence because there is nothing unique about these properties that would be different from similar plastic turn signal lenses on many other cars.

RELATIONSHIPS AND CONTEXT

The relationships between the people, places, and things involved in crimes are critical to deciding what to examine and how to interpret the results. For example, if a sexual assault occurs and the perpetrator and victim are strangers, more evidence may be relevant than if they live together or are sexual partners. Strangers are not expected to have ever met previously and, therefore, would not have transferred evidence before the crime. People who live together would have some opportunities to transfer certain types of evidence (head hairs and carpet fibers from the living room, for example) but not others (semen or vaginal secretions). Spouses or sexual partners, being the most intimate relationship of the three examples, would share a good deal of more information. The interaction of these evidence environments is shown in Figure 3.4.

Stranger-on-stranger crimes beg the question of **coincidental associations**; that is, two things which previously have never been in contact with each other have items on them which are analytically indistinguishable at a certain class level. Attorneys in cross-examination may ask, "Yes, but couldn't [insert evidence type here] really have come from *anywhere*? Aren't [generic class-level evidence] very *common*?" It has

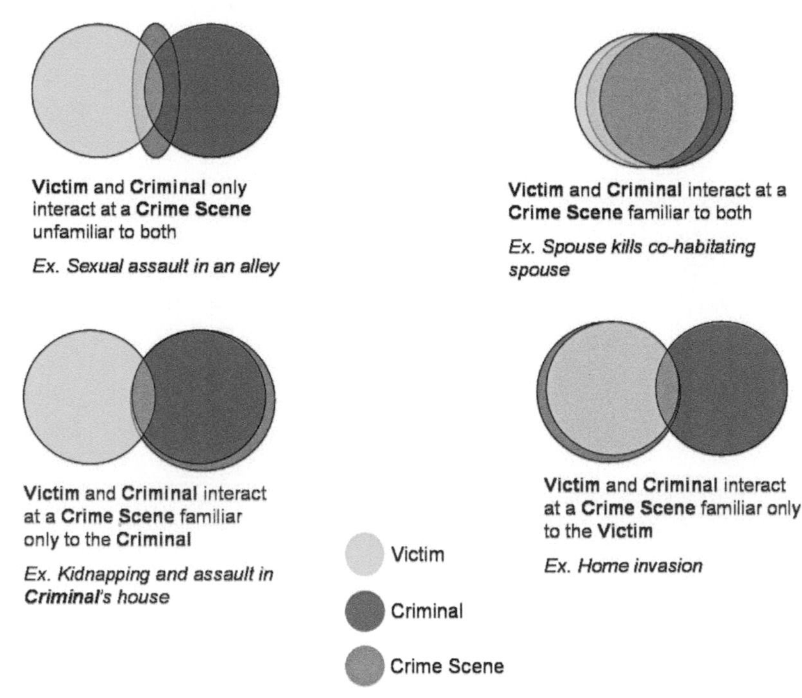

FIGURE 3.4

The significance of the interaction between the victim(s) and the criminal(s) at one or more crime scenes is largely determined by the relationships between the people, places, and things involved. Strangers have a different relationship than do spouses or family members. People who live together have more opportunities to transfer evidence on a regular basis than do strangers. Spouses or sexual partners, being more intimate, would share more information.

been proven for a wide variety of evidence that coincidental matches are extremely rare. The variety of mass-produced goods, consumer choices, economic factors, and other product traits creates a nearly infinite combination of comparable characteristics for the items involved in any one situation. Some kinds of evidence, however, are either quite common, such as white cotton fibers, or have few distinguishing characteristics, such as indigo-dyed cotton from denim fabric. "Common," however, is a word to be used with caution and even then only after a thorough knowledge of how that material is produced, either naturally or artificially and how it varies. Even materials that are thought to be "common" can have a high variance (see Figure 3.5).

It is important to establish the context of the crime and those involved early in the investigation. This sets the stage for what evidence is significant, what methods may be most effective for collection or analysis, and what may be safely ignored. Using context for direction prevents the indiscriminate collection of items that clog the workflow of the forensic science laboratory. Every item collected must be transferred

FIGURE 3.5

Forensic scientists need to learn the details about the materials they study and analyze as evidence—even something perceived to be very common, like sand, can have a wide variation. Top to bottom: Rodeo Beach, Marin County, CA; Agate Beach, OR; Daytona Beach, FL; Bermuda; Sanorini, Greece; Ayers Rock (Uluru), Australia; Sahara Desert, Mauritania; Old Course Beach, St. Andrews, Scotland.

Holman (2009).

to the laboratory and catalogued—at a minimum—and this takes people and time. Evidence collection based on intelligent decision-making, instead of fear of missing something, produces a better result in the laboratory and the courts.

COMPARISON OF EVIDENCE

There are two fundamental processes in the analysis of evidence. The first has already been discussed: identification. Recall that identification is the process of discovering physical and chemical characteristics of evidence with an eye toward putting it into successively smaller classes. The other process is **comparison**. Comparison is done to try to establish the source of evidence. The questioned evidence is compared with objects whose source is known. The goal is to determine whether or not sufficient common physical and/or chemical characteristics exist between the samples. If they do, it can be concluded that an association exists between the questioned and known evidence. The strength of this association depends on a number of factors, including the following:

- Kind of evidence;
- Intra- and inter-sample variation;
- Amount of evidence;
- Location of evidence;
- Transfer and cross-transfer;
- Number of different kinds of evidence associated to one or more sources.

Individualization occurs when at least one unique characteristic is found to exist in both the known and the questioned samples. Individualization cannot be accomplished by identification alone.

CONTROLS

Controls are materials whose source is known and which are used for comparison with unknown evidence. Controls are often used to determine if a chemical test is performing correctly. They may also be used to determine if a substrate where evidence may be found is interfering with a chemical or instrumental test. There are two types of controls: positive and negative.

Consider a case in which some red stains are found on the shirt of a suspect in a homicide. The first question that needs to be answered about these stains is: Are they blood? A number of tests can be performed to determine whether a stain may be blood. Suppose one of these tests is run on some of the stains and the results are *negative*. There are a number of reasons why this might happen:

- The stain isn't blood.
- The stain is blood, but the reagents used to run the test are of poor quality.
- Something in the shirt is interfering with the test.

Before concluding that the stain isn't blood, a number of additional steps could be taken. One might run a different presumptive test and see whether the results change. Another is to run the first test on a sample that is known to be blood and that should yield a positive test. This known blood is a **positive control**. It is a material that is expected to give a positive result with the test reagents and serves to show that the test is working properly. In this case, if the positive control yields a correct result, then it can be presumed that the reagents are working properly and there must be another reason for the negative result obtained on the blood-soaked shirt. It could be proposed that the shirt fibers contain some dye or other material that deactivates the blood test so that it will fail to react with blood. To test this hypothesis, some fibers from the shirt that have absolutely no stains on them could be collected and run the test on them. This would be a **negative control** for the shirt; it is expected that the results of the test would come out negative. If the test results are negative as expected, they could still mean that the shirt contains something that interferes with the test. This presumption could only be verified by running a different test on the stain. Other negative controls can be run on "blank" samples, that is, those prepared similarly to the test materials being used but without any sample present.

If the initial test for blood was done on the stained shirt and came out positive, we should not immediately assume that the stain is definitely blood. A sample of the unstained shirt fibers should be tested as a negative control. A negative result here would mean that the positive result on the stain most likely means that the stain is blood.

What is the consequence of not running a positive or negative control? If a negative control is not used, a **false positive** may be the result; that is, it may be concluded that the stain is blood when it is not. This gives rise to what statisticians call a **Type I error**. Type I errors are serious because they can cause a person to be falsely incriminated in a crime.

Failure to run a positive control can cause a **false negative** result. This can give rise to what is called **Type II error**. This type of error means that a person may be falsely exonerated from a crime that he or she really did commit. Any error is problematic, but from the criminal justice standpoint, a Type II error is less serious than a Type I error. It is better to have someone falsely released than falsely accused. Positive and negative controls are usually easy to obtain and should be used to minimize the chance of errors.

ANALYSIS OF EVIDENCE: SOME PRELIMINARY CONSIDERATIONS

Science is a way of examining the world and learning about it. The process of science, the **scientific method,** is proposing and refining of plausible explanations about any unknown situation. It involves asking and answering questions in a formal way and then drawing conclusions from the answers. Science, through its method, has two hallmarks. The first is the questions that are asked must be testable (or have **testability**). Asking "How many angels can dance on the head of a pin?" or "Why do ghosts haunt this house?" is not scientific because a test cannot be constructed to answer either of these questions. The second hallmark of science is **repeatability**. Science is a public endeavor, and its results are published for many reasons, the most important of which is for other scientists to review the work and determine whether it is sound. If nobody but you can make a particular experiment work, it isn't science. Other scientists must be able to take the same kinds of samples and methods, repeat your experiments, and get the same results for it to be science (see "History: The Method of Science" for a discussion of scientific models).

HISTORY: THE METHOD OF SCIENCE

[An important person in the history of science] was not a scientist at all, but a lawyer who rose to be Lord Chancellor of England in the reign of James I, Elizabeth's successor. His name was Sir Francis Bacon, and in his magnum opus, which he called Novum Organum, he put forth the first theory of the scientific method. In Bacon's view, the scientist should be a disinterested observer of nature, collecting observations with a mind cleansed of harmful preconceptions that might cause error to creep into the scientific record. Once enough such observations have been gathered, patterns will emerge from them, giving rise to truths about nature.

Bacon's idea, that science proceeds through the collection of observations without prejudice, has been rejected by all serious thinkers. Everything about the way we do science—the language we use, the instruments we use, the methods we use—depends on clear presuppositions about how the world works. At the most fundamental level, it is impossible to observe nature without having some reason to choose what is worth observing and what is not worth observing.

In contrast to Bacon, [Sir Karl] Popper believed all science begins with a prejudice, or perhaps more politely, a theory or hypothesis. Popper was deeply influenced by the fact that a theory can never be proved right by agreement with observation, but it can be proved wrong by disagreement with observation. Because of the asymmetry, science makes progress uniquely by proving that good ideas are wrong so that they can be replaced by even better ideas. Thus, Bacon's disinterested observer of nature is replaced by Popper's skeptical theorist.

Popper's ideas…fall short in a number of ways in describing correctly how science works. Although it maybe impossible to prove a theory is true by observation or experiment, it is nearly just as impossible to prove one is false by these same methods. Almost without exception, in order to extract a falsifiable prediction from a theory, it is necessary to make additional assumptions beyond the theory itself. Then, when the prediction turns out to be false, it may well be one of the other assumptions, rather than the theory itself, that is false.

It takes a great deal of hard work to come up with a new theory that is consistent with nearly everything that is known in any area of science. Popper's notion that the scientist's duty is then to attack that theory at its most vulnerable point is fundamentally inconsistent with human nature. It would be impossible to invest the enormous amount of time and energy necessary to develop a new theory in any part of modern science if the primary purpose of all that work was to show that the theory was wrong.

Another towering figure in the twentieth century theory of science is Thomas Kuhn. A paradigm, for Kuhn, is a sort of consensual world view within which scientists work. Within a given paradigm, scientists make steady, incremental progress, doing what Kuhn calls "normal science."

As time goes on, difficulties and contradictions arise that cannot be resolved, but one way or another, they are swept under the rug, rather than be allowed to threaten the central paradigm. However, at a certain point, enough of these difficulties have accumulated so that the situation becomes intolerable. At that point, a scientific revolution occurs, shattering the paradigm and replacing it with an entirely new one.

If a theory makes novel and unexpected predictions, and those predictions are verified by experiments that reveal new and useful or interesting phenomena, then the chances that the theory is correct are greatly enhanced. [However, science] does undergo startling changes of perspective that lead to new and, invariably, better ways of understanding the world. Thus, science does not proceed smoothly and incrementally, but it is one of the few areas of human endeavor that is truly progressive. [Science] is, above all, an adversary process. The scientific debate is very different from what happens in a court of law, but just as in the law, it is crucial that every idea receive the most vigorous possible advocacy, just in case it might be right.

Excerpted from Goodstein, D., 2000. How science works. In: Reference Manual on Scientific Evidence, second ed. Federal Judicial Center, Washington, DC, pp. 67–82.

In the language of science, the particular questions to be tested are called **hypotheses**. Suppose fibers are found on the bed where a victim has been sexually assaulted. Are the fibers those of the victim, the suspect, or someone else? The hypothesis could be framed as follows: "There is a significant difference between the questioned fibers and the known fibers from the suspect's clothes." Notice that the hypothesis is formed as a neutral statement that can be either proven or disproven.

After the hypothesis has been formed, the forensic scientist seeks to collect data that shed light on the hypothesis. Known fibers from the suspect are compared with those from the scene and the victim. All relevant data will be collected without regard to whether it favors the hypothesis. Once collected, the data will be carefully examined to determine what value they have in proving or disproving the hypothesis; this is the **probative value** of the data. If the questioned fibers are analytically indistinguishable from the known fibers, then the hypothesis is rejected. The scientist could then conclude that the questioned fibers could have come from the suspect.

But suppose that *most* of the data suggest that the suspect is the one who left the fibers there, but there are not enough data to associate the fibers to that source. It cannot be said that the hypothesis has been *disproved* (there are some similarities), but neither can it be said that it has been *proved* (some differences exist, but are they significant?). Although a scientist would like to be able to prove unequivocally that the garment is or is not the source of evidence, doing so is not always possible. As previously mentioned not all evidence can be individualized. The important point to note here is that evidence analysis proceeds by forming many hypotheses and perhaps rejecting some as the investigation progresses.

Some preliminary questions must be answered before we even begin to formulate hypotheses. Is there sufficient material to analyze? If the amount of evidence is limited, then choices have to be made about which tests to perform and in what order. The general rule is to perform nondestructive tests first because they conserve material. Most jurisdictions also have evidentiary rules that require that some evidence be kept for additional analyzes by opposing experts; if the entire sample will be consumed in an analysis, then both sides must be informed that not enough evidence will be available to have additional analyzes performed.

If extremely large amounts of material are submitted as evidence, how are they sampled? This situation often happens in drug cases in which, for example, a 50-pound block of marijuana or several kilograms of cocaine are received in one package. The laboratory must have a protocol for sampling large quantities of material so that samples taken are representative of the whole. In other kinds of cases in which this situation occurs, many exhibits may appear to contain the same thing, for example, 100 0.5-ounce packets of white powder. The laboratory and the scientist must decide how many samples to take and what tests to perform. This decision is especially important because the results of the analyzes will ascribe the characteristics of the samples to the whole exhibit, such as identifying 1000 packets of powder as 23% cocaine based on analysis of a fraction of the packets.

What happens in cases in which more than one kind of analysis must be done on the same item of evidence? Consider a handgun received into evidence from a

FIGURE 3.6

Even one small item of evidence can be subjected to multiple examinations and may travel through most of a forensic laboratory. A threat letter, like this one, could pass through bacterial diagnosis, trace evidence, DNA, questioned documents, latent print analysis and content analysis.

© Yahoo News, with permission.

shooting incident; it has red stains and possible fingerprints on it. This means that firearms testing, serology, latent print, and possibly DNA analysis must be performed on the handgun. These analyzes should be put into an order such that one exam does not spoil or preclude the subsequent exam(s). In this case, the order should be first serology, then latent print, and finally firearms testing.

It is important to note that one seemingly small piece of evidence can be subjected to many examinations. Consider the example of a threatening letter, as depicted in Figure 3.6, one that supposedly contains anthrax or some other contagion. The envelope and the letter could be subjected to the following exams, in order:

- *Disease diagnosis*, to determine if it really contains the suspected contagion;
- *Trace evidence*, for hairs or fibers in the envelope or stuck to the adhesives (stamp, closure, tape used to seal it);
- *DNA*, from saliva on the stamp or the envelope closure;
- *Questioned documents*, for the paper, lettering and other aspects of the form of the letter;
- *Ink analysis*, to determine what was used to write the message, address, etc.;
- *Handwriting*, *typewriter*, or *printer analysis*, as appropriate;
- *Latent fingerprints*;
- *Content analysis*, to evaluate the nature of the writer's intent and other investigative clues.

In this example, the ordering of the exams is crucial to ensure not only the integrity of the evidence, but also the safety of the scientists and their co-workers. Other evidence can also be very, very large—ocean currents, for example (see "In More Detail: Rubber Duckies and Human Remains"). It is important to realize that *anything* can become evidence and forensic scientists must keep open minds if they are to solve the most difficult of crimes.

IN MORE DETAIL: RUBBER DUCKIES AND HUMAN REMAINS

In January 1992, a container ship en route from Hong Kong to America encountered a storm, and several containers broke free from their moorings and dropped into the water. At least one, containing 29,000 plastic bath toys, split open. Drifting at the whim of the wind and ocean currents, the ducks, along with red beavers, green frogs and blue turtles, moved up the western coast of North America, crossed the waters of the North Pole and headed toward the United Kingdom, as shown in Figure 3.7.

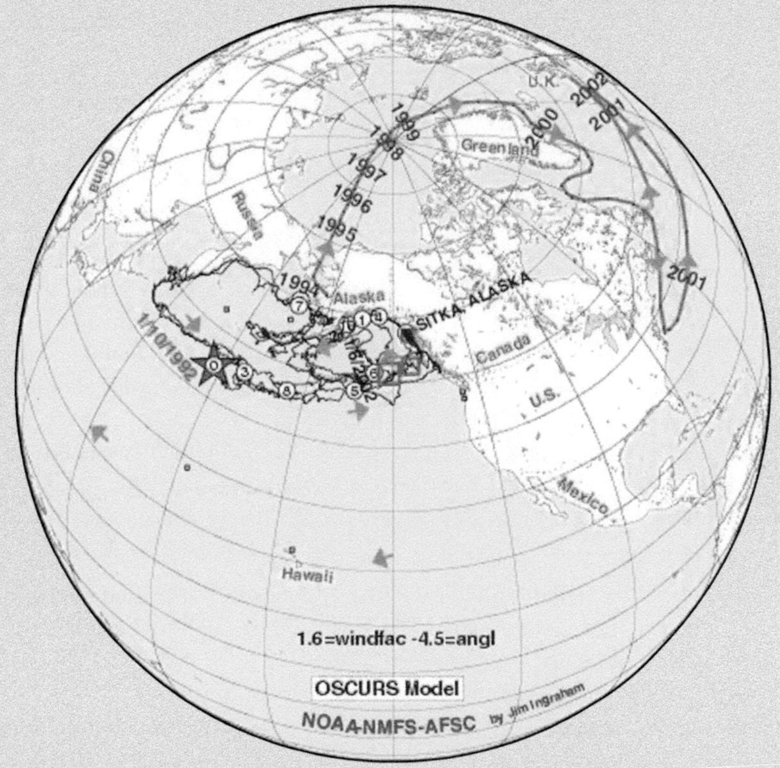

FIGURE 3.7

Calculated drifts of bathtub toys lost at sea. Even seemingly obscure information like this can be of use in solving crimes and finding victims.

C. Ebbesmeyer, with permission.

(Continued)

IN MORE DETAIL: RUBBER DUCKIES AND HUMAN REMAINS—cont'd

Oddly, very little is known about how winds and currents move drifting objects. Two scientists, Curtis Ebbesmeyer, an oceanographer in Seattle, and James Ingraham, a scientist at the National Marine Fisheries Service, carefully recorded each reported sighting of the plastic toys to better understand the phenomena. Beachcombers reported sightings of finds to http://beachcombersalert.org/, and the data were entered into Ingraham's ocean modeling program, OSCUR (**O**cean **S**urface **C**urrents **S**imulation). OSCUR uses air pressure metrics dating back to 1967 to calculate wind speed, direction, and surface currents. The floating toy finds helped the scientists to check and improve the performance of OSCUR.

Ebbesmeyer and Ingraham have tracked the journeys of everything from toy cars, balloons, ice hockey gloves, even five million pieces of Lego, all lost from ships over the years. They even processed data from 33,000 Nike shoes that fell off a ship near California. OSCUR estimated a landing for about 1600 of the shoes (roughly 2% of the dunked shoes)—this is as accurate an estimate as that of oceanographers who deliberately release objects to measure currents.

But are cute bath toys and scientific ingenuity *forensic*? Using OSCUR, Ebbesmeyer predicted the final resting place of George Karn, a crewman lost from the *Galaxy*, a freezer longliner that caught Pacific cod with miles of baited hooks, which sunk in the Bering Sea in 2002. Starting from the location of the *Galaxy's* sinking, the model ran forward in time and came up with a location—an island 430 nautical miles southwest of the disaster. On June 9, 2003, while working at Portage Bite, a seldom-visited site on Tanaga Island far west in the Aleutians and 1400 nautical miles due north of Hawaii's Midway Island, a beachcomber spotted a lower jawbone—the extensive dental work told him it was human. Upon subsequent search of the area, an orange survival suit was discovered. State troopers traced the suit's serial number to the *Galaxy*. Karn's body drifted in an unusual way, possibly leading to his delayed discovery. The two calculated where Karn would have drifted if lost on the same day (October 20) of each year from 1967 to 2002. These drifts terminate after 3.5 months, the time interval between the disaster and Tanaga Island. All but 3 of the 36 drifts headed west toward Siberia, nearly the opposite direction of where Karn drifted. If George had perished in most years except 2002, he would have drifted west toward Kamchatka and then south into the wide North Pacific, never to be found.

SUMMARY

Anything can be submitted for scientific analysis in an investigation, becoming the samples that yield data for forensic scientists to interpret. As evidence, however, these samples and data follow different rules than in other scientific, non-forensic laboratories. The context of the evidence is central to how it is analyzed and interpreted in the reconstruction of the criminal events. The scientific method still applies, however, and forensic scientists still employ that approach as do other non-forensic scientists. These differences and similarities will follow forensic scientists into the courtroom and either support, if done well, or weaken, if done poorly, the fruits of their scientific labors.

TEST YOUR KNOWLEDGE

1. What is a "trier-of-fact?"
2. What is evidence?
3. Name four kinds of evidence.

4. What is exculpatory evidence?
5. What are "proxy data?"
6. How is direct transfer different from indirect transfer? Give an example.
7. What is persistence in relation to evidence?
8. Is contamination evidence? Why or why not?
9. What is class-level evidence?
10. What does it mean to identify something?
11. What is a "common source?"
12. If you have individualized two pieces of evidence, how many common sources could they have come from?
13. What is the difference between questioned and known evidence?
14. What is a control? How is it different from known evidence?
15. What is the probative value of an item of evidence?
16. What is the difference between a Type I and a Type II error?
17. What are the two hallmarks of science?
18. What is a cross-transfer?
19. Name three ways an association between a questioned and known item can be strengthened.
20. Name three ways an association between a questioned and known item can be weakened.

CONSIDER THIS...

1. How do transfer and persistence relate? How would this relationship affect the collection of evidence? What would be the difference in processing a crime scene 1 h after the crime and 48 h afterward?
2. Why is context important to forensic science? How does this determine what evidence should be collected and analyzed?
3. Why is forensic science a historical science? Does this make it inferior to non-historical sciences? What are the limits of historical sciences?

BIBLIOGRAPHY AND FURTHER READING

Champod, C., 2013. Overview and meaning of identification/individualization. In: Siegel, J., Saukko, P. (Eds.), Encyclopedia of Forensic Sciences, second ed. Elsevier, Amsterdam, pp. 303–309.

Collins, H.M., Pinch, T., 1998. The Golem: What You Should Know about Science. Cambridge University Press, Cambridge, UK.

Crispino, F., Houck, M., 2013. Principles of forensic science. In: Siegel, J., Saukko, P. (Eds.), Encyclopedia of Forensic Sciences, second ed. Elsevier, Amsterdam, pp. 278–281.

Dawson, P., Han, I., Cox, M., Black, C., Simmons, L., 2007. Residence time and food contact time effects on transfer of *Salmonella typhimurium* from tile, wood and carpet: testing the five second rule. Journal of Applied Microbiology 102, 945–953.

Federal Judicial Center, 2000. Reference Manual on Scientific Evidence, second ed. Washington, DC.

Goodstein, D., 2000. How Science Works. Reference Manual on Scientific Evidence, second ed. Federal Judicial Center, Washington, DC. pp. 67–82.

Garner, B.A. (Ed.), Black's Law Dictionary 2000, seventh ed. West Group, St. Paul, MN.

Holman, R., 2009. Many worlds in tiny grains. Science 323, 1291.

Houck, M., 2013a. Interpretation/the comparative method. In: Siegel, J., Saukko, P. (Eds.), Encyclopedia of Forensic Sciences, second ed. Elsevier, Amsterdam, pp. 314–317.

Houck, M., 2013b. Forensic classification of evidence. In: Siegel, J., Saukko, P. (Eds.), Encyclopedia of Forensic Sciences, second ed. Elsevier, Amsterdam. pp. 318–317.

Locard, E., 1930. Analysis of dust traces. American Journal of Police Science 1 (3), 276–298.

McGee, H., May 9, 2007. The Five-Second Rule Explored, or How Dirty Is that Bologna? New York Times. page F3.

Millen, P., 2013. Contamination. In: Siegel, J., Saukko, P. (Eds.), Encyclopedia of Forensic Sciences, second ed. Elsevier, Amsterdam, pp. 337–340.

Ou, C., Ciesielski, C.A., Myers, G., Bandea, C.I., Luo, C., Korber, B.T.M., Mullins, J.I., Schochetman, G., Berkelman, R.L., Economou, A.N., Witte, J.J., Furman, L.J., Satten, G.A., MacInnes, K.A., Curran, J.W., Jaffe, H.W., Laboratory Investigation Group, Epidemiologic Investigation Group, 1992. Molecular epidemiology of HIV transmission in a dental practice. Science 256, 1165–1171.

Poole, F., 2013. Collection and chain of evidence. In: Siegel, J., Saukko, P. (Eds.), Encyclopedia of Forensic Sciences, second ed. Elsevier, Amsterdam, pp. 333–336.

Pounds, C.A., Smalldon, K.W., 1975. The transfer of fibres between clothing materials during simulated contacts and their persistence during wear, Part II—fibre persistence. Journal of the Forensic Science Society 15, 29–37.

Rose, S., Schlager, N., 2003. How Things Are Made: From Automobiles to Zippers. Black Dog, London.

Schullar, Y., Crispino, F., 2013. Semiotics, heuristics, and inferences used by forensic scientists. In: Siegel, J., Saukko, P. (Eds.), Encyclopedia of Forensic Sciences, second ed. Elsevier, Amsterdam, pp. 310–313.

Schum, D.A., 1994. Evidential Foundations of Probabilistic Reasoning. John Wiley and Sons, New York.

Thornton, J.I., 1986. Ensembles of subclass characteristics in physical evidence examination. Journal of Forensic Sciences 31 (2), 501–503.

Zobel, H.B., 1996. The Boston Massacre. W.W. Norton, New York City.

PART

Analytical Tools

2

CHAPTER

Microscopy

4

CHAPTER OUTLINE

KEY TERMS

- Achromatic objectives
- Analyzer
- Anisotropic
- Apochromats
- Astigmatism
- Binocular
- Birefringence
- Chromatic aberration
- Compound magnification system
- Condenser
- Condenser diaphragm
- Coverslips
- Critical illumination
- Curvature of field
- Empty magnification

- Eyepiece
- Field diaphragm
- Field of view
- Fluorescence
- Fluorites
- Fluorophores
- Focal length
- Focus
- Infinity-corrected lens systems
- Isotropic
- Köhler illumination
- Lens
- Mechanical stage
- Monocular
- Mountants
- Mounting media
- Numerical aperture
- Objective
- Ocular
- Phosphorescence
- Plan achromats
- Polarization colors
- Polarizer
- Polarizing light microscope
- Real image
- Resolution
- Rotating stage
- Semi-apochromats
- Simple magnification system
- Snell's Law
- Spherical aberration
- Stage
- Tube length
- Virtual image

INTRODUCTION

The microscope is a nearly universal symbol of science, representing our ability to explore the world below the limits of our perception. Forensic science is equally well represented by the microscope; illustrations in Sir Arthur Conan Doyle's Sherlock

Holmes stories show the great detective peering through a microscope at some minute evidence. As Dr Peter DeForest (2002, p. 217) has stated, "Good criminalistic technique demands the effective use of the microscope."

The microscope may seem to be a relic of an antiquated age of science when compared with some of today's advanced instrumentation. But, as the life's work of Dr Walter McCrone and others has shown, microscopy is applicable to every area of forensic science (see Table 4.1). Microscopy can be as powerful as many current technologies and, in some cases, more powerful. For example, microscopy can easily distinguish between cotton and rayon textile fibers, whereas to an infrared spectrometer they both appear to be cellulose.

Forensic microscopy is more than simply looking at small things. It requires the student (and the expert) to know a great deal about many things, how they are made, how they are used, and their physical and chemical natures. Chamot and Mason, in their classic text *Handbook of Chemical Microscopy, Volume I*, succinctly describe the role of the forensic (or technical, in their words) microscopist:

> *The technical microscopist is concerned with form, but also with formation and function. He needs to know, as completely as possible, the existing structure of the specimen, but he frequently has to investigate or at least postulate how that structure developed or was produced, how it can be controlled, and how it affects performance. The correlation of these three aspects of his studies is too specific to the material involved to be dealt with here .... But even descriptive microscopy often requires more than superficial observation, or the ordinary arts of varying focus and illumination that experience makes habitual. And there are many properties closely governing non-microscopical behaviour that can be usefully explored, as a background for understanding it and as an adjunct to tests on a larger scale.*
>
> **(1940, 1958, p. 173)**

Table 4.1 Microscopy Has Nearly Unlimited Application to Forensic Sciences

Art forgeries	Minerals
Asbestos	Paint
Building materials	Paper
Bullets	Photographic analysis
Chemistry	Pollen
Drugs	Polymers
Dust	Product tampering
Fibers	Questioned documents
Fingerprints	Serology
Food poisoning	Soil
Glass	Tapes
Hairs	Toolmarks
Handwriting	Wood

A full explanation of microscopy and the optical principles involved is beyond the scope of this book; the physics and geometry get complicated. Additional details will be listed throughout this chapter, but only the core information necessary for an understanding of the fundamentals of microscopy will be presented. For a fuller treatment of the optical theory of microscopy, see DeForest (2002) or McCrone et al. (1978).

MAGNIFICATION SYSTEMS

To see more detail in an object—a postage stamp, for example—the image needs to be magnified as shown in Figure 4.1. The easiest way to do this is with a common pocket magnifier or hand lens; this is a **simple magnification system**, a single lens used to form an enlarged image of an object. A similar system is used to project the image of a 35-mm slide or transparency in a lecture hall. If the screen where the focused image is projected was removed and, say, a hand lens was put in its place, a second, larger image, as shown in Figure 4.2, would be produced. This is the basic principle of all microscopy—a **compound magnification system**, where magnification occurs in two stages and the total magnification is the product of the magnification of the first lens and the second lens. The observer looks at the first image with a lens that produces an enlarged image called a **virtual image**. This is the image the eye perceives—a real, projectable image does

FIGURE 4.1

To see more detail in an object, here a postage stamp, the image must be magnified. This is accomplished with a simple hand lens, which enlarges the image 10 times, or 10×.

FIGURE 4.2

In a compound magnification system, magnification occurs in two stages, and the total magnification is the product of the first lens and the second lens. So, a 10× lens and a 4× lens would produce a 40× image (10 × 4 = 40), or one that has been magnified 40 times. The observer looks at the first image with a lens that produces an enlarged image called a "virtual image." This is the image the eye perceives and is visible only as a result of the compound magnification system.

not exist where the virtual image appears to be—and is visible only as a result of the compound magnification system. A more commonplace example of a virtual image is that seen in a mirror: Standing 2 ft away from the mirror, our image in the mirror looks as if it is standing 2 ft away from the other side of the mirror. Where a white screen or glass plate substituted for the mirror, no image would be visible. In contrast, a **real image** is the one that could be seen *on* the screen—that is, projected *onto* the screen.

THE LENS

Most people are familiar with the lenses in our daily lives: eyeglasses, reading magnifiers, and the like. In microscopy, a **lens** means a very specific thing: a translucent material that bends light in a known and predictable manner. For example, an ideal converging lens causes all light entering the lens from one side of the lens to meet again at a point on the other side of the lens, as shown in Figure 4.3. In doing so, an image of the original object is produced.

The size and position of an image produced by a lens can be determined through geometry based on the **focal length** of the lens, which is the distance between the two points of focus on either side of the lens, as shown in Figure 4.4. Focal length is important in microscopy because it determines much of the image quality. Think of it this way: If one eye is too far or too close, it is difficult to see a clear image of an object. Why? Human

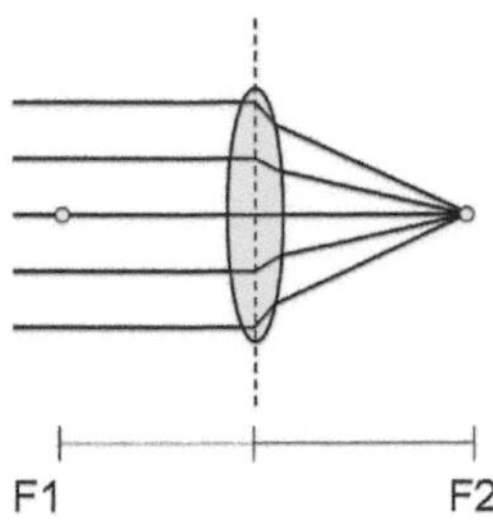

FIGURE 4.3

An ideal converging lens causes light entering it from one side to meet again (converge) at a point on the other side of the lens.

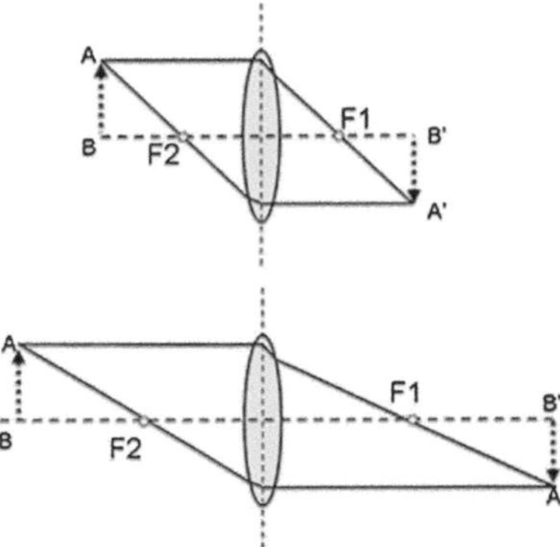

FIGURE 4.4

The focal length is the distance from the two focal points (F1 and F2) of a lens. F2 sits on a plane where the image will appear to be in focus when the object being viewed is at F1.

eyes, being curved, cannot maintain a clear point of focus for all distances: About 10 in or 25 cm is the distance that a human eye can easily distinguish between two objects next to each other. Lenses are made using this "ideal" viewing distance, or focal length.

At 25 cm, the **resolution**, or the minimum distance two objects can be separated and still be seen as two objects, of the human eye is between 0.15 and 0.30 mm. Therefore, this is the limit of human eyes without assistance; if better resolution is required (that is, to see more detail in the postage stamp), the image must be magnified. If a hand lens magnifies an image 4 times (the shorthand for this is "4×"), then the viewer will be able to resolve two objects that are about 0.05 mm apart (for the math used to obtain this value, see "In More Detail: Why Resolution Is More Important Than Magnification"). Magnification with one lens cannot continue indefinitely, however. As magnification *increases*, lens diameter *decreases* to bend the light more to make a larger image. A simple lens that magnifies 1000× would be only 0.12 mm in diameter! Therefore, about 10× to 15× is the practical limit of magnification for simple lenses.

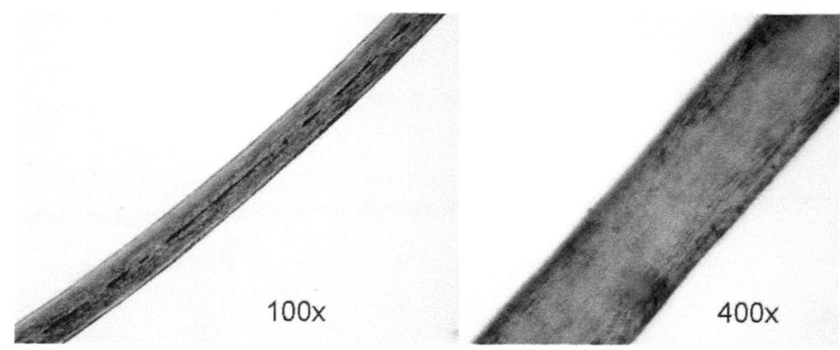

FIGURE 4.5

Empty magnification results from an increase in magnification without an increase in resolution.

COMPOUND MAGNIFYING SYSTEMS

A compound microscope, as the name implies, employs a magnification system that exceeds the limits imposed by simple lenses. A second lens is placed in line with the first lens, and this further enlarges the image. The total magnification of the microscope is the product of the two lenses. A 10× lens and a 4× lens would produce a 40× image (10 × 4 = 40), or one that has been magnified 40 times. Lenses of up to 40× can be used in a compound microscope, and higher magnifications are possible with special lenses.

Even lenses in compound microscopes have resolution limits, however, and it is possible to continue to magnify an image but not improve its resolution—this is called **empty magnification**. The result of empty magnification is a larger but fuzzier looking image, as shown in Figure 4.5.

THE MICROSCOPE

The fundamental design of the microscope has not changed much since its original invention; improvements to nearly every component, however, have made even the most inexpensive microscopes suitable for basic applications. In this section, refer to Figure 4.6 for a diagram of the important parts of a microscope.

Starting at the top, the **eyepiece** or **ocular** is the lens that the observer looks into when viewing an object microscopically. A microscope may be **monocular**, having one eyepiece, or **binocular**, having two eyepieces; most microscopes found in laboratories today are binocular. Many microscopes today are trinocular; they have an eyepiece that accommodates a video or digital camera. Typically, the eyepiece(s) will have a magnification of 10× and may be focusable; this allows the viewer to adjust the eyepieces if one eye is stronger than the other. The area seen when looking through the eyepieces is called the **field of view** and will change if the specimen is moved or the magnification is changed.

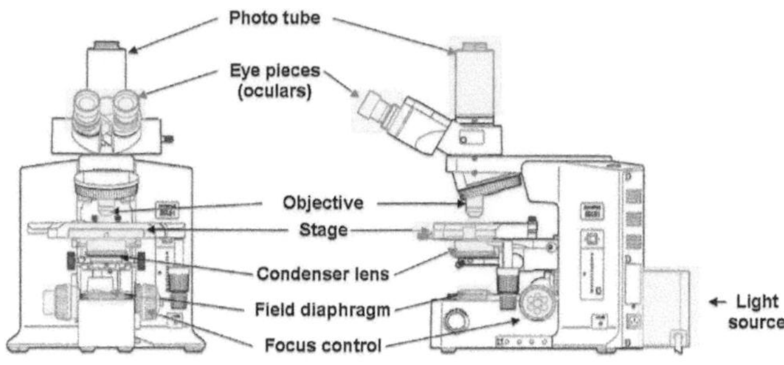

FIGURE 4.6

The various parts of the microscope.

Courtesy Olympus USA.

FIGURE 4.7

The objective lens, so called because it is closest to the object or specimen being viewed. The objective is the most important part of the microscope and comes in many types and magnifications. The information on the lens is very specific: "10×" is the magnification, "0.25 na" is the numerical aperture, "170 mm" is the tube length (some objectives are now infinity-corrected and are labeled "∞"), and "0.17 mm" is the recommended thickness of cover slip to use.

The next lens in the microscope is called the objective lens (or just the **objective**) because it is closest to the object or specimen being studied. The objective is the most important part of the microscope. Objectives come in many types (see "In More Detail: Lens Corrections") and magnifications (typically, 4×, 10×, 15×, 20× and 25×; higher magnifications are possible). Each objective will have information about it engraved into its body in a specific format, as shown in Figure 4.7. Although the information may vary by manufacturer, objectives will usually have the magnification, the numerical aperture (NA), the tube length, and the thickness of coverslip that

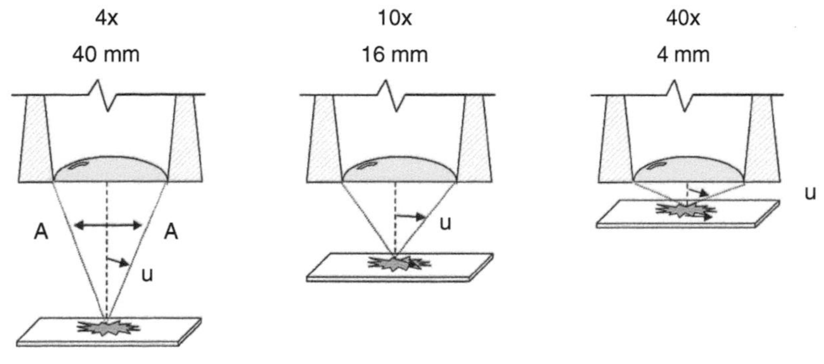

FIGURE 4.8

The numerical aperture is an angular measure of the lens' light-gathering ability. It is an indication of the lens' resolving power.

should be used with the objective. The **numerical aperture** is an angular measure of the lens's light-gathering ability and, ultimately, its resolving quality, as shown in Figure 4.8 (see "In More Detail: Why Resolution Is More Important Than Magnification"). The **tube length** is the distance from the lowest part of the objective to the upper edge of the eyepiece; this has been standardized at 160 mm in modern microscopes. Because the tube length determines where the in-focus image will appear, objectives must be designed and constructed for a specific tube length (however, read about "infinity-corrected" lenses in "In More Detail: Lens Corrections"). **Coverslips**, the thin glass plates that are placed on top of mounted specimens, protect the specimen and the objective from damage. They come in a range of thicknesses measured in millimeters (0.17 mm, for example). All of this information is important to the microscopist's proper use of a particular objective.

IN MORE DETAIL: WHY RESOLUTION IS MORE IMPORTANT THAN MAGNIFICATION

In the card game of microscopy, numerical aperture (NA) always trumps magnification. This short aside should provide a better understanding of why that is so.

The minimum distance d which must exist between two separate points in the specimen in order for them to be seen as two distinct points is

$$d = \lambda/2\text{NA}$$

or the wavelength of light divided by twice the NA. The NA is further defined as

$$\text{NA} = n \text{ sine } u$$

where n represents the refractive index (RI) of the medium between the coverslip and the front lens, and u is half the angle of aperture of the objective (refer to Figure 4.8). The RI of air is 1.0; practically speaking, this means the NA of any lens system with air as the intermediate medium (so-called dry systems; other systems use oil as the intermediate medium, improving their NA) will be less than 1 because half of the angle u in air cannot be more than 90°.

(Continued)

IN MORE DETAIL: WHY RESOLUTION IS MORE IMPORTANT THAN MAGNIFICATION—cont'd

The resolving power of the human eye or the objective lens is not enough for a magnification of, say, 10,000×, because two points on the object can be seen as separate only if the distance between them is within the limit of the resolving power. If the distance is below the resolving power, then two objects would not be visible; if it were higher, only two (and not several) points would be visible with no more detail than before. The maximum useful magnification available is about 1000 times the NA of the objective.

Source: *Davidson and Abromowitz (2005).*

IN MORE DETAIL: LENS CORRECTIONS

Achromatic objectives are the least expensive objectives, and they are found on most microscopes. These objectives are designed to be corrected for **chromatic aberration**, where white light from the specimen is broken out into multiple colored images at various distances from the lens. Achromats are corrected for red and blue only, and this can lead to substantial artefacts, such as colored halos. Because of this, it may be necessary to use a green filter and employ black-and-white film for photomicrography.

A simple lens focuses a flat specimen on a microscope slide onto the lens, a rounded surface. This results in an aberration called **curvature of field** and results in only part of the image being in focus. Regular achromats lack correction for flatness of field, but recently most manufacturers have started offering flat-field corrections for achromat objectives, called **plan achromats**.

Astigmatism or **spherical aberration** results from a lens not being properly spherical. This makes specimen images seem to be "pulled" in one direction when focusing through it. Most modern microscope objectives are corrected for spherical aberration.

A step up in corrected lenses is **fluorites** or **semi-apochromats**, so called because the mineral fluorite was the original method used for correction. Fluorites are also corrected for spherical aberration, where the light passing near the center of the lens is less refracted than the light at the edge of the lens. Fluorite objectives are now made with advanced glass formulations that contain fluorspar or synthetic substitutes. These materials give fluorites a higher numerical aperture (NA), better resolution, and higher contrast. The cost for fluorite objectives, of course, is higher than that for achromats.

The most highly corrected objectives are the **apochromats**, which contain several internal lenses that have different thicknesses and curvatures in a specific configuration unique to apochromats. Apochromats are corrected for three colors (red, green, and blue) and, thus, have almost no chromatic aberration. They are very costly but provide even better NA and resolution than fluorites.

In the past decade, major microscope manufacturers have all migrated to **infinity-corrected lens systems**. In a typical microscope, the tube length (distance from the top of the eyepiece to the bottom of the objective) is set to 160 mm, but in these systems, the image distance is set to infinity, and a lens is placed within the tube between the objective and the eyepieces to produce the intermediate image. Infinity-corrected lens systems produce very high-quality images and allow for the addition of a variety of analytical components to the microscope. More information on infinity-corrected lenses and microscopy can be found on the Web at www.microscopyu.com.

The microscope **stage** is the platform where the specimen sits during viewing. The stage can be moved up or down to **focus** the specimen image, meaning that portion of the specimen in the field of view is sitting in the same horizontal plane; typically, stages are equipped with a coarse and fine focus. Stages may be **mechanical** (that is, having knobs for control of movement), **rotating** (able to spin in 360° but not move back and forth), or both.

The **condenser** is used to obtain a bright, even field of view and improve image resolution. Condensers are lenses below the stage that focus or condense the light onto the specimen field of view. Condensers also have their own **condenser diaphragm** control to eliminate excess light and adjust for contrast in the image. The condenser diaphragm is different from the **field diaphragm**, a control that allows more or less light into the lens system of the microscope.

The illumination of the microscope is critical to a quality image and is more complicated than merely turning on a light bulb. Two main types of illumination are used in microscopy, critical and Köhler. **Critical illumination** concentrates the light on the specimen with the condenser lens; this produces an intense lighting that highlights edges but may be uneven. **Köhler illumination**, named after August Köhler in 1893, sets the light rays parallel throughout the lens system, allowing them to evenly illuminate the specimen. Köhler illumination is considered the standard setup for microscopic illumination (Davidson and Abromowitz, 2005).

REFRACTIVE INDEX

The refraction of visible light is an important characteristic of lenses that allows them to focus a beam of light onto a single point. Refraction (or bending of the light) occurs as light passes from one medium to another when there is a difference in the index of refraction between the two materials, and it is responsible for a variety of familiar phenomena such as the apparent distortion of objects partially submerged in water.

Refractive index (RI) is defined as the relative speed at which light moves through a material with respect to its speed in a vacuum. By convention, the RI of a vacuum is defined as having a value of 1.0. The index of refraction, N (or n), of other transparent materials is defined through the equation

$$N = C/v$$

where C is the speed of light and v is the velocity of light in that material. Because the RI of a vacuum is defined as 1.0 and a vacuum is devoid of any material, the refractive indices of all transparent materials are therefore greater than 1.0. For most practical purposes, the RI of light through air (1.0008) can be used to calculate refractive indices of unknown materials. Refractive indices of some common materials are presented in Table 4.2.

Table 4.2 The Refractive Indices of Several Materials

Material	Refractive Index
Air	1.0008
Water	1.330
Ice	1.310
Glass, soda lime	1.510
Diamond	2.417
Ruby	1.760

When light passes from a less dense medium (such as air) to a more dense medium (such as water), the speed of the wave decreases. Alternatively, when light passes from a more dense medium (water) to a less dense medium (air), the speed of the wave increases. The angle of refracted light is dependent on both the angle of incidence and the composition of the material into which it is entering. The *normal* is defined as a line perpendicular to the boundary between two substances. Light will pass into the boundary at an angle to the surface and will be refracted according to **Snell's Law**:

$$N_1 \times \sin(q_1) = N_2 \times \sin(q_2)$$

In this equation, N represents the refractive indices of material 1 and material 2 and q are the angles of light traveling through these materials with respect to the normal. There are several important points that can be drawn from this equation. When $N(1)$ is greater than $N(2)$, the angle of refraction is always larger than the angle of incidence. Alternatively, when $N(2)$ is greater than $N(1)$, the angle of refraction is always smaller than the angle of incidence. When the two refractive indices are equal ($N(1) = N(2)$), then the light is passed through without refraction. The concept of RI is illustrated in Figure 4.9 for the case of light passing from air through both glass and

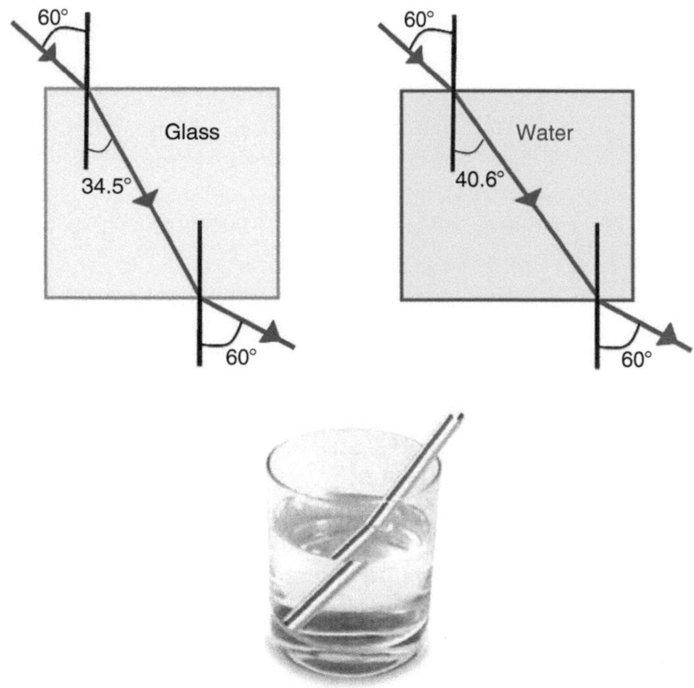

FIGURE 4.9

Samples to be viewed microscopically must be mounted in a material that has a refractive index (RI) near their own. If the RI of the sample and the mountant are too different, like this straw in water (RI = 1.33), then optical distortion results. The RI of glass is about 6° more than that for water, meaning that a light ray gets bent more passing through glass than water.

water. Notice that while both beams enter the more dense material through the same angle of incidence with respect to the normal (60°), the refraction for glass is almost 6° more than that for water due to the higher RI of glass.

Samples to be viewed in transmitted light must be in a material with a RI that is close to their own. Numerous materials are commercially available to use as **mounting media** or **mountants**. The RI of water is about 1.33 and therefore makes a poor mounting medium because it refracts the light so much less than a hair, which has a RI of about 1.5.

POLARIZED LIGHT MICROSCOPY

One of the most powerful tools forensic scientists have at their disposal is the **polarizing light microscope**, a tool of nearly infinite uses and applications. Sadly, in this age of computerized instrumentation, few scientists routinely use a polarized light microscope, or PLM. Something can be learnt about almost every kind of sample, from asbestos to zircon, by using PLM. The PLM exploits optical properties of materials to discover details about the structure and composition of materials, and these lead to its identification and characterization.

Materials fall into one of two categories. The first are materials that demonstrate the same optical properties in all directions, such as gases, liquids, and certain glasses and crystals. These are **isotropic** materials. Because they are optically the same in all directions, they have only one RI. Light, therefore, passes through them at the same speed with no directional restrictions.

The second category is **anisotropic** materials, which have optical properties that vary with the orientation of the incoming light and the optical structure of the material. About 90% of all solid materials are anisotropic. The RIs vary in anisotropic materials depending both on the direction of the incident light and on the optical structure. Think of anisotropic materials as having a "grain," like wood, with preferential orientations, as illustrated in Figure 4.10.

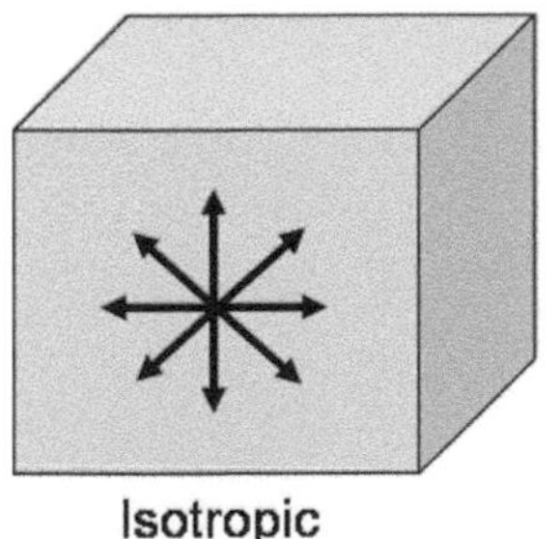

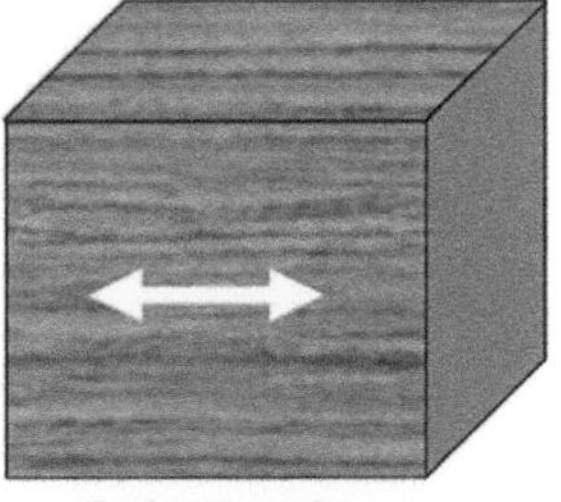

FIGURE 4.10

Isotropic materials have the same optical properties in all directions, whereas anisotropic ones have differing properties based on the incident light and the internal structure of the material. Anisotropic materials can be envisioned as having a "grain."

Because of their inhomogeneous internal structure, anisotropic materials divide light rays into two parts. PLM uses this to cause the light rays to interact in a way that yields information about the material. Light is emitted from a source in all directions; in the wave model of light, all directions of vibration are equally possible. If the light passes through a special filter, called a **polarizer**, then the only light that passes is that which vibrates in that "preferred" direction; light that vibrates in only one direction is called polarized light (see Figure 4.11). Human eyes are "blind" to the vibrational direction of light; it can be seen only by a color effect or by intensity. This may sound complicated, but chances are good that most people have seen polarized light—through polarized sunglasses! They reduce the glare, like off of a car hood on a sunny day, by filtering out all the light except for that which is traveling in the direction preferred by the orientation of the treated sunglass lens.

All light that reflects off a flat surface is at least partially polarized. The easiest way to visualize polarization is to imagine a wave vibrating perpendicular to the direction in which it's traveling. The light can move in two directions or vectors (the x and y components). In this simple example, assume the two components have exactly the same frequency (occurrence over time). The x and y components can differ in two other ways. The two components may differ in amplitude, and the two components may not have the same phase (they may not hit their peaks and troughs at the same time). When the shape is traced as the light wave, the light's polarization state can be described as illustrated in Figure 4.11.

A PLM uses two polarizing filters (or polarizers, sometimes called "polars," for short), one called the "polarizer" (that's obvious, isn't it?) and the "analyzer" (for reasons that will become obvious). The polarizer sits beneath the stage and has its

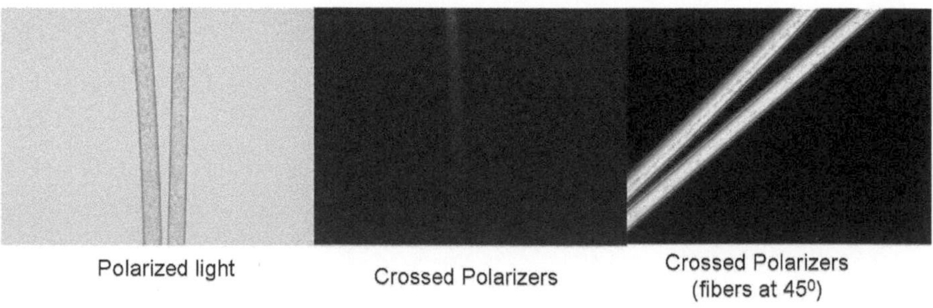

FIGURE 4.11

Because of the orientation of the polarizing filter, only light rays that are in line with its orientation can pass through. This is how polarized sunglasses work, by filtering out scattered light rays and allowing only certain ones through. When the preferred orientations of the filters, sometimes called "polars," are at right angles to each other, no light can pass through. Varying degrees of rotation will allow progressively more light through until the polars are aligned.

Wikipedia, retrieved from www.wikipedia.com, with permission.

preferred vibration direction set left-to-right (sometimes called the "east–west"). The **analyzer**, aligned opposite to that of the polarizer (i.e., north–south), is located above the objectives; the analyzer can be manually slid into or out of the light path. If the analyzer is inserted with its orientation opposite to that of the polarizer (at right angles), what should be seen? Nothing. The filters are said to be crossed, and no light can pass through the microscope to the viewer's eyes. The field of view appears black or very, very dark, as shown in Figure 4.12. Information can be obtained both in plane-polarized light (only the polarizer in place) or with crossed polarizers (polarizer *and* analyzer in place).

Anisotropic materials split light into component light rays. **Birefringence** is the result of this division of light into at least two rays (the ordinary ray and the extraordinary ray) when it passes through certain types of material, depending on the polarization of the light. Two different refractive indices are assigned to the material for different polarization orientations (rotating the sample under the polarizing filter). Birefringence is quantified by

$$\Delta n = n_e - n_o$$

where n_o is the RI for the ordinary ray and n_e is the RI for the extraordinary ray.

The difference in velocity of the ordinary and extraordinary rays is called retardation and increases linearly with both the thickness of a specimen and with the birefringence. The greater the thickness, the greater the retardation (the thicker the specimen, the farther one ray lags behind the other) and the greater the difference between the refractive indices (that is, the higher the birefringence) to begin with, the greater the retardation. This can be related in an equation

$$r = t(n_2 - n_1)$$

where r is retardation, t is thickness, and $n_2 - n_1$ is birefringence.

FIGURE 4.12

When an anisotropic material is placed under crossed polarizers and rotated on the optical axis of the microscope, **polarization colors** result. (left) A grain of sillimanite, a mineral component found in a soil sample from a crime scene *(Academic Press, by permission).* (middle, right) A section of brass metal with a fracture in polarized light and under cross-polarizers *(Carl Zeiss, with permission).*

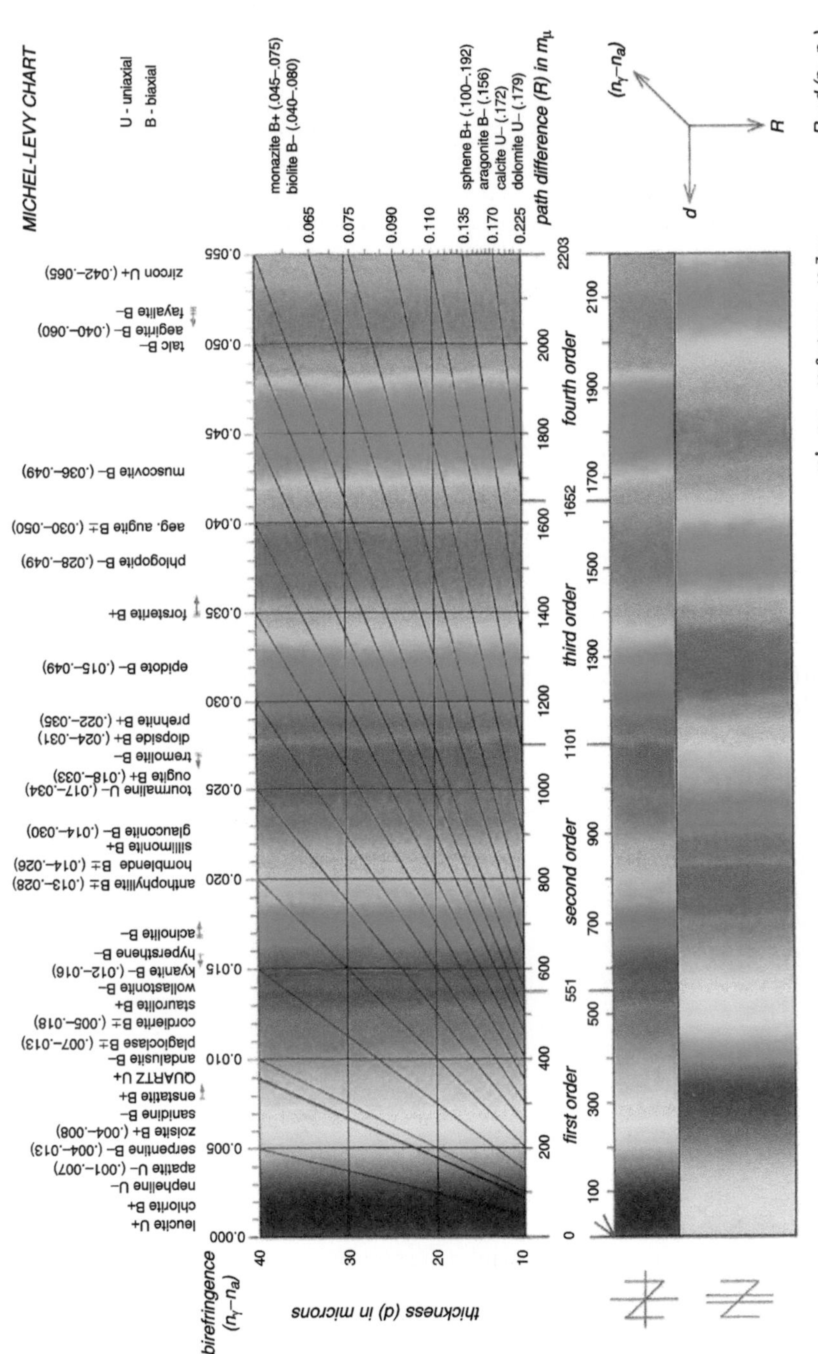

FIGURE 4.13

The Michel-Levy Chart devised in 1888 by a French geologist, August Michel-Levy.

When these out-of-phase waves of light strike the analyzer, it diffracts them into various colors depending on the wavelengths being added and subtracted through interference; they are called "interference colors." These colors are caused by the interference of the two rays of light split by the anisotropic material interfering destructively with each other; that is, they cancel each other out to a greater or lesser degree. The colors produced are indicative of the specimen's molecular organization. The birefringence of a specimen can be determined with the polarizing microscope by examining it between crossed polars. The characteristic birefringence of a given substance is the numerical difference between the maximum and minimum refractive indices. Birefringence will be greatest when the specimen's molecular structure is aligned along its longitudinal axis and will be zero if they are randomly organized. A chart of diameter, birefringence, and retardation, pictured in Figure 4.13, is called a Michel-Levy Chart, after its inventor, Auguste Michel-Lévy (1844–1911). Michel-Levy, a French geologist, was born in Paris and became inspector-general of mines and director of the Geological Survey of France. He was distinguished for his research into the microscopic structure and origin of eruptive minerals; importantly, Michel-Levy was a pioneer in the use of the polarizing microscope for the determination of minerals. The chart assists in the identification of birefringent materials. One of the ingenious things about the chart is that if two of the parameters are known, the third can be calculated (using the equation listed previously). For more information about the Michel-Levy Chart, see Delly (2003). For more information on microscopy, see "On the Web: Microscopy."

ON THE WEB: MICROSCOPY

MicroscopyU, a Web site operated by Nikon providing free tutorials on microscopy and related topics at www.microscopyu.com.

Molecular Expressions, a Web site at www.microscopy.fsu.edu, and *Microscopy Resource* Center, a website operated by Olympus providing free tutorials on microscopy and related topics at www.olympusmicro.com.

Modern Microscopy, an online journal for microscopists, at www.modernmicroscopy.com.

OTHER MICROSCOPICAL METHODS

FLUORESCENCE MICROSCOPY

Fluorescence is the luminescence of a substance excited by radiation. Luminescence can be subdivided into **phosphorescence**, which is characterized by long-lived emission, and fluorescence, in which the emission stops when the excitation stops. The wavelength of the emitted fluorescence light is longer than that of the exciting radiation. In other words, a radiation of relatively high energy falls on a substance. The substance absorbs and/or converts (into heat, for example) a certain, small part of the energy. Most of the energy that is not absorbed by the substance is emitted again. Compared with the exciting radiation, the fluorescence radiation has lost energy, and its wavelength will be longer than that of the exciting radiation. Consequently, a fluorescing substance can be excited by near-UV invisible radiation, and its fluorescent components (**fluorophores**) are seen in the visible range.

In a fluorescence microscope, the specimen is illuminated with light of a short wavelength, for example, ultraviolet or blue. Part of this light is absorbed by the specimen and re-emitted as fluorescence. To enable the comparatively weak fluorescence to be seen, despite the strong illumination, the light used for excitation is filtered out by a secondary (barrier) filter placed between the specimen and the eye. This filter, in principle, should be fully opaque at the wavelength used for excitation, and fully transparent at longer wavelengths so as to transmit the fluorescence. The fluorescent object is therefore seen as a bright image against a dark background.

It follows that a fluorescence microscope differs from a microscope used for conventional light microscopy mainly in that it has a special light source and a pair of complementary filters. The lamp should be a powerful light source, rich in short wavelengths. A primary or excitation filter is placed somewhere between the lamp and the specimen. The filter, in combination with the lamp, should provide light over a comparatively narrow band of wavelengths corresponding to the absorption maximum of the fluorescent substance. The secondary, barrier, or suppression filter prevents the excitation light from reaching the observer's eye and is placed anywhere between the specimen and the eye. A fluorescence microscope and filter sets are shown in Figure 4.14.

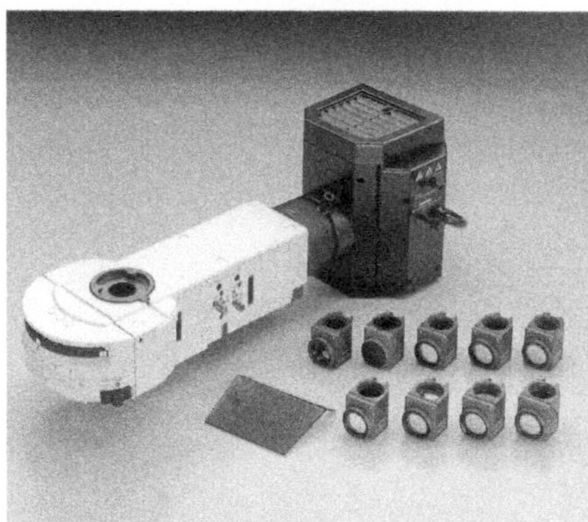

FIGURE 4.14

A fluorescence microscope uses various filters to exclude and excite specific wavelengths of light to induce fluorescence. Most microscope companies now package filters in sets, or cubes, to make choosing combinations easier.

Courtesy Olympus USA.

> **2014 NOBEL PRIZE IN CHEMISTRY**
>
> A German and two Americans won the 2014 Nobel Prize in Chemistry for their research into super-resolution microscopy which will allow breakthroughs in disease and cellular research. Eric Betzig, Stefan Hell and WE Moerner developed a technique that enables extremely high-resolution images by circumventing the diffraction limit of visible light (about 200nm). This advance will allow researchers to visualize nanoscale activities, such as molecular processes, in real time. Using one laser to excite fluorescent-tagged molecules, a second laser quenches the entire signal except for a nanometer-sized strip. Multiple strips are imaged and combined to build extremely high-resolution images. The new technique will allow researchers to watch organelles in action, visualize molecular changes, and perhaps even view how brains develop, leading to potentially massive advances in medicine, treatment and science.
>
> *Stoye, E., October 2014. Super-resolution light microscopy wins chemistry Nobel. Chemistry World. http://www.rsc.org/chemistryworld/2014/10/super-resolution-light-microscopy-wins-chemistry-nobel.*

ELECTRON MICROSCOPY

A completely different type of microscopy is well known to many forensic scientists which does not use light; instead, it uses electrons. Electron microscopy employs a particle beam of electrons focused by magnetic lenses. Electron microscopes have a much higher resolving power and greater depth of field (i.e., more of the image is in focus at one time) than light microscopes and can magnify a specimen hundreds of thousands of times (see Figure 4.15). Electron microscopes are either transmission or scanning. In a transmission electron microscope, or TEM, the electron beam passes through a specimen that has been very thinly sectioned

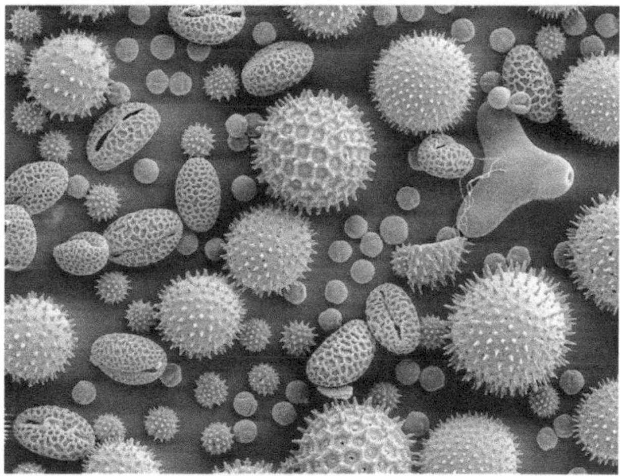

FIGURE 4.15

Pollen from a variety of common plants: sunflower (*Helianthus annuus*), morning glory (*Ipomoea purpurea*), hollyhock (*Sidalcea malviflora*), lily (*Lilium auratum*), primrose (*Oenothera fruticosa*), and castor bean (*Ricinus communis*). The image is magnified some 500×; the grain in the bottom left corner is about 50-μm long.

Public domain image, courtesy Dartmouth Electron Microscope Facility, Dartmouth College.

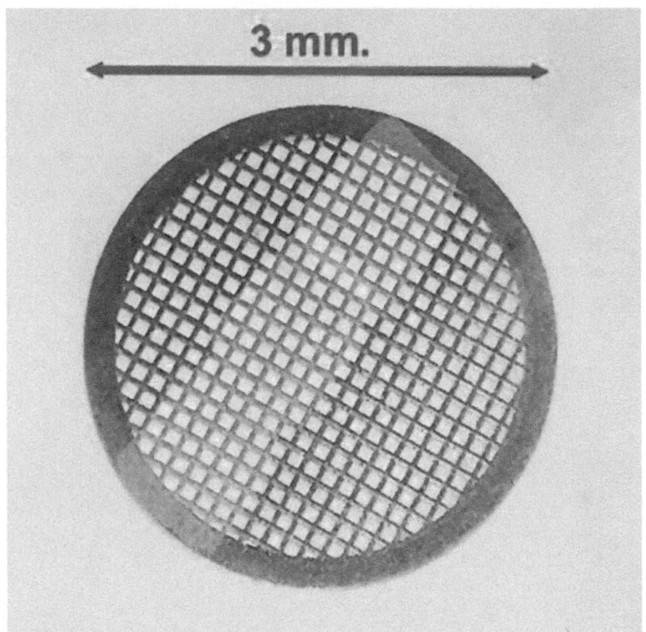

FIGURE 4.16

A transmission electron microscope sample grid. Samples are mounted in supporting material and sectioned on an ultramicrotome down to only a few nanometers in thickness. A rectangular sample can be seen faintly on the grid.

Public domain image.

and projects the beam onto a specially treated plate that transmits the image to a monitor. In this sense, TEM images are much like light microscope images in that they provide information about the internal structure of the specimen. A TEM can resolve extremely fine details, down to the atomic scale. Sample preparation for a TEM is complicated, and the samples must be very small to fit on the support grid for viewing (see Figure 4.16), which is only a few millimeters in diameter.

A scanning electron microscope, or SEM, rasters a beam of electrons across a specimen and provides a noncolored image of its surface (see Figure 4.17). SEMs can reveal details only a few nanometers in size; their magnification ranges from very low (around 2×) to up to 250,000× or more. SEMs are used in forensic laboratories to analyze a wide variety of samples, including paint, particles, fractures, toolmarks, and gunshot residue (see Figure 4.18). This analysis is enhanced by additional analytical instrumentation that can be attached to an SEM (or, in many cases, a TEM), such as:

- *Back-scattered electron detector (BSED):* Not all electrons bounce off the surface of the sample: Many penetrate the sample and are ejected at a rate and energy proportional to the material's average atomic number. Thus, lead would

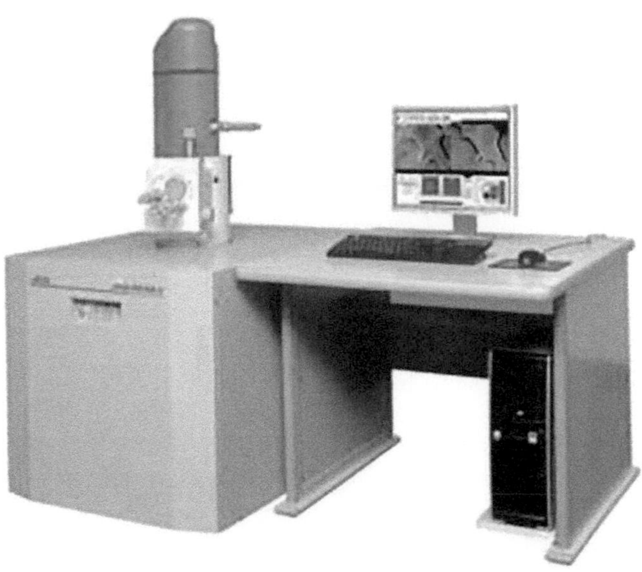

FIGURE 4.17

A modern scanning electron microscope is a highly computerized instrument. The sample would be introduced to the chamber through the airlock at the base of the blue column.

Courtesy JEOL.

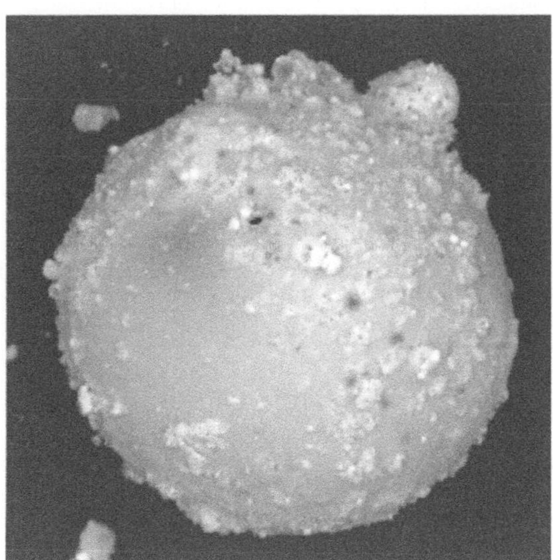

FIGURE 4.18

A particle of gunshot residue is formed in the discharge of ammunition in a firearm. The molten materials congeal into rough spheres with a particular elemental content.

Image courtesy Doug DeGaetano, Virginia Department of Forensic Services.

appear brighter than aluminum in a BSED image. BSEDs assist analysts in detecting materials of interest, like gunshot residue particles.

- *Energy-dispersive spectrometer (EDS):* Electrons from the beam are not the only thing ejected from the sample. The electron beam excites the sample creating electromagnetic radiation from atomic exchanges in the various bands of electrons. Because each element has a particular atomic structure, the X-rays emitted are characteristic of that element. Nearly all the elements in a sample and their respective weight percentages can be determined with a high degree of accuracy (around ±0.5%).
- *Wavelength-dispersive spectrometer (WDS):* Unlike EDS, wavelength-dispersive spectroscopy measures the wavelength of the emitted radiation using a tightly spaced crystal lattice. The wavelength and the lattice spacing are related using Bragg's law. WDS, unlike EDS, can detect only one wavelength at a time (EDS measures all elements in a sample simultaneously). This limitation is moderated by WDS's greatly increased detection limit of 100 parts per million (ppm) in most cases, lower in others.

SEMs are fairly common in many forensic laboratories; electron microscopy centers at universities are good sources of information about the instruments and their applications.

SUMMARY

The microscope is a nearly universal symbol of science, and forensic science is equally well represented by the microscope. For all its power and simplicity, microscopy is sometimes neglected in modern laboratories in favor of expensive and complicated instrumentation. Microscopy provides fast, low-cost, and definitive results to the trained scientist. The wise forensic scientist would learn and develop strong microscopy skills to ensure successful scientific investigations.

TEST YOUR KNOWLEDGE

1. What is a simple magnification system? How is it different from a compound magnification system?
2. What is a virtual image?
3. What is focal length?
4. What is resolution?
5. Why is resolution more important than magnification?
6. What are the main parts of a microscope?
7. If you saw "10×/0.54/170/0.17" on an objective, what would it mean?
8. What is astigmatism?
9. What does a condensing lens do?
10. What's the difference between a real image and a virtual image?

11. What is the RI of air? Of water? Of a diamond?
12. Why is microscopy so important to forensic science?
13. What is a mounting medium?
14. Name three materials besides air that are isotropic.
15. What does a polarizing filter do?
16. Why do crossed polarizing filters create a black field of view?
17. If you had a pair of polarizing sunglasses, how could you tell their polarization direction?
18. What is birefringence?
19. A fluorescing substance contains _______.
20. What materials can be accurately analyzed by microscopy?

CONSIDER THIS...

1. Why do you see polarization (interference) colors *only* when the analyzer is placed into the light path?
2. What do you think Chamot and Mason meant when they said, "But even descriptive microscopy often requires more than superficial observation?"
3. Polarizing sunglasses cancel out the glare from surfaces. All polarizing filters have a preferred orientation, even the sunglasses. What is the preferred orientation of polarizing sunglasses? Why?

BIBLIOGRAPHY AND FURTHER READING

Chamot, E.M., Mason, C.W., 1940, 1958. Handbook of Chemical Microscopy, vols. 1 and 2. John Wiley and Sons, Inc., New York.

Davidson, M.W., Abromowitz, M., 2005. Optical Microscopy. Olympus America, Inc., and Florida State University. Retrieved from http://micro.magnet.fsu.edu.

DeForest, P.R., 2002. Foundations of forensic microscopy (Chapter 5), In: Saferstein, R. (Ed.), Forensic Science Handbook, second ed. vol. 1. Prentice-Hall, Englewood Cliffs, NJ.

Delly, J.G., July 2003. The Michel-Levy interference color chart: microscopy's magical color key. Modern Microscopy. Online at: http://www.modernmicroscopy.com.

Goldstein, J., Newberry, D., Joy, D., Lyman, C., Echlin, P., Lifshin, E., Sawyer, L., Michael, J., 2003. Scanning Electron Microscopy and X-ray Microanalysis, third ed. Springer, New York.

McCrone, W.C., McCrone, L.B., Delly, J.G., 1978. Polarized Light Microscopy. Ann Arbor Science Publications, Inc., Ann Arbor, MI.

Wheeler, B., Wilson, L., 2008. Practical Forensic Microscopy: A Laboratory Manual. Wiley-Blackwell, West Sussex, UK.

CHAPTER

Light and Matter

5

CHAPTER OUTLINE

KEY TERMS

- Atomic absorption
- Atomic Emission
- Electromagnetic radiation
- Fluorescence
- Frequency
- Infrared light
- Mass Spectrometry
- Microspectrophotometry
- Photon
- Raman Spectroscopy
- Spectrum

- UV/visible light
- Wavelength
- Wavenumber

INTRODUCTION

One of the most important chemical properties of matter is how it reacts to exposure to **electromagnetic radiation**, which is often referred to as "light." The electromagnetic spectrum covers a whole range of energy levels from television and radio waves, which are harmless and contain very low energy, to gamma radiation, which is lethal to living organisms and which contains large amounts of energy. Matter reacts with electromagnetic radiation in various ways depending upon the energy content of the radiation. In this chapter, we will study the effects of certain categories of electromagnetic radiation on materials that often occur as evidence. We will be concerned mainly with **ultraviolet/visible** and **infrared (IR)** sectors of the electromagnetic spectrum. As we will see, these types of radiation have different effects on matter. Within a given type of radiation, the effects may differ slightly from substance to substance. This opens the door to characterizing and differentiating among different forms of the same type of material. For example, IR radiation reacts slightly differently to different types of fibers such as nylon and cotton. Measurement of these interactions provides evidence of the fiber type present. This chapter will discuss the effects of ultraviolet, visible, and IR radiation on various types of evidence.

The term **electromagnetic radiation** refers to various forms of energy in the form of waves. Humans and animals are sensitive to certain types of this radiation. We refer to this as **light**. Light radiation strikes the optic nerves of our eyes and we sense it as color. Different wavelengths of the light register in our brains as different colors. This type of reaction to electromagnetic radiation is only one type of interaction of radiation with matter. Various types of matter react with different waves of light in a number of ways. These interactions begin with radiation being absorbed by matter. All types of electromagnetic radiation contain energy. When radiation strikes matter, the energy from the radiation is absorbed by the matter. This causes any of several types of responses. In some cases, the color of the matter is revealed. In other cases, the radiation can cause the matter to heat up and even cook. Radiation can affect living cells, causing mutations that can give rise to cancer. From an analytical and forensic chemistry standpoint, it is not so important what effects that the light has on matter, but what types of light are absorbed by matter.

In this chapter, the properties of electromagnetic radiation will be described. Then the interaction of radiation and matter will be discussed. We will be concerned with certain regions of the electromagnetic spectrum and how specifically these regions interact with matter. Methods of measuring the absorption of radiation will be described and also how this is done in a forensic science laboratory. Along the way, we will show how these properties of materials are used in forensic chemistry.

ELECTROMAGNETIC RADIATION

Electromagnetic radiation can be visualized in a number of ways. One way is to think of it as existing in **sine waves** irradiating out from a source in all directions. There are many sizes of waves that can be described by their **wavelength** (λ), which is the distance between corresponding points on two adjacent waves. This is shown in Figure 5.1. Some types of radiation can have extremely short wavelengths such as X-rays. Others can be very long. Radio carrier waves have wavelengths that exceed 2 m.

Sometimes it is more convenient to measure light in terms of its **frequency (ν)**, which is the number of waves that passes a given point in 1 s. Frequency is measured in **cycles per second** (**Hertz**). Since light travels very fast and the wavelengths are generally very short, the number of waves that passes a given point in 1 s is generally very high and most light has high numbers of cycles per second. There is a simple inverse relationship between wavelength and frequency, as shown in Equation (5.1).

$$c = \lambda\nu \qquad \text{(Equation 5.1)}$$

In Equation (5.1), "c" is the speed of light (3×10^8 m/s or about 186,000 miles/s). This equation shows that, as frequency increases, wavelength decreases and vice versa. Given the speed of light and either the frequency or wavelength, the other variable can be calculated. For example, your favorite FM radio station might be located at 90.5 on the dial. This is shorthand for a broadcast frequency of 90.5 MHz (millions of Hertz) or 9.05×10^7 Hz. Using Equation (5.1), the wavelength of this light would be about 3.1 m, which is about 10 ft. Radio waves are very long waves compared to other types. Frequency can also be expressed in other units. One of the more common measurement units is **wavenumbers**. A wavenumber is the inverse of the wavelength measured in centimeters. Thus, one wavenumber is 1 cm^{-1}. Another way of expressing the broadcast frequency of the above-mentioned radio station (0.5 MHz) would be in wavenumbers. To convert Hertz to wavenumbers, change the wavelength from 3.1 m to 310 cm and then take the reciprocal; the result is 3.2×10^{-2} cm^{-1}. Likewise wavelength can be expressed in any unit of length. As you study various regions of the electromagnetic spectrum, you will see that sometimes the radiation is described

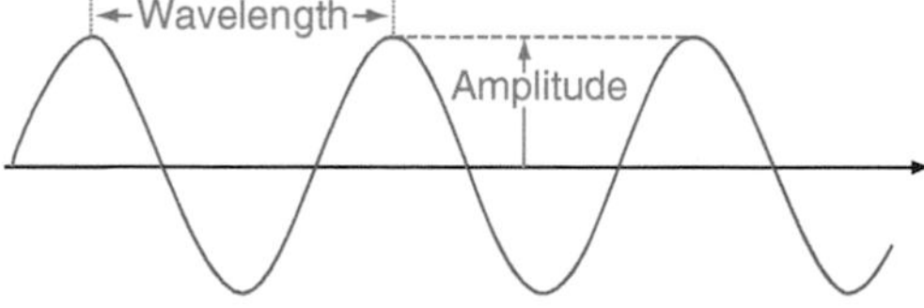

FIGURE 5.1

Electromagnetic radiation can be viewed as a sine wave. The wavelength is the distance between two corresponding peaks or valleys and is denoted by the Greek letter λ. The number of waves that passes a given point in 1 s is referred to as the frequency of the light and is denoted by the Greek letter υ.

Courtesy: William Reusch, 1999. www.chemistry.msu.edu/~reusch/virtualtext/intro1.htm#contnt.

in wavelength units and sometimes as frequency. Also, you will see that different units of wavelength or frequency are used depending upon the type of radiation. These conventions have arisen over time purely as a convenience. Spectroscopists (scientists who study light and matter) like to work in small, whole numbers if possible. They choose units of wavelength or frequency for a particular region so that they can work with small numbers. For example, in the ultraviolet and visible region of electromagnetic radiation, scientists generally use wavelengths as a measuring unit. In particular, they measure wavelength in billionths of meters (10^{-9} m or nanometers (nm)). Using this unit, ultraviolet light comprises 200 to about 450 nm and visible light runs from 450 to about 750 nm.

Electromagnetic radiation can be thought of as consisting of tiny packets of **energy (E)** called **photons**. The energy of a photon can be described in terms of the wavelength or frequency of the radiation as shown in Equations (5.2) and (5.3).

$$E = h\nu \qquad \text{(Equation 5.2)}$$

$$E = hc/\lambda \qquad \text{(Equation 5.3)}$$

In these equations, "h" is a constant of proportionality called Planck's constant. It ensures that the units are the same on both sides of the equation. These equations show that, as the frequency of light increases, so does its energy and as the wavelength increases, the energy decreases. Electromagnetic radiation exists as a continuum of wavelengths from the very short to very long. It is probable that there exists radiation of wavelengths that are too short for modern measuring instruments to even detect. The continuum of electromagnetic radiation that we are aware of and can measure is depicted in a chart in Figure 5.2.

At the far left of this electromagnetic spectrum are **gamma rays**. These are very energetic and can pass through matter. They can be dangerous to life in that they can damage or destroy cells. Next lower in energy are **X-rays**. These rays can also pass through most matter but are deflected by dense matter such as bones. This is the principle behind the cameras that are used to take X-ray pictures of peoples' insides. The X-rays reflect off the bone and other dense tissue and are detected while the others pass through soft tissue. The next major region of the electromagnetic spectrum is called the ultraviolet. This region contains ultraviolet radiation and visible light. These two areas are lumped together because both UV and visible light have the same effects on matter. Light in this region is not energetic enough to pass through matter. Instead, when a molecule absorbs this light, electrons are shifted from one **orbital** to another. An orbital is an energy level where an electron resides. The ultraviolet region is so-called because it borders on the violet area of the visible region, which is the light that human eyes can detect and see as color. As frequencies of visible light decrease, the light changes from violet down to red at the lowest frequencies. Figure 5.3 shows the color spectrum produced by visible light. Only certain types of molecules will absorb ultraviolet light. Most substances do not. The UV/visible region has many applications in the analysis of forensic evidence.

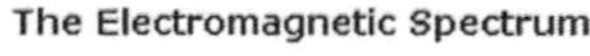

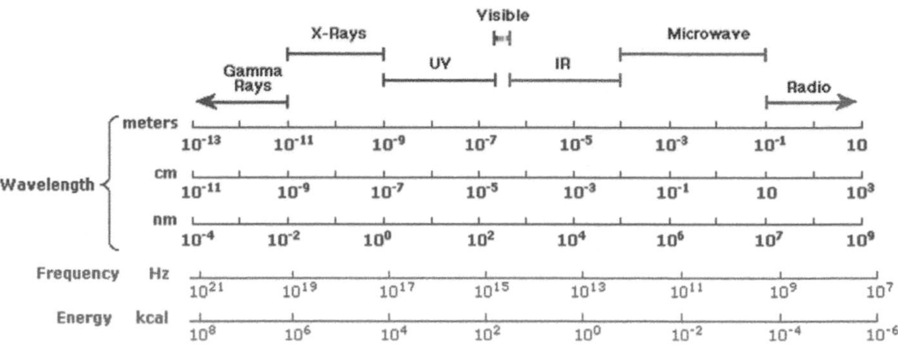

FIGURE 5.2

The electromagnetic spectrum. At the top of the chart are the frequencies of electromagnetic radiation or light in decreasing order. Scientists divide the spectrum into regions. Within each region, electromagnetic radiation has different effects on matter that it comes in to contact with. For forensic science purposes, the most important regions are the ultraviolet/visible (UV/visible) and the infrared (IR).

Courtesy: William Reusch, 1999. www.chemistry.msu.edu/~reusch/virtualtext/intro1.htm#contnt.

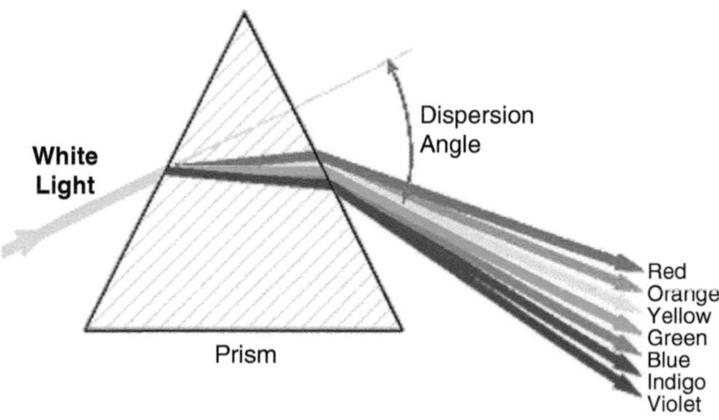

FIGURE 5.3

The color spectrum. When white light is refracted by a prism, it breaks up into various colors. Light of these wavelengths is called the visible spectrum because when photons reach our eyes, our optic nerves send images to our brain that registers as a color. The highest frequency (shortest wavelength) light is violet and the lowest is red. Frequencies higher than violet are in the ultraviolet region. We do not see this light as colored. Frequencies below the red are in the infrared region. We do not see this light as being colored either.

Courtesy: William Reusch, 1999. www.chemistry.msu.edu/~reusch/virtualtext/intro1.htm#contnt.

Lower in energy than the red region of visible light is the **IR** (infrared) region (*infra* means "below"). When absorbed by matter, this type of light causes bonds between atoms in a molecule to vibrate like two weights on either end of a spring. Every substance absorbs light in the IR region. Taken as a whole, the wavelengths of IR radiation absorbed are different for every substance. This makes it useful as a tool for the identification of a pure substance. The IR region is also very important in the analysis of chemical evidence in forensic science. At still lower frequencies than IR light is the **microwave** region. These light waves cause molecules to rotate or spin.

IN DEPTH: THE MICROWAVE REGION

Microwaves serve a number of purposes. They are used as carrier waves for some transmissions of audio devices. Their major effect chemically is to cause molecules to rotate or spin. The practical effect of this is that, when adjacent molecules absorb microwave radiation and spin, they rub against each other and cause friction. This friction in turn, generates heat. This is the principle behind microwave ovens. When food is put in a microwave oven and the oven is turned on, the food is bombarded with microwaves. The water molecules in the food absorb the microwaves and begin to spin, creating heat that cooks the food. Because of the energy of the microwaves, not enough heat is produced to caramelize or char the sugars in the food, so the food doesn't "brown" like it would in a conventional radiative or convection oven. When microwave ovens first came out, people thought that they weren't really cooking food, especially meats because they didn't turn brown. This spawned the production of "browning sauces" that would cause the food to turn brown when being cooked in a microwave oven. Some people believed that these ovens cooked food from the inside out. This cannot be true, of course, because the microwaves are absorbed by the first molecules they encounter, which would be on the outside surface.

At the lowest end of the light spectrum are **radio** waves. These have very long wavelengths and thus very low frequencies and relatively little energy. Some of these waves are meters long! They carry radio and TV signals. Remember the example of the radio station at 90.5 MHz. Its wavelength is more than 10-feet long! Radio waves are transported through the air to the radio receiver by a carrier wave. This process is called "modulation". Modulation can be accomplished using either amplitude (AM) or frequency (FM). Once the waves reach the radio receiver, the radio wave and the carrier wave are separated using a process called demodulation. Radio waves are not commonly used in forensic science as analytical tools.

INTERACTION OF MATTER WITH SPECIFIC REGIONS OF ELECTROMAGNETIC RADIATION

For many years, analytical chemists have exploited the ways that radiation interacts with matter. As it turns out, the particular effects that matter has upon light (and vice versa) depend upon the energy content of the radiation and the type of matter. Forensic and analytical chemists are interested in the wavelengths and/or frequencies of radiation absorbed by matter. When a substance is exposed to electromagnetic radiation, it undergoes changes that may or may not be reversible and which depend upon the energy of the radiation. For example, gamma radiation can cause matter to lose electrons and undergo irreversible changes. In the case of living matter, radiation of this high energy can cause mutations in tissue that may result in cancer or some other disease. Forensic science, however, is more concerned with what happens to a substance when it is exposed to light of much lower frequencies and energies. There are two principal regions of light that are most important in characterizing evidence: the ultraviolet/visible (UV/visible) and the IR. Remember, a forensic scientist is most interested in comparing evidence from a crime scene (unknown evidence) to some object or material (known evidence) to see to what extent they may be associated with each other. This is accomplished principally by comparing as many physical and chemical properties as possible. The more characteristics the known and unknown samples have in common, the higher the degree of association. Behavior of matter when exposed to light is a very important chemical property and is greatly exploited by forensic scientists.

UV/VISIBLE SPECTROPHOTOMETRY

Ultraviolet Light and Matter

All matter consists of atoms that are made up of negatively charged electrons that inhabit orbitals that exist in approximately concentric spheres around the nucleus, which is made up of positively charged protons and neutral neutrons. In a neutral atom, there are equal numbers of electrons and protons, so there is no net positive or negative charge. When atoms combine to make molecules (the building blocks of compounds, materials, or substances), they do so by sharing or donating/accepting electrons to form covalent or ionic bonds. The electrons that are shared are those that are farthest from the nucleus, called the valence electrons. Valence electrons in atoms and in molecules can be promoted to a higher energy level by absorbing energy from light or other energy sources. This process is said to be **quantized**, because the atom or molecule can only absorb the exact amount of energy that corresponds to the difference in energy between the occupied and unoccupied energy level. This packet of energy is called a **photon**. In other words, a molecule will absorb energy and promote an electron if it is exposed to a photon of the proper energy. One can visualize these energy levels to be like stairs on a staircase; you can be on one stair or the next stair, but cannot occupy the space between stairs. Figure 5.4 illustrates this.

A photon that causes electron promotion in atoms and molecules is in the UV/visible region of the electromagnetic spectrum. When a substance is exposed to UV/visible radiation, it will absorb certain photons of particular energy (and thus particular frequencies or wavelengths). If the amount of each wavelength of light that is absorbed by a substance throughout the UV/visible region is plotted, a **spectrum** is generated. See Figure 5.5 for the UV/visible spectrum of heroin.

Note that the peaks in the UV/visible spectrum of a typical substance tend to be few in number and quite broad in shape. This is due to the nature of the absorbance of this type of energy—there are not too many electrons that can be promoted in a typical molecule so there are not very many wavelengths where an appreciable number of photons are absorbed. The broadness of the peaks is due to the temperature; at very low temperatures, UV absorptions are narrower. The practical effect of these

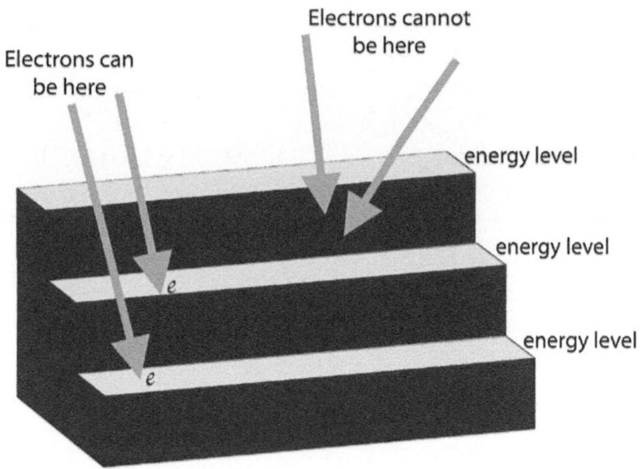

FIGURE 5.4

Electronic energy levels (orbitals) surround the nucleus of an atom. One of their properties is that they are quantized. An electron must reside in an energy level. It cannot be between two of them. In that sense, energy levels are like stairs on a staircase. A person who is climbing a staircase can stop on any stair but cannot stop between stairs.

Courtesy: Meredith Haddon.

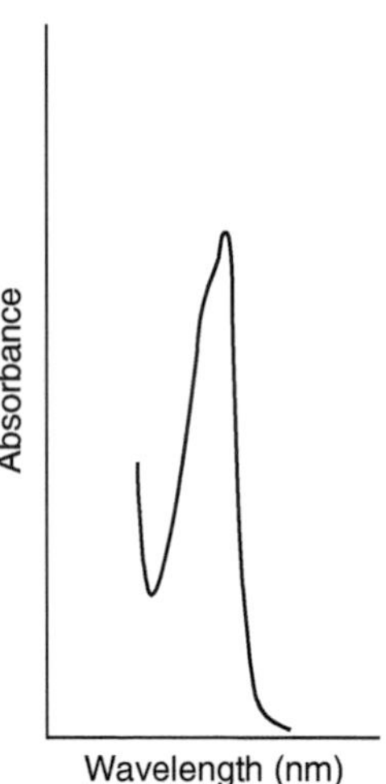

FIGURE 5.5

The ultraviolet spectrum of heroin. The benzene ring backbone of heroin gives the UV spectrum its characteristic shape. Substituted benzene structures all have their major absorbance near 265 nm.

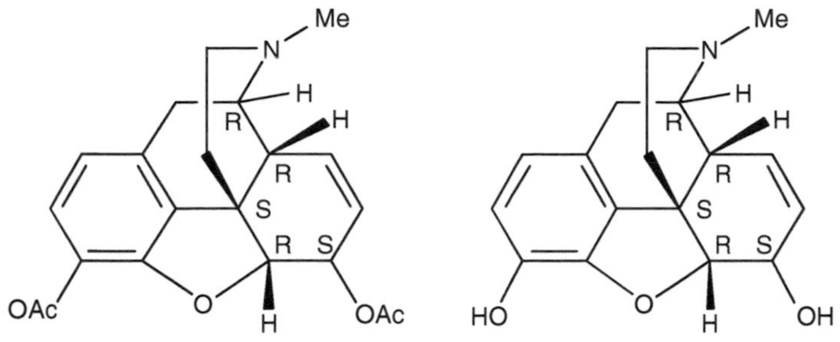

Heroin

Morphine

FIGURE 5.6

Structures of morphine and diacetylmorphine (heroin). The structures of these two substances are very similar, differing only in that the two OH groups on morphine have been replaced by AcO (acetate) groups on heroin. Because of their similarity in structure, their UV spectra are very similar.

characteristics of UV/visible spectra is that they are not commonly used for absolute identification of a pure chemical substance. Closely related substances exhibit UV/visible spectra that are practically indistinguishable. For example, morphine and heroin (which is derived from morphine and is similar in structure) have very similar UV/visible spectra. Not every substance will absorb energy in the UV/visible range. Certainly, any substance that appears to the human eye as possessing a color will absorb in this region because the sensation of color is caused by light reflection from a substance that is received by our optic nerves, which in turn, send a signal to the brain that is registered as the quality of color. Many organic substances will also have a UV/visible spectrum because they usually possess a number of **conjugated carbon/carbon double bonds**. These are alternating single and double (or triple) bonds in the molecule. Any compound that is based on the benzene ring, for example, will absorb strongly in the UV/visible region. It is conceivable that several substances could have the same chromophore and thus the same UV/visible spectrum. This is one reason why UV/visible spectra cannot be used for unequivocal identification of a substance. This can be seen in Figure 5.6, which shows the structures of morphine and diacetylmorphine (heroin). As mentioned above, these two substances have practically indistinguishable UV/visible spectra.

Obtaining a UV/Visible Spectrum

The UV/visible spectrum of a substance is obtained by using a UV/visible spectrophotometer. A simplified diagram of a spectrophotometer is shown in Figure 5.7.

The source emits all of the wavelengths of UV or visible light. Most often, this is a deuterium (heavy hydrogen) lamp for UV light and an incandescent light for visible wavelengths. Next, there is a **monochromator**. This is a device that selects one particular wavelength (or a small packet of wavelengths) to be exposed to the sample. The monochromator is a prism or grating (see Figure 5.3) that is rotated,

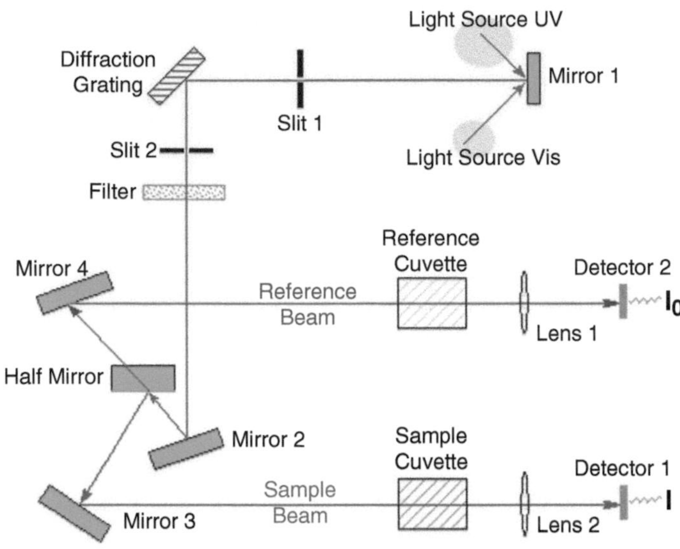

FIGURE 5.7

A diagram of an ultraviolet/visible spectrophotometer. There are two light sources; one for ultraviolet light and one for visible light. A mirror is used to select the proper light source. The diffraction grating is the monochromator that selects specific wavelengths of light. The two detectors are coupled so that reference absorptions can be subtracted from sample absorptions.

Courtesy: William Reusch, 1999. www.chemistry.msu.edu/~reusch/virtualtext/intro1.htm#contnt.

thus exposing the sample to steadily increasing or decreasing wavelengths of light throughout the entire spectrum. The monochromator is coupled to the detector so that the amount of transmitted light at each wavelength is known. The sample holder comes next. Most samples are run as solutions in a solvent that does not absorb light in the UV/visible range. Methyl alcohol is a popular solvent for many substances such as drugs. The liquid sample holder is a rectangular, quartz glass cuvette, usually with a 1 cm square base. Spectra of gases can also be obtained using a special gas-tight holder. Finally, there is the detector. The detector must be sensitive to changes in the intensity of UV/visible light that reaches it. The most commonly used UV/visible detector is the **photocell**. A photocell is a device that converts UV or visible light into an electric current. The more intense the light, the more current will be created. At a wavelength where the sample does not absorb any light, the detector will produce the maximum electric current because all of the light from the source reaches the detector. When the sample absorbs some or all of a wavelength of light, less light reaches the detector and thus, less current is created. Modern spectrophotometers are computer controlled. The computer stores the wavelength and corresponding electric current and then, when the entire spectrum has been obtained, will construct a graph of wavelength (or frequency) versus intensity of transmitted light. This is called the **transmission spectrum**. The computer can also convert this to the wavelength versus amount of light absorbed by the sample, the **absorption spectrum**. In practice, a spectrum of the analyte will be obtained and then a spectrum of just the solvent will be obtained. The latter will be subtracted from the former, resulting in the sample spectrum.

UV/Visible Microspectrophotometry

There are many types of evidentiary materials that are too small to be accommodated by an ultraviolet spectrophotometer. For example, one may wish to determine the exact color of a tiny paint chip and compare it to paint taken from a car suspected of being involved in a hit and run case. This could be accomplished by determining the exact wavelengths of light that are absorbed or reflected by the paint. A tiny paint chip could not be made to fit properly into a conventional spectrophotometer. The solution is to combine a powerful microscope with a UV/visible spectrophotometer. Light that travels through the microscope onto the paint chip is detected by a photocell, just as in a normal spectrophotometer. The ultraviolet and visible spectra are thus obtained and comparisons can be made. Figure 5.8 shows a UV/visible microspectrophotometer.

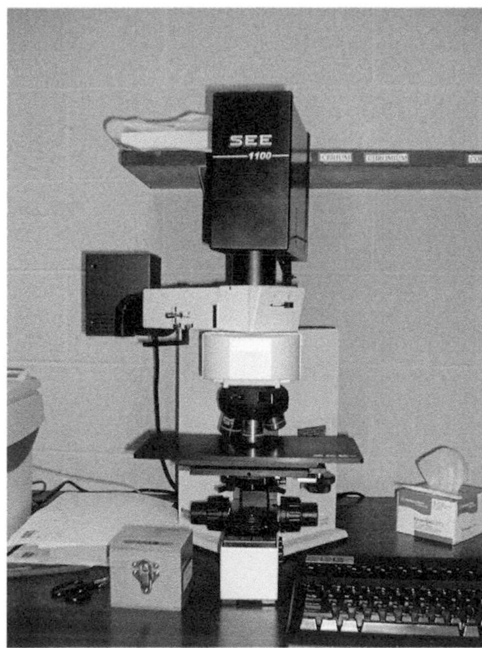

FIGURE 5.8

A UV/visible microspectrophotometer. The rectangular module on top is the UV/visible spectrophotometer. It sits upon the microscope, which focuses the light onto the sample. It is capable of absorption or reflectance spectroscopy.

Applications of UV/Visible Spectroscopy in Forensic Science

One major application of this type of spectroscopy is the determination of the exact color of an object or substance. The paint chip described previously is an example of when this would be needed. UV/visible spectroscopy is also widely used in the analysis of textile fibers. See Chapter 15 for a discussion on textile fibers. A microspectrophotometer can be employed to compare the colors of two fibers. In a murder case that occurred in Michigan more than 20 years ago, purple fibers were transferred from a sweater worn by the victim to the seat of a car driven by the suspected killer. Samples taken from the sweater were compared to those lifted from the car seat and the exact colors were determined. Microspectrophotometry has also been used for determining the color characteristics of hair dyes. The same hair dyes were put on different color hairs and the colors were compared to see if the natural color of the hair affected the dye color. Another experiment determined if the color of the dyes changed with time. Microspectrophotometry has also been widely used to compare plastic fragments from the covers on lights on cars.

Sometimes it is important to obtain the ultraviolet spectrum of objects of evidence that are colorless. One example is automobile paint clear coats. A clear coat is the top, colorless layer of coating that is applied to automobile paints to protect the color coats from exposure to the sun's ultraviolet light. The clear coat contains UV "scavengers"—chemicals that absorb large quantities of UV light. Different paint manufacturers use different chemical formulations in their clear coats. The ultraviolet spectrum of the clear coat can be important in associating paint chips from an incident scene to a suspect automobile. Colorless plastic items such as certain automobile light covers, plastic bags used to transport drugs and plastic films can also be analyzed by ultraviolet spectroscopy. Powder forms of illicit drugs are generally white and have no visible spectrum but might have a characteristic ultraviolet spectrum. This is illustrated in Figure 5.5, the ultraviolet spectrum of heroin.

UV/visible spectrophotometry can also be used to determine the amount of a substance in a mixture. This is because of its adherence to **Beer's Law**. This law relates the amount of an absorbing substance present to the quantity of absorbed light. The absorbance can be obtained directly from the spectrum of the substance. It is related to the height of the absorbance peak. In general, the concentration of a UV/visible absorber is directly proportional to its absorbance. So if heroin is dissolved in a solvent that doesn't absorb UV light, the concentration of the heroin can be determined from the UV spectrum.

MOLECULAR FLUORESCENCE

Transportation safety experts tell people to wear fluorescent tape or articles of clothing at night when walking or riding a bicycle. Some road signs fluoresce at night when automobile headlights shine on them. Many homes and businesses use

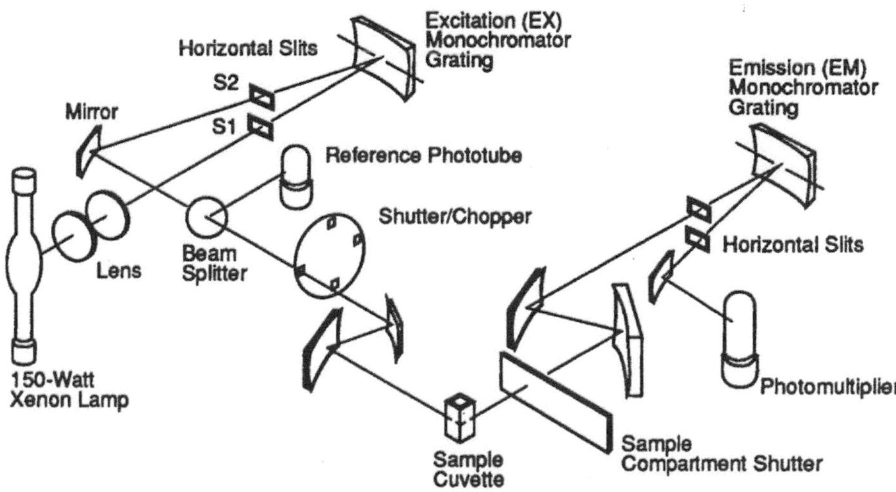

FIGURE 5.9

Diagram of a UV fluorescence spectrophotometer. The source light passes through a monochromator that selects wavelengths of light for excitation of the analyte. The emission monochromator is stationed at right angles to the excitation light. Light emitted by the sample passes through the emission monochromator and is detected by the photomultiplier.

Courtesy: William Reusch, 1999. www.chemistry.msu.edu/~reusch/virtualtext/intro1.htm#contnt.

fluorescent lighting. Most incandescent light bulbs have been replaced by compact fluorescent lights. Some nightclubs use "black lights" (ultraviolet lights) and fluorescent paint to jazz up the dance floors with wild, fluorescent colors. All of these are examples of the phenomenon of **fluorescence**. This occurs when a substance absorbs energy and then emits it in the form of (usually) visible light. In the fluorescent tape and paint examples above, the dyes in the tape and pigments in the paint absorb ultraviolet or visible light and then emit light of a different wavelength. In the case of fluorescent lights, a gas absorbs electrical energy and emits visible light. Most substances do not fluoresce. They absorb light and then emit the same wavelength back. Those substances that fluoresce will always emit light of a longer wavelength (lower energy) than they absorb. Most substances of forensic interest that fluoresce do so when the light absorbed is in the visible or ultraviolet range. Some substances such as certain inks undergo IR fluorescence, where the light absorbed and emitted is in the IR region. (See the next section of this chapter for a discussion on IR spectroscopy.)

Fluorescence is measured similarly to UV/visible spectrophotometry. A fluorescence spectrophotometer looks a lot like a UV/visible spectrophotometer with some important differences. Figure 5.9 is the internal diagram of a fluorescence spectrophotometer.

Figure 5.7 above showed a UV/visible spectrophotometer. The detector of that instrument is in a straight-line path from the source through the sample. In fluorescence spectroscopy, the detector is at a right angle to the source, with the sample at the apex, so that the detector does not see any light that leaves the source and is directly transmitted by the sample. The detector sees only light that is fluoresced by the sample. In addition, in fluorescence spectroscopy, there are two monochromators; one between the source and the sample, so the wavelengths of light that reach the sample can be selected and there is another between the sample and the detector, so that the wavelengths of light that reach the detector can be selected. Using the two monochromators, the specific wavelengths the sample absorbs (excitation) and emits (emission) can be determined. The excitation and emission wavelengths are very characteristic of a particular substance.

A surprising variety of evidence types have fluorescent characteristics that are used in their analysis. Certain illicit drugs exhibit ultraviolet fluorescence. The most common example is LSD, which will absorb light strongly at 320 nm and then emit light at 400 nm. Like UV/visible spectrophotometry, fluorescence spectroscopy also obeys Beer's Law. Thus the concentration of LSD in a sample can be determined from its fluorescence spectrum. Some pigments and dyes used in automobile and decorative paints, some inks, fibers and tape materials will exhibit fluorescence. Some fabrics and cleaning agents contain optical brighteners that exhibit fluorescence. In many of these cases, UV/visible spectrophotometry and fluorescence spectroscopy can both be used to characterize these substances.

IN DEPTH: FLUORESCENCE SPECTROSCOPY

Comparatively few substances exhibit luminescence, which includes fluorescence and phosphorescence. An example of phosphorescence is the light emitted by lightning bugs. In organic chemistry, the types of molecules that luminesce are generally organic and contain conjugated carbon–carbon double bonds. These are double bonds that alternate with single bonds as shown below:

$$C{=}C{-}C{=}C{-}C{=}C$$

The double bonds between carbon atoms are called **pi** (Π) bonds. The conjugation allows the Π bonds to be delocalized over several carbon atoms. This has the effect of lowering the energy of these orbitals. As a result, the energy needed to promote electrons from their ground state into these orbitals is in the UV/visible range. When an electron is promoted, it will eventually fall back to its lowest ground state. The particular mechanism by which this happens determines whether the molecule will fluoresce or phosphoresce. In both cases, some of the energy absorbed by the molecule to promote the electrons into excited Π orbitals is lost by vibrations or some other mechanism. Then the electron drops back to lower levels, emitting photons of light as it does so. These photons are of lower energy than the light that the molecule absorbed in the first place. This is why a molecule will always fluoresce at a longer wavelength than it absorbs. Measurement of fluorescence can be a powerful tool in characterizing those substances that have this property. Fluorescence is very efficient and thus very sensitive. Small amounts of such substances can be detected by their fluorescence. It is also a good quantitative technique. Fluorescence is a short-lived phenomenon, lasting just fractions of a second. Phosphorescence, on the other hand is a longer lasting process. It may persist for seconds or even minutes.

IR SPECTROSCOPY

IR Light and Matter

Recall that the IR region of the electromagnetic spectrum contains less energy (lower frequency, higher wavelength) than the UV/visible region. Each photon of IR radiation contains less energy than a UV/visible photon. Recall that when photons of UV/visible light are absorbed by a substance, electrons are promoted to higher energy levels. In the case of photons of IR radiation, there is not enough energy to promote electrons. Instead each bond between all atoms that make up a given molecule will vibrate much like two weights connected by a spring. The particular wavelengths of light that are absorbed by chemical bonds depend upon the atoms on each side of the bond and the strength of the bond that holds them together. This is analogous to the weights and spring model of bonds. The frequency of vibration of two weights and a spring depends upon the mass of each weight and the strength of the spring. The weight and spring model is shown in Figure 5.10.

The chemical bond is the spring and the atoms on either side of the bond are the weights. When the weights attached to a spring are pulled apart the spring will vibrate back and forth at a frequency that depends upon the strength of the spring and the amount of weight on either side. When IR radiation of the proper energy strikes a molecule, one of its bonds may absorb it and cause a vibration to take place. Like UV/visible interactions with matter, IR absorptions are also quantized. The energy of a photon must exactly match the proper energy of vibration of one of the bonds in the molecule. Each different chemical bond in the molecule has its own characteristic vibrations and each bond can undergo a number of different kinds of vibrations. Some of the most common vibrations of molecules are shown in Figure 5.11.

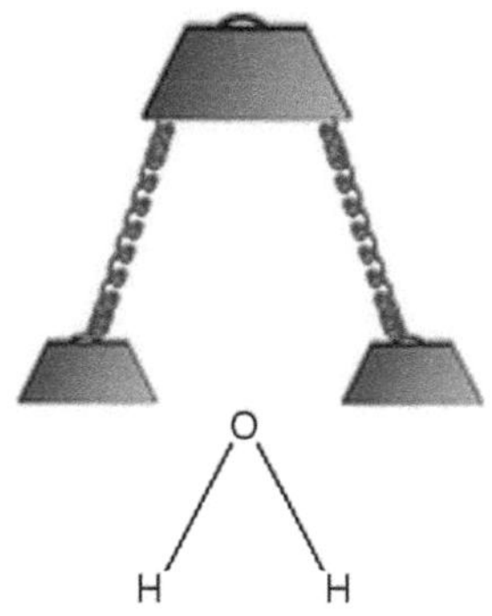

FIGURE 5.10

A molecule can be visualized as a set of weights connected by springs. The springs are the chemical bonds made up of shared electrons. This diagram shows a molecule of water (H_2O) and a model using weights and springs. When the springs are pulled or bent, they contract and expand or wag back and forth. When the bonds between two atoms absorb energy, they vibrate back and forth at characteristic frequencies.

Courtesy: Meredith Haddon.

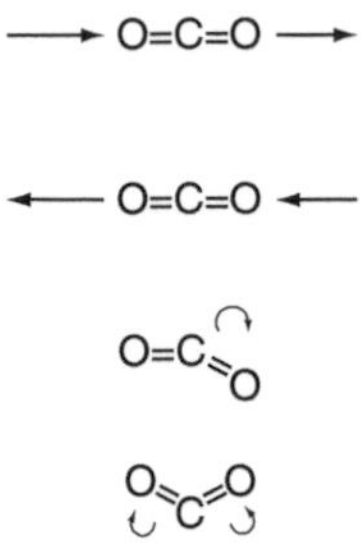

→ O=C=O →

← O=C=O ←

O=C=O

O=C=O

FIGURE 5.11

Each chemical bond in a molecule can undergo several types of vibrations as shown in the figure. These vibrations absorb energy and give rise to the infrared (IR) spectrum. More complex molecules contain more bonds, which results in a more complex IR spectrum. Each molecule has a unique set of vibrational absorptions.

The result is that, unlike UV/visible absorptions, there are many IR absorptions in each type of molecule. Even the slightest change in the composition of a molecule will result in a different IR spectrum. Thus, the IR spectrum of substance is unique and can be used to unequivocally identify that substance. IR spectrophotometry is one of the two analytical techniques, along with gas chromatography/mass spectrometry, that can be used for identification of pure substances, such as drugs. So, thus far we have seen two important differences between UV and IR radiation; IR is of lower energy and causes bond vibrations rather than electron promotion and all substances absorb IR radiation whereas only some substances absorb UV radiation.

Obtaining an IR Spectrum

The process of obtaining spectral data for IR spectrophotometry is quite different than with UV/visible techniques. There is a source of IR radiation that emits all wavelengths simultaneously. There is a detector that is designed to respond only to radiation in the IR region. Sample preparation is quite different. Also, there are no monochromators that select various wavelengths of light. All of the light reaches the sample at the same time. Through a mechanical and mathematical process known as **Fourier Transform**, the wavelengths of light that are absorbed by the sample are sorted out and displayed as either a function of absorbance or transmittance. Sampling for IR spectrophotometry is more flexible than for UV/visible spectrophotometry. Since all substances absorb light in the IR, it is necessary to purify the sample before IR analysis. So, for example, a street drug sample of cocaine is almost never found as pure drug. It is always cut (diluted) with inert powders such as sugars. These diluents will also absorb IR light and the resulting spectrum will be a very complex mixture of peaks that will not be easily interpretable. In order to identify the cocaine in the sample, it must first be separated from all of the diluents. Solid spectra can be easily obtained by preparing potassium bromide (KBr) pellets. KBr, which is a white powder, becomes a hard, solid, transparent pellet when subjected to high pressure. It also does not absorb IR radiation in the same regions where organic compounds commonly absorb. If one has a solid, pure drug sample, such as heroin, an IR spectrum can be obtained by making a 10% solid solution of the drug with KBr, grinding it to a fine powder, and then forming a small pellet using high pressure and a die. This pellet contains small particles of the drug dispersed throughout the solid KBr. The pellet can be put directly in the beam of the IR and an excellent spectrum can be obtained. Pure liquid sample spectra can be obtained by putting a thin film of the pure substance between two premade KBr plates. Vapor spectra can be made using a special gas-tight cell with KBr windows. Sometimes the sample is too small to be made into a KBr pellet. In such cases, a **diamond cell** can be used. The sample is squeezed between two tiny diamond chips (diamond is practically transparent in the IR where most substances absorb). This flattens out the sample making it easier to obtain a spectrum. The light from the source is focused on the diamond windows to get a high-quality spectrum.

Ordinarily it is necessary for the analyte sample to be transparent to IR radiation. IR spectrophotometers are constructed to measure transmitted radiation—light that passes through the sample. Thus opaque materials cannot be analyzed by ordinary means. It is possible, however, to obtain **reflectance** spectra. There are two common methods for obtaining reflectance spectra. One, called **diffuse reflectance** uses a set of mirrors that direct the IR source light at the sample at an oblique angle to the surface of the material, which then absorbs some of the light. The light that is not absorbed, but is reflected off the surface, reaches the detector. The other reflectance method, **attenuated total reflectance (ATR)**, uses a special crystal that is brought into direct contact with the sample. The source radiation is directed at the sample through the crystal. Because of the nature of the crystal, the radiation bounces off the sample several times before reaching the detector.

Detectors are also different than those used in UV/visible spectrophotometry. IR detectors are usually some type of **thermocouple**—a device that converts heat into electricity. To increase the sensitivity of these detectors, they are often housed in a flask that has liquid nitrogen circulating around it to make it very cold. This makes the detector very sensitive to even slight changes in temperature and thus it can detect very small amounts of material. One of the advantages of having computers that control IR spectrophotometers is the ability to create libraries of IR spectra. Most IR spectra are unique and the ability of computerized instruments to compare spectra with library entries is an excellent method of identification. This type of analysis is tempered, however, by the fact that some IR spectra of similar substances are almost indistinguishable. Examples include isomers called enantiomers, which have the same exact chemical structure but are mirror images of each other. Modern computers are capable of searching a library containing thousands of spectra in just a few seconds. It will return a list of the substances whose spectra most closely match the unknown. Figure 5.12 shows the IR spectra of an unknown white powder and a known sample of cocaine overlaid. It can be seen that these two IR spectra are virtually identical.

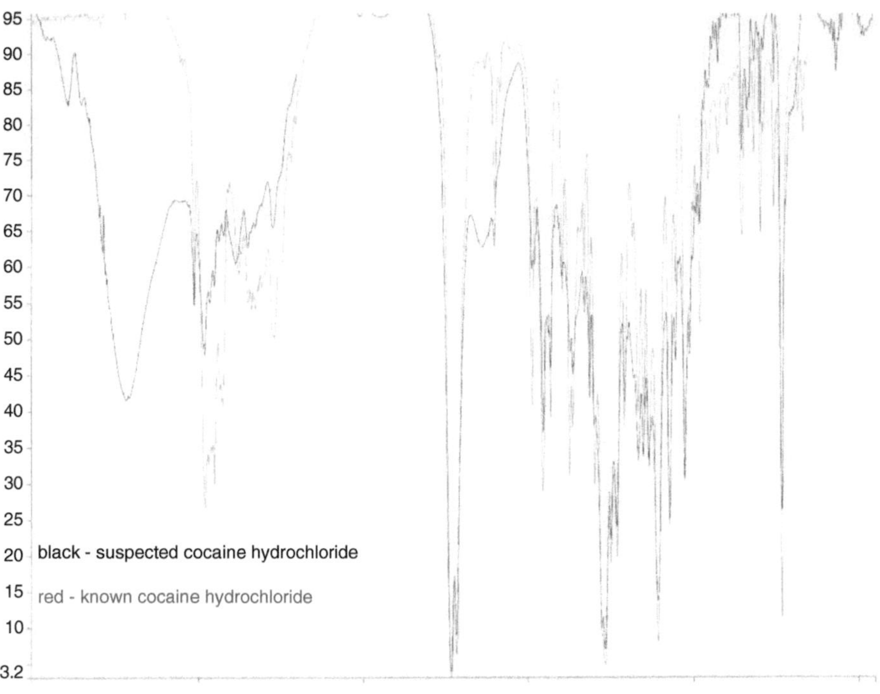

FIGURE 5.12

Overlaid IR spectra of known cocaine and a sample of suspected cocaine.

IN THE LAB: FOURIER TRANSFORM IR SPECTROPHOTOMETRY

Modern analytical IR spectrophotometers represent a great improvement over classical instruments. In the classical setup, the sample is exposed to each frequency or wavelength of light individually. This is accomplished using a monochromator. A series of mirrors is used to focus the light on the sample and then the transmitted light is further focused on the detector. The light must be attenuated (reduced) by a slit before reaching the detector to avoid overloading it. The result is that obtaining a spectrum takes a long time and involves a lot of moving parts and a degradation of sensitivity because of all of the mirrors and slits. Modern instruments take advantage of a mathematical concept called the Fourier Transform. The light from the source is split into two beams by a beam splitter. A moving mirror is used to change the path length of one of the beams. When the beams recombine they are in phase or out of phase, depending upon the position of the moving mirror. This apparatus is called a Michelson Interferometer. The resultant beam is called an interferogram. The entire range of wavelengths of light from the source are put through the interferometer and then exposed to the sample, which absorbs some of the light as usual. The interferogram is sent to the detector where it is subjected to a mathematical reconversion to individual wavelengths of light using a Fourier Transform. This process has only one moving part and it takes around 1 s to obtain a complete IR spectrum!

IR Microspectrophotometry

Just as with UV/visible spectrophotometry, it is possible to obtain IR spectra of microscopic pieces of evidence. Instruments can be obtained that have a microscope attached to the spectrophotometer. Through a light path, the source radiation is channeled through the microscope and the object and then to the detector. Both transmittance and reflectance spectra can be obtained. Some microscopes are outfitted with micro-reflectance objectives so that small amounts of opaque material can be analyzed directly. A large number of evidence types can be analyzed by IR microspectrophotometry. These include single fibers, paint chips including cross sections, drugs, inks, copier toners, polymers, and dyes and pigments. Figure 5.13 is an IR spectrophotometer with attached microscope.

Applications of IR in Forensic Science

Because every substance absorbs radiation in the IR region of the electromagnetic spectrum, theoretically IR spectrophotometry is a practically universal technique for the analysis of evidence. There are limitations, however, on this technique that are mostly sampling related. Remember that IR analysis relies upon the presence of a pure substance. IR spectra of mixtures are difficult to interpret and are not suitable for identification. For very small amounts of impure material, purification can be impractical and IR is not used. In such cases, gas chromatography/mass spectrometry (GC/MS) is more suited. There have been attempts to marry a gas chromatograph

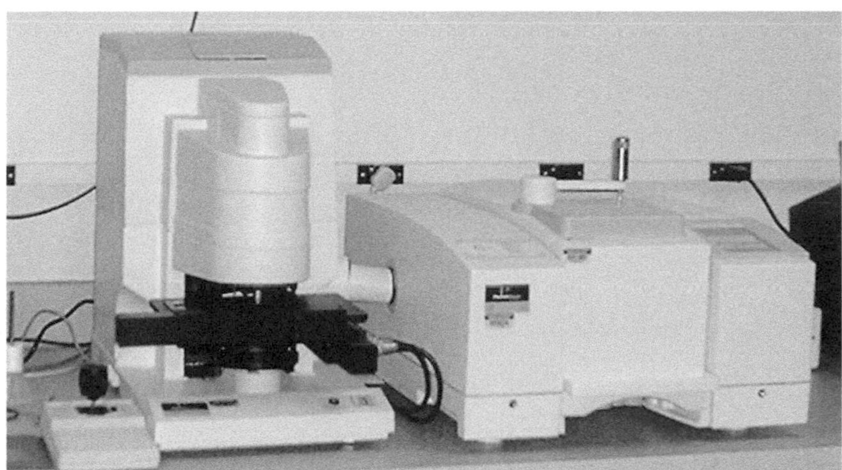

FIGURE 5.13

A Fourier Transform infrared Spectrophotometer with attached microscope. Small objects such as single fibers can be mounted under the microscope and high quality infrared spectra can be obtained. Note that there is no ocular to see the sample through. Instead there is a high-resolution camera mounted on top of the microscope. This is linked to the computer which visualizes the image of the sample.

(see Chapter 6) to an IR spectrophotometer so that small amounts of material can be purified first and then analyzed. These instruments have not been very successful and have not been widely adapted to forensic use. Having said that, it is true that IR spectrophotometry is very versatile and there are a number of applications. Solid materials such as purified drugs are easily confirmed using IR. Paint samples can be ground up or analyzed by diamond cell or ATR. Liquid hydrocarbons such as gasoline can be easily characterized by IR. Plastics and other polymers can be analyzed by transmitted or reflected light.

RAMAN SPECTROSCOPY

Recall that the absorption of IR radiation by a molecule causes the bonds to absorb energy and vibrate. A plot of the amount of energy absorbed versus the wavelengths of radiation absorbed comprises the IR spectrum. There are rules that these absorptions must obey in order for them to show up in the IR spectrum (called IR active transitions). Some vibrations are IR inactive. These vibrations may however, be active in **Raman spectroscopy**, which is a companion technique to IR spectrophotometry. The Raman effect involves radiation in the UV/visible range. Instead of absorbing this radiation, the molecule causes it to be scattered. The vast majority of the scattering incidents are **elastic**; that is the energy of the scattered photon is the same as that of the incident or absorbed photon. Approximately one out of a million of the scatterings are **inelastic**; the energy of the scattered photon can be greater (anti-Stokes line) or less (Stokes line) than that of the incident one. The Raman spectrum is measured as the **chemical shifts** of the emitted photons, which is the difference in energy between the incident photon and the inelastically scattered emitted photon. The scattering of the radiation causes molecular vibrations in the IR region that are called Raman active. In general, Raman active vibrations are IR inactive and vice versa. One of the significant advantages of Raman over IR is in sampling. Many types of glass and plastic polymers are Raman inactive. So, for example, a pure drug sample inside a plastic bag can be analyzed by Raman spectroscopy without interference from the bag. This can be useful if it is necessary to obtain fingerprints from the bag.

A few years ago, one of the authors of this book was involved in a somewhat bizarre case that was solved with Raman spectroscopy. Personnel from a police bomb squad were dismantling a safe when they found a steel cage containing a sealed glass tube that had about 75 ml of a clear liquid inside. There was a metal button on the cage that, if pressed, would break the glass and release the liquid. The bomb squad suspected that this might be a "booby trap". They brought the glass vessel to the forensic science laboratory at Michigan State University. The liquid was tested using Raman spectroscopy inside the sealed glass tube and the liquid was identified as CS gas (a type of tear gas), with the help of the FBI. CS is a liquid at room temperature but is very volatile. The glass vessel was indeed a trap. If a safe cracker hit that button, CS gas would have spread all over the place, driving away the burglar without damaging the contents of the safe!

Since Raman spectroscopy is a light scattering method, materials can be analyzed as they are. Inks and dyes can be tested while still on paper. A paint chip can be cross sectioned and laid on a piece of aluminum foil (transparent in the Raman region) and each layer can be sampled. As with IR and UV/visible spectrophotometry, Raman spectroscopy can be used in conjunction with a microscope. In this case, a laser is used as the light source and laser light passes through the microscope and the sample. Raman spectroscopy is routinely used in the analysis of drugs, paints, inks and dyes, and fibers.

MASS SPECTROMETRY

Thus far we have discussed the interactions of electromagnetic radiation with matter. In the regions of the spectrum that are the main interest of forensic science; UV/visible and IR, energy is absorbed, electrons are promoted or bonds are caused to vibrate, but there is no lasting change to the substance. Electromagnetic radiation is not the only type of energy that can be absorbed by molecules which then undergo changes. Energy from lasers, a beam of electrons, or a beam of small molecules can be transferred to matter. The result of this energy absorbance is usually the loss of one or more electrons by the substance, normally creating positive ions (although negative ion mass spectrometry is also sometimes employed). Depending upon the amount of energy from the source, these ions may stay intact or may undergo fragmentation into more stable ions. The resultant array of ions is called the mass spectrum and the techniques used to create the mass spectrum are collectively called **mass spectrometry**. Mass spectrometry has two very important properties that make it a valuable tool in analytical chemistry and thus in forensic chemistry.

1. If the energy of the source is carefully controlled then the fragmentation pattern for a given substance will be very reproducible.
2. The fragmentation pattern for a given substance is unique. The mass spectrum of a pure substance is a reliable way of identifying it.

The basic components of a mass spectrometer are shown in Figure 5.14. There are several types of instruments that vary by sampling method, type of source energy, and methods of separating the fragment ions formed. These are described briefly below.

SAMPLE INTRODUCTION

Mass spectrometers are very versatile. Samples can be introduced in almost any form. Solids and liquids and even gases can be directly injected into the instrument. A mass spectrometer can be designed as a detector for a gas chromatograph or liquid chromatograph (see Chapter 6). As each analyte component is separated by chromatography, it is introduced into the ionization chamber of the mass spectrometer. In the case of liquid chromatography, the mobile phase liquids are stripped off before the analyte is ionized. Even intractable or

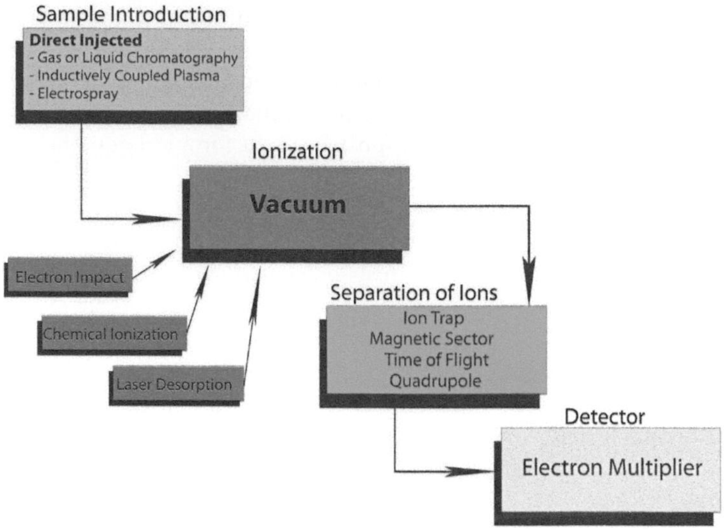

FIGURE 5.14

Diagram of the major parts of a mass spectrometer. There are several ways that analytes can be ionized and sometimes fragmented as shown in the diagram. The ionization is accomplished in a vacuum. There are also a number of ways that the ions can be separated. Detection is done by an electron multiplier.

Courtesy: Meredith Haddon.

insoluble materials such as glass can be introduced into a mass spectrometer. The elemental composition of glass samples can be identified and quantified by inductively coupled plasma mass spectrometry (ICPMS). In ICPMS, the glass is digested and is transformed into an aerosol by a nebulizer that breaks up the sample into very small droplets. The aerosol is heated to 8000 °C by argon plasma, in which it is vaporized, molecular bonds are broken, and the resulting atoms are ionized.

Ionization

Once the sample has been introduced it is sent to an ionization chamber that has been evacuated so that there is a vacuum of approximately 10^{-5} Torr. There are a number of mechanisms for ionizing the sample molecules. One method, ICPMS was discussed above.

Electron Impact

In the most common method if mass spectrometry, the analyte is bombarded by a stream of energetic electrons. The molecules absorb the energy of the electrons and then lose an electron to form a positively charged cation. Depending upon the nature of the analyte and the energy of the electrons, the parent ion may undergo decomposition into smaller ions. These in turn may further decompose or may react with other energetic species to form new daughter ions. If the ionization conditions are kept constant, the fragmentation pattern formed by a given substance will be highly reproducible, both qualitatively and quantitatively. Except for very similar substances such as enantiomers, each substance will form a unique mass spectrum by electron impact.

Chemical Ionization

Electron impact ionization tends to treat molecules harshly and they decompose extensively. Sometimes it is important for the scientist to know the molecular weight of the original analyte. In such cases small molecules such as methane or butane can be used to ionize the analyte. These molecules are much less energetic than electrons and do not impart as much energy to the analyte, so decomposition is much less extensive and more of the molecular ions remain intact.

Laser Desorption

Laser desorption mass spectrometry uses a laser to ionize the analyte. In some cases, the laser can be applied directly to the sample. It will remove molecules from the surface of the material and then ionize them. Very little decomposition of the parent ion takes place so molecular ions are always prominent. There are situations where the laser is unable to directly desorb substances. In such cases, a matrix is used. The analyte is embedded in the solid or liquid matrix. The matrix absorbs the laser energy and transfers it to the analyte. This technique is called **matrix-assisted laser desorption ionization** or MALDI. A diagram of the MALDI ionization system is shown in Figure 5.15.

SEPARATION OF IONS

After the ions have been formed they must be separated. Separation of the ions generated in the MALDI experiment is accomplished in the same way that this is done in other types of mass spectrometry.

Magnetic Sector Mass Spectrometry

In the magnetic sector mass spectrometer, the ions are accelerated through a curved magnetic field toward the detector. Smaller ions are deflected to a greater extent as they pass through the field.

Quadrupole Mass Spectrometry

The quadrupole mass spectrometer has a set of four rods arranged in the corners of a square. Diagonally opposite rods have positive charges and the others, negative. As ions pass between the rods, the strength of the fields created by the rods are altered. This allows only certain mass/charge ratio ions to get through. Continual changing of the voltages across the rods permits all ions within a given range to be analyzed.

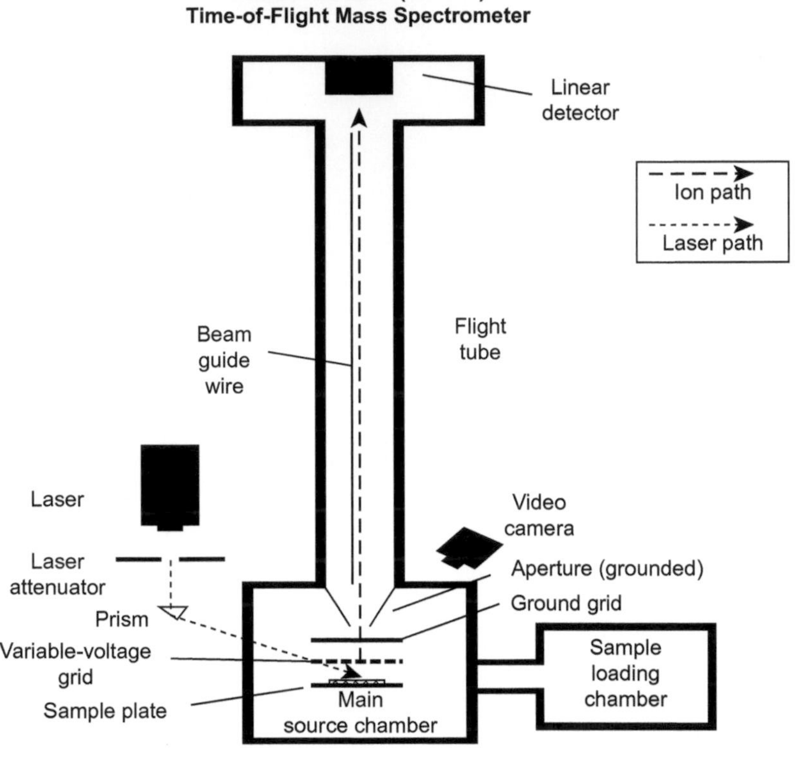

FIGURE 5.15

Diagram of a matrix-assisted laser desorption ionization (MALDI) mass spectrometer. A laser beam is focused on the sample chamber. The sample is embedded in a matrix that absorbs the energy from the laser and then transmits some of it to the sample. The sample ionizes and then is sent to the detector through a time-of-flight tube that separates the ions by their weight. One advantage of MALDI is that very little fragmentation of the ions takes place and molecular ions are very prominent.

Ion Trap Mass Spectrometry

In this type of instrument, ions are focused by a quadrupole into an ion trap where they are collected. They are then ejected toward a conventional detector.

Time-of-Flight Mass Spectrometry

In the time-of-light mass analyzer, the ions are accelerated by a magnetic field of known strength. The time it takes for a given ion to reach the detector is then used to determine the mass/charge ratio.

DETECTION OF IONS

Detectors in mass spectrometry are based on electron multipliers. After being separated, the ions from the mass analyzer are put through an amplifier to boost their signal. They then strike the surface of the detector, kicking loose electrons that are then measured. The more ions of a given mass/charge ratio, the more electrons are released and the stronger the signal.

ATOMIC SPECTROSCOPY

All of the spectroscopic methods discussed thus far are for the characterization of molecules. At times it may be necessary to focus on particular elements in a piece of evidence. For example, it may be important to know how much lead is present in a particular bullet so that it may be compared with others. Sometimes the nature of a metallic particle is completely unknown and it would be helpful to know which elements are present. The pigments in automotive paints are mostly inorganic and it is helpful to be able to determine what elements are present and in what concentration. Since the focus of this analysis is on particular elements within a molecule, a different type of spectroscopy is called for. There are two types of so-called atomic spectroscopy: **atomic absorption spectroscopy** (**AA**) and **emission spectroscopy** (**ES**).

ATOMIC ABSORPTION SPECTROSCOPY

In AA spectroscopy, substances are analyzed in the vapor phase. The elements that are to be analyzed must be known in advance. The material is dissolved in a suitable solvent and then introduced into a flame or furnace so that it can be vaporized. For illustration purposes, assume that the chemist is going to determine the amount of lead in a bullet. A weighed portion of the bullet is dissolved and vaporized. A source lamp is chosen that emits light of wavelengths that lead is known to absorb. This lamp is directed at the vaporized solution of the bullet material. The amount of light absorbed by the vapor is determined at each wavelength. From this data, the amount of lead in the bullet can be determined by Beer's Law. If the chemist then wants to determine how much copper, if any is in the bullet, she must choose a different lamp, one that is specific for copper. AA spectroscopy is very sensitive but the analyte must be vaporized and a separate experiment must be done for each element.

ATOMIC EMISSION SPECTROSCOPY

Atomic ES is an alternative to AA. It is not as sensitive as AA but does have the advantage of being able to analyze multiple elements simultaneously.

The analyte solution is introduced into a flame, oven or plasma to vaporize it. The high temperature atomization of the analyte drives the atoms to high energy levels. As they return to ground states, they emit photons of characteristic wavelengths. A high-resolution spectrometer is used to determine the emission wavelengths and thus the elements present. AE is used when the material being analyzed has a large number of elements that are being analyzed such as an unknown metallic material or sometimes an automotive paint chip.

SUMMARY

When light strikes a material, it can cause a number of effects, depending upon the nature of the material and the characteristics of the light. Light can be thought of as packets of energy (photons), which can be described in terms of their wavelengths or frequencies. When the energy reaches matter it can cause effects to the nucleus or the electrons that surround it. This is manifested by the absorption of certain wavelengths of the light. The exact number of type of wavelengths of light absorbed are characteristic of the material and the molecules from which it is made. This information helps to characterize materials.

Although there are many different types of light that can interact with matter, forensic science is chiefly concerned with two types: ultraviolet (and visible) and IR. Ultraviolet light causes electrons in atoms and molecules to be promoted to higher energy levels, resulting in the absorption of light. Since visible light is also in this range, accurate information about the color of an object from its absorption of visible light can be collected. If a material is not colored, it will only absorb ultraviolet light if it has certain chemical characteristics.

IR light is absorbed by all molecules. It causes the bonds that hold atoms together to vibrate and/or rotate. Since there are many different types of bonds within a given molecule, there are many different absorptions of IR light for even simple molecules. IR spectra are so complex that each one is unique to a particular molecule. In order for light absorption to be measured, an instrument must be used. All instruments for measuring light absorption are pretty similar. They consist of a source of light, a sample holder, a way of breaking the light into individual wavelengths, and a detector to tell when light has been absorbed.

TEST YOURSELF

1. What is wavelength? What units of measure does it have?
2. Define frequency? What are its units? What is a wavenumber?
3. How is the relationship between wavelength and frequency expressed?
4. How is the relationship between the energy of a photon and its frequency expressed?
5. Rank the following regions of the electromagnetic spectrum in the order of decreasing energy (list the highest energy one first):
   Infrared Radio Visible X-ray

6. What happens to the molecules of a substance when X-rays strike it? Why are X-rays called 'ionizing radiation'?
7. Why is visible light spectroscopy always measured at the same time as UV/visible light spectroscopy? What happens to molecules when light in these regions strikes them?
8. What happens to molecules when light in the infrared region strikes them?
9. What is the most common type of detector used in UV–visible spectrophotometry?
10. What is the most common type of detector used in infrared spectrophotometry?
11. What type of light interactions with molecules give rise to molecular fluorescence?
12. What does the unit 'Hertz' measure?
13. The absorption of light by molecules is said to be quantized. What does this mean?
14. What is a monochromator? How is it used in spectroscopy?
15. If one had two fibers that appeared to be the same color to the naked eye, what spectroscopic technique would you use to determine if they were?
16. Briefly describe the purpose of the Michelson Interferometer in FTIR.
17. What is diffuse reflectance? On what types of samples is it used?
18. What is a diamond cell? When is it used?
19. What spectroscopic technique would you use to identify a pure sample of an illicit drug?
20. All spectrophotometric detectors measure the amount of light that passes through a sample (or reflects off its surface). How can we determine what light is absorbed by the sample?

FURTHER READING

Humecki, H.J. (Ed.), 1995. Practical Guide to Infrared Microspectroscopy. Marcel Dekker.

Perkampus, H.-H., Grinter, H.C., 1992. UV-vis Spectroscopy and its Applications. (Springer Laboratory), Springer Verlag.

Skoog, D.A., Holler, F.J., Nieman, T.A., 1997. Principles of Instrumental Analysis, fifth ed. Brooks Cole.

ON THE WEB

http://molit.concord.org/database/activities/256.html – interactive site on molecular fluorescence.

http://www.files.chem.vt.edu/chem-ed/spec/spectros.html – Good introduction to spectroscopy.

http://www.cem.msu.edu/~reusch/VirtualText/Spectrpy/spectro.htm – Excellent introduction to mass, UV/visible and infrared spectroscopy.

http://www.mtholyoke.edu/~mlyount/MySites/ForensicSpectroscopy/ForensicApps.html – forensic applications of infrared spectroscopy.

CHAPTER

Separation Methods

CHAPTER OUTLINE

KEY TERMS

- Analyte
- Chromatography
- Electrophoresis
- Gas chromatography
- High Performance Liquid Chromatography
- Polarity
- Pyrolysis
- Reverse phase
- Solvent
- Stationary phase
- Stationary phase mobile phases
- Thin layer chromatography

INTRODUCTION

The most important types of examinations done in a crime laboratory involve the identification of evidence. This broad goal of evidence analysis can mean identifying the source of a fingerprint or a bullet, the identity of a particular illicit drug, the type of explosive used in a terrorist bombing, or the kind of paint used on an automobile in a hit-and-run incident. The association of a fingerprint or bullet to its source involves mainly a physical examination of the evidence itself. The others all involve some sort of chemical examination. The latter types of identifications are the subject of this chapter. In Chapter 5, you learned of two types of instrumental techniques that are suitable for the unequivocal identification of substances: mass spectrometry (MS) and infrared spectrophotometry. You also learnt that it is necessary to have the substance being identified in pure form, free of adulterants. Since chemical evidence seldom occurs in a pure state, it is usually necessary to separate it from the matrix in which it is found at a crime scene. In some cases, it is possible to physically pick out the substance of interest from a mixture but most often, it is necessary to use chemical or instrumental means to effect separations. There are a wide variety of separation methods in analytical and forensic chemistry. They range from the very basic, such as gravity filtration, to the complex, such as capillary electrophoresis. There is no single, universal method for separation of evidence from its surroundings. The separation method used in a material depends on what and how much evidence needs to be separated. For example, the separation of drugs from cutting agents may involve a liquid extraction if there is a large amount of material, or gas chromatography (GC) or liquid chromatography (LC) if only small amounts are involved. The separation of the components of gasoline in fire residues normally is accomplished by GC. The choice of the best extraction method is dependent upon the nature of the analyte and whether or not further testing such as confirmation of a pure substance is desired. If a particular substance is to be unequivocally identified (confirmed), it must be pure. It must be separated from all impurities, substrates, cutting agents, etc. Although there are a great variety of separation methods available to a forensic chemist, three of the most common and versatile families of techniques used to purify evidentiary materials will be discussed in this chapter:

- Liquid phase extraction
- Solid phase extraction
- Chromatography

Throughout the chapter the term **analyte** will be used to describe the substance or substances being separated. The term **solvent** is used to describe a liquid or liquid solution that is used to dissolve all or part of an analyte. The term **solute** is used to describe a substance that is dissolved in a solvent and, in this case is synonymous with analyte.

LIQUID PHASE EXTRACTION

Liquid phase extraction involves the separation of two or more substances in an analyte through a process where two solvents are employed. The two solvents are chosen so that they do not mix with each other (they are immiscible). An example of immiscible solvents would be chloroform and water. The solvents are also chosen such that the analyte is much more soluble in one than the other. The competition between two solvents for an analyte is called **partitioning**. This involves analytes being distributed between the two solvents according to certain chemical properties, mainly **polarity** and **pH**. A diagram of the partitioning process is shown in Figure 6.1.

POLARITY

Polarity is the tendency of the compound to behave like a miniature magnet, with a positive side and a negative side. Not all compounds have this property. It depends upon their structure and symmetry. Figure 6.2 gives examples of polar and nonpolar compounds. Figure 6.2(a) shows examples of nonpolar compounds and Figure 6.2(b) shows polar compounds.

Most organic compounds tend to be nonpolar or slightly polar, whereas inorganic compounds can range from nonpolar to very polar. Compounds that are symmetric tend to be nonpolar. Polarity is caused by an excess of electron density on one side of a molecule and therefore a deficiency on the other side. The side with the excess electron density has a net negative charge and the other side has a net positive charge because it is deficient in electrons. The degree of polarity exhibited by a substance determines its solubility in a given solvent. A simple rule about solubility and polarity is **like dissolves like**. This means that polar compounds have a greater affinity

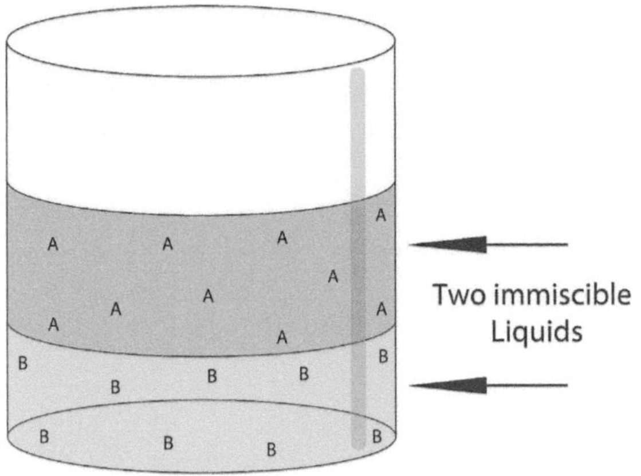

FIGURE 6.1

Immiscible liquids. The two liquids do not mix with one another. The less dense liquid sits on top of the more dense one. One is more polar than the other. The more polar analytes tend to dissolve in the more polar liquid.

Courtesy: Meredith Haddon.

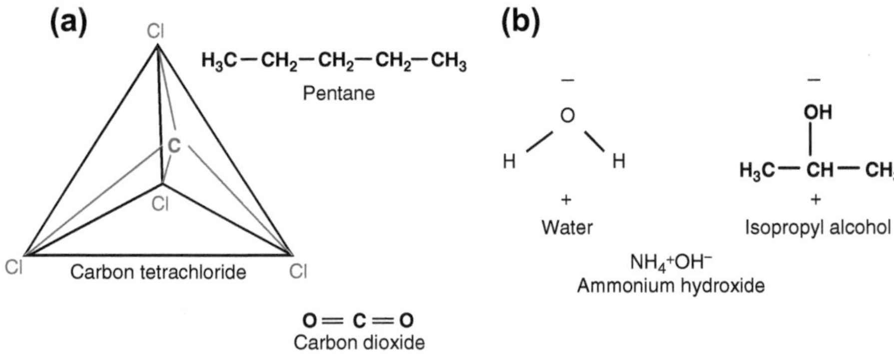

FIGURE 6.2

Polar and nonpolar compounds. Compounds that exhibit certain types of symmetry are nonpolar. The electrons pull equally in all directions in nonpolar compounds. Examples are shown in (a). Polar compounds have an unequal pull of electrons in one direction. This creates positive and negative sides of the molecule. This can be most easily seen in the water molecule in (b).

for other polar compounds and, in the case of solubility, it means that polar solutes will dissolve more readily and to a greater degree in polar solvents. This property is exploited in liquid extractions. If an analyte contains a mixture of substances where some are polar and others are nonpolar, they can be separated into two groups using a polar solvent such as water to dissolve the polar substances and a nonpolar solvent such as methylene chloride to dissolve the nonpolar substances. Sometimes the polarity of a substance can be manipulated chemically in such a way so as to not change its basic nature. For example, cocaine is, like most organic compounds, fairly nonpolar. It can be made more polar by reacting it with a dilute acid, forming a salt. Salts are generally quite polar substances. The free cocaine can be recovered at any time with the use of an alkaline substance that reverses the action of the acid.

pH

Another property of certain chemical compounds is their acidity or alkalinity relative to water. An acidic substance is the one that releases hydrogen ions H^+ (they become hydrated in the presence of water, so they are in the form of H_2O. H^+ or H_3O^+ called hydronium ions) when dissolved in water. The amount of H_3O^+ in an aqueous solution is measured by its pH. This is the negative logarithm of the H_3O^+ concentration in moles per liter. Acids have pH values between 0 and 7. An alkaline or basic substance is the one that releases hydroxide (OH^-) ions when dissolved in water. Its pH is between 7 and 14. A neutral substance is the one that releases neither H_3O^+ nor OH^- ions when dissolved. Its pH is 7. Drugs, for example, can be classified as acidic, basic, or neutral. Cocaine is a basic drug. When it is dissolved in water or an aqueous solvent, it attracts H^+ from the solvent leaving OH^- behind. On the other hand, barbiturates are acidic drugs. They attract hydroxide ions leaving behind excess hydrogen ions. Caffeine is an example of a neutral drug. Sugars and carbohydrates (common cutting agents in street drugs) are also neutral. Figure 6.3 is an example of the reaction of a basic compound, in this case, cocaine in water making it an acidic salt.

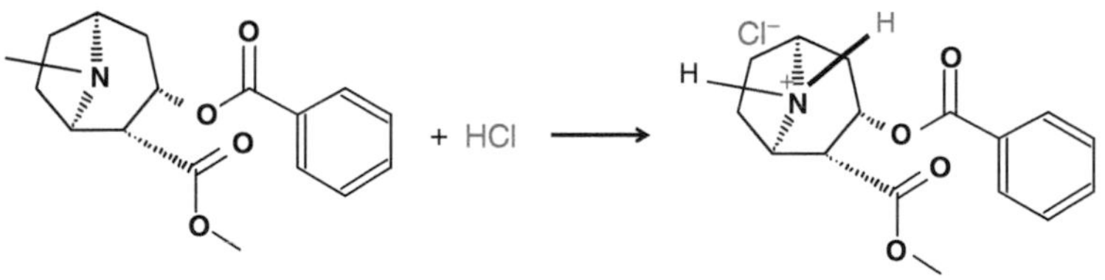

FIGURE 6.3

Cocaine hydrochloride. If cocaine is dissolved in an acidic solution, an extra proton (H^+) attaches itself to the amine group (NH_2R) on the cocaine. This makes the cocaine much more polar than it is in its free form.

IN THE LABORATORY: SEPARATION OF A DRUG MIXTURE BY LIQUID PHASE EXTRACTION

Both the properties of polarity and pH can be used to advantage when trying to purify a drug. Suppose that a forensic scientist receives a drug sample that turns out to be 50% cocaine hydrochloride and 50% sucrose, a sugar used as a cutting agent or diluent. Cocaine hydrochloride is a salt form of cocaine that is much more polar than cocaine free base, the naturally occurring form of cocaine. Sucrose is a neutral, nonpolar substance. The task is to separate the cocaine from the sucrose, saving the cocaine and getting rid of the sucrose. Two immiscible solvents will be employed in this process. This is an example of a liquid phase extraction. A diagram of how this works is shown in Figure 6.4.

(Continued)

IN THE LABORATORY: SEPARATION OF A DRUG MIXTURE BY LIQUID PHASE EXTRACTION—cont'd

1. The mixture is dissolved in water and filtered. All of the cocaine hydrochloride will dissolve. It is fairly polar and water is a polar solvent (remember: like dissolves like). Some of the sucrose will dissolve. The filtration step removes the sucrose that doesn't dissolve.
2. The filtered liquid (the filtrate) is then put into a glass **separatory** funnel. Then some weakly alkaline liquid such as ammonium hydroxide is added to the water. This gives the solution a high pH. The H^+ and Cl^- that are attached to the cocaine hydrochloride react with the ammonium hydroxide to form ammonium chloride and the cocaine hydrochloride is converted to the free base form of cocaine, which is much less polar than cocaine hydrochloride and much less soluble in water, causing it to precipitate out. The sucrose that originally dissolved in the water remains in solution.
3. Now an equal volume of a nonpolar solvent such as chloroform ($CHCl_3$) is added to the separatory funnel. The nonpolar cocaine free base dissolves readily in the chloroform, but the somewhat polar sucrose stays in the water.
4. The chloroform and water layers are separated. The chloroform can then be evaporated, leaving the purified cocaine free base.

The foregoing is called a basic extraction. The solvent containing the dissolved analyte is made basic and then extracted with a nonpolar solvent. An acidic extraction can be used on mixtures containing an acidic drug.

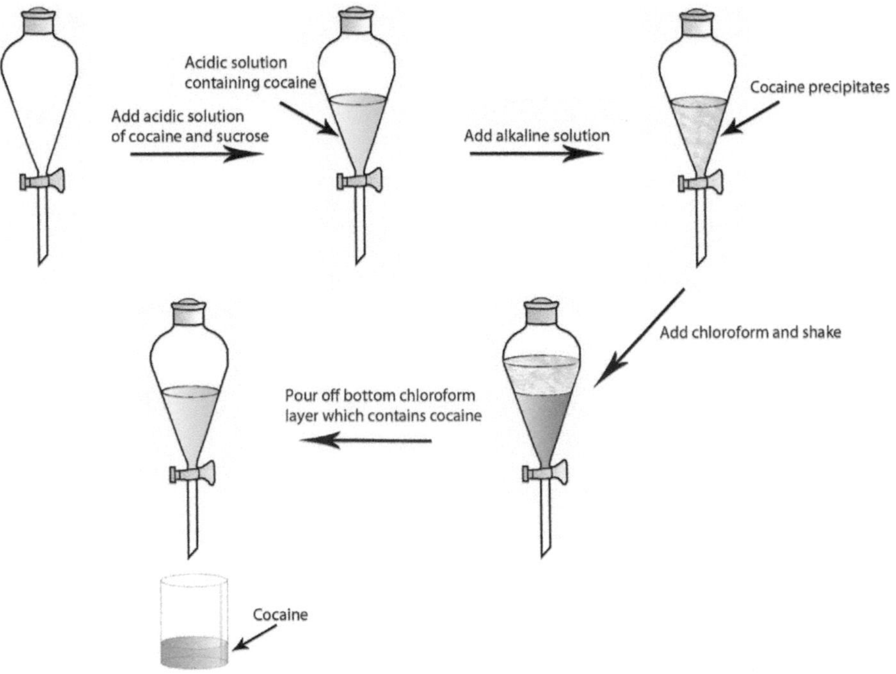

FIGURE 6.4

A liquid extraction process. Making use of a separatory funnel, this process takes advantage of the tendency of polar solutes to dissolve in polar solvents. The same holds true for nonpolar solutes and solvents.

Courtesy: Meredith Haddon.

Note that in Figure 6.3 above, the cocaine has been converted to a salt form. The cocaine molecule has obtained a positive charge and the chloride ion from the hydrochloric acid (HCl) has a negative charge. This form of cocaine is much more polar than free cocaine. This property can be exploited in separating cocaine from a mixture.

Liquid phase extractions are commonly used to separate mixtures of solids. They are ideal for separating substances where one is much more soluble than the rest or if they are of different polarity and pH. If, however, the mixture contains two substances of similar polarity and both are acidic or basic, such as cocaine and heroin, then a liquid phase extraction would likely fail to achieve a good separation. A different type of separation process would be required for such mixtures.

SOLID PHASE EXTRACTION

There are times when a liquid phase extraction is not suitable. A relatively large amount of material, at least a few grams, is normally required for an effective liquid phase extraction. Because of similarities in pH or polarity, it may not be feasible to separate two substances by liquid phase extraction. In such cases, there is another technique that can overcome these limitations. It is called **solid phase extraction**. Solid phase extraction does not involve a partitioning mechanism. Instead, it relies on **adsorption**, a process whereby a solid, liquid, or gaseous analyte is attracted to the surface of a solid adsorbing material. The analyte molecules adhere to its surface. If just one component of a mixture is adsorbed onto the surface of the adsorbent, it can be separated using this method. In some cases, two or more components of an analyte mixture can be separated this way if they have different affinities for the adsorbent. A number of chemical processes affect the tendency and tenacity of the adsorption including polarity.

One example of solid phase adsorption is the trapping of a hydrocarbon accelerant that was used to start a fire, on the surface of a plastic strip coated with finely divided charcoal, a potent adsorbing material. The strip is immersed in a can containing the residue from a fire suspected to contain the accelerant. As the can is heated, the accelerant molecules evaporate into the air space above the debris (called the headspace) and adsorb on to the surface of the coated strip. When it is removed from the can, the strip can be heated or added to a solvent to elute (remove) the adsorbed accelerant.

Another example of a solid phase extraction is the "cleanup" process of a biological sample containing a drug. A column of adsorbing material is inserted into a large tube and a blood or urine sample is then added. It flows through the tube under a vacuum and the drug is adsorbed on to the surface of the adsorbing material whereas the rest of the blood or urine passes through. The drug can then be eluted from the adsorbent with a compatible solvent. There are a variety of solid phase adsorbing materials available for different types of drugs and other substances. In the section on chromatography in this chapter, the pioneering chromatography experiment, separating plant pigments on a solid column is described. It is an example of solid phase extraction.

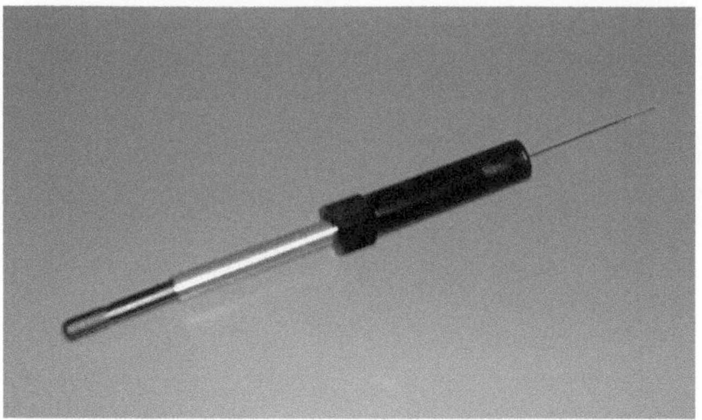

FIGURE 6.5

The solid phase microextraction (SPME) apparatus. The fiber at the end of the wand can be coated with a particular polymer or other coating so that it will efficiently adsorb certain types of analytes. For example, there are SPME fibers that will adsorb molecules of flammable liquids mixed in with debris from a fire.

SOLID PHASE MICROEXTRACTION

The early methods of solid phase extraction required a relatively large amount of analyte to get an effective separation. Much of the evidence at crime scenes exists in only small quantities. In recent years, a modification of solid phase extraction has been developed. This is called **solid phase** microextraction (SPME). This technique is used for very small samples. A small wire is coated with an adsorbent such as charcoal and attached to a holder that can extend or withdraw the wire. The wire is extended into a vapor or liquid where adsorption takes place. Then the wire can be introduced into a gas chromatograph (see the next section) where the adsorbed materials are eluted and analyzed. An apparatus used for SPME is shown in Figure 6.5.

CHROMATOGRAPHY

Solid and liquid phase extractions have proven to be reliable, versatile methods of separation of many types of analytes. However, they are by no means universal and even the microextraction methods developed for solid phase extraction are not suitable for extremely small amounts of material. These techniques work best with solid samples that are soluble in at least one volatile solvent. Neither of these techniques are quantitative; one cannot easily determine the concentration of an analyte by these methods. At the turn of the last century, a Russian botanist revolutionized analytical chemistry by developing a separation method that has evolved into a whole family of analytical techniques applicable to a huge variety of mixtures of solids, liquids, and vapors, over a large temperature range, whether they are soluble in solvents or not. This family is collectively known as **chromatography**. The term "chromatography" means literally "to write with color." This seems like an odd name for a family of techniques that seem to have little to do with color, and everything to do with separating mixtures of substances. The reason for the name is that the technique was originally developed by a Russian botanist, Michael Tswett (whose name in Russian means color!) in 1901, who was interested in separating colored pigments in plants. He purified a fine, sand-like substance and filled a long column with it. He then prepared a solution of the pigments that he wanted to separate and poured this through the column. He found that the pigments were divided into colored bands at various points along the length of the column. Each band represented a component of the pigments. The bands were identifiable by their different colors. This column was able to separate the pigments this way. He could then take each band of the column and elute off the pigment. This technique worked only for substances that had a native color. The "detector" was the naked eye. Transparent pigments could not be detected by this method. Chromatography evolved and developed over the next century. It would have had much more limited uses if it depended on color to detect substances and could only have been operated at ambient temperature. Since these original experiments, however, chromatography has come a long way. The term has come to represent a family of techniques that all do essentially the same thing: separate complex mixtures of substances into their individual components and then display these components so that the analyst can get information about their number and chemical nature and sometimes concentration. There are many advantages of chromatography over solid and liquid phase extractions and a huge variety of materials may be separated by one type of chromatography or another. Chromatography methods are also generally more sensitive than extractions. Some chromatography methods can separate millionths or billionths of a gram of material.

HISTORY OF CHROMATOGRAPHY

Chromatographic separations may have been performed as far back as the fifteenth century, but there are no written records about how they were done. In 1906, Mikhail Tswett, a Russian botanist, published his first paper on his technique of liquid–solid separation of plant pigments. He was clearly the father of chromatography. It wasn't until 1941, with the development of alumina as a dependable stationary phase, that scientists finally recognized chromatography as a reliable and versatile separation technique.

In 1941, Martin and Synge, working with amino acid separations, developed a technique that used two liquids rather than a liquid and a solid. This became the foundation for LC. They also developed the first theoretical framework for describing how chromatography could be optimized by measuring its efficiency. They also speculated that a gaseous mobile phase could be paired with a liquid stationary phase to achieve effective separations. This foreshadowed the development of gas–liquid chromatography, or simply GC. For all of this developmental work, they won the 1952 Nobel Prize.

In 1958, new detectors were announced for GC, thus greatly extending its usefulness. These were the flame ionization and electron capture detectors. At about the same time, Golay proposed the use of narrow-bore capillaries that would have their inside walls coated with a liquid as the stationary phase. This revolutionized GC because it greatly improved separations and efficiencies. Capillary GC is universally used today.

High performance liquid chromatography (HPLC) wasn't developed until the 1970s. Reverse phase chromatography using long-chain hydrocarbons coated on the surface of silica beads was developed about this time. HPLC started with long thin columns like GC but it was soon discovered that shorter, thicker columns containing small particles could improve resolution. This technology is widely used in forensic science today.

HOW CHROMATOGRAPHY WORKS

Almost all chromatographic methods work on the same principle. They differ in how the experiment is set up and some of the analytical details. The components of the analyte will show some differences in at least one property that is exploited by the chromatography experiment. That will be the basis for the separation. The original experiment, cited above, where plant pigments are separated in a column of silica, illustrates the principles.

In all forms of chromatography, there are two phases present: a **stationary phase** and a **mobile phase**. The stationary phase is a finely divided solid material or a viscous liquid that is contained within a long column. The mobile phase is a liquid (or liquid solution) or a gas under pressure. The mobile phase moves through the stationary phase carrying the analyte mixture with it. Depending upon their affinity for the stationary phase, the components of the analyte move quickly or slowly through the column, separating from other components along the way.

In the plant pigment separation cited above, the column of silica is an example of a stationary phase. The plant pigment mixture is dissolved in a solvent that is then poured through the stationary phase. The solvent is the mobile phase. If the stationary phase had no affinity for the analyte components, then they would all travel together right along with the mobile phase and emerge at the bottom together. The stationary phase is designed to attract or, in some cases, repel, certain members of the analyte, each one in a different way. This means that the progress of each component of the analyte will be affected by the stationary phase, hopefully in a different way from all of the others. When the mobile phase has completed its journey through the column, the various pigments have been held up by the stationary phase and form colored bands at various points in the column. To recover one or more of the pigments, they would have to be eluted off the column using a suitable solvent. Each pigment has a distinct visible color and can thus be detected visually. In modern applications of chromatography, most analytes have no color and there are such small quantities being separated, that no color would be visible anyway. Therefore each type of chromatography has its own types of **detectors** that use various properties of the analytes to signal their presence.

In chromatography, the relationship between the stationary phase and mobile phase is often described as **normal** or **reverse** phase. In normal phase chromatography, the

IN MORE DEPTH

One way of visualizing how chromatography works to separate components of a mixture is to consider a group of tourists who are visiting a large city. They decide to go sightseeing one day. The city runs tour buses that leave a central point every few minutes. Passengers can board or alight from any bus any time. All the buses make a circuit of the city, stopping at a number of points of interest. A group of tourists all board a bus in the morning (the mixture). Along the way, some of the tourists stop and get off the bus to see an art gallery or the state capitol, or a performing arts center, etc. They get back on a tour bus after seeing the sights. Some of the passengers may stay on the bus for the whole tour as a way of getting the lay of the land. At the end of the day, all of the tourists will eventually make it to the end of the tour, but at different times. They would have been separated by their different preferences for one sight or another or for the tour bus. In this analogy, the tour buses are the mobile phase and the various points of interest are locations on the stationary phase.

mobile phase is less polar than the stationary phase. This is always the situation with GC, where the mobile phase is a nonpolar inert gas. In reverse phase chromatography, the opposite is true. The mobile phase is more polar than the stationary phase. In LC and thin-layer chromatography (TLC), either normal or reverse phase can be used.

GAS CHROMATOGRAPHY

STATIONARY AND MOBILE PHASES

The most versatile chromatography method is called **gas chromatography** (GC), sometimes called gas–liquid chromatography. Many people call the method simply **GC**. Modern GC is called **capillary GC** because the stationary phase is contained within a very narrow, hollow tube that is made of glass or a synthetic polymer and is often coated with a plastic to add strength. The inside of the column contains the stationary phase, a thick, high boiling, viscous liquid, that has the consistency of molasses. The stationary phase forms a thin coating on the inside of the capillary. The columns in capillary GCs can be up to 30 m long or on rare occasions, even longer. The development of capillary columns in the late 1970s was a huge improvement in GC because it resulted in great increases in column efficiencies and separation of even similar substances. The older generation of GC columns was glass or copper tubes usually from 1/8″ to 1/4″ (or sometimes even wider) in diameter and generally 1 or 2 m long. They were filled with tiny, polymeric spheres that were coated with the same kind of stationary phase described above for capillary columns. These were called packed columns. They were orders of magnitude less efficient in separating complex mixtures.

The mobile phase in GC is an inert gas. The most commonly used gas is helium. Nitrogen is also used but gives inferior results. The best gas is hydrogen but it is more expensive than helium and is quite flammable. If there is a leak in the system, an explosion or fire can result. In a gas chromatograph, the mobile phase is forced through the stationary phase under pressure. Since the analytes are carried through the stationary phase by the gaseous mobile phase, they too have to be in a vapor state. This results in one of the limitations of GC. The analytes have to be heated until they vaporize. GC stationary phases are only stable to about 350 °C so the analyte must be able to be converted to a vapor (at least partially) at this temperature. In addition, the analytes must be thermally stable at such temperatures. Some substances decompose at high temperatures and would not be suitable for GC analysis. Forensically important substances that are not stable at high temperatures include many explosives. The presence of the inert gas as the mobile phase purges the entire system of oxygen so there is no chance for analytes to burn when they are heated inside the instrument.

PARTS OF THE GAS CHROMATOGRAPH

A gas chromatograph is an instrument that is used to separate components of an analyte mixture using the principles of GC. It consists of several parts. A diagram of a gas chromatograph is shown in Figure 6.6.

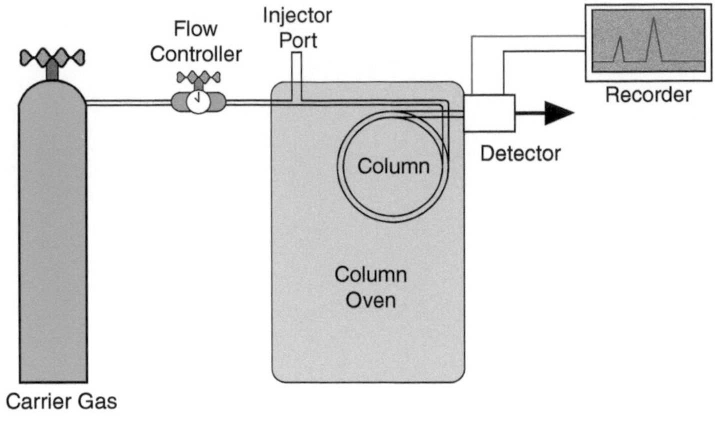

FIGURE 6.6

The gas chromatograph.

Courtesy: Meredith Haddon.

For illustrative purposes, the separation of a mixture containing cocaine, caffeine, and sugar will be described below. GC can be used to determine the concentration of the cocaine in the mixture. If this is to be done, the amount of mixture that is dissolved must be accurately known.

The Injector

The injector is a heated chamber where the analyte mixture is introduced and combined with the mobile phase. The mobile phase continually passes through the injector under pressure. In a typical GC experiment, the analyte mixture is dissolved in a volatile solvent. For the cocaine/caffeine/sugar analyte, methyl alcohol is a good choice for the solvent. Cocaine, caffeine, and sugar are all solids at room temperature. Sugar is mostly insoluble in methanol so it must be filtered out before the experiment is run. This leaves only the cocaine and caffeine to be separated. The injector is generally heated to about 250 °C. At this temperature at least some of the cocaine and caffeine will vaporize as will all of the alcohol. The solution is introduced into the injector using a syringe, through an airtight septum. The vaporized mixture is mixed immediately with the flowing mobile phase and carried into the capillary column. Injectors can be configured as **split** or **splitless**. Capillary columns are very narrow and easily overloaded with analyte so the mobile phase will be split so that some of it is vented away and only part of it goes through the column. If the analytes are very dilute or there is very little, then the entire amount is sent through the column in a splitless configuration.

The Stationary Phase

The column containing the stationary phase was described above. As the mobile phase passes through the stationary phase, the various components of the analyte mixture are exposed to the surface of the stationary phase. There are two principles that determine

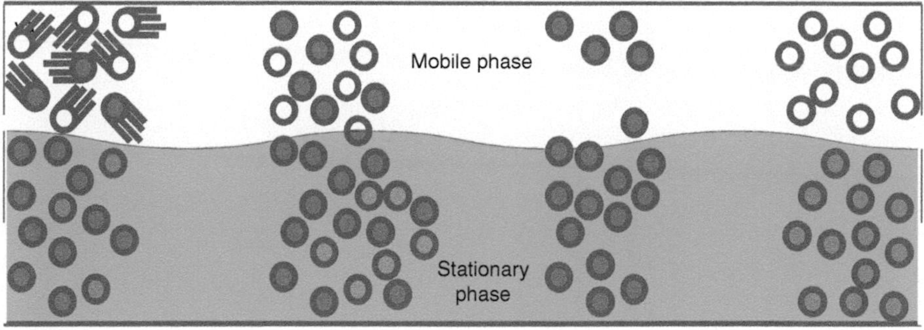

FIGURE 6.7

The partitioning process of analyte molecules between a stationary phase and a mobile phase. The partitioning depends upon the polarities of the analyte components and the relative polarities of the stationary and mobile phases.

how long it will take a substance to traverse the entire column: its molecular weight and its polarity. All other factors being equal, a lower molecular weight substance will traverse the column faster than a heavier one. The degree of influence that polarity has on the time depends upon the polarity of the stationary phase and the polarities of the analytes. Because of their differences in structure, cocaine and caffeine have different weights and polarities and are easily separated by GC. Figure 6.7 is a diagram that shows how an analyte mixture is separated by a GC stationary phase.

The operator has quite a bit of control over the conditions of the GC experiment. The time it takes for analytes to traverse the stationary phase (**the retention** time) and the degree of separation of the analyte components can be controlled by varying the polarity of the stationary phase, the speed of the mobile phase as it passes through the stationary phase and, most importantly, the temperature of the stationary and mobile phases. The rule of thumb for GC is that every 10 °C rise in temperature of the experiment halves the retention time of a material. This is a powerful factor in designing an experiment to separate a complex mixture. If the mixture contains substances that are low molecular weight and high molecular weight and of varying polarity, one can use temperature programming to vary the temperature of the experiment during its progress. For example, gasoline contains more than 300 different compounds. Their polarities are generally similar but there is a large variation in the weights of the compounds. If the separation is done at a low temperature, the lower weight compounds will separate from each other but the process will take a long time. If the temperature is raised so that the process takes a short time, the low weight compounds will all elute together and won't separate. This is where temperature programming comes in. The oven can be set at a low temperature (around 50 °C) at the beginning and then it is allowed to gradually rise during the run. This provides good separation of low weight compounds and completes the run in a reasonable time. Figure 6.8 shows a chromatogram of a sample of gasoline that was partially burned in a fire. The chart proceeds from left to right, with the lowest weight components on the left side.

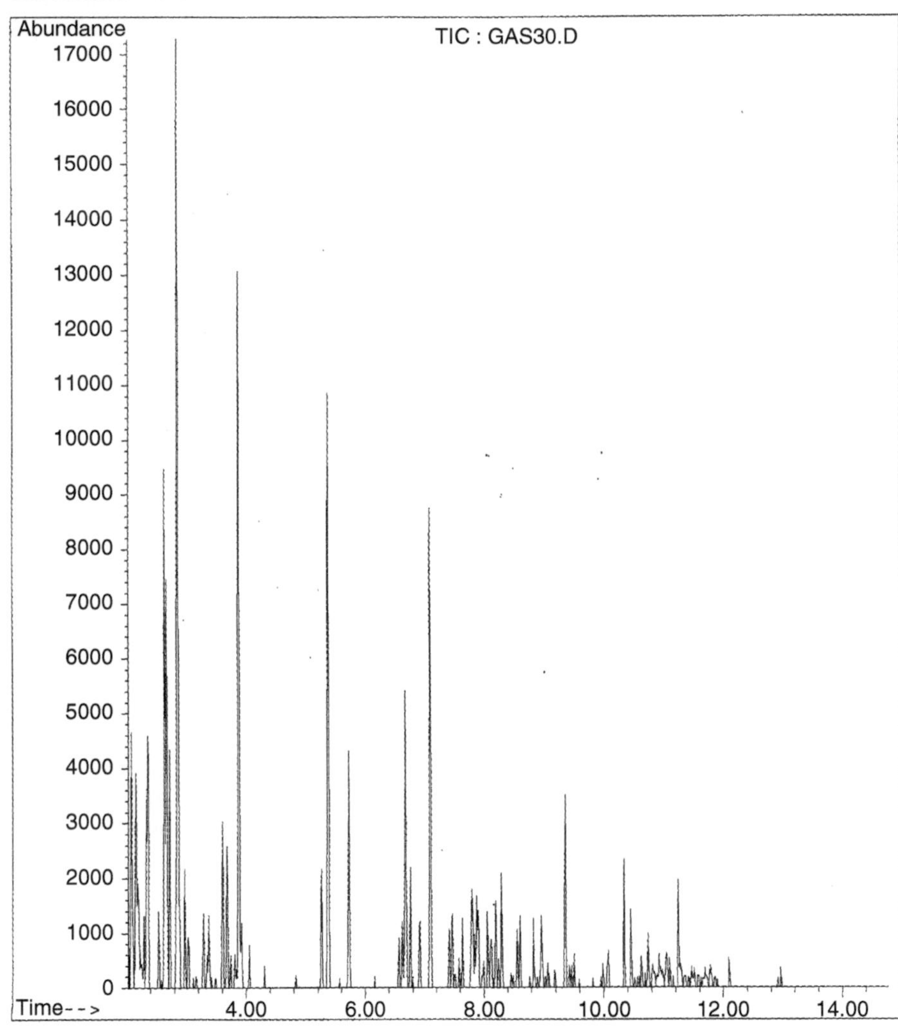

FIGURE 6.8

A gas chromatogram of partially burned gasoline. Each peak represents a component of the gasoline. Whole gasoline contains more than 300 substances. The most volatile substances evaporate when the gasoline is subjected to heat.

The Detector

Once a component of the analyte makes it all the way through the stationary phase it has to be detected. Remember that each component is a vapor mixed with the inert mobile phase. Thus detectors in GC have to be able to detect changes in the composition of a vapor solution. These detectors are designed so that they do not respond to pure mobile phase and so they do not show any activity until the mobile phase contains one of the analyte components. GC detectors work by converting the signal they receive when analyte reaches them into a small electric current. This is amplified and then computerized so that it can be seen on a monitor and printed. Each component is displayed as a triangular peak. The retention time of each component is the time it takes for that component to traverse the injector and column, and is measured to the top of the peak. The area under the peak is proportional to the amount of that component in the mixture so that GC can be used for quantitative analysis.

Ideally, each substance in the mixture would take a different amount of time to traverse the column and reach the detector. A **chromatogram** is a plot of the response of the detector versus the retention time. Every time GC analyzes the same substance under the same conditions, its retention time should be about the same, as long as the conditions of the experiment are not changed. Thus, the retention time gives a tentative identification of the substance. It is important to understand that the retention time is not a characteristic that definitely identifies a substance. For example, an exhibit may show a peak at 2.4 min in a gas chromatogram. A sample of known heroin also has a retention time of 2.4 min using the same instrument under the same conditions. The fact that both the unknown and the known have the same retention time is indicative of their being the same substance, but it does not prove it. There are millions of substances in the world and several might have the same retention time. This is why chromatography is a separation technique and not an identification technique. A few of the more common types of GC detectors are described below.

Flame Ionization Detector

This detector produces a small flame from the reaction of hydrogen taken from a tank and oxygen from the air. This flame does not affect the mobile phase carrier gas; however, when a component of the analyte reaches the flame it loses an electron and becomes ionized. These ions create an electric current that is amplified and sent to a computer for display. The magnitude of the current is proportional to the amount of substance present. This is a nonselective detector. It responds pretty much to all organic compounds. The gas chromatogram in Figure 6.8 above was generated on an instrument using a flame ionization detector.

Mass Spectrometer Detector

In Chapter 5, MS was discussed as a stand-alone instrument for the identification of pure substances. One of the concepts mentioned there was combining a chromatograph such as a gas chromatograph with a mass spectrometer. As each substance elutes from the stationary phase of the GC, it is sent immediately to the ionization chamber of mass spectrometer. A mass spectrometer can detect and identify each analyte component as it elutes from the column. A mass spectrum of each substance can be generated very quickly.

The identification process can be very efficient if the gas chromatography/mass spectrometry (GC/MS) system contains a spectral library. This is a collection of up to thousands of mass spectra of known compounds. A reasonably powerful personal computer can take the mass spectrum of an unknown substance and use it to search the spectral library. This process may take less than 1 min for 50,000 compounds. The result of the search will usually be a list of about 10 compounds whose mass spectra most resemble the unknown and a number that indicates how closely each one matches. A very high match number indicates that there is a high likelihood that the known and unknown are the same substance. The MS detector is also a quantitative tool. A chromatogram can be produced that is developed by plotting the total ions produced in the mass spectrometer versus retention time. The area under the peaks in this **total ion chromatogram** are proportional to the amount of material in each component of the analyte.

Other GC Detectors There are several other types of GC detectors that are not as widely used in forensic applications. They are listed here for completeness. The responses of all of these detectors, like those discussed above are displayed as peaks that can be used for quantitative analysis.

- **Nitrogen–phosphorous** – This type of detector is similar to the flame ionization detector except that it can detect only substances that contain nitrogen or phosphorous. This type is widely used in biological, toxicological, and environmental applications and is very sensitive.
- **Thermal conductivity** – This type of detector relies on the change in the ability of the mobile phase gas to conduct heat as it is mixed with an analyte. It is simple to engineer and use and is very versatile.
- **Electron capture** – This is an extremely sensitive detector that is used on substances that have a halide such as chloride or bromide, or oxygen in the molecule.

GAS CHROMATOGRAPH QUANTITATIVE ANALYSIS BY GAS CHROMATOGRAPHY

As previously noted, the size of the peak on a gas chromatogram is proportional to the amount of material that reaches the detector. Strictly speaking, it is the area under the peak (geometrically speaking), which is the important quantity. Suppose, in the case with the heroin and cocaine, one wanted to determine the percent cocaine in the drug exhibit. The following steps would be taken:

1. A sample of the exhibit would be weighed out and dissolved in a suitable solvent that also contained an internal standard. An internal standard is a compound that elutes near the analyte and is used to standardize the procedure.
2. A sample of known cocaine would be weighed out and dissolved in the same solvent with the same amount of internal standard.
3. Both would then be chromatographed and the areas under the cocaine and internal standard peaks for both the known cocaine and case exhibit are calculated. Through simple proportions, the weight of cocaine in the exhibit can be

calculated and then the percent can be determined by knowing the weight of the powder that was dissolved.

In most jurisdictions, the percent of a drug is not a legal issue in the sense that the penalty for possession or distribution does not depend on the percent of cocaine. Why then would a drug chemist do this quantitative analysis? In some cases, the investigative agency asks for these data because it can help in determining how far up the distribution chain the seized drugs are. For example, if normal "street" cocaine is 40% pure and this particular exhibit is 80%, it means that the person arrested for possession of this exhibit is probably not an ultimate user, but is more likely a distributor. Also, sometimes judges want to know the purity of a drug exhibit so that they can impose appropriate sentences when someone is found guilty of possession or distribution.

PYROLYSIS GAS CHROMATOGRAPHY

GC is always operated at elevated temperatures. As discussed previously in the section on stationary phases above, GC experiments can be run at temperatures of up to about 350 °C. At higher temperatures, the stationary phase will begin to bleed off the sides of the capillary and destroy the column. Any substance which is stable at these temperatures and which can easily be vaporized is a good candidate for GC. There are, however, many substances that could be otherwise analyzed by GC except that they do not vaporize to any appreciable degree at these temperatures and cannot be analyzed by normal GC methods. These substances include fibers, paints, plastics, hairs, and other polymers. A modification of GC, called **pyrolysis gas chromatography** (PGC), can make it possible for a gas chromatograph to analyze polymers.

The term "pyrolysis" means essentially "to heat in the absence of air." If a polymer such as a fiber is heated to very high temperatures, up to 1000 °C, in the absence of oxygen, it will not burn but instead will decompose into stable fragments, called **pyrolyzates**. If this process is done repeatedly under the same conditions, the number, size, and relative amounts of the pyrolyzates will be the same for a particular polymer type. In PGC, an apparatus that can hold a small fragment of polymer is inserted directly into the injector of the gas chromatograph. There is no oxygen present in the injector because of the inert mobile phase gas, so only pyrolysis and not combustion takes place. The pyrolyzer is then heated to high temperatures, generally 700–1000 °C and the polymer decomposes. The fragments are then separated, the same as the components of any analyte. The resulting chromatogram is called a **pyrogram**. Figure 6.9 shows a typical apparatus used in pyrolysis. The wand has a coil made of platinum wire at the tip. A quartz glass tube is used to hold the sample. The tube is plugged at both ends with quartz glass wool. The tube is threaded into the platinum coil and then the tip of the wand is inserted directly into the inlet of the gas chromatograph. The coil is heated and the sample pyrolyzes, forming vapor phase pyrolyzates that are swept into the stationary phase by the mobile phase.

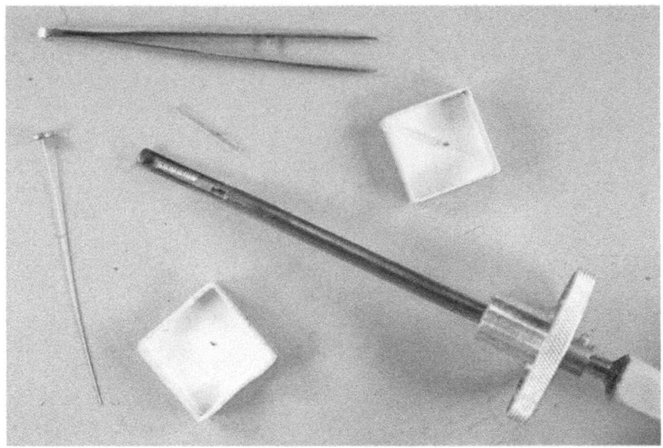

FIGURE 6.9

A pyrolysis unit. The quartz tubes hold the samples and can fit inside the platinum coil on the end of the probe. The probe is then inserted into the inlet of a gas chromatograph and then the platinum coil is heated under controlled conditions. The sample in the quartz tube pyrolyzes and the fragments are separated by the GC.

Figure 6.10 is a pyrogram of a polyester fiber. The fiber is heated to 700 °C. The GC is temperature programed. There are many different types of polyester fibers. This pyrogram is characteristic of this particular type.

IN MORE DEPTH: HYPHENATED ANALYTICAL TECHNIQUES

GC/MS is an example of a hyphenated technique. This is a colloquial term used in analytical chemistry to denote two instruments that are engineered to act as a single entity. In the case of GC/MS, the individual substances separated by the GC are sent directly into the mass spectrometer where they may be identified. The mass spectrometer can be thought of as a detector for the GC or the GC can be thought of as an inlet device for the MS. There are also other hyphenated techniques used in analytical chemistry and forensic science. For example, there is GC-FTIR. FTIR stands for **Fourier transform infrared spectrophotometer**. In this instrument, the GC separates a mixture into individual components and then each one can be introduced into a special sample compartment in an FTIR (see Chapter 5).

High performance liquid chromatography or HPLC-MS (see below) can also be mated to a mass spectrometer. It works in much the same way as GC/MS.

Pyrolysis GC, discussed above is another hyphenated technique. This one is a bit different than the others in that the pyrolysis unit cannot work by itself and must have a GC, whereas the other instrument pairs can stand alone.

HIGH PERFORMANCE LIQUID CHROMATOGRAPHY (HPLC)

At the beginning of this chapter the original experiments involving separation of plant pigments were described. These are early examples of LC. The analytes were dissolved in a liquid and then poured through a bed of silica. The liquid is the mobile

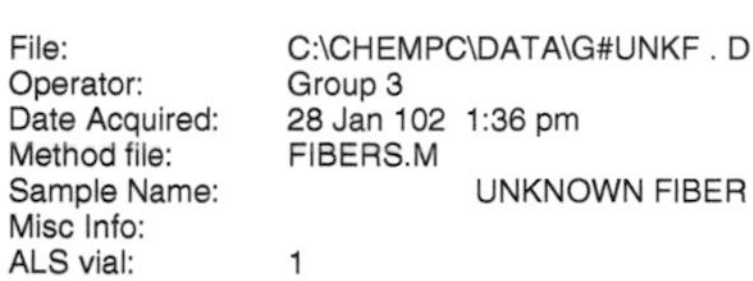

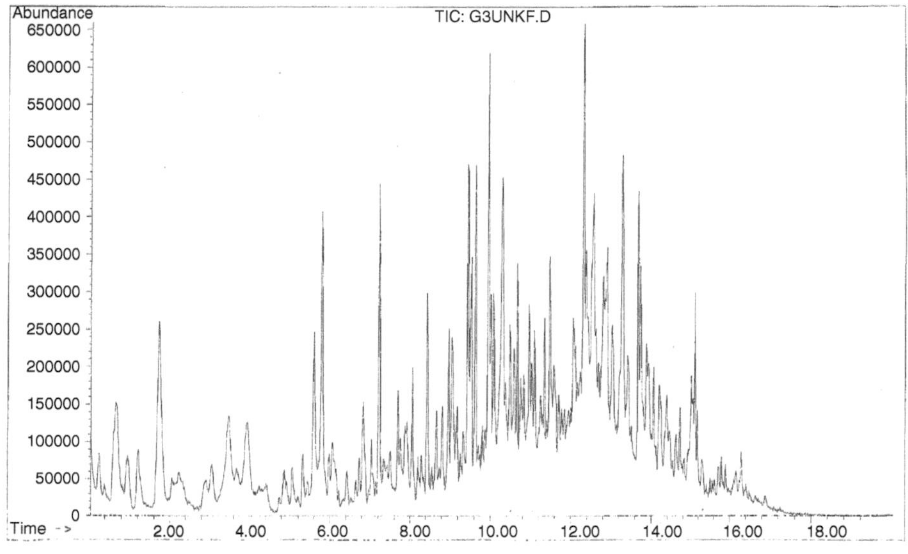

FIGURE 6.10

A pyrogram of a polyester fiber. Each peak represents a product of the pyrolysis. The extreme heat of the pyrolysis in the absence of oxygen causes decomposition of the polyester polymers into smaller fragments. These, in turn may further decompose or react chemically with other fragments, creating new substances that may react or degrade further. This results in a large number of substances and a large amount of data for comparison of known and unknown substances.

phase and the silica is the stationary phase. This process is relatively slow because it depends upon gravity to get the mobile phase through the stationary phase. Vast improvements have been made in LC since the first experiments. Stationary phases have become much more efficient in separating components of an analyte and they are much more sensitive. As a result, the process can be sped up by having the mobile phase pushed through the stationary phase using pumps. This makes the experiment go much faster while keeping the high resolving power of the technique. This type of chromatography is called **high performance liquid chromatography** or HPLC. Some people refer to this technique as high pressure liquid chromatography, but this is technically not correct. In HPLC, packed columns are routinely used and the stationary phase can be similar to those in packed column GC or can be very different. In fact, one of the most popular HPLC stationary phases used in forensic science is a C_{18} hydrocarbon (octadecane). This material has the approximate consistency of candle wax. Mobile phases can be either a single liquid or a solution containing two or more miscible liquids.

HPLC has some significant advantages over GC. In GC, for example, the stationary phase is always more polar than the mobile phase (nothing can be less polar than an inert gas such as nitrogen or helium). In HPLC, stationary phases and mobile phases can be designed so that the stationary phase is less polar than the mobile phase. Octadecane is an example of a very nonpolar stationary phase. In such cases, the chromatography is referred to as being **reverse phase**. This can be a great help in separating a mixture of nonpolar substances that would not separate well using a polar stationary phase. Another advantage of HPLC over GC is that the composition of the mobile phase can be altered during the run. This is called **gradient** chromatography. At times it is desirable to start with a relatively nonpolar mobile phase and then gradually increase its polarity by adding more and more of a polar solvent. This can be easily accomplished using two or more solvents and two or more pumps. A computer controls the amounts of each solvent, thus changing the polarity of the mobile phase on the fly. Gradient chromatography is used when the analyte contains components of varying polarity. Its use can help separate similar low weight substances while keeping the experiment to reasonable time. It is somewhat analogous to temperature programming in GC. When the mobile phase stays constant during an HPLC run, it is called **isocratic** chromatography. Because liquids are used as the mobile phase, HPLC is commonly run at room temperature to remove the danger of pressure build-ups that can occur when liquids get near their boiling point.

PARTS OF AN HPLC

Figure 6.11 is a schematic of an HPLC. Each part is described below.

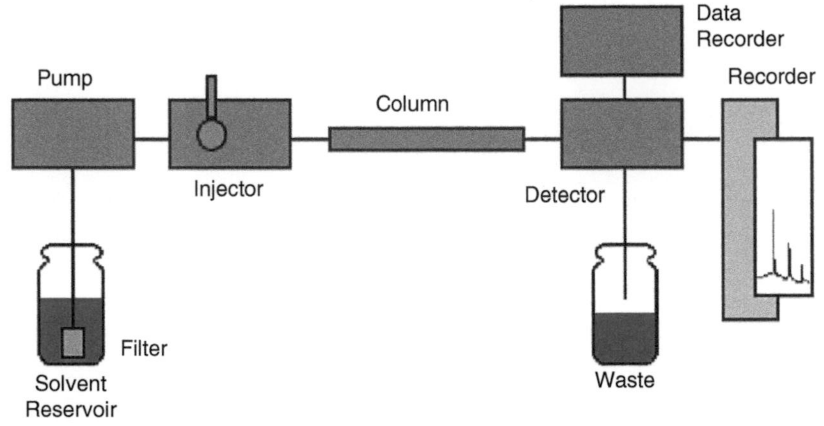

FIGURE 6.11

A high performance liquid chromatograph. The most common detector is a UV visible diode array detector computer for display and manipulation of data from detector.

The Injector

A liquid chromatograph has the same parts as a gas chromatograph. They differ in how they work because the mobile phase is a liquid or liquid solution. As in GC, the analyte is dissolved in a suitable solvent, in this case one that is miscible with the liquid mobile phase. The injector usually consists of a sample loop, a small piece of hollow tubing that is isolated from the mobile phase stream until the analysis is ready to be done. Then the sample loop is joined to the stream and the analyte is introduced. The mobile phase is pumped into the column containing the stationary phase by way of very accurate and precise liquid pumps. An auto sampler unit can be used with HPLC, as it can with GC. The liquid samples are loaded into small vials, which in turn, are put into a carousel. The computer controlling the process directs the introduction of the samples into the instrument.

The Stationary Phase

Today, most stationary phases are in packed columns. There are capillary HPLC columns but they are not yet commonly used in forensic applications. Typically columns are around 5 mm in diameter. The stationary phase is either a solid or a viscous liquid coated onto spherical, solid particles. The columns are generally much shorter than GC columns—usually around 25 cm. Even with this short length, efficient separations can be achieved.

Detectors

The detectors in an HPLC are quite different than those for a GC. Whereas GC detectors must detect solutions of gases, HPLC detectors must detect liquid solutions. When there is no analyte component present, the mobile phase flows through the detector by itself. When an analyte component is present, the properties of the liquid mobile phase change. Detectors are designed to detect changes in the concentrations of substances in the mobile phase. The most popular detector for HPLC is a UV/visible spectrophotometer, usually a special type called a **diode array detector** (DAD). This detector measures the ultraviolet and visible spectrum of the solution as it flows through. Most mobile phases are not active in the UV or visible spectral range, so the detector does not respond to pure mobile phase. A DAD simultaneously measures all of the wavelengths of UV and visible absorption of the analyte, so there are many ways that the data can be presented. For example, a simple chromatogram of retention volume (similar to retention time) versus absorption can be plotted. This will look similar to a gas chromatogram. In addition, however, many HPLC systems are capable of plotting absorption versus retention volume versus wavelength. This "3-dimensional" (3-D) plot presents a great deal more information than a simple 2-dimensional plot. An example of a 3-D plot is given in Figure 6.12.

There are also other detectors that can be used for HPLC. They are briefly discussed below.

- **Fluorescence** – This detector will detect only those substances that exhibit fluorescence, such as the illicit drug LSD. This limits its utility, but it is

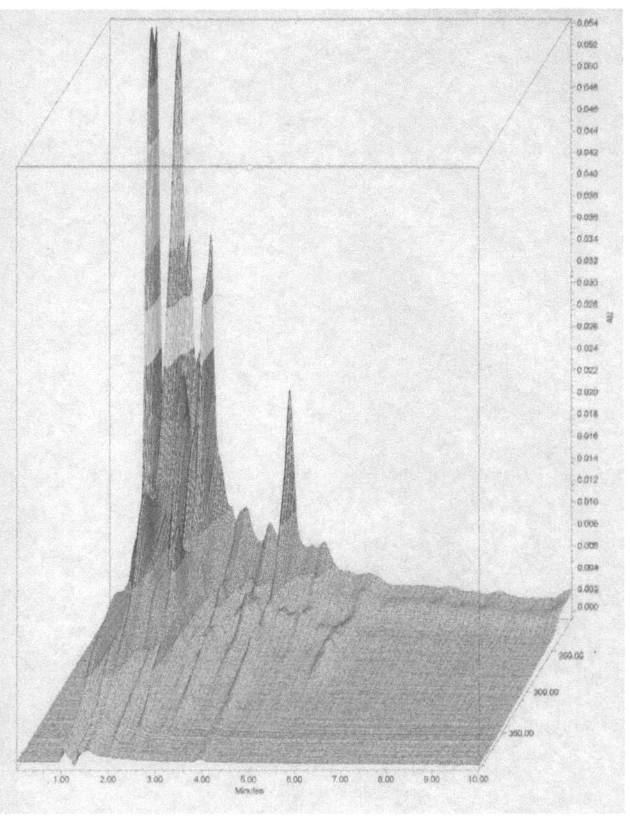

FIGURE 6.12

A "3-Dimensional" high performance liquid chromatography plot. The X-axis is time, the Y-axis is wavelength from the detector, and the Z-axis is absorbance units from the detector.

extremely sensitive. Ultraviolet or visible light is used as the source. A discussion of fluorescence spectroscopy can be found in Chapter 5.

- **Conductivity** – Most liquids will conduct electricity to a greater or lesser extent. A small electric current is continuously being passed into the mobile phase and the ability of the solution to conduct the electricity is measured. When an analyte, especially a polar one is introduced into the mobile phase, the conductivity changes, thus enabling detection of the analyte. This works best if the mobile phase contains at least some water because water is a very good conductor of electricity.
- **Refractive index** – The ability of liquids and other transparent materials to bend and decrease the velocity of light as it passes through, is called refraction. All liquids refract light differently. A mobile phase with an analyte dissolved in it will refract light differently than the mobile phase alone. A refractive index detector can measure this change.

- **Mass Spectrometry** – LC/MS has not been around nearly as long as GC/MS, in part because of some formidable engineering hurdles that had to be overcome. When the mobile phase and analytes reach the mass spectrometer the mobile phase is stripped away and the mass spectrum of each component of the analyte is measured. As in GC, this permits separations and identifications to take place in one step.

APPLICATIONS OF HPLC

HPLC has become increasingly popular in forensic science laboratories. Some of the same materials that are separated by GC methods can also be analyzed by HPLC. Also, HPLC may be the method of choice for separating analytes that are sensitive to temperature, such as explosives, which decompose, sometimes violently, when subjected to heat. Some of the more popular applications to evidence analysis are given below.

- **Drugs** – Many controlled substances are analyzed by HPLC. In addition drugs taken from body fluids can also be analyzed. Drugs are more often identified by GC because of the ease with which a mass spectrometer can be used. Although HPLC/MS instruments are now commercially available, they are not widely used in forensic science laboratories.
- **Soils** – Organic extractions can be done on soils and the various substances can be separated. The result is a profile of the soil. The substances in the mixture are usually not identified but the profile is a useful way of determining if a soil found at a crime scene could have come from a particular location.
- **Explosives** – It may not be safe to run explosive extracts by GC because of the high heat, but HPLC is an ideal method for separation of explosive residues.
- **Inks and dyes** – Determination of the visible and UV spectra of inks is useful in comparing a writing instrument to writing on a document. It can also be used to follow the aging of the ink as it dries and degrades. Fiber dyes can be extracted from fibers and separated by HPLC also.

THIN-LAYER CHROMATOGRAPHY

If you have ever cleaned up an ink spill with a paper towel and noted that the ink dyes separated on the surface of the paper, you are actually performing a type of chromatography. Paper chromatography is one of the oldest methods of separation and is still used in some applications. The paper acts as a stationary phase and the ink solvent is the mobile phase. The method is somewhat crude and in recent years has largely been replaced by more sophisticated stationary phases and more complex mobile phases. This technique is now called **thin-layer chromatography** because the stationary phase consists of a thin layer of solid material that is coated onto a small glass or plastic plate. TLC is very much like HPLC. The stationary and mobile phases are similar. In TLC it is not possible to change the characteristics of the mobile phase on the fly, but by proper mixing, a large variety of polarities can be achieved in the mobile phase. Stationary phases of various polarities are also available commercially.

THE STATIONARY PHASE

The stationary phase is a thin layer of a solid material combined with binders that are coated on to the surface of either a glass or plastic plate. These range in size from a microscope slide to more than 6″ on a side. The coatings range from a few microns up to 1–2 mm for preparative scale work. For many samples of forensic science interest, the stationary phase coating may contain an internal fluorophore. This is a substance that will fluoresce when exposed to UV light. When a nonfluorescent sample is loaded onto the stationary phase, it will quench or blot out the fluorescence under the sample and it will be seen as a dark spot. This helps in determining how heavily a spot has been made and its position. Stationary phases can range from moderately polar to very nonpolar so that both normal and reverse phase chromatography are possible.

THE MOBILE PHASE

As in HPLC, the mobile phase in TLC is an organic liquid (or water) or a solution of two or more liquids. The polarity of the mobile phase ranges from the very nonpolar to very polar. It can also be buffered to maintain a particular pH or ionic strength. Although the mobile phase cannot be altered during a TLC run, sometimes 2-D TLC is done. The plate is developed using one mobile phase and then turned 90° and developed in a different mobile phase.

THE TLC PROCESS

TLC is carried out in a chamber. Its dimensions depend upon the size of the coated plastic or glass plate. The plate must fit so that it does not touch the sides of the chamber. The plate must also fit entirely within the chamber. A typical arrangement may use a 5 × 10-cm plate and a 400-ml beaker. A piece of filter paper is put inside the chamber up against the side. This will absorb some of the mobile phase so that the entire inside of the chamber is saturated with the mobile phase. The top of the chamber is tightly covered. In many cases, Parafilm® works well as a sealer. An apparatus used for performing TLC is shown in Figure 6.13.

The analyte is dissolved in a small amount of a suitable solvent. The solvent must be volatile. Chloroform or methanol is often used. A well of a spot plate can be used for this. A spot of the dissolved analyte is put onto the TLC plate about 1 cm up from the bottom. This spot is kept as tiny as possible. A very narrow capillary can be used to make the spot. If necessary, the spot can be over spotted, but the original spot should be dried first by blowing on it. This will keep the spot as small as possible. One of the advantages of TLC over other forms of chromatography is that more than one sample can be run at the same time. There is generally room for several spots along the bottom of the TLC plate even with the need to keep some space between each spot. For example, in a drug case containing three exhibits where cocaine is suspected, one TLC plate can hold spots of each of the three exhibits as well as a sample of known cocaine and perhaps lidocaine, a common cutting agent for cocaine. After the plate is loaded with samples, a small amount of the mobile phase is put in the

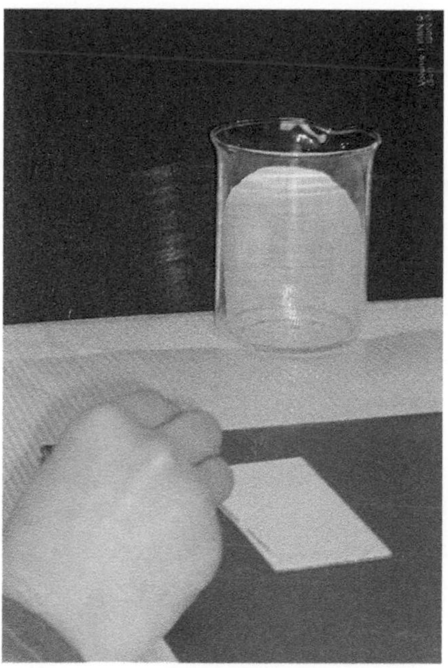

FIGURE 6.13

A thin-layer chromatography (TLC) apparatus. Note the piece of filter paper in the chamber (beaker). A small amount of mobile phase will be put in the chamber. The filter paper helps to saturate the space in the chamber. After the TLC plate is added, the chamber is tightly sealed.

chamber. There must be enough to travel up the plate but not enough to cover the spots. The chamber is covered and the mobile phase travels up through the stationary phase, carrying with it the analyte spots. Using the same principles that govern all chromatographic separations, the components of the analyte will be differentially retarded by the stationary phase. When the mobile phase front as nearly reached the top of the plate, the process is stopped by removing and drying the plate.

DETECTION

Detection of the components of the analyte is different than with other types of chromatography. Some of the spots may show up under UV light. Some may fluoresce. Most will quench the native fluorescence of the plate and will show up as dark spots. In other cases there may be reagents that can be added to the spots, usually by spraying an aerosol. These reagents react with the analyte component to form a characteristic color. For example, tetrahydrocannabinol, the active ingredient in marihuana, shows up as a bright, orange-red spot when sprayed with a reagent known as Fast Blue BB. Most nitrite (NO_2) containing compounds, such as most explosives, will turn red when a two-step reagent sequence, known collectively as Griess reagent is sprayed on them.

Once the spots are visualized, their positions are measured as a **retention factor (Rf)**. The Rf is the distance that the sample component travels up the plate divided by the distance that the mobile phase traveled. This is done in an attempt to make the results of a TLC experiment portable so that other laboratories can use the Rf data in their work. Using a ratio can eliminate many of the variables that are present in this process so that one laboratory can rely on the results of another laboratory.

APPLICATIONS OF TLC

TLC can be used in all of the applications than HPLC and to some extent, GC are used for. In fact TLC is often used to "model" an HPLC experiment. If one has a need to optimize a separation, it can often be done quickly and cheaply using TLC. Then the parameters such as stationary and mobile phase compositions can be transferred to HPLC.

ADVANTAGES AND DISADVANTAGES OF TLC

Compared to GC and HPLC, TLC is much cheaper. No instrument is required. In addition, multiple samples can be run simultaneously on TLC, whereas only one sample can be run at a time on GC or HPLC. On the other hand, quantitative analysis can be easily performed using GC and HPLC, whereas this is much more difficult with TLC. TLC is also less sensitive than the others—more sample is required. Finally, a method of visualization is needed for analyte components separated by TLC, whereas the other methods result in visible peaks on a chart.

ELECTROPHORESIS

Electrophoresis is a type of chromatography that relies upon somewhat different principles than the others previously discussed. Stationary phases are usually quite different in electrophoresis, although there are some examples where conventional stationary phases can be used. There are two major types of electrophoresis: gel and capillary. Gel electrophoresis is similar in some respects to TLC, whereas capillary electrophoresis is similar to HPLC. The major advantage of electrophoresis over conventional chromatography is resolution; even very similar components of an analyte can be easily separated by electrophoresis whereas they cannot be separated at all by other forms of chromatography. The best example of this resolution power is DNA. In order to accomplish forensic DNA analysis, it is necessary to separate fragments of DNA and determine their size. These fragments are virtually identical in chemical composition except for their size. Capillary electrophoresis is capable of separating DNA fragments that differ by only one base pair in size. In such cases, the entire separation process is accomplished by mass action—larger fragments of DNA travel slower. The major difference between electrophoresis and conventional chromatography is the role of an electric field.

THE STATIONARY PHASE

In gel electrophoresis, the stationary phase is a slab of a gel material such as agarose or polyacrylamide. This slab is immersed in a buffer solution to maintain a particular pH and ionic strength. Small wells are made in the gel and the analyte, which may be extracted DNA or blood or another body fluid, is put in the well. As in TLC, many samples can be run at the same time and in the case of DNA, several positive and negative controls are run with each case. In capillary electrophoresis, the stationary phase is a thin column, similar to a capillary used in GC. The capillary itself may be the stationary phase or it may be filled with another material.

THE MOBILE PHASE

The mobile phase in electrophoresis is an electric current. When the capillary or gel slab is immersed in the buffer, a power supply is connected that will deliver hundreds or thousands of volts to the system. This will give one end of the stationary phase a strong positive charge and the other a strong negative charge. The buffer serves to put a positive or negative charge on the analyte components. During the separation, the analyte components will migrate toward the side with the charge opposite to their own. In DNA analysis, for example, the DNA fragments usually have a negative charge and they migrate toward the positive side of the capillary or gel. DNA fragments that differ only slightly in size will still have different rates of migration and will be separated. A gel electrophoresis apparatus is shown in Figure 6.14.

DETECTORS

Detection in gel electrophoresis is usually by staining the analyte components so that they can be seen with visible or UV light. In the case of capillary electrophoresis, the detection is usually by UV absorption of light by the analyte components, although

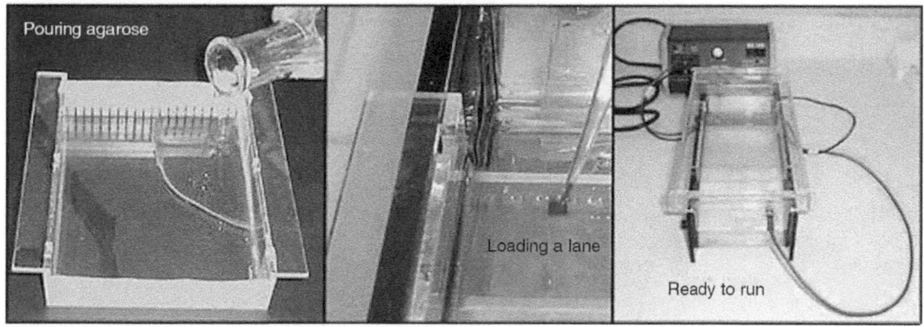

FIGURE 6.14

A gel electrophoresis apparatus.

Courtesy: R. Bowen at Colorado State University: arbl.cvmbs.colostate.edu/hbooks/genetics/biotech/gels/agardna.html. Email: rbowen@lamar.colostate.edu.

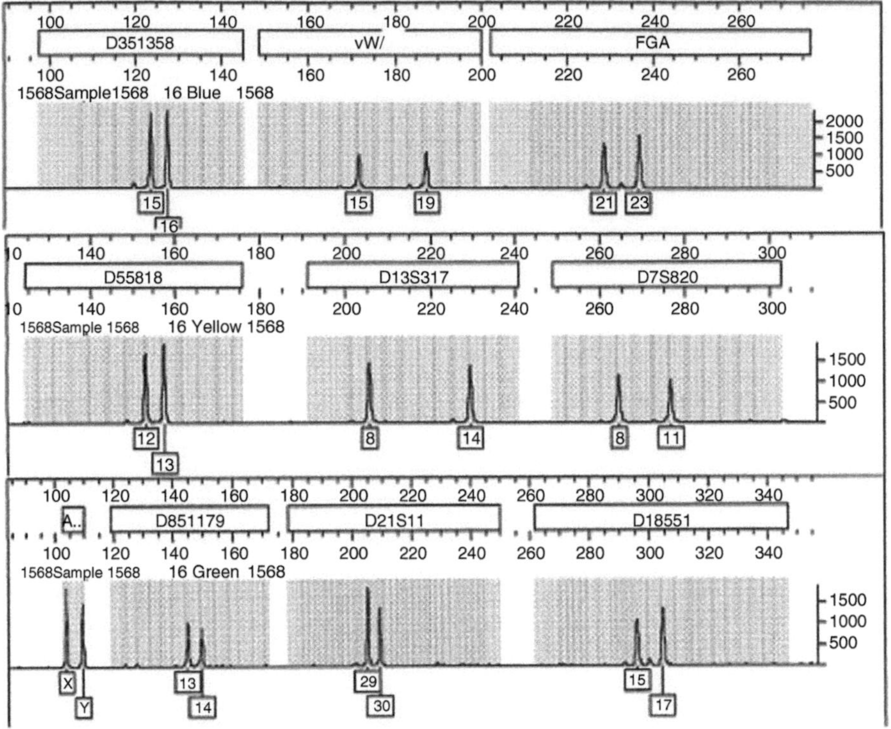

FIGURE 6.15

A capillary electropherogram. This is very similar to a gas or liquid chromatogram. Each peak represents a different substance, in this case a piece of DNA. This process is discussed in detail in Chapter 11.

there are other detection methods available. The result is a chromatogram with a peak for each component. This is similar to the output from GC or HPLC. This type of chromatogram is called a capillary electropherogram and an example is shown in Figure 6.15. The topic of detection of DNA fragments in capillary electrophoresis is discussed in more detail in Chapter 11.

APPLICATIONS OF ELECTROPHORESIS

- DNA typing—This is the only method available for separating DNA fragments suitable for forensic DNA typing. Either gel or capillary electrophoresis can be used.
- Drugs—Although drugs can be analyzed by a number of types of chromatography, capillary electrophoresis is the most sensitive of the methods.
- Explosive residues—Capillary electrophoresis has been employed because it is more sensitive and has higher resolution than HPLC. Most organic explosives can be separated by this method.

- Gunshot residues—Again, capillary electrophoresis is very sensitive. It must be optimized for detection of inorganic substances in this application.
- Questioned documents—Capillary electrophoresis has just begun to be used for the separation of ink components used in pens.

SUMMARY

Forensic science evidence seldom appears in a pure form. Very often the material of interest must be separated from other substances that are present. Such evidence commonly includes drugs, fire residues, and explosive residues. When a large amount of the material of interest is present, then a bulk extraction method can be used that takes advantage of the solubility or insolubility of materials in certain solvents. More commonly, however, the important evidence occurs in very small quantities; too small to be handled without losing it. In such cases, separation techniques that can separate and detect very small quantities of material are necessary. These techniques are collectively called chromatography. Chromatography is a family of techniques that separate materials using a stationary phase and a mobile phase. The basis for the separation is that different substances will have different affinities, or attractions, for the stationary or mobile phase. In GC and LC, the stationary phase is put into a long column. The mobile phase travels through the column under pressure. It carries with it the mixture that is to be separated. As the components of the mixture interact with the stationary and mobile phases, they are separated and emerge from the column at different times. The instrument contains a detector that reacts to the presence of the components of the mixture. In TLC the sample is placed onto a thin plate that is coated with the stationary phase and then the plate is dipped into a reservoir containing the mobile phase. This travels up the plate, carrying the mixture whose components are then separated by interaction with the stationary phase. The type of chromatography used depends upon the nature and form of the mixture. A specialized type of chromatography, called electrophoresis, is used for the separation of substances that are so similar to each other, that they cannot be separated by using conventional chromatography. In electrophoresis, a strong electric charge is used to carry the analytes through the stationary phase. Very specialized types of stationary phases are used in electrophoresis. In forensic science, the major use of electrophoresis is in the separation of fragments of DNA.

TEST YOUR KNOWLEDGE

1. What is normal phase chromatography? What types of substances are best separated this way?
2. What does the term "stationary phase" mean? What types of stationary phases are used in gas chromatography?
3. What type of substance is the mobile phase in gas chromatography?

4. List two advantages of HPLC over GC.
5. Explain how a flame ionization detector works. What other types of detectors are used in gas chromatography?
6. What is reverse phase liquid chromatography? What types of substances are best separated using this technique?
7. In HPLC, why would one want to use two pumps for the mobile phase?
8. List and describe three types of detectors used in HPLC.
9. Describe three advantages of thin-layer chromatography over other types.
10. Give at least two advantages of HPLC over TLC.
11. What are the two general requirements for an analyte in order for it to be separated by GC.
12. In electrophoresis, what are the stationary phase and mobile phase?
13. What is the major advantage of electrophoresis over other types of chromatography?
14. Define pH. Why is it important in liquid extractions?
15. How do extractions differ from chromatography?
16. What is the difference between liquid phase extraction and solid phase extraction?
17. What is the difference between adsorption and partition chromatography?
18. Why is it that HPLC can be used for the quantitation of an analyte but TLC cannot?
19. How are the spots obtained from TLC visualized?
20. How does capillary electrophoresis differ from gel electrophoresis?

CONSIDER THIS...

1. Polymers are found in many types of evidence such as paints, fibers, plastics, etc. What type of chromatography is performed on these polymers? How is it done? What is the principle that permits comparison of knowns and unknowns this way?
2. Explosive residues are generally not analyzed by GC. Why? What method(s) can be used for separation of explosive residues? Certain drugs, like amphetamines are difficult to separate by GC because of their interaction with the stationary phase and their thermal instability. What can be done to drugs like these to make it easier for them to be separated by GC?
3. In gas chromatography, resolution of complex mixtures of analytes can be improved by temperature programming. Explain how and why this helps. Likewise, in HPLC, mobile phase programming can be used to achieve a similar purpose. How does this work?

FURTHER READING

Siegel, Jay A., Knupfer, Geoffrey, Sauko, Pekka (Eds.), 2001. The Encyclopedia of Forensic Sciences, vol. 1. Academic Press.

Saferstein, Richard (Ed.), 1983. Forensic Science Handbook, vol. 1. Prentice-Hall.

Saferstein, Richard (Ed.), 1988. Forensic Science Handbook, vol. 2. Prentice-Hall.

ON THE WEB

http://www.shsu.edu/~chemistry/primers/gcms.html Good site on gas chromatography/mass spectrometry

http://www.rpi.edu/dept/chem-eng/Biotech-Environ/CHROMO/chromintro.html a primer on chromatography

http://teaching.shu.ac.uk/hwb/chemistry/tutorials/chrom/chrom1.htm more advanced explanation of chromatography theory

PART

Biological Sciences

3

CHAPTER

Pathology

7

CHAPTER OUTLINE

KEY TERMS

- Algor mortis
- Asphyxia
- Autolysis
- Autopsy
- Blunt force trauma
- Carboxyhemoglobin
- Cause of death
- Contact gunshot wound
- Contusion

- Coroner
- Defensive wounds
- Defibrillatory
- Distant gunshot wound
- Embalming
- Exhumation
- Exsanguination
- Hematoma
- Histology
- Hyperthermia
- Hypothermia
- Immediate cause of death
- Incised wounds
- Intermediate gunshot wound
- Lacerations
- Ligatures
- Livor mortis
- Manner of death
- Mechanical trauma
- Medical examiner
- Medico-legal autopsy
- Microtome
- Petechiae
- Postmortem clock
- Primary cause of death
- Putrefaction
- Rigor mortis
- Secondary cause of death
- Sharp force trauma
- Shored exit wound
- Smears
- Stippling
- Tardieu spots
- Tetany
- Toxicology screen
- Ventricular fibrillation

CASE EXAMPLE: GLORIA RAMIREZ

The strange and still unsolved case of Gloria Ramirez, unfairly dubbed 'The Toxic Lady', stands as a precautionary tale about the unpredictability of events during an investigation. Ramirez, diagnosed with advanced cervical cancer, was having nausea, heartbeat, and breathing difficulty at her home in Riverside, California on the evening of 19 February 1994. She was rushed to Riverside General Hospital by paramedics who administered oxygen along the way. At the hospital, she was in respiratory and cardiac distress, which caused a critically low blood pressure. Despite this, Ramirez responded to questions but acted lethargic and vomited in the emergency room (ER). The doctors gave her drugs to calm her down (Valium, Versed, and Ativan) and to restore a normal heart rate (Lidocaine and other antiarrhythmic drugs). Shortly after her arrival, Ramirez went into full cardiac arrest.

The ER staff applied a breathing tube to provide oxygen, and she was defibrillated (an electric shock delivered to restore a normal heart rhythm). After this, accounts vary as to what exactly happened.

As a nurse drew blood for routine tests, one of the doctors smelled ammonia and felt dizzy. The nurse keeled over. The senior medical resident checked on the nurse to make sure she was not hurt; the doctor took the syringe and smelled ammonia. She noticed the blood had funny manila-colored crystals in it; then she passed out and went into convulsions. Other ER staff were also affected and the ER was cleared. The fire department's Hazardous Materials team was called in and incoming patients were rerouted to other hospitals. Attempts to revive Ramirez failed and she was pronounced dead. As many as 23 staff were affected, reporting nausea and headaches. The senior medical resident was in the hospital for two weeks with breathing disorders, hepatitis, and pancreatitis, in addition to other maladies.

An autopsy was later conducted by professionals wearing protective suits with respirators. Ramirez had been suffering from a urinary blockage as well as the cervical cancer; she had died of kidney failure. No known toxic chemicals were found, neither in Ramirez nor the hospital's plumbing or ventilation systems.

INTRODUCTION

A pathologist is a medical doctor who studies and diagnoses disease in humans. A *forensic* pathologist is a pathologist who has studied not only disease, but also trauma (wounds and damage) that leads to the death of an individual. The modern **autopsy**, from the Greek *autopsia*, meaning "seeing with one's own eyes" (*Oxford English Dictionary*, 2005), involves the standardized dissection of a corpse to determine the cause and manner of death. Regrettably, the number of autopsies has steadily declined in the past 50 years; less than 5% of hospital deaths are routinely autopsied, compared to 50% in the years after World War II. This is a shame, really, because autopsies are a quality control tool for doctors; they provide a "reality check" on their diagnoses and give them feedback on the effectiveness of treatments. Autopsies done to help solve a murder, however, are different in many ways, such as who conducts them, when and how they are conducted, and what purpose they serve to society.

CAUSE AND MANNER OF DEATH

The **cause of death** is divided into the primary and secondary causes of death. The **primary cause of death** or **immediate cause of death** is a three-link causal chain that explains the cessation of life starting with the most recent condition and going backward in time. For example,

1. *Most recent condition* (coronary bypass surgery, for example), due to or as a consequence of;
2. *Next oldest condition* (a rupture of the heart's lining due to tissue death from lack of oxygen, for example), due to or as a consequence of;
3. *Oldest* (original, initiating) *condition* (coronary artery disease, for example).

Each condition is a result of the one before it. At least one cause must be listed, but always using all the three is not necessary. The **secondary cause of death**, which includes conditions that are not related to the primary cause of death but contribute substantially to the individual's demise, such as extreme heat or frigid temperatures, is typically listed.

A distinct difference exists between the standard hospital autopsy and a **medico-legal autopsy**. The hospital autopsy is conducted based on a doctor's request and the family's permission. If the family denies the request for personal or religious reasons, the autopsy is not performed. A medico-legal autopsy, however, is performed pursuant to a medical investigation of death for legal purposes. For more information on the history of the autopsy, see "History: The Autopsy" later in this chapter.

If a person dies unexpectedly, unnaturally, or under suspicious circumstances, the coroner or medical examiner (ME) has the authority to order an examination of the body to determine the cause of death. The **manner of death** is the *way* in which the causes of death came to be. Generally, only four manners of death are acknowledged: homicide, suicide, accidental, and natural. The deceased may have met his or her end in a way that appears suspicious to the authorities, and therefore, the cause and manner of death must be established. Other purposes for a medico-legal autopsy may be to identify the deceased, establish a time of death, or collect evidence surrounding the death. The cause of death is often known, but the manner and mechanism of death may not be immediately obvious and are crucial to the goals of a medico-legal autopsy. Imagine a body found at the base of a cliff: The cause of death may be the *obvious* cause of death (a fractured skull), but was the individual pushed, did the person jump, or did he or she slip? The pathologist may never know from the results of the autopsy alone. An important consideration to keep in mind is that if an unnatural event starts a chain of direct consequences, then the manner of that initial event determines the ultimate manner of death. A simple example would be an elderly individual who falls, suffers a hip fracture, and subsequently dies in the hospital of a blood clot in the lung (pulmonary embolus); that is an accidental death. Somewhat more difficult to determine might be the case of a young person who suffers a severe, closed head injury as a result of an assault and dies in a chronic care facility three years later, having never recovered consciousness. The manner of death in this instance is homicide.

While a pathologist can perform a hospital autopsy, more than normal medical training is required to interpret morbid anatomy and fatal trauma. In one study by Collins and Lantz (1994), trauma surgeons misinterpreted both the number and the sites of the entrance and exit wounds in up to half of fatal gunshot wounds (GSWs).

CORONERS AND MEs

THE CORONER SYSTEM

The office of **coroner** was first granted by England's "Charts of Privileges" to St. John of Beverley in AD 925, and before the 1194 publication of the "Articles of Eyre," the office of coroner had become an official position throughout the country. These individuals were called "keepers of the pleas of the crown," a phrase later shortened to "crowner" and then "coroner." The position was initially that of a formidable and prestigious judicial officer in charge of collecting monies due to the king, trying felony cases, and gradually narrowed to the investigation of unusual, untimely, or suspicious deaths. By the thirteenth century, coroners had to examine all bodies before burial and appraise all wounds, bruises, and other signs of possible foul play (Thorwald, 1964) (see "History: The Origins of the Coroner System").

HISTORY: THE ORIGINS OF THE CORONER SYSTEM

The position of coroner dates from September 1194 and was initiated about 800 years ago. During the last decade of Henry II's reign, discontent had developed over the corruption and greed of the sheriffs, the law officers who represented the Crown in each English county. At that time, they were "reif of the shire." Later they became known as the "shire's reif" and then "sheriff." Sheriffs were known to extort and embezzle the populace and manipulate the legal system to their personal financial advantage: They diverted funds that should have gone to the king. A new network of law officers who would be independent of the sheriffs was established to thwart their greedy ways and return the flow of money to the king.

The edict that formally established the coroners was Article 20 of the "Articles of Eyre" in September 1194. The King's judges traveled around the country side, holding court and dispensing justice wherever they went; this was called the "General Eyre." The Eyre of September 1194 was held in the County of Kent, and Article 20 stated:

In Every County Of The King's Realm Shall Be Elected Three Knights And One Clerk, To Keep The Pleas Of The Crown

And that is the only legal basis for the coroner. Coroners had to be knights and men of substance—their appointment depended on their owning property and having a sizeable income. Coroner was an unpaid position; this was intended to reduce the desire to adopt any of the sheriffs' larcenous habits.

(Continued)

HISTORY: THE ORIGINS OF THE CORONER SYSTEM—cont'd

The most important task of the coroner was the investigation of violent or suspicious deaths; in the medieval system, this task held great potential for generating royal income. All manners of death were investigated by the coroner. Interestingly, discovering the perpetrator of a homicide was not of particular concern to the coroner; the guilty party usually confessed or ran away to avoid an almost certain hanging. The coroner was, however, concerned to record everything on his rolls so that no witnesses, neighbors, property, or chattels escaped the eagle eyes of the Justices in Eyre. There was a rigid procedure enforced at every unexpected death, any deviation from the rules being heavily fined. The rules were so complex that probably most cases showed some slip-up, with consequent financial penalty to someone. It was common practice either to ignore a dead body or even to hide it clandestinely. Some people would even drag a corpse by night to another village so that they would not be burdened with the problem. Even where no guilt lay, to be involved in a death, even a sudden natural one, caused endless trouble and usually financial loss.

Sources: *Thorwald (1964); Wilson and Wilson (2003).*

The first American coroner was Thomas Baldridge of St. Mary's, Maryland Colony appointed on 29 January 1637. He held his first death inquest two days later. It was not until 1890 that Baltimore appointed two physicians as the United States' first MEs (Thorwald, 1964).

The position of coroner can be appointed or elected, and typically no formal education or medical training is required. Today, many coroners are funeral directors, who get possession of the body after the autopsy. This can be a major source of income to such officials.

A **medical examiner**, in contrast, is typically a physician who has gone through four years of university, four years of medical school, four years of basic pathology training (residency), and an additional one to two years of special training in forensic pathology. These positions are appointed. Some states' have a mixture of MEs and coroner systems whereas others are strictly ME or coroner systems (see Figure 7.1):

	Coroner	Medical Examiner
Required to be a physician	Usually not required	Almost always
Investigates death	Yes	Yes
Performs autopsies	No	Yes
Determines cause of death	Yes	Yes
Death certificates	Yes	Yes
Appointed or elected	Either	Appointed
Pathologist or forensic pathologist	Not required	Almost always

The beginning and end of life are socially bounded by a certification process on which major monetary and legal issues often turn. Any licensed physician is permitted and expected to sign death certificates in cases of natural death of patients which that physician is treating. Unlike the mosaic of ME and coroner systems, there is a

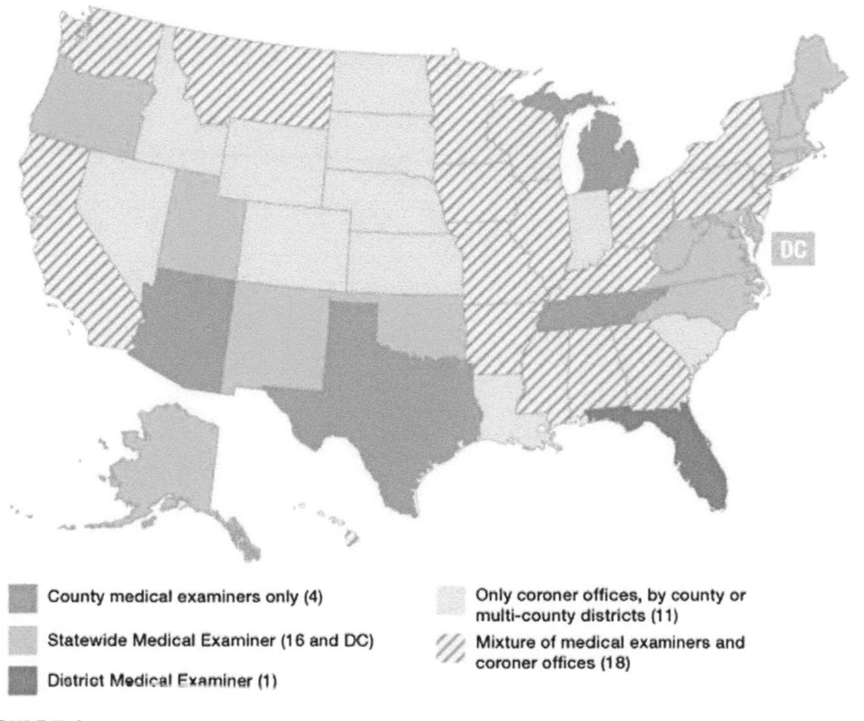

FIGURE 7.1

Map of coroner and ME systems in the United States.

National Public Radio, with Permission.

United States Standard Certificate of Death on which all 50 states closely base their individual death certificates. Additionally, some printed guidelines exist to assist physicians in the completion of this form, which is not necessarily straightforward, even for natural deaths (Council of American Pathologists, 2006).

THE POSTMORTEM EXAMINATION (AUTOPSY)

EXTERNAL EXAMINATION

The Visual Examination

The visual or external examination of a body starts with a careful description of the deceased's clothing, photographs (including close-ups) of the body both clothed and unclothed, and a detailed examination of the entire body. The attention to detail during the external examination is one important way in which the forensic autopsy differs from a hospital autopsy. Any trauma is noted on a form where the pathologist can make notes, sketches, or record measurements (see Figure 7.2); damage to clothing should correlate to trauma in the same area on the body. GSWs are recorded, for example,

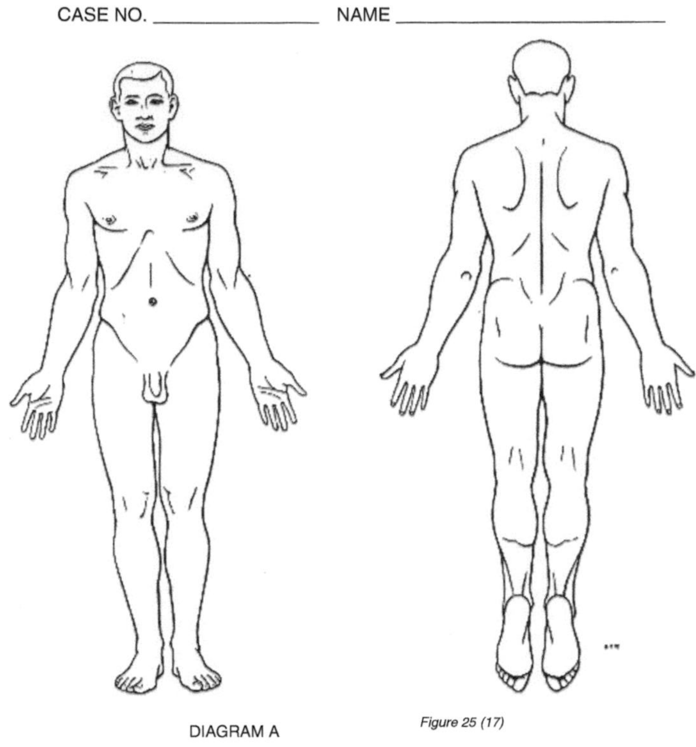

FIGURE 7.2

Diagrams like this are used to mark wounds, bruises, and other trauma; they also allow the examiner to take notes during the visual examination.

to indicate entrance and exits wounds and the path of the bullet through the body, as shown in Figure 7.3. Also noted are **defensive wounds**, like those shown in Figure 7.4, that are traumas caused by victims trying to defend themselves against an attacker.

CLASSIFICATION OF TRAUMA

Traumatic deaths may be classified as mechanical, thermal, chemical, or electrical. It should be noted that medical doctors and surgeons may classify wounds differently than MEs and forensic pathologists.

Mechanical Trauma

Mechanical trauma occurs when the force applied to a tissue, such as skin or bone, exceeds mechanical or tensile strength of that tissue. Mechanical trauma can be described as resulting from sharp or blunt force. **Sharp force trauma** refers to injuries caused by sharp implements, such as knives, axes, or ice picks. Significantly less force is needed for a sharpened object to cut or pierce tissue than what is required with a blunt object.

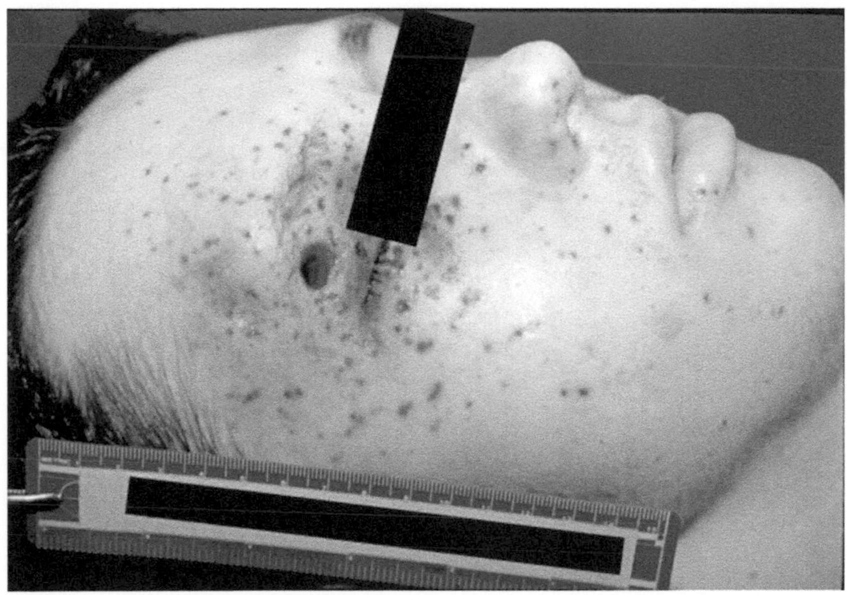

FIGURE 7.3

A gunshot wound to the head typically shows a small, clean entrance; note the stippling of gunpowder burns around the wound.

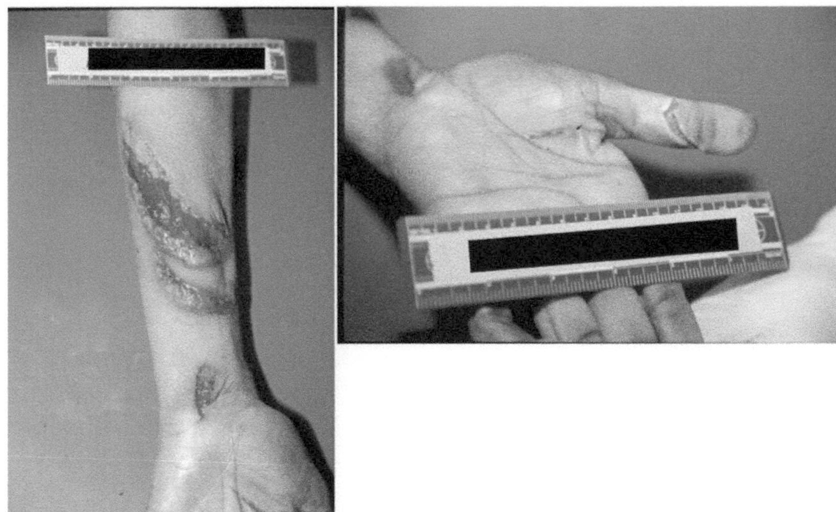

FIGURE 7.4

In protecting themselves from attack by a sharp object, victims often have wounds indicating their attempt to ward off their attacker.

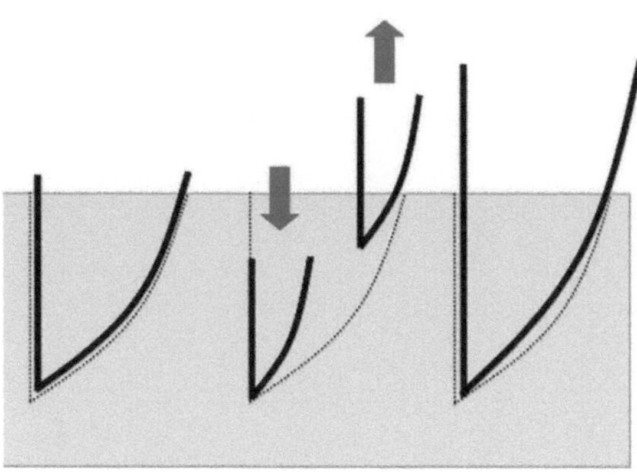

FIGURE 7.5

Determining the size and shape of the weapon by the size and shape of the wound may be difficult. Here, the same-size wound could be caused by a knife of the same, smaller or larger size. Education, training, and experience are important for the forensic pathologist to make a proper interpretation.

Blunt force trauma is caused by dull or nonsharpened objects, like baseball bats, bricks, or lamps. Blunt objects produce **lacerations**, or tears in the tissue, typically the skin, whereas sharp objects produce **incised wounds**, wounds that have more depth than length or width. The size, shape, and kind of wound may allow the forensic pathologist to determine if a sharp or blunt object caused it. Judicious interpretations and caution are required because of the flexible nature of many of the body's tissues and the variability of the violent force. For example, a stab wound 1-inch wide, 1/8-inch thick, and 3-inches deep could have been produced by (1) a sharp object of the same dimensions, (2) a sharp object that is 1/2-inch wide, 1/8-inch thick, and 2-inches long that was thrust in with great force and removed at a different angle, or (3) a sharp object larger than the stated dimensions but was only pushed in part of its length, as represented graphically in Figure 7.5. Occasionally, the injury may be patterned and reflect the specific nature of the causative agent: For example, the threaded end of lead pipe used to beat an individual may transfer a set of parallel contusions with uniform spacing that corresponds to the pipe's thread pattern. Death from blunt and sharp trauma results from multiple processes, but sharp trauma most commonly causes death from a fatal loss of blood (**exsanguination**) when a major artery or the heart is damaged. Blunt trauma causes death most often when the brain has been severely damaged. A **contusion** is an accumulation of blood in the tissues outside the normal blood vessels and is most often the result of blunt impact. The blood pressures the tissues enough to break small blood vessels in the tissues and this leaks blood into the surrounding area. Importantly, the pattern of the object may be transferred to the skin and visualized by the blood welling up in the tissues.

Table 7.1 Descriptions of the Major Classes of Gunshot Wounds (GSWs)

GSW Class	Distance	Characteristics
Contact (entrance)	0	Blackening of the skin; lacerations from escaping muzzle gases; bright-red coloration of the blood in wound from carbon monoxide gases reacting to hemoglobin in blood (**carboxyhemoglobin**).
Intermediate (entrance)	0.5 cm–1 m	Unburned gunpowder penetrates skin and burns it, causing small red dots called **stippling**; the stippling pattern enlarges as the muzzle-to-target distance increases.
Distant (entrance)	>1 m	Speed of gunpowder is insufficient to cause stippling at this distance; lack blackening; no carboxyhemoglobin; circular defect with abraded rim; distance indeterminate.
Shored exit	–	Skin is supported or shored by some material, such as tight clothing, wall board, or wood, as bullet exits; may look very similar to entrance GSW *except* pattern of shoring material (such as the weave of cloth) may be transferred to skin as it expands when bullet exits.

An extreme contusion, a **hematoma**, is a blood tumor or a contusion with more blood. Abrasions, scraping of the skin surface, while rarely fatal in themselves can often corroborate or help explain the circumstances surrounding death.

Asphyxia is a type of mechanical trauma in which the body is deprived of oxygen. The brain is the most susceptible organ to asphyxia, and unconsciousness typically follows loss of oxygen flow in 10 s with irreversible coma resulting in a matter of a few minutes. Asphyxia can occur as a result of three main mechanisms. Suffocation occurs by covering the nose and mouth blockage of the major airways with a foreign object. Strangulation occurs by manual or ligature compression of the structures of the neck, often leaving characteristic physical evidence, such as the fracture of the hyoid bone and bruising. Finally, chemical asphyxiation occurs when the oxygen in the air is replaced by some other gas, such as carbon monoxide (CO).

Gunshot Wounds

The projectile from a discharged firearm produces a special kind of blunt force trauma. Deaths due to firearm (handguns, rifles, and shotguns) are a commonly encountered entity, especially in the United States, where they form the bulk of the homicidal and, to lesser degree, suicidal manners of death. Table 7.1 lists the major classes of GSWs and their characteristics. The factors surrounding a GSW can be quite complex and are beyond the scope of this chapter; see DiMaio and DiMaio (2001).

> **ON THE WEB**
>
> The Website for the National Association of Medical Examiners is www.thename.org.
>
> A virtual autopsy, presenting a series of interactive cases and histories, written by Ajay Mark Verma at the University of Leicester, UK. This Web site won the Scientific American 2002 SciTech Web Award (www.le.ac.uk/pathology/teach/va).
>
> Virtopsy is a visualizing scanner system that allows for multimodal viewing of a body, both internally and externally, for autopsy purposes. It provides computed tomography, magnetic resonance, 3D surface scanning, and 3D photogrammetry. This technology provides full documentation of the examination, allowing for observer-independent review of what is normally a one-time event. Patterned injuries of difficult-to-examine areas, like flailing fractures of ribs, can be easily visualized and recorded. Additionally, in cases where the body cannot be traditionally autopsied due to medial, legal, or social reasons, the Virtopsy technique can provide sufficient medico-legal examination for cause and manner of death (www.virtopsy.com).

Chemical Trauma

Chemical trauma refers to damage and death which results from the interaction of chemicals with the human body. This is the domain of the forensic toxicologist and is discussed later in this chapter. If the damage from chemicals is external, as in the case of acid or alkaline burns, then this is still the purview of the pathologist.

Thermal Trauma

Extreme heat or cold also may produce death. **Hypothermia** is too much exposure to cold, and **hyperthermia** is excessive heat. Either condition can interfere with the normal physiological mechanisms that keep body temperature at about 98 °F/37 °C. In both cases, the forensic pathologist may encounter few signs at autopsy that will indicate either of those mechanisms; more commonly, external or environmental factors, as well as what is *not* found, may lead to this determination. Individuals in a vulnerable state of health, typically the sick, the very elderly or the very young, most often succumb to hypo- or hyperthermia. Other factors may contribute, such as alcohol, which reduces sensitivity to cold and dilates (opens) the blood vessels, speeding the cooling of the body. Hyperthermia deaths are common in elderly people in northern cities and infants left in automobiles during the summer. The inside temperature of a closed car in the sun can exceed 140 °F/60 °C and can be fatal to an infant in 10 min. Thermal burns tend to be localized; persons who die in a fire do so generally because of the inhalation of combustion products, like carbon monoxide (CO). Additionally, the level of CO in the tissues and the presence of soot in the throat tissues can determine whether the person was alive or dead when the fire burned him or her. A body from a burned building with 1 or 2% CO is presumed to have been dead (or at least not breathing) at the time the fire started. True deaths from thermal injuries do occur due to either massive tissue damage and/or swelling of the airway causing suffocation.

Electrical Trauma

Electricity can cause death by a number of means. Circuits of alternating current (AC) at low voltages (<1000 V) that cross the heart cause **ventricular fibrillation**, a random quivering that does not pump the blood through the body properly. A person in ventricular fibrillation for even a few minutes cannot be resuscitated. The heart fibrillates because the current is acting like a (faulty) pacemaker. AC in the United States alternates from positive to negative at 3600 times/minute and at 2500 times/minute in Europe; the heart can only beat about 300 times/minute at maximum. At high voltages, the amount of current causes the heart to *stop* beating (it becomes **defibrillatory**), pushing the heart into **tetany**, a sustained contraction that is broken only when the circuit is broken. While the heart will generally start beating normally again, high voltages produce severe burns and cellular damage within a fraction of a second.

When the clothing is removed, care is taken to preserve any trace evidence that may be later submitted to a forensic science laboratory. Wet clothes are suspended to air dry at room temperature. Folding wet clothes may obscure important evidence patterns, such as bloodstains, and promote the growth of bacteria, which, besides smelling bad, can damage potential DNA evidence.

The age, sex, ancestry, height, weight, state of nourishment, and any birth-related abnormalities are noted during the external exam. The body is also checked for death-related phenomena that may provide information to the investigation. For example, the presence of rigor mortis and livor mortis, if present, is noted. **Rigor mortis** is the stiffening of the body after death due to the membranes of muscle cells becoming more permeable to calcium ions. Living muscle cells expend energy to transport calcium ions outside the cells; calcium plays a crucial role in muscle contraction. Without this calcium transport, the muscle fibers continue to contract until they are fully contracted; the muscles release only when the tissues begin to decompose. Onset typically begins 2–6 h after death and releases after 24 h. The rate of rigor mortis depends on activity before death and the ambient temperature; these must be taken into account by the pathologist when estimating a time since death.

Livor mortis, also known as postmortem lividity, is the settling of blood due to gravity after the heart no longer circulates it through the body. This results in a purplish discoloration in the skin, shown in Figure 7.6; the blood also is not reaching the lungs to be oxygenated and the settled blood takes on a bluish tone. This is not true, however, of people who have died from poisons or substances that alter the color of the blood—for example, carbon monoxide, which colors the blood a bright, cherry red. Lividity begins to set in about an hour after death and peaks in about 3 or 4 h. The blood settles in accordance with gravity and, once coagulated, does not move. The only exception to this is where pressure is applied—for example, a body lying on its back will have light patches where the blood couldn't settle, like around the shoulder blades and the buttocks. Because of this, lividity can indicate if a body has been moved: The pattern of lividity does not match the position of the body as it was found, illustrated in Figure 7.7.

The eyes are also examined for a variety of indications that will provide clues to the pathologist. **Petechiae**, shown in Figure 7.8, are pinpoint hemorrhages found around the eyes, the lining of the mouth and throat, as well as other areas often seen in hanging or strangulation victims. But petechiae are by no means conclusive evidence of strangulation or asphyxiation because other phenomena, such as heart attacks or cardiopulmonary resuscitation, can induce them. In older pathology literature, petechiae may be referred to as Tardieu spots, after the doctor who first described them. The mouth area and oral cavity (the inside of the mouth) are also examined for trauma, trace evidence, and indications of disease.

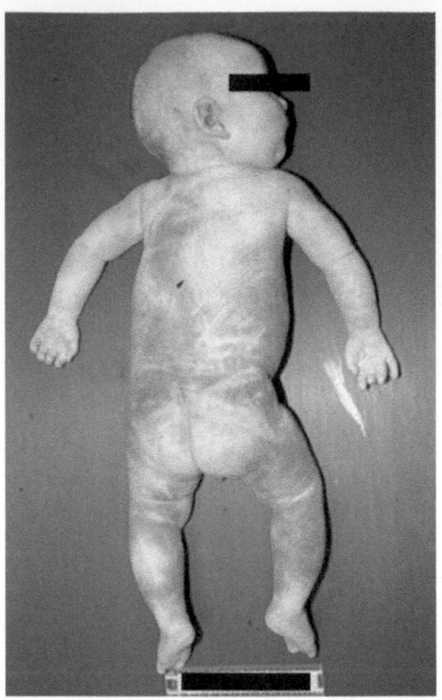

FIGURE 7.6

Lividity is the settling of blood cells once the heart stops pumping.

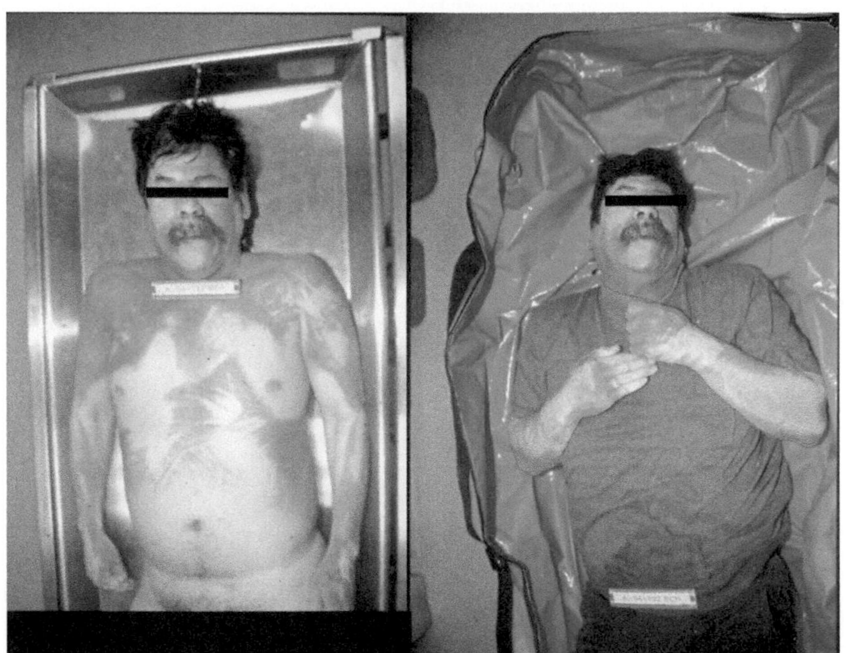

FIGURE 7.7

Lividity becomes fixed and, if a body is moved after this point, that fact becomes clear: The pressure of the body's weight keeps blood cells away from areas in contact with a surface. The position of the body as found (clothed) is confirmed once the clothes are removed.

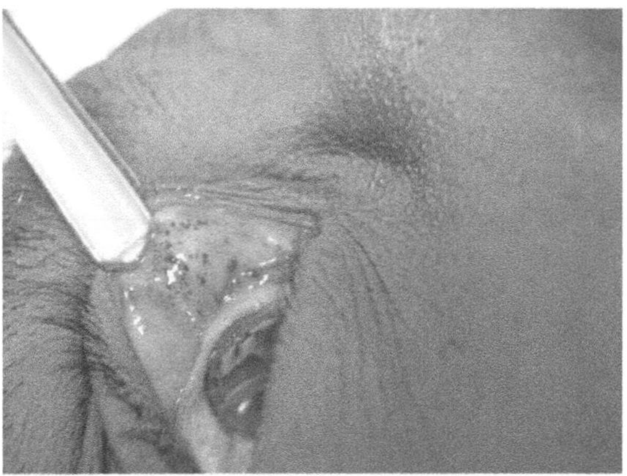

FIGURE 7.8

Petechiae, tiny blood vessels that burst often due to strangulation, are seen in the eyelids as well as other places.

HISTORY: THE AUTOPSY

Physicians have been performing autopsies for thousands of years. A Chinese text, *Hsi Yuan Chi Lu, The Washing Away of Unjust Wrongs*, written in 1247, describes various trauma patterns, how to identify weapons from the wounds they leave, and how to tell if a victim was drowned or died in a fire.

Greek physicians, including the famous Galen who lived during the second century, performed autopsies as early as the fifth century on criminals, war dead, and animals. Christian Europe discouraged and even forbade autopsies until the sudden death of Pope Alexander V in 1490; it was questioned whether his successor had poisoned him. An examination found no evidence of poisoning, however. During the reign of Pope Sixtus IV (1471–1484), the plague raged through Europe, causing millions of deaths. The Pope allowed for medical students at the universities in Bologna and Padua to perform autopsies in hopes of finding a cause and cure for the savage disease.

In 1530, the Emperor Charles V issued the *Constitutio Criminalis Carolina,* which promoted the use of medical pathology by requiring medical testimony in death investigations. Complete autopsies were not performed, however, but this did signal an advance by mandating some medical expertise to perform the inquest.

In the 1790s, the first English pathology texts were published: Baille's *Morbid Anatomy* (1793) and Hunter's *A Treatise on the Blood, Inflammation, and Gun-Shot Wounds* (1794). The next great advance came from the legendary Rudolf Virchow (1821–1902), who added microscopic examinations of diseased body tissues to the gross visual exam in his 1858 *Cellular Pathology*. Virchow's work signals the beginning of the modern autopsy process.

The first ME's office in the United States was instituted in Baltimore in 1890. New York City abolished the coroner system in 1915 and established the ME's office headed by Milton Helpern. Helpern added toxicological exams with the help of Alexander Gettler. In 1939, Maryland established the first state-wide ME system in the United States and, in doing so, set the position of ME apart from the political system in the state.

Sources: *Iverson (2001); Thorwald (1964).*

OTHER EVIDENCE COLLECTED

Other evidence is routinely collected at autopsy for submission to a forensic or toxicological laboratory. In cases in which sexual assault is known or suspected, three sets of swabs will be used to collect foreign body fluids. For females, a vaginal swab, an oral swab, and a rectal swab are collected; for males, oral and rectal swabs alone are taken. One set will be for **smears**, where the collected fluid on each swab is wiped across a separate clean glass microscope slide. Smears are microscopically examined for the presence of spermatozoa. The second and third sets are for serological examinations, including testing for the acid phosphatase in seminal fluid and possible blood typing. Any other stains on the decedent's clothing or body may also be swabbed for later analysis.

Known head hairs and pubic hairs are collected during the autopsy procedure. These will be forwarded to the forensic science laboratory for comparison with any questioned hairs found on the decedent's clothing or at the crime scene. A pubic hair combing is also taken to collect any foreign materials that may be associated with the perpetrator of a sexual crime.

Any **ligatures** (for binding victims), such as electrical cords, ropes, or duct tape, are extensively photographed, sketched, and then collected. The knots should be retained for later examination by the forensic science laboratory because hairs, fibers, or other trace evidence may have been trapped in the knot when it was tied. The ligature is cut away from the knot and then labeled to distinguish that cut from any others that may have existed when the body was brought to the morgue. Be alert—not all cuts may be due to the perpetrator! Emergency medical technicians may have cut the ligatures, or clothes for that matter, in an effort to free or unbind the victim.

If the decedent's identity is unknown, a full set of fingerprints are taken to be referenced against any databases. For badly decomposed remains, the jaws may be removed to facilitate a forensic dental examination and identification.

INTERNAL EXAMINATION AND DISSECTION

The pathologist then removes the internal organs, either all together or individually; this latter method is called the Virchow method, after the famous pathologist Rudolph Ludwig Carl Virchow, known for his meticulous methodology. In the Virchow method, each organ is removed, examined, weighed, and sampled separately to isolate any pathologies or evidence of disease (Dolinak et al., 2005). The stomach contents, if any, are examined in detail because they can provide crucial clues to the decedent's last actions. The nature, amount, size, and condition of the contents are described, including the possibility of microscopic analysis to identify partially digested or difficult-to-digest materials (see "In More Detail: Cereal Killer in Spokane"), including tablets or foreign objects. The small intestines may also be examined for undigested materials (corn kernels, tomato peels, among others) to determine the rate of digestion. Liquids digest faster than solids; 150 ml of orange juice empties from the stomach in about 1.5 h, whereas the same amount of solid food may empty in 2 h or more, depending on the density of the food. Finally, a toxicological exam may be requested.

Each organ is sectioned and viewed internally and externally. Samples for microscopic analysis of the cellular structure (**histology**) and for toxicology screening tests are taken. After all the organs have been examined, they are placed in a plastic bag and returned to the body cavity.

IN MORE DETAIL: CEREAL KILLER IN SPOKANE

In February 1999, the residence of James Cochran* was found engulfed in flames, and Kevin, the 11-year-old son of James Cochran, was missing. Cochran claimed no knowledge of his son's location, suggesting Kevin had started the fire while playing with matches and had run off. Two days later, the fully clothed body of Kevin Cochran was found along a road north of Spokane (see Figure 7.9). Kevin's clothing, face, and mouth exhibited a large amount of creamy brown vomit. Kevin's shoes were tied but were on the wrong feet. At autopsy, the pathologist determined the cause of death to be strangulation. The boy's stomach contents, fingernail clippings, hand swabs, and clothing were collected as evidence for laboratory examination. That same week, James Cochran was arrested for embezzling funds from his employer.

FIGURE 7.9

The victim was found along a lake road by a snowplow driver. Note that the victim's shoes are tied on the wrong feet.

James Cochran's pickup truck was seized and searched. Several droplets of light brown to pink material were observed on the driver's side wheel well hump and in various locations on the midportion of the bed liner. The scientist collecting these droplets noted the smell of possible vomit while scraping to recover the stains (see Figure 7.10).

Stains from the bed of the pickup truck were compared to the vomit and gastric contents of Kevin Cochran. One of Kevin's sisters stated in an interview Kevin was last seen eating cereal in the kitchen the morning of the fire. Investigators recovered known boxes of cereal from the Cochran's kitchen. Two opened and partially consumed plastic bags labeled *Apple Cinnamon Toastyo's®* and *Marshmallow Mateys®*, among others, were submitted, pictured in Figure 7.11. If the cereal found

(Continued)

IN MORE DETAIL: CEREAL KILLER IN SPOKANE—cont'd

FIGURE 7.10

The bed liner of the suspect's pickup truck. Arrows point to suspected vomit stains.

FIGURE 7.11

Marshmallow Mateys® breakfast cereal. The anchor-shaped particles contain oat flour, whereas the colored particles contain processed corn starch and sugar.

in the kitchen of the Cochran residence "matched" the cereal in the vomit on Kevin's clothing and was found to be similar to stains in the pickup truck, investigators may have a connection linking James Cochran to the death of his own son.

All the cereal brands could be distinguished microscopically. The microscopical examination and comparison of stains found on the pickup truck bed liner revealed the presence of vomit with

IN MORE DETAIL: CEREAL KILLER IN SPOKANE—cont'd

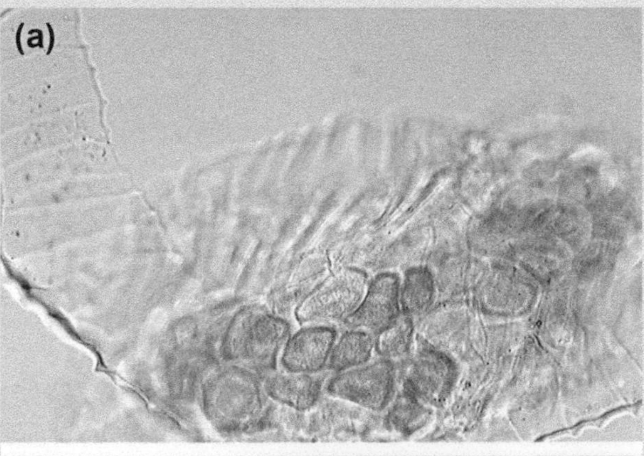

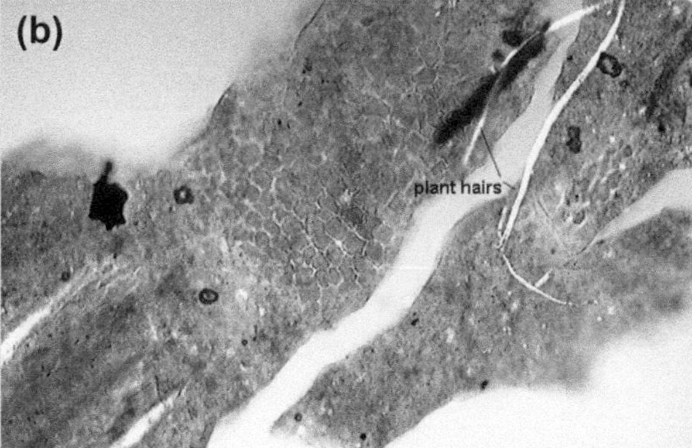

FIGURE 7.12

Microscopic structures in oat flour. (a) The lower portion of the photomicrograph shows cells in the coating of the oat bran. (b) Microscopic structures in vomit containing oat flour. The elongated fibrous structures are plant hairs common in oat flour.

cereal ingredients similar to that found in the vomit on Kevin's clothing and gastric fluid, as shown in Figure 7.12. The cereal ingredients were consistent with *Marshmallow Mateys®*, the final meal of Kevin Cochran. The vomit in Cochran's truck, along with other trace evidence, linked him to the death of his son, as well as the arson of his home. Investigators learnt that Cochran gave a file folder containing documents, specifically the homeowners and life insurance policies of his children, to a neighbor the night after the fire.

On Memorial Day of 1999, James Cochran committed suicide in his jail cell using a coaxial cable from a television set. Investigators theorized Cochran killed his son and set fire to his house for the insurance money.

*Names have been changed.

Source: *Schneck (2003).*

DETERMINING TIME SINCE DEATH (POSTMORTEM INTERVAL)

Following death, numerous changes occur that ultimately lead to the dissolution of all soft tissues. The importance of these changes to the forensic pathologist is that they provide a sequence of events that may allow an estimate of time since death ensued. This determination is based on the principle of sequential changes called the **postmortem clock**. The evaluation may include the following phenomena:

- Changes evident upon external examination of the body, such as temperature, livor, rigor, and decomposition;
- Chemical changes in body fluids or tissues;
- Physiological changes with progression rates, such as digestion;
- Survival after injuries, based on the nature, severity and other factors such as blood loss.

This hypothetical "postmortem clock" factors in various phenomena, such as stiffness of the joints (rigor mortis), settling of blood on the skin surface (livor mortis), and decrease in body temperature (**algor mortis**), with additional laboratory findings, such as chemical measurements of body fluids and physiological changes such as digestion, to provide an estimate of how long it has been since the person died. Any attempt at this type of evaluation is best described as difficult, imprecise, and often not possible (DiMaio, 1999). As the postmortem interval increases, all these estimates become increasingly more inaccurate.

Having started with that precautionary note, we must say that these observations are an integral part of the autopsy and can, in individual cases, provide valuable information. Because of the variation inherent in each of these processes, an initial time range of death is established and modified as more information becomes available. This initial time range is the interval prior to which it may be asserted with some evidence that the victim was alive, based on witness sighting, signed documents, or other established events. This initial time range is then modified by various methods of evaluating postmortem changes.

Postmortem cooling (algor mortis) is often evaluated by various "rules of thumb" that state various degrees of cooling per hour. The best comment on these rules is by the eminent British forensic pathologist Bernard Knight who states, "The only thing that can be said about these rules is that, if they happen to be right it is by chance and not science" (Saukko and Knight, 2004).

The eyes are also an indicator of postmortem changes. Because the circulation of blood ceases, blood settles in the innermost corners of the eyes. If the eyes remain open, a thin film forms on the surface within minutes and clouds over in 2–3 h; if they are closed, it may take longer for this film (an hour or more) and cloudiness (24 h) to develop. Postmortem lividity can be seen as early as 20 min after death, peaking in about 3–4 h. In its early stages, lividity will blanch when pressed (nonfixed), but in advanced stages it will not change under pressure (fixed). If the pattern of lividity does not match the position of the body as it was found (refer to Figure 7.7), it indicates that the body has been moved after death. In more advanced stages, the eventual pressure will burst the skin capillaries, causing petechiae.

Stomach contents may be helpful in the determination of time since death. This determination is based on the assumption that the stomach empties at a known rate, which speeds or slows with the various types of food in it. Light meals last in the stomach for 1.5–2.0h, with heavier meals or meals mixed with alcohol taking a longer period of time. Food moves from the stomach in small amounts, after having been chewed, swallowed, and ground into tiny pieces. A meal eaten hurriedly or gulped will last longer because it hasn't been properly chewed. Alcoholic beverages also delay the stomach's evacuation. The range of variation is quite large, and estimates must be taken with caution.

Decomposition of the body begins almost immediately after death and consists of two parallel processes:

- **Autolysis**, the disintegration of the body by enzymes released by dying cells; and
- **Putrefaction**, the disintegration of the body by the action of microorganisms, such as bacteria.

The body passes through four main stages of decomposition: fresh, bloated (as the gaseous by-products of bacterial action build up in the body cavity), decay (ranging from wet to mushy to liquid), and dry. These changes depend in large part on the environmental factors surrounding the decedent, such as geographical location, seasonality, clothing, sun exposure, and animals and insects in the area. Insect activity, when present, greatly assists the decomposition process.

LABORATORY ANALYSIS

HISTOLOGY

The pathologist typically requests a histology examination for evidence of cellular pathologies resulting from disease, trauma, or preexisting conditions. Small samples of the tissues of interest are taken, embedded in plastic, and sectioned using a **microtome** (a machine that makes very thin, very precise slices) to a thickness of only a few microns. A medical technologist or histologist will then examine the sections microscopically, write a report, and pass this along to the pathologist.

TOXICOLOGY

Another routine examination requested by pathologists in medico-legal autopsies is a broad-based screen test, called a **toxicology screen**, or "tox screen" for short. These tests help the forensic toxicologist determine the absence or presence of drugs and their metabolites, chemicals such as ethanol and other volatile substances, carbon monoxide and other gases, metals and other toxic chemicals in human fluids and tissues. The results help the toxicologist and the pathologist evaluate the role of any drugs or chemicals as a determinant or contributory factor in the cause and manner of death. The common perception is that drug overdoses are predominantly illicit drugs such as heroin, cocaine, and amphetamines, and occur in a limited societal group. In reality, the problem now is much broader and increasingly involves legal drugs (or sometimes illegally manufactured copies of legal drugs, or counterfeits). Furthermore, the problem is complicated by an increasingly complex mixture of legal and illicit drugs, requiring not a tox screen but a complete toxicological testing.

ON THE WEB: SOCIETY OF FORENSIC TOXICOLOGISTS

The Society of Forensic Toxicologists, Inc. (SOFT) is an organization composed of practising forensic toxicologists and those interested in the discipline for the purpose of promoting and developing forensic toxicology. Its website is located at www.soft-tox.org.

AUTOPSY REPORT

The autopsy report is a crucial piece of information in a death investigation. No standard method for reporting autopsy results exists, although guidelines and headings have been suggested by the College of American Pathologists. Because the results of an autopsy, hospital, or medico-legal, may end up in court, it is imperative that certain basic and specific information be included in every autopsy file, such as

- Police report,
- Medical investigator report,
- Witness reports,
- Medical history of the decedent.

EXHUMATIONS

Humans have always had particular practices for dealing with the dead. Rituals, ceremonies, and wakes are all a part of how society acknowledges a person's passing life. One of the most common funereal practices in the United States is the embalming and burial of the dead. If questions about cause or manner of death arise once the deceased is buried, he or she must be dug up or removed from his or her mausoleum; this process is called an **exhumation**. The changes wrought by death, time, and embalming practices can obliterate or obscure details that otherwise might be easily examined. **Embalming** is a process of chemically treating the dead human body to reduce the presence and growth of microorganisms, to retard organic decomposition, and to restore an acceptable physical appearance. Formaldehyde or formalin is the main chemical used to preserve the body. These chemicals are highly reactive and can alter or mask drugs or poisons in the body at the time of death. Toxicologists Tim Tracy of the University of Minnesota and Pete Gannett at West Virginia University have developed special methods to analyze embalmed tissues for drugs, poisons, and medications. These methods have been successfully applied in casework; more methods for other drugs of abuse in embalmed tissues are being researched (Gannet et al., 2001; Tracy et al., 2001).

CONSULTATIONS

The forensic pathologist, when presented with challenging cases of burned, decomposed, or dismembered bodies, may consult with any of a variety of forensic specialists. Forensic anthropologists, entomologists, and odontologists all may play a role in a death investigation. Some ME offices or forensic laboratories have one or more of these specialists on staff due to regular caseload demands. This is especially true of offices that cover a large geographical area or large metropolitan areas.

BACK TO THE CASE: GLORIA RAMIREZ

Various agencies have come up with explanations of what happened in the Riverside ER, from the laughable (the ER staff were overcome by the "smell of death") to the bizarre (the hospital was running a secret methamphetamine lab). Scientists at Livermore National Laboratory have provided the most scientific explanation to date, but it still has weaknesses. Dimethyl sulfone ($DMSO_2$) was found in Ramirez's blood. $DMSO_2$ is a metabolic product of dimethyl sulfoxide (DMSO), a solvent sometimes used by cancer patients and athletes as a pain remedy. The theory runs like this: Due to Ramirez's use of DMSO and her urinary blockage, DMSO accumulated in her bloodstream and the oxygen the paramedics gave her in the ambulance converted the DMSO in her blood into a high concentration of $DMSO_2$. Some unknown catalyst, perhaps the electric defibrillation, converts the $DMSO_2$ into $DMSO_4$ and induces the unhealthy effects. When the nurse draws the blood and it cools to room temperature, the straw-colored crystals form. The $DMSO_4$ evaporates, leaving no clues behind. Beyond this theory, no credible explanation has ever been offered for the strange case of Gloria Ramirez.

Sources: *Adams, 1996; Pilkington, 2004.*

SUMMARY

MEs study disease and trauma that lead to the death of an individual. When these examiners conduct autopsies, the dissection of a dead body to determine the cause and manner of death, they greatly assist death investigations. It is a sad fact, however, that the number of autopsies has steadily declined in the past 50 years; the medical profession loses its most valuable quality control tool when autopsies are not performed. Many times, the morgue is as important as the crime scene.

TEST YOUR KNOWLEDGE

1. What's the difference between cause and manner of death?
2. What is the primary cause of death?
3. Name the four manners of death.
4. What is the difference between a coroner and a ME?
5. What is livor mortis?
6. What is another name for postmortem cooling?
7. How long does rigor mortis last?
8. What are petechiae? Where do they appear?

9. What are Tardieu spots?
10. Who was Milton Helpern?
11. What is autolysis?
12. How many stages are there to decomposition?
13. Histology is the study of what?
14. What is an exhumation?
15. What is the difference between blunt and sharp force trauma?
16. What is stippling?
17. Where does the term 'sheriff' come from?
18. What causes rigor mortis?
19. What is putrefaction?
20. How accurate is algor mortis?

CONSIDER THIS...

1. How does an autopsy differ from a medico-legal autopsy? Why?
2. What specialists might assist a ME? Why? What other specialties in this textbook might aid a pathologist in his or her investigation?
3. Why do you think the number of hospital autopsies has declined? Do you think the number of medico-legal autopsies has similarly declined? Why or why not?

BIBLIOGRAPHY AND FURTHER READING

Adams, C., 1996. What's the Story on the 'Toxic Lady'? The Straight Dope. March 22, Retrieved from: www.straightdope.com.

Collins, K.A., Lantz, P.E., 1994. Interpretation of fatal, multiple, and exiting gunshot wounds by trauma specialists. Forensic Science International 65, 185–193.

Council of American Pathologists, 2006. Cause of Death and the Death Certificate. Council of American Pathologists, Northfield, IL.

DiMaio, V., 1999. Gunshot Wounds, second ed. CRC Press, Boca Raton, FL.

DiMaio, V., DiMaio, D., 2001. Forensic Pathology, second ed. CRC Press, Boca Raton, FL.

Dolinak, D., Matshes, E., Lew, E., 2005. Forensic Pathology: Principles and Practice, Elsevier, Amsterdam.

Gannett, P.M., Hailu, S., Daft, J., James, D., Rybeck, B., Tracy, T.S., 2001. In vitro reaction of formaldehyde with fenfluramine: conversion to *N*-methyl fenfluramine. Journal of Analytical Toxicology 25, 88–92.

Hanzlick, R., 2000. The autopsy lexicon. Archives of Pathology and Laboratory Medicine 124, 594–603.

Hanzlick, R., 2006. Death Investigation: Systems and Procedures. CRC Press, Boca Raton, FL.

Hutchins, G., Berman, J., Moore, W., Hanzlick, R., 1999. Practice guidelines for autopsy pathology. Archives of Pathology and Laboratory Medicine 123, 1085–1092.

Kanchan, T., Krishan, K., 2013. Forensic pathology principles and overview. In: Siegel, J., Saukko, P. (Eds.), Encyclopedia of Forensic Sciences, second ed. Elsevier, Amsterdam, pp. 193–196.

Pilkington, M., 2004. Deadly Miasma. The Guardian. Thursday July 1. Available: http://www.guardian.co.uk/science/2004/jul/01/science.research.

Saukko, P., Knight, B., 2004. Knight's Forensic Pathology. Arnold Publishers, London.

Saukko, P., Pollak, S., 2013a. In: Siegel, J., Saukko, P. (Eds.), Autopsy Encyclopedia of Forensic Sciences, second ed. Elsevier, Amsterdam, pp. 205–209.

Saukko, P., Pollak, S., 2013b. In: Siegel, J., Saukko, P. (Eds.), Histopathology Encyclopedia of Forensic Sciences, second ed. Elsevier, Amsterdam, pp. 210–216.

Schneck, W., 2003. Cereal murder. In: Houck, M.M. (Ed.), Microscopic Evidence: Mute Witnesses 2 More Trace Evidence Cases. Academic Press, New York.

Thorwald, J., 1964. The Century of the Detective Harcourt. Brace & World, New York City.

Tracy, T.S., Rybeck, B.F., James, D.G., Knopp, J.B., Gannett, P.M., 2001. Stability of benzodiazepines in formaldehyde solutions. Journal of Analytical Toxicology 25, 166–173.

Wilson, C., Wilson, D., 2003. Written in Blood: A History of Forensic Detection. Carroll and Graf Publishers, New York City.

CHAPTER

Anthropology and Odontology

CHAPTER OUTLINE

KEY TERMS

- Acetabulum
- Anterior
- Appendicular skeleton
- Axial skeleton
- Biological profile

Fundamentals of Forensic Science

- Buccal
- Calipers: spreading, sliding
- Carpals
- Centers of ossification
- Clavicle
- Coccyx
- Compact bone
- Cortical bone
- Cranial skeleton
- Cranium
- Diaphysis
- Distal
- Enamel
- Endochondral bone
- Epiphyses
- Femur
- Fibula
- Forensic odontologists
- Frontal sinus
- Humerus
- Ilium
- Interstitial bone
- Intervertebral disk
- Intramembranous
- Ischium
- Lacuna
- Lingual
- Mandible
- Marrow
- Mastoid processes
- Medullary cavity
- Mesial
- Metacarpals
- Occlusal surface
- Os coxae/innominates
- Osteoblasts
- Osteoclasts

- Osteon
- Patella
- Phalanx, phalanges
- Postcranial skeleton
- Posterior
- Preauricular sulcus
- Proximal
- Pubis
- Radius
- Ribs
- Sacrum
- Scapula
- Sciatic notch
- Skull
- Sternum
- Superimposition
- Sutures
- Symphysis
- Taphonomy
- Tibia
- Trabecular bone
- Ulna
- Vertebrae

THE CASE: "BUCKY"

Children in Pennsylvania found a five-gallon bucket in a stream bed dried from a recent drought. Inside the bucket, they saw what appeared to be part of a skull. They called their parents, who called the police, who submitted the bucket to the medical examiner (ME). The skull was partially encased in a gray material. The ME used a reciprocating bone saw to try to remove the gray material; the material was so hard that it burned out the motor on the saw. The ME took an X-ray of the skull (see Figure 8.1) and, in desperation, sent it to the FBI Laboratory.

Technicians and anthropologists at the Smithsonian Institution's National Museum of Natural History and the FBI eventually removed the material using a pneumatic drill (see Figure 8.2). The material that surrounded the skull was determined by FBI chemists to be a synthetic material used to make kitchen countertops—very hard, durable, and difficult to obtain in large quantities. Typically, only 1-ounce tubes are commercially available for repairing chips in countertops and this was a *bucket* full of the material.

Looking at the X-ray and considering the nature of the encasing material, what seems to be the nature of this case? Refer to the X-ray throughout this chapter. What clues are in this image?

(Continued)

THE CASE: "BUCKY"—cont'd

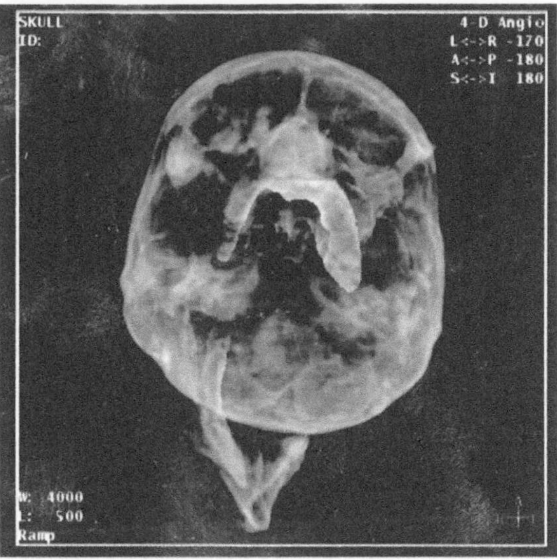

FIGURE 8.1

X-ray of skull.

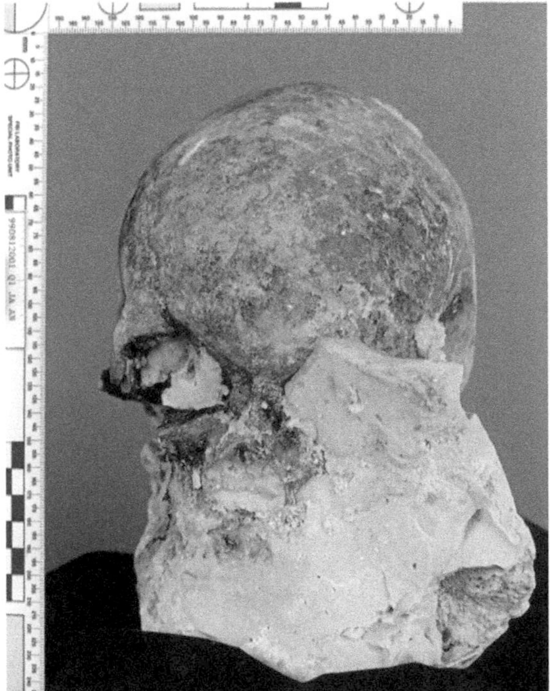

FIGURE 8.2

Skull with gray material partially removed.

INTRODUCTION

Anthropology is the study of humans, their cultures, and their biology. Anthropology can be divided into the study of human biology and human culture, and these can be further divided into the study of the past and the study of the present. This presents us with four main disciplines within anthropology, as shown in Table 8.1.

Paleoanthropology: The *biological* study of *past* human populations.
Bioanthropology: The *biological* study of *current* human populations.
Archaeology: The study of *past* human *cultures*.
Ethnology: The study of *current* human *cultures*.

Forensic anthropology is the application of the study of humans to situations of modern legal or public concern. This typically takes the form of collecting and analyzing human skeletal remains to help identify victims and reconstruct the events surrounding their deaths. Why wouldn't a medical doctor or pathologist perform these analyzes? As medical doctors, pathologists learn about the body's various organ systems; additionally, forensic pathologists learn what makes these systems stop working. Forensic anthropologists are taught about only one system in the body: the skeleton. They learn to identify minute pieces of bone, recognizing hints that might indicate what portion of what bone they are holding. Pathologists require assistance from the advanced, focused knowledge of skeletal anatomy that anthropologists have just as anthropologists require assistance from the detailed and extensive medical training that pathologists gain in medical school. Pathologists generally do not learn about the bits and pieces that are the clues forensic anthropologists use to identify human remains.

Forensic anthropology involves methods from all the anthropological disciplines but mostly from paleoanthropology and bioanthropology because of the study of the human skeleton. Archaeological methods are employed to collect the remains and paleoanthropological techniques are used to identify and analyze the bones to determine sex, age, race, and other biological descriptors. Forensic anthropology is therefore multidisciplinary in nature and requires a professional with the proper education, training, and experience to assist investigators.

Table 8.1 The Traditional Disciplines of Anthropology

	Past	**Present**
Biological	Paleoanthropology	Bioanthropology
Cultural	Archaeology	Ethnology

The four main disciplines of anthropology are derived from the combinations of studying human biology, human culture, the past and the present. Forensic anthropology principally applies the methods of paleoanthropology to present populations, but also employs archaeological methods and, perhaps, some ethnological techniques as well.

THE HUMAN SKELETON

The human skeleton consists of 206 bones, most of which are paired (left and right) or grouped by area (the skull or the spine, for example), as shown in Figure 8.3.

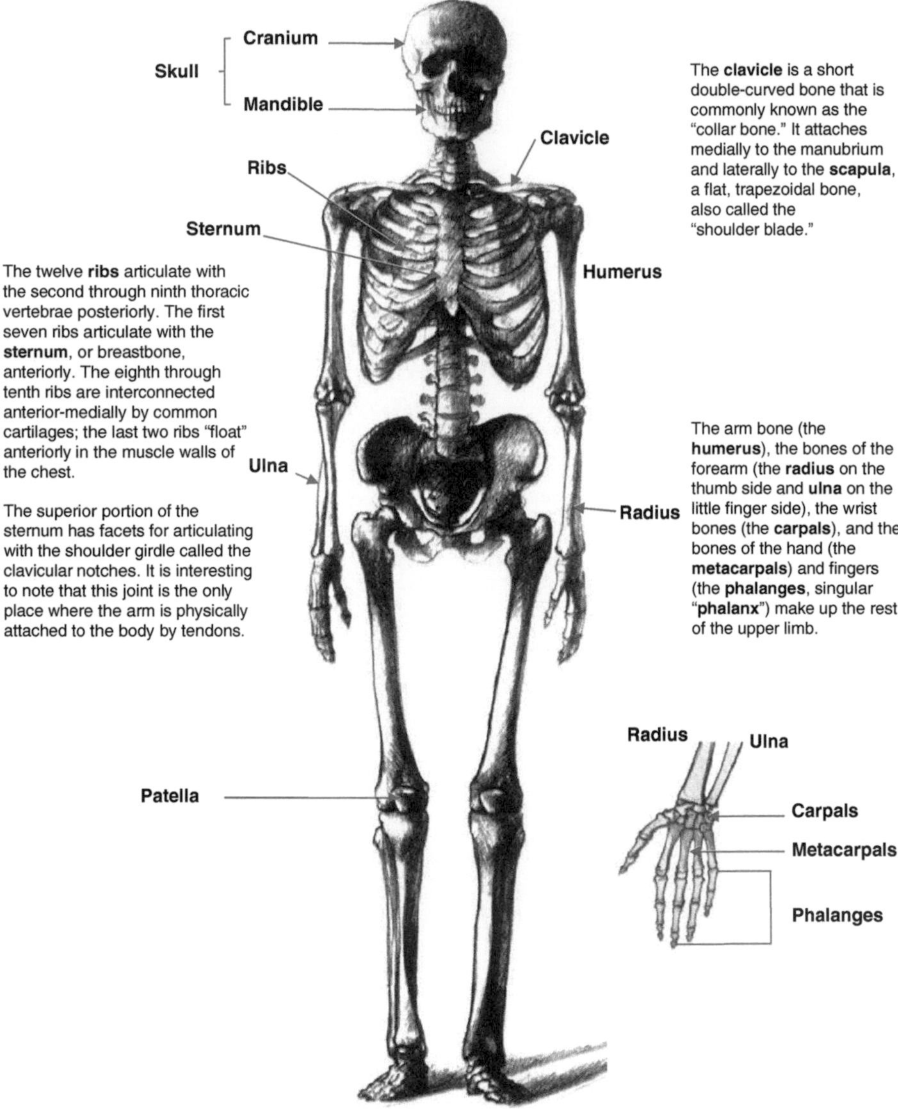

FIGURE 8.3

The human skeleton consists of 206 bones that are paired or grouped by area.

Humans have twenty-four **vertebrae** (singular **"vertebra"**) that constitute the spine, made up of seven **cervical** (neck), twelve **thoracic** (chest), and five **lumbar** (lower back). Regardless of the type, all vertebrae share some common characteristics. The vertebrae stack in a flexible integrated column, held upright by tendons and muscles.

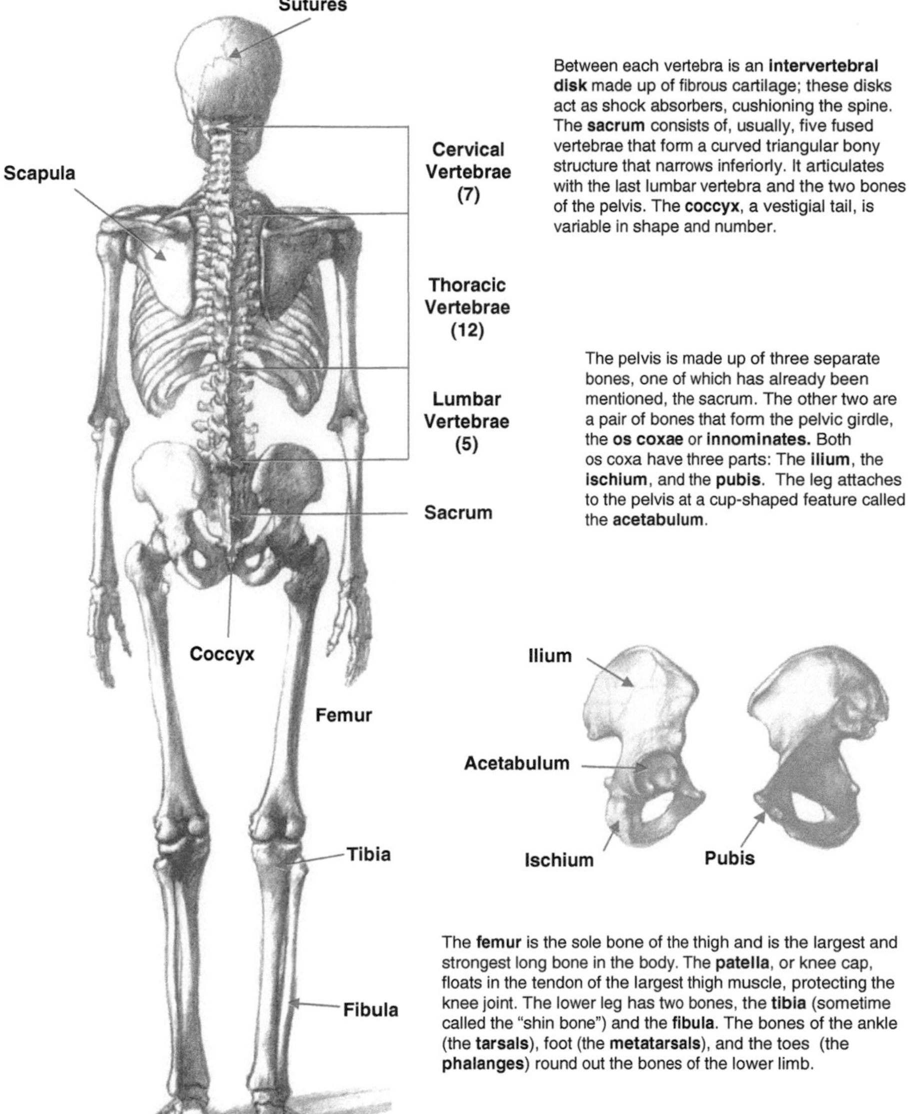

Between each vertebra is an **intervertebral disk** made up of fibrous cartilage; these disks act as shock absorbers, cushioning the spine. The **sacrum** consists of, usually, five fused vertebrae that form a curved triangular bony structure that narrows inferiorly. It articulates with the last lumbar vertebra and the two bones of the pelvis. The **coccyx**, a vestigial tail, is variable in shape and number.

The pelvis is made up of three separate bones, one of which has already been mentioned, the sacrum. The other two are a pair of bones that form the pelvic girdle, the **os coxae** or **innominates.** Both os coxa have three parts: The **ilium**, the **ischium**, and the **pubis**. The leg attaches to the pelvis at a cup-shaped feature called the **acetabulum**.

The **femur** is the sole bone of the thigh and is the largest and strongest long bone in the body. The **patella**, or knee cap, floats in the tendon of the largest thigh muscle, protecting the knee joint. The lower leg has two bones, the **tibia** (sometime called the "shin bone") and the **fibula**. The bones of the ankle (the **tarsals**), foot (the **metatarsals**), and the toes (the **phalanges**) round out the bones of the lower limb.

FIGURE 8.3—cont'd

Bone may seem like a "dead" material because it is so hard and inflexible. In reality, the skeleton is a very active organ system that can repair itself and alter its form over time. Bone, as a tissue and a structure, responds to the stresses placed on it, adding or subtracting boney material as needed. This activity that takes place throughout our lives, plus the genetic potential we inherit from our parents, results in the biological and anatomical variation we see between and within populations and individuals.

Bones perform four main functions for the body: support, motion, protection, and growth.

First, the skeleton provides the infrastructure for attachment and support of the softer tissues in our bodies. Second, these attachments allow the bones to act as levers, providing motion, powered by muscles, at the joints. The structure and arrangement of our bones sets the range of motion for our limbs and bodies. Third, the hard bones protect our soft organs from physical damage; this is especially true of the brain (encased by the **skull**) and the heart and lungs (enclosed within the spine and rib cage). Fourth and finally, the bones are centers of growth from infancy to early adulthood; they also continue important physiological functions throughout our lives by housing the tissue that makes red blood cells. Bones supply us with a ready source of calcium if our dietary intake of that mineral is too low for a too long period.

BONE ORGANIZATION AND GROWTH

Bone growth and maintenance are complex processes that continue throughout our lives. Our skeletons must grow, mature, and repair at the macro- and microscopic levels even as we use them. An understanding of how bones grow and are organized is central to many of the analyzes that forensic anthropologists perform (see "In More Detail: Bone Growth").

IN MORE DETAIL: BONE GROWTH

Two types of bone growth characterize the human skeleton: endochondral and intramembranous. **Endochondral bone** growth starts with a "model" of a bone consisting of cartilage and **centers of ossification** (see Figure 8.4). From these centers, bone is produced and infiltrates the cartilage

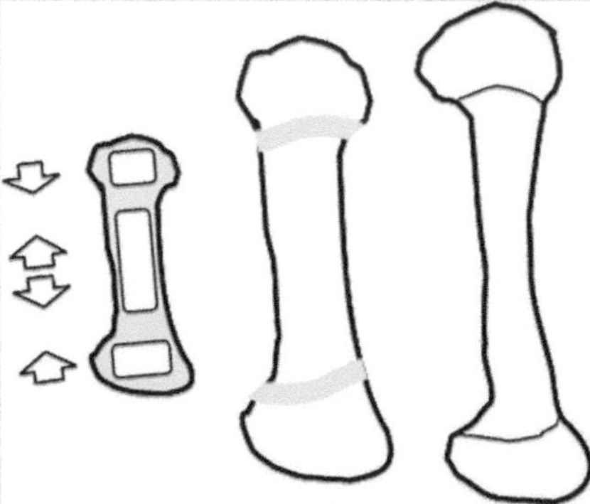

FIGURE 8.4

Bone growth starts in centers of ossification and these spread out to meet each other.

IN MORE DETAIL: BONE GROWTH—cont'd

model, which itself continues to grow. The developing shaft of the bone is called the **diaphysis** and the ends are called **epiphyses**. The growing areas eventually meet and the bone knits together. Not all epiphyses unite at the same time and the sequence of union is important for estimating age at death for individuals younger than about 25 years. In **intramembranous** bone growth, instead of a cartilage model, the ossification occurs within a membrane and this occurs in many bones of the skull. Bone differs from cartilage by having its collagenous connective tissue matrix impregnated with inorganic salts (primarily calcium phosphate and lesser amounts of calcium carbonate, calcium fluoride, magnesium phosphate, and sodium chloride). The osteoblasts, which form the osseous tissue, become encapsulated in lacunae but maintain contact with the vascular system via microscopic canaliculi. When they become encapsulated, they are referred to as osteocytes.

A characteristic feature of a cross section of the shaft (diaphysis) of a long bone is its organization in concentric rings around a central canal containing a blood vessel. This is called a Haversian system (osteon). Between neighboring Haversian systems are nonconcentric lamellae, devoid of Haversian canals, termed interstitial lamellae. Vascular canals, called Volkmann's canals, traverse the long axis of the bone; they are always at right angles to Haversian canals. Their function is to link vascular canals of adjacent Haversian systems with each other and with the periosteal and endosteal blood vessels of the bone. The outer perimeter of a long bone, beneath the osteogenic connective tissue (called periosteum), is composed of circumferential lamellae, which also lack Haversian canals. This thick-walled hollow shaft of **compact bone** (the diaphysis) contains bone marrow. At the distal ends of long bones, where Haversian systems are not found, the bone appears spongy and is therefore called cancellous, or spongy, bone. The spongy appearance is misleading because careful examination of the architecture reveals a highly organized trabecular system providing maximal structural support with minimal density of bony tissue.

The epiphyses at the ends of the diaphysis or shaft contain the spongy bone covered by a thin layer of compact bone. The cavities of the epiphyseal spongy bone are in contact with the bone marrow core of the diaphysis except during growth of long bones in young animals. Interposed between the epiphysis and the diaphysis is the cartilaginous epiphyseal plate. The epiphyseal plate is joined to the diaphysis by columns of cancellous bone; this region is known as the metaphysis.

When bone is formed in and replaces a cartilaginous "model," the process is termed endochondral ossification. Some parts of the skull develop from osteogenic mesenchymal connective tissue, however, without a cartilaginous "model" having been formed first. This is termed intramembranous ossification and these bones are called membrane bones. In both instances, three types of cells are associated with bone formation, growth, and maintenance: osteoblasts, osteocytes, and osteoclasts. The osteoblasts produce osseous tissue (bone), become embedded in the matrix they manufacture and are then renamed osteocytes, to reflect their change of status. They remain viable because they have access to the vascular supply via microscopic canaliculi through which cellular processes extend to receive nutrients and oxygen. Osteoclasts actively resorb and remodel bone as required for growth; these are giant, multinuclear, phagocytic, and osteolytic cells.

Bones consist of an outer layer of hard, smooth compact bone, also called **cortical bone**, pictured in Figure 8.5. The inner layer is an infrastructure of sponge-like bone called **trabecular bone** in long bones, which increases the structural strength of the bone without additional weight. In the very center of long bones is the **medullary cavity**, which contains **marrow**, a fatty material that also houses blood-generating tissues. In life, this composite architecture creates a very strong but resilient framework for our bodies.

The microstructure of bone is quite complex and organized, as shown in Figure 8.6. Specialized growth cells (**osteoblasts**) produce bone and deposit it in layers, eventually becoming encapsulated in a self-made chamber (**lacuna**; plural lacunae).

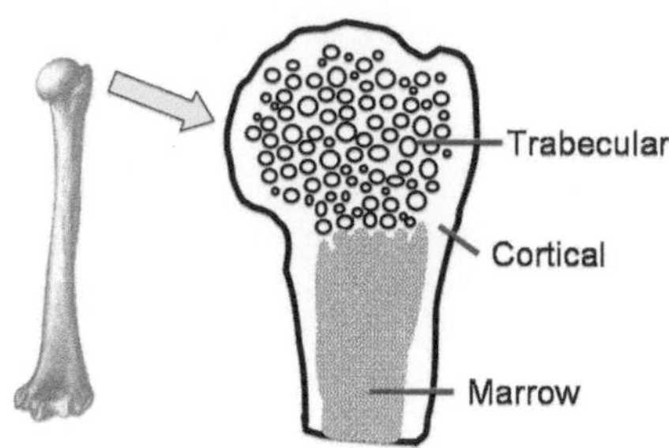

FIGURE 8.5

The outer portion of a bone is the compact or cortical bone and is very dense. The inner portion of a bone is trabecular bone, which is made up of a fine web work of thin, boney spines. The center of a long bone contains marrow, where blood is made.

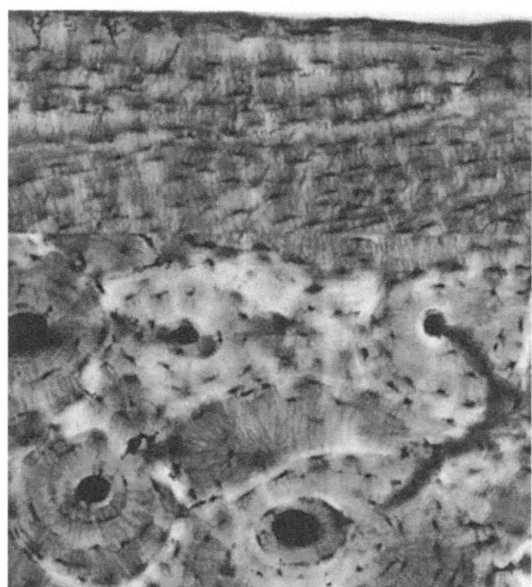

FIGURE 8.6

Bone grows much in the way a brick wall is made and repaired. Bone is laid down by osteoblasts (bone-generating cells) and then, in response to the stresses it undergoes, is torn down by osteoclasts (bone-destroying cells, shown here) before being reworked by the osteoblasts. Bone may seem dead, but it is a very active tissue during life.

Image © Alan Boyde with permission.

They maintain contact with the circulatory system and other bone cells through microscopic vascular channels through which cellular processes extend to receive nutrients and oxygen. When an osteoblast becomes fully encapsulated, it is referred to as an **osteon**.

The third main type of bone cell, **osteoclasts**, actively breaks down and remodels bone as required for growth. When an osteocyte reaches the end of its productivity, it dies and the bone around is reworked and made available to new osteoblasts. In response to the stresses our activities place on our skeletons, the interaction between osteoblasts, osteocytes, and osteoclasts model and shape our bones. Because new osteons are formed by remodeling existing structures, bone has a patchwork appearance at the cellular level. Bone that lies between recently reworked bone is called **interstitial bone**; the amounts of new, reworked, and old bone provide an indication of how old someone is; we will see later how this can provide an estimate of age at death.

SKELETAL ANATOMY

Before describing the human skeletal anatomy, we need to discuss the proper handling of human remains. Most people encounter skeletons only on Halloween or at a costume party. Given that they are potent symbols of death (which is what they represent in those contexts), it is only natural that people feel nervous or anxious when presented with the real thing. The urge to gesture, joke around, or taunt others with a bone or skull is simply a way of expressing that unease, by laughing at "the Grim Reaper." What must be kept in mind, however, is that the material being handled was once part of a human being, like yourself, with a life, family, feelings, and dignity. Additionally, every specimen is unique and irreplaceable, so care must be taken with how it is handled. Bones should always be held over a table, preferably with a padded or protected surface. The skull is of special consideration due to its delicacy and centrality to a forensic examination. The bones of the nose and the eye orbits and also the teeth are fragile. The skull should be handled by the sides and base in both hands with a firm grasp. As the noted osteologist Tim White says, "Common sense and both hands should always be used" (2000, p. 53).

Figure 8.3 shows the human skeleton in a variety of anatomical views. The **cranial skeleton** refers to the skull only; everything else is called the **postcranial skeleton** (meaning below the cranial skeleton). The **axial skeleton** describes the spine (**vertebrae**), **ribs**, and breastbone (**sternum**). The grouping of either upper limb bones (including the shoulder) or lower limb bones (excluding the pelvis) is called the **appendicular skeleton**.

BACK TO THE CASE: "BUCKY"

After having learnt about human skeletal anatomy, review the image of the X-ray in this case (Figure 8.1). Notice that the **mandible** is disarticulated (meaning, it is not in anatomical orientation) and is at a more-or-less right angle to the **cranium**. This means that the skull was not encased in the plastic as a single item. Also, look at the image of the skull partially removed from the plastic (Figure 8.2); notice the margin between the skull and the plastic: There's no gap. When the skull was placed in the plastic, therefore, there was no flesh on it. One might think the skull was buried (and natural processes defleshed it) and then it was placed in the plastic; however, FBI geologists examined the skull and found no evidence of soil whatsoever.

The plastic countertop material was invented in the late-1990s, so the skull could not have been encased in it before then. Anthropologically, the skull presented characteristics of a 50-plus-year-old African-American male. But if the skull was encased in the 1990s, the question remains: When did the *individual* die?

COLLECTING HUMAN REMAINS

Forensic anthropologists rarely find skeletal remains that are aboveground. It is often a hiker, hunter, or some other civilian in a remote or uninhabited area who stumbles across the bones at a crime scene. Because the "evidence" has been found by untrained persons, securing the scene is the most effective way of initiating evidence protection. The subsequent searching of an area for bones is similar to processing other crime scenes, however, and proceeds as an orderly, careful search by trained personnel. This search may be aided by various detection methods, such as probes that detect the gases produced by decomposition, radar that penetrates into the ground, or even dogs trained to sniff for the smells of human decomposition, so-called cadaver dogs.

If the remains are scattered, each bone fragment should be flagged or marked. This provides a view of the pattern of dispersal and where missing bones might lie. Context is even more important with skeletal remains and the individual bones should not be disturbed until the entire scene has been photographed and documented. All the bones on the surface, even animal bones, should be collected.

Buried remains require more time and skill to retrieve, as pictured in Figure 8.7. Archaeological techniques are employed to excavate buried skeletal materials and should be performed only by trained personnel under the supervision of an experienced archaeological excavator. A grid is set up with one point set as a datum, or reference point, from

FIGURE 8.7

Some crime scenes are very similar to archaeological excavations, where shovels and trowels replace magnifying lenses and fingerprint powder. Professional archaeologists or forensic anthropologists are skilled at locating and removing buried remains and should be consulted before any digging starts.

From Ubelaker (1999), © Taraxacum Press, with permission.

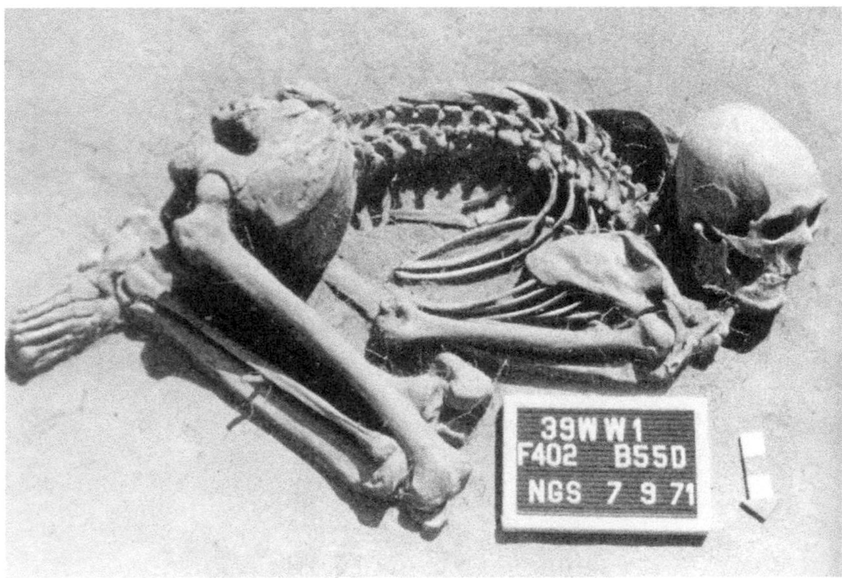

FIGURE 8.8

To gain a clear picture of the body's last resting position, it is useful to clean down to the bottom of the remains and then clear out all the soil around the bones. This process is called "pedestalling" the body.

From Ubelaker (1999), © Taraxacum Press, with permission.

which all measurements originate. Each unit in the grid is excavated separately; they may be processed at the same time or done in series. Soil and materials are removed by a thin layer at a time (usually 2–5 cm) slowly exposing the buried items. Figure 8.8 shows how each bone is carefully delineated and cleaned in place to preserve the final position of the body. Only after the bones have all been found, excavated, photographed, and documented, they will be removed and transported for analysis.

Sometimes, humans, animals, and nature are not kind enough to skeletal remains. A skull or bone may not be whole when recovered and it must be reconstructed prior to analysis. Thin wooden sticks and glue usually do the trick, although other means may need to be used depending on how damaged the bone is. Subsequent analyzes need to be kept in mind (carbon-14 dating, DNA, X-rays, etc.) to minimize any obstacles to their successful completion.

ANALYSIS OF SKELETAL MATERIALS

The first question the anthropologist must ask is, "Is the submitted material really bone?" With whole bones, the answer is obvious. A surprising number of materials can superficially resemble a bone fragment, so even professionals need to be careful, especially with very small fragments. It may be necessary to take a thin section of the

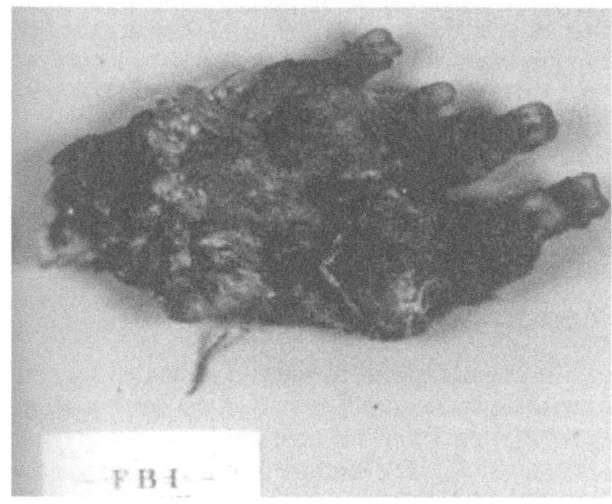

FIGURE 8.9

If a questioned material is bone, it still may not be human; some animal bones look very much like human bones at first glance (like this bear paw). A professional trained in nonhuman skeletal anatomy may need to be consulted.

From Ubelaker (1999), © Taraxacum Press, with permission.

material and examine it microscopically for cell morphology. Elemental analysis is also very useful for small fragments because few materials have the same elemental ratios as bone.

Once the material is determined to be bone, the second question is whether the bone is animal or human. This can present a greater challenge than it may appear at first. Pig bones, bear paws, and some sheep bones can, at first, appear similar to human bones, as illustrated in Figure 8.9. A comprehensive knowledge of human anatomy and a solid grounding in animal osteology will answer most of these questions. A comparative collection of catalogued skeletal remains is crucial to an accurate taxonomical assessment: It can be as useful to know what something is, not just what it is not (see "In More Detail: When Is a Doctor Not a Doctor?").

IN MORE DETAIL: WHEN IS A DOCTOR NOT A DOCTOR?

Dr Douglas Ubelaker writes of the following example in his book, *Human Skeletal Remains* (1999). A bone fragment had been found in a remote part of Alaska. The bone displayed a fracture that had been repaired surgically with a metal plate (see Figure 8.10). The extensive bone growth over the surgical plate indicated the patient had received the surgery long before death. Given the nature of the surgery and the surgical efforts, the authorities began to search for the surgeon who had performed the operation. After these efforts failed, the bone was sent to Dr Ubelaker at the Smithsonian Institution, where a microscopic section revealed the bone to have a nonhuman bone cell morphology, one that closely matched that of a large dog. This explains why the surgeon couldn't be found—because the doctor was a veterinarian! This is an excellent example of why assumptions are dangerous and one should not come to a conclusion until all the facts are in.

IN MORE DETAIL: WHEN IS A DOCTOR NOT A DOCTOR?—cont'd

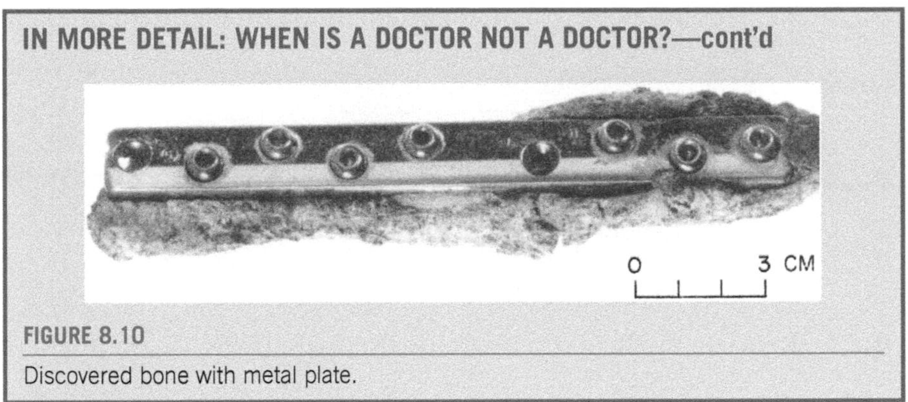

FIGURE 8.10

Discovered bone with metal plate.

THE BIOLOGICAL PROFILE

Once the remains are determined to be human, then a **biological profile** can be developed for the individual(s) represented. The biological profile consists of assessing the sex, age at death, racial affinity, height, and any other aspects that would describe the individual-class-level information. The biological profile is the first step toward identifying whom the remains represent. It is a waste of time to immediately start comparing the dental X-rays or sequencing DNA samples of a 20-year-old woman when the bones recovered are from a 50-year-old man. Which bones are present and their quality will determine what methods can be applied and, in part, the accuracy of those methods.

The criteria that help determine the biological profile are either qualitative, that is, morphological (the presence or absence of a trait, or the shape or size of a landmark) or quantitative. Physical anthropologists use many different measurements as a way of discriminating among individuals, samples, and populations. Some of these information have been catalogued (e.g., at the University of Tennessee's Forensic Data Bank) and used to provide virtual "comparative collections" of measurements that can be used by anyone with a computer (FORDISC is an example of commercially available software for forensic anthropologists). As more museums and universities surrender their osteological collections for repatriation and reburial, collections of data instead of bones will become increasingly crucial to future anthropologists' research. Quantitative physical anthropology is dominated by statistical analysis and sometimes these analyzes, such as principal component analysis, are quite complex involving many measurements, samples, and relationships.

IS THIS PERSON MALE OR FEMALE?

Although in life the differences between males and females are almost always obvious, these differences are not always so apparent, especially when the visual cues of the flesh provides are gone. Males can be up to 20% larger than females, but in some instances, there is little or no difference in size. Many of the quantitative skeletal traits overlap in the middle of the distribution of their values and statistical analysis is required to sort out equivocal examples.

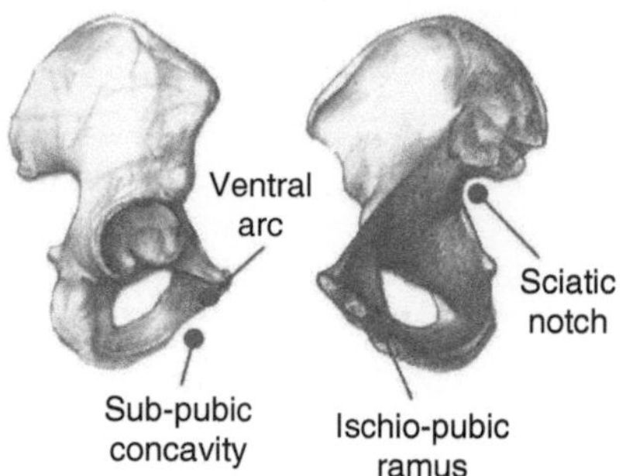

FIGURE 8.11

The main differences between males and females in the pelvis are due to females' biological ability to bear children. The most reliable method is the Phenice method, which uses three areas and the presence and absence of certain characteristics.

Drawing from Barcsay (2001), © heirs of Jeno Barcsay, with permission.

Sexual differences in the human skeleton begin before birth although they are not truly diagnostic until after puberty. In general, females' postcranial skeleton develops faster than males and this difference in rate can be used to infer sex in prepubertal individuals. Typically, however, sex should not be estimated unless the individual is of an age when puberty has begun; above 18 years of age, sex can be determined with confidence.

The significant differences between males and females are size- and function-related morphology.

The two areas that are used most often to determine the sex of an individual in life are also the most diagnostic in death: the pelvis and the skull. Other bones can be very useful for estimating sex as well, and with only a few measurements, an experienced forensic anthropologist can be accurate 70–90% of the time.

The largest number of and most accurate traits for determining sex reside in the pelvis, illustrated in Figure 8.11. The major reason that male and female skeletal anatomy differs so much in the pelvic region is that only females carry and bear babies; human pelvic anatomy reflects this functional difference. Thus, the male pelvis tends to be larger and more robust, whereas the female pelvis is broader and can exhibit pregnancy-specific traits. A useful trait for distinguishing between the male and female pelvis is the **sciatic notch**, located on the inferior lateral border of the **ilium**. The sciatic notch is wide (an angle of about 60°) in females and narrow in males (about 30°).

A very reliable method for determining the sex from pelvis is the Phenice method, developed by Dr Terrell Phenice in 1969, which uses three characteristics: the ventral arc, the subpubic concavity, and the ischiopubic ramus (see Table 8.2). The ventral arc is a ridge on the **anterior** surface of the pubic bone that is present in females but absent in males. The subpubic concavity is a depression on the medial border of the ischiopubic ramus, just inferior to the pubic symphysis. The concavity is wider and deeper in females and is only slight, if at all present, in males. Finally, the ischiopubic ramus itself is flatter and thinner in males, whereas in females it is wide and may

Table 8.2 Traits Useful for Estimating Sex from the Pelvic bones, Including Those Detailed by Phenice: The Subpubic Angle, the Ventral Arc, and the Ischiopubic Ramus

Method	Male Characteristics	Female Characteristics
Pelvis in general	Large, rugged	Smaller, gracile
Subpubic concavity	Narrow	Wide
Acetabulum (hip socket)	Large	Medium to small
Sciatic notch	Narrow	Wide
Preauricular sulcus	Not present	May be present
Ventral arc	Not present or very small	Present, sometimes strongly
Subpubic concavity	Not present or shallow	Present, sometimes deep
Ischiopubic ramus	Thin, narrow	Wide, possible ridge

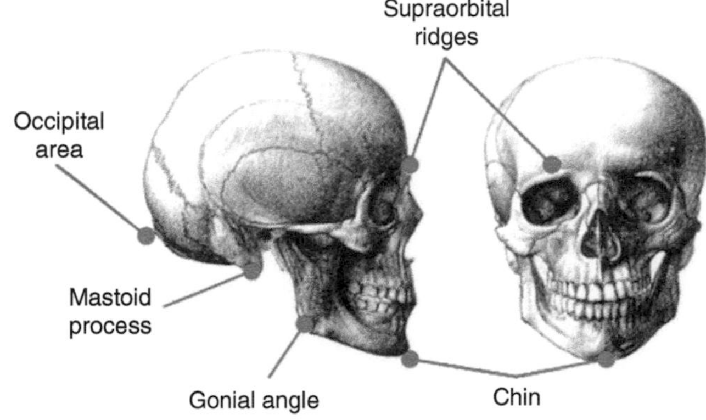

FIGURE 8.12

The skull has many indicators of maleness or femaleness on it, but they are not as clear as those on the pelvis. It therefore takes training and experience to become a good judge of variations in populations. A very slender male or a very robust female may have skeletal traits that fall into an overlap between the sexes.

even have a ridge on it. It is possible to be accurate in sexing a pelvis with only these three traits. The Phenice method cannot be relied upon all by itself, however, because the pelvic remains may be fragmentary and the pubic bone may be absent. Numerous measurements have been used along with statistical analysis to derive more objective sexing methods than descriptive anatomy. Often, these methods are as accurate as morphological traits, but they are important for gauging slight differences between anatomically similar populations.

Sex can be estimated from the cranium as well as the pelvis, but the traits may not always be as obvious. As shown in Figure 8.12, males tend to be larger and have larger muscle attachments than females. The specific areas of interest are the brow ridges, **mastoid processes** (bony masses just behind the ears for attachment of neck muscles), occipital area at the rear of the skull, upper palate, and the general architecture of the skull.

The skull is one of the most, if not the most, studied, measured, and examined part of the skeleton. This metric enthusiasm extends to the determination of sex. Thirty-four standard measurements are the minimum for inclusion of a skull into the National Forensic Data Base, and from these, sex (and race, as we'll see later) can be estimated. These measurements are taken with specialized rulers, called **calipers**, that are either **spreading calipers** or **sliding calipers**. The measurements are taken from various landmarks around the skull. Complicated statistical techniques are used to sort out the measurements, relate them to each other, and then compare them against an appropriate reference population. Software developed at the University of Tennessee, called FORDISC, provides an easy way to analyze and compare data from skeletons, as graphically represented in Figure 8.13.

Postcranial bones can also provide information about a person's sex, but most of this information is based on size and therefore is quantitative. Many of the postcranial bone measurements will yield an accuracy of between 58% and 100%. The measurement may be straightforward, but the interpretation may not be. For example, if the head of the **femur** is greater than 48 mm, then the person was most likely male; a measurement of less than 43 mm indicates a female. The area between 43 and 48 mm indicates that the size of the person was such that estimating sex from this measurement alone would

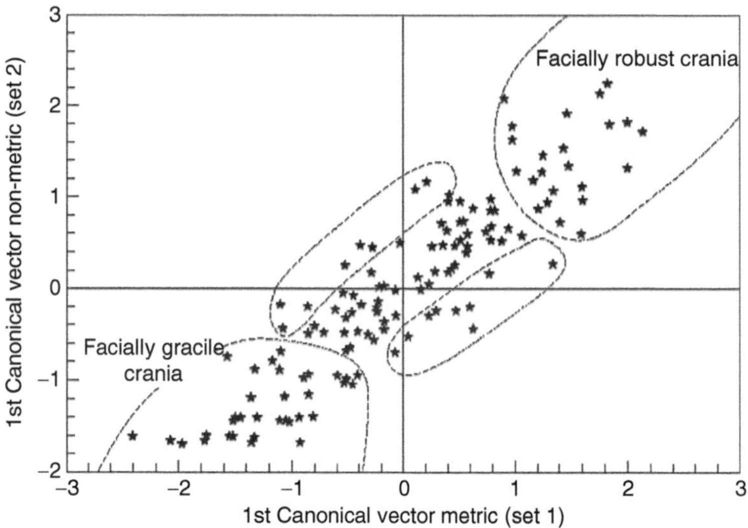

FIGURE 8.13

This is a plot of the calculations taken from a skull to determine its racial ancestry. The circular areas indicate the range of the populations against which the skull was compared; the skull's location is shown with an "X." Given the amount of overlap between some of the circles, it is apparent that even numerical data can sometimes lead to a "fuzzy" answer with race.

give an inconclusive result. This example illustrates why it is very important to consider all the recovered bones before making a judgement, and in turn, this emphasizes the need for a comprehensive search and collection of the remains at the scene.

HOW OLD WAS THIS PERSON?

As we develop in the womb, grow into adults, and age over the years, our skeletons change in known and predictable ways. For infants and children, this is the appearance and development of skeletal growth areas that spread, meet, and fuse into whole bones. As adults, our skeleton's growth shifts to maintenance functions, responding to new stresses, such as exercise (or lack thereof) and job-related activities. Our later years bring with them the loss of bone mass, the slowing of our physiology, and the general degradation that accompanies our senior years. These changes are all recorded in our skeletons and forensic anthropologists use these alterations to estimate a person's age at death.

Estimating age is conceptually different from estimating sex: There are only two sexes, but age is a continuum of 70, 80, or 90 (sometimes more) years. The age-related changes in our skeletons are predictable but not specific enough to allow for an estimate of "31 years and 8 months." The natural variation within a population and between individuals in a population prohibits a precise determination of age. Estimated age ranges, bracketed around the most likely age (25–35 years, for example), are the most acceptable way of reporting age at death. This bracketing necessarily leads to imprecision while retaining accuracy, but only up to a point. If an individual's age is always estimated to be between 1 and 95 years, those estimates will almost always be correct. That estimate, however, would not be very useful to investigators. By balancing the natural variation in ageing and the anthropologist's skill with the methods used, an estimate that accurately reflects the precision of the sample *and* technique can be produced.

For the sake of convenience and organization, the range of human ages has been broken into various classes with associated years: fetal (before birth), infant (0–3), child (3–12), adolescent (12–20), young adult (20–35), adult (35–50), and old adult (50+). These classes represent the significant phases of growth, maturation, and decline in the skeleton and related tissues.

Bones can indicate the stage of development attained by the appearance and fusion of the various epiphyses throughout the body. Nonunited epiphyses are easy to observe because the diaphyseal surface is characteristically rough and irregular in appearance. Epiphyseal appearance and union occurs over the course of years and is a process, not an event; the degree of union (usually scored on a multipoint scale) must be carefully assessed because this could indicate which extreme of an age range is being observed. The three main stages of union are shown in Figure 8.14: First, the epiphysis is open; second, the epiphysis is united, but the junction is still visible; and, third, the epiphysis is completely fused. Epiphyses can be small, so every effort should be made during collection to make sure none are overlooked.

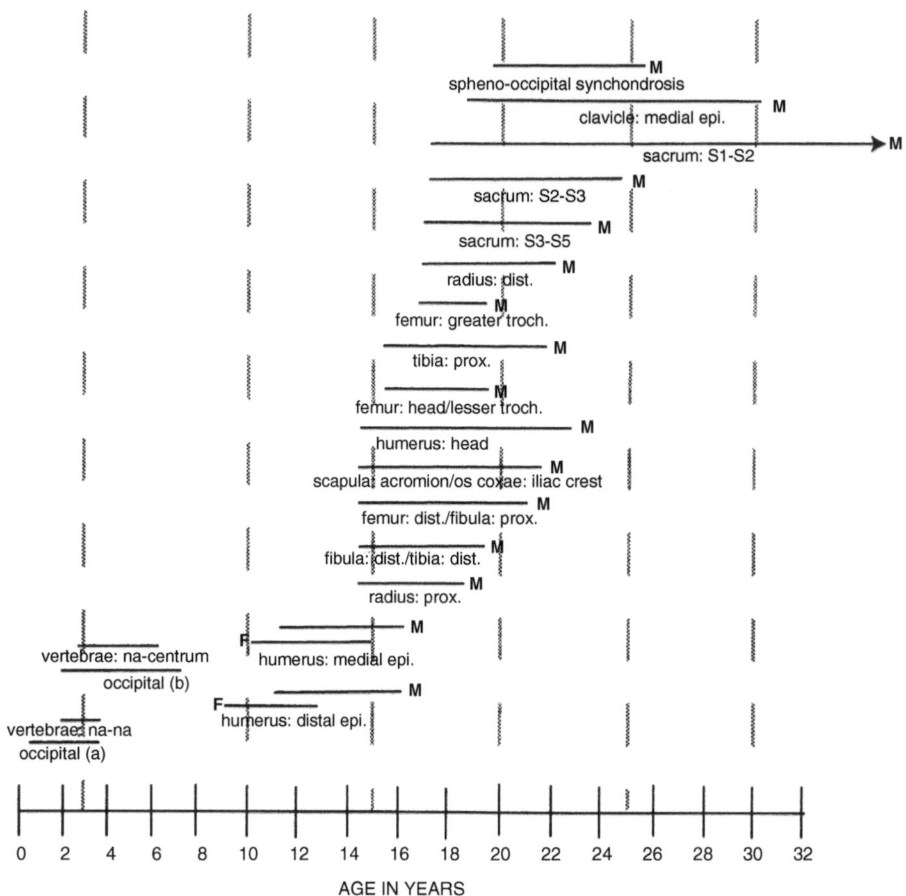

FIGURE 8.14

Different epiphyses unite with the main portion of a bone gradually, so the forensic anthropologist must evaluate the degree of union to correctly estimate age. Epiphyses fuse to the main portions of bone at different times and this pattern of bone growth is an important technique for estimating age in younger individuals.

From Buikstra and Ubelaker (1994), with permission.

Although epiphyses all over the body are uniting from infancy onward, the major epiphyses of the bones of modern populations fuse between 13 and 18 years of age. Union typically occurs in the order of elbow, hip, ankle, knee, wrist, and shoulder. Note that the beginning of epiphyseal union overlaps with the end of dental development, and therefore, these two methods complement one another. The last epiphysis to fuse is usually the medial **clavicle** (collarbone) in the early 1920s. Once all the epiphyses have fused, by about age 28 for most of the population, the growth of the skeleton stops and other age indicators must be used.

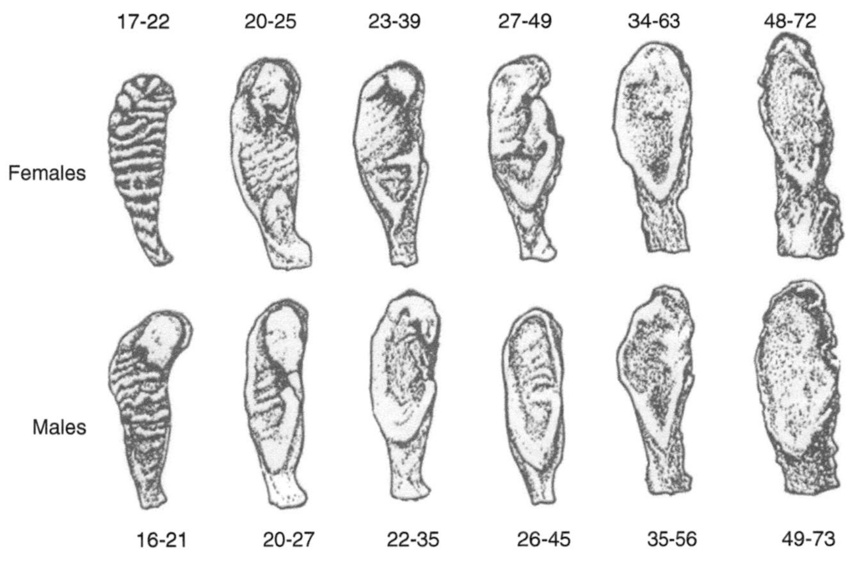

FIGURE 8.15

The face of the pubic symphysis is an important characteristic for estimating age in adults. The surface starts out rugged and bumpy with no defined rim. Gradually, the surface flattens out and a rim develops around the edge of the face. With advanced age, the rim begins to disintegrate although the face remains smooth.

A few areas of the skeleton continue to change in subtle ways (compared with the appearance and union of epiphyses) throughout the remainder of adulthood. The main areas used for estimating adult age are found on the pelvic bones, the ribs, and the continuous remodeling of bone's cellular structure. These few, relatively small areas of the human skeleton have been intensely studied and restudied over the years by researchers trying to fine-tune the estimation of age at death for adults. Any one method alone, however, runs the risk of misleading the investigator, so all available information must be considered, including physical evidence not of an anthropological nature (clothing, personal effects, etc.).

The pubic symphysis (a **symphysis** is a "false" joint) is the junction of the two pubic bones lying roughly 4–5 in below the navel. This junction is bridged by cartilage that acts as a cushion between the two bones. The symphyseal face shown in Figure 8.15 is a raised platform that slowly changes over the years from a rough, rugged surface to a smooth, well-defined area. The morphological changes of the pubic symphysis are considered by the majority of anthropologists to be among the most reliable estimators of age at death. This area was first studied in-depth by Todd, who divided the changes he saw into 10 phases, each defined phase relating to an age range. Todd's work was later advanced by McKern and Stewart, who broke Todd's holistic method into a sectional evaluation to simplify the process. McKern and Stewart's work was based on young males who were killed in the Korean War, and this may have unintentionally biased their results; their work was, after all, focused on identifying soldiers of that very same sex/age category. Nevertheless, the McKern and Stewart method held sway for a number of years until Judy Suchey and Allison Brooks began a large-scale collection and analysis project on the pubic symphysis by collecting samples from the Los Angeles County morgue. The intention was to collect a wide-ranging, demographically accurate sample that could be assessed not only for age but also for variations due to an individual's sex. Their results are more akin to Todd's than McKern and Stewart's, although with fewer phases of development (Ubelaker, 1999).

Another area of morphological change with advancing adulthood is the sternal end of the fourth left rib. As the cartilage between the sternum and the ribs ages, it begins to ossify at a known and predictable rate. Another method of estimating age at death is the examination of the changes in the auricular surface, where the ilium attaches to the **sacrum** (the so-called sacroiliac joint). As age progresses, the surface of the bone becomes less bumpy and more smooth, with smallish pores opening up, creating a decrease in the organization of the surface traits.

Finally, bone never rests. It is constantly remodeling in response to the stresses placed upon it. This remodeling can be seen in the microscopic structure of bone. In approximately the same way as a wall would be rebuilt, bone first needs to be torn down before it can be built up. This constant erosion and renewal leave permanent markers in bone: Once we die, these changes cease. Therefore, a correlation exists between the amount of bone reworking and the amount of time the body has expended energy on this remodeling. A thin section of bone is cut, specific areas are viewed microscopically, and the various structural elements (whole osteons, fragmented osteons, interstitial bone fragments, etc.) are counted. Various formulae have been developed and are among the most accurate methods available for estimating age at death. A major disadvantage of this method is that some amount of bone must be removed, which may or may not be allowed because of case requirements.

ANCESTRY

Many of the cues we use to assess someone's ancestry in life are not well demonstrated in the skeleton. Moreover, ancestry or "race" is a difficult concept, both biologically and socially: Human physical variation is often a subtle thing and people are sensitive to the labels other people place on them. While it is true that no pure ethnic groups exist (or have ever existed), we identify people based partly on what we perceive their "race" to be. This combination of blurred ancestral categories and popular perception, not to mention people's racial self-identity, makes ancestry one of the most difficult estimations in a forensic anthropologist's examination. Nonetheless, forensic anthropologists routinely are called upon to assess skeletal remains for clues as to that person's ancestral affiliation to help lead police toward identification. The terms forensic anthropologists use to designate ancestry are typically those of the United States Census, namely, Whites, Blacks, Hispanics, Asians, Native Americans, and Other (www.census.gov).

Ancestry can be estimated by morphological or quantitative analysis and both of these methods are centered on the skull. Features of the skull, such as the general shape of the eye orbits, nasal aperture, dentition, and surrounding bone and the face, can offer indications of ancestry. Other features are more distinct, such as the scooped-out appearance of the lingual (tongue) side of the upper central incisors often found in individuals of Asian ancestry (so-called "shovel-shaped" incisors). But even indicators like this are not as clear as they may appear at first glance: Prehistoric Native Americans migrated into North America across the Bering Strait from Asia and some of them showed shovel-shaping on their incisors.

In hopes of rendering ancestral assessment more objective, physical anthropologists sought metric means of categorizing human populations. Currently, these means consist of numerous measurements that are then placed in formulae derived from analysis of known populations. While fairly accurate, these formulae suffer from being based on historically small samples that are not necessarily representative of modern populations. These concerns aside, given a complete skull or cranium, ancestral affiliation can be assessed with enough accuracy to make them useful for forensic investigations.

STATURE

Our living stature directly relates to the length of our long bones, especially those of our lower limbs. Calculating stature from long-bone lengths is relatively simple and even partial bones can yield useful results. The only difficulty is that sex and ancestry must be known to correctly estimate height (see Table 8.3) because humans vary within and between these categories.

For example, a White male with a femur length of 55.88 cm would be estimated to have been between 189 and 196 cm ($(2.38 * 55.88) + 61.41 \pm 3.27$, rounding up) tall during life or about 6 ft 1 in to 6 ft 3 in.

FACIAL REPRODUCTIONS

To identify someone, premortem records, such as X-rays, are necessary. To get those, the investigator must have an idea of who the remains under study might belong to. Sometimes, bones are found and law enforcement investigators have no good leads as to whose they might be. In these cases, forensic science has to turn to the world of art for assistance.

Because the shape of our faces is based on our skulls, if we were to reconstruct the soft tissues of a face on top of a skull, we could create a likeness of that individual. This is what happens in **facial reproductions**: An artist recreates the likeness of a person either by sculpting the soft tissues with clay in three dimensions or by drawing, as shown in Figure 8.16. Facial reconstructions require a high degree of artistic skill, a good knowledge of human anatomy and variation, and an appreciation of the human face. These likenesses are not used for identification purposes but are meant to stir the public's recognition of otherwise unidentifiable remains. Flyers, images on television or in newspapers and police bulletins are used to distribute the likenesses in the hopes that someone will recognize them.

Table 8.3 Estimating Stature Is a Straightforward Procedure

White Males	
Stature	3.08 * Humerus + 70.45 ± 4.05
	3.78 * Radius + 79.01 ± 4.32
	3.70 * Ulna + 74.05 ± 4.32
	2.38 * Femur + 61.41 ± 3.27
	2.52 * Tibia + 78.62 ± 3.37
	2.68 * Fibula + 71.78 ± 3.29
Black Males	
Stature	3.26 * Humerus + 62.10 ± 4.43
	3.42 * Radius + 81.56 ± 4.30
	3.26 * Ulna + 79.29 ± 4.42
	2.11 * Femur + 70.35 ± 3.94
	2.19 * Tibia + 86.02 ± 3.78
	2.19 * Fibula + 85.65 ± 4.08
Asian Males	
Stature	2.68 * Humerus + 83.19 ± 4.25
	3.54 * Radius + 82.00 ± 4.60
	3.48 * Ulna + 77.45 ± 4.66
	2.15 * Femur + 72.75 ± 3.80
	2.40 * Fibula + 80.56 ± 3.24

The trick is that an estimate of sex and race is necessary to determine the proper formula to use. All measurements are in centimeter.

FIGURE 8.16

Based on science and anatomy but completed through art, facial reconstructions are helpful in approaching the public for investigative leads to a person's identity. Although they can be quite accurate, as in this example, they are not used for identification.

From Taylor (2001), © CRC Press, with permission.

ODONTOLOGY

The most common role of the forensic dentist is the identification of deceased individuals. Dental identification can be conducted through comparison of dental remains to either ante-mortem or postmortem records. The most frequently performed examination is comparing the dentition of a deceased person to those of a person represented by ante-mortem to determine if they are the same individual. The biological profile developed by the forensic anthropologist is very helpful in narrowing down the potential choices for selecting the ante-mortem records. If the ante-mortem records are available, any postmortem X-rays should replicate the view and angle in the ante-mortem X-rays. If ante-mortem records are not available, a postmortem record is created by the forensic dentist for possible future comparisons. The forensic dentist produces the postmortem record by careful charting and written descriptions of the dental structures and by taking radiographs.

Once the postmortem record is complete, a comparison between it and any ante-mortem records can be conducted. The comparison is methodical and systematic: Each tooth and structure is examined and compared. Fillings, caps, and restorations play the largest role in the identification process. Other features play a role in those individuals with good dental hygiene and few restorations. Similarities should be noted during the comparison process, as well as explainable and unexplainable discrepancies. Those differences that can be explained typically encompass dental restorations that occurred in the time elapsed between the ante-mortem and postmortem records. The person had a tooth pulled or a cavity filled, for example. If a discrepancy is unexplainable, such as a postmortem tooth that is not present on the ante-mortem record, then the odontologist will conclude that two different people are represented (an exclusion).

ON THE WEB

American Board of Forensic Odontology	www.abfo.org
British Association of Forensic Odontology	www.bafo.org.uk

DENTAL ANATOMY

The anatomy of the mouth is important to forensic science for a number of reasons. First, the teeth are made of **enamel**, the hardest substance that the body produces, and teeth can survive severe conditions and still be viable for analysis. Second, the teeth are the only part of the skeletal anatomy that directly interacts with the environment and, therefore, can reflect conditions the person experienced during life. Finally, teeth and their related structures have the potential to be used in the identification of the deceased. Because of these reasons and the complexity of fillings, braces, and other dental work, **forensic odontologists**, dental health professionals who apply their skills to legal investigations, are a specialty often relied upon in cases of unidentified bodies, mass disasters, and missing person cases.

TEETH

Forensic odontologists use a variety of methods to organize and uniquely name each tooth in the mouth. The common names of teeth are also useful, but they refer to a group of teeth with the same characteristics. Typically, a numbering method is used and one of the most common is to number the teeth from the lower right molar, moving anteriorly, to the lower left molar; the next tooth would then be the upper left molar and then back around to the upper right molar (see Figure 8.17). This numbering scheme sections the mouth into four quadrants: upper right, lower right, upper left, and lower left.

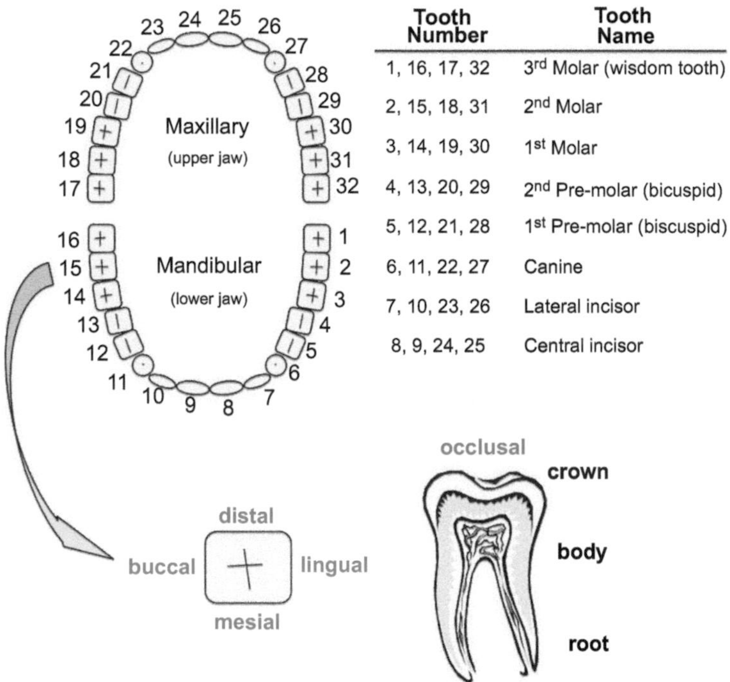

Tooth Number	Tooth Name
1, 16, 17, 32	3rd Molar (wisdom tooth)
2, 15, 18, 31	2nd Molar
3, 14, 19, 30	1st Molar
4, 13, 20, 29	2nd Pre-molar (bicuspid)
5, 12, 21, 28	1st Pre-molar (biscuspid)
6, 11, 22, 27	Canine
7, 10, 23, 26	Lateral incisor
8, 9, 24, 25	Central incisor

FIGURE 8.17

Because the terminology for teeth overlaps between top and bottom and right and left, it is important to have a unique identifier for each tooth. This aids in clear communication between forensic professionals.

Each tooth has five sides: **buccal**, the side toward the cheek; **lingual**, the side toward the tongue; **mesial**, toward the midline of the body; **distal**, the side away from the midline; and the chewing surface, called the **occlusal surface**. These orientations help to describe where a cavity or filling is located. Individually, each tooth has similar structures but is shaped differently due to their functions. Every tooth has a crown, body, and root.

TOOTH DEVELOPMENT

Teeth grow from the chewing surface, or cusps, downward to the roots. This continual process is usually broken up into phases that relate to the amount of tooth development. Humans have two sets of teeth, one when we are children, called "baby" teeth but more properly termed "deciduous" teeth, and one when we are adults, our permanent teeth. Dentists often have a dental development chart in their offices, like the one in Figure 8.18. Different teeth develop at different rates, with incisors developing faster than molars. Teeth erupt through the gums when they are about one-half to three-fourth developed. Notable landmarks in tooth eruption are the first deciduous incisor at about 9 months, the first permanent molar at about 6 years, the first permanent incisor at about 7 years and the third permanent molar at sometime between 15 and 21 years; this latter tooth is notorious for irregular eruption and is not necessarily a reliable indicator of age.

IDENTIFICATION

The goal of a forensic anthropological examination is individualizing a set of human remains, often referred to as a "positive identification." This moves beyond class characteristics, no matter how narrow a classification, into the realm of uniqueness. To achieve this level of certainty, the data have to support the conclusion that the remains represent those of one, and only one, person to the exclusion of all other people.

Because most people regularly visit their dentists, dental records and X-rays are the most common form of ante-mortem record that leads to a positive identification, as demonstrated in Figure 8.19. Because many years may have passed since the last X-ray and the forensic comparison, having a skilled forensic odontologist consult on the examination may be necessary. Any differences between the X-rays taken before death and after death must be explainable and not be significant for the identification to be positive.

Other X-rays can lead to positive identifications as well. A structure in the frontal bone, the **frontal sinus**, is considered to be unique to a reasonable degree of scientific certainty. Likewise, the internal structure of postcranial bones is considered to be unique as well. Surgeries, healed fractures, and disease may all be documented radiographically and also can lead to positive comparisons.

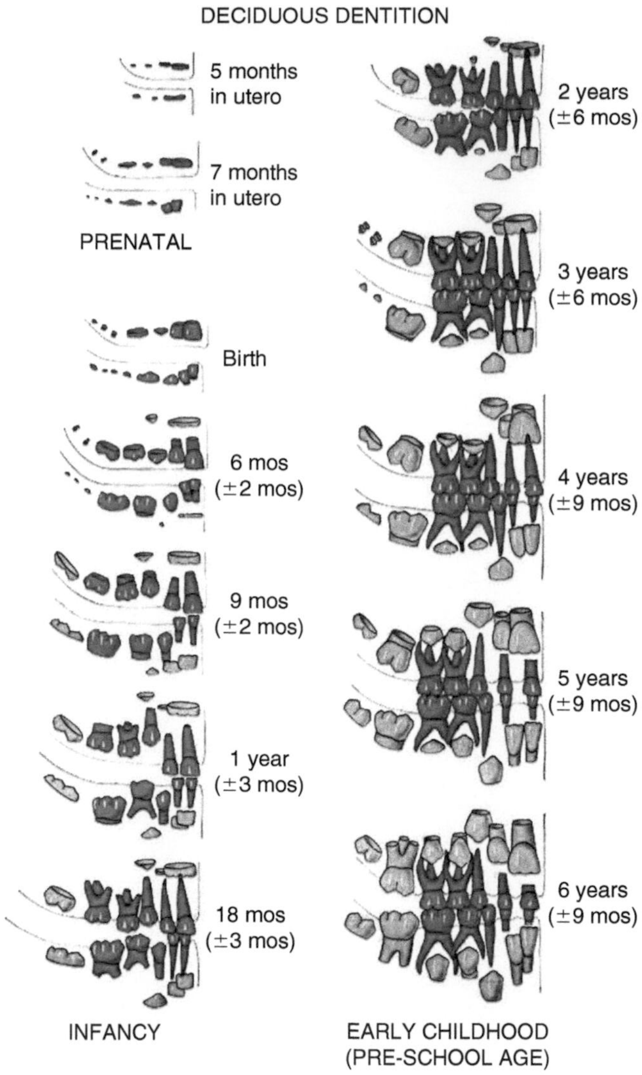

FIGURE 8.18

Teeth grow from the cusps downward to the roots. Humans have one set of teeth as children (deciduous) and one when we are adults (permanent). Tooth development is differential depending on the type of tooth it is.

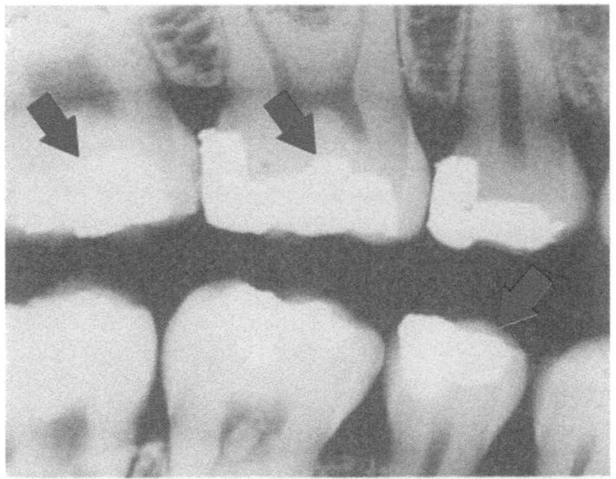

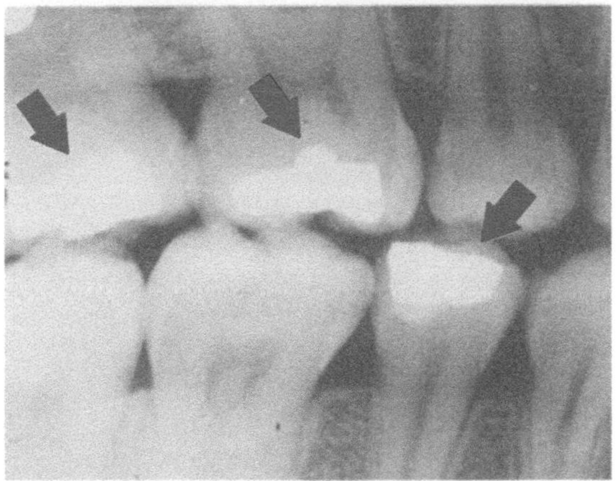

FIGURE 8.19

For a forensic odontologist to identify someone, he or she must have dental X-rays taken prior to the person's death. It is then a simple matter of comparing these with X-rays taken of the remains and looking for points of comparison, shown with arrows in the figure.

Identification through the comparison of ante- and postmortem X-rays is considered the best method for skeletal remains. People's teeth vary in size, number, and position and the amount, size, type, location, and extent of dental work also varies enormously from person to person. Taken in combination, this natural and medical variation is such that it would be unthinkable to find two people whose teeth *and* dental work were exactly the same. X-rays can also document other individualizing traits, such as the habitual wear mentioned earlier, and some of these may be corroborated by family or friends.

INTERPRETATIONS

CAUSE VERSUS MANNER OF DEATH

The cause of death is the action that initiates the cessation of life; the manner of death is the way in which this action came about. There are, literally, thousands of causes of death, but there are only four manners in which to die: natural, accidental, suicide, and homicide. Forensic anthropologists can sometimes assist a ME with assessing the manner of death (e.g., see Sauer, 1984), but only rarely can one assist with the cause of death. Just because a skull exhibits an entrance and exit bullet hole doesn't mean that it is what caused the person to die; many people get shot each year, but only some of them die from their wounds. Likewise, a person may be strangled to death (cause: asphyxiation), but this activity may leave no markers on the skeleton. Forensic anthropologists must be very careful to stay within the bounds of their knowledge and training in order to provide the most useful information to MEs, investigators, and others who require their services.

TAPHONOMY

Taphonomy is the study of what happens to an organism from the time it dies until the time it ends up in the laboratory. In recent years, taphonomy has blossomed into a full-fledged area of study in its own right (e.g., see Haglund and Sorg, 1997); this expansion has greatly assisted the various forensic sciences that relate directly to the study of the dead. This information greatly increases the ability of investigators to assess time since death, discern premortem from postmortem effects, as shown in Figure 8.20, and detect subtle clues that might help lead to a killer's identity or activity.

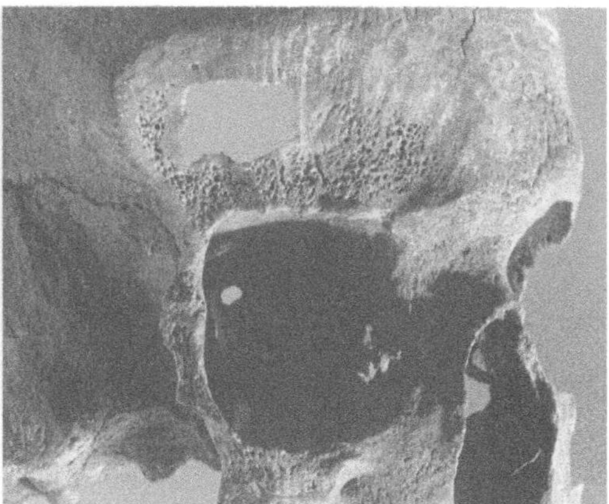

FIGURE 8.20

Taphonomic marks, such as these rodent-chewing marks, can help the forensic anthropologist to determine the order of events after a deceased person is exposed to the environment.

From White (2000), © Academic Press, with permission.

PATHOLOGY

Forensic anthropologists work closely with forensic pathologists and may often be able to provide information beyond what a pathologist may know. Certain aspects of the pathologist's and anthropologist's work necessarily overlap, however, and these most often are in the areas of wounding and healing of bone.

The distinction of greatest importance for forensic anthropologists is the differences between premortem (before death) and postmortem (after death) injuries. Living bone has different mechanical properties than dead, dried bone and this leads to different reactions to traumatic events. Any sign of healing in bone is definitive of a premortem injury. Wounds or breaks that occur near the time of death (called perimortem injuries) may be difficult to distinguish from trauma that occurs shortly after death because the body will not be alive long enough to begin noticeable healing. It is possible to distinguish between perimortem and long-term postmortem cuts using electron microscopy: At the edge of a fresh cut, the soft tissue will have dried and pulled back from the edge of the cut, whereas in a bone cut, after the soft tissue has dried, it will be at the edge of the cut, as pictured in Figure 8.21.

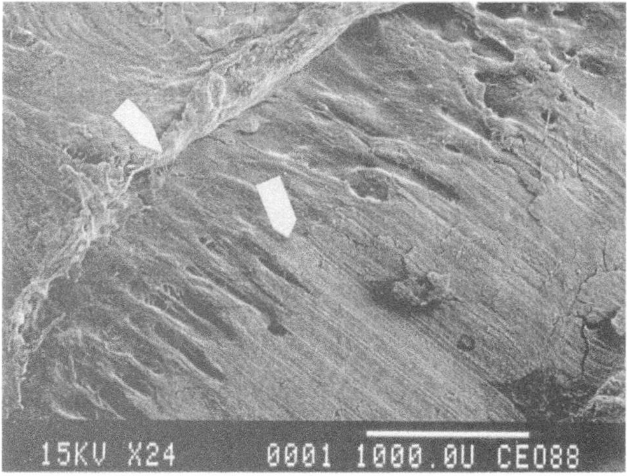

FIGURE 8.21

It may be possible to distinguish between cuts made when bone was fresh (perimortem) and when it was dry (postmortem). The soft tissue from a fresh cut will dry and pull back from the cut in the bone (arrow on the left), whereas it will remain at the edge of the cut in the dry bone (arrow on the right) because it was already dried.

BACK TO THE CASE: "BUCKY"

To determine when the individual in this case died, carbon-14 (C-14) testing was used. Living things take in C-14 (a radioactive isotope of carbon) throughout their life and maintain an equilibrium of it; when they die, the C-14 slowly degrades at a specified rate (its half-life is 5730 years). By measuring the amount of C-14 that is active, the amount lost can be calculated. Normally, C-14 testing is used on very old samples, such as archaeological artifacts. But, because of nuclear weapons testing between 1952 and 1963, a "bomb curve" exists that is used to demarcate between "older" (pre-1950) and "newer" samples. C-14 testing on a sample from the skull indicated that the individual died between 1680 and 1740, meaning that the case was *historic* and not *forensic* (at least not currently).

Why would someone encase a historic skull in plastic and dump it in a river? Who would have access to that much liquid plastic countertop material? Where did the skull come from? Because the case was historic and not current, the submitting police agency declined to pursue the investigation further. Therefore, the mystery of "Bucky's" origin remains unsolved.

SUMMARY

Forensic anthropology plays a central role in the identification of people who are not identifiable by fingerprints or photographs: Nature has taken its course. Using their knowledge of human anatomy and variation, forensic anthropologists develop biological profiles of skeletal remains and look for individualizing traits in the hopes that the victim can be identified. They also assist other investigators, such as forensic odontologists and MEs, to help with the interpretation of taphonomic information and trauma.

TEST YOUR KNOWLEDGE

1. What is forensic anthropology?
2. How is forensic anthropology different from archaeology?
3. What is a datum and how is it used?
4. How can you tell if something is bone?
5. What is a biological profile?
6. Name the two areas of the body that are the most accurate for estimating sex.
7. What is an epiphysis?
8. What is the last epiphysis to fuse?
9. Where is the pubic symphysis located?
10. What is the fourth left rib used for in forensic anthropology?
11. What needs to be known about a person before you can calculate his or her stature?
12. What's another term for a bicuspid?
13. What is forensic odontology?
14. How many teeth do humans typically have?
15. When does the first adult molar erupt?
16. What are two methods of identification for skeletal remains?
17. What is taphonomy?

18. What are some differences between the pelvises of males and females?
19. What bone is the most accurate for estimating height?
20. Name three ways to estimate age.

CONSIDER THIS...

1. Why is ancestry such a complex concept?
2. How does forensic anthropology differ from pathology?
3. If you had only the pelvic bones of a deceased individual, what could you tell about that person?

BIBLIOGRAPHY AND FURTHER READING

Barcsay, J., 2001. Anatomy for the Artist. Metrobooks, London.

Brooks, S., Suchey, J., 1990. Skeletal age determination based on the os pubis: a comparison of the Acsadi-Nemeskeri and Suchey-Brooks methods. Human Evolution 5, 227–238.

Buikstra, J.E., Ubelaker, D.H., 1994. Standards for data collection from human skeletal remains. Arkansas Archeological Society, Fayetteville. Arkansas Archeological Survey Research Series Number 44.

Cattaneo, C., 2013. Forensic anthropology: an introduction. In: Siegel, J., Saukko, P. (Eds.), Encyclopedia of Forensic Sciences, second ed. Elsevier, Amsterdam, pp. 9–11.

Clement, J., 2013. In: Siegel, J., Saukko, P. (Eds.), Encyclopedia of Forensic Sciences, second ed. Elsevier, Amsterdam, pp. 106–113.

Haglund, W., Sorg, M., 1997. Forensic Taphonomy. CRC Press, New York.

Houck, M.M., 1998. Skeletal trauma and the individualization of knife marks in bone. In: Reichs, K.J. (Ed.), Forensic Osteology: Advances in the Identification of Human Remains, second ed. C.C. Thomas Publishers, Springfield, IL, pp. 410–424.

Jantz, R., 2013. Ancestry. In: Siegel, J., Saukko, P. (Eds.), Encyclopedia of Forensic Sciences, second ed. Elsevier, Amsterdam, pp. 54–59.

Krishan, K., Kanchan, T., 2013. Stature and build. In: Siegel, J., Saukko, P. (Eds.), Encyclopedia of Forensic Sciences, second ed. Elsevier, Amsterdam, pp. 42–48.

Lahr, M.M., Wright, R.V.S., 1996. The question of robusticity and the relationship between cranial size and shape in *Homo sapiens*. Journal of Human Evolution 31, 157–191.

Sauer, N., 1984. Manner of death. In: Rathbun, T., Buikstra, J. (Eds.), Human Identification: Case Studies in Forensic Anthropology, Charles C. Thomas Publishers, Springfield, IL, pp. 176–184.

Steyn, M., 2013. Sexing. In: Siegel, J., Saukko, P. (Eds.), Encyclopedia of Forensic Sciences, second ed. Elsevier, Amsterdam, pp. 34–41.

Suchey, J.M., Wiseley, D.V., Katz, D., 1986. Evaluation of the Todd and McKern-Stewart methods for aging the male os-pubis. In: Reichs, K.J. (Ed.), Forensic Osteology: Advances in the Identification of Human Remains. C.C. Thomas Publishers, Springfield, IL, pp. 33–67.

Taylor, K.T., 2001. Forensic Art and Illustration. CRC Press, Boca Raton, FL.

Ubelaker, D., 1999. Human Skeletal Remains. Taraxacum, Washington, DC.

Ubelaker, D.H., Scammell, H., 1992. Bones: A Forensic Detective's Casebook. Edward Burlingame Books, New York, NY.

White, T.D., 2000. Human Osteology. Academic Press, London.

CHAPTER

9 Entomology

CHAPTER OUTLINE

KEY TERMS

- Abdomen
- Ametabolous metamorphosis
- Antennae
- Arthropods
- Chitin
- Exoskeleton
- Head
- Holometabolous metamorphosis
- Incidental species
- Instar
- Key
- Killing jar
- Larva
- Larvaposits

- Maggot mass effect
- Maggots
- Mesothorax
- Metamorphosis
- Metathorax
- Molting
- Necrophagous species
- Necrophilous
- Nymph
- Omnivorous species
- Oviposits
- Paurometabolous metamorphosis
- Postmortem interval
- Predatory and parasitic species
- Prothorax
- Pupal stage
- Puparium
- Segments
- Spiracles
- Subspecies
- Taphonomy
- Taxa: kingdom, phylum, class, order, family, genus, and species
- Taxonomy
- Thorax

THE CASE: DANIELLE VAN DAM

The homicide of 7-year-old Danielle Van Dam in 2002 shocked the nation and brought forensic entomology into the limelight. On February 1, 2002, Danielle's parents realized she went missing while they thought she was asleep in her room. On February 27, 2002, Danielle's naked and decomposing body was found alongside a road. A neighbor of the Van Dam, David Westerfield, came under suspicion when he could not account for his whereabouts the morning of Danielle's disappearance. Westerfield was placed under surveillance and was seen taking bedding and clothing to a dry cleaner's. Later analysis identified Danielle's blood on those items. Hairs and fibers microscopically like those from Danielle, as well as her fingerprints, were found in Westerfield's vehicle and recreational vehicle.

Westerfield was arrested and, when the trial started in June of 2002, he pleaded not guilty. The various types of evidence were proffered by the prosecution. Because Westerfield did not have a supportable alibi for the morning of Danielle's disappearance, the time of death became a critical issue. Forensic entomology, therefore, was central to the arguments of both the prosecution and the defense. Anthropologists, pathologists, and entomologists were called on both sides to testify about the postmortem interval (PMI).

INTRODUCTION

Forensic entomology is the application of the study of **arthropods** (order Arthropoda), including insects, arachnids (spiders and their kin), centipedes, millipedes, and crustaceans, to criminal or legal cases. This field has been divided into three topics: urban entomology (involving insects that affect houses, buildings, and similar human environments), stored products entomology (involving insects infesting stored goods such as food or clothing), and medicolegal entomology (involving insects and their utility in solving criminal cases). Typically, the use of insects and their life cycles helps to establish a PMI, which is an estimate of how much time has passed since a person died. This estimate depends on the entomologist's knowledge of the ecology of insects and ability to accurately identify insects. Medicolegal, or forensic, entomology is what this chapter will cover and what most professionals think of when they hear the term "forensic entomology." While a "speciality" science in many ways, forensic entomology is intimately linked with the disciplines of medical entomology (insects and the diseases they transmit), pathology, and taxonomy (the classification of living things).

Initially, insects and the law may seem an odd pairing, but wherever humans choose to live on the planet, insects are already there waiting for them. Found in nearly every habitat on land or in water, insects are the only group of animals to evolve true wings; the wings of birds and bats are modified upper limbs. This adaptation has provided insects with the means to travel far and to inhabit diverse ecologies for food and reproduction, including on and in dead animals. This fact may strike the average person as disgusting, but insects, particularly flies, play a vital role in the "recycling" of animal carcasses and other decomposing organic material. Often, insects are the first to find a corpse, and they colonize it in a predictable pattern. Forensically important conclusions may be drawn by analyzing the phase of insect invasion of a corpse or by identifying the life stage of **necrophagous** (dead-flesh eating) insects found in, on, or around the body. Knowledge of insect (especially fly) biology and habitats may provide information for accurate estimates of how much time a body has been exposed to insect activity. A knowledgeable entomologist will be able to tell if the insects are from the local area where the body was found; if they are not, this is a good indication that the body may have been moved. The absence of insects on a corpse is also a situation requiring the attention of a forensic entomologist.

The study of an organism from the time it dies until the time it reaches the laboratory is called **taphonomy**. The term was coined to describe the analysis of what happened to prehistoric animals, like dinosaurs, from the time they died until they became fossils sitting in a museum case. Investigating how different processes, such as wind, rain, animal, or insect activity, affected them, researchers could distinguish natural phenomena (animal tooth marks) from those caused by human intervention (injury) or healing. In this sense, paleontologists are a type of detective looking for clues of a prehistoric "crime." The knowledge gained from the taphonomic study of fossilized animals has been adopted by modern detectives and scientists who have applied it to modern crimes. Forensic entomology is a good example of the application of the principles of taphonomy to legal investigations.

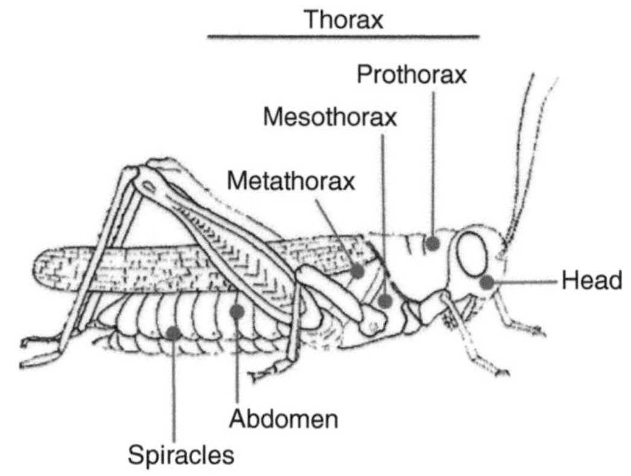

FIGURE 9.1

Insects have three main body parts: the head, thorax, and abdomen; the thorax is further divided into the prothorax, mesothorax, and metathorax. Insects are the only animals to have evolved true wings, as opposed to specialized front limbs.

INSECTS AND THEIR BIOLOGY

Insects are the largest group of arthropods and are defined by having six legs and a three-segment body. Although small individually, insects are the most numerous and diverse group of organisms known, with nearly one million species described. The total number of plants and (noninsect) animals combined comprise fewer species than insects.

Unlike other animals, insects have an external skeleton, or **exoskeleton**, composed of a material called **chitin** and protein. This outer shell protects the animal's internal organs, conserves fluids, and acts as the structure for muscle attachment. Insect's bodies are divided into three **segments**, which are joined to each other by flexible joints. These segments are the **head**, **thorax**, and **abdomen**, as shown in Figure 9.1. The head contains the insect's eyes, sensory organs (including specialized **antennae**), and mouth parts. The thorax is further divided into the **prothorax**, **mesothorax**, and **metathorax**; each of these subsegments has a pair of legs. In addition, the mesothorax and metathorax are sites of wing attachment, if the insect has them. The abdomen carries much of the insect's internal organs and is segmented. Each of these segments bears a pair of holes, called **spiracles**, which the insect uses for breathing (Resh and Carde, 2003).

LIFE CYCLES OF INSECTS

Distinctive of the arthropods is their variety of immature forms. As an insect grows, it passes through a series of maturation phases, and each phase can look quite different from the previous or subsequent one, as demonstrated in Figure 9.2. Over millions of years of evolution, insects have developed three patterns of growth. The first and simplest is **ametabolous** ("without change") **metamorphosis**, where the eggs yield

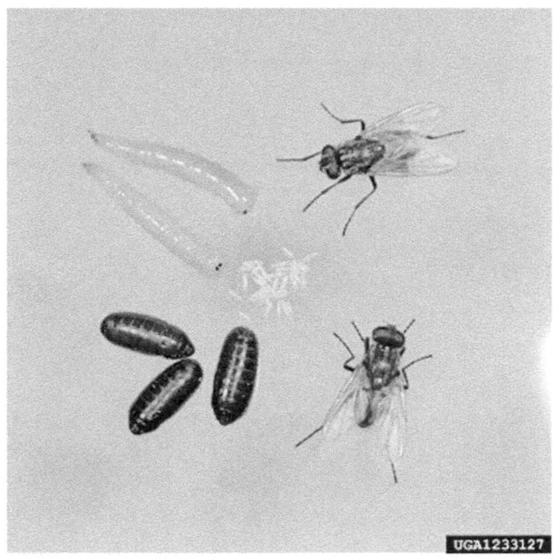

FIGURE 9.2

Insects develop through various life stages, depending on the type of metamorphosis they experience. Ametabolous insects have immature forms that appear to be small adults. Paurometabolous insects emerge from hatching into a nymph form, which progresses to adult through a series of moltings. Holometabolous insects develop from eggs into larva, which then go through a separate growth stage to reach adult form. The caterpillar spinning a cocoon and emerging as a butterfly is a common example, as is the housefly shown here.

Courtesy: James Amrine.

immature forms that look like smaller forms of the adults. Eventually, these juveniles develop in size and mature sexually but otherwise undergo little structural change. This type of metamorphosis is limited to more primitive wingless insects (Apterygota).

The second type of metamorphosis is **paurometabolous**, or gradual, **metamorphosis**. The hatchlings emerge in a form called a **nymph**, which generally resembles a wingless version of the adult of the species. The nymphs and adults will occupy the same habitat and exploit the same food sources. Nymphs grow by **moulting** (shedding their skin), and each successive moult produces a new **instar** or growth phase. As the nymph passes through each instar, it increasingly resembles the adult form and eventually develops wings. Different species pass through specific numbers of instars, and this can be useful in identifying immature forms. Cockroaches (Blattaria) and various predatory bugs (Hemiptera), for example, develop this way.

Holometabolous (or complete) **metamorphosis** is the third type of arthropod growth, and it is the most complex format of the three. The adult lays an egg (**oviposits**) or deposits a **larva** (**larvaposits**) onto a food source. The larvae (plural) start eating or hatch from the egg and then begin eating immediately and increase in size by molting through instars. The larval form is very different from the adult form, both in appearance and in its habitat. At the end of the instars, however, the larvae transition into an inactive phase, called the **pupal stage**. The pupa is a hardened outer shell or skin that protects the larva while it undergoes its final growth stage to the adult form. Butterflies (Lepidoptera) are a common example of holometabolous insects as they change from caterpillar into cocoon to their final, colorful adult form. There are several types of pupa in holometabolous insects, but the type most frequently encountered by forensic entomologists is that evidenced in flies (Diptera), the **puparium**. The puparium is the hardened skin of the last larval instar and tends to be darker than the normal larval skin (Resh and Carde, 2003).

Depending on the species of insect, the time it takes to go from egg to adult varies greatly: Some insects may have a few or many generations in 1 year. The weather, environment, season, food (abundance or lack), rainfall, humidity, and other such factors all can affect the timing of insect reproduction. In the case of **necrophilous** insects ("dead loving," or those associated with decomposition), many other factors, such as location (indoors, outdoors, on land, in water, etc.), shade, slope, and where the body lays (on soil, cement, in a tree, in an attic, etc.), can have an influence on the number and timing of successive generations.

Necrophilous insects are very sensitive to chemical changes in a dead body and can detect even the slightest hint of decomposition, sometimes within minutes of death. The chemicals are by-products of the decomposition process and signal to the insect that a new food source is available. As the body decays, the signals it sends out change and communicate "food" to the different species that inhabit the body at different times and conditions. Dermestid beetles, for example, prefer dry flesh and won't colonize a body until the tissues are no longer wet or even moist; by that time, the odors and chemicals coming off the remains are very different from those emitted, say, 2 weeks prior. The habitat of a decomposing body is a finely tuned environment, and insects have evolved to make the most of each stage of decay.

COLLECTING INSECTS AT A CRIME SCENE

Not all the insects mentioned here will appear on a body in equal numbers or even be present at all. The number, type, and distribution of insects drawn to a dead body will vary by the environmental conditions, time since death, location, geography, weather, and many other factors. This is why it is important for a professional forensic entomologist to collect, process, and analyze the insect data from a death scene: It is a complicated and specialized discipline. Because of this variability in the number and kind of insects, the information they provide can sometimes be quite precise as no two scenes are exactly alike in time or space.

Forensic entomologists encounter a diverse range of habitats and conditions when assisting with crime scenes. It is important that all personnel from the various agencies at a death scene cooperate with the primary investigating agency and be aware of each person's assigned responsibilities. This is especially true for the forensic entomologist because many police agencies are not familiar with this science and its requirements for evidence collection. The entomologist should discuss with the evidence technicians and the primary investigator the plan for evidence collection and the role the entomologist intends to play. The following is a suggested sequence of stages for a forensic entomological investigation (Haskell et al., 2002):

Visually observing and taking notes of the scene
Recording notes
Approximating the number and kinds of insects
Recording locations of major insect infestations
Noting immature stages
Identifying the precise location of the body
Observing any other phenomena of note (trauma, coverings, etc.)
Collecting climatological data from the scene
Recording ambient air temperature
Measuring ambient humidity
Taking ground surface temperature
Taking body surface temperatures
Taking below-body temperatures
Taking maggot mass temperatures
Taking postbody removal subsoil temperature

Collecting specimens from the body before its removal from the scene

- The area surrounding the body (up to 20 ft) before its removal
- Directly under the body after the body has been removed

Necrophilous insects, particularly flies, are attracted to dark, moist areas: On fresh bodies, this means the face (nostrils, mouth, eyes, etc.) or any open wounds, shown in Figure 9.3. The genital or rectal areas, if exposed or traumatized, will sometimes

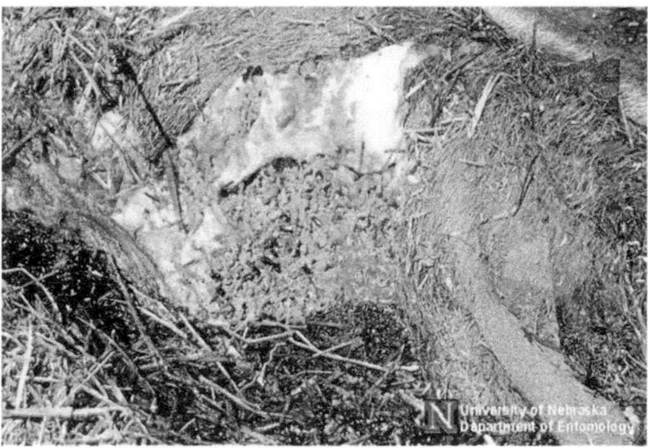

FIGURE 9.3

Insects that are attracted to dead animals as an environment for food and reproduction (necrophilous) usually inhabit dark, moist areas first, like the eyes, mouth, nose, and open wounds.

Courtesy: James Amrine.

provide shelter and moisture for ovipositing flies. The entomologist should record the patterning and number of ovipositing and larvae with notes, drawings, and photographs.

Insects can be collected in a variety of ways, most of which will be employed at every death scene. Flying insects can be trapped in a net by sweeping it back and forth repeatedly over the body. The end of the net, with the insects in it, can then be placed in a wide-mouth **killing jar**, a glass jar containing cotton balls soaked in ethyl acetate. Several minutes of exposure to the ethyl acetate will kill the insects; they should then be placed in a vial of 75% ethyl alcohol (ETOH) to preserve them. Two labels should be prepared for each specimen (one for inside the vial and one for the outside), and they must be written in pencil; ink may dissolve in the ETOH.

Crawling insects on and around the body can be collected with forceps or fingers. The entomologist must be careful not to disturb any other potential evidence while collecting insects. If the body will be put into a body bag, it is a good idea to check for any insect activity before the body is placed inside it. Eggs and a mixture of larvae of various sizes (several hundred in total) should be collected, as well as any adults. A portion of the larvae should be preserved the same as described for flying insects; another portion should be kept alive to rear to adulthood. If the entomologist is collecting the insects in the morgue, a careful inspection of the clothing must be made in conjunction with the forensic pathologist's observations.

Once the body has been removed, the soil under the body should be sampled. An approximately 4″ × 4 × 4″ cube of soil (about the size of a one-pint ice cream container) should be taken from areas associated with the body, such as the head, torso, limbs, or wherever seems appropriate given the body's position. Additional soil samples should be taken up to 6 ft from the body in each direction. Any plant materials associated with the body or its location should also be collected for possible botanical examination.

Buried or enclosed remains present particular problems for the entomologist because insects' access to a body is limited. Some flies are barred from a body by as little as one inch of soil. Burial also slows the process of decomposition due to lower and more constant temperatures, fewer bacteria, and limited access to the body. A building can also prevent some types of insects from gaining access to a body or slow down their recognition of the chemical odors that signal decomposition. This alters the entomologist's estimation of time since death because the "clock" of insect succession rate has been altered. However, the odors may escape, but the insects may not be able to gain access: Finding a cloud of flies hovering above a car trunk may indicate that a dead body has been in there for some time. If the structure is a house or an apartment, then weather data probably will not help the entomologist devise a time since death. Rather, the thermostat settings could be substituted for "climate" data. Another example would be a car with the windows up during the summer, where the internal temperature even on a mild day can easily reach in excess of 110 °F. In short, any environmental change, whether natural or artificial, needs to be measured and noted for the entomologist to make an accurate estimate.

Wide-angle and close-up photographs should also be taken, with emphasis on specific areas of insect activity. The forensic entomologist should, after returning to the laboratory from the scene, begin collecting weather data for the period of time in question.

THE POSTMORTEM INTERVAL

The forensic entomologist's main contribution to death investigation is an estimate of the **PMI**. Being able to provide a time range for when the crime occurred is of great importance in limiting the number of suspects who may or may not have an alibi. If the victim is unidentified, the PMI may also assist in narrowing the number of potential missing persons. Calculating an estimated PMI sets a minimum and maximum time since death based on the insect evidence collected and developed. The maximum limit is set by the insects present on and around the body at the time of collection; this limit is moderated by the recent weather conditions that could help or hinder those species' development. A minimal PMI is estimated by the age of developing immature insects and the time needed for them to grow to adulthood under the conditions surrounding the crime scene. A maximal PMI can be difficult to estimate because the uncertainty widens as time and decomposition continues. It is imperative that forensic entomologists conduct outdoor studies with local species in various seasonal conditions to establish a baseline reference. These data can provide invaluable information in estimating PMIs, especially in circumstances where the environmental indicators may be vague.

THE CLASSIFICATION OF INSECTS

Estimating a PMI requires that the forensic entomologist be able to precisely identify the insects on and around a body. This can only be properly performed by an experienced forensic entomologist with the proper reference collections. Differentiating between closely related insects, especially certain species of flies, requires the recognition of minute anatomical details and should be attempted only by qualified professionals. The science of identifying and classifying organisms is called **taxonomy**. All organisms are categorized by their relatedness through the recognition of significant evolutionary traits. The order of relatedness is broken into these **taxa**, or related groups: **Kingdom**, **Phylum**, **Class**, **Order**, **Family**, **Genus**, and **Species**.[1] When we refer to a specific type of organism, describing it by the genus and species (and sometime subspecies) is sufficient to set it apart from all other organisms. Thus, when talking about *Calliphora vicina*, *Canis familiaris*, or *Homo sapiens*, we

[1] For example, humans have the classification Kingdom: Animalia, Phylum: Chordata, Class: Mammalia, Order: Primates, Family: Hominidae, Genus: *Homo* and Species: *sapiens*.

Table 9.1 Insects That May Be Found on or Near Decomposing Bodies

Order	Common Names	Families	Figure(s)
Collembola	Springtails		9.4(a)
Blattaria	Cockroaches		9.4(f)
Coleoptera	Beetles	Necrophagous Silphidae (carrion beetles) Dermestidae (dermestid beetles) Cleridae (checkered beetles)	9.4(d)
		Predatory Staphylinidae (rove beetles) Scarabaeidae (scarab beetles) Histeridae (clown beetles)	9.4(b)
Dermaptera	Earwigs		
Diptera	Flies	Calliphoridae (blow flies)	9.4(e)
		Muscidae (house flies) Piophilidae (skipper flies) Sarcophagidae (flesh flies) Scathophagidae (dung flies)	9.4(c)
Hemiptera	True bugs	*Predatory*	9.4(g); Assassin bug (Reduviidae)
Hymenoptera	Ants, bees, wasps	*Predatory/necrophagous*	9.4(h); Hymenopter

know we're discussing the blue-bottle fly, the domesticated dog, and humans. These terms are formal so the genus is capitalized and, because they are Latin, it is proper to format genus and species designations in italics. Some species, especially among insects, have well-defined variants or **subspecies**. A taxonomic **key** is a method for classifying organisms where each trait identified separates otherwise similar groups of organisms. By following a detailed key, a forensic entomologist can identify, or "key out," all of the forensically important insects that may be found on or around a body (see Table 9.1 and Figure 9.4).

REARING INSECTS

A significant step in identifying immature insects, especially flies, is the rearing of larvae into adult insects. This process is not as easy as it may initially sound. Because these immature insects are the reference materials for the forensic entomologist's estimation of PMI, their growth environments (temperature, humidity, space, light, etc.) must be closely controlled and monitored. A vent hood is a necessity: Because their food source is rotting meat (typically beef, pork, or liver), the smell can become unpleasant. Depending on how many cases the entomologist works on at one time,

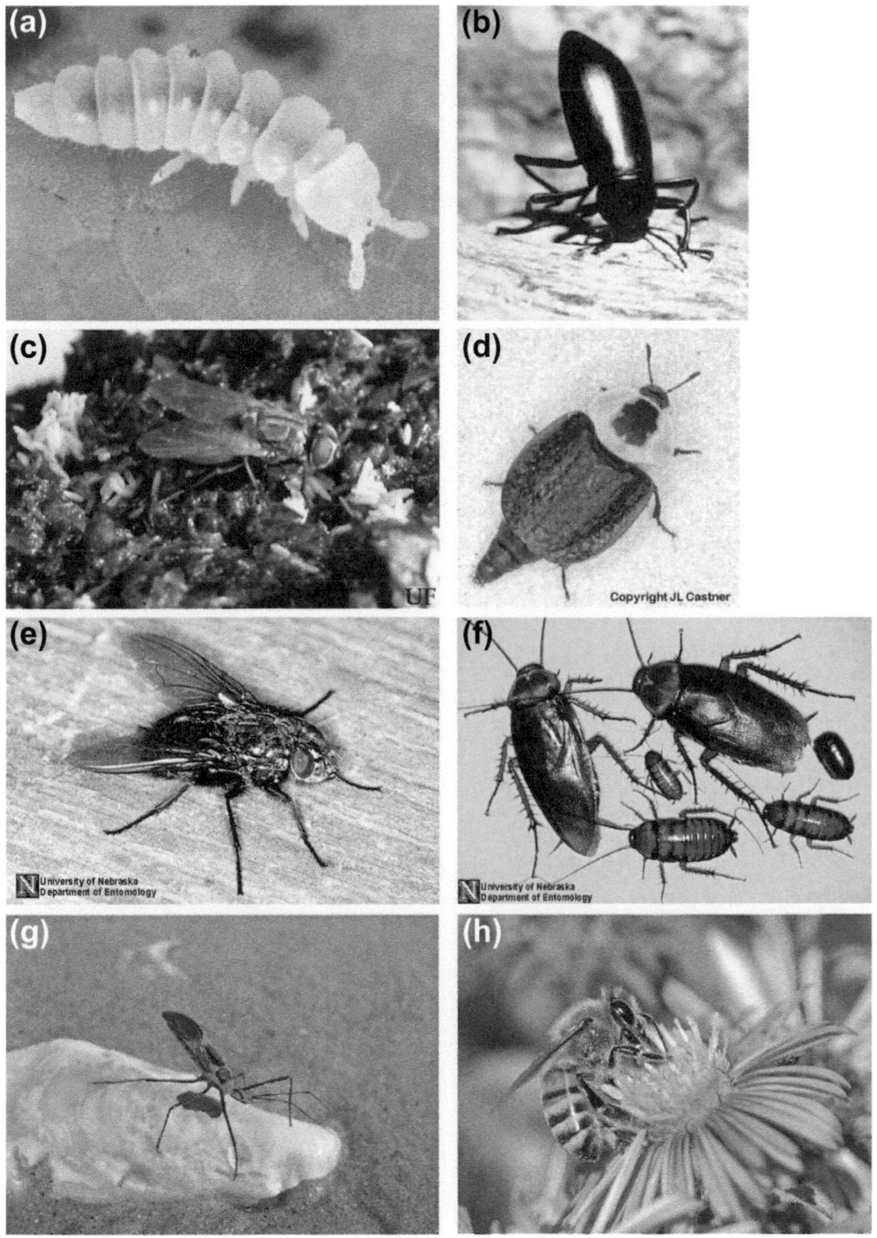

FIGURE 9.4

Insects commonly found on or near dead bodies. (a) Springtail, (b) Rove Beetle, (c) Housefly, (d) Carrion Beetle, (e) Blow Fly (blue), (f) Cockroach (American), (g) Assassin bug (Hemiptera, Reduviidae), (h) Hymenopter (Hymenoptera).

Public domain photos from Wikipedia.

the rearing laboratory must be able to keep all the samples and insects separate. It is important to remember that fly larvae grow into adult flies, and they must be kept from zipping across the laboratory! And, finally, the laboratory must be designed so that it is easy to clean after the case work is completed.

Specially devised chambers for insect rearing can be purchased, but they are very expensive. Many entomology laboratories use large aquariums, disposable containers (often, pint-sized ice cream or plastic containers with holes punched in the lid for ventilation), and pie tins as inexpensive but effective larval growth chambers. Some insects require special conditions for growth that mimic the phase of decomposition that the insects recognize as appealing, such as dermestid beetles, which colonize remains only after they have become dry and desiccated.

DNA AND INSECTS

DNA analysis is used outside forensic science to identify insect species. In the forensic sciences, this method has only recently gained interest. Dr Paul Hebert of the University of Guelph in Ontario, Canada, identified a mitochondrial gene (cytochrome *c* oxidase I, or COI) used in cell respiration that is common to all species but differs slightly in each one. That gene can be used to distinguish between species of animals, including insects; the project to collect information on all known species is called the Barcode of Life. DNA identification of species cannot replace traditional taxonomic methods for unknown species: What would it be compared against? But once a species is identified, species identification via DNA becomes rapid and reliable. DNA barcoding has not been adopted as a routine method for forensic entomology casework but may be in the future.

Another use of DNA with insects is to extract the gut contents of maggots in the hopes that nuclear or mitochondrial DNA from the deceased can be extracted, analyzed, and compared. Not only can this potentially assist in the identification of decedents, but this approach has relevance to identifying maggots that were actually on a particular corpse—if the maggot was not on that body, then its stage of development is not relevant to estimating how long the decedent had been dead. This topic of estimating time since death is a key task of forensic entomologists.

CALCULATING A PMI

The main reason for studying the presence and life stages of insects on a corpse is to establish the time since death. A method for establishing a PMI is based on an ecological and faunal study of the cadaver, demonstrated in Figure 9.5. Data collection must be detailed and precise if the PMI is to be accurate. The basis of the method is to study which insects, or their young, inhabit a dead body and in what sequence they do so. A body that has been dead only 1 or 2 days will have infestations primarily of blowflies, such as *Cochliomyia macellaria*, because these insects are attracted to a

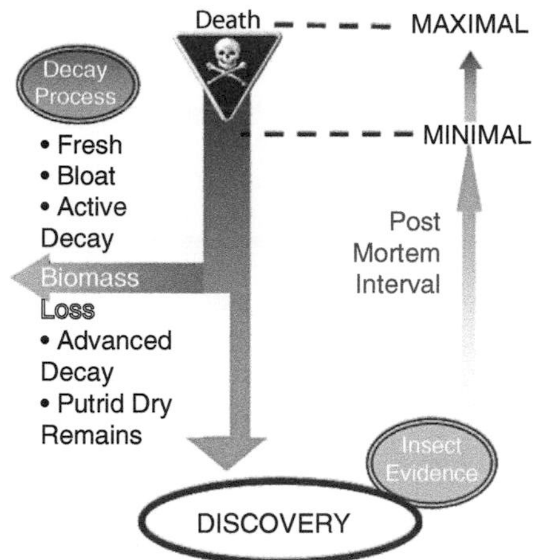

FIGURE 9.5

Data collected by entomologists and other biologists, as well as weather data, all contribute to the estimation of a postmortem interval, the time since death occurred.

corpse almost immediately. The recognition of each species in all stages and knowledge of the time occupied in each stage allow a time since death to be estimated. Other information could be gleaned from the faunal composition, such as whether the body has been moved.

Four ecological categories exist in the cadaver community. The first are the **necrophagous species**, which feed on the carrion itself, contributing directly to the estimation of PMI. Examples of necrophagous insects are diptera, coleoptera, silphidae, and dermestidae. The second most important group, forensically speaking, is the **predatory and parasitic species**, such as certain coleoptera, silphidae, and some diptera. These insects prey on other insects, including the necrophagous ones, which inhabit the cadaver. Some of the species in this group, however, may be necrophagous while immature but become predatory in later instars. **Omnivorous species** make up the third category. Wasps, ants, and some coleoptera fit into this group because they may eat material from the body, other insects or whatever food source presents itself. The last category of insects uses the cadaver simply as an extension of their normal habitat, such as spiders, butterflies, collembola, and others. This group can be referred to as the **incidental species**.

The faunal succession on carrion is linked to the natural changes that take place in a body following death. After death, the body temperature falls to that of its ambient environment. Cellular breakdown begins after several hours, which results in the release of gases such as ammonia (NH_3), hydrogen sulfide (H_2S), carbon dioxide (CO_2), and nitrogen (N_2). Putrefaction follows due to the activity of microbes, especially those from the body's own intestinal flora. These chemical and microbiological consequences of death are the earliest, and tend to be the most accurate, indicators of time since death. Their accuracy and utility diminish as time moves forward, however, and other information, namely ecological, must be used.

At a minimum, the estimated age of an immature insect can provide a PMI, but this estimate does not provide a maximum limit because the amount of time between death and egg/larval deposition is unknown. Necrophagous insects appear almost immediately as the cellular breakdown begins; some species of flies are so sensitive to the chemistry of death that they appear within minutes of the cessation of life. The level of larval development can provide an estimate that is accurate from less than 1 day to just over 1 month, depending on conditions and the species reared.

A more complete, although more complicated, method of PMI estimation involves the study of the succession of insect species on and within a body. The forensic entomologist employs a model that is based on information about the ecological and environmental events between the time of death and the appearance of a particular insect species. The simplest model would be one in which the forensic entomologist estimates the age of a larva and the time between death and the insect landing on the body. The activities of the insects, especially fly larvae, accelerate the putrefaction and disintegration of the body. The number of waves of insects in the succession on a body has been interpreted to be between 2 and 8. Such a model provides both a minimum and maximum PMI and yields much more accurate estimates. Many environmental factors, such as whether the body is on the surface, buried, or in water; the temperature, weather, humidity, amount of light/shade, season and even manner of death, influence the number, type, appearance, and life cycles of necrophagous insects. Regardless of the complexity, the forensic entomologist must choose a model of insect development or succession, sometimes drawn from published experimental data. For an example, see "In More Detail: PMI in Hawaii."

IN MORE DETAIL: PMI IN HAWAII

One of the first cases forensic entomologist Lee Goff worked involved the death of a woman in Honolulu in 1984. She had last been seen over 2 weeks before her body was found near the shore by an abandoned brewery; her car, with blood on the interior, was found 30 miles away. Goff and a graduate student collected maggots, hide beetles and scene information. "There were three species of maggots on the body, in different locations and in different stages of development," Goff notes in his book, *A Fly for the Prosecution* (2001, p. 3). "I sorted each type into two sub-lots. I measured the length of each of the maggots in one of the lots, and used the average of these lengths to give me some idea of their stage of development. Then I preserved them in ethyl alcohol. I put the other sub-lot of maggots into a rearing chamber to complete their development to the adult stage."

Initially, Goff used a home-grown computer approach for calculating the PMI, the first time he had done so in a real case (remember, this was 1984). The result was disappointing: It told him that the body either didn't exist or there were two bodies! The conflicting results were caused by the computer not being able to resolve the dilemma of flesh flies, which like soft, moist tissues to eat, being on a body whereas the hide beetles' preference is for dried flesh. To investigate a solution, Goff visited the crime scene. He found that the victim had been lying on her back, partially submerged in about 5 in of water. This accounted for soft, moist tissues to remain on the victim's back while the Hawaii sun dried out the front.

Returning to the lab, Goff began his calculations with this new data. "For *Chrysomya rufifacies*, egg laying can begin quite soon after the adult females reach the body and will continue, under Hawaiian conditions, for approximately the first 6 days following death (and) completion of development...usually requires 11 days. Since the only evidence of this species on the body was the

IN MORE DETAIL: PMI IN HAWAII—cont'd

empty pupal cases, discarded when the flies reach adulthood, I was confident that all *Chrysomya* maggots maturing on the body had completed development before it was discovered" (2001, p. 6). Goff noted that another fly species, the cheese skipper, which does not invade a body until days after death, were all at the same stage as samples from a test he had conducted: 19 days old.

The hide beetles were also very useful. "In lowland habitats on Oahu, (the beetles) begin to arrive between 8 and 11 days after the onset of decomposition, and during decomposition studies I have gathered larvae comparable in size to those collected from this case beginning on day 19. The remaining species…were consistent with a post-mortem interval of 19 to 20 days but did not yield more precise information" (2001, pp. 6–7). Goff gave an official estimate of 19 days to the medical examiner.

The victim had been missing precisely that many days, since she was seen leaving with a tall man from the restaurant she co-owned. This man was later identified, tried, and convicted of second-degree murder—all because of some flies and beetles.

Source: *Goff (2001).*

If no data are available that take into account the parameters that the forensic entomologist faces, then experimentation is required. The experimental conditions should be as close to those at the crime scene as possible; this logically means that a forensic entomologist should be collecting data on decomposition in his or her ecological zone(s) year round. The closer the experimental data are to the crime scene conditions, the lower the margin of error will be in the PMI estimate. The subjects for these decomposition studies are typically small pigs (under 50 pounds), which have been shown to be appropriate stand-ins for humans despite their smaller size. In the second part of a study funded by the National Institute of Justice, Haskell et al. (2002) showed that both pigs and humans attract a large majority of the same arthropod species, but also the most common and moderately common species. This was true regardless of the pigs' size, but small pigs are easier to physically handle than large ones, practically speaking. Importantly, their work also indicates that cross-comparison of "pig studies" from differing geographical zones may be a viable research interest.

One of the most influential factors in estimating PMI is temperature. Temperature has a direct effect on the metabolism and development of insects. This is true not only of ambient (air) temperature, but also the amount of sun or shade to which a body is exposed. The larvae of necrophagous flies (**maggots**) are essentially "eating machines," and they have a metabolism and feeding rate that is much higher than other immature insect forms. When a group of maggots is living, feeding, and moving all in approximately the same area, the temperature can soar by many degrees: This is termed the **maggot mass effect**. The temperature at the center of a maggot mass can be 100 °F while the ambient temperature is in the 30 °F range, and this could obviously bias a forensic entomologist's PMI estimation.

The forensic entomologist studies insect samples that were killed and preserved at the time of collection as well as those kept alive for rearing. The time when the

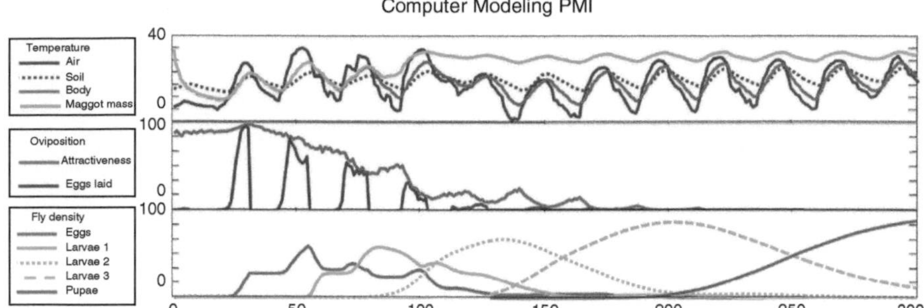

The purpose of a forensic PMI model is to predict the timing of a past event. The ending point of the model is always the point where the sample was obtained: in this hypothetical case at 1:00 AM on April 30, 2001, in Farewell, Texas. Using historical hourly temperature data from a nearby weather station that was conveniently found on the internet, we run the model, here starting at a point 300 hours in the past (above).

Because the ending point of the simulation is known, but the starting point is not, it is necessary to run the model at all possible starting points using historical environmental data to generate possible solutions from each hour in the past. Each model run assumes a time of death at the point where the model starts.

FIGURE 9.6

Computers logically lend themselves to calculations involving a large amount of data, such as a PMI. This example shows the data collected, graphed, and interpreted using specific mathematical models for the particular geographical area in question. Other models would need to be employed if the victim were found in another area or at another time of year.

Courtesy: D.H. Sloane.

preserved samples were collected is the starting point for the PMI, and it is from here forward that the entomologist makes his or her calculations for the maximal time since death. Because every death scene has unique circumstances and environs, no one algorithm best calculates all PMI estimates. As shown in Figure 9.6, computers are now being used to create very complex but highly realistic models that provide forensic entomologists with improved models for PMI estimates. As humans and computers become more adept at handling large amounts of complex data, the estimates of PMI based on entomological information will become more realistic and accurate.

BACK TO THE CASE: DANIELLE VAN DAM

The chart in Figure 9.7 shows the various timelines offered by different witnesses in the Westerfield trial. Each entomologist based his or her estimates on slightly different methods which yielded PMI estimates that either overlapped or came within 4 days of doing so. The other experts used various methods and ancillary data that provided even greater ranges of variation. To better understand the variations and control them, some entomologists have conducted blind proficiency studies; this kind of information will be increasingly helpful to validate and support the forensic activities of entomologists (see VanLaerhoven, 2008, for example).

This case illustrates the importance of education, training, and methodology in forensic entomology casework. More on the Danielle Van Dam case and the trial can be found at http://www.signonsandiego.com/news/metro/danielle/transcripts.html.

Source: *VanLaerhoven (2008).*

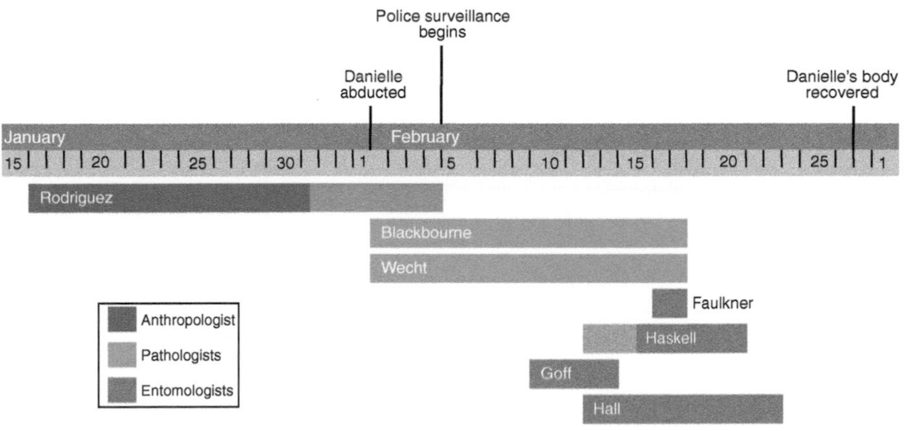

FIGURE 9.7

Chart of the various timelines in the Westerfield trial. During the trial, an anthropologist, two pathologists, and four entomologists offered estimates of PMI for Danielle Van Dam; the lighter colored areas indicate times conceded to on the stand. Methodology and expertise played a role in the range of variation of their estimates.

OTHER FORENSIC USES FOR INSECTS

Insects are important evidence in ways other than estimating PMI. Because they ingest portions of the bodies they inhabit, insects can ingest drugs, toxins, or other substances that are in the body at the time of death. Additionally, DNA from the victim may be obtained from the gut of insects that feed on the body. These tiny samples can offer critical evidence of poisoning or identity, for example, when no other evidence is available. Insects can also give indications of location (many species are habitat-specific), travel, or geography if associated with items, such as crates or shipments.

SUMMARY

Although forensic entomology may seem to be a narrow specialty, it is applicable in a wide variety of cases. Forensic entomologists identify insects associated with dead bodies and estimate time since death. They also play an important role in other areas where insects and crime intersect, such as drugs, poisons, and location of stolen goods.

TEST YOUR KNOWLEDGE

1. What is an insect? Is it the same as an arthropod?
2. How many kinds of insect development are there and what are they?
3. What is the protective outer covering on an insect called?

4. What is an instar?
5. What is taxonomy?
6. What are the categories, in order, used to describe an organism's taxonomy?
7. In "PMI in Hawaii," Lee Goff used a particular fly, *Chrysomya rufifacies*, in his PMI estimate. What are the words *C. rufifacies*?
8. What does "necrophilous" mean?
9. What are the uses of forensic entomology?
10. What is the difference between insects that larvaposit and those that oviposit?
11. Name three factors that go into calculating a PMI.
12. What are the four kinds of species that can be found on a dead body?
13. How many waves of insect invasion are there on a dead body?
14. What does "necrophagous" mean?
15. What are the larvae of necrophagous insects called?
16. What is the "maggot mass effect?"
17. What is the role of insects in decomposition?
18. What goes into the calculation of a PMI?
19. How would a forensic entomology case in Montana differ from one in Florida?
20. What is "molting?"

CONSIDER THIS...

1. Early in this chapter, we mentioned that the complete absence of insects from a dead body is a good reason to contact a forensic entomologist. What do you think some of the reasons for this might be?
2. If a person was killed in Florida in a train's freight car and the body wasn't discovered until it reached its destination in New York days later, how might a forensic entomologist assist investigators? Would the time of year matter?

BIBLIOGRAPHY AND FURTHER READING

Byrd, J.H., Castner, J.L. (Eds.), 2001. Forensic Entomology: The Utility of Arthropods in Legal Investigations. CRC Press, Boca Raton, FL.

Catts, E.P., Haskell, N.H. (Eds.), 1990. Entomology & Death: A Procedural Guide. Joyce's Print Shop, Clemson, SC.

Goff, M.L., 2001. A Fly for the Prosecution. Harvard University Press, Cambridge, MA.

Haskell, N.H., Schoenly, K.G., Hall, R.D., 2002. Testing reliability of animal models in research and training programs in forensic entomology, part II. In: NIJ Office of Science and Technology, Investigative and Forensic Sciences Division, 2002 Grantees Meeting, February 12, Atlanta, GA.

Herbert, D., Cywinska, A., Ball, S., deWaard, J., 2003. Biological identifications through DNA barcodes. Proceedings of the Royal Society of London 270, 313–321.

Resh, V., Carde, R., 2003. Encyclopedia of Insects. Elsevier, Amsterdam.

Smith, K.G.V., 1986. A Manual of Forensic Entomology Comstock Printing Associates. Cornell University Press, Ithica, NY.

VanLaerhoven, S., 2008. Blind validation of post-mortem interval estimates using developmental rates of blow flies. Forensic Science International 180, 76–80.

Wells, J., Introna, F., Di Vella, G., Campobasso, C., Hayes, J., Sperling, F., 2001. Human and insect mitochondrial DNA analysis from maggots. Journal of Forensic Sciences 46 (3), 685–687.

Wells, J., Linville, J., 2013. In: Siegel, J., Saukko, P. (Eds.), Overview Encyclopedia of Forensic Sciences, second ed. Elsevier, Amsterdam, pp. 387–393.

CHAPTER

10 Serology and Bloodstain Pattern Analysis

CHAPTER OUTLINE

KEY TERMS

- ABO blood group
- Acid phosphatase (AP)
- Agglutinate
- Angle of impact
- Anti-A and anti-B
- Antibodies
- Antigen
- Arterial spurts/gushes
- Back spatter
- Benzidine
- Blood
- Blood group

- Bloodstain pattern analysis
- Brentamine fast blue B
- Cast-off stains
- Christmas tree stain
- Confirmatory test
- Direction angle
- Directionality
- Electrophoresis methods
- Enzyme-linked immunosorbent assay (ELISA)
- Erythrocytes
- Fluorescein
- Fly spots
- Forward spatter
- Genome
- Hemoglobin
- Human antiserum
- Immune response
- Leucomalachite green
- Leukocytes
- Luminescence
- Luminol
- Lymphocytes
- Macrophages
- Neutrophils
- Parent stain
- Passive bloodstains
- Phenolphthalein
- Plasma
- Platelets
- Point-of-origin
- Precipitin test
- Presumptive test
- Projected or impact bloodstains
- Prostate-specific antigen or p30
- Proteome
- Proteomics
- Saliva

- Satellite droplets
- Semen
- Serology
- Skeletonized stains
- Spatter
- Spermatozoa
- Takayama test/hemochromogen test
- Tetramethylbenzidine
- Time since intercourse (TSI)
- Transfer bloodstains
- Urine
- Voids
- Wipe stain

THE CASE: THE CHAMBERLAIN CASE

One of the most famous and infamous serology cases is that of the disappearance of Azaria Chamberlain in Australia in 1980. The case is a difficult one to consider because the courts, police, and scientists all failed at their tasks. The Chamberlains, Michael and Lindy, had taken their two sons, Aidan and Reagan, and their infant daughter, Azaria, on a camping trip in the Northern Territory of Australia, including Ayer's Rock (now known as Uluru). One evening, Lindy cried out as she saw a dingo, a wild dog, leave their tent and then discovered that 9-week-old Azaria was missing. Hundreds of people searched the area around the campsite but found nothing. Days later, a tourist found a bloodstained jumpsuit, T-shirt, and a diaper near a dingo lair close to the Chamberlains' campsite. The tourist called the police. When the officer arrived, he handled the heavily stained jumpsuit, removing the T-shirt from it; after calling his superior officer, he pushed the T-shirt back into the jumpsuit, the first of many errors with the evidence and the scene.

When Lindy was questioned about the garments that Azaria had on at the time of her disappearance, she stated that the baby wore a jacket over the jumpsuit. No jacket had yet been found. The baby's T-shirt was found inside out; when asked about this, Lindy maintained that she never dressed her children like that. This conflicted with the way the evidence was recovered (it later turned out that the clothing had been arranged by the investigating officer for a photograph).

The prosecution's case was built on forensic evidence of blood testing on the Chamberlains' car, Azaria's clothing, and the statements taken from the Chamberlains, especially Lindy. The Crown (the phrase for the state government in trials in Australia) maintained that Lindy had cut Azaria's throat in the front seat of the car, hid the body, and then joined her family at the campsite; later, she raised the alarm about the dingo. The Crown contended that she later hid the baby's body while the others were searching the area for her. The missing jacket was considered evidence that Lindy had hidden.

The main piece of physical evidence supporting the Crown's prosecution was the jumpsuit, which appeared to have been cut, and alleged fetal bloodstains on the front seat of the Chamberlains' car. Infants younger than 6 months of age still have fetal hemoglobin in their system. A crime of this horrific nature shocked Australia and the evidence seemed damning—the baby's clothing had been slashed and fetal blood found in the family automobile. What more could a prosecutor ask for?

INTRODUCTION

As DNA roared into the forensic laboratory in the late 1980s and into the public consciousness in the early 1990s, the study of bodily fluids left at crimes scenes, **serology**, nearly became a casualty of scientific advancement. While most forensic laboratories still perform serology examinations, some have abandoned them and send potential biological stain samples directly to DNA analysis. But serology still has an important place in the modern forensic science laboratory for several reasons. First, finding someone's DNA on an item of evidence doesn't necessarily provide the *source* of that DNA: It could be skin flakes, saliva, or semen, each of which may have different implications in the context of the case, alleged sexual contact versus mere presence, for example. Second, as a preliminary test, serology is fast, efficient, and inexpensive, thereby saving much time and effort by identifying biological fluid stains and avoiding needless DNA analysis of nonbiological materials. Remember, sorting evidence by relevance is the key to interpretation, and serology does a good job of that. And, finally, many pre-DNA serology cases are being re-examined in the light of current DNA methods. The reinterpretation of historical cases through the lens of modern methods—without an appreciation or understanding of the "state-of-the-art" at the time of the first analysis—is fraught with potential pitfalls for scientists, attorneys, and law enforcement officers alike. The work of today's forensic scientists will be judged by methods that may not even currently exist, and serology offers a good example of the dangers of incautious reanalysis. How is this so? Several hundred of these reanalyzes have resulted in wrongly imprisoned people being released.

The review and re-examination of past forensic biology cases poses a danger of historical misinterpretation in regards to the specificity of serology versus DNA analysis. If a pre-DNA serology case included an individual (both the known and the questioned samples are A, for example), it is certainly possible for DNA analysis to later exclude that individual. Does this mean the serologist was wrong, incompetent, or, worse, malicious in his or her examination? Certainly not; DNA is a far more specific comparison method than serology for many reasons. While DNA analysis is based on the groups of base units that make up our genetic code, serology identifies proteins associated with specific body fluids. Proteins are a more complicated form of biological material and are coded for by DNA. But, while proteins are specific to a body fluid type, they are generic biologically; that is, the proteins that are used to detect semen in one body are the same proteins that exist in any other semen stain. Nevertheless, the combination of blood grouping and protein variation testing that was common in forensic laboratories pre-DNA could be quite specific but still not as specific as forensic DNA analysis. This doesn't make serology a poor test; traditional DNA methods, for example, are largely blind to the type of body fluid being tested and are not faulted for this weakness. The serology tests used today work well for their intended purpose: the quick and simple identification of body fluids. To look back and judge serology a bad test in the light of DNA analysis is to ignore the science upon which both methods are based.

Serology is a major component of crime scene processing and analysis. It also plays a large role in the processing of items of evidence in the laboratory, presumptively identifying blood, semen, saliva, and urine prior to further analysis. It is a conservative method, in that, while the stain may be identified, only a portion of that stain is further analyzed and the identified remainder is reserved for future testing. Given the intense interest in the analysis of proteins (the discipline is called proteomics; see "In More Detail: Proteomics—The New Serology?"), serology may be due for some exciting scientific and technological advances.

IN MORE DETAIL: PROTEOMICS—THE NEW SEROLOGY?

The term **proteome** was first coined to describe the set of proteins coded in the genetic makeup of an individual, the **genome**. The study of the proteome, called **proteomics**, covers all the proteins in any given cell, their various forms and modifications, interactions, structure, the higher order complexes they form, and pretty much everything that happens "post-genome." This is an enormous and complicated area of study in biology and chemistry. And the goal of proteomics is no less enormous: a full description of cellular function.

The study of proteins would be impossible without the success of the study of the genome, notably the Human Genome Project (http://www.ornl.gov/sci/techresources/Human_Genome/home.shtml), which provided the "blueprint" of possible gene products (i.e., proteins). But despite having a successful template, proteomics faces several daunting challenges. While scientists who studied the genome with DNA sequencing, polymerase chain reaction, and automated methods, proteomics has to work with samples that are limited and variable, degradation of proteins over time, the huge range of protein abundance (more than 10^6-fold), not to mention the modifications and changes proteins go through after they are constructed by a cell. Realizing that most of the results of proteomic research are intended for medical applications, researchers must consider disease and drug effects as well.

But the potential payoff is astounding. Disease-specific drugs that target only those cells or cell proteins responsible for devastating or deadly diseases, highly accurate diagnoses, therapeutic treatments that are not debilitating for the patient (as are some current treatments, like radiation or chemotherapy), and even treatment of genetic diseases by targeting the proteins involved are all realizable goals of proteomics.

What could proteomics do for forensic science? It could improve the accuracy and broaden the scope of serology, for example. Imagine a device like a personal digital assistant with a detection and viewing screen. A biological stain is swabbed at a crime scene, and the swab is smeared across the detection screen. In a few seconds, the results of a highly specific protein analysis appear: The person in question is male, late 40s, probably Hispanic, diabetic, and has a blood protein complex with a frequency of 1 in 1,340,000 in the US population, for example. The next generation of forensic biologists needs to watch what happens in the rapidly advancing discipline of proteomics.

For more information about proteomics, see Sali et al. (2003) and Tyers and Mann (2003).

COLLECTION OF BODY FLUIDS

Serological analysis, like other forensic analyzes, has two types of tests. The first is a **presumptive test**, which is highly sensitive to but not specific for a particular substance. For example, a color test may indicate that a stain may be blood, but not what kind of blood (human or nonhuman). It may even give a false positive result; that is, the substance may not be blood but something that reacts with the chemicals used in the test. The idea of presumptive tests is that some false positive results are acceptable as long as no false negative results are obtained. False negative results are possible, of course. The presumptive positive results can be more specifically tested with the second type of test, a **confirmatory test**, which tests positive for the substance in question and only that substance. Therefore, it is known in advance that some presumptive positive results will not be confirmed. Confirmatory tests lack sensitivity, in that a relatively large amount of the substance must be available for the test to be positive, but a few false negatives are acceptable as long as no false positives are obtained. Generally, confirmatory tests are performed in a laboratory rather than in the field because they require more controlled conditions and additional equipment than presumptive tests.

The presumptive/confirmatory test structure allows crime scene and laboratory personnel to sort potential evidence into processing categories, such as "Test for DNA" and "No DNA Testing." Because of the demands on reconstructive sciences to sort out what is relevant from what is irrelevant, a testing structure like this greatly aids the laboratory to more efficiently process and analyze evidence.

THE MAJOR BODY FLUIDS

BLOOD

By definition, **blood** is a tissue, composed of several types of cells in a matrix called **plasma**. Plasma consists of about 90% water and 10% of a long list of other substances (7% protein, 3% urea, amino acids, carbohydrates, organic acids, fats, steroid hormones, and other inorganic ions). Within the plasma are three types of cells: erythrocytes (red blood cells), leukocytes (white blood cells), and platelets.

Red blood cells, **erythrocytes**, are legion in the blood—roughly 5 million per *milliliter* of blood! The purpose of these 6–8 μm diameter cells is to transport oxygen and carbon dioxide throughout the body via the circulatory system; this is accomplished by hemoglobin. **Hemoglobin**, the respiratory pigment of many animals, is a conjugated protein consisting of four polypeptides, each of which contains a heme group. The heme groups contain iron and have the ability to bind with oxygen; this association is reversible, allowing for respiration. Erythrocytes are produced in the bone marrow and have about a 4-month life span. They discard their nuclei as they mature and, therefore, contain no DNA.

White blood cells, or **leukocytes**, are active in the immune system but are not as numerous as erythrocytes, about 10–15,000 per milliliter of blood. The two types of leukocytes differ in their specific functions but work in a coordinated fashion to provide the body's defense against disease. The first type, **neutrophils**, is part of the first line of defense and offers up a complicated response to invaders: the **immune response**. Neutrophils, which are the most abundant type of white blood cell, work in conjunction with **lymphocytes**, which are produced in the bone marrow and the thymus gland, to engender the immune response. Lymphocytes produce **antibodies**, which are protein molecules that can bind to foreign molecules. Any foreign molecule that induces antibody formation is called an **antigen**. **Macrophages** support the immune response. Once bacteria or damaged platelets are identified, macrophages swarm the area and consume the offending materials until they literally eat themselves to death. The dead cells are exuded from the body as pus. Finally, **platelets** are

Table 10.1 The Blood Groups in the ABO System and Their Antigens, Antibodies, and Frequency in the Population

Blood Group	Antigen	Antibody	Population Frequency (%)
A	A	Anti-B	40
B	B	Anti-A	10
AB	A & B	None	5
O	H	Anti-A & Anti-B	45

only fragments of cells and contain no nuclei; they number around 15–300,000 per milliliter of blood. Platelets are involved in the clotting process.

Genetic Markers in Blood

A **blood group** is a class of antigens produced by allelic genes at one or more loci and inherited independently of other genes. Genetically controlled and invariant throughout a person's life, blood groups are a robust biological marker. About 20 human blood groups are known to exist. The practical meaning of this is that a blood group is a permanent genetic trait—one that is controlled by genes and unchanging throughout a person's life. This makes blood potentially excellent evidence for classification and possible inclusion or exclusion.

Several systems are used to characterize and classify blood. The first and best known is the **ABO blood group**, discovered in 1900 by Karl Landsteiner. The letters A, B, and O refer to the antigens on the surface of the red blood cells; corresponding antibodies, **anti-A** and **anti-B**, are present in the plasma (www.nobel.se) (see Table 10.1).

A person with Type B blood will have anti-A antibodies in his or her plasma. If the plasma is mixed with Type A blood, the cells will **agglutinate**, or clump together, from the reaction of the Type A antigens and the anti-A antibodies. Very few forensic laboratories currently perform blood group testing. If a stain is tested and is presumptively positive for blood, it is sent for DNA analysis (see "History: Landsteiner's Breakthrough").

HISTORY: LANDSTEINER'S BREAKTHROUGH

Karl Landsteiner was awarded the Nobel Prize for Medicine or Physiology in 1930 for his discovery of human blood groups. A portion of the presentation speech by Professor G. Hedrén, Chairman of the Nobel Committee for Physiology or Medicine of the Royal Caroline Institute, made on December 10, 1930 is below (full text available at www.nobel.se).

Thirty years ago, in 1900, in the course of his serological studies Landsteiner observed that when, under normal physiological conditions, blood serum of a human was added to normal blood of another human the red corpuscles in some cases coalesced into larger or smaller clusters. This observation of Landsteiner was the starting-point of his discovery of the human blood groups. In the following year, i.e. 1901, Landsteiner published his discovery that in man, blood types could be classified into three groups according to their different agglutinating properties. These agglutinating properties were identified more closely by two specific blood-cell structures, which can occur either singly or simultaneously in the same individual. A year

(Continued)

HISTORY: LANDSTEINER'S BREAKTHROUGH—cont'd

later von Decastello and Sturli showed that there was yet another blood group. The number of blood groups in man is therefore four.

Landsteiner's discovery of the blood groups was immediately confirmed but it was a long time before anyone began to realize the great importance of the discovery. The first incentive to pay greater attention to this discovery was provided by von Dungern and Hirszfeld when in 1910 they published their investigations into the hereditary transmission of blood groups. Thereafter the blood groups became the subject of exhaustive studies, on a scale increasing year by year, in more or less all civilized countries. In order to avoid, in the publication of research on this subject, detailed descriptions which would otherwise be necessary—of the four blood groups and their appropriate cell structures, certain short designations for the blood groups and corresponding specific cell structures have been introduced. Thus, one of the two specific cell structures, characterizing the agglutinating properties of human blood is designated by the letter A and another by B, and accordingly we speak of "blood group A" and "blood group B". These two cell structures can also occur simultaneously in the same individual, and this structure as well as the corresponding blood group is described as AB. The fourth blood-cell structure and the corresponding blood group is known as O, which is intended to indicate that people belonging to this group lack the specific blood characteristics typical of each of the other blood groups. Landsteiner had shown that under normal physiological conditions the blood serum will not agglutinate the erythrocytes of the same individual or those of other individuals with the same structure. Thus, the blood serum of people whose erythrocytes have group structure A will not agglutinate erythrocytes of this structure but it will agglutinate those of group structure B, and where the erythrocytes have group structure B the corresponding serum does not agglutinate these erythrocytes but it does agglutinate those with group structure A. Blood serum of persons whose erythrocytes have structures A as well as B, i.e. who have structure AB, does not agglutinate erythrocytes having structures A, B, or AB. Blood serum of persons belonging to blood group O agglutinates erythrocytes of persons belonging to any of the groups A, B, or AB, but erythrocytes of persons belonging to blood group O are not agglutinated by normal human blood serum. These facts constitute the actual basic principles of Landsteiner's discovery of the blood groups of mankind.

However, the discovery of the blood groups has also brought with it important scientific advances in the purely practical field—first and foremost in connection with blood-transfusion therapy, identification of blood, and establishing of paternity.

The transfer of blood from one person to another for therapeutic purposes began to be practiced on a considerable scale during the 17th century. It was found, however, that such blood transfusion involved serious risks and not infrequently resulted in the death of the patient. Therapeutic application of the blood transfusion had therefore been almost entirely given up by the time of Landsteiner's discovery. As a result of the discovery of the blood groups it was now possible, at least in the majority of cases, to explain the cause of the dangers linked with this therapeutic measure as previous experience had shown, and at the same time to avoid them. A person from whom blood is taken must in fact belong to the same blood group as the patient [universal donors and recipients notwithstanding]. *Thanks to Landsteiner's discovery of the blood groups, blood transfusions have come back into use and have saved a great many lives.*

Already at the time of publishing his discovery of the blood groups in 1901, Landsteiner pointed out that the blood-group reaction could be used for investigating the origin of a blood sample, for instance of a bloodstain. However, it is not possible to prove by determining the blood group that a blood sample comes from a particular individual, but it is possible to prove that it is not from a particular individual. If, for instance, the blood of a bloodstain is from an individual belonging to blood group A, then it cannot be from an individual who is found to belong to group B, but a blood-group determination will not tell us from which person of blood group A the blood came.

Retrieved from www.nobel.se.

PRESUMPTIVE TESTS FOR BLOOD

Presumptive tests for blood react with the hemoglobin present in blood. If hemoglobin is present, one of two general results occurs, depending on the test. Either a colorless reactive substance changes to a colored form (from clear to pink, for example) or light of a specific wavelength is emitted (fluorescence or chemiluminescence) in the presence of hemoglobin.

In the first type of test, the testing chemical is added to the suspected stain and then an oxidant is added, usually 3% hydrogen peroxide. The hydrogen peroxide reacts (oxidizes) with the hemoglobin and changes the color of the testing chemical; hemoglobin acts as the catalyst, speeding up the reaction. The most commonly used catalytic color tests are **phenolphthalein**, **benzidine**, **leucomalachite green**, and **tetramethylbenzidine** (TMB). For sensitivity and safety reasons among these tests, the phenolphthalein test is used more often than the other tests. The sensitivity of the phenolphthalein test can detect blood diluted down to 10^{-7} (1 part in 10 million) and even decades-old bloodstains can yield positive results. Phenolphthalein is cross-reactive with other substances, such as some vegetables. The test is performed by moistening a clean cotton swab with distilled water and rubbing it on the suspected stain. A drop of phenolphthalein solution is added to the swab's tip; it should remain colorless. A drop of hydrogen peroxide is then added; if the tip turns pink, the test is presumptively positive for blood. If the swab tip remains colorless, then the result is negative for blood. The hydrogen peroxide would continue to react with the hemoglobin and degrade it if it were not for an enzyme called catalase found primarily in red blood cells that destroys hydrogen peroxide and frees water and oxygen; this makes the local pH more basic and turns the phenolphthalein pink. The color change must be within several seconds because the tip may turn pink through normal oxidation after several minutes of exposure to air.

At times, it is not only the presence of blood that is of interest, but also the pattern or distribution of the blood. The area to be tested may be large or intricate, such as floors, walls, and automobile interiors. In these instances, the testing chemical is sprayed onto the surface(s) and then observed for any emitted light (glowing). Because the light output is faint, the treated surfaces must be viewed in the dark or with an alternate light source (ALS). Specialized photographic techniques must be used to capture the images because the effect of emitted light is temporary. These types of tests may affect subsequent tests; therefore, caution must be employed in their use (see Table 10.2). A noted expert in serology, Robert Spaulding (2002), has suggested that if the stain can be seen and collected, then this type of test should not be used.

Two chemicals, luminol and fluorescein, are predominantly used for large-scale serology testing. **Luminol** (3-aminophthalhydrazide) reacts in the presence of hemoglobin, much like phenolphthalein, when an oxidizer is applied. The reaction, however, results in a blue-white to yellow-green **luminescence** (light emitted as a by-product of a chemical reaction) if blood is present. Luminol is very sensitive to hemoglobin and will detect blood in dilutions of 1 in 5,000,000. Luminol, a suitable oxidant, and water are mixed and sprayed over the area of interest.

Table 10.2 The Effects of Various Presumptive Serology Tests on Subsequent Tests

References	Chemical Test	Effects on Subsequent Tests
Laux (1991)	Luminol	Does not significantly affect presumptive, confirmatory, species origin, and ABO tests. Does interfere with some enzyme and protein genetic marker systems, such as acid phosphatase, esterase D, peptidase A, and adenylate kinase.
Gross et al. (1999)	Luminol	Does *not* affect polymerase chain reaction of DNA.
Hochmeister et al. (1991)	Ethanolic benzidine Phenolphthalein Luminol	Does not affect recovery of DNA for restriction fragment length polymorphism but does lower the yield somewhat.
Budowle et al. (2000)	Fluorescein	Does *not* affect short tandem repeat analysis of DNA.

The pattern will be visible for up to 30 s before additional treatment is required; overspraying, however, will result in "bleeding" of the patterns and a loss of detail.

Fluorescein is another chemical that is used to check for the presence of blood and is prepared much in the same way as luminol except that the commercial preparation contains a thickener. This makes fluorescein stay on the surface better than luminol, making it easier to use on walls and other vertical surfaces. Unlike luminol, fluorescein produces fluorescence (light emitted as energy loss at a longer wavelength than it is illuminated with) and must be illuminated at 450 nm via an ALS to be seen.

Both luminol and fluorescein are characterized as irritants but are not known to be carcinogens. Nevertheless, safety precautions and protective equipment should be employed during their use.

Confirmatory Tests for Blood

Confirmatory tests for blood utilize the formation of crystals through the application of heat and testing chemicals. For example, the **Takayama test** (also known as the **hemochromogen test**) is performed by taking a small sample of the presumptive stain and placing it under a coverslip. The sample is heated briefly and, while being observed through a microscope, pyridine under alkaline conditions in the presence of a reducing sugar is added with a pipette. If blood is present, salmon-colored crystals form. The Takayama test is very sensitive, and even very old bloodstains may give a positive reaction. Heating the sample properly is key: Even when blood is present, improper heating of the sample can result in a false negative. Historically, the Teichmans test was used as a confirmatory test for blood; it is essentially the same procedure with different chemicals. A modification of the Takayama test appeared in the *Journal of Forensic Sciences* in 1993; the author, Hatch, used a reagent (dithiothreitol) to increase the rate of crystal formation (Hatch, 1993).

Practically speaking, most forensic laboratories today do not conduct confirmatory tests for blood—the sample, if presumptively positive, will go straight to the DNA unit. A sensitive and simple test card (such as the ABAcard® HemaTrace®) is a cost-effective way to confirm blood on a stain too small for DNA analysis. Forensic laboratories are learning that it is simply not possible to send all potential evidence to the DNA unit; doing so creates the backlogs that currently burden those same laboratories. Some type of intelligent, evidence-based selection is necessary to route relevant evidence for the proper analyzes as well as determine which analysis should be conducted.

Species Origin

Tests that determine the species from which a blood sample originated fall into two general categories: diffusion reactions and electrophoretic methods. The most common diffusion reaction test, the Ouchterlony test, is based on an antibody–antigen reaction between human blood and human antiserum. **Human antiserum** is typically produced by injecting rabbits with human blood. The rabbit's immune system, reacting to the foreign blood, produces antibodies to neutralize it. When the rabbit's human-sensitized blood is drawn and the serum isolated, it can be used to detect human blood because it now has antibodies that will react specifically with human blood. Other antisera, for dogs, cats, and horses, for example, can be produced in a similar way.

The Ouchterlony test is performed as follows. An agarose gel is poured into a small petri dish. A circular pattern of six wells is cut out of the gel with an additional well in the center. The antihuman serum is placed in the center well with a known human control placed in every other well. The sera and samples are allowed to diffuse. The human controls test positive (of course) with a diffusion line; if the unknown tests positive, the line extends between the adjoining known samples (see Figure 10.1). The Ouchterlony test is being supplanted by the Hematrace™ card, where a positive test is indicated by a color change.

Electrophoresis methods are based on the diffusion of antibodies and antigens on an electrically charged gel-coated plate. The bloodstain extract and the human antiserum are placed in separate wells on opposite sides of the plate. When the plate is charged, a zone of precipitation forms at the juncture of the antibodies and antigens; Figure 10.2 shows an electrophoresis device.

SEMEN

Semen is a complex gelatinous mixture of cells, amino acids, sugars, salts, ions, and other materials produced by postpubescent males and is ejaculated following

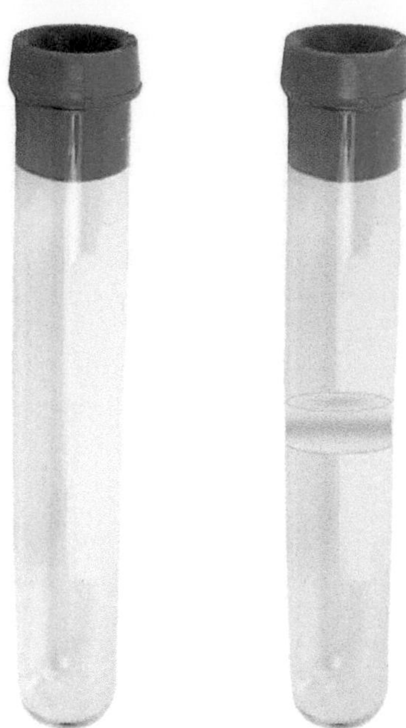

FIGURE 10.1

This is an Ouchterlony Double Diffusion method gel. The central well contains an antibody and the surrounding wells contain the corresponding antigen in decreasing concentration ("Neat," "(1:1)," "1:2," "1:4," "1:8," "1:16," and "1:32"). The line that runs from top center to bottom center stops at the titer value, 1:8.

Public domain image.

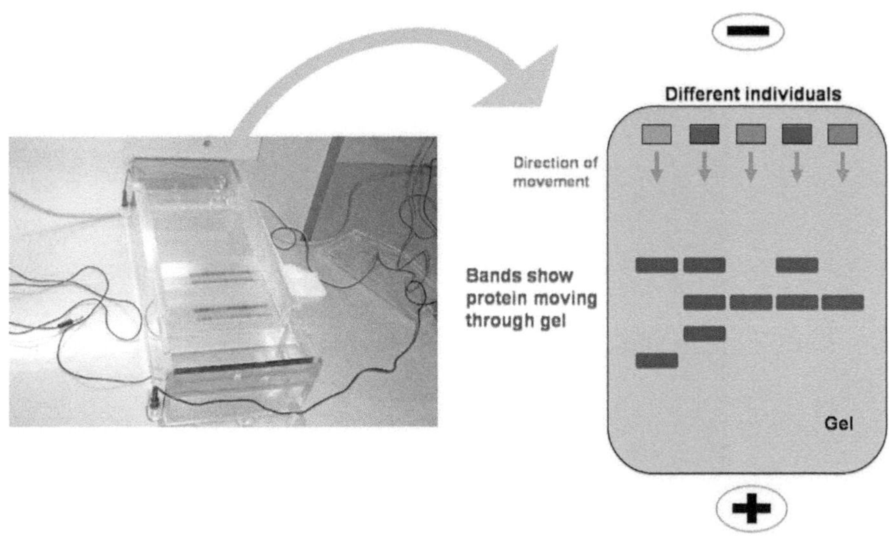

FIGURE 10.2

In electrophoresis antibodies and antigens diffuse on an electrically charged gel-coated plate forming a juncture.

sexual stimulation. The volume of ejaculate varies from 2 to 6 mL and typically contains between 100 and 150 million **spermatozoa**, or sperm cells, per milliliter. Sperm cells, shown in Figure 10.3, are a specialized structure approximately 55 μm in length with a head containing DNA and a tail that wiggles, or flagellates, to produce movement. The presence of semen (or, by extension, intact sperm) is considered presumptive evidence of sexual contact.

Presumptive Tests for Semen

Semen contains **acid phosphatase** (AP), a common enzyme in nature that occurs at a very high level in semen. This allows for a test, with a high AP threshold, to presumptively identify semen. The most common test is **Brentamine Fast Blue B** applied to the sample on an alpha-naphthyl phosphate substrate (see "In More Detail: Presumptive Test for Acid Phosphatase"). Brentamine Fast Blue B is a known carcinogen and must be handled accordingly. A piece of filter paper or cotton swab is moistened with sterile water and applied to the questioned stain. The reagent is added, and if an intense purple color is seen, the test is positive; if no color reaction occurs within 2 min, the test is negative. If a sample is known or suspected to be "old," a negative result should be cautiously interpreted because AP becomes less active over time. Positive results are presumptive, remember, because many biological fluids, including vaginal secretions, contain some amount of AP. Commercial test kits are available for semen.

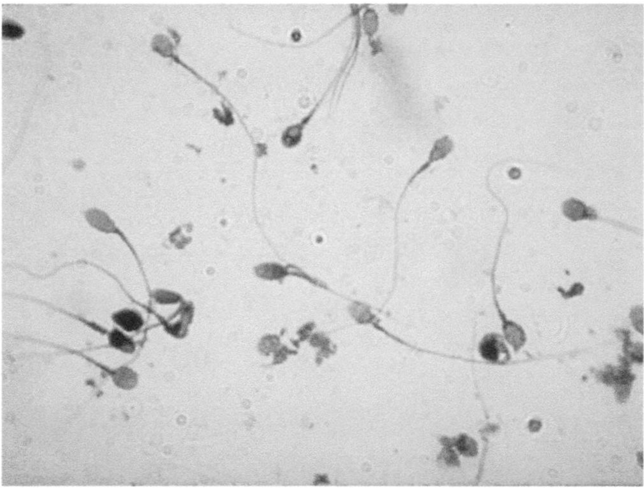

FIGURE 10.3

Between 100 and 150 million spermatozoa are found per milliliter of ejaculate. Semen (or, by extension, sperm) is considered presumptive evidence of sexual contact.

IN MORE DETAIL: PRESUMPTIVE TEST FOR AP

Reagent Preparation

Buffer

8.21 g anhydrous sodium acetate, pH 5.5

Reagent

- Step 1. Dissolve 5 mg alpha-naphthyl phosphate in 5 mL buffer.
- Step 2. Dissolve 5 mg Fast Blue B in 5 mL buffer.

  Prepare a single reagent by adding equal volumes of reagents from Steps 1 and 2.

Procedure

Perform the test on a portion of the stain, an extract, or a "wipe" made from the stained area. Always test an unstained substrate control and a positive control at the same time as the unknown samples.

Two-Step Method

Apply a drop of the alpha-naphthyl solution to the unknown sample and wait 60 s.
Apply a drop of the Fast Blue B solution to the unknown sample.
An immediate purple color is a positive reaction.

One-Step Method

Apply a drop of the combined reagents to the unknown sample. A purple color that develops within 60 s is a positive reaction.

From Shaler (2002, p. 537).

Semen can be visualized by alternative light sources at 450 nm and viewed with amber goggles. The method is useful because it works on light or dark surfaces, covers large areas, and is quick; the disadvantage is that some other fluids will also fluoresce, such as saliva and urine. Semen exhibits a blue-white fluorescence, so this test can help narrow down which stains to test for AP. Just because no fluorescence occurs, however, it cannot be assumed that no semen is present.

Confirmatory Tests for Semen

The presence of intact spermatozoa in a biological stain has historically been the conclusive test for semen; they are abundant in semen and should be plentiful. A lack of sperm doesn't necessarily mean the stain isn't semen, only that sperm are not present.

The traditional method for sperm identification is to use the **Christmas tree stain**, which turns the tip of the sperm's head pink, the bottom of the head dark red, the middle portion blue and the tail yellowish-green; skin cells stain green to blue-green and are easily distinguished. See "In More Detail: Using the Christmas Tree Stain to Visualize Sperm" for a description of the method. An extract of the stain is dissolved in water, and then a portion is applied to a microscope slide, heat-fixed, and then colored with the Christmas tree stain. The slide is then scanned at magnifications of 400× to 1000×. Even if detached sperm heads are the only structure on the slide, and the Christmas tree stain assists in distinguishing them, this is still confirmative for the presence of semen. Phase contrast or dark field microscopy may also be used. The hematoxylin-eosin stain is also used but operates on the same premise (the stain colors are purple for heads and pink for the rest).

IN MORE DETAIL: USING THE CHRISTMAS TREE STAIN TO VISUALIZE SPERM

Reagents

Nuclear Fast Red

2.5 g aluminum sulfate

50 mg nuclear fast red

Dissolve the aluminum sulfate in 100 mL warm deionized water and then add the nuclear fast red. Stir.

After cooling, filter the solution.

Picro Indigo Carmine

1.30 g picric acid

0.33 g indigo carmine

Dissolve the picric acid in 100 mL of warm deionized water, yielding a saturated solution. Add the indigo carmine and stir overnight.

Procedure

Apply a portion of the extract to a microscope slide and heat fix.

Cover the dried extract with a few drops of nuclear fast red and allow to sit for at least 10 min.

Wash the excess reagent away with deionized water.

Add a drop of picro indigo carmine (PIC) to the still-wet slide and allow to sit for 30 s or less.

Wash away the excess PIC with absolute ethanol.

Observe the slide microscopically.

From Shaler (2002, p. 541).

In 1978, George Sensabaugh published a paper outlining the forensic use of a **prostate specific antigen** that he named **p30** (*p* for *p*rostate, *30* for its molecular weight of 30,000) (Sensabaugh, 1978). A method called **enzyme-linked immunosorbent assay (ELISA)** is typically used to detect p30 at levels as low as 0.005 ng/mL (the threshold for rectal samples is 2 ng/mL because of reactions with other substances found there). ELISA is based on the antigen–antibody reaction: The reagent is added to the filter paper or swab, and if an intense purple color is seen, a reaction has occurred and p30 is present. The labeled p30 is attached to the antibody. In ELISA, the label is an enzyme that catalyzes a reaction where the substrate changes color; the deeper or more intense the color, the more label, and therefore the more p30, is present. ELISA is a good method for mass-testing of samples; in forensic laboratories, ABA semen detection cards or similar types of tests are now used.

Depending on the crime, it may be useful to determine the **time since intercourse (TSI)** to assist in the sequence of events. Typically, this means the detection of spermatozoa, but because of natural variations, the timing is rarely exact. Motile (moving) sperm can survive in the vagina for about 3 h, ranging from 1 to 8 h; they survive longer in the cervix, up to several days in some cases. By the time a case gets to the forensic serologist, however, the sperm are rarely motile. Time lags inevitably occur between the occurrence of the crime, collection, submission, and analysis. Forensic serologists therefore look for *intact* sperm. These can persist in the vagina up to 26h, and the heads alone can last up to 3 days; again, the persistence is greater in the cervix. Intact sperm can be found from 6 to 65h post coitus in the rectum (or until the next bowel movement) but rarely more than 6h in the mouth. Levels of p30 have been used to estimate TSI, and most p30 is eliminated within 24–27h after intercourse.

SALIVA

Saliva can be evidence in a number of crimes. Bite marks, licked adhesives (like envelopes and stamps), eating and drink surfaces, or even expectoration (spitting) can yield important DNA evidence. Saliva stains may be difficult to see, and detection can be tricky.

The problem is that although the enzyme amylase occurs in saliva, and tests exist for amylase, amylase also occurs in many other body fluids. It occurs in higher amounts in saliva, so the intensity of a test result could be considered presumptively positive for saliva. An old test, the radial diffusion test, used to be employed to confirm the presence of saliva, but now the sample is considered presumptively positive for saliva and simply sent on for DNA analysis. Saliva has large amounts of skin (epithelial) cells from the inner cheek walls and therefore is easy to type for DNA analysis.

URINE

Urine, the excreted fluid and waste products filtered by the kidneys, can be presumptively tested for through the presence of urea (with urease, an enzyme) or creatine (with picric acid). Also, when heated, a urine stain gives off a characteristic odor that everyone is familiar with. Urine has few skin (epithelial) cells in it, and a sample must be quite concentrated for DNA typing to be successful.

BLOODSTAIN PATTERN ANALYSIS

One of the most explicit methods of forensic science that exemplifies its reconstructive nature is the analysis and interpretation of bloodstain patterns. Bevel and Gardner, in the second edition of their *Bloodstain Pattern Analysis* (2002), define **bloodstain pattern analysis** (BPA) as the analysis and interpretation of the dispersion, shape characteristics, volume, pattern, number, and relationship of bloodstains at a crime scene to reconstruct a process of events. A combination of geometry, physiology, physics, and logic, BPA requires extensive training coupled with a solid scientific education to be properly applied. The International Association for Identification (IAI, www.theiai.org), for example, requires the following for its certification in BPA:

- An applicant for certification must be of good moral character, high integrity, good repute, and must possess a high ethical and professional standing.

- A minimum of 40 h of education in an approved workshop providing theory, study, and practice, which includes oral and/or visual presentation of physical activity of blood droplets illustrating blood as fluid being acted upon by motion or force, past research, treatise, or other reference materials for the student; laboratory exercises that document bloodstains and standards by previous research.
- A minimum of 3 years of practice within the discipline of bloodstain pattern identification, following the required 40-h training course, must be documented.
- The applicant for certification must have a minimum of 240 h of instruction in associated fields of study related to bloodstain pattern identification in any of photography (evidence/documentary), crime scene investigation technology, evidence recovery, blood detection techniques/presumptives, medico-legal death investigation, forensic science, and technology.
- The course requirements must include a 40-h Basic Bloodstain Evidence Course as previously outlined.

As can be seen from this brief overview of the process, a great deal of work must be accomplished to be considered certified (more details can be found at the IAI's website).

TERMINOLOGY IN BPA

Bloodstains can be grouped into three main classes: passive, transfer, and projected or impact stains. **Passive bloodstains** include clots, drops, flows, and pooling. **Transfer bloodstains** include wipes, swipes, pattern transfers, and general contact bloodstains. Finally, spatters, splashes, cast-off stains, and arterial spurts or gushes are examples of **projected** or **impact bloodstains**. Other patterns include fly spots, voids, and skeletonized stains.

A **wipe stain** is created when an object moves through a pre-existing bloodstain. An example would be the stain resulting from a clean rag being moved through a blood pool on a floor. In contrast, a "swipe stain" is the transfer of blood onto a target by a moving object that is itself bloodstained. Blood-soaked clothing being dragged over unstained vinyl flooring would result in a swipe, not a wipe. An easy way to remember this difference is that an object that is *s*tained creates a *s*wipe; an unstained object makes a wipe (no stain, no "s").

Spatter is a technical term in BPA that describes a stain that results from blood hitting a target. Two types of spatter are recognized. The first, **forward spatter**, results when blood droplets are projected away from the item creating the impact, such as a hammer. **Back spatter**, in contrast, is caused by droplets being projected toward the item; in general, back spatter will be lighter and the stains smaller than forward spatter (Figure 10.4). Note that the word "splatter" has no technical meaning in BPA and should not be used.

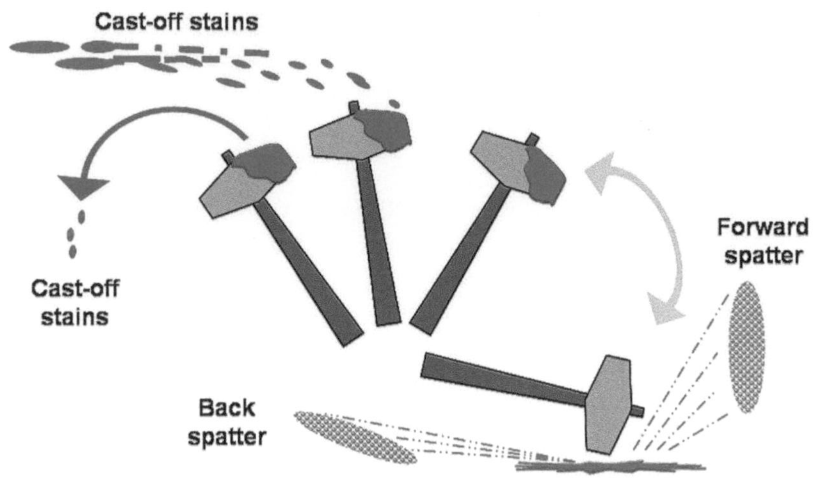

FIGURE 10.4

Forward spatter results from droplets being projected to the front of the object hitting the blood; back spatter is the opposite. Cast-off stains result from blood being flung from a bloodied object; note that cast-off stains can occur *behind* the item as well—for example, on the back of the assailant's shirt.

Cast-off stains are the result of blood being flung or projected from a bloody object in motion or one that stops suddenly (see Figure 10.4). Cast-off stains are linear and reflect the position of the person moving the bloody object. If a criminal bludgeons a victim with a baseball bat, as the criminal's arm comes back to swing again, any blood on the end of the bat will be projected by centrifugal force in an arc. Remember that cast-off stains can arc directly behind the object and land, for example, on the back of the assailant's shirt.

The blood flowing through the arteries is under high pressure. When an artery is breached while the heart is pumping, blood will spurt or gush from the wound, as depicted in Figure 10.5. **Arterial spurts/gushes** can vary due to the pumping action and variable pressure of the blood as it exits the wound, producing a zig-zag, up-and-down pattern.

Fly spots are stains resulting from fly activity—and may mimic other relevant BPA patterns. Flies may regurgitate and defecate when consuming blood at a crime scene, and these spots, as well as small amounts of blood that are tracked, can be confusing or misleading.

Voids are an indicator that some secondary object came between a blood spatter and the final target; this leaves an outline or "shadow" on the final target, illustrated in Figure 10.6. Voids are important clues about items that may have been moved or discarded after an attack but were present during the criminal process.

FIGURE 10.5

The arterial spurt pattern from the victim (a) can be seen in detail on the round ottoman (b).

Courtesy: John Black, South Carolina Law Enforcement Division.

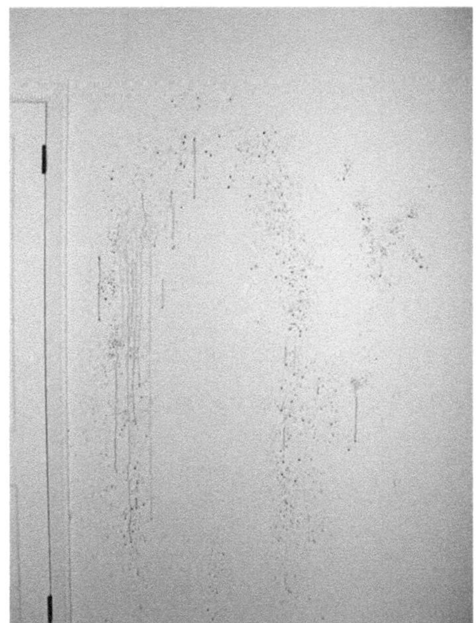

FIGURE 10.6

Voids indicate that some object came between a blood spatter source and the final target. The outline or "shadow" is an important clue that some item that was present during the incident may have been moved or discarded afterward.

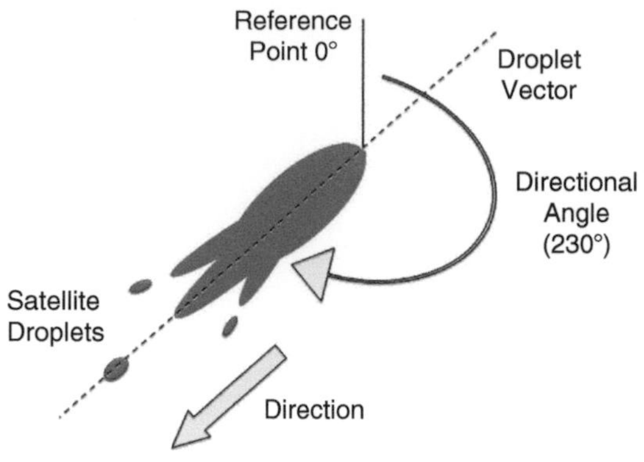

FIGURE 10.7

The "tail" of the stain indicates direction; the angle from a 0° reference point shows the directional angle. The satellite droplets are small "splashes" from the parent stain.

As a stain dries, the edges and borders dry first due to surface effects. If the bloodstain is wiped, these dried areas, called **skeletonized stains**, remain behind. Skeletonized stains retain the size and shape of the original stain and indicate the passage of time.

Figure 10.7 shows some of the basic measurements for BPA. The **angle of impact** is the acute angle created by the intercept of the target with the droplet's vector. This is different from the **direction angle**, which is the angle between the long axis of the stain and a standard reference point, usually 0° vertical. The **directionality** demonstrates the vector of a droplet when it hits the target; the tail points in the direction of travel. **Satellite droplets** are small amounts of blood that detach from the **parent stain** and "splash" onto a surface.

DETERMINING POINT-OF-ORIGIN

Although it may seem a macabre game of connect-the-dots, determining the point-of-origin of one or more bloodstains is central to the reconstruction of a blood-related event. Whenever the direction of a bloodstain can be determined, it can be expected to have originated at a point somewhere along that line. Doing this for a number of bloodstains can demonstrate a convergence of lines (paths), indicating a possible **point-of-origin** for the stains, as shown in Figure 10.8. The more paths converge to this point, the more confidence the analyst has in that point being the origin of the pattern (Figure 10.8(a)). The analyst must be aware that multiple paths may cross, generating a confusing or conflicting pattern (Figure 10.8(b)).

A bloodstain scene may be particularly difficult to interpret. Visual aids, from simple strings and pins to advanced forensic software, are available to assist the

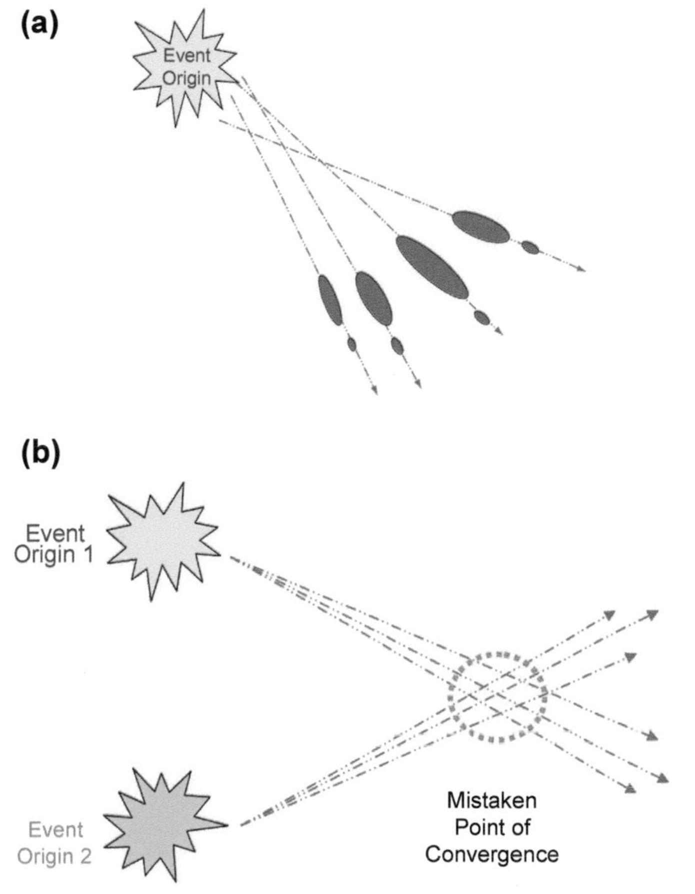

FIGURE 10.8

By finding the path for each bloodstain in a pattern, the analyst can interpret a point-of-origin (a); the more paths that converge to this point, the more likely it is the actual point-of-origin. The analyst must not be confused by multiple adjacent patterns, however, just because points converge doesn't mean that is the point-of-origin, (b).

analyst. Stringing a scene, depicted in Figure 10.9, is the easiest and cheapest method to interpret multiple bloodstain patterns. The path of a bloodstain is established, and a string is run from that point backward using pushpins or masking tape to fasten the ends; this process is repeated for numerous stains until the pattern's origin becomes clear. Rulers, protractors, and even laser pointers can be used in this method. Software, such as *Backtrack/Images*® and *Backtrack/Win*®, available through Forensic

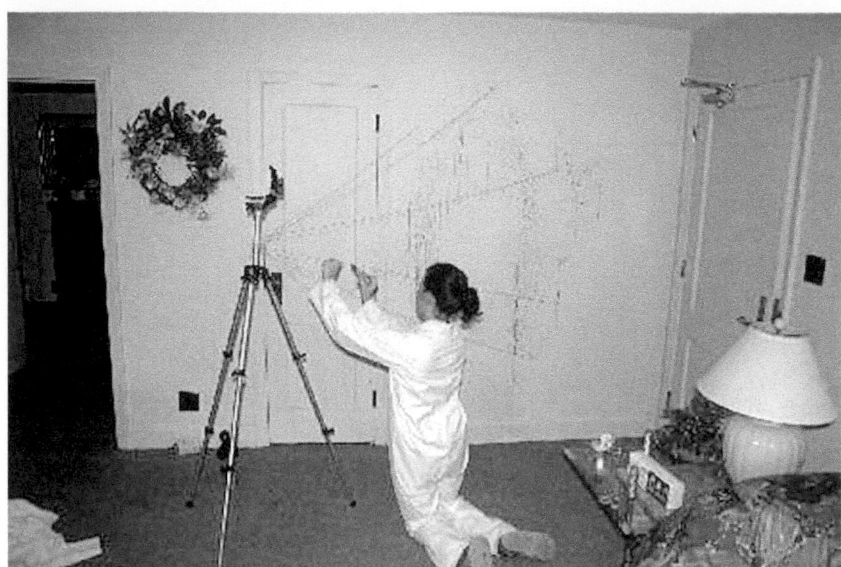

FIGURE 10.9

The easiest and cheapest method of interpreting bloodstain patterns is stringing. A string is run from the presumptive source to the target, using pushpins or masking tape to fasten the ends. Rulers, protractors, and even laser pointers can be used in this method.

Computing of Ottawa (www.physics.carleton.ca/~carter/index.html), can assist through the automated calculation of vectors and angles; an example is shown in Figure 10.10.

DOCUMENTING BLOODSTAINS AT THE SCENE

Presumptive serological tests can be employed to discover if the stain in question is truly blood; if it's tomato sauce, then it's probably not worth the analyst's time. Additionally, many of the enhancement techniques used for visualizing blood discussed earlier in this chapter can be used to visualize bloodstain patterns.

The documentation of bloodstains is painstaking work but crucial to a successful reconstruction. Tom Bevel and Ross Gardner (2002), two well-known bloodstain pattern analysts, recommend the following photographic guidelines:

- Document the entire scene as discovered, including "establishing" photographs.
- Photograph pattern transfers, pools, and other fragile patterns first.

(a)

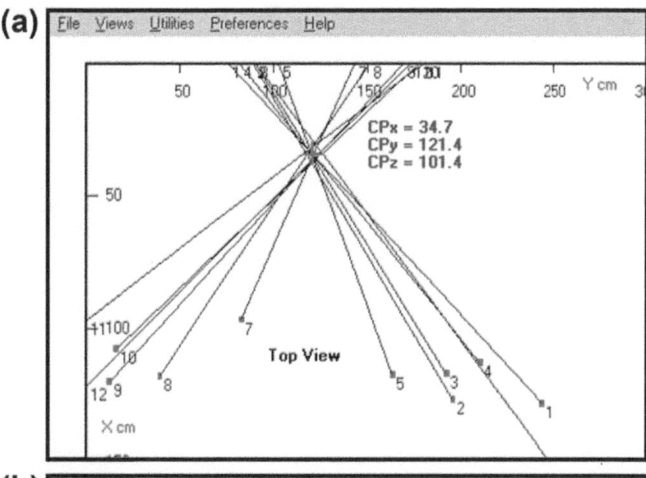

(b)

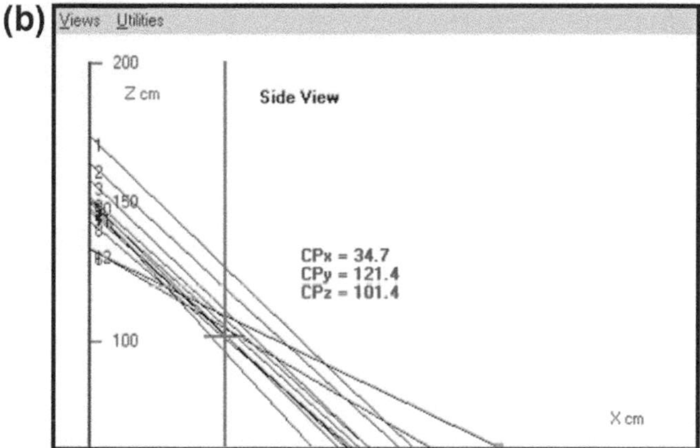

FIGURE 10.10

Computer software can assist in the reconstruction of bloodstain patterns by automatically calculating angles and vectors.

Courtesy: Forensic Software of Ottawa.

- Document patterns with "establishing" photographs that show the pattern's relationship to landmarks or other items of evidence.
- Take macro and close-up photographs; *include a scale in every photograph.*
- When reconstructing point-of-origin, document individual stains used in the reconstruction.

Note-taking, sketching, and measurements must accompany photographic documentation to help organize and describe the stains at the scene.

BACK TO THE CASE: THE CHAMBERLAIN CASE

Lindy Chamberlain was found guilty of murder in 1982 and sentenced to life imprisonment; Michael was found guilty of being an accessory after the fact, but his sentence was suspended. The case was a lightning rod for years in Australia and around the world. The trial was the most publicized in Australian history. The Chamberlains appealed several times, all unsuccessful.

In 1986, a tourist was killed in a fall while climbing Ayers Rock/Uluru. The vast and remote nature of the area meant that it was several days before his remains were found. While searching the area, police discovered a small jacket, badly weather-beaten. It was identified as Azaria's missing garment. Numerous dingo dens were in the area where the jacket was found. This odd discovery began a review of the entire case investigation, including the serology. Doubts had been raised over the years about the case, the way the scene was handled, and the testing of the evidence.

Two of the problems eventually discovered with the physical evidence were the test for fetal hemoglobin and preconceptions about dingos; there were other issues in the case, to be sure. The fetal hemoglobin test could render a false positive result on a variety of materials, including mucus and chocolate milkshakes. These materials had been in the car previous to Azaria's disappearance. A spray-on soundproofing used on that particular make and model of the vehicle's wheel wells also produced similar positive results. Remember, this was in 1980 and well before the advent of DNA analysis in forensic science. Also, many Australians had misconceptions about dingos. Dingos are canines that were previously domesticated thousands of years ago but have over time become wild again. They look like household pets but are in fact fairly dangerous wild animals. At the time, many people thought it preposterous that a dingo would attack and carry off a child. An engineer who had researched dingos for many years testified that a dingo's teeth are sharp enough to cut through a car's seat belts; they are also wily enough to remove meat from a package and leave the paper intact. His testimony was rejected. Dingos are strong enough to carry away an adult kangaroo (120–200 lbs); in fact, a child had been pulled from a vehicle weeks before while the parents watched in horror. The child was rescued as the dingo ran away.

In a legal review, Lindy was released from prison and cleared of all charges. Azaria's manner of death was ruled "unknown." The Chamberlain case changed the way forensic science operated in Australia and sparked many questions about forensic scene work, testing, and testimony. It stands today not only as an example of justice gone wrong but also as a warning about how science works in the service of the courts.

SUMMARY

Far from being obsolete, serology is still a significant part of the forensic biologist's toolkit. Testing for body fluids can save a great deal of time and effort later in the analytical stream of things (i.e., DNA analysis). There can be no argument that serology has taken a backseat to DNA, but the argument should be made for retaining a battery of serology tests in the modern forensic laboratory. New methods being researched, such as proteomics, offer serology a renewed life and application as biologists discover more and different ways to identify the substances that make up our bodies.

TEST YOUR KNOWLEDGE

1. What is serology?
2. What is the proteome?
3. What's the difference between a presumptive and confirmatory test?

4. Name the components of blood.
5. What are leukocytes and what do they do?
6. What is a blood group?
7. List three presumptive tests for blood.
8. What's luminol?
9. What does the precipitin test determine?
10. What is the most common presumptive test for semen?
11. What does "ELISA" stand for?
12. How long can motile sperm survive in the vagina?
13. Name the presumptive test for saliva.
14. What's the difference between a wipe and a swipe?
15. What is a cast-off stain?
16. How is point-of-origin determined?
17. Is there a presumptive test for urine?
18. What is angle of impact?
19. What is the difference between forward and backward spatter?
20. What is acid phosphatase?

CONSIDER THIS...

1. Why would you perform presumptive serology tests? Why not send everything straight to the DNA unit?
2. Why would two (or more) experts disagree about bloodstain pattern interpretations? Isn't it just geometry and physics?

BIBLIOGRAPHY AND FURTHER READING

Bevel, T., Gardner, R.M., 2002. Bloodstain Pattern Analysis, second ed. CRC Press, Boca Raton, FL.

Budowle, B., et al., 2000. The presumptive reagent fluorescein for the detection of dilute bloodstains and subsequent STR typing of recovered DNA. Journal of Forensic Science 45, 1090–1092.

Gaensslen, R.E., 1983. Sourcebook in Forensic Serology, Immunology, and Biochemistry. U.S. Government Printing Office, Washington, DC.

Grispino, R.R.J., 1990. The effect of luminol on the serological analysis of dried human bloodstains. Crime Laboratory Digest 17, 13–23.

Gross, A.M., Harris, D.A., Kaldun, G.L., 1999. The effect of luminol on presumptive tests and DNA analysis using the polymerase chain reaction. Journal of Forensic Sciences 44, 837–840.

Hatch, A.L., 1993. A modified reagent for the confirmation of blood. Journal of Forensic Sciences 38, 1502–1506.

Hochmeister, M.N., Budowle, B., Baechtel, F.S., 1991. Effects of presumptive test reagents on the ability to obtain restriction fragment length polymorphism (RFLP) patterns from human blood and semen stains. Journal of Forensic Sciences 44, 656–661.

Laux, D.L., 1991. Effects of luminol on subsequent analysis of bloodstains. Journal of Forensic Sciences 36, 1512–1520.

Ponce, A.C., Verdu Pascual, F.A., 1999. Critical revision of presumptive tests for bloodstains. Forensic Science Communications 1 (2). Online at: www.fbi.gov.

Sali, A., Glaeser, R., Earnest, T., Baumeister, W., 2003. From words to literature in structural proteomics. Nature 422, 216–225.

Sensabaugh, G., 1978. Isolation and characterization of a semen-specific protein from human seminal plasma: a potential new maker for semen identification. Journal of Forensic Sciences 23, 106.

Shaler, R.C., 2002. Modern forensic biology. In: Saferstein, R. (Ed.), Forensic Science Handbooks, vol. I. Prentice-Hall, Inc., Englewood Cliffs, NJ, pp. 525–613.

Spaulding, R.P., 2002. Identification and characterization of blood and bloodstains. (Chapter 11). In: James, S.H., Nordby, J.J. (Eds.), Forensic Science: An Introduction to Scientific and Investigative Techniques. CRC Press, Boca Raton, FL.

Sutton, T.P., 1999. Presumptive blood testing. (Chapter 4). In: James, S.H. (Ed.), Scientific and Legal Applications of Bloodstain Pattern Interpretation. CRC Press, Boca Raton, FL.

Tyers, M., Mann, M., 2003. From genomics to proteomics. Nature 422, 193–197.

CHAPTER

DNA Analysis

11

CHAPTER OUTLINE

KEY TERMS

- Allelle
- Chromosome
- CODIS

- Deoxyribonucleic acid (DNA)
- Gene
- Genetic code
- Genotype
- Heterozygous
- Homozygous
- Mitochondria
- PCR
- Phenotype
- Polymorphism
- RFLP
- Short Tandem Repeats (STRs)

INTRODUCTION

THE CASE: THE EXONERATIONS OF HENRY LEE MCCOLLUM AND LEON BROWN

The case and the eventual exonerations were reported in the New York Times on September 2, 2014.

Henry Lee McCollum and Leon Brown, two mentally disabled half brothers, were released from prison in North Carolina, 30 years after their convictions in the murder and rape of an 11-year-old girl. Their convictions were based upon confessions that both men said were coerced. The case against them was destroyed by DNA evidence that implicated another man who lived near the victim and who had confessed to committing a similar rape and murder. McCollum was on death row for the crime and Brown was serving a life sentence at the time they were exonerated. During the time that this case was prosecuted, it stood as an example of the difficulties that many people have with the death penalty and the issue of invoking it in cases where the defendant is mentally defective. In 1994, the United States Supreme Court turned down a request to review the case. One justice commented that the crime was so shocking that the death penalty was warranted. Another justice declared that one defendant had the mental age of a child and invoking the death penalty would be unconstitutional. The case also gave graphic evidence of the power of DNA typing to provide compelling evidence to overturn verdicts, especially in cases where confessions are suspect. The DNA evidence was brought into the case by the North Carolina Center for Death Penalty Litigation.

McCollum was 19 and Brown was 15 when they were picked up by police who were investigating the rape and murder of Sabrina Buie, age 11. The body was discovered in a soybean field. After 5 h of intense questioning, McCollum confessed to the crime, indicating that his half brother and two other youths had raped and murdered Buie. McCollum later recanted his confession, citing the terrible pressure he was put under and how he made up the story just so he could go home. Brown, upon being told that McCollum had confessed, also signed a confession. The other two people named by McCollum were never prosecuted for the crime. At the trial, both McCollum and Brown were sentenced to death. At a second trial ordered by the State Supreme Court, Brown's sentence was reduced to life imprisonment.

When the Center for Death Penalty litigation became involved in the case, they pressed for DNA analysis of evidence from the crime. Chief among these items was a cigarette butt found at the scene. DNA recovered from the butt was matched to Roscoe Artis, who lived near the victim and had a history of sexual assault convictions. At the exoneration hearing a witness from the innocence inquiry commission testified that there was no evidence that tied Brown or McCollum to the crime and that the DNA recovered from the cigarette butt matched Roscoe Artis. The district attorney did not dispute the evidence. This paved the way for McCollum and Brown to be released from prison.

Chapter 10—"Serology and Bloodstain Pattern Analysis"—discussed biologic markers present in blood and other body fluids. These include red and white blood cell antigens and enzymes in red and white blood cells. Many of these antigens and enzymes are polymorphic. This means that each of them exist in a number of different, but similar chemical configurations. Each person has one or two (depending upon which ones they inherited from their parents) forms of each of these substances. Thus, a population of people may be separated into groups based upon which forms of these antigens and enzymes they possess. The size of each group will depend upon the frequency of occurrence of each particular marker. This **binning** of human populations was used for many years in characterizing certain biologic evidence from crime scenes. It has also been used in establishing paternity in disputed cases. The grouping of human populations by determining the frequencies of red blood cell antigens and red and white blood cell enzymes, although useful, suffers from a number of problems. These include a lack of stability of many of these proteins, especially if blood is allowed to dry, and their limited ability to discriminate among a population of people.

The discovery of DNA, its structure and how it carries genetic information, has had profound effects on our understanding of the development of plants and animals and how some diseases are caused and perhaps cured. In addition, it has caused a revolution in forensic science. Today, a successful DNA profile makes it possible to associate a DNA sample to a specific person with a high degree of certainty that allows for conclusions of individuality under certain circumstances, giving law enforcement and forensic science a new, powerful identification tool that complements fingerprints and other methods of identification.

In this chapter, the development of DNA typing methods and how they help in the comparison of blood, semen, and other body fluids and tissues generated by criminal activity will be explored. The application of DNA databases to crime scene evidence will also be presented. It should be noted that only basic descriptions of DNA typing methodologies and genetics are presented in this book. A discussion of exceptions to the rules and assumptions made about DNA typing, genetic mutations, and many of the scientific issues that inevitably arise with something as complicated as amplifying and analyzing DNA are beyond the scope of this book. The reader is directed to the further readings suggested at the end of the chapter for a more detailed explanation of the topics covered in this chapter.

THE NATURE OF DNA

Deoxyribonucleic acid (DNA) is a complex molecule found in nearly all cells in all animals and plants. Notable exceptions in humans include red blood cells that have no nucleus. DNA is a special type of molecule known as a **polymer**, a molecule made up of repeating simpler units, called **monomers**. DNA is located in two regions in a cell, the nucleus and mitochondria. Both can be used in DNA typing; however, mitochondrial DNA (mtDNA) is of a different length and shape and is used differently than nuclear DNA in the characterization of biologic evidence. Unlike nuclear DNA, it is inherited only from the mother. mtDNA will be covered later in this chapter.

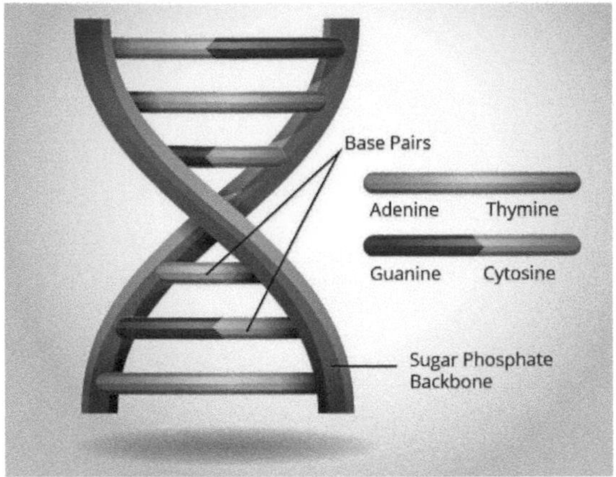

FIGURE 11.1

The DNA double helix. The backbone of the DNA polymer is made up of sugar molecule (deoxyribose) and phosphate. The bases bind in pairs. Only C and G can bind with each other and only T and A can bind with each other. There are more than 3 billion base pairs in the human genome.

NUCLEAR DNA

Nuclear DNA has a geometric shape called a **double helix**. A helix is a spiral-shaped geometric figure. DNA looks like two helices wrapped around each other. Consider a ladder, made up of two poles held together by a series of rungs. Now consider taking the ladder at both ends and twisting it until it looks more like a spiral staircase—this is what the DNA molecule looks like. This is shown in Figure 11.1.

The poles of the ladder are identical in all living things. They are made up of alternating sugar molecules (deoxyribose) and phosphates. Dangling off of each sugar molecule is one of four **bases** or **nucleotides**: **adenine** (**A**), **guanine** (**G**), **cytosine** (**C**), and **thymine** (**T**). When an adenine base and a thymine base comes into proximity, they form a bond to each other. Likewise, when cytosine and guanine get near each other, they will bond. Neither T nor A can link with G or C. The DNA molecule then, consists of the sugar phosphate backbones connected by linked base pairs and the linkages must be A–T, T–A, G–C, or C–G. Although base pairing is governed by the above rules, the order in which these pairs of with bases is the principle of genetics and inheritance. The order of the base pairs comprises a blueprint or **genetic code** that determines many of the characteristics of a person. An apt analogy would be one's telephone number. Everyone has a ten-digit phone number but, in order to get your individual phone to ring, someone has to dial the digits in the correct sequence.

DNA in Cells

Most cells in the human body have a **nucleus**. This is where most of the cell's functions are controlled. Within the nucleus, the DNA is arranged into 46 structures called **chromosomes**. The chromosomes are arranged in 23 pairs. One member of each pair

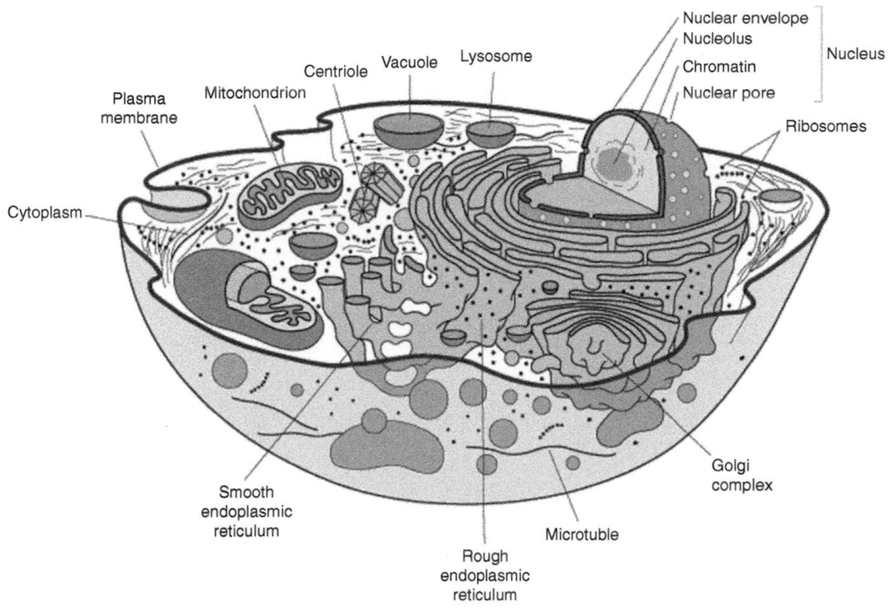

FIGURE 11.2

A cross-section of a human cell. The nucleus contains the genomic DNA. One of the mitochondria present in the cytoplasm is also shown.

of chromosomes comes from the father's sperm cells and the other member comes from the mother's egg cells. Male sperm contains 23 chromosomes and the female ovum (egg) also contains 23. When a sperm and an egg unite, the 23 chromosomes from the sperm and the egg pair up, forming the 46 found in every nucleated cell in the offspring. One of the 23 pairs of chromosomes determines the sex of the individual. For females, both chromosomes are of the "X" type. In males, one of the chromosomes is X and the other is Y. A cutaway diagram of a human cell is shown in Figure 11.2. Figure 11.3 shows a diagram of the 23 pairs of chromosomes.

GENES AND THE GENETIC CODE

There are billions of base pairs within the 46 chromosomes. Certain sections of these base pairs have special functions in inheritance and the development of an embryo after conception. These sections of chromosomes are called **genes**. The ordering of the base pairs in genes provides the chemical instructions to manufacture particular proteins. These genetic instructions are copied onto RNA (ribonucleic acid) that transmits this information to protein manufacturing sites in the cell. Each gene provides instructions for building a particular protein. Virtually all human characteristics (and those of other animals) are defined and controlled by genes. Sometimes a single gene determines a trait as in the case of certain blood types such as ABO (this describes

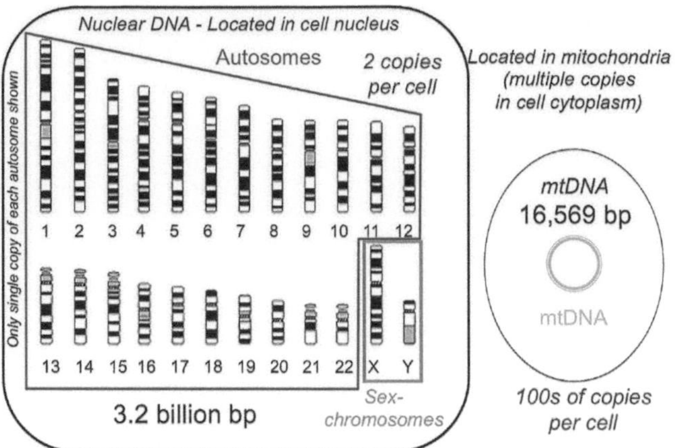

FIGURE 11.3

The human genome contained in every cell consists of 23 pairs of chromosomes and a small circular genome known as mitochondrial DNA. Chromosomes 1–22 are numbered according to their relative size and occur in single copy pairs within a cell's nucleus with one copy being inherited from one's mother and the other copy coming from one's father. Sex chromosomes are either X,Y for males or X,X for females. Mitochondrial DNA is inherited only from one's mother and is located in the mitochondria with hundreds of copies per cell. Together the nuclear DNA material amounts to over 3 billion base pairs (bp) while mitochondrial DNA is only about 16,569 bp in length.

Courtesy: The National Institute of Standards and Technology, 2010.

the presence of A or B antigens on red blood cells). In the case of some other characteristics such as hair color or eye color, several genes, acting in concert, determine the characteristics of the trait. At one time there were estimated to be up to 100,000 genes in a human being. Since the "Human Genome Project" was completed, it has been determined that there are only about 30,000 protein coding genes. It has also been shown by the Genome Project, however, that these 30,000+ genes are able to manufacture between 100,000 and 1 million proteins. The Human Genome Project has been a global effort to map the entire human genome. The ultimate goal of this project is to find all genes on all chromosomes and determine their functions.

VARIATIONS OF GENES: ALLELES

Genes that determine a person's characteristics are found in particular locations on the 46 chromosomes. Each individual has two copies of each gene. One copy comes from the person's father and the other copy comes from the mother. Some traits are determined by a single gene on one chromosome. Others, such as eye color, are determined by multiple genes at several locations. Simple observation of peoples' eyes indicates that there must be considerable variation in these genes. Some people have brown eyes, others have blue or green eyes, and many people have eye colors that are intermediate between two or more of these. A more basic example of how gene inheritance works to produce a particular characteristic is with the ABO blood type. There are four different blood types in this system: A, B, O, and AB. Everyone has one of these types and there is a single gene that determines which type will be inherited from each parent. If a person inherits the same form of a gene from the mother and the father, that person is said to be **homozygous** with respect to that gene. For example, if a person inherits the type A form of the ABO gene from the mother and from the father, the person is homozygous AA. If, on the other hand, the person receives different forms of the same gene (A and B), then that person is said to be **heterozygous**; he or she has different forms of the genes for ABO blood type, and he or she will be type AB. Each form of a particular gene at a particular locus in the genome is called an **allele**. Thus, the A and B antigens are each alleles. In addition, some alleles are **dominant**, while others are **recessive**. If a person receives a dominant allele from one parent and a recessive allele from the other, the dominant one will usually prevail and the person will exhibit that characteristic. If there are a large number of such alleles, then the potential exists for a great deal of variation among human beings at this location (locus). This situation provides the basis for a DNA profile wherein the variation of alleles at several loci can be combined to provide a statistical evaluation of the likelihood of a particular set of alleles in a given population.

What is meant by "different forms of an allele?" The observed characteristic expressed by the gene is called the **phenotype**. The observed blood type of a person is his or her phenotype. The alleles that make up that gene constitute the **genotype** of the person. For example, a person with the genotype "AB" (inheriting the A gene from one parent and the B gene from the other) would have the phenotype AB. In DNA analysis, loci that are polymorphic are purposely chosen. These loci exhibit variation among members of a population. The more the variation at a locus, the more discriminating the analysis will be. For example, in the ABO blood system, type A blood is present in about 42% of the Caucasian population, type O is present in about 43%, type B is about 10%, and type AB in about 5%. Thus the locus for ABO blood type does show polymorphism, but by itself is not very discriminating, since even the rarest form of the gene would still include 5% of individuals as being the source of a blood sample.

There are two types of variability in alleles. The first type is called **sequence polymorphisms**. An example is shown below. This type of sequence polymorphism is called a **single nucleotide polymorphism (SNP)**.

```
CTCGATTAAGG          CTCGGTTAAGG
:::::::::::    and   :::::::::::
GAGCTAATTCC          GAGCCAATTCC
    ↑                    ↑
```

The two sequences of double-stranded DNA are exactly the same except at the location indicated by the arrows.

The other type of variation in DNA is called **length polymorphism**. Consider the following variation in a part of Lincoln's Gettysburg Address:

Four Score and Seven Years Ago
Four Score and and Seven Years Ago

Four Score and and and and Seven Years Ago
Four Score and and and and and and Seven Years Ago

These phrases are all the same except for the "and," which repeats a different number of times in the various phrases. Now consider the length polymorphism that occurs in the short tandem repeat (STR) marker TH01 (T C A T or its complementary strand, A G T A). This four base repeating sequence is highly polymorphic. In the figure below, the sequence repeats twice:

```
T C A T - T C A T
: : : :   : : : :
A G T A - A G T A
```

The next figure shows the same sequence repeating four times:

```
T C A T - T C A T - T C A T - T C A T
: : : :   : : : :   : : : :   : : : :
A G T A - A G T A - A G T A - A G T A
```

The actual TH01 marker has between 3 and 14 repeats in the human genome.

Because the repeats are right next to each other, without any intervening base pairs, these are referred to as **tandem repeats**. When variation in the number of repeats occurs from one individual to the next, then this locus is described as having a **variable number of tandem repeats** (VNTR). A person's **DNA type** is a description of the type of alleles at all of the loci being analyzed on the genome.

POPULATION GENETICS

In Chapter 10 on serology, remember that the distribution of ABO blood types is about

Type A = 42%
Type O = 43%
Type B = 10%
Type AB = 5%

These population statistics are very important in the interpretation of serologic evidence. They add significance to conclusions about the association between biologic evidence between people. As we will see, the population statistics that can be derived from modern DNA typing have been determined accurately and thus, reliable, scientific associations between DNA evidence and a suspect, for example, can be made. Determination of the frequencies with which particular genetic markers occur in a given population is called **population genetics**. This branch of statistics can shed light on crucial questions that arise during the admission of biological evidence such as "If the DNA type of the evidence and the accused are the same, what are the chances (probabilities) that this is a coincidence—that someone else could have the same DNA type?" The answers to such questions permit the jury or judge to make meaningful conclusions about the role of this type of evidence in reaching decisions of guilt or innocence.

In forensic DNA analysis multiple loci are evaluated, giving rise to many degrees of association. Consider the situation where there are several alleles at a particular locus.

In DNA analysis today, the frequency of occurrence in the population can be determined for each allele. Now consider this situation at several loci. By determining which allele is present at each locus, the frequency of occurrence of all of these alleles can be determined by simply multiplying the frequency of occurrence of each one. This can be illustrated with the familiar coin toss routine. If a coin is tossed once, the probability (frequency of occurrence) for it coming up head is ½ since there are only two equally probable outcomes from one coin toss: head (H) or tail (T). If the coin is tossed twice, the probability of it coming up heads both times is ¼. This is because there are four possible outcomes from tossing a coin twice: H–H, T–T, H–T, and T–H. Only one of these outcomes results in heads coming up twice in a row (H–H). This probability can be determined by multiplying the probability of each toss: $\frac{1}{2} \times \frac{1}{2} = \frac{1}{4}$. Likewise the probability of getting three heads in a row is 1/8 ($\frac{1}{2} \times \frac{1}{2} \times \frac{1}{2}$). The technique of multiplying probabilities together is known as the **product rule**. The product rule for calculating the probabilities of multiple events can only be used when each event or condition is independent of all of the others. An honest coin has no tendency toward head or tail and has no memory of whether head or tail came up the last time it was tossed. Thus, each toss of the coin is independent of all others and the product rule can be used to determine the probability of each possible outcome of multiple tosses. As we will see later in this chapter, multiple pieces of data about a DNA type are determined during an analysis and the population statistics for each allele of each data point have been determined. In order to arrive at an overall DNA type by invoking the product rule, each data point (each allele present at each locus being studied) is independent of the other data points. The loci used in today's DNA typing methods have been extensively tested to check for independence. Using the product rule in such cases yields DNA types that are so rare that the chances of finding more than one person at random within a population who has the same DNA type is extremely small. This means that if DNA derived from biological evidence is of the same type as a suspect in the case, the probability of the evidentiary DNA arising from a different individual (other than an identical twin) is extremely remote.

DNA TYPING

The first DNA typing method to be widely adopted by forensic biologists in the analysis of crime is called **restriction fragment length polymorphism** (**RFLP**). It is not used any longer in forensic applications, having been supplanted by methods with higher powers of discrimination and whose results can be obtained faster using much less biologic material. RFLP was eventually supplanted by methods derived from the **polymerase chain reaction** (**PCR**), a technique that is used primarily to increase the amount of DNA by amplification. For a period of time, many forensic science laboratories used both RFLP and PCR methods in tandem. Today, most laboratories use a typing method known as **Short Tandem Repeats** (**STRs**), which combines some of the attributes of both PCR and RFLP. Since RFLP is no longer used in modern forensic DNA laboratories, it will be only briefly discussed for historic purposes. Methods based upon PCR technologies will be discussed in greater detail.

RESTRICTION FRAGMENT LENGTH POLYMORPHISM

In RFLP, DNA is extracted from biologic material and then **restriction enzymes** are used to isolate small fragments of DNA called **minisatellites** or **variable number tandem repeats (VNTRs)** using **restriction enzymes**. These VNTRs are length polymorphisms of 10–100 base pairs. In forensic analysis, 4–6 of these highly polymorphic loci are analyzed and the results enable forensic scientists to generate DNA profiles that permit a high degree of discrimination of DNA types.

How RFLP Works

The DNA sequences of the target VNTRs are known in advance. Specific restriction enzymes are chosen so that they will cut strands of DNA at specific base pair sequences that correspond to the ends of the target VNTRs. These regions are **hypervariable** in that they have a large number of alleles. In 1980, the first DNA polymorphism was discovered that was suitable for forensic purposes. It is a gene known as D14S1. Over the next few years, other hypervariable genetic markers were developed for RFLP. Some of the VNTRs are found only at one locus in the genome whereas other hypervariable regions can be found at several loci at the same time. These were called **multilocus** VNTRs. Because multilocus VNTRs are subject to problems in interpreting mixed samples and problems with limited or degraded DNA, RFLP typing in the United States predominately used single-locus VNTR analysis. In this more limited technique, the result consists of one or two bands of DNA fragments depending upon whether the subject is homozygous or heterozygous for that particular locus. Figure 11.4 shows single- and multilocus probes.

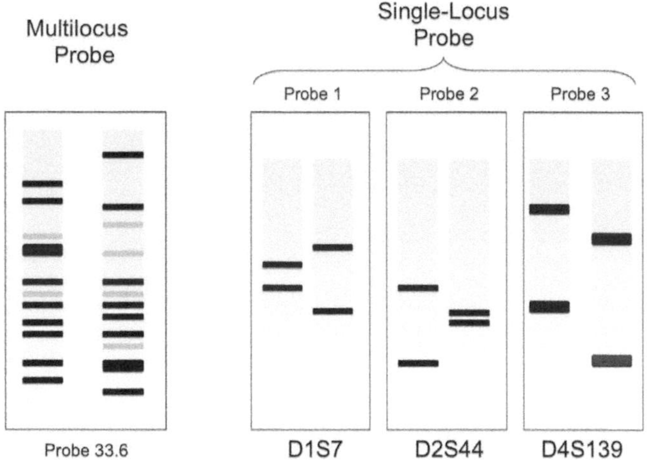

FIGURE 11.4

Illustration of patterns that might be seen with two DNA samples using multilocus versus single-locus VNTR probes. Multilocus probes produce a more complex pattern than the sequentially processed single-locus probes.

Courtesy: The National Institute of Standards and Technology, 2010.

Separation of VNTR Fragments

In Chapter 6—"Separation Methods," various methods of separating mixtures of substances were described. Recall that separation of biologic material often requires a high-resolution technique because the analyte components are so similar to each other that conventional chromatographic methods won't suffice. For this reason, electrophoresis is used for separation of DNA fragments. Recall that gel electrophoresis uses a slab of agarose gel to separate the different size DNA fragments by sieving them through pores in the gel. Each DNA sample is loaded into a well at one end of the gel slab. Other wells contain calibration standards known as **ladders**. Ladders are made up of pieces of DNA that cover the size range that spans the DNA fragments being analyzed. These ladders are used to help in ensuring that the process is working correctly and in determining the length of each of the VNTRs. Once the electrophoretic separation of the DNA fragments has taken place, the next step is to transfer them to a piece of nylon membrane because the gel slab is too fragile to be used for subsequent steps in the analysis. The technique used for this transfer is known as Southern Blotting, named after Dr Edward Southern, who developed the technique in the 1970s. The Southern Blotting technique is shown in the diagram in Figure 11.5.

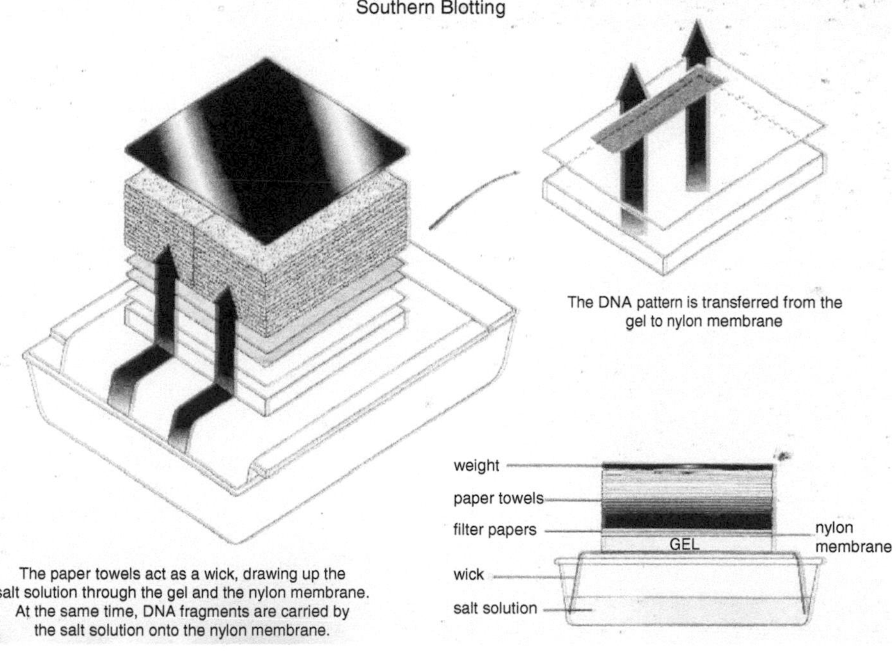

FIGURE 11.5

The Southern Blotting technique. The DNA fragments on the gel from the electrophoresis are transferred to a nylon membrane, which is more stable and easier to manipulate.

Visualization of VNTRs

Once the DNA has been transferred to the nylon membrane, a technique called **probe hybridization** is used to visualize the VNTRs. When RFLP was first developed for forensic use, short strands of DNA that are complementary to the core-repeating units of the VNTRs, were radioactively labeled. These short sequences of single-stranded DNA (probes) were given the opportunity to bind (hybridize) to complementary single-stranded sequence on the membrane.

When the membrane was brought in contact with photographic or X-ray film, the labeled fragments exposed the film, creating an autoradiogram or **autorad**. In recent years, radioactive labeling has given way to the use of chemiluminescence, whereby the probes are labeled with a chemical that will react with a chemiluminescent substrate to produce visual VNTRs. Figure 11.6 illustrates probe hybridization using a radioactive label.

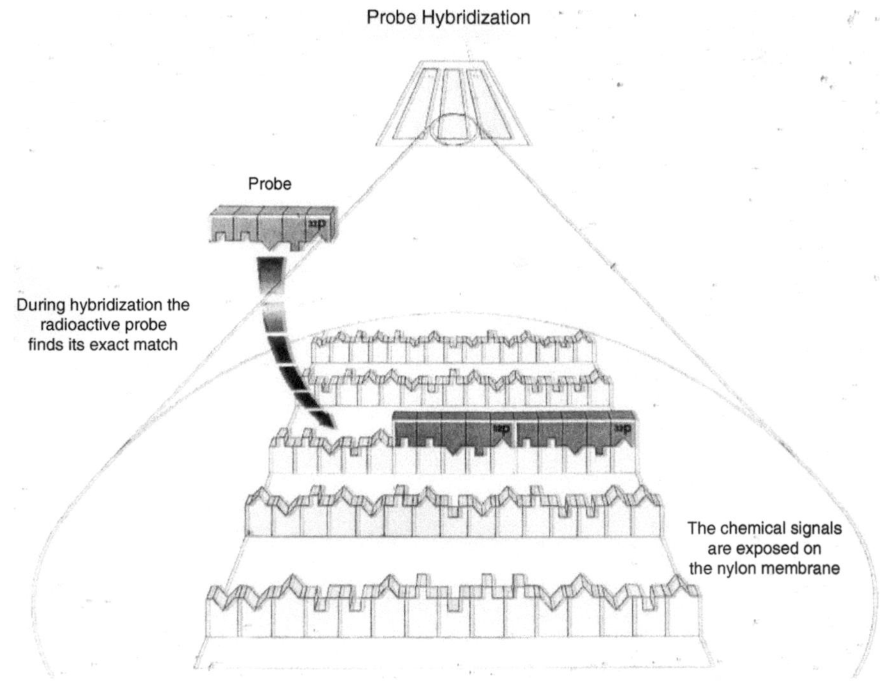

FIGURE 11.6

The probe hybridization process. After the DNA fragments have been separated, they are single–stranded. Special probes, short sequences of DNA that are complementary to the VNTR's are put onto the membrane and they will attach to their complementary sequences. These probes are labeled either radioactively or by chemiluminescence so that they can be easily visualized.

With the help of the calibration ladder, the lengths of each of the VNTRs can be determined. As RFLP was developed, the more number of VNTRs were isolated and analyzed and more data were collected that determined the population frequencies of occurrence of each band of each VNTR. One of the limitations of RFLP typing is that it is not possible to resolve a band into an exact VNTR length. A band consists of a small group of fragments whose lengths differ by a few base pairs. Thus, VNTR fragments cannot be viewed as discrete alleles. Because of this, scientists have been conservative in interpreting RFLP results. Instead of treating a fragment as a unique allele, they are put into bins of various sizes that take measurement errors into account. When an RFLP was run on a case and a match occurred between a known and unknown DNA sample, the probability that this match was a coincidence could be determined.

THE POLYMERASE CHAIN REACTION

Around the same time in the 1980s that RFLP was being developed for forensic use, another major advance was the development of forensic applications of the **polymerase chain reaction** (**PCR**). PCR had been used since the 1970s for making copies (amplifying) of DNA using polymerase enzymes. PCR overcame one of the major problems facing forensic biologists: RFLP methods of DNA typing required relatively large quantities of DNA. A bloodstain about the size of a dime was needed to ensure that there would be enough DNA to complete an RFLP analysis. Kary Mullis adopted PCR (see the box below) to amplify DNA fragments of forensic interest in an automated process. Later, polymorphic PCR products were themselves typed. The first marker to be amplified and used forensically was DQ α (now called DQA1).

HISTORY OF DNA TYPING: DR KARY MULLIS

In 1983 a biochemist, Dr Kary Mullis, developed a way to employ high temperatures to automate PCR for amplification of DNA fragments. He was awarded the *Nobel Prize* for his discovery in 1993. Mullis' idea was to develop a process by which DNA could be artificially multiplied through repeated cycles of heat and cold using an enzyme called DNA polymerase. DNA polymerase is a naturally occurring substance in all living organisms. Its function is to aid in the replication of DNA as a cell divides. During the cell division process, the double-stranded DNA unzips to become single-stranded. DNA polymerase acts by binding to each single strand and directs the formation of the complementary strand, thus making exact duplicates of the DNA. Originally, the DNA polymerase that Mullis used for the reaction was temperature sensitive and it would decompose at high temperatures that are needed to cause the DNA double helix to unzip. His big breakthrough came when he developed thermal cycling and employed polymerase that is found in organisms that live in or near geysers that can survive at temperatures well above those needed for PCR. Originally he employed DNA polymerase from a bacterium known as *Thermas acquaticus* (Taq). This is still widely used during the PCR replication process.

THE PCR PROCESS

PCR methods are very sensitive to contamination by foreign DNA. For this reason, DNA extractions are always done in a location physically isolated from the place where the subsequent amplifications will be performed. Once the scientist enters the amplification room with the extracted DNA, she will usually not leave until preparation of PCR reaction vials and placement in the thermal cycler is complete so as to minimize carrying foreign material into or out of the amplification environment.

The PCR process involves three steps. They all take place within a **thermal cycler**. This is essentially an apparatus capable of achieving and maintaining preset temperatures very precisely. The DNA samples are added to a reaction buffer, which is a salt solution that is buffered at the optimal pH for the polymerase enzyme. The four nucleotides (building blocks of DNA) are added to the mixture along with the polymerase enzyme that catalyzes the extension step. There are several DNA polymerases that can be employed. The most commonly used one in the United States is **Taq**. Under the control of a computer, the thermal cycler heats the vials up to predetermined temperatures for each step of the process (see below). These temperatures can be held for precise amounts of time and then quickly changed to the next level. Each set of temperatures constitutes a thermal cycle. The thermal cycler can be programmed to run through as many cycles as necessary for proper amplification. Figure 11.7 shows the temperature program of a DNA amplification.

The steps in the PCR reaction are:

1. **Denaturation**—The DNA is added to the PCR tube that contains the reaction mixture and is then heated to 94 °C. Under these conditions the double-stranded DNA denatures. The bonds between the base pairs that hold the strands together break, resulting in single-stranded DNA. As long as this temperature is maintained, the strands will remain apart. Each strand will be the template for the formation of a new piece of double-stranded DNA.
2. **Annealing**—The next step in the PCR process is to attach a short strand of synthetic DNA to each of the separated strands. These are called **primers** because they will mark the starting points for addition of new bases to complete the reproduction of each strand. The thermal cycler temperature drops to 60 °C for this step.
3. **Extension**—The temperature of the reaction is raised to 72 °C. Under the influence of Taq polymerase, single bases (**nucleotides**) are added to the primer, one-by-one. Each base is complementary to a single nucleotide present on the strand being duplicated. In this way the entire complementary strand is built up and a new piece of double-stranded DNA is produced. This process occurs at each of the complementary single strands created by the denaturation process, so the end result is that two identical pieces of double-stranded DNA are produced. This completes one PCR cycle. The temperature is raised once again to 94 °C and the process repeats.

The two strands of DNA denature and forms four single strands. These are, in turn, subjected to annealing and extension, forming four new double strands. The

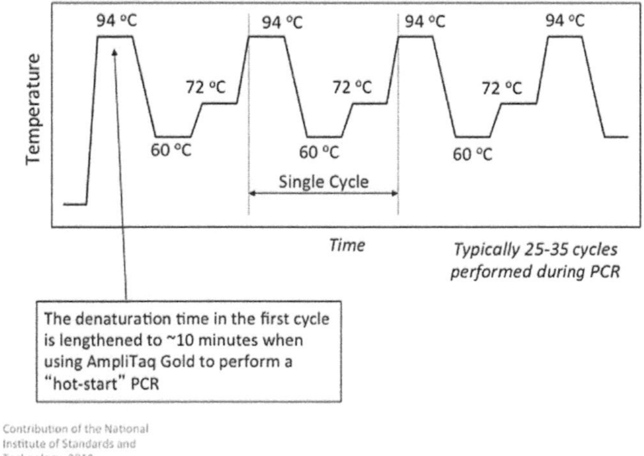

Contribution of the National Institute of Standards and Technology, 2010

FIGURE 11.7

Thermal cycling temperature profile for PCR. Thermal cycling typically involves three different temperatures that are repeated over and over again 28 to 32 times. At 94 °C, the DNA strands separate or "denature." At 60 °C, primers bind or "anneal" to the DNA template and target the region to be amplified. At 72 °C, the DNA polymerase extends the primers by copying the target region using the deoxynucleotide triphosphate building blocks. The entire PCR process is about 3 h in duration with each cycle taking ~5 min on conventional thermal cyclers: 1 min each at 94, 60, and 72 °C and about 2 min ramping between the three temperatures.

Courtesy: The National Institute of Standards and Technology, 2010.

process continues until a sufficient amount of DNA is produced, typically 28–32 cycles, which takes about 3 h. This produces about one billion copies of the original DNA, enough for additional typing. The steps in PCR are shown in Figure 11.8.

DNA Typing of PCR Product

After the amplification process is complete, the products must be detected. There are a number of ways to do this. Because so much product is made relative to that produced by RFLP, it is not necessary to employ very sensitive detection methods such as radioactive labeling. One can simply run a yield gel experiment on agarose and stain the product with ethidium bromide. The first DNA region that was widely subjected to amplification and typing for forensic purposes by PCR is the **HLA** (**Human Leukocyte Antigen**) **DQ alpha** (now called DQA1) gene. This gene exhibits sequence polymorphisms. DQ alpha and a number of other genes collectively called **polymarker** are typed using a method called **reverse dot blot**. This process involves identifying the particular alleles present by reacting them with color-forming reagents on specially treated nylon strips. Neither DQ alpha nor polymarker DNA typing are used in forensic science anymore. They have been largely supplanted by STRs. One reason for this is that the alleles in these markers do not vary to a great

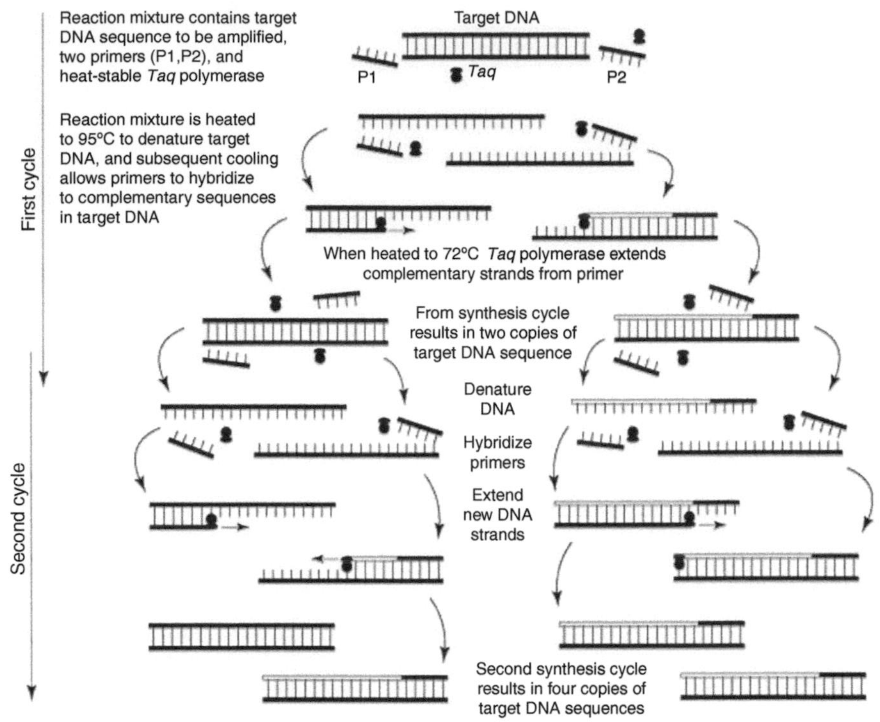

FIGURE 11.8

The PCR amplification process. Each cycle doubles the amount of DNA. Under ideal conditions, 30 cycles would produce over a billion copies. The process takes around 3 h.

extent in the human population. As a result, it is not possible to generate a DNA type that is rare enough to associate with just one individual. A more important reason is that this method of DNA typing is not capable of resolving multiple DNA types that are present in mixtures such as vaginal swabs obtained after a rape. A reverse dot blot of DQA1 is shown in Figure 11.9.

SHORT TANDEM REPEATS

Recall that the technique of RFLP involves the isolation of minisatellites of 10–100 base pair VNTRs. During the 1980s another type of repeating unit containing 2–6 base pairs was developed. These are designated as **microsatellites** and are called short tandem repeats (STRs). They have the same basic arrangement as VNTRs in that they contain repeating units of base pair sequences in tandem. STRs have certain advantages over VNTRs that make them attractive for forensic comparison purposes. STR markers exhibit high variability in a population, thus giving rise to high degrees of association of evidence with a suspect. The small size of the repeats makes STRs

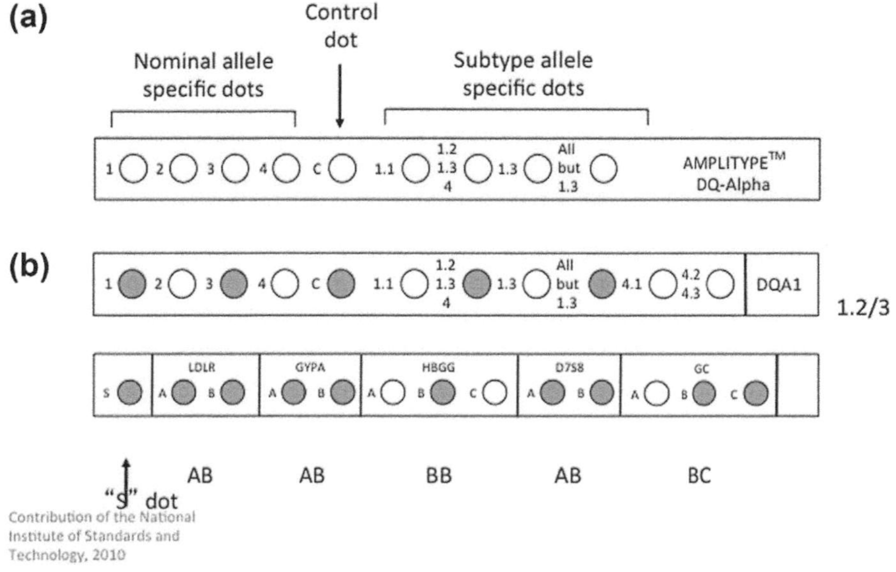

FIGURE 11.9

Reverse dot blot tests: (a) original AmpliType DQ alpha with nine probes to detect six alleles and (b) the AmpliType PM + DQA1 kit released a few years later with expanded DQA1 probes and the additional five PolyMarker loci. The control and "S" dot serve as positive controls to test that the sample is above the PCR stochastic threshold and allele dropout should not be an issue. In (b) the DQA1 and PolyMarker genotypes for the standard cell line 9948 are illustrated: 1.2/3, AB, AB, BB, AB, BC.

Courtesy: The National Institute of Standards and Technology, 2010.

much less sensitive to degradation of the DNA. Finally, there are many microsatellites to choose from for forensic purposes. Thousands of them have been identified and many are used for commercial and medical purposes.

In the intervening years since STR was developed for forensic purposes, a number of different loci have been suggested and kits containing the necessary materials have been commercialized. Finally, in 1996 an effort was led by the FBI to develop a standard database called **Combined DNA Index System (CODIS)**. This will be discussed later in the chapter. After more than a year of work, 13 loci were chosen for CODIS by consensus of the forensic DNA typing community. The 13 loci are designated by standard nomenclature used in genetics as follows: D3S1358, VWA, FGA, D8S1179, D21S11, D18S51, D5S818, D13S317, D7S820, D16S539, THO1, TPOX, and CSF1PO. In recent years, this suite of loci has been expanded to the current 15 with the addition of Penta E and Penta D. All of these use four base pair repeats. In addition, the gender of the subject is determined by analyzing the Amelogenin locus, which indicates the presence of the X and Y chromosomes. This is explained in the section below "Gender Identification." Figure 11.10 shows a capillary electropherogram of a DNA typing of all 15 loci and Amelogenin.

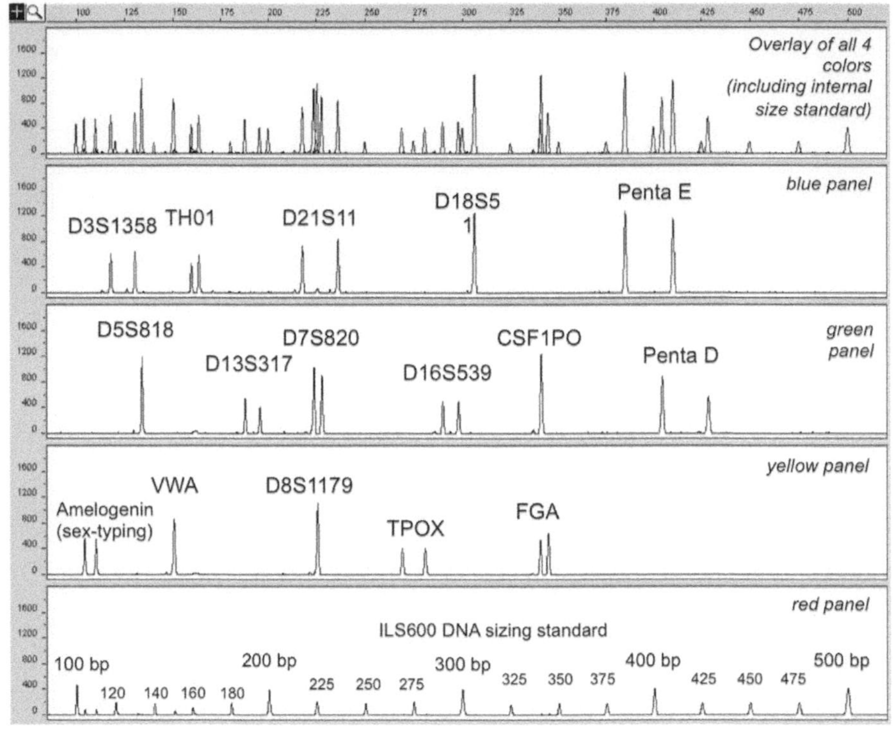

FIGURE 11.10

PowerPlex 16 result from 1 ng genomic DNA.

Courtesy: The National Institute of Standards and Technology, 2010.

The DNA is amplified at these loci by the PCR. Primers are chosen so that they will anneal with DNA just outside each side of the STR. Separation was done initially by using gel electrophoresis. Modern practice usually employs capillary electrophoresis using a capillary filled with a polymer similar to polyacrylamide. The DNA is detected by means of laser-induced fluorescence. The alleles are divided into four or five groups (depending upon the system used). Each group is labeled with a different colored fluorescent dye. The dyes are then detected by a UV/visible detector. The result is one or two peaks (homozygous or heterozygous) for each locus. Chapter 6 has an explanation of the workings of capillary electrophoresis. **Allelic ladders**, which are strands of DNA made up of all common alleles present at each STR locus, are used for calibration, thus enabling the computer to estimate the size of the alleles at each locus. As in other DNA typing methods, the population frequency ranges for each allele at each locus have been previously determined and, using the product rule, population frequencies for the entire genotype can be estimated. This means that the probability of having any given DNA type from all of the loci is extremely small; on the order of one in several billion or even trillion. When one considers that the population of the United States is about 260 million people, the chances of any two of them selected at random, having the same exact DNA type at all of the loci is extremely remote. Around 1998, the FBI laboratory made a policy decision to count as individualized, any DNA type whose odds of a chance occurrence exceeded 1000 times the US population (or about 260 billion to one). Today, virtually all DNA types exceed this threshold. It should be pointed out that the concept of individualization as it is commonly meant does not apply to DNA typing. First, all DNA associations are expressed as probabilities of a chance occurrence. This means that there is always a chance, however improbable, that there will be another individual with the same DNA as the subject. Second, identical twins have the same DNA; at least insofar as forensic DNA methods are concerned. Finally, it should be noted that extreme care should be taken when evaluating such statistics of rare occurrences. For example, in a room of 50 people, the chances that two have the same month and day of birth date is more than 37%. Most people believe that it would be rare for two people out of 50 to have the same birth date given that there are 366 possibilities. As long as the forensic biologist is able to put the statistics generated by an STR analysis in proper context, the jury should not be misled.

GENDER IDENTIFICATION

There are two approaches to gender identification using DNA typing. On each of the sex determination chromosomes, there is a locus called **Amelogenin**. One of the regions of this locus is six-base-pairs longer in males than in females. Females have two X chromosomes and will thus show only one band for Amelogenin. Males have one X and one Y chromosome and will thus show two bands, one six-base-pairs longer than the other. This locus is not an STR but can be analyzed at the same time as STR and is printed out on the electropherogram with the results of the analysis of the 13 STR loci. The other approach to gender ID utilizes Y-STRs. The Y chromosome, found only in males, also contains STRs. These can be typed even on small or degraded samples or mixtures with large quantities of female DNA. Y-STRs are quite useful when typing mixed samples that contain sperm and are thus guaranteed to have a male fraction. It should be noted, however, that Y-chromosome analysis produces only a haplotype (a trait inherited from only one parent) and is thus not as informative as common STR analysis.

MITOCHONDRIAL DNA

Mitochondria are small structures located within practically all animal and plant cells (human red blood cells being one of the exceptions). They function as energy mediators of the cell. They take energy released by metabolism of sugars, fats, and proteins and store it in energetic molecules such as adenosine triphosphate (ATP) where it can be used to drive virtually all cell processes. Each cell in a human being contains hundreds or thousands of mitochondria. There are a number of differences between mtDNA and genomic DNA. The more important ones are listed below.

1. mtDNA is circular in shape, containing 26,569 base pairs and codes for 37 genes.
2. Cells contain many mitochondria and each one has up to 10 copies of mtDNA. Thus, each cell contains hundreds or thousands of copies of mtDNA, whereas there are only two copies of nuclear (genomic) DNA.
3. mtDNA contains a noncoding region of 1100 base pairs that, in turn, contains two hypervariable regions. These regions exhibit a high mutation rate so that over a period of many generations, sequence variations can occur at these sites. As a result, these regions can be quite useful in comparing known and questioned DNA samples.
4. All male and female mtDNA comes from the mother. There is no mtDNA from one's father. This means that, except for the mutations mentioned above, every descendent of a woman should have the same mtDNA. This makes mtDNA very powerful for tracing family lines back through the maternal side.
5. mtDNA often shows a high degree of variation between unrelated people, making it a powerful tool in forensic typing, however, because there are only two hypervariable regions in mtDNA, the population statistics are not nearly as discriminating as with nuclear DNA.
6. Because of the large number of copies per cell, mtDNA can be useful in typing samples that have low quantities of DNA or in exhibits that are degraded or very old.

Figure 11.11 shows the arrangement of mtDNA.

Many forensic science laboratories that perform genomic DNA analysis do not perform mtDNA analysis. Those that do mtDNA analysis generally use DNA sequencing; they determine the entire base pair sequence in the two hypervariable regions, rather than relying on length polymorphism.

COMPARISON OF DNA SAMPLES

The goal of all forensic analysis is to associate a piece of evidence with as few people or objects as possible and ideally for there to be only one possible source. For evidence in general, there is no scientific basis for a conclusion of individuality and the very concept may not have a true meaning when referring to comparing evidence to its possible source. DNA typing as practiced today is unique among all physical evidence in that valid, rigorous scientific testing has been done that validates the concepts and testing methodologies for human DNA typing. Likewise, valid scientifically determined statistical frequencies for the alleles at the loci that are used in DNA typing have also been calculated. Once the particular allele(s) are identified at each locus, genotype frequencies and the product rule are used to determine the overall frequency of the DNA profile. If the DNA types of

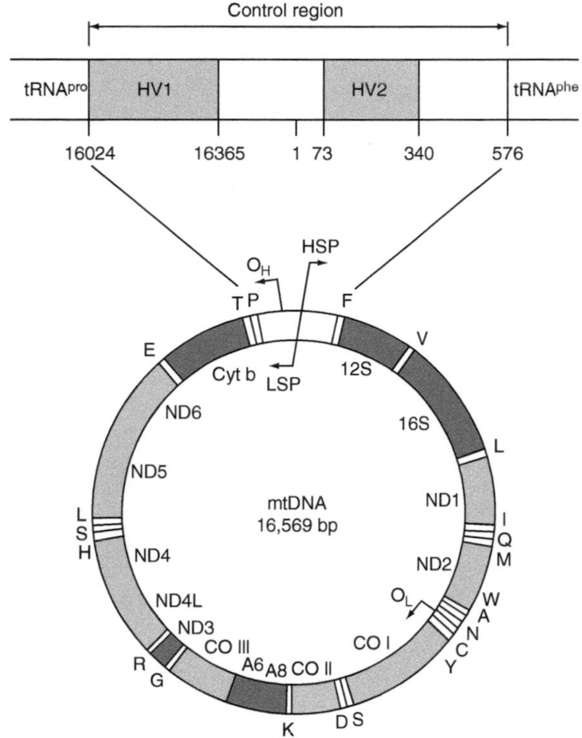

FIGURE 11.11

Mitochondrial DNA (mtDNA) is circular and contains 16,569 base pairs. The white region at the top of the figure contains the two hypervariable loci, HV1 and HV2. These are used to generate mtDNA profiles.

the evidence and of a suspect (or victim or other person of interest), then the odds that this is a coincidence can be computed. The term commonly used to express this comparison is **match**. The DNA in the biological evidence found at the crime scene is said to have "matched" the DNA from the suspect. But the term "match" may not be understood by a jury in the same way it is by scientists. Scientists define match to mean that there are no significant or unexplainable differences between the known and unknown materials. Thus the term "match" is used to describe the relationship between two fingerprints or shoeprints. In DNA typing, not all of the evidence is examined. The methods used for DNA typing today look at only small, select parts of the DNA.

It is possible that, if an exact "match" between two samples for all of the loci tested is achieved, then further examination of additional loci might reveal differences. For this reason, the term "match" should not be used to describe the relationship between two samples of DNA. Scientists instead use the term **genetic concordance**.

ESTIMATION OF POPULATION FREQUENCIES

The population frequency for an allele is the number of times that it appears divided by the total number of alleles in a given population. For example, if an allele occurs four times in a population of 1 million, then the population frequency for that allele would be 1/500,000 (remember that human chromosomes are diploid—there are two copies, one from each parent). Determining a population frequency at one locus is usually pretty straightforward. Large numbers of people are tested and the number of times each allele appears in that population is determined. It may take a large number of people in the database to have all of the alleles represented at a locus, especially if some are very rare. Determining a population frequency for an entire DNA profile is not so simple, especially if a large number of loci are being analyzed and the number of alleles at a given loci is large. Under these conditions, a particular DNA profile may never show up in a database even if the number of people tested is large. It would then not be possible to determine the population frequency of that profile. In order to get population frequencies in such situations, estimates are made. Population frequencies of genotypes made up of multiple loci can be calculated by taking product of the population frequencies of each individual locus.

Table 11.1 is an actual example of the calculation of population frequency for a DNA profile using 13 loci.

INTERPRETATION OF DNA TYPING RESULTS: PURITY ISSUES

If biological material from a crime scene is relatively clean, fresh, nondegraded, and from only one individual, then interpretation of the results of DNA typing will usually be straightforward. The majority of problems occur when the DNA is compromised in some way. A few of the more common situations are given below:

CONTAMINATION

If care is not used in DNA extractions and typing, then biologic material from an extraneous source, such as the evidence technician, scientist, or laboratory technician, can be introduced accidentally. This can be a serious problem, especially with PCR-based methods, because the DNA from the contamination may also be amplified and can overwhelm the DNA from the sample. In most cases, sufficient biological material is present to provide enough DNA so that the problem occurs only rarely; however, there has been an increase in recent years because of the smaller amounts of biologic material needed to determine a DNA type. Forensic biology laboratories take extraordinary steps and precautions to minimize contamination and detect it if it occurs. For example, DNA extraction is performed in a completely different environment than amplification.

Table 11.1 Match Statistic for a Random African-American Individual Typed at 13 CODIS Loci

Locus	Genotype	Allele Frequencies	Match Statistic
CSF1PO	10, 12	0.257; 0.298	0.153
D13S317	11, 11	0.306	0.09036
D16S539	11, 12	0.318; 0.096	0.125
D18S51	14, 18	0.072; 0.123	0.0177
D21S11	27, 37	0.078; 0.002	0.000831
D3S1358	15, 17	0.302; 0.205	0.123
D5S818	8, 12	0.048; 0.353	0.0338
D7S820	8, 10	0.236; 0.331	0.156
D8S1179	12, 12	0.141	0.0199
FGA	22, 22	0.196	0.0384
THO1	6, 9	0.124; 0.151	0.0374
TPOX	10, 11	0.089; 0.219	0.0389
vWA	15, 16	0.236; 0.269	0.127

Random Match Statistic: 2.327×10^{-18} or one person in 427,800,000,000,000,000 chosen at random from the black population would be expected to match by chance.
The first column is the locus where the STR is found. The second column (genotype) is the particular alleles that the particular individual possesses. Note that he/she is heterozygous at 10 loci and homozygous at D13S317, D8S1179, and FGA. The third column (allele frequencies) contains the allele frequencies for each allele. For example, in CSF1P0, the 10 allele is found in 257 out of every 1000 people in the black population. The fourth column (match statistic) is two times the product of the allele frequencies when the locus is heterozygous and the square of the allele frequency in homozygous cases. To find the random match statistic, all 13 match statistics are multiplied (rule of multiplication). The final number, just of 7 septillion, is astronomic. As a point of reference, it is estimated that there have been no more than 100 billion (100,000,000,000) people that have ever lived on earth. Note: The National Research Council specifies that corrections in frequency calculations be made in cases where the genotype is homozygous at a given locus.
Courtesy: Orchid Genescreen, East Lansing, Michigan.

DEGRADATION

DNA is a remarkably stable substance but it can degrade from a number of causes. These include strong ultraviolet light around 260 nm, humidity, strongly acidic conditions, and oxidizing agents such as strong bleaches and hydrogen peroxide. When DNA degrades, long strands may become fragmented. This fragmentation process is exacerbated by exposure to extreme conditions for longer time periods. The RFLP technique is particularly sensitive to degradation. Successful RFLP analysis requires long intact strands of DNA. Degradation may break up the DNA into pieces that are too small for RFLP. STR analysis is better adapted to degraded DNA and in fact, STR was developed with this problem in mind.

DNA DATABASE: THE FBI CODIS SYSTEM

The **CODIS** is a set of local, state, and national databases of DNA profiles. CODIS consists of three sets of databases. There is the national NDIS administered by the FBI. It began as a pilot project in 1990. There are also state CODIS systems (SDIS) that regularly contribute data to CODIS and they contain many thousands of DNA profiles. For an up-to-date list of participating states, see http://www.fbi.gov/hq/lab/codis/partstates.htm. Many large cities also have local databases (LDIS). All profiles originate at the local level. These are then fed into the state-level database. Finally, the states input their data into the national-level database. This allows a crime laboratory to search the database at whatever level is necessary for that particular case. Only crime laboratories which are ISO- or ASCLD-accredited may have access to the CODIS databases. This has caused some consternation among academic researchers and others who would be interested in mining data from these databases.

The CODIS system consists of types of three databases categorized by the type of information they contain. The first contains DNA profiles that are obtained from crime scenes (the forensic database). In most cases, the source of this DNA is not known. The second database consists of profiles of criminal offenders and sometimes even those arrested for felonies and misdemeanors. Different states have different criteria for what DNA types will be contributed. If a crime occurs where DNA evidence is generated such as the sexual assault described in the case at the beginning of the chapter, CODIS may be searched to see if the offender's DNA is on file or if the DNA recovered from the scene is also found at another scene, indicating possibly that a serial criminal is at large. The third and most recent database in CODIS is that of missing persons. Efforts are being made to make this database as inclusive as possible nationwide so as to maximize the chances of identifying a missing person who may have crossed state lines.

There are three levels to the CODIS database system. They are the local, state, and national levels. This arrangement increases efficiency in database searches in that one need only search at the appropriate level and thus not consume unnecessary resources. Figure 11.12 is a diagram of how the levels of the CODIS system are arranged.

CODIS SUCCESS STORIES

Following are just a few of the hundreds of success stories of crimes that have been solved, at least in part, by the CODIS Database system. Many of these cases are "cold"; they have been investigated until there are no more leads and then they are shelved until a useful lead arises. Sometimes this takes years.

Richmond Virginia, July 1998

A rape and homicide had baffled the police since the body was discovered in 1994. Although the police had samples of blood and semen found in the victim's apartment, they were unable to develop a solid suspect in the case. A recent routine computer search on the state's DNA database identified a

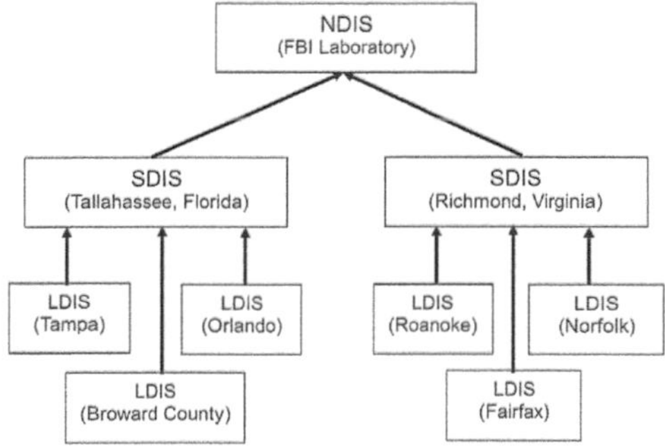

FIGURE 11.12

Schematic of the three tiers in the Combined DNA Index System (CODIS). DNA profile information begins at the local level, or Local DNA Index System (LDIS), and then can be uploaded to the state level, or State DNA Index System (SDIS), and finally to the national level, or National DNA Index System (NDIS). Each local or state laboratory maintains its portion of CODIS while the FBI laboratory maintains the national portion (NDIS).

Courtesy: The National Institute of Standards and Technology, 2010.

suspect in the case. A 20-year-old convicted offender, already serving a sentence for a different rape and murder, was arrested for the 1994 crime.

Oklahoma City, Oklahoma, February 1997

In 1992, five women were bound, gagged, and stabbed in a reported drug house in Oklahoma City. The Oklahoma State Bureau of Investigation developed a DNA profile for the killer in 1995, based on evidence at the crime scene. The California Department of Justice used CODIS to match the evidence profile against Danny Keith Hooks, who was convicted of rape, kidnapping, and assault in California in 1998.

Tallahassee, Florida, February 1995

The Florida Department of Law Enforcement linked semen found on a Jane Doe rape–homicide victim to a convicted offender's DNA profile. The suspect's DNA was collected, analyzed, and stored in the CODIS database while he was incarcerated for another rape. The match was timely; it prevented the suspect/offender's release on parole scheduled eight days later.

St Paul, Minnesota, November 1994

A man wearing a nylon stocking over his face and armed with a knife jumped out from behind bushes and forced a woman who was walking by to perform oral sex. Semen recovered from the victim's short skirt and saliva was analyzed using DNA technology. The resulting profile was searched against Minnesota's CODIS database. The search identified Terry Lee Anderson, who confessed to the crime and is now in prison (http://www.fbi.gov/hq/lab/codis/index1.htm).

DNA CASE BACKLOG

The success of DNA typing and the CODIS database has resulted in nearly all states passing laws that require some or all people arrested for crimes to be DNA typed and the data stored in CODIS. Most of the time, these laws do not make provision for hiring additional DNA analysts or building more facilities to handle this large caseload. In most cases, the so-called CODIS samples greatly outnumber criminal DNA evidence and cause huge backlogs in many forensic science laboratory systems. Dr Joseph Peterson of the California State University at Los Angeles conducts a census and survey of publically funded crime laboratories every three years. The latest year for which data is complete is 2005. At that time, the nationwide backlog in DNA cases represented less than 10% of all requests that were backlogged. At the beginning of 2005, a typical laboratory had 86 backlogged requests for DNA analysis. At the end of that year, the backlog was 152 cases. The total number of backlogged cases in 2005 of all types was over 435,000. For DNA, the number was about 40,000. This data, however, does not tell the whole story. In 2005, California law mandated a widening of the types of offences for which people arrested or convicted would have to supply DNA. As a result, there were more than 235,000 database DNA samples backlogged at the end of 2005 in California alone. In some states, separate CODIS laboratories are being created; in others, CODIS samples are being sent to private laboratories at considerable expense. There is little question that the number of database and case samples will continue to increase as more laboratories bring DNA typing online and more states mandate DNA collection and processing for CODIS for additional arrests and convictions.

DNA ANALYSIS AT WORK: THE INNOCENCE PROJECT

In 1992, Barry Scheck and Peter Neufeld established the Innocence Project at Benjamin Cordoza School of Law in New York. According to the Mission Statement of the Innocence Project (http://www.innocenceproject.org/about/Mission-Statement.php), "it was established to assist prisoners who could be proven innocent through DNA testing." To date, "more than 300 people in the United States have been exonerated by DNA testing, including more than 20 who served time on death row. These people served an average of 12 years in prison before exoneration and release." The cases of wrongful convictions in Illinois caused the governor to suspend the death penalty there and the suspension remains in force today. The Innocence Project has a network of more than 40 law schools that participate by using full-time staff attorneys and law students to provide assistance to these cases. These cases, which include murder, rape, and other violent crimes, were all tried before DNA typing was available in that jurisdiction. The biological evidence is reanalyzed by modern DNA typing methods and, if the testing shows that the prisoner was not the source of the DNA, motions are made for *habeas corpus* release and/or a new hearing or trial. Researchers with the Innocence Project claim that faulty forensic testing or testimony is implicated in more than half of the wrongful conviction cases investigated. Some forensic scientists dispute these claims and counter that ineffective counsel is more to blame than Innocence Project statistics show. Regardless, there is no doubt that the Innocence Project has had a profound effect on the criminal justice system in the United States and will continue to do so. As the Illinois experience with the death penalty illustrates, these effects will go beyond the individual wrongful convictions and exonerations.

BACK TO THE CASE

The exoneration case described at the beginning of the chapter is illustrative of more than 300 cases where innocence projects and their offspring throughout the country have orchestrated reversals of guilty pleas and verdicts, resulting in the release of prisoners who have served decades in prison in some cases. Many of these people were on death row awaiting execution when DNA evidence from the crime showed that they were not guilty. In a disturbing number of these cases, the defendants were convicted based in large part to either a coerced confession or a misidentification by the victim (in the cases of sexual assaults or other violent crimes where the victim survived). Such cases have called into question the practice of relying on victim identifications without sufficient corroborative evidence, especially physical evidence. In many jurisdictions today, victim identifications and eyewitness identifications are not used by themselves for convictions. Coerced confessions are also problematic because they illustrate the practice of overzealous police and prosecutorial pursuit of a suspect without sufficient checks and balances. It is also interesting to note that in the past decade or so, DNA typing has become routine practice in criminal investigations where there is biologic evidence available. This, by itself, should decrease the instances of faulty convictions because the biologic evidence will include or exclude the suspect on the front end of the case. Also, many jurisdictions now have a policy of retaining biologic evidence until there is no longer any judicial need for it. It is also interesting to note that there is a strong trend in the United States and in other countries to require increased numbers of people have their DNA typed for inclusion in the CODIS databases. In some locations, these include everyone convicted of any crime. In others, all arrestees are typed. The results have shown that this policy has increased clearance rates of crimes, especially those where one person is responsible for many crimes across a large geographic area.

SUMMARY

Each individual has billions of cells that contain a nucleus. Within the nucleus is genetic material arranged in 23 pairs of chromosomes. These contain the polymeric molecule, DNA, that is responsible for genetic inheritance of all characteristics of the person. The DNA molecule is arranged in the form of a double helix containing base pairs linked to a chemical backbone. There are approximately 3 billion base pairs in the human genome and less than one percent differ from person to person. DNA typing methods utilize these differences in DNA to help identify people from biological evidence. The first method that was used commercially for DNA typing was RFLP. This method isolates certain regions of DNA that are made up of core base pair sequences that are characterized by repeating a different number of times throughout the human population. The RFLP process isolates these sequences by the use of restriction enzymes and separates them by gel electrophoresis. They are visualized by radio-labeling or chemiluminescence.

Modern methods of DNA typing rely on the PCR. Using enzymes, nucleotides, and DNA primers, sequences of DNA can be replicated automatically using a thermal cycler. The standard method for DNA analysis today exploits some of the thousands of STRs. These are 4 base pair polymorphic repeating sequences. The STRs are fluorescently labeled and separated by capillary electrophoresis. Currently 15 loci are being typed for forensic purposes. Reliable population statistics have been developed for the various alleles of each of the 15 STRs. Since the DNA types at all 15 loci have been shown to be independent, the product rule can be used to calculate the probability of a chance occurrence of a given DNA profile within a chosen population. Each multilocus genotype derived from the 15 loci being used today is so rare that it is improbable that two people in the world would have the same exact type. This has resulted in forensic biology laboratories to conclude in STR cases, that a match of the DNA type of the evidence and the suspect (or other person of interest) is essentially an identification, except in the case of identical twins.

Under the auspices of the FBI, a three-tiered (local, state, and national) CODIS database has been created that contains nearly 10 million DNA profiles. Starting at the local LDIS database, any accredited forensic science laboratory can mount a CODIS search to see if a DNA sample recovered from a crime matches an entry in the database. This has resulted in hundreds of hits, some of which have come in cold cases that have been open for many years.

The ability to test biologic evidence for DNA years after it was collected (as long as it has been properly preserved) has given rise to the Innocence Project that uses DNA typing to reexamine criminal convictions where the case was originally adjudicated without the benefit of DNA typing. In more than 300 instances, prisoners have been exonerated by postconviction DNA typing.

mtDNA is present in all cells. There are two hypervariable regions in mtDNA. Unlike nuclear DNA which has only one copy per cell, there are hundreds of copies of mtDNA in each cell. All mtDNA comes from the mother and each person has the same DNA as his or her mother. mtDNA is useful for typing old, degraded samples and in cases where nuclear DNA may not be present such as in old bones, hairs with no root, teeth, etc.

TEST YOUR KNOWLEDGE

1. What are the four bases that make up human DNA?
2. What is a gene?
3. What is an allele?
4. List three ways that mitochondrial DNA differs from genomic DNA?
5. What is a restriction enzyme? In what kind of DNA typing is it used?
6. What are some of the advantages of DNA typing over other methods for identifying a person, such as fingerprints?
7. In one of the early DNA typing cases in England (Colin Pitchfork), the police went to all males in a town to collect DNA samples to be tested against crime scene evidence. What are the problems with such an approach?
8. What does PCR stand for? For what purpose was it developed?
9. What is an STR? Why has it become the method of choice for forensic DNA typing?
10. What is the importance of Amelogenin?
11. What is polymarker? How is it typed?
12. What is a reverse dot blot? How is it used in DNA typing?

13. Of the DNA testing methods you have learnt about in this chapter, which one has the potential of generating a profile that can be considered to be unique? How is this possible?
14. What types of electrophoresis are used for the separation of DNA fragments in STR analysis?
15. What is Taq polymerase? How is it used in DNA typing?
16. What are the advantages and disadvantages of mtDNA typing compared to genomic DNA analysis?
17. What is length polymorphism? Give an example?
18. What is sequence polymorphism? Give an example?
19. What does heterozygous mean in DNA? Give an example?
20. What are the two ways that VNTRs can be visualized?

CONSIDER THIS...

1. Forensic DNA typing has evolved over time by developing analytical methods for smaller and smaller fragments that, at the same time, are increasingly variable in the human population. At this time, the standard STR method in the United States uses 15 loci for comparing DNA. Yet there are systems that use 16 or 17 loci. Since present methods permit a conclusion that a DNA exhibit can be individualized to a person, what are the advantages, if any of going on to ever increasing numbers of loci? Is this continued development cost-effective? What is the logical end for this process?
2. What are the common objections to the use of DNA databases such as CODIS? Are these rational objections at this time? Do they have the potential of being serious problems in the future? What protections can be put into place to minimize objections?
3. Techniques such as capillary electrophoresis do not have infinite resolution and there may arise questions about whether a peak really represents just a single base pair segment. How do we know, for example, that a peak is 29 or 30 base pairs? How is this problem, if it is one, handled in case work? Remember that any assumptions should favor the accused.

FURTHER READING

Butler, J.M., 2010. Fundamental of Forensic DNA Typing. Academic Press, Boston.

Farley, M.A., Harrington, J.J. (Eds.), 1991. Forensic DNA Technology. Lewis Publishers, Chelsea, MI.

Rudin, N., Inman, K., 2002. An Introduction to Forensic DNA Analysis, second ed. CRC Press, Boca Raton, FL.

Waye, J.S., Fourney, R.M., 1993. Forensic DNA typing of highly polymorphic VNTR loci. In: Saferstein, R. (Ed.), Forensic Science Handbook, vol. III. Prentice-Hall, Englewood Cliffs, NJ.

ON THE WEB

http://www.ornl.gov/sci/techresources/Human_Genome/elsi/forensics.shtml, Homepage of the Human Genome Project.

http://74.125.47.132/search?q=cache:6srimOgaLqwJ:www.cstl.nist.gov/strbase/ppt/intro.pdf+dna+typing&cd=4&hl=en&ct=clnk&gl=us, History of DNA typing.

http://dna-trace-analysis.suite101.com/article.cfm/forensic_dna, Good overview of DNA methodologies.

http://www.fbi.gov/congress/congress01/dwight061201.htm, The FBI DNA program.

http://www.fbi.gov/hq/lab/html/codis1.htm, CODIS system.

CHAPTER

Forensic Hair Examinations

12

CHAPTER OUTLINE

KEY TERMS

- Anagen
- Buckling
- Catagen
- Club root
- Cortex
- Cortical fusi
- Cortical or medullary disruptions
- Cuticle
- Epidermis
- Eumelanin
- Follicle
- Fur hairs
- Fusiform
- Guard hairs
- Hairs
- Imbricate

- Keratin
- Keratinization
- Melanin
- Melanocytes
- Monilethrix
- Ovoid bodies
- Pheomelanin
- Pigment
- Pigment granules
- Pili annulati
- Pili arrector
- Pili torti
- Root
- Root bulb
- Scale cast
- Scale patterns
- Scales
- Sebaceous glands
- Shaft
- Shield
- Shouldering
- Sub-shield stricture
- Telogen phase
- Tip
- Transitional body hairs
- Vibrissa

THE CASE: ARE HAIRS JUNK SCIENCE?

Santae Tribble, Kirk L. Odom, and Donald Gates are now free because DNA analysis refuted the results offered by FBI hair examiners that crime scene hairs could have come from the men in question. Thousands of other cases – including many on death row – await review in what is now the U.S. government's largest post-conviction review of forensic evidence. Some examiners testified beyond the limits of good practice ('high degree of probability') but even those that explained their results properly have to face the fact that their results were wrong as to the source of the hairs. The larger issue remains: How does the criminal justice system address weaknesses in past forensic testimony and methods without damning methods that were considered acceptable at the time? For example, if blood typing (like ABO) includes a person but DNA excludes them, was the blood typing wrong? Technically, because the person's blood type is, in fact, A or B or O, the answer is correct as far as it goes; blood types cover only certain percentages of the population and the

THE CASE: ARE HAIRS JUNK SCIENCE?—cont'd

individual is in that group. But the blood typing is wrong as to the *source* of the blood and that leads to the concept of resolution. Some methods (like DNA) are more specific than others (like blood typing) and even methods within a category are more specific than other similar methods (nuclear DNA is more specific than mitochondrial DNA (mtDNA), for example).

The questions revolve around two issues: What is the resolution of hair examinations and how can that specificity be communicated to others?

Source: *Hsu, S., July 29, 2014. Federal Review Stalled after Finding Forensic Errors by FBI Unit Spanned Two Decades. The Washington Post.*

INTRODUCTION

One of the most often recovered types of evidence is also one of the most misunderstood. Hairs make good forensic evidence because they are sturdy and can survive for many years, they carry a lot of biological information, and they are easy and cost-effective to examine. DNA can also be extracted from hairs, and this adds to their forensic utility. Nonhuman or animal hairs are also potentially useful evidence, given the number of domestic animals kept as pets. With over 150 dog breeds and nearly 100 cat breeds—not to mention 'mutts' or mixed breeds—animal hair can be quite diagnostic of an environment, like a house. As we will see, hairs can offer strong investigative and adjudicative information, but only when examined properly, reported on conservatively, and testified to accurately.

GROWTH OF HAIRS

Hairs are a particular structure common only to mammals; they are the fibrous growths that originate from their skin. Other animals have structures that may appear to be or are even called hairs but they are not: Only mammals have hairs (see Figure 12.1). Humans use hairs as signs of culture, status, and gender, as well as for personal or artistic expression.

Hairs grow from the skin or, more precisely, **epidermis**, of the body, as shown in Figure 12.2. The **follicle** is the structure within which hairs grow; it is a roughly cylindrical tube with a larger pit at the bottom. Hairs grow from the base of the follicle upward. In the base of the follicle, the hair is still very soft; as the hair proceeds up the follicle, it slowly begins to harden and dry out. Hair is made of **keratin**, a tough protein-based material from which hair, nails, and horns are made in animals. The hardening process of hair growth is therefore called **keratinization**. Hair is one of the most durable materials produced by nature; hairs from mummies, both natural and cultural in origin, have been found thousands of years after the person's death. Keratinization also explains why it doesn't hurt when hair is cut: Hair is "dead" from the moment it peeks above the skin. The only place hair is "alive" is in the base of the follicle, which is why it *does* hurt when a hair is pulled out.

FIGURE 12.1

Hairs are fibrous growths that originate from the skin of mammals. Other animals have structures that are called hairs (like the tarantula), but only mammals have true hairs. Humans use hair as cultural and personal signs of status, gender, and art.

Beach photo courtesy of philg@mit.edu.

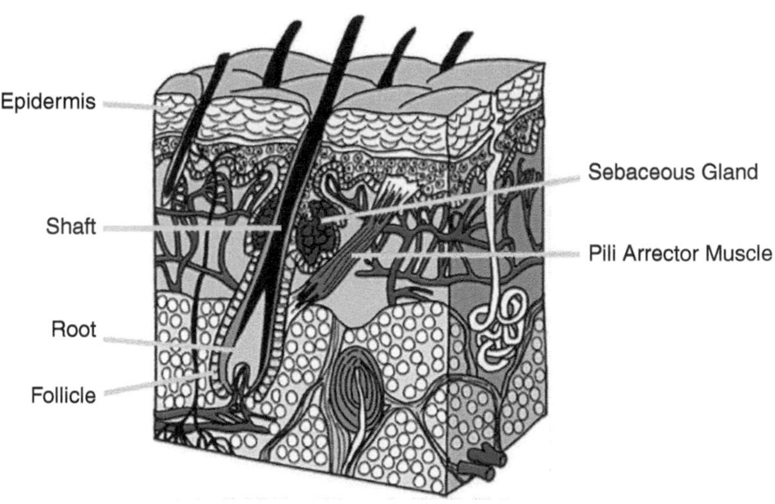

FIGURE 12.2

The epidermis is a complicated structure, containing many different structures. The hair, composed of the tip, shaft, and root, develops within the follicle. As the hair grows, it slowly hardens and is fully keratinized by the time it reaches the surface of the skin. Sebaceous glands open into the follicle to secrete oils onto the hair. The pili arrector muscle controls the position of the hair, creating the "goosebump" effect when a person gets chilled by contracting and pulling the hair upright.

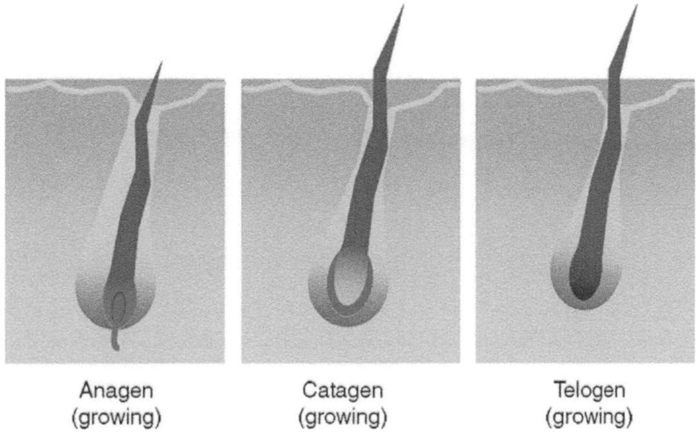

FIGURE 12.3

Hairs grow in three phases. In the anagen, or actively growing, phase, the follicle produces new cells and pushes them up the hair shaft. After 2–7 years, the follicle transitions into the catagen phase. The follicle begins to shut down and quits producing hair in about 2–3 weeks. The final phase, the telogen or resting phase, which lasts about 100 days, the follicle is shut down completely and the root is dried to a bulb. At this point, the hair is only attached mechanically and will be shed naturally.

The follicle contains other structures, such as blood vessels, nerves, and **sebaceous glands**, the latter producing oils that coat hairs, helping to keep them soft and pliable. Hairs even have muscles, called **pili arrector** muscles (*pilius* is the Latin word for "hair") that raise hairs when a person gets chilled (so-called goose bumps).

Hairs go through three phases of growth, as depicted in Figure 12.3. In the **anagen**, or actively growing, phase, the follicle produces new cells and pushes them up the hair shaft as they become incorporated into the structure of the hair. The hair is moved up the shaft by a mechanical method. As the cells are produced, they "ratchet" up the shaft by opposing scales—much like gears in a machine! Between this mechanical method and the upward pressure from the growth of the cells in the follicle, the hairs grow outward from the skin.

Specialized cells in the follicle produce small colored granules, called **melanin** or **pigment**, that give hairs their particular color; these cells are called **melanocytes**. Only two types of melanin are found in hairs: a dark brown pigment called **eumelanin** and a lighter pigment called **pheomelanin**. The combination, density, and distribution of these granules produce the range of hair colors seen in humans and animals.

After the active growth phase, the hair transitions into a resting phase; this transitional phase is called the **catagen** phase. During the catagen phase, the follicle begins to shut down production of cells, the cells begin to shrink, and the root condenses into a bulb-shaped structure called, understandably, a **root bulb** or a **club root**.

The **telogen phase** is the resting phase for the follicle. Cell production has ceased completely; the root has condensed into a bulb and is held in place only by a mechanical connection at the base of the root/follicle. When this mechanical connection breaks (through combing, brushing, or normal wear), the follicle is triggered into the anagen phase again and the cycle renews. On a healthy human head of hair, about 80–90% of the hairs would be in the anagen phase, about 2% in the catagen phase, and about 10–18% in the telogen phase. When the telogen hairs are removed, new hairs begin to grow at once; clipping and shaving have no effect on growth. The time required for human follicles to regrow hairs varies from 147 days for scalp hairs to 61 days for eyebrow hairs. Humans, on average, lose about 100 scalp hairs a day; this provides for an adequate and constant source of potential evidence for transfer and collection.

Forensic hair examiners are sometimes asked whether they can determine if a hair was removed forcibly, during a struggle or assault, for example, to document the severity of the assault. This is a difficult question. Obviously, if the hair has a bulb root (meaning it was removed during the telogen phase), then the question can't be answered. If tissue from the follicle is attached to the root, then the hair was removed during the anagen or possibly catagen phase, that is, while the hair and the follicle were attached through active cellular growth. Because the actively growing hair is still soft and unkeratinized, the root may stretch before it is torn out of the follicle. Therefore, if the root is stretched *and* has follicular tissue attached, the examiner may state that the hair was forcibly removed, as shown in Figure 12.4. That does not,

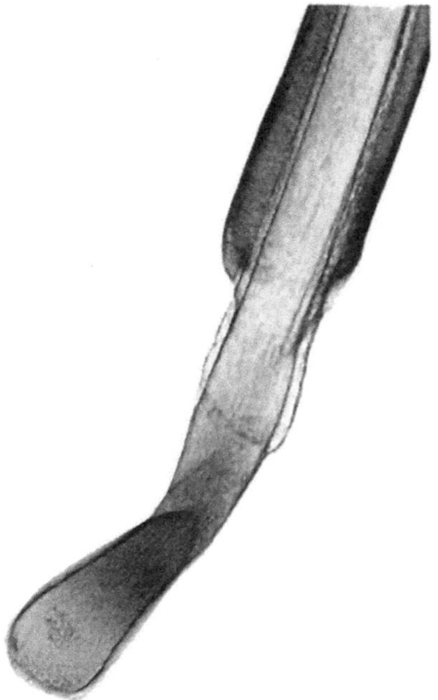

FIGURE 12.4

Roots that are stretched *and* have follicular tissue attached were probably removed by force; otherwise, this anagen phase hair would have stayed in the follicle. This does not, however, tell the examiner what *kind* of force was used—a violent assault, hair being caught in something or a friendly wrestling match—and the examiner must be cautious about making unsupportable statements.

however, tell the examiner what *kind* of force was used—a violent assault, hair being caught in something or a friendly wrestling match—and the examiner must be cautious about making unsupportable statements. Plucking hairs does not guarantee follicle tissue on the root. King, Wigmore, and Twibell showed in 1981 that only 65% of forcibly removed hairs yielded sheaths. Moreover, of the hairs removed by fast plucking, 53% had sheaths, while of those that were pulled slowly, only 11% had sheath tissue. Sheath cells were always associated with anagen and catagen hairs in this study. This study also suggests that in a bulk sample submitted as evidence, the anagen/telogen ratio may be more significant to the investigator than the presence or absence of sheath material.

MICROANATOMY

A hair is a complicated, composite material with many intricately organized structures—only some of which are visible under the microscope. A single hair on a macroscale has a root, a shaft, and a tip, as depicted in Figure 12.5. The **root** is that portion that formerly was in the follicle, the proximal (the direction toward the body) most portion of the hair. The **shaft** is the main portion of the hair. The **tip** is the distal (the direction away from the body) most portion of the hair.

Internally, hairs have a variable and complex microanatomy. The three main structural elements in a hair are the cuticle, the cortex, and the medulla. The **cuticle** of a hair

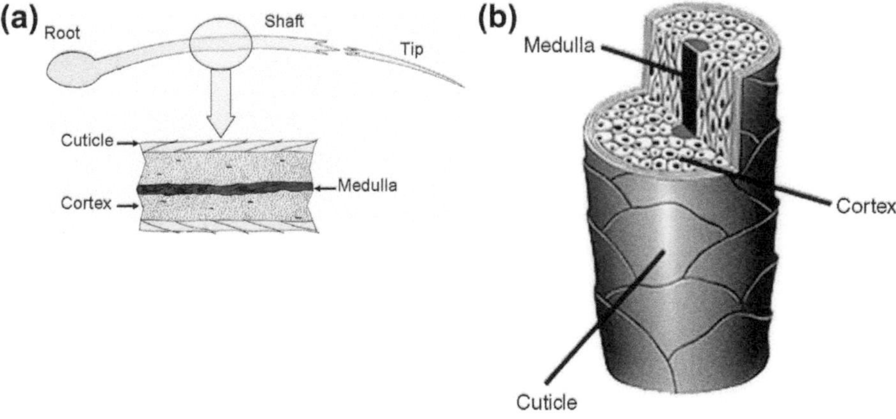

FIGURE 12.5

Macroscopically, a single hair has a root, a shaft, and a tip (a). The root is that portion that formerly was in the follicle, the proximal (the direction toward the body) most portion of the hair. The shaft is the main portion of the hair. The tip is the distal (the direction away from the body) most portion of the hair. Microscopically, a hair consists of three main portions (b). The cuticle is an outer covering of overlapping scales, like shingles on a roof. The cortex is the main mass of the hair and contains numerous microanatomical features. The medulla is the central portion of the hair and consists of air- or fluid-filled cells.

FIGURE 12.6

The cuticle of a hair is a series of overlapping layers of scales that form a protective covering. Animal hairs have scale patterns that vary by species, and these patterns are a useful diagnostic tool for identifying animal hairs. Humans have a scale pattern called imbricate (outlined in red), but it occurs among animals as well. Despite attempts to use scales as an individualizing tool for human hairs, they are not generally useful in forensic examinations.

is a series of overlapping layers of **scales** that form a protective covering. Animal hairs have **scale patterns** that vary by species, and these patterns are a useful diagnostic tool for identifying animal hairs, shown in Figure 12.6. Humans have a scale pattern called **imbricate**, but it is fairly common among animals and, despite attempts to use scales as an individualizing tool for human hairs, is not generally useful in forensic examinations.

The next structure is the **cortex** and makes up the bulk of the hair. The cortex consists of spindle-shaped cells (sometimes called **fusiform**) that contain or constrain numerous other structures. **Pigment granules** are found in the cortex and are dispersed variably throughout the cortex. The granules vary in size, shape, aggregation, and distribution—all excellent characteristics for forensic comparisons. Small bubbles, called **cortical fusi**, may appear in the cortex; when they do appear, they may be sparse, aggregated or evenly distributed throughout the cortex. Cortical fusi also vary in size and shape. Many telogen root hairs will have an aggregate of cortical fusi near the root bulb; it is thought that this is related to the shut down of the growth activity as the follicle transitions from catagen to telogen phase. This "burst" of fusi, then, is most likely related to physiology, so it is not necessarily useful for forensic comparisons, as pictured in Figure 12.7.

Odd structures that look like very large pigment granules, called **ovoid bodies**, may appear irregularly in the cortex. They may, in fact, *be* large, aggregated, or

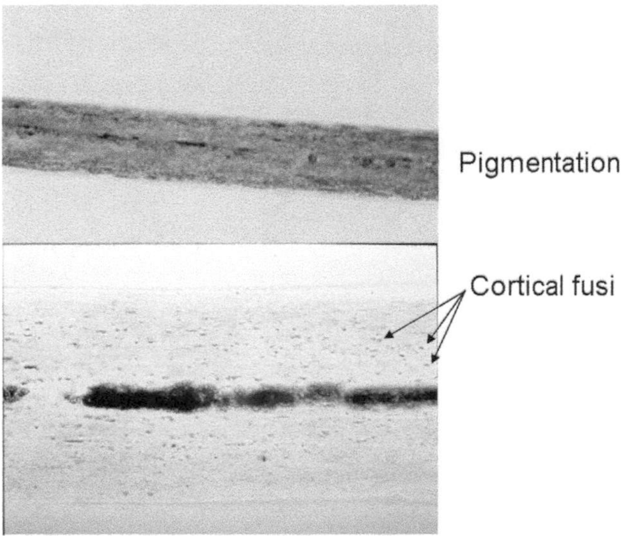

FIGURE 12.7

Numerous microanatomical features are useful in the examination of hairs, including pigment granules, cortical fusi, and ovoid bodies (odd structures that look like very large pigment granules).

aberrant pigment granules, but no one knows; little if any research has been conducted on what ovoid bodies are. Another phenomenon that can be found in hairs is **cortical** or **medullary disruptions**. These appear as if a small explosion occurred in the middle of the hair and may be found singly or in multiples.

HUMAN VERSUS NONHUMAN HAIRS

It is relatively easy to determine whether a hair is human or "nonhuman" (this term is often used instead of "animal" because, technically, humans are also animals) by a simple microscopic examination, as shown in Figure 12.8. Determining *what kind* of nonhuman hair it is, however, may be in some circumstances quite tricky because certain animals' hairs can be similar. Animal hairs have several macroscopic characteristics that distinguish them from those of humans.

First of all, animals have three types of hairs. **Guard hairs** are large, stiff hairs that make up the outer part of the animal's coat. Guard hairs are the hairs that should be used for microscopic identification. Guard hairs may have a widening in the upper half of the shaft, called a **shield**. Below the shield, if it is present, may often be found a **sub-shield stricture**, a narrowing of the hair to slightly less than the normal, nonshield shaft diameter. A sub-shield stricture may be accompanied by a bend in the shaft at the stricture.

Thinner, softer **fur hairs** fill in the rest of the coat providing warmth and bulk. Fur hairs are generic in their appearance and are typically useless for microscopic identification. The root may give an indication as to taxonomic origin, but it may also be misleading; it is best not to use fur hairs for microscopic evaluations.

Finally, animals have **vibrissa**, the technical term for whiskers, the short to long, stiff, often white hairs around the snout and muzzle. No comprehensive study has been made on the identification of taxonomic origin by vibrissa, probably because these hairs have a long life cycle and are lost comparatively less often than the myriad guard and fur hairs of a typical animal.

Some nonhuman hairs are **color banded**, showing abrupt color transitions along the shaft of the hair, including the tip. Raccoons, for example, have four color bands in their guard hairs; incidentally, they are the only animals known to have this many bands.

As noted earlier, scale patterns also may be useful in identifying animal hairs. The best ways to visualize scale patterns are with a scanning electron microscope or

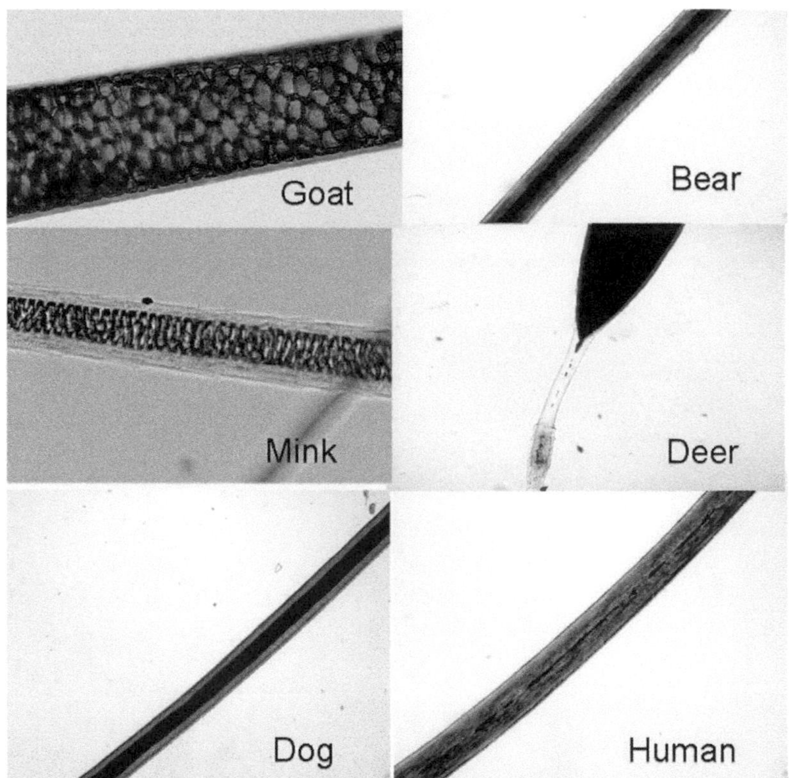

FIGURE 12.8

It is relatively easy to determine whether a hair is human or nonhuman by a simple microscopic examination. Animals have several macroscopic characteristics that distinguish their hairs from those of humans.

by making a **scale cast** and viewing it with a light microscope. The simplest method of making a scale cast is to brush clear nail polish onto a glass microscope slide and lay the hair in the still-wet polish. Before the polish dries completely, the hair should be gently "peeled" from the polish; a cast of the exterior of the hair remains in the polish. This cast can then be examined on a light microscope.

BODY AREA DETERMINATION

Unlike other animals, humans exhibit a wide variety of hairs on their bodies; why humans have hair where they do is of interest to evolutionary biologists, and one recent theory is discussed in "In More Detail: Hairless and Flea-free." The characteristics of these hairs may allow for an estimation of body area origin. The typical body areas that can be determined are head (or scalp), pubic, facial, chest, axillary (armpits), eyelash/eyebrow, and limb; typically, only head and pubic hairs are suitable for microscopic comparison, as shown in Figure 12.9. Hairs that do not fit into these categories may be called **transitional body hairs**, such as those on the stomach, between the chest and the pubic region. Table 12.1 lists the characteristics generally associated with the different body hair types.

Buckling is an abrupt change in direction of the hair shaft with or without a slight twist. **Shouldering** is an asymmetrical cross section of hairs.

In some instances, it may be difficult or impossible for the forensic scientist to make a clear decision as to whether a hair is "chest" or "axillary" in origin; it may also not matter to the circumstances of the crime. Labeling the hair as a "body hair" is sufficient and may be the most accurate conclusion given the quality and nature of the hair.

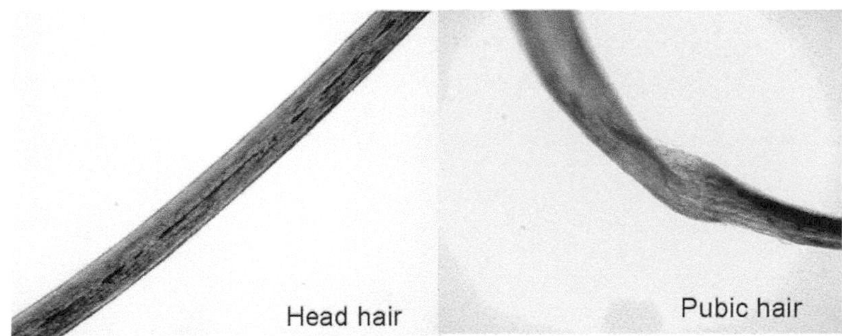

FIGURE 12.9

Unlike other animals, humans exhibit a wide variety of hairs on their bodies. The characteristics of these hairs may allow for an estimation of body area origin. The typical body areas that can be determined are head (or scalp), pubic, facial, chest, axillary (armpits), eyelash/eyebrow, and limb. Hairs that do not fit into these categories may be called transitional body hairs, such as those on the stomach, between the chest and the pubic region.

Table 12.1 General Descriptions of Human Body Area Hair Traits

Area	Diameter	Shaft	Tip
Head	Even	Straight or curly; some waviness; may be very long	Usually cut
Pubic	Varies	Buckling; sometimes extreme waviness or curl	Usually pointed; may be razor cut
Facial	Wide; even	Triangular in cross section; some shouldering	Usually cut; may be scissors or razor cut
Chest	Even to some variation	Wavy to curly; some more straight	Usually pointed
Axillary	Even; some variation	Less wavy/curly than chest	Usually pointed; may be colorless
Limb	Fine; tapering	Slight arc	Usually pointed
Eyebrow/eyelash	Tapering	Arc; short	Pointed

Compare with the Photographs in Figure 12.9.

This determination may have important consequences for a case: One of the authors (MMH) worked a case involving the identification of an adult pubic area hair on a preadolescent victim. A girl of that age could not have produced a pubic area hair: Those hairs are generated by the hormones associated with puberty. DNA from the hair was the same as that from the suspect; this, in addition to overwhelming trace evidence associating the suspect with the crime, led to a guilty plea (see Ryland and Houck (2000) for more information).

IN MORE DETAIL: HAIRLESS AND FLEA-FREE

Did humans lose their thick fur to cut down on parasites or to lose heat more efficiently? A new theory comes down on the side of being bug-free, not staying cool. "The nakedness of humans is a glaring difference between humans and other mammals," says evolutionary biologist Mark Pagel of the University of Reading. U.K. Pagel and Walter Bodmer, a geneticist at the University of Oxford, believe hairlessness is tied to humans' uniquely civilized behavior. When early humans began to don clothing and build shelters, they no longer needed protective fur, the researchers say. And those with less hair may have been healthier because it was easier to keep free of parasites, which thrive where animals make permanent homes.

Sexual selection might have speeded up the evolution of hairlessness, as exposed skin signaled a healthier prospective mate, Pagel and Bodmer argued in a paper published online June 9, 2003, in *Biology Letters*.

Evolutionary biologist Robin Dunbar of the University of Liverpool notes that the theory needs testing—for example, by seeing if people in high parasite areas have less hair. He adds that it would radically change our image of early humans. The cooling-off theory suggests that we lost most of our hair more than 2 million years ago, after taking to two legs; if the parasite idea is correct, nakedness would likely have evolved 1.5 million years later.

Source: *From Holden (2003).*

ANCESTRAL ESTIMATION

Estimating the ethnicity or ancestry of an individual from his or her hairs is just that: an estimate. A study of forensic hair examiner trainees conducted by one of the authors (MMH) showed that their accuracy for racial estimation on a standard set of tests was 85%, not bad for trainees, considering that this was based on a microscopical examination alone. Anthropologists can be more accurate using skeletal measurements, but they use several measurements on different bones and then compare them to a large population of similar measurements. This approach makes the anthropologists' estimate more accurate, but regrettably these are not options for microscopical hair examinations.

The general morphology and color of a hair can give an indication of a person's ancestry. Humans are more variable from one to another in their hair morphology than any other primate. This variation tends to correlate with a person's ancestry (see Table 12.2) although it is not an exact correlation. For simplicity and accuracy, three main ancestral groups are used: Europeans, Africans, and Asians. In the older anthropological and forensic literature, these groups were referred to as, respectively, Caucasoids, Negroids, and Mongoloids; these terms are archaic now and should probably not be used. They are no better at describing the intended populations than the geographic terms listed previously—Caucasoid/European hair descriptions include some Hispanics and peoples of the Middle East, for example—but the geographic terms are as accurate and less potentially offensive.

Typically, head and pubic hairs provide the clearest evidence for ancestral estimates. It may be possible with certain other hairs, especially facial hairs, but body hairs should be viewed with a cautious eye. Asians, for example, have less body hair than other populations and, in some areas, may have none.

Some examiners include a fourth category: mixed race. Technically, everyone is "mixed race," so this term is a misnomer; "other" might be more accurate. In one study, two researchers, one experienced in hair examinations (>14 years) and one not as experienced (<1 year), did a blind study of hair from children of known "mixed" marriages. Both researchers showed positive correlation between non-Black ancestral assessment and increasing European ancestry. The less experienced examiner had a correlation of 0.23 (1.0 being a perfect 1:1 correlation), whereas the experienced examiner had a stronger correlation of 0.61. This point is important to remember: Just

Table 12.2 Various Characteristics of Hair by Ancestry

Ancestry	Diameter (μm)	Cross Section	Pigment Distribution	Cuticle	Undulation
African	60–90	Flat	Dense; clumped	Thin	Prevalent
European	70–100	Oval	Even	Medium	Uncommon
Asian	90–120	Roun	Dense to very dense	Thick	Never

because an examiner estimates a hair to be from a person of a certain ancestry doesn't mean that is how that person identifies himself or herself racially.

DAMAGE, DISEASE, AND TREATMENTS

Humans do many different things to their hair depending on their culture—cutting, dyeing, braiding, even shaving—and this isn't limited to just the scalp. Some diseases affect the hairs or the follicles and are distinctive but rare.

The tips of hairs can provide good information about how the hair has been treated. Scissor-cut hair has a clean, straight border, whereas razor-cut hair is angled, as depicted in Figure 12.10. In a hit-and-run incident or an explosion, flying glass cuts hair in a unique way, leaving a long curved "tail." Burned hair is blackened and may appear bubbled or expanded. Crushed hair is also easy to recognize.

Bleaching of the hair oxidizes the pigmentation and removes its color. The treatment may stop at this point or a new color may be added to the hair. Coloring hair is much like dyeing wool fibers (both are hair) or other textile fibers. As the hair continues to grow, the point where the bleaching/coloration was applied is visible as an abrupt color change, as shown in Figure 12.11. If the length of the natural hair color portion is measured, the examiner can make an estimate of the time interval between the cosmetic treatment and the time the hair was lost. Head hairs grow an average of 1/2 in (1.3 cm) per month, so the natural portion length in inches would be multiplied by 0.5 to yield the approximate number of months.

The diseases that affect the hair morphology are rare, but this makes them excellent evidence for identifying a source. **Pili annulati** refers to hairs with colored rings. In pili annulati, the hair has alternating light and dark bands along its length, like tiger or zebra stripes. People with dark hair may have pili annulati but not know it because their hair color masks the condition. **Monilethrix** makes hairs look like a string of beads (the name comes from the Greek words for "bead" and "hair"). Along the length of the hair are nodes and constrictions making the hair vary in diameter. This hair beading weakens the hair, and people suffering from monilethrix have patchy hair loss. **Pili torti** is, as the name suggests, a twisting of the hair along its length, creating a spiral morphology. There may be several twists in one hair. The cuticle is present, but the twisting creates stress that leads to fractures in the cuticle and cortex.

Vermin (such as lice), dandruff, or fungus may also be present on hairs, and this fact should be noted. These factors add to the classification of the hairs as coming from individuals with these traits.

Misconceptions abound about hairs and what can be derived from their examination. Age and sex cannot be determined from looking at hairs; gray hairs may occur from a person's 20s onward, and long hair doesn't mean "female" just as short hair doesn't mean "male." Hairs do not grow after people die (how could they?)—the skin shrinks from loss of water, making the hairs more prominent (likewise with nails). And, some studies to the contrary, shaving does not stimulate hair growth.

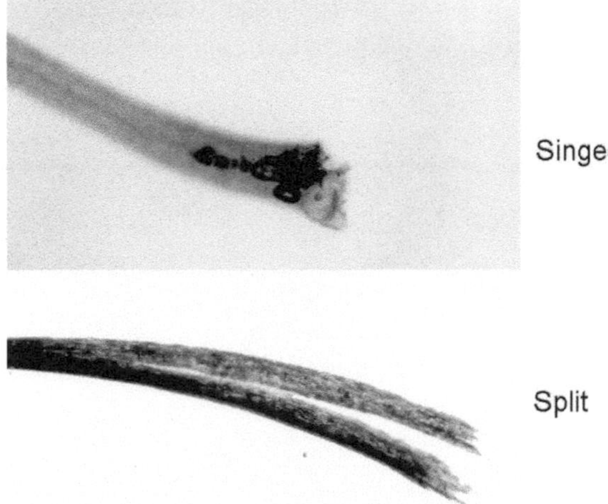

FIGURE 12.10

The tips of hairs can provide good information about how the hair has been treated. Scissor-cut hair has a clean, straight border, whereas razor-cut hair is angled. In a hit-and-run incident or an explosion, flying glass cuts hair in a unique way, leaving a long curved "tail." Singed hair is blackened and may appear bubbled or expanded. Split tips may be due to cosmetic treatment or weakened hair.

FIGURE 12.11

Coloring hair is much like dyeing wool fibers (both are hair) or other textile fibers. As the hair continues to grow, the point where the bleaching/coloration was applied is visible as an abrupt color change. This hair has been bleached.

HOW ACCURATE ARE HAIR COMPARISONS?

Historically, the goal of most forensic hair examinations is the microscopic comparison of a questioned hair or hairs from a crime scene to a known hair sample using a comparison microscope (Figures 12.12 and 12.13) based upon a list of characteristics that cover the root, the microanatomy of the shaft, and the tip (see Chart 12.1). The evaluation of microscopic traits within and between samples is key to the comparison process; Figure 12.13 shows hairs that are positively and negatively associated.

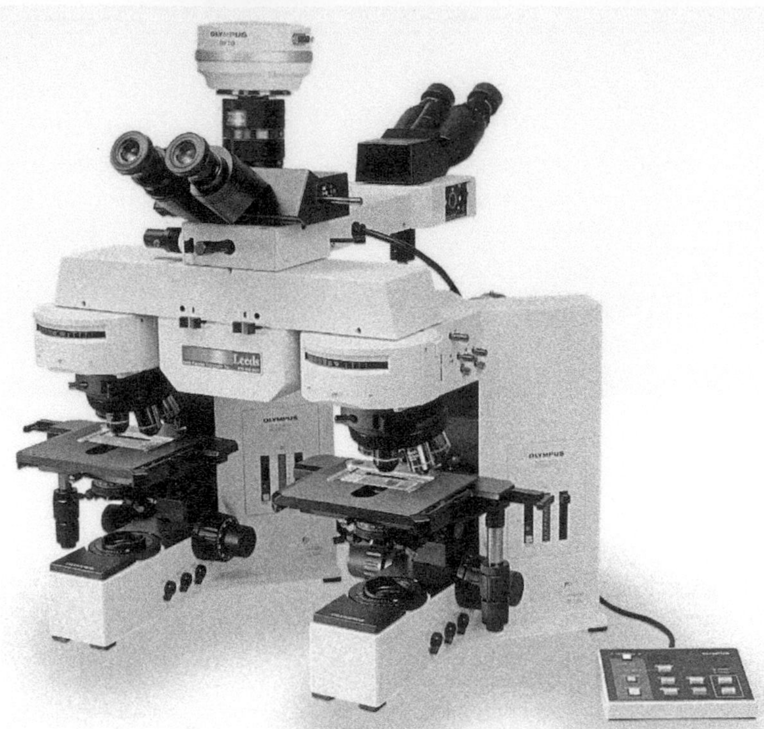

FIGURE 12.12

A comparison microscope is used for the examination. A comparison microscope is composed of two transmitted light microscopes joined by an optical bridge to produce a split image. The sample on the right appears in the right-hand field of view, and the sample on the left appears in the left-hand field of view. This side-by-side, point-by-point comparison is central to the effectiveness and accuracy of a forensic hair comparison. Hairs cannot be compared properly without one.

Courtesy: Olympus USA.

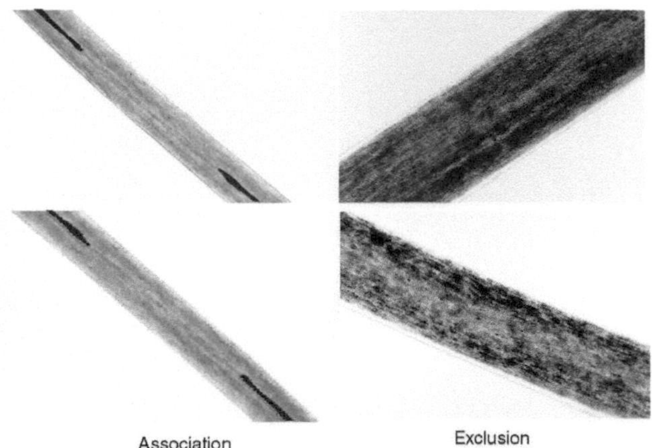

FIGURE 12.13

A hair comparison is a good method of demonstrating possible association between questioned hairs and individuals. A suitable known sample of hairs from the same body area is necessary to conduct a comparison. Hairs are not a means of positive identification, however; statistics or frequency estimates cannot currently be applied to microscopic hair comparisons.

But how to interpret the results of a forensic hair comparison? This process is not as simple as might be imagined. Wording of microscopic hair examination results usually takes the following forms:

- …a hair sample from the crime scene and another taken from (the defendant) were "similar" and "consistent."
- …the pubic hairs from the crime and (the defendant's) pubic hairs exhibited "similar microscopic characteristics."
- …that hairs from the crime scene were "similar" to (the defendant's).
- …hairs from the crime scene exhibited "the same microscopic characteristics" as (the defendant's) hair.

A fundamental misunderstanding about what can and cannot be said with hair evidence lies at the heart of this issue; none of the preceding statements are beyond the realm of what is considered reasonable testimony. But how specific are these statements and what notions do they convey to laypersons? Given the list of traits in Chart 12.1, it seems that hairs could be coded, entered into a database, and eventually frequency information could be derived. A hair's traits could be entered as a query, and at the push of a button, a frequency of occurrence for a population could be calculated. But it's not that easy.

Exploratory research has been conducted to evaluate hair results statistically (Gaudette and Keeping, 1974; Wickenheiser and Hepworth, 1990) but, to date, no universal approach for calculating significance has been published. And probably none will be (Gaudette, 1978, 1982). Hairs are a very complicated composite biological material and the expression of hair traits across the population is highly variable. Being three-dimensional makes quantifying the traits that much more difficult; characteristics would need to be recorded in X, Y, and Z dimensions, none of which are easily measured under a microscope. And now that DNA analysis is more accessible, a statistical approach based on microscopic examination is hardly justified.

DNA AND HAIRS

The advent of forensic mtDNA in the mid-1990s heralded a new era of biological analysis in forensic science. This was especially true for hairs because it offered a way to add information to microscopic hair examinations; in 1996, the FBI instituted a policy that all positive microscopic associations of hairs were to be checked by DNA analysis. mtDNA sequencing added another test for assessing the significance of attributing a hair to an individual. Neither the microscopic nor molecular analysis alone, or together, provides positive identification. The two methods complement each other in the information they provide. For example, mtDNA typing can often distinguish between hairs from different sources although they have similar, or insufficient, microscopic hair characteristics.

In the only study of its kind to date, the results of microscopic and mitochondrial examinations of human hairs submitted to the FBI Laboratory for analysis were reviewed (Houck and Budowle, 2002). Of 170 hair examinations, there were

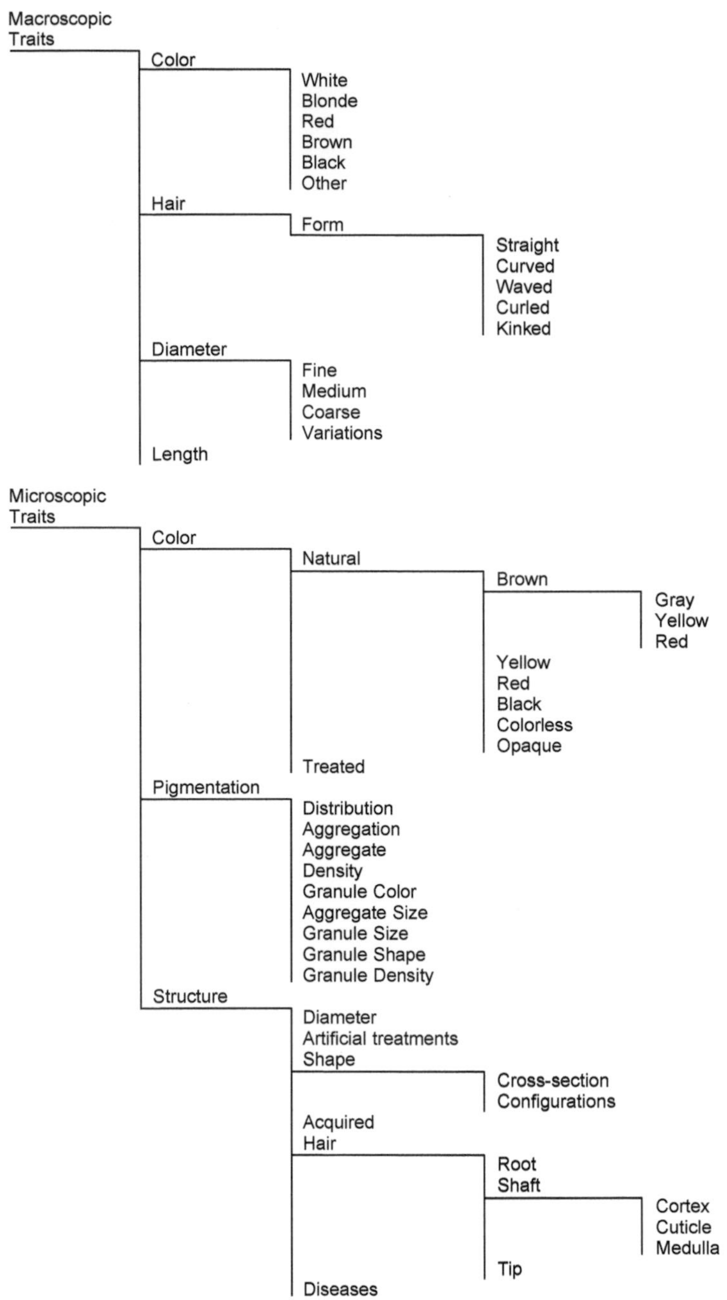

CHART 12.1

Chart traits. A sample list of hair characteristics used to describe known and questioned hairs. Some of the traits can be further defined, such as "scissor-cut tip," "razor-cut tip," "glass cut tip," etc.

This list was produced by the Forensic Resource Network Hair Project (a National Institute of Justice-funded program).

Table 12.3 Results of Houck and Budowle (2002)

		Mitochondrial Results			
		Association	**Inconclusive**	**Exclusion**	**Insufficient**
Microscopic results	Association	69	1	9	1
	Inconclusive	15	1	20	1
	Exclusion	0	1	17	1
	Insufficient	13	0	18	3

80 microscopic associations; importantly, only 9 were excluded by mtDNA. Also, 66 hairs that were considered either unsuitable for microscopic examinations or yielded inconclusive microscopic associations were able to be analyzed with mtDNA. Only six of these hairs did not provide enough mtDNA, and another three yielded inconclusive results. This study demonstrates the strength of combining the two techniques (Table 12.3).

Both methods, or either, can provide important information to an investigation because they both analyze different characteristics. The only question left, then, as posed by James Robertson of the Australian Federal Police, is:

> *to what extent preliminary microscopic examinations should be conducted prior to DNA analysis …it may well be the case that there will be little if any reduction in the level of microscopic examination as it will be both necessary and desirable to eliminate as many questioned hairs as possible and concentrate mtDNA analysis on only key hairs.*
>
> (1999, p. 127)

The data in the FBI study support the usefulness of both methods.

BACK TO THE CASE: ARE HAIRS "JUNK SCIENCE"?

Despite its critics, hair is a potentially important type of physical evidence, and the combination of microscopical and mtDNA examinations has made it far more powerful and reliable than ever before. Aristotle said, "It is the mark of an educated man to look for precision in each class of things just so far as the nature of the subject admits," and, thus, to look for more precision in microscopic hair comparisons than is in the nature of hairs is foolish. But how to assess its accuracy?

Sensitivity and specificity are performance measures of binary classification tests (true/false, correct/wrong, present/absent) and use the following terminology:

- **Sensitivity**: True positive rate
- **Specificity**: True negative rate
- **Precision** (positive predictive value, or PPV): Proportion of true positives against all positive results

- **Negative predictive value** (NPV): Proportion of true negatives against all negative results
- **Accuracy**: Proportion of true results

As an example of sensitivity and specificity analysis, the results from the Houck and Budowle, study are shown in Table 12.4. The insufficient results were excluded from the following analyzes. Based on the difference between the associations and exclusions called by mtDNA that were called inconclusive by microscopic comparison being less than 3% of the sample size, the inconclusive results were also excluded from this example. Removing insufficient and inconclusive results, microscopic hair comparisons (as judged against mitochondrial results) perform as shown in Table 12.4.

The value of microscopic hair comparisons in exclusion (NPV = 1.0) is higher than in associations (PPV, or precision = 0.88), as has been noted anecdotally in the literature (Houck and Bisbing, 2005). Microscopic hair comparisons are a highly sensitive (1.0) but only moderately specific test (0.65). An accuracy of 0.91 and a precision of 0.88 would argue in favor of the method, all things being equal. The numbers from the Houck and Budowle study are based on the results of FBI hair examiners, although not those involved in the exonerations mentioned. The recent revelations of FBI hair examiners overstating results or misleading juries has harmed the science of microscopic hair examinations, perhaps forever (Hsu, 2015). Given that hairs are more reliable in exclusions than inclusions, they still have a role to play in addressing wrongful convictions. The accuracy of microscopic hair examinations (0.91) has been overshadowed by the willingness of some examiners to testify outside the bounds of acceptable science.

The exonerations of Tribble, Odom, and Gates would argue that something is amiss in the case-specific application of the method. Thus, microscopic hair examinations have utility in forensic investigations (largely through description and exclusions) but positive associations of any significant evidence should be the provence of DNA analysis.

Table 12.4 Calculations of Sensitivity and Selectivity from Houck and Budowle (2002)

		Mitochondrial Results		
		Condition Positive	**Condition Negative**	
Microscopic result	Test outcome positive	69 True positives	9 False positives	0.88 Precision
	Test outcome negative	0 False negatives	17 True negatives	1.00 Negative predictive value
		1.00 Sensitivity	0.65 specificity	0.91 Accuracy

SUMMARY

Hairs are among the most often encountered types of trace evidence. Information about people and animals is readily apparent from a simple microscopical examination. Comparisons by microscopy for positive associations have potential pitfalls, so comparisons should be conducted by DNA analysis after the hairs have been described by microscopy.

TEST YOUR KNOWLEDGE

1. What types of hairs do animals have?
2. What are the growth stages of hairs?
3. How can you tell if a hair may have been forcibly removed?
4. What are some of the differences between human and animal hairs?
5. What characteristics are used to determine body area?
6. Why is estimating ancestry from hairs difficult?
7. Name three ways in which a hair can be cosmetically treated.
8. Why are hairs stronger in exclusion than in inclusion?
9. What is a comparison microscope?
10. What is a guard hair?
11. How does the use of mtDNA assist in hair comparisons?
12. How would you distinguish between males and females using hair?
13. Can you tell how old people are by looking at their hair?
14. What are cortical fusi?
15. What are the three macroscopic parts of a hair?
16. What are three main microscopic parts of a hair?
17. How would you distinguish between a head hair and a pubic hair?
18. Can you use statistics to describe the significance of hair comparisons?
19. What is specificity? What is selectivity?
20. How could you tell if a "hair" is really a synthetic fiber from a wig? What would you look for?

CONSIDER THIS...

1. Why are hairs *not* a form of positive identification? What prevents them from being so?
2. If hairs are not a form of positive identification, how can they aid an investigation?

BIBLIOGRAPHY AND FURTHER READING

Bisbing, R., 2001. The forensic identification and association of human hair. In: Saferstein, R. (Ed.), Forensic Science Handbook, second ed. Prentice Hall, Inc, Englewood Cliffs (NJ).

Christensen, A., Crowder, C.M., Ousley, S.D., Houck, M.M., 2014. Error and its meaning in forensic science. Journal of Forensic Sciences 59 (1), 123–126.

Gaudette, B.D., 1976. Probabilities and human pubic hair comparisons. Journal of Forensic Sciences 21, 514–517.

Gaudette, B.D., 1978. Some further thoughts on probabilities and human hair comparisons. Journal of Forensic Sciences 23, 758–763.

Gaudette, B.D., 1982. A supplementary discussion of probabilities and human hair comparisons. Journal of Forensic Sciences 27, 279–289.

Gaudette, B.D., Keeping, E.S., 1974. An attempt at determining probabilities in human scalp hair comparison. Journal of Forensic Sciences 19, 599–606.

Holden, C. (Ed.), 2003. Random Samples. Science 300, 2028–2029.

Houck, M.M., Budowle, B., 2002. Correlation of microscopic and mitochondrial DNA analysis of hairs. Journal of Forensic Sciences 45 (5), 1–4.

Houck, M.M., Bisbing, R.E., 2005. Forensic human hair examination and comparison in the 21st century. Forensic Science Review 17 (1), 51–66.

Hsu, S., 2015. FBI admits flaws in hair analysis over decades, The Washington Post, April 18.

King, L.A., Wigmore, R., Twibell, J.M., 1981. The morphology and occurrence of human hair sheath cells. Journal of the Forensic Science Society 22, 267–269.

Lepez, T., Vandewoestyne, M., Van Hoofstat, D., Deforce, D., 2014. Fast nuclear staining of head hair roots as a screening method for successful STR analysis in forensics. Forensic Science International: Genetics 13, 191–194.

Melton, T., et al., 2005. Forensic mitochondrial DNA analysis of 691 casework hairs. Journal of Forensic Sciences 50, 1–8.

Ryland, S., Houck, M., 2000. Only circumstantial evidence. In: Houck, M. (Ed.), Mute Witnesses. Academic Press, San Diego (CA).

Tridico, S., Houck, M.M., Kirkbride, K.P., Smith, M.E., Yates, B.C., 2014. Morphological identification of animal hairs: myths and misconceptions, possibilities and pitfalls. Forensic Science International 238, 101–107.

Wickenheiser, R.A., Hepworth, D.G., 1990. Further evaluation of probabilities in human scalp hair comparisons. Journal of Forensic Sciences 35, 1323–1329.

Wilson, M.R., DiZinno, J.A., Polanskey, D., Replogle, J., Budowle, B., 1995. Validation of mitochondrial DNA sequencing for forensic casework analysis. International Journal of Legal Medicine 108, 68–72.

PART

Chemical Sciences

4

CHAPTER

Illicit Drugs

13

CHAPTER OUTLINE

KEY TERMS

- Barbiturate
- Comprehensive Controlled Substances Act of 1970
- Controlled substance
- Crack
- Drug
- Drug abuse
- Excipients
- Flashbacks
- Harrison Act

- Narcotics
- Narcotic Drug Control Act
- Pure Food and Drugs Act
- Stimulants
- Uniform Controlled Substances Act
- Useable quantity

THE CASE: THE FRENCH CONNECTION AFFAIR

One of the most famous global drug smuggling and selling operations in history was the famous **French Connection** affair. This case involved gangs in Corsica, Italy, organized crime in the United States, farmers in Turkey, and the New York City Police Department. The case was the subject of two movies, one of which "The French Connection" won several Academy Awards including Best Picture. The French connection was a scheme of heroin cultivation in Turkey, processing in France, and smuggling into the United States. At its height, the Connection supplied nearly all of the white heroin that was being smuggled into the United States. It started in the 1930s in Turkey where farmers had licenses to grow opium poppy plants and sell them to legitimate drug companies, but they often grew more than they needed and the excess was sold to the illegitimate market. The opium was partially processed in Turkey whereby the naturally occurring morphine was extracted from the opium and the resultant paste was shipped to Marseille, France where the morphine was converted in one chemical step to heroin. This was smuggled into the United States, chiefly through New York. After the World War II, heroin shipments picked up as did seizures at United States ports. On one occasion in 1949, more than 45 pounds was seized from one French ship. By the 1960s, more than 5000 lbs of heroin was coming into the United States from France.

After many years of negotiations with the Turkish government, opium growing was completely banned in Turkey in 1971. United States and French authorities stepped up efforts to interdict heroin shipments in France. Hundreds of pounds of heroin were seized and major French Connection arrests made. In the 1970s, many illicit drug laboratories that made heroin from morphine were dismantled and the operators were arrested in and around Marseilles. In the United States, corrupt New York Police officers were arrested after they permitted access to the property storage room where thousands of pounds of heroin were stored. The thieves substituted flour and similar substances for the heroin. They were caught when insects were discovered eating the "heroin." This completed the dismantling of the French Connection. It is interesting to note that, when this heroin route went down, much of the heroin being smuggled into the United States came from Mexico and Central and South America. This heroin was refined differently than the French variety and was tan to light brown in color instead of white. It was sometimes called "Mexican Mud" on the street.

INTRODUCTION

More than 50% of the evidence submissions to most crime laboratories are drug cases and the drug unit is usually the largest in the laboratory in terms of the number of forensic scientists, space, instrumentation, and case submissions. This has been the situation for more than 50 years. The United States Government has been attempting to control illicit drugs for nearly a century on a number of fronts, including helping other countries with their efforts to suppress the growing and manufacture of illicit drugs, interdiction of drug shipments from foreign countries, manufacture and sale within the United States borders, and prevention programs aimed at children and adults. The success of these efforts has been disappointing over the years and the fact is that a small fraction of foreign drug shipments are stopped at the borders. Today, drug use in the United States remains unabated and certain classes of drugs are abused at higher levels than ever. Recently, even United States Justice Department officials have admitted that the so-called "war on drugs" has been largely a failure and should be curtailed. Federal and state efforts in drug control as well as forfeiture laws that make it easy for governments to seize property that is involved in drug enterprises, have resulted in the availability of millions of dollars for crime laboratories to outfit themselves with the latest in analytical chemistry instruments and with more trained scientists to analyze drugs and provide court testimony. In many laboratories, the drug unit is responsible for nearly all of the analytical instrumentation in the laboratory. In this chapter, we will explore some of the history of drug use and abuse and law enforcement of illicit drugs as well as survey the major classes of drugs and discuss how laboratories analyze them.

WHAT IS AN ILLICIT DRUG?

A **drug** is a natural or synthetic substance that is designed to produce a specific set of psychological or physiological effects on the human body or, in some cases, other animals. Most drugs are produced legitimately by drug manufacturers and are prescribed for particular illnesses, injuries, or other medical problems. These drugs are most often taken and used for an intended purpose. Sometimes, however, they have effects that people find pleasurable, and thus are taken for other than their intended purposes. **Drug abuse** occurs when people take drugs for purposes other than for which they are intended; usually for their psychoactive effects.

In addition to legally produced pharmaceutical drugs, there are also substances that have no legitimate, recognized medicinal purpose, but are produced and ingested entirely for their psychoactive effects. Many of these drugs are naturally occurring substances or are extracted or derived from natural substances, usually plants. Others are purely synthetic compounds. Legally produced drugs that are abused and drugs produced for no reason other than abuse are called abused drugs, drugs of abuse, or illicit drugs. In the United States, many of them are **Controlled Substances**, which refer to their inclusion in a part of the Federal Code called the *Controlled Substances Act* (Act 21 United States C. 812). Throughout the world, many of these terms are used to describe abused drugs. The most common one is **illicit drugs** and that is the term that will be used in this chapter.

THE CONTROL OF ILLICIT DRUGS IN THE UNITED STATES

Why are some drug substances prohibited or controlled in the United States while others are taken freely? The reasons are complex and have to do with how people perceive the notion of the public interest. In addition, questions of morality, personal choice, social order, and health are part of the debate. Over time, the issue of drug control has been complicated by the emergence of facts and fallacies about certain drugs. What is clear is that historically our drug control laws and regulations have been disjointed and uncoordinated and have resulted from society's responses to various social crises throughout our history.

Prior to the beginning of the twentieth century, there was little in the way of drug control in the United States. This changed with the passage of two Federal laws, one in 1906 and the other in 1914. In part, these were due to public reaction to opium smoking among Chinese immigrants, the rise of cocaine use and increased activity by purveyors of patent medicines. The result, in 1906, was the passage of the *Pure Food and Drugs Act*, which prohibited interstate commerce in mislabeled or adulterated food or drugs. Among the substances targeted by the law were marihuana, cocaine, heroin, and opium. This act was administered by the Department of Agriculture. In 1914, Congress passed the *Harrison Act*, which is properly known as "An act to provide for the registration of, with collectors of internal revenue, and to impose a special tax upon all persons who produce, import, manufacture, compound, deal in, dispense, or give away opium or coca leaves, their salts, derivatives, or preparations, and for other purposes." This law was enforced and administered by the Bureau of Internal Revenue in the Treasury Department. It gave the Federal Government broad control over cocaine and narcotics traffic in the United States. At the time the Harrison Act was passed, the climate in the country seemed to favor continuing to supply addicts with their needed drugs, while simultaneously closing down dealers and purveyors of the illegal drugs. This was the way that the Act was enforced early on. Later, in the late 1920s, the mood shifted and it was felt that drug addicts could be easily cured if their drugs were taken away. This resulted in a crackdown on physicians who had been heretofore legally supplying addicts with drugs. Slowly the view was changing from drug abuse being a medical problem to a law enforcement problem.

In 1930, Congress formed the Bureau of Narcotics within the Treasury Department. The Bureau stepped up law enforcement against illicit drugs, particularly narcotics and cocaine and marihuana. At this time, anyone who wanted to buy or import or sell any of these drugs had to register and pay a tax. Because marihuana was included, it was labeled a narcotic in all relevant Federal laws, a label that stuck until the early 1970s. After World War II, testimony before Congress indicated that half of all crime in cities in the United States was related to illegal drug use. This led, in 1956, to the *Narcotic Drug Control Act*, which called for the increased penalties for illicit use of these drugs. Stiff jail sentences went to all but first-time offenders and anyone who sold drugs to a minor faced the death penalty. This law also had another important feature. If a new drug came into the marketplace that had a potential for abuse, a recommendation to control it could be made by the Food and Drug Administration to the Secretary of Health, Education, and Welfare. Drugs such as amphetamines, barbiturates, and D-lysergic acid diethyl amide (LSD) were brought under control during this time. Rather than labeling them narcotics, they were referred to in the law as "dangerous drugs." The Bureau of Narcotics was changed to the **Bureau of Narcotics and Dangerous Drugs** and they became the chief enforcers of the new laws.

In 1970, the Congress passed the *Comprehensive Controlled Substances Act of 1970*. This comprehensive law repealed or updated all previous laws that controlled both narcotics and dangerous drugs. This law put all controlled substances in the federal realm. This meant that the Federal Government could prosecute anyone for a drug offence regardless of whether interstate trafficking was involved and irrespective of state laws.

This new law resulted in a number of major changes in drug enforcement in the United States:

1. Control of drugs became a direct law enforcement activity, rather than through registration and taxation.
2. Enforcement was moved from the Treasury Department to the Justice Department and the Bureau of Narcotics and Dangerous Drugs became the **Drug Enforcement Administration** (**DEA**).
3. The decision on which drugs should be controlled rests with the Secretary of Health and Human Services, which delegates to the Food and Drug Administration (FDA) the determination of which drugs should be controlled. In making decisions about whether a drug should be controlled, the FDA evaluates such factors as: pharmacological effects, ability to induce psychological dependence or physical addiction, and whether there is any legitimate medical use for the substance (as defined and recognized by the FDA).

Under this law, tobacco and alcohol products are excluded. Controlled drugs are put into five schedules. See Table 13.1 for a summary of the schedules and the drugs that are found in each one. More comprehensive information about the federal schedules can be found on the DEA website at: http://www.dea.gov/concern/abuse/chap1/contents.htm.

The penalties for the use, manufacture, and sale of Controlled Substances are linked to its Schedule. The drugs in Schedules 1 and 2 carry higher penalties for possession, manufacture, and sale than do drugs in the higher numbered schedules. Table 13.2 summarizes the penalties for the five drug schedules.

Notice that Table 13.2 does not include marihuana. This plant has had an interesting and colorful history in the United States and has been treated in different ways over the years by the Federal and many state governments. As a result, sanctions for possession, manufacture (growing), and sale are subject to a different scheme than the other Controlled Substances. This is set out in Table 13.3.

Table 13.1 Federal Schedules of Controlled Substances

Schedule I

- The drug or other substance has a high potential for abuse.
- The drug causes physical addiction or psychological dependence.
- The drug or other substance has no currently accepted medical use in treatment in the United States.
- There is a lack of accepted safety for use of the drug or other substance under medical supervision.
- Some Schedule I substances are heroin, LSD, marihuana, PCP, and methaqualone.

Schedule II

- The drug or other substance has a high potential for abuse.
- The drug or other substance has a currently accepted medical use in treatment in the United States or a currently accepted medical use with severe restrictions.
- Abuse of the drug or other substance may lead to severe psychological or physical dependence.
- Schedule II substances include morphine, PCP, cocaine, methadone, and methamphetamine.

Schedule III

- The drug or other substance has a potential for abuse less than the drugs or other substances in Schedules I and II.
- The drug or other substance has a currently accepted medical use in treatment in the United States.
- Abuse of the drug or other substance may lead to moderate or low physical dependence or high psychological dependence.
- Anabolic steroids, codeine, and hydrocodone with aspirin or Tylenol and some barbiturates are Schedule III substances.

Schedule IV

- The drug or other substance has a low potential for abuse relative to the drugs or other substances in Schedule III.
- The drug or other substance has a currently accepted medical use in treatment in the United States.
- Abuse of the drug or other substance may lead to limited physical dependence or psychological dependence relative to the drugs or other substances in Schedule III.
- Included in Schedule IV are Darvon, Talwin, Equanil, Valium, and Xanax.

Schedule V

- The drug or other substance has a low potential for abuse relative to the drugs or other substances in Schedule IV.
- The drug or other substance has a currently accepted medical use in treatment in the United States.
- Abuse of the drug or other substance may lead to limited physical dependence or psychological dependence relative to the drugs or other substances in Schedule IV.
- Over-the-counter cough medicines with codeine are classified in Schedule V.

LSD, D-lysergic acid diethyl amide; PCP, Phencyclidine.

Table 13.2 Current Penalties for Offences for the Various Schedules of Controlled Substances

CSA	Second Offence	First Offence	Quantity	Drug	Quantity	First Offence	Second Offence
I and II	– Not less than 10 years, not more than life – If death or serious injury, not less than life	– Not less than 5 years, not more than 40 years – If death or serious injury, not less than 20 years, or more than life	10–99 g pure or 100–999 g mixture	Methamphetamine	100 g or more pure or 1 kg or more mixture	– Not less than 10 years, not more than life – If death or serious injury, not less than 20 years, or more than life	– Not less than 20 years, not more than life – If death or serious injury, not less than life
			100–999 g mixture	Heroin	1 kg or more mixture		
			500–4999 g mixture	Cocaine	5 kg or more mixture		
			5–49 g Mixture	Cocaine base	50 g or more mixture		
			10–99 g pure or 100–999 g mixture	PCP	100 g or more pure or 1 kg or more mixture		
	– Fine of not more than $4 million individual, $10 million other than individual	– Fine of not more than $2 million individual, $5 million other than individual	1–9 g mixture	LSD	10 g or more mixture	– Fine of not more than $4 million individual, $10 million other than individual	– Fine of not more than $8 million individual, $20 million other than individual
			40–399 g mixture	Fentanyl	400 g or more mixture		
			10–99 g mixture	Fentanyl analogue	100 g or more mixture		

Continued

Table 13.2 Current Penalties for Offences for the Various Schedules of Controlled Substances—cont'd

	Drug	Quantity	First Offence	Second Offence
I and II	Others (law does not include marijuana, hashish, or hash oil)	Any	– Not more than 20 years – If death or serious injury, not less than 20 years, not more than life – Fine $1 million individual, $5 million not individual	– Not more than 30 years – If death or serious injury, life – Fine $2 million individual, $10 million not individual
III	All (includes anabolic steroids as of 2-27-91)	Any	– Not more than 5 years – Fine not more than $250,000 individual, $1 million not individual	– Not more than 30 years – If death or serious injury, life – Fine $2 million individual, $10 million not individual
IV	All	Any	– Not more than 3 years – Fine not more than $250,000 individual, $1 million not individual	– Not more than 30 years – If death or serious injury, life – Fine $2 million individual, $10 million not individual
V	All	Any	– Not more than 1 year – Fine not more than $100,000 individual, $250,000 not individual	– Not more than 30 years – If death or serious injury, life – Fine $2 million individual, $10 million not individual

CSA, Controlled Substances Act; LSD, D-lysergic acid diethyl amide; PCP, Phencyclidine.

Table 13.3 Current Penalties for Marihuana Abuse

Description	Quantity	First Offence	Second Offence
Marijuana	1000 kg or more mixture; or 1000 or more plants	– Not less than 10 years, not more than life – If death or serious injury, not less than 20 years, not more than life – Fine not more than $4 million individual, $10 million other than individual	– Not less than 20 years, not more than life – If death or serious injury, not more than life – Fine not more than $8 million individual, $20 million other than individual
Marijuana	100–999 kg mixture; or 100–999 plants	– Not less than 5 years, not more than 40 years – If death or serious injury, not less than 20 years, not more than life – Fine not more than $2 million individual, $5 million other than individual	– Not less than 10 years, not more than life – If death or serious injury, not more than life – Fine not more than $4 million individual, $10 million other than individual
Marijuana	50–99 kg mixture; or 50–99 plants	– Not more than 20 years – If death or serious injury, not less than 20 years, not more than life – Fine $1 million individual, $5 million other than individual	– Not more than 30 years – If death or serious injury, not more than life – Fine $2 million individual, $10 million other than individual
Marijuana	Less than 50 kg mixture	– Not more than 5 years – Fine not more than $250,000 $1 million other than individual	– Not more than 10 years – Fine $500,000 individual, $2 million other than individual
Hashish	10 kg or more		
Hashish	1 kg or more		

The Comprehensive Controlled Substances Act of 1970 remains the law of the land today. The only major changes in the law have been an increase in the number of controlled substances and changes in penalties associated with possession and distribution of the drugs. In addition, the DEA developed and recommends a model state law entitled the *Uniform Controlled Substances Act*. Most states have adopted this as a framework to replace their existing drug laws. Under this Act, states use the same scheduling system for controlling illicit drugs. Some states have added schedules, changed the specific drugs within a schedule, or have changed penalties for possession or distribution of drugs, but the basic framework remains the same as for the Federal laws.

DRUGS AND PUBLIC POLICY: WHY ARE CERTAIN DRUGS REGULATED

As mentioned previously, there are number of reasons why governments seek to control the use of illicit drugs—why some substances are labeled "illicit" while others are not. The major reason seems tot be our notion of the "public interest." There is strong sentiment that everyone should be a productive member of society so that it will prosper and grow. If people spend their otherwise productive time in pursuit of the hedonistic pleasures derived from the abuse of substances such as illicit drugs, then they are not acting in the public interest. Of course, rationales for penalizing drug abuse go beyond the nature of the public interest. There is also a widespread belief that drug abuse is an immoral activity like prostitution. Of course, there are those people who believe that a person should be free to engage in such "victimless" pursuits as recreational drug use in their own homes; that no one is being hurt by this practice and the government is making an unwarranted intrusion into people's lives when it punishes casual drug users. But then, on the other side of this coin are those that espouse economic, social, and health arguments against drug abuse. Many people become "hooked onto" (addicted to) certain illicit drugs and much of their lives are spent in pursuit of the drugs they need. This leads to a marked increase in crime as people steal, burgle, and rob to support their habit. In many prisons and jails, more than half of the inmates are there because of some drug offence. The argument goes that if you take the profit out of marketing illegal drugs by legalizing them, you take away the crime that accompanies the need that results in the high cost of the drugs. In addition to this social cost of drug abuse, there are the health arguments. Drug abuse, especially serious situations where someone is addicted, can cause great harm to physical and mental health. If such people cannot afford health insurance, then they become a public burden on the health system, to the detriment of everyone in society.

From all of these considerations arises a dilemma that has been here as long as our society has been regulating drugs; namely, should our resources be put into stopping the flow of drugs into the hands of users, or should society concentrate on prevention of drug abuse through education and treatment? Should we treat drug abuse as a crime or as a physical and mental illness? Many countries have vacillated back and forth among these strategies, sometimes preferring one to the other and then, with a new administration, changing tactics. These are fundamental public policy questions that are not easily answered. One of the major concerns that muddies these arguments is the extent to which illicit drugs are addictive as opposed to "merely" causing (psychological) dependency. An addiction occurs when the body makes profound physiological and biochemical changes to accommodate a drug. When the addict stops taking the drug, especially suddenly or "cold turkey," a set of physical symptoms (withdrawal syndrome) occurs. This syndrome can be intensely uncomfortable and painful, and in some cases, can even cause death. An addicted drug user will do almost anything to avoid withdrawal and his or her life may be consumed by a constant search for a reliable source of the drug. On the other hand, when a drug user does not become physically addicted to the drug, it may still exert powerful psychological effects (dependence). The user finds the effects of the drug so pleasurable or satisfying that he or she becomes dependent upon the drug. This craving is not physical, but psychological. Such users may exhibit similar behaviors to addicts; they constantly seek the drug, but there are no physical symptoms of withdrawal when the drug is stopped. In either case, drug users in the grip of an addictive or dependence causing drug may exhibit the same behaviors that are considered anti-social by governments. The cost of drug prevention and treatment is extremely high, thus there is the tension between interdicting drugs and prevention. The fact is that, for more than a century, the focus has been on regulation and distribution of illicit drugs. In the forensic science context, however, the task is not to settle the issue of whether or how drugs should be controlled, but rather to describe how drugs are classified and how forensic scientists identify and characterize them.

RECENT DEVELOPMENTS IN ILLICIT DRUG POLICY

In the second decade of this century, there have been some remarkable changes to attitudes and policies regarding illicit drugs. As of 2015, three states, California, Alaska and Washington, have legalized growing, possession, and sale of small amounts of marihuana. It is possible that more states will do this in the future. The legalization of marihuana at the state level is in opposition to Federal laws that prohibit possession and sale of marihuana. The current federal administration has indicated that it will not interfere with these initiatives at the state level as long as the state has enacted such laws.

In recent years, marihuana has been shown to have some beneficial effects to people who are suffering from glaucoma or in the treatment of cancer with drugs as well as a half dozen other diseases. Although the United States Food and Drug Administration does not officially recognize these benefits of marihuana, the Federal Government has not interfered with those states that do acknowledge the benefits and that have passed legislation permitting people who petition the courts, to possess small amounts of marihuana or an extract. As of 2015, more than 30 states and the District of Columbia have passed medical marihuana laws.

A quarter century ago, when crack cocaine exploded onto the drug scene, the United States Congress tried to stem the tide by enacting laws that provided for greatly increased penalties for possession and distribution of crack compared to flake cocaine. In some cases, the prison sentences are 10 times as long for possession of the same quantity of crack compared to flake cocaine. Many states followed this lead by enacting similar legislation. Within the past few years, the United States Justice Department has begun to signal that these penalties are unfair and unduly affect minority drug offenders. It seems likely that the Congress will soon enact legislation that will minimize the differences between the sanctions for crack and flake cocaine.

In the past few years, the abuse of so-called "synthetic narcotics" such as oxycodone and hydrocodone has exploded in the United States. These and other similar drugs have been around for a long time and some are contained in legal prescriptions as painkillers, but their abuse has risen dramatically in the past decade or so. The problem has become so severe that the government is calling for strong limitations to be put on prescription of these drugs and for increased prosecution of physicians who overprescribe them. As it has become more difficult to procure these synthetic narcotics, the use of heroin has recently shown a major uptick.

CLASSIFICATION OF ILLICIT DRUGS

There are a wide variety of illicit drugs. They range from synthetic to naturally occurring and can have a wide variety of psychoactive effects. They occur in a number of forms from plant materials and plant extracts to powders, tablets and capsules, liquids, and solids. Some can be easily grown, whereas others are manufactured using sophisticated chemistry. In order to make sense of all of these drugs, it is necessary to develop a useful classification system. In fact, there are several ways of classifying illicit drugs. As mentioned previously, the Federal laws put them in one of five schedules based upon their abuse potential and pharmacology, and the existence of a legitimate medical use. Another convenient way of classifying drugs is by origin. Under this scheme, drugs are put in one of four classes:

1. **Naturally occurring**. These substances are found in nature in plants. Part of the plant is ingested and the drug is extracted and used by the person. Examples include:
   a. **Marihuana** – The leaves are dried and smoked
   b. **Psilocybin mushrooms** – These are eaten. They contain psilocybin and psilocin, which cause hallucinations (hallucinogen)
   c. **Peyote cactus** – The cactus buttons are eaten. They contain mescaline, a hallucinogen
2. **Plant extracts**. These are naturally occurring substances that are extracted from plants and then ingested. Examples include:
   a. **Cocaine** – extracted from the coca plant
   b. **Morphine and codeine** – extracted from the opium poppy
3. **Semisynthetic**. These substances are derived chemically from a naturally occurring substance. Examples include:
   a. **Heroin** – manufactured from morphine
   b. **LSD** – manufactured from lysergic acid
4. **Synthetic**. These substances are totally manmade. Examples include:
   a. Amphetamines
   b. Barbiturates
   c. Phencyclidine (PCP)
   d. Oxycodone

This classification system is useful from the forensic chemistry standpoint as it helps in determining the proper scheme of analysis. Outside of the forensic science field, the most popular way of classifying drugs is by their psychoactive effects. Under this scheme, illicit drugs are put into one of four classes: **stimulant**, **depressant**, **narcotic**, and **hallucinogen**. Because of its popularity and acceptance by the public, this classification system will be discussed in more detail.

STIMULANTS

Stimulants are drugs that elevate one's mood. They help people feel better who are sad or depressed. They give people extra energy. Other claims are also made for stimulants; they make you stronger, faster, have better sexual experiences, even smarter. Stimulants can range in power from mild, such as caffeine, which is not an illicit drug, to strong. The most common examples of the latter are **amphetamine** and **cocaine**. Both of these drugs have been abused for many years and are still quite popular. They are excellent representatives of abused stimulants and will be discussed in more detail below.

Amphetamines

There are many drugs derived from amphetamine. Although amphetamine itself has been abused for many years around the world, a derivative called **methamphetamine** is far more popular as an illicit drug. Amphetamine arose from the desire of pharmacologists to find a substitute for **ephedrine**, the active ingredient in a group of herbs that have been used for thousands of years. Ephedrine is used today to dilate bronchial passages in treatment of asthma and this was one of the early uses of amphetamine. Amphetamine has also been used in the treatment of narcolepsy, a disease that causes its victims to fall asleep suddenly many times a day. It has also been used as an appetite suppressant and in the treatment of hyperkinesia, a disease that causes hyperactivity, mainly in children. Although still in Federal Schedule II, amphetamine is no longer widely prescribed for any of these purposes, having been replaced by drugs that are more effective with fewer side effects. Figure 13.1 shows the chemical structures of amphetamine and methamphetamine.

In the 1960s, amphetamine and methamphetamine began to be widely abused for their stimulant properties. Instead of taking the drugs orally, which was the preferred route of administration for pharmaceutical users, abusers started taking them intravenously, which magnified their effects. Even today, clandestine methamphetamine laboratories flourish in many parts of the country. There are many routes to the preparation of methamphetamine and they can be found in underground publications and on the web. Because of its potent stimulant effects, methamphetamine has been called "speed" since the 1960s and the stimulants in general are called "uppers."

In recent years, the widespread abuse of the amphetamines has led to increasingly tighter control of legitimately manufactured doses, so more of the abused drugs have been made clandestinely. In an attempt to overcome the unpleasant habit of intravenous injection of these drugs, some users developed a smokeable form of methamphetamine called "ice." Ice is made by slowly evaporating a solution of methamphetamine, forming large crystals. One of the forms of clandestine methamphetamine tablets is shown in Figure 13.2. There are a number of synthetic routes to manufacture amphetamine. As new ones crop up, the Federal Government responds by putting some of the precursors under control, making them more difficult to obtain. Clandestine chemists then develop new ways to manufacture "meth." An example of this phenomenon is the simple synthesis of methamphetamine from pseudoephedrine, an over-the-counter allergy medicine. Combining this with lithium, which can be obtained from small batteries, and ammonia that can be obtained from farms, where it is used in the manufacture of fertilizers, forms methamphetamine. The ease of obtaining these materials turned clandestine methamphetamine

$-CH_2-CH-CH_3$ / NH_2

Amphetamine

$-CH_2-CH-CH_3$ / $HN-CH_3$

Methamphetamine

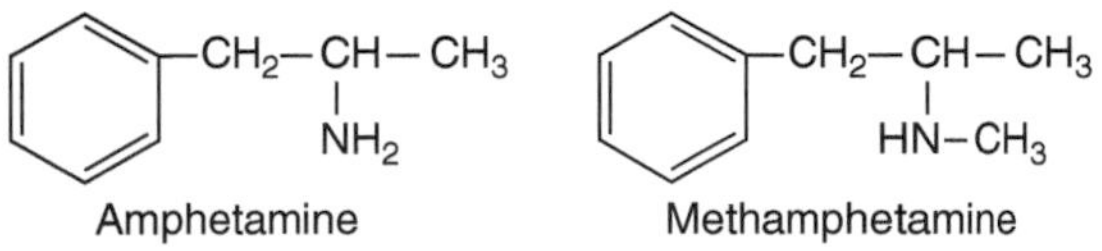

FIGURE 13.1

The chemical structures of amphetamine and methamphetamine. Note that the only difference between these two substances is that the amine group in methamphetamine has a methyl (CH_3) group. This is enough to alter the pharmacology of the molecule.

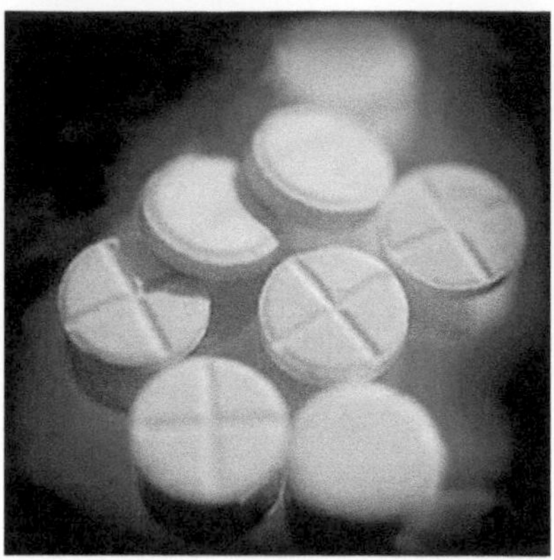

FIGURE 13.2

Clandestine Methamphetamine Tablets. These have been around for more than 50 years. They used to be called "minibennies" or "cartwheels" on the street. There have also been a number of knockoffs of these tablets, many of which contain caffeine.

manufacture into an epidemic during the 1990s and 2000s. Finally many states and the Federal Government retaliated by putting pseudoephedrine behind pharmacy counters and requiring purchasers to furnish identification and sign for the drug. People who illegally manufacture methamphetamine did not want to have to identify themselves and thus, this method of meth manufacture has been drastically curtailed. As a result, there has been a return to previous times when most methamphetamine entered the United States from large, well-organized laboratories located mainly in Mexico.

There is some disagreement as to whether amphetamine and methamphetamine are addictive. It is now generally believed that when taken intravenously, these substances become addicting, whereas when taken orally or smoked, they cause strong psychological dependence, but not addiction.

Cocaine

The other major stimulant that is abused heavily in the United States is cocaine. Cocaine is a naturally occurring substance that is found only in the *Erythoxylon coca* plant that grows almost exclusively on the Amazon slopes of the Andes Mountains in South America. Evidence from as far back as 500 AD indicates that indigenous people were using coca leaves. Five hundred years later, coca plants were being extensively cultivated in Peru. Today it is believed that more than 50 million kilograms (about 110 million pounds) are produced annually in South America, chiefly in Bolivia, Peru, and Columbia, and only a small fraction of that is used domestically or legally exported. Cocaine is extracted from the coca leaves domestically and then exported to the United States and other countries. It takes about 500 kg of coca leaves to produce 1 kg of cocaine powder. In those countries where it is grown, cocaine has been used for hundreds of years by chewing the leaves of

FIGURE 13.3

(a) Cocaine hydrochloride. This is sometimes called "snow" or "flake" or "blow." It is made by extracting cocaine from the coca plant and then treating the extract with hydrochloric acid. It is called "blow" because a popular route of ingestion is by inhaling it into the nose with a straw or small spoon. (b) The coca plant.

the coca plant, rather than by extracting the cocaine chemically. Figure 13.3(a) is a photograph of cocaine hydrochloride refined powder. Figure 13.3(b) is a photograph of coca leaves.

One of the early proponents of cocaine for its medicinal effects was Sigmund Freud, who experimented with it extensively and praised its stimulant effects and the feelings of well-being that it caused. He especially recommended it as a method for curing morphine addiction. In his famous Sherlock Holmes detective fiction books, Arthur Conan Doyle wrote about cocaine as a habit forming drug, describing Holmes' experimentation with it. A motion picture in the 1980s, "The Seven Percent

Solution" is a fictional account of how Sigmund Freud cured Sherlock Holmes' addiction to cocaine. In 1886, John Pemberton developed a new soft drink that contained coca leaves and cocaine. The stimulant and euphoric effects of the cocaine made this drink an overnight success. In 1903, Pemberton removed the cocaine from his elixir because of government pressure on the heels of medical evidence of the dangers of taking cocaine. He replaced it with caffeine. For a time, he continued to add decocainized coca leaves for flavoring. Beverages derived from his formulations are still popular today.

By the turn of the twentieth century, cocaine was extremely popular in the United States as a pleasure drug. A large number of products containing cocaine were available. These could be imbibed by drinking, sniffing through the nose, or injecting. In 1906, with the Pure Food and Drugs Act and the Harrison Act of 1914, cocaine use was severely curtailed and the drug became heavily controlled. As amphetamines became easy to obtain in the 1930s, cocaine use declined and then rose again when amphetamines became strictly controlled in the 1970s. For many years, it was believed that cocaine was not a physically addictive drug. This opinion has changed, however, with the advent of **crack**, a form of crystalline cocaine. Crack became popular because as the freebase, its melting point is lower than powdered cocaine, enabling crack to be smoked. This enables crack to be absorbed more easily by the body and its effects are greatly magnified. When smoked, crack cocaine can cause physical addiction. Sniffing powdered cocaine, on the other hand, does not lead to addiction although a strong psychological dependence can occur. Crack cocaine is shown in Figure 13.4.

FIGURE 13.4

Crack cocaine. This is a form of cocaine freebase. It is smoked rather than snorted. It is made from flake cocaine by treating it with sodium bicarbonate or other alkaline substances.

Cocaine provides an excellent case study of the huge profits that are to be made in illegal drug trafficking. A major drug trafficker can obtain 500 pounds of coca leaves from a farmer for about $500. This in turn, will produce about one pound of pure cocaine. This is sold to a refiner/exporter for about $3000. Broken down into smaller packages and diluted, the final product, up to 5 pounds of diluted cocaine can sell for as much as $100,000 on the streets of the United States. Much of this increase in price can be traced to the fact that cocaine is illegal to manufacture, possess, or distribute in the United States. Since lengthy imprisonment and heavy fines await violators, they charge a lot of money for the product because of the risk they are taking.

DEPRESSANTS

When one thinks of abused depressant substances, the first one that comes to mind is ethyl alcohol, used to make beer, wine, and spirits. It is important to note, however, that alcohol is not a controlled substance in the United States, and thus is not covered under the laws that control drugs. Alcohol is covered under a separate set of regulations. This topic will be covered in the chapter on forensic toxicology in Chapter 14. Over the years, a number of depressant substances have been abused. These have been mostly legitimate prescription medicines taken because of their depressant effects. In many cases, they are taken along with stimulants to try to mediate their depressant effects. A few of the more popular abused depressants are described below.

The Barbiturates

Depressant drugs are known by a variety of names including sedatives, hypnotics, and the street drug term "downers." They all have the common effect to one degree or another, of decreasing brain activity. In small doses, these drugs may be taken to reduce anxiety and are termed "sedatives." In larger doses, the same drugs are taken as sleeping pills and are called "hypnotics." The major class of illicit depressants in the United States is the **barbiturates**. This is a group of chemical substances based on the compounds **barbituric acid** and **thiobarbituric acid**. Barbituric acid itself is not a central nervous system depressant, but over 2500 derivatives have since been produced. Barbiturates are grouped pharmacologically into three groups: short, intermediate, and long acting.

As a group, the barbiturates can be highly addictive and withdrawal can be difficult and dangerous. Sudden ("cold turkey") withdrawal of some of the more powerful barbiturates can be fatal. There is also a great danger of the interaction of alcohol and barbiturates. Several people, including some celebrities have died from an accidental (or deliberate) overdose of alcohol and "barbs." Other people become addicted to barbiturates and amphetamines, taking both in great quantities. Detoxification from this potentially lethal combination of drugs can take many months or even years.

IN MORE DETAILS: BARBITURATES AND DEATH PENALTIES

The United States and other countries have been carrying out death penalties for many years. Traditional methods for executions include firing squad, hanging, electrocution, and chemicals. In the United States, some methods of execution have been outlawed because they are in violation of the Eighth Amendment of the Constitution, which prohibits "cruel and unusual punishment." Most states and Federal statutes now require a lethal injection for executions. For years, the regimen has included the following:

1. Sodium pentothal or pentobarbital to render the prisoner unconscious
2. Pancuronium bromide to cause muscle paralysis
3. Potassium chloride to stop the heart and cause death by cardiac arrest

Although in most of the instances where lethal injection has been used and been effective, there have been some cases where the prisoner took a long time to become unconscious, or death was greatly delayed or the prisoner was in agony. Several high-profile lawsuits have been filed for "botched executions" and Eighth Amendment violations. This has caused some jurisdictions to take another look at lethal injections as a means of execution. In addition, several of the few laboratories worldwide who manufacture the sodium pentothal or pentobarbital have either stopped making them or refuse to sell them if they are to be used in lethal injections. This has caused a shortage of the drugs, which has delayed some executions.

Other Depressants

Besides the barbiturates, other depressants have been abused over the years. One of the more popular of these used to be **meprobamate** (Miltown), which was introduced in the 1950s. This never became a widely used or abused drug except for a short time in the 1960s and 1970s. Since barbiturates became popular, scientists have searched for alternative drugs that would be less toxic and addicting. They thought they had one with **methaqualone**, marketed as "Quaalude" and as "Sopor," thus earning the drug the nicknames of "ludes" and "sopers." College students heavily abused the drug in the 1960s and 1970s and it didn't take long to prove that it was just as dangerous as the barbiturates. It was finally taken off the market in 1985 and abuse today is almost nonexistent. Another attempt to develop a more suitable drug to replace the barbiturates was the **benzodiazepines**. The first one was called "Librium" (chlordiazepoxide). Librium was so-called because it liberated people from their anxieties. It rose to become the most often prescribed drug in the United States in the late 1960s. It was later supplanted by "Valium" (diazepam), which is more potent. Valium soon became the country's most popular prescribed drug. It also became a very popular illicit drug and before long, doctors discovered that withdrawal was causing addiction and dependence-like symptoms. Overdose deaths rose markedly and Valium soon became more tightly controlled by the Federal Government and enforced by the DEA. Today, Valium is still prescribed for anxiety but at greatly reduced rates. Valium injections are used today as an anesthetic in some medical procedures and minor surgeries.

NARCOTICS

Do you ever wonder why, in the classic movie, *The Wizard of Oz*, Dorothy fell asleep in the field of beautiful red flowers on her way to the castle of Oz? Those were the flowers of the **opium poppy**; *Papaver somniferum*, a plant with more than 5000 years history as a medicinal plant. Opium, the resin from the poppy plant, has been, at least until the past 100 years or so, the one reliable, naturally occurring substance that physicians could use for pain and suffering, and for diarrhea and dehydration from dysentery. It has also given users pleasure, peace, rest, and relief from anxiety. These latter effects have caused opium and its derivatives to be abused throughout its history. Its highly addictive nature has also placed many of these people in its grip for much of their lives. An opium poppy pod is shown in Figure 13.5. Opium resin is contained within the pod. One of the ancient ways that opium resin is harvested is for the farmer to make slits in the pods. As the resin oozes out, workers run through the fields wearing clothing to which the resin will cling. The clothing is laid out to dry and then resin is then removed. It can be smoked as is, or extracted to remove naturally occurring narcotics such as morphine or codeine.

Narcotics Derived from Opium

Because of their ability to relieve pain and cause sleep, opium and its derivatives became known as **narcotics**. This is derived from the Greek word *narkotikos*, which means, "sleep." During the early part of the twentieth century, the term "narcotic" became synonymous with all drugs that were considered dangerous and in need of control. Because of this, "narcotic" became a pejorative label and any drug that was classified as a narcotic was painted with this negative image.

Some states labeled marihuana and cocaine as narcotics and this became incorporated into state laws until as recently as the 1970s. Today, some narcotics are still used as legitimate pharmaceuticals. Morphine, which is extracted from opium, is a powerful analgesic (painkiller), used in surgical procedures. It is interesting to note that **heroin**, a drug that is easily made from morphine, is approximately ten times more potent, and is used legitimately as an analgesic in some other countries. But heroin has such a bad name in the United States that it is a Schedule I controlled substance and has no legitimate medical use here. Besides morphine, **codeine** is the

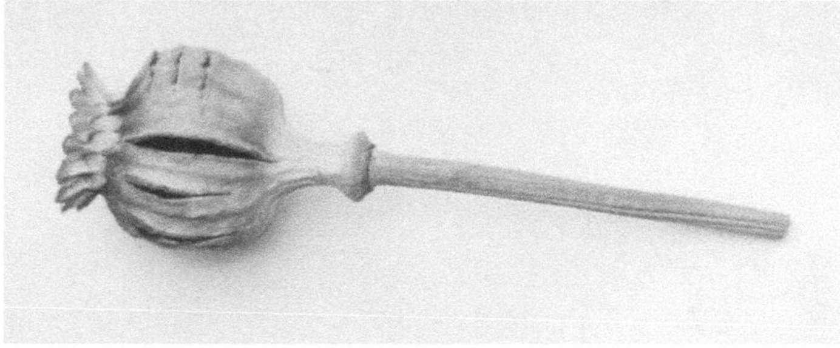

FIGURE 13.5

A pod from the opium poppy plant. At harvest time, the pods are slit open, allowing the resin to ooze out. This is gathered and dried. It contains about 10% morphine and a lesser amount of codeine. The resin itself has been smoked for thousands of years.

other popular derivative from opium. Codeine is a popular cough suppressant in liquid preparations and is also mixed with mild analgesics such as aspirin or Tylenol® to boost their analgesic (pain management) effects. Figure 13.6 shows some elixirs containing Schedules I and II controlled substances. These were stolen from a drug store during an overnight robbery.

Synthetic Narcotics

Besides the naturally occurring narcotics, there are also a number of synthetic narcotics that are still prescribed for pain. These include Demerol (meperidine), oxycodone, hydrocodone, fentanyl, and many others. Of the members of this group, a few bear special mentioning. Methadone is a synthetic narcotic that is used in the United States as a heroin substitute to get addicts off of heroin under close medical supervision. Fentanyl (China White) is the backbone of a series of **designer drugs**, illegal substances that are synthesized with particular pharmacological characteristics designed for abuse purposes. Oxycodone (Percodan), is, at the time this is being written, making a large comeback in the United States as an abused drug and is known as "Oxycontin." Fatal overdoses among young users are skyrocketing.

The preferred illicit narcotic for many years in the United States has been heroin. The preferred mode of ingestion of heroin has been by intravenous injection. Because addicts often have difficulty getting sterile needles, they often contract blood-borne diseases such as hepatitis or AIDS from sharing contaminated syringes. Another problem with heroin use over the years has been purity. Over the years purity has varied from less than 3% to more than 10%. This has led to many problems

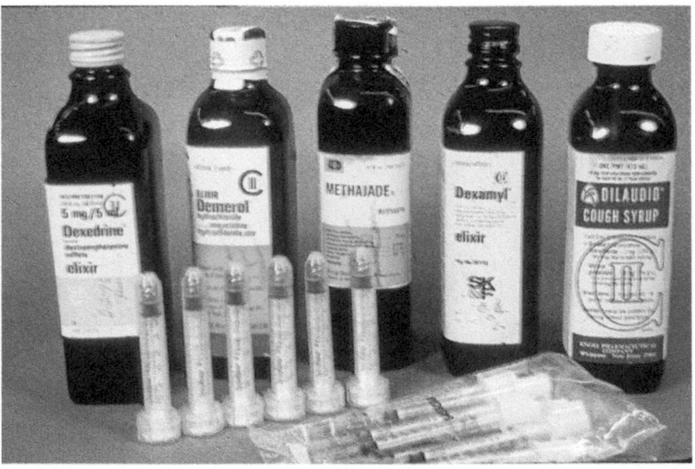

FIGURE 13.6

Some elixirs containing controlled substances. Demerol, Methajade, and Dilauded are all synthetic narcotics. Dexedrine is an amphetamine and Dexamyl is a combination of an amphetamine and a barbiturate. These bottles were seized from a thief who was trying to steal them from the storage room of a drug store.

with overdosing, where the user may take a more potent dose than he or she is used to. Along with this is the often bizarre variety of cutting agents used in heroin, some of which can cause illness or even death. Heroin addiction is also expensive and because some addicts cannot hold down a job or earn money, they must steal to support their habit. This causes inflated crime rates traceable to the drug abuse and fills our prisons with addicts.

HALLUCINOGENS

The types of drugs that have been discussed thus far; stimulants, depressants, and narcotics all have at least some members that have accepted, legitimate medical uses. This is not the case with the hallucinogens. Most of the important members of this class are naturally occurring substances, although a few, such as PCP are synthetic. None of the prominent members of this class have any legitimate medical use in the United States. Many plants contain substances that can cause pain, suffering, sickness, and even death if ingested in sufficient quantity. This is, no doubt, part of their evolution that gives them an edge for survival. People and animals are not likely to try these plants twice if doing so results in unpleasant experiences. It is also true, however, that man has learned to ingest some plants or plant substances in amounts and ways that cause pleasant effects without the dangerous or uncomfortable side effects. These make up the illicit hallucinogens, virtually all of which are in Federal Schedule I. Hallucinogens fall into a number of classes based on the chemical structure of the psychoactive substance. A few of the more common ones will be discussed below.

D-Lysergic Acid Diethyl Amide

LSD is not a naturally occurring substance but is derived from ergot alkaloids which themselves are derived from a grain fungus. This mold, if incorporated into bread products made from infected grain, can result in a disorder called **ergotism** or **St Anthony's Fire** (see box below). LSD is the most potent and certainly the most famous of the hallucinogens and the one that is most responsible for popularizing this genre of drugs. As little as 50 μg (a droplet smaller than a period on this page) of LSD can cause auditory and visual hallucinogens that can last up to 12 h. LSD is not addictive and psychological dependence has been rarely recorded, but it can cause psychosis in borderline cases and often gives rise to **flashbacks**, episodes of hallucinations months or years after a dose of the drug was taken. It has also been implicated in liver damage among regular users. LSD is normally taken in unusual dosage forms. It is a colorless, odorless, tasteless liquid. It may be dissolved in a volatile solvent and then impregnated onto absorbent paper, which is often decorated with colorful cartoon characters. Once dried, the paper is cut up into small squares and ingested. This form is called "blotter acid." This is shown in Figure 13.7. Other forms of LSD include tiny colorful tablets (microdots) or small pieces of impregnated, dried gelatin (window panes). There have been cases where a dose of LSD was put behind a postage stamp on a letter and mailed to another user.

ST ANTHONY'S FIRE

If not properly stored, rye grain is susceptible to attack by a fungus known as *Claviceps purpurea*. One of the major alkaloids in this fungus is lysergic acid, the parent compound of LSD. If lysergic acid is ingested in large quantities, **ergotism**, or St Anthony's fire results. As far back as the ninth century, there have been reports of people suffering a plague of blisters and a sensation that their arms and legs were falling off (they weren't). Ergot poisoning is characterized by gangrene and extreme pain and burning sensation. Convulsions, hallucinations, and even death can result from acute ergot poisoning.

St Anthony is the patron saint of victims of ergotism and the Order of St Anthony treated many of the sufferers. There have been sporadic reports of outbreaks of ergotism throughout the middle ages, some of them called "dancing mania." Some historians claim that women accused of witchcraft had St Anthony's fire and that explained their behavior. This has never been proven, however.

In the seventeenth century, the ergot fungus was identified as the cause of St Anthony's fire. Damp growing conditions in Europe contributed to outbreaks of the disease. The most recent reported outbreak took place in Pont St. Esprit in France in 1951. Four people died and several hundred exhibited symptoms.

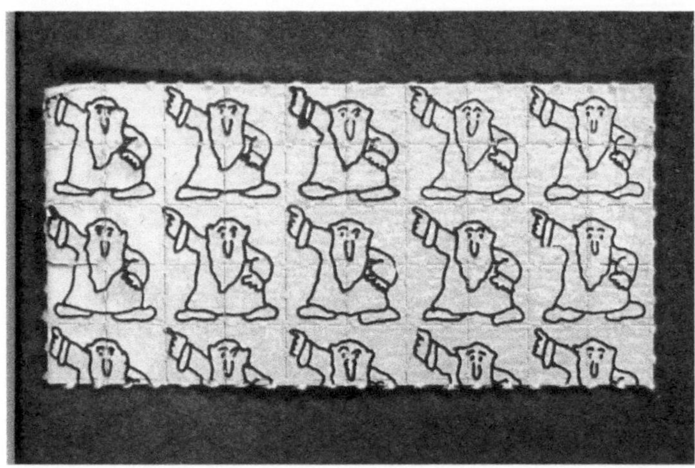

FIGURE 13.7

Blotter acid. D-Lysergic acid diethyl amide (LSD) is dissolved in a solvent and poured onto absorbent paper. The solvent is allowed to evaporate, leaving the LSD. The paper is cut into small squares and eaten.

Psilocybin

Psilocybin is similar to LSD in that its chemical structural backbone is the same (a substance called an "indole"). It is found in a variety of mushrooms with the most potent one being *Psilocybe mexicana*. Psilocybin's effects are similar to both LSD and mescaline and there appears to be some cross-tolerance among these three hallucinogens. Dried mushrooms contain approximately 0.5% psilocybin. The most effective dose seems to be about 5 mg, with higher doses causing some unpleasant effects. One of the more serious problems with psilocybin abuse is collecting the proper

FIGURE 13.8

Marihuana leaves. There are always an odd number of leaves. The leaves are primarily dried and smoked. They contain considerable amounts of Δ^9-tetrahydrocannabinol (THC), the active hallucinogenic substance in these plants.

types of mushrooms. There are more than 15 varieties of psilocybe mushrooms, but some of them resemble highly toxic varieties. A few poisonings are reported every year among people who ingest the wrong types.

Marihuana

Marihuana is unique among the controlled substances. It has some analgesic properties, albeit mild, and was, at one time, classified as a narcotic for pharmacologic and political reasons. It also has some sedative properties, also mild. It is most famous for its mild hallucinogenic effects and here is where it seems to be best classified. Marihuana leaves are shown in Figure 13.8.

Unlike the other hallucinogens discussed in this section, marihuana has been purported to have beneficial medical effects. These include antiemetic (relieves nausea and upset stomach) effects for symptoms caused by anticancer drugs. It has also been linked to the reduction of eye pressure caused by glaucoma. It is important to note that as of now, the FDA does not recognize any of these or other medical effects of marihuana and therefore, the Federal Government maintains the position that marihuana has no accepted medical use.

The marihuana plant grows worldwide. It belongs to the genus *Cannabis*. In the 1960s, there was controversy over how many species there are in this genus. Some botanists felt that there was evidence for 4 species; *sativa, indicus, gigantis, and ruderalis*. Others believed that there is only one species, *sativa*, and the others are regional variants of this plant. When the Federal Government first controlled marihuana, the legal literature and statutes referred to it as *Cannabis sativa*. In the 1960s and 1970s there were many legal problems with prosecutions of marihuana cases in state and federal courts because it is virtually impossible to determine which species is present if one is presented with dried, chopped up leaves. Forensic scientists were being challenged to prove that what was seized met the requirements of the law, namely that it was *C. sativa* and not a different species. To respond to these challenges, Congress and state legislatures took note that all marihuana, no matter what species it might be, contains the active ingredients that give the plant its hallucinogenic properties; the cannabinoid alkaloids, chiefly Δ^9-tetrahydrocannabinol (THC). They changed the legal description of marihuana to include all members of the genus *Cannabis*, and that ended the legal skirmishing. Marihuana is currently controlled as a Federal Schedule I substance. For many years there has been an active legalization lobby in the United States and elsewhere. In the United States, the most enduring group is called the *National Organization for the Reform of Marihuana Laws* (NORML). They advocate and lobby for decriminalization and legalization of marihuana.

Marihuana has been used for thousands of years. The bark of the plant is especially useful for making a type of rope called hemp and marihuana is sometimes called the hemp plant. In some countries (e.g., Japan), marihuana is still grown for its hemp. In the United States colonial times, George Washington was known to cultivate marihuana for hemp! Some "counterculture" shops in the United States and elsewhere sell clothing that is woven out of hemp. The THC content of marihuana varies regionally. In some low-grade plants it is less than 1%. With careful breeding and cultivation and removal of male plants a form of female, seedless marihuana called **sinsemilla**, can be grown with THC content as high as 10%. There is also a Federal Government that supported experimental farm in Mississippi, where marihuana with THC content over 30% has been cultivated. The THC in marihuana is concentrated in the resin, which is most abundant in the flowering tops and leaves of the plant. The stalks, seeds, and roots contain almost no THC and are generally removed. The leaves and flowers are dried and then smoked. In many jurisdictions, marihuana stems and stalks are not controlled and seeds are only controlled if they are viable (they can be germinated). Concentrated forms of marihuana are prepared in various ways and known by different names all over the world. In the United States, the plant material can be boiled in methyl alcohol, filtered, and then evaporated down to a thick, gooey liquid known as **hashish (hash) oil**. High quality hash oil may contain more than 50% THC. Another preparation, hashish (hash) is prepared by collecting the resin from the live plants with leather straps and cloths. It consists of resin and hairs from the plant. It is a solid and is often sold in bricks. Hash oil and hash are generally smoked in small pipes that are designed for this purpose. The dish in the center of Figure 13.9 shows some pieces of hashish.

Marihuana has some interesting effects on some people in that it appears that smoking and enjoying the drug involves a learning process. This consists of learning just how long to keep the smoke in the lungs before exhaling and learning how to recognize and cultivate the mild hallucinogenic effects. These behavioral characteristics may lead to a type of "reverse tolerance" whereby the effects seem to be stronger as one gets more experienced in smoking. Some of this reverse tolerance may be due to

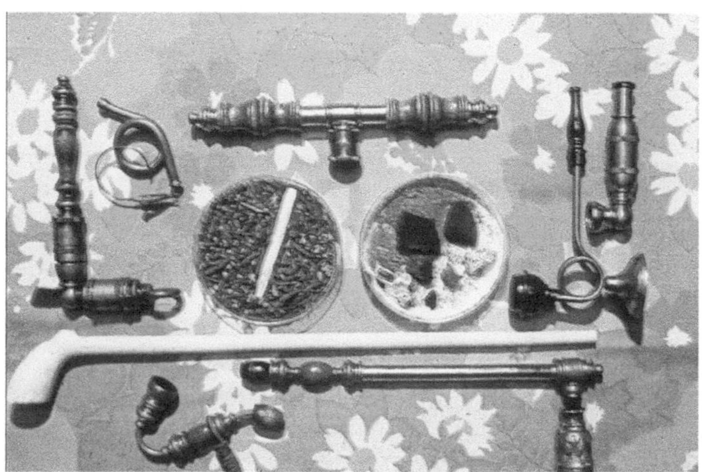

FIGURE 13.9

Hashish (in dish in center), marihuana leaves and some of the different types of pipes that are used to smoke it. Hash is made by extracting marihuana with a solvent such as methanol and then allowing it to evaporate. The residue is generally formed into bricks and allowed to dry.

a very long half-life for THC, which has been found in some tissues for months after the last ingestion. Marihuana also seems to have an appetite stimulating effect on many people, especially inexperienced users who report that they get the "munchies" and want to eat great quantities of food after smoking marihuana.

Synthetic Marihuana

Within the past decade, a new form of marihuana has appeared on the drug scene. It is synthetic marihuana and is called "Spice" or "K2" or any of hundreds of other names on the street. It is basically a blend of herbs and plant material that has been sprayed with one or more synthetic cannabinoids. These are substances that mimic the effects of THC. Synthetic marihuana products seem to have the same effects and side effects as marihuana. In 2011, the DEA temporarily classified some of the synthetic cannabinoids as Schedule I controlled substances. Today, more than half of the states have passed legislation that controls synthetic marihuana. Synthetic marihuana preparations do not react to the typical laboratory tests for marihuana.

Spice has grown in popularity over the past few years although in 2013, poison control centers determined that calls concerning poisonings were leveling off.

Mescaline

Mescaline is one of a group of substances (see below for more examples) whose chemical structure is similar to amphetamine but because of substitutions on the benzene ring, have hallucinogenic, rather than stimulant properties. Mescaline is found in the upper crown of the **peyote cactus** that grows extensively in Mexico and the southwest part of the United States. These mescal buttons are harvested and then sliced into wafers. These are then softened in the mouth and then rolled up into balls and swallowed. Intense hallucinations follow which can last for many hours. Mescaline use has been part of the religious ceremonies of certain tribes of Native Americans for many hundreds of years and remains so today. Figure 13.10 shows peyote cactus buttons obtained during a law enforcement raid on a house in Virginia.

3,4-methylenedioxy-methamphetamine (MDMA) (Ecstasy)

This amphetamine derivative has been around for many years and is considered by some psychiatrists to be a true hallucinogen. It has even been used in psychotherapy, at least until the mid-1980s when the Congress moved to control it. Since then its use has exploded in the United States. It has become the drug of choice in the popular drug and alcohol parties known as "raves." It is a Schedule I controlled substance.

Phencyclidine

PCP was first marketed by Parke, Davis & Company as one of a new class of intravenous anesthetics. It was first used in surgical procedures on both large mammals and on humans. It turned out to be an excellent anesthetic for animals, principally monkeys, but did not work well on humans. It also appeared to cause hallucinations. It also caused some bizarre side effects in humans that include a feeling of no pain sensations, superhuman strength, rage, loss of memory, and paranoia. In the 1970s it was taken off the market even as an anesthetic for animals because of the side

FIGURE 13.10

Peyote cactus buttons. Peyote contains a potent hallucinogen, mescaline. The buttons are usually eaten and the mescaline is absorbed into the blood stream. This seizure contained over 300 cactus buttons, one of the largest seizures of this drug in Virginia at that time.

effects. It is now considered to have no legitimate medical use and is in Federal Schedule I. PCP is abused in a variety of forms. It showed up in the 1960s as a small, white tablet called the "peace pill." At about the same time, it was sprinkled or recrystallized onto marihuana, which was then fraudulently sold as high-grade marihuana such as "Acapulco Gold," or "Colombian" and was also known as "wobble weed" or "sherms" (the drug hit you like a Sherman tank). In the 1970s, someone got the bright idea that contaminating marihuana with PCP was a waste of good marihuana and started impregnating otherwise nonhallucinogenic plant material such as oregano or parsley with PCP. In this context, the drug is the aforementioned "wobble weed." On the East Coast in the 1960s and 1970s, clandestine PCP laboratory activity was intense. PCP is among the easiest of the illicit drugs to manufacture in a home laboratory. A typical laboratory raid netted many pounds of the drug and great quantities of dried parsley. Some of this activity financed other illegal and illicit activities of motorcycle gangs.

DRUG ANALYSIS

There are a number of important considerations in designing methods for drug analysis. Chief among these is the desired information that is to be gained from the analysis. A number of questions should be answered before embarking on a scheme of analysis:

1. How are the controlled drugs defined and described in this jurisdiction?
2. Are the weight of the drug and/or the aggregate weight of the exhibit important? Does the case involve unusually large amounts of drug or a large number of exhibits or a very small amount of the drug?
3. Must the identity of the drug be established and then confirmed?
4. Is it necessary to determine the purity of the drug exhibit (quantitative analysis)?
5. Is it necessary to identify any of the cutting agents present in the exhibit?

Each of these questions will be taken up in turn. From the answers, it can be shown how an acceptable scheme of analysis can be developed that will stand up to the scrutiny of a courtroom.

HOW ARE DRUGS DESCRIBED LEGALLY?

Even though most states subscribe to some form of the model controlled substance legislation propounded by the Federal Government, there are still some differences in how drugs are defined by a state legislature. For example, as explained above, there were many legal problems for drug chemists when marihuana was narrowly defined as the specific species *C. sativa*. Likewise, cocaine was at one time, subject to legal challenges over its description as having to be derived from coca leaves. Cocaine can occur as two mirror image isomers, only one of which is derived from coca leaves. It is then left to the drug chemist to prove that an exhibit is not the other isomer. These examples reinforce the necessity that the drug chemist knows how the law defines a particular controlled substance so that the chosen scheme of analysis takes the definition into account.

WEIGHT AND SAMPLING

In some jurisdictions, not only is the identity of the illicit drug important, but also the quantity. This can be understood in three contexts. First, there is a desire among prosecutors and police to concentrate their law enforcement efforts on major drug dealers rather than the low-level user. If the possession of large quantities of drugs is punished more harshly than small amounts, then this might discourage large-scale drug dealers from plying their trade. The important question here is what constitutes the weight of the drug? Illicit drugs are seldom sold in a pure form. They are almost always adulterated, or cut with other substances. In most states that have weight laws, it is the aggregate weight that counts. This is the weight of the drug and any cutting agents present. So, for example, many states have laws that penalize someone with life imprisonment who possesses a substance containing cocaine or heroin that is over a certain aggregate weight. The cocaine or heroin doesn't have to weigh that much, it is the total weight that counts. So an exhibit that contains 1 g of cocaine cut with 650 g of sugar, can still qualify under this law. Of course, it goes without saying that there must be proof that the balance that is used to determine these aggregate weights is accurate. Another context where weight is important is where a government wishes to punish the possession of one form of a drug more harshly than another. This is the way that the Federal Government sanctions cocaine. Under Federal law, the possession of equal weights of cocaine flake (or salt) and crack carry vastly different penalties, with the crack form carrying a much higher penalty. Weight considerations also come into play at the opposite end of the spectrum, where there is very little material present. In some states, there must be a **useable quantity** of a drug present in order for a law to be broken. A useable quantity is defined as an amount of a drug that is likely to have a demonstrable psychoactive effect on an average person. Mere traces are not enough.

There is also another weight-related consideration and that is sampling. This comes into play when there are very large exhibits or when there are a large number of exhibits, and the question arises as to how much of the material must actually be analyzed. In the case of large exhibits, it is usually not necessary to identify every particle in the exhibit. However, if the entire mass of substance is to be characterized as being or containing a controlled substance, the samples taken for analysis must be representative of the whole exhibit. For example, the exhibit depicted in Figure 13.11 is a brick of marihuana that was compressed in a trash compactor. Several samples were taken from the exterior and interior of the brick and independently tested in order to show that the entire 38 pounds was marihuana.

Another major sampling issue arises with cases that have a large number of exhibits. Many times a drug chemist will receive a case that consists of hundreds or thousands of exhibits. It would be unduly consumptive of time and effort to fully analyze

FIGURE 13.11

A 38.5 lb brick of marihuana. This solid mass of plant material was formed in a trash compactor and left in a stairwell in a college dormitory basement. Prior to analysis, the brick was X-rayed to make sure that it wasn't booby trapped.

every exhibit. However, if one is to report that all of the exhibits contain a particular illicit drug, then it is necessary to show that the samples that were taken for analysis are representative of the whole. Let's look at one possible approach. Suppose that a case contains 1000 exhibits. Five hundred exhibits consist of white powders, each wrapped in foil. Each appears to be approximately the same size and weight. The other 500 exhibits are small, plastic baggies each containing approximately the same amount of white powder. At the start, these would be treated as two types of exhibits. A random sample of the foil-wrapped drugs would be opened, examined, and weighed. If they all appeared the same and weighed approximately the same, then one might assume for now that all 500 contain the same thing. The same would then be done on a random sample of the plastic-wrapped exhibits. Then a random sample of each of the two types would be tested and the drugs identified. The total weight of each 500 exhibits would then be estimated and the qualitative and quantitative results would be reported for the whole case. If, at any time, one or more of the randomly selected exhibits appeared to be different in appearance or chemical properties than the rest, then the analysis scheme would have to be changed.

Finally there is the opposite situation, where there is very little of a drug present in an exhibit. Examples of this are "roaches" (marihuana cigarette butts), "cookers" (usually bottle caps containing the residue of injected heroin), or even bloody syringes that were used to inject heroin that may contain traces of the drug. States that have useable quantity laws require that a certain minimum amount of a drug be present in order to prosecute someone for possession of an illicit drug. It is unlikely that any of the three examples given above would qualify as useable quantities of drug under these statutes. In states where there are no useable quantity laws, then these exhibits could be analyzed and reported out as controlled substances. In some cases, there may not be enough material to do a complete analysis and a confirmatory test may not be done. This will be discussed later.

DRUG PURITY

As mentioned previously, drugs are nearly always contaminated by impurities. These fall into two categories: excipients and diluents. **Excipients** are substances that may mimic the activity of the main illicit drug present in order to make it more difficult for the user to know just how much of the drug there really is in the exhibit. For example, a common excipient in cocaine exhibits is lidocaine. Lidocaine, like cocaine, is a topical anesthetic. When cocaine is snorted, it numbs the nasal membranes, as does lidocaine. Thus, if lidocaine is present, the user cannot determine, at least by the numbing action, how much cocaine is present. **Diluents**, on the other hand, are chemicals that are used to dilute an illicit drug and to give it more bulk. This is done to cut the purity of the drug, and increase the amount and thus the profits. In most states, there is no requirement that cutting agents be identified in drug exhibits. In some areas including in some federal cases, it is necessary to identify and quantify all cutting agents present with an illicit drug. This is done chiefly for intelligence purposes so that the law enforcement agents can track a case up through the distribution chain and identify the possible origin of the drugs.

DEVELOPING AN ANALYTICAL SCHEME

Once the weight and sampling issues have been settled, then it is necessary to develop a scheme of analysis for the exhibits. This scheme will ordinarily proceed from general types of tests toward specific tests. For most drug analyses, the goal is to unequivocally identify all controlled substances in an exhibit. There are certain cases where this **confirmation** may not be done. These situations will be discussed later. Each exhibit should be treated as an unknown substance. Police officers or drug enforcement agents may already have a good idea what is contained in a drug exhibit and will usually relay this information to the drug chemist. Sometimes this information is based in part on some field-testing that the officer may have performed. Several companies sell field test kits that contain the chemicals necessary to perform a preliminary or presumptive test on a suspected controlled substance. These tests may be necessary for the law enforcement agency to establish probable cause to obtain a search warrant or for other purposes. Even if this test is performed the results are only preliminary and cannot be relied on for identification purposes. Therefore, although information about a drug case may be interesting and perhaps useful, it should not dissuade the drug chemist from treating each case as an unknown situation.

One of the most important advances in the development and validation of analytical tests and schemes for drug analysis has been the work of the **Scientific Working Group on Seized Drugs** (SWGDRUG). This international committee of drug experts has been working for nearly 10 years on developing standards for the analysis of illicit drugs. SWGDRUG was formed and is funded by the United States DEA. It has developed standards for schemes of analysis, education and professional development of drug chemists, quality assurance and control, sampling and statistical analysis. Its work is ongoing. Check their website at: www.swgdrug.org for more information and a listing of their standards.

Preliminary Tests

The first test done on a drug exhibit is visual. The package should be opened (protective gloves should be worn. LSD can be absorbed through the skin, causing significant hallucinations.) The appearance of the exhibit should be noted. Plant materials may be treated differently than white powders or marked tablets. The exhibit is then weighed. Over the past 50 years or so, a number of presumptive tests have been developed that react with various common controlled drugs, usually resulting in a visual color change to the reagent when the drug is added. These are valuable tests in that they can give the examiner some possible avenues for further examination. For example, the **Ruybal** (**or Scott**) test consists of three reagents that are added in turn to an exhibit suspected to be or contain cocaine. The final result of the test is a turquoise color in a chloroform layer at the bottom of the test tube where the test is run. This test is said to be presumptive for cocaine. It is not specific, there are other substances that give similar results to this test, but it does give the analyst a direction to proceed, namely to continue to test for the presence of cocaine. Some of the more common presumptive tests and the drugs they are used on are given below.

Presumptive Test	Drug(s)	Results
Duquenois–Levine	Marihuana	Purple bottom layer
Ruybal (Scott)	Cocaine	Turquoise bottom layer
Marquis	Opium derivatives	Purple
Marquis (+water)	Amphetamine	Bright orange fluorescence
Dillie-Koppanyi	Barbiturates	Purple
Ehrlich's	LSD	Purple

LSD, D-lysergic acid diethyl amide.

Figure 13.12 is a field test kit commonly used by narcotics and other law enforcement agents.

Microcrystal Tests

In this test, a reagent or series of reagents are added to a suspected drug under carefully controlled conditions so that the drug forms a complex with the reagent(s) and is allowed to slowly recrystallize. The appearance, color, shape, and speed of crystallization are characteristic of particular types of drugs. Not all drug laboratories use microcrystal tests—their use has been declining over

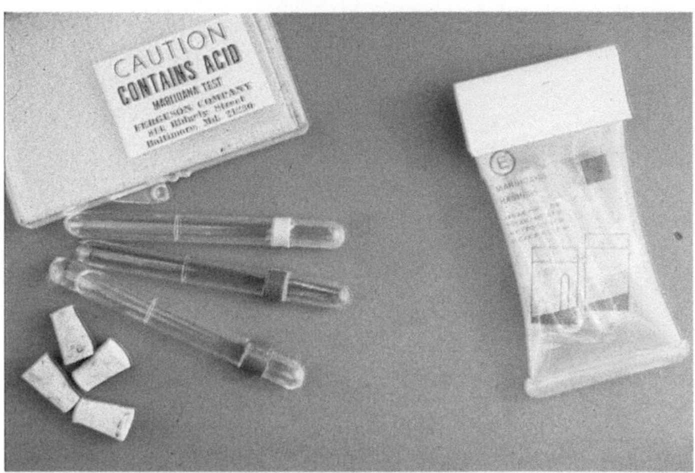

FIGURE 13.12

A field test kit. There are a number of different types of kits. In the type pictured here, a sample of suspected marihuana leaf is put into the thick, plastic envelope. There are three vials in the envelope. The envelope is squeezed so that each vial breaks. The contents are then shaken and, if marihuana is present, will turn purple. The vials on the left of the figure are single vial tests for different types of drugs.

the past 25 years. In some parts of the country, especially in certain laboratories in California, microcrystal tests are used as confirmatory tests for a few selected drugs. In these situations, at least two different microcrystal tests are run along with other presumptive tests before a confirmation is declared. A certain percentage of these cases are also checked by another confirmatory test to make sure that the microcrystal tests are working properly. In other laboratories where microcrystal tests are used, they are considered to be presumptive tests that require further testing for confirmation. SWGDRUG considers microcrystal tests to be presumptive.

Chromatography

As discussed in Chapter 6, chromatography tests are utilized for separation purposes. They are not used for confirmation of a drug. Once the preliminary tests have been run on an exhibit, the drug chemist may run a thin-layer chromatography (TLC) test to determine how many substances are present in the exhibit and what they might be. TLC will usually show a spot for each drug and most excipients, but will usually not indicate any diluents. Some laboratories will utilize gas chromatography or liquid chromatography for these purposes. Chromatography may be used as an essential part of confirmation by methods such as gas chromatography/mass spectrometry (GC/MS) where compounds that have identical mass spectra may have different retention times.

Quantitative Analysis

When quantitative analysis of a drug exhibit is called for, gas chromatography (or GC/MS) is almost always used. High performance liquid chromatography (HPLC) will work just as well on many drugs. To get accurate results by chromatography, an internal standard must always be used.

Confirmation

Most drug exhibits must be confirmed. There are two tests that are generally recognized as confirmatory for controlled substances. It is only necessary to run one of these tests. The most common one in modern drug laboratories is GC/MS. If one has a white powder that is suspected of containing cocaine, then a small portion of the powder is dissolved in a suitable solvent such as chloroform and then filtered. The cocaine will be separated by the GC and then identified by the mass spectrometer. Many commercial GC/MS instruments have computer-based libraries of mass spectra of illicit drugs that can be compared to the spectrum of the drug exhibit. The retention time of the drug peak and its mass spectrum may give an absolute identification of the drug. The other confirmatory test for drugs is infrared spectrophotometry (usually FTIR). An infrared spectrum is unique to each individual chemical compound (except certain isomers and homologs). Infrared spectrophotometers often come with computerized, searchable spectral libraries that aid in identification of the spectrum. One drawback to FTIR relative to GC/MS is that the drug must be separated from the cutting agents prior to obtaining the IR spectrum. In the case of small or dilute samples, this can pose a problem. Some analytical chemists who are familiar with the operation and interpretation of nuclear magnetic resonance spectroscopy use this technique for the identification of certain drugs.

Some Unusual Situations

There are some situations where the usual schemes of analysis may not be used. These occur where there is visual or other evidence that the controlled substance present is most probably of a certain type. The most common situation that illustrates this is marihuana. As was previously mentioned, marihuana is most often used by smoking the dried, crushed leaves, and flowers of the cannabis plant. This plant material has some distinctive features that can be used to help in identification. These features include the presence of **cystolith** hairs on one side of the leaf surface and numerous, small white hairs on the other side. The seeds of the cannabis plant are also quite distinctive in appearance. Once the drug analyst recognizes these characteristic features, then it is necessary only to show that the cannabinoid alkaloids that are associated with cannabis are present. These include THC, cannabinol, and cannabidiol, as well as others. This is accomplished by using the presumptive color test for marihuana, the **Duquenois–Levine** test, followed by some form of chromatography, usually TLC. The vast majority of crime laboratories throughout the world consider this scheme to be sufficient to declare that such plant material is marihuana. If the exhibit occurs as suspected hash oil, where there is virtually no plant material to identify, then this is usually treated as more of an unknown and a confirmatory test must be done.

Another situation that is often treated in a different manner than the usual drug is LSD cases. Most often, LSD occurs as blotter acid—impregnated into absorbent paper, which is then eaten. There is no other controlled substance that looks like this. LSD is intensely fluorescent and measurement of the fluorescence spectrum is highly indicative of LSD or one of its known isomers such as LAMPA (lysergic acid methylpropyl amide). There is also a good presumptive color test for LSD; **Ehrlich's** test. The Ehrlich's reagent is also a good spray reagent for thin layer plates and colors LSD light purple. A combination of Ehrlich's test, TLC, and fluorescence is considered a valid scheme of analysis for LSD by many laboratories.

Another important exception to the confirmation rule for drugs is marked tablets and capsules. Legitimately manufactured tablets and capsules are normally marked with a logo and some identifying numbers and/or letters. The size, shape, and color of the tablet or capsule can provide valuable and helpful information about the identity of that drug. There are compendia such as the *Physician's Desk Reference* that have pictures of many common tablets and capsules and which are helpful in identification. In many laboratories, such an identification coupled with one test such as TLC, is all that is needed to identify the tablet or capsule. It must be recognized, however, that there are some very good counterfeit tablets and that many capsules can be easily opened and adulterated, so the physical identification is not enough for forensic confirmation.

CLANDESTINE DRUG LABORATORIES

Illicit drugs that do not occur naturally must be manufactured somewhere. If legitimate drug companies manufacture them, then they can be obtained for abuse by either stealing them from the manufacturing plant or warehouse or from a doctor or pharmacy or by forging a prescription. Drugs that are manufactured in other countries can be smuggled into this country. For some drugs there are no legitimate manufacturing plants or, if there are, it may still be difficult to obtain these drugs by the aforementioned route. The alternative is then the clandestine drug laboratory. For LSD, PCP, ecstasy, and other popular abused drugs, clandestine manufacture is the only way to get them. For amphetamine and methamphetamine, which are legally manufactured, the clandestine laboratory is still the most popular source. There are numerous books and internet sites that have recipes for manufacturing various drugs. Using these recipes and some fairly rudimentary chemicals, glassware, containers, and appliances, one can manufacture huge quantities of illicit drugs—if one has a source for the chemicals. It used to be fairly easy to obtain precursor chemicals from chemical supply houses or chemistry laboratories, but in recent years, this has become much more difficult. Chemical suppliers are more particular about who they will furnish drugs to and will report large sales of chemicals that are suspected to be precursors of popular illicit drugs to the Drug Enforcement Administration or the police. In addition, the Federal Government and many state governments now control the distribution of precursor chemicals by putting them in a Federal Schedule, making their distribution much more difficult. In spite of all of these efforts, illegal manufacture of illicit drugs goes on and in some areas of the country, is on the rise.

As one might expect, the sophistication of clandestine laboratories varies widely. Some laboratories are extremely modern and would be the envy of a legal manufacturer. Most, however, are rudimentary, dangerous, filthy places with virtually no health and safety precautions. In fact, this characteristic is one of the more prominent reasons why clandestine laboratories are discovered. Huge piles of trash containing many chemical containers or strange smells emanating from the drug laboratory can tip off neighbors who then call the police. Fires and explosions also occur occasionally in clandestine laboratories. Some clandestine laboratories can be set up in the trunk of an automobile or station wagon. Sometimes laboratories will be set up in rented motel rooms or apartments or even abandoned buildings. A typical clandestine drug laboratory is shown in Figure 13.13.

When drug enforcement agents are alerted to the possible presence of a clandestine laboratory by neighbors or by reports of the purchase of precursor chemicals, they will generally set up surveillance or use undercover agents to discover what is being produced and at what stage the production is. The best strategy is to wait until the final product has been produced. If the arrest takes place at this point, the doers can be charged with manufacture of an illicit drug and possession with an intent to distribute that drug. These offences carry the stiffest penalties. If, however, the laboratory is raided before the final product has been made, then the government can only charge the suspects with attempted manufacture. This

FIGURE 13.13

A portion of a clandestine methamphetamine laboratory. Note the messy, dangerous conditions, conducive to a destructive fire.

crime generally carries lesser charges than does manufacture, and the government must prove that the final product could have been produced with the chemicals, apparatus, and recipes that were found at the laboratory. Such prosecutions are much more difficult than those for manufacture. It is worth noting that people who grow marihuana plants, peyote cactus, or psilocybin mushrooms in their home or on their property are also charged with manufacture if they are caught.

BACK TO THE CASE

The "French Connection" case described at the beginning of this chapter illustrates several important facts about drug use and abuse. First, it is a global phenomenon. Except for marihuana and some synthetic hallucinogens such as PCP and MDMA, most of the illicit drugs that are abused in the United States come from outside. Second, it is extremely difficult to stop the flow of drugs into the United States because the borders are so porous and busy. Third, one of the major reasons that drug trafficking is so active is because of the profit. The illegality of possession and distribution of drugs increases the cost many multiples of what it takes to produce the drugs. Since the chances of getting caught smuggling drugs are slim, and the profits are so great, getting caught and doing jail time are considered part of the cost of doing business for traffickers. Everyone who is involved in drug enforcement agrees that the best and easiest way to curb drug trafficking and abuse is to lesson demand. If demand drops, the price and profits drop. This can only reasonably be accomplished by education and treatment.

The last point about the French Connection is about heroin itself. It is easy to grow opium poppies. They have been cultivated for thousands of years in many locales throughout the world. The resin contains about 10% morphine that is used as a painkiller throughout the world in major surgeries and injuries. It can be easily converted to heroin in one simple chemical step. Heroin is much more powerful as a pain reliever and its abuse effects are much stronger than morphine. Although heroin is used in some countries legitimately the way morphine is used in the United States, it has such a bad connotation in the United States that it is never used as a legal pain reliever and remains in Federal Schedule 1.

SUMMARY

Illicit drugs represent the largest volume of criminal cases that are examined by forensic science laboratories. They can occur naturally as with marihuana or cocaine, or they can be prepared from naturally occurring substances such as the case with heroin, or they can be totally synthetic as is the case with amphetamines and most other prescription drugs. Illicit drugs can also be classified by major effects. There are four major types: stimulants, depressants, narcotics, and hallucinogens. Illicit drugs in the United States are controlled both by the Federal and all 50 state governments. The model laws adopted by the Federal Government are embodied in the Uniform Controlled Substances Act, which put drugs in one of 5 Schedules, according to potential for abuse and approved medical use. Illicit drugs seldom occur as pure substances and therefore must be separated from the cutting agents. This can be accomplished by liquid extraction or by some form of chromatography. Virtually all illicit drug cases much have a confirmatory test, such as GC/MS in order to be presented in court.

TEST YOUR KNOWLEDGE

1. What are the four major classes of illicit drugs? Give an example of each.
2. What is a semisynthetic drug? Give an example of one.
3. What are the two major criteria for deciding if a drug shall be put in a Federal Schedule?
4. When will a drug be put in Schedule 1?
5. What schedule would drugs that require a doctor's prescription and which are not listed in another schedule, be put in?
6. What is "speed?" What family of substances does it belong to? Where is it scheduled?
7. What was the first act passed by Congress to control drugs? What were its main provisions?
8. What was the Harrison Act? What was its purpose? What drugs was it aimed at principally?
9. What is the significance of a "useable quantity" in drug control? Give an example.
10. What is an excipient? What is its purpose?
11. What is a diluent? Why are they used? Give an example?
12. What is meant by the term "aggregate weight" as it applies to drug control? Give an example.
13. Give an example of a spot or field test and the drug or class of drugs it is used on. When are these tests used?
14. What type of test is used to determine the percentage or quantity of a drug in a mixture?
15. What tests are used for the confirmation of drugs?
16. The analysis of marihuana is considered an exception to the general scheme of analysis of drugs, especially those in powdered mixtures. Why is this so? What are the differences?
17. Explain how mass spectrometry is used for confirmation of illicit drugs?
18. LSD is considered unique in the family of illicit drugs. Why? How does its occurrence differ from other drugs?
19. When a clandestine laboratory is raided and no final product is found, what charge is usually levied against the perpetrators? What must be proven in such cases?
20. Under what conditions may it not be possible to perform a confirmatory test upon a drug exhibit? How might one's conclusion about the exhibit be altered in such cases?

CONSIDER THIS...

1. The Federal Government and many states treat "crack" differently than cocaine. What is crack? How is it made? Why do law enforcement agencies and courts treat them differently? How do the penalties for possession and distribution differ federally?

2. Some forensic chemists maintain that tablets and capsules that contain stamped or printed manufacturer's markings can be treated differently than powdered mixtures of drugs? Why would this be the case? How would you take these markings into account in an analytical scheme? Why are marked capsules (two piece) treated more like unknown powders than are marked tablets?
3. What are some of the important considerations that come into play when confronted with large exhibits, e.g., a bale of 25 pounds of suspected cocaine? How would this be sampled? What about the case where one receives 25 pounds of suspected cocaine in the form of 400, 1 ounce packages?

FURTHER READING

Siegel, J., 2003. Forensic identification of controlled substances. In: Saferstein, R. (Ed.), Forensic Science Handbook, vol. 2. Prentice-Hall.

Ray, O., Ksir, C., 1987. Drugs, Society and Human Behavior, fourth ed. Times Mirror/Mosby.

Blachford, Stacey L., Krapp, Kristine (Eds.), 2002. Drugs and Controlled Substances Information for Students. Gale Group.

ON THE WEB

http://www.nida.nih.gov/. The portal for the National Institute on Drug Abuse, one of the National Institutes of Health.

http://www.usdoj.gov/dea/concern/concern.htm. An excellent source of information about many illicit drugs from the United States Drug Enforcement Administration.

http://www.swgdrug.org/. The home page of the Scientific Working Group for the Analysis of Seized Drugs.

http://www.drugs.com/. Comprehensive source for information about many prescribed drugs.

http://www.norml.com/. The home page of the National Association for the Reform of Marihuana Laws.

CHAPTER

Forensic Toxicology

14

CHAPTER OUTLINE

KEY TERMS

- Addiction
- Alcohol
- Blood alcohol concentration (BAC)
- Breath alcohol concentration (BrAC)
- Dependence
- Distribution
- Drug screen
- Drugs
- Forensic toxicology
- Metabolite
- Pharmacokinetics
- Pharmacology
- Syneregism
- Tolerance
- Toxicology
- Withdrawal

THE CASE

A Caucasian male was stopped for driving 50 mph in a 30 mph zone at 8:43 pm. The officer who stopped him administered a breath alcohol test at 10:04 pm. The result was 0.14 g/210 l. The legal limit is 0.08 g/210 L. The officer then administered a number of field sobriety tests, including the horizontal gaze nystagmus, the walk and turn and other balance tests, and a finger touch to the nose test. The subject had difficulty with all of the tests. When questioned, he admitted to having 2 beers between 1 pm and 5 pm that day. Then he changed his story twice, finally admitting having 5 beers during that time. He claimed that he had been working that morning sealing a cement garage foundation, using a sealant that he claimed to have been working with for more than 20 years. He did not use a respirator during this job. This sealant contains approximately 50% naptha aromatics and 25% trimethylbenzene. He was charged with drunk driving. In his defense, his expert witness claimed that the breath test was faulty, having been contaminated by the presence of the volatile solvents in the sealant that he inhaled. The defense further claimed that the defendant's failure to pass the field sobriety tests was due to his impairment brought on by the effects of these solvents. The government testing laboratory did an infrared breath test that failed to detect the presence of the solvents in the sealant. The government laboratory determined that 5 beers could cause a breath alcohol reading of 0.14%.

Courtesy: Michael Wagner.

INTRODUCTION

Many people think of poisons when they hear the term **toxicology**. But actually, toxicology includes the study of virtually any nonfood substance taken by a living organism. It is concerned not only with how much of a substance was taken, but also the physiological and psychological effects of these substances. Since this book is about forensic science, this chapter will be concerned with **forensic toxicology**, which is about humans and how drugs and poisons affect them. When someone ingests a drug or poison, it is absorbed into the bloodstream, circulates throughout the body where it has its intended and/or unintended effects, and then is eliminated from the body by a variety of processes. Forensic toxicologists become involved in a case when a person has died under suspicious circumstances. The toxicologist works with the forensic pathologist to help determine the cause and manner of death. This can be a complex problem. Chapter 7—Forensic Pathology, includes a discussion of the determination of cause and manner of death. The toxicologist must learn the person's medical history, drug use patterns, physical condition at the time of ingestion, the amount and duration of ingestion, and the identities and amounts of other drugs that are in the body at the same time. Forensic toxicologists also work on certain cases where people have taken drugs or poisons but don't die. These cases mainly involve drunk or drugged driving. The job of the forensic toxicologist in these cases is to determine the amount of alcohol in the body and its likely effects on the person while operating a motor vehicle.

This chapter contains material on how drugs get into the body, how they are distributed, and eliminated. It does not discuss the effects of drugs on humans. That part of **pharmacology** is beyond the scope of this introductory forensic science book. Because it is so prevalent in our society and takes up so much of the forensic toxicologist's time and effort, alcohol in drunk-driving cases will be used to illustrate the principles of forensic toxicology in this chapter.

FORENSIC PHARMACOLOGY AND FORENSIC TOXICOLOGY

In the broadest sense, pharmacology is the science that studies the relationships between drugs and living things. There are many branches of pharmacology, but the one that is applicable to forensic science is **clinical pharmacology**, which is concerned with the effects of drugs on humans. This branch of pharmacology is called **toxicology**. A forensic toxicologist is a scientist who works on cases where drugs are involved in death or injury.

DRUGS AND POISONS

A **drug** is a chemical or chemical mixture that is designed to have one or more physiological and/or psychological effects upon a person. See Chapter 13 for a discussion of illicit drugs and their major effects upon humans. The difference between licit drugs and other substances is that the drug is manufactured or designed to cause a particular response. A poison, on the other hand, is a substance that has a toxic (life threatening) effect on a person. Drugs can also be poisons if too much of a drug is ingested or if two or more drugs are taken such that their cumulative effects cause a toxic response. Actually, nearly any substance can be a poison if taken in excessive quantities that can cause harm to living beings. Direct effects of drugs are those that are intended by the drug's maker. These are distinguished from unintended side effects. These may be mild or severe and do not occur in everyone who takes the drug. For example, some drugs meant to treat some of the symptoms of allergies may have the side effect of causing drowsiness. Some side effects may even cause death. From a toxicology standpoint side effects may be as important as direct or intended effects from some drugs.

THE FORENSIC TOXICOLOGIST

The forensic toxicologist has a number of tasks that must be accomplished in order to reach conclusions about the role of a drug in causing death.

- Determine the identity of all drugs and poisons present in the body
- Determine the quantities of all drugs and poisons present at the time of death
- Determine which **metabolites** (secondary products of drugs as they are acted on by the liver) of these drugs are present
- Determine what interactions (e.g., synergisms) may exist among the particular combination of drugs that are present
- Help determine the history and patterns of drug use by the person involved and the role that **drug dependence** or **addiction** may play
- Help determine the role that **tolerance** may play

Of all of these tasks the most critical ones are the first two; the identification of the drugs and determination of their quantities. Drug identification will be covered later on in this chapter. For now, the factors that affect the ultimate concentration of drug in the human body will be discussed.

PHARMACOKINETICS

The science of **pharmacokinetics** is concerned with how drugs move into and out of the body. Four processes define pharmacokinetics. At times, only one or two of these processes are taking place; at other times all four are going on simultaneously. The four processes are **absorption, distribution, metabolism**, and **elimination**. Once the drug is ingested and all four processes are operating, a dynamic equilibrium is set up within the body. This means that the drug concentration at any given time in any given part of the body is dependent on all of the processes acting simultaneously. It is dynamic because the concentration at any time is determined by which of the processes is dominant at that time. Depending upon the amount of drug taken and the time since ingestion, any of the processes may predominate and the drug concentration changes with time, sometimes rapidly.

ABSORPTION

Drugs may be introduced into a body by a number of means. These include oral, intramuscular, intravenous, rectal, topical, subcutaneous, and inhalation. Different methods are used for different drugs and there is usually a preferred method for a given drug. All methods involve the passage of the drug through a tissue barrier such as stomach or intestine, nasal passages, skin, etc. The chemical nature of the drug dictates how easily the drug can cross the barrier. In addition, the form of the drug can affect its rate of absorption. For example, some drugs including aspirin, for example, may be coated with a substance that slows down absorption so that the drug is gradually absorbed over time. This prevents side effects that may occur if a dose of a drug is suddenly introduced into the body. Once the barrier has been breached the drug will enter the bloodstream. Although a drug may be distributed locally by diffusion through tissues, global distribution through the body is accomplished by way of the bloodstream. When a drug is taken orally it is generally absorbed through the stomach and/or small intestine into the bloodstream. The rate of absorption will depend in part upon what else is already in the stomach at the time of ingestion.

DISTRIBUTION

Blood reaches every cell in the body and drugs are distributed via the bloodstream. Some portion of a given drug may be bound to blood proteins and would be unavailable for interacting with the brain or other organs and this must be taken into account when determining the effective concentration of a drug. Although a drug in the bloodstream will reach all tissues in the body, this doesn't mean that the concentration of the drug is the same everywhere. Some organs, such as the brain, heart, and liver receive more of a blood supply than less vital organs so they would be exposed to more of a given drug. Also many drugs have a chemical structure that causes them to preferentially collect in particular types of tissue. For example, some pesticides tend to be attracted to adipose (fatty) tissue. Once the tissue absorbs these drugs, they are very hard to remove. Over time, large concentrations can build up. This can cause great harm or even death. If pesticides are dumped into lakes and rivers and fish ingest them, the pesticides will collect in the fatty tissues of the fish. When humans eat the fish, large doses of the pesticides can be transferred to them.

METABOLISM

Metabolism is a process whereby a drug or other substance is chemically changed to a different but related substance, called a **metabolite**. Metabolism serves at least three purposes:

1. It may deactivate the drug so that it has fewer or milder effects on the body.
2. The metabolite may be more water soluble than the parent drug. This makes it easier to eliminate the drug through urination.
3. It may convert the drug into a substance that can be used by the body's cells for energy. This also aids in elimination of the drug.

Most metabolism takes place in the liver where enzymes cause chemical changes. A drug may undergo a series of metabolic reactions whereby a first metabolite undergoes further changes to form additional metabolites. An example of metabolism that renders a substance less harmful than the primary drug or substance can be found in alcohol. Ethyl alcohol, the substance that is found in beer, wine, and spirits, is a neurotoxin (kills nerve cells). The liver metabolizes alcohol to acetaldehyde, which is then metabolized to acetic acid (vinegar is a dilute form of acetic acid). Neither acetaldehyde nor acetic acid is a neurotoxin. Acetic acid is very water soluble and can be easily removed from the body in urine. It is also easily used by the cells in oxidation to produce energy.

ELIMINATION

There are a number of ways that the body can eliminate drugs. The predominant mechanism is by excretion in urine. Since urine is mainly water, the drug must be water soluble before it can be effectively eliminated this way. As mentioned above, metabolism by the liver often accomplishes the task of rendering a drug more water soluble. If a drug is volatile (easily converted to a vapor) it can also undergo elimination by respiration; it can be exhaled from the lungs. Some volatile substances can also be partially eliminated by perspiration. Again, an example of a substance that is somewhat eliminated by perspiration and respiration is alcohol. Even so, the vast majority of alcohol is eliminated by metabolism followed by urination.

DRUG ACTIONS—PHARMACODYNAMICS

The study of how drugs act in the body is called **Pharmacodynamics**. Certain organs in the body, such as the brain contain cells that have active sites called **receptors**. Drugs are designed to bind to a particular type of receptor. When the drug finds and binds to its receptor, the receptor causes the cell to fulfil a particular function or process. For example, when a drug binds to a certain receptor on the pancreas, insulin is secreted into the bloodstream. A drug that binds to a receptor and causes it to exert its function on the cell is called an **agonist**. Some drugs may bind to a receptor but not cause it to exert the action of the cell to which the receptor is attached. These substances are called **antagonists**. Antagonists can serve to block or reverse the actions of agonists. An example of this agonist/antagonist relationship can be found in heroin or other narcotics. Heroin is a powerful central nervous system (CNS) depressant. An overdose of heroin can cause death by depressing the CNS so much that respiration ceases and the person dies. A person who has such an overdose can be given Nalaxone, a heroin antagonist. Nalaxone will compete with heroin for the same receptor sites in the brain, but as an antagonist will not cause CNS depression. Determining the effective dose of a therapeutic drug can be a very complex process. It depends upon the person and his/her physical condition and the severity of the illness being treated. The whole process is based upon knowledge of pharmacodynamics and the characteristics of the receptors for the drug being tried. A great deal of research continues today in the search for better antagonists for a wider variety of drugs, including alcohol. There are also drugs that cause a violent reaction in a person who has imbibed alcohol. These drugs are not antagonists; they are designed to prevent a person from drinking alcohol.

DEPENDENCE, TOLERANCE, AND SYNERGISM

A forensic toxicologist must make a determination of the contribution that drugs make to death, injury, or incapacitation. This can be a very complex task, especially in the case where the person has been admitted to a hospital or clinic and is unable to tell doctors what drugs or how much of a drug they have ingested. Some of the criteria that enter into decisions about the role of drugs include the degree to which the subject is addicted or dependent upon the drug, what their experience has been with the drug over time, and the cumulative effects of multiple drugs on the subject. Sometimes only educated guesses can be made about these factors. The major factors that inform these decisions are discussed below.

Addiction and Withdrawal

When a person becomes addicted to a drug, there will be a potent craving for it. The person's whole life becomes a constant search for the money to buy the drug or for the drug itself. This dependence can be more than psychological. There may be an actual physical dependence on the drug. How can you tell if a person is psychologically dependent on a drug or physically addicted? Outward actions and reactions may not reveal this since they cause similar behaviors in the victim. The way to find out is for the subject to suddenly stop taking the drug. If there is a physical dependence on the drug then the person will undergo a withdrawal syndrome. This is a well-defined set of physical symptoms, including high temperature, physical discomfort, pain, etc. In certain cases, such as severe addiction to barbiturates, sudden or "cold turkey" withdrawal can be fatal. If the person is psychologically dependent on the drug, there will be no withdrawal syndrome but the subject will be quite uncomfortable and will demonstrate symptoms of deprivation of the drug.

Tolerance

Chemical **tolerance** is a phenomenon whereby the body's organ systems adapt to the drug. Then it takes ever-increasing doses to achieve an equivalent psychoactive effect. Most drugs will eventually exhibit tolerance to one degree or another, but it is more pronounced in some types, including opium-based narcotics such as morphine and heroin, as well as cocaine and barbiturates.

The cause of tolerance appears to be a decrease in sensitivity or number of receptors for the drug. It usually takes many repeated doses of the drug over an extended period of time for tolerance to be manifested. If the drug is stopped, it may take a long time period for the body to recover. In some cases of extreme tolerance build-up, sudden withdrawal of the drug can be fatal. This has been demonstrated with barbiturate addiction. In the case of marihuana, there seems to be a sort of "reverse tolerance" taking place. Some users report that they don't need to take more and more marihuana to achieve the same effects and, in some cases, they can decrease the dosage. The reasons for this are not well understood. It may be that the reactions that a person has to taking marihuana may be partly learned behavior and it takes time to learn to expect certain reactions. Another reason may be that marihuana may collect and persist in the body for a very long time—perhaps months, and the build-up of its psychoactive components may be the cause of the reverse tolerance.

In the case of LSD, there is no evidence of drug tolerance but there is evidence that the drug may persist in the body for months or even years. Some regular users have experienced so-called "flashbacks." This is an instance where the person experiences hallucinations months or years after the drug was last taken. This is all the more surprising since the dose of LSD that can cause hallucinations is about 50 μg, a very small amount by drug standards.

Synergism

You may have heard the expression; "The whole is greater than the sum of the parts." In pharmacology, this means that the total effects on the body of two or more drugs taken together is greater than the effects would be if the drugs are taken separately. The drugs work together to magnify their effects or create effects that would not have occurred otherwise. This is called **synergism**. A forensic toxicologist must be aware of synergism when making conclusions about the role of a drug in the cause and manner of death. The toxicologist must know what drugs were taken and what drugs were already present when another one is taken and must be aware of synergistic effects. Many new drugs come onto the market every year to treat various diseases and ailments. It is not possible to test these drugs against all other drugs that a person might be taking at the same time. As a result, synergisms might occur that are unanticipated.

One of the most well-known synergisms in toxicology is that of alcohol and barbiturates. Barbiturates are CNS depressants. They slow down many functions of the body and may induce drowsiness or sleep. Alcohol is also a CNS depressant, but its mechanism of action is different than barbiturates. When alcohol and barbiturates are taken together, the depressant effects are greatly magnified over what they would be if the alcohol and drugs were taken separately. The effects can be magnified to the point where a person may die even from sublethal quantities of both the alcohol and barbiturates. This combination of substances was apparently the cause of death of rock stars Janice Joplin and Jimi Hendrix, for example. There have been many reports of both accidental and deliberate cases of overdose by alcohol and barbiturates in the United States each year.

Sometimes it is difficult to determine if two drugs are acting synergistically. For example, if someone takes two CNS depressant drugs and has a significant reaction, it may be that the drugs' effects were merely additive, rather than enhanced. Synergism is easiest to detect if someone takes two drugs and has effects that would not be expected from either one of the drugs.

IDENTIFICATION OF DRUGS IN THE BODY

Once a drug is ingested and has been distributed throughout the body, identification can be a difficult process. There may be little or no information about what drug or drugs a person may have taken or when or how much was taken. This makes designing or implementing an analytical scheme difficult. Many drugs require only small doses to be effective and once distributed, their concentrations may be very low. Some drugs have a preference for certain tissues or organs and may be hard to find. The process of drug identification involves several important steps. They include sampling, extraction, screening, and confirmation.

SAMPLING

The types of samples taken from the body for drug identification are dictated by the condition of the body and the most likely place for the drug to congregate. If the person is alive, then blood, urine, and, increasingly, hair are the preferred samples. If the person is dead then all of the above may be available. In addition, other tissues such as brain, liver, vitreous humor (eyes), or spinal fluid can be used. If the person took the drug and then died shortly thereafter, some of the undigested or partially digested drug may remain in the stomach. Urine concentrations of drugs and metabolites may be much greater than blood and so urine makes an ideal medium for screening for most drugs. On the other hand, the concentration of the drug in urine may not correlate well with blood concentrations and using urine concentrations may lead to misleading conclusions about the magnitude of the drug's effects. Therefore, it is usually good scientific practice to use urine samples to screen for the possible presence of a drug, but to use blood for determination of the concentration of the drug and for confirmation of its presence.

In the past few years, hair has become an increasingly important specimen for drug analysis. Unlike blood or urine, hair can trap and hold drugs for as long as the hair is on the body, thus yielding information about drug use patterns and frequency of ingestion. Caution must be used in hair analysis for drugs owing to the possibilities for direct uptake by hair from the outside and to the effects on hair treatments such as bleaching on drug concentrations. The subject of using hair for the analysis of certain drugs will be discussed further in the section on "Drug Testing in the Workplace."

EXTRACTION

Once a tissue or fluid has been identified and removed, the drug must be extracted. There are two main reasons for this. First, the extract is "cleaned up" so that there are few substances other than the drug present. This makes analysis easier and keeps the instrumentation from becoming fouled and contaminated. The other reason is to concentrate the drug in a small amount of matrix so it will be easier to detect. There are several effective methods for extraction of drugs. The one chosen in a particular case depends upon the drug and the tissue or fluid.

Liquid Phase Extraction

In order to accomplish an efficient separation, the pH range of the drug must be known. Most drugs are either acidic or basic in aqueous solutions. A few drugs, such as caffeine are neutral. An acidic drug is one whose pH is between 1 and 7, and a basic drug has a pH between 7 and 14. The pH dictates the method of extraction. As an example, consider a urine sample containing cocaine. Urine is very acidic and cocaine is a basic drug. In an acidic medium, then, cocaine would exist in what is known as the salt (ionic) form. The cocaine has an H^+ attached to it and there would be an anion such as Cl^- present. This form of cocaine is very soluble in urine. If the solution is made basic, the cocaine reverts to its free base form as plain cocaine. This form is not soluble in urine or other aqueous solutions and the cocaine would precipitate out. An organic solvent is then added in which the cocaine is very soluble. This solvent doesn't mix with the urine and thus the cocaine can be efficiently separated from the urine this way. Acidic drugs such as the barbiturates can be extracted from urine using an acid extraction rather than a basic extraction. Liquid phase extraction is not a suitable technique where two or more acidic or basic drugs are known to be present. This is because all of the acidic or basic drugs will be extracted together and they cannot be separated by this method. More information concerning liquid phase extractions can be found in Chapter 6, Separation Methods.

Solid Phase Extraction

To overcome the limitations of liquid phase extraction and increase sensitivity, solid phase extraction of drugs has become popular in recent years. In solid phase extraction a small column or coated wire is used to extract the drug out of the urine or blood. The blood or urine is poured through a special solid matrix that selectively removes the drug. The matrix is then washed or eluted to strip the drug off for further analysis. A recent refinement of solid phase extraction is solid phase microextraction (SPME). Here a specially coated wire, strip, or fiber is inserted into the fluid that contains the drug or drugs. The drugs are selectively adsorbed onto the wire, which is then removed. The drug can then be eluted for further analysis. SPME is capable of capturing and measuring very small amounts of drug, so it is ideal for situations where there is limited sample available. Even if there are many substances dissolved in the liquid, there are coatings that can be used to adsorb a particular type of substance. Figure 14.1 shows how the SPME process works.

SCREENING

Screening tests are a type of preliminary test for drugs in body fluids. They are designed to give a preliminary result that indicates that a drug may be present but they do not confirm the presence of a particular drug. Screening tests are important in cases where it is not known what drug or drugs have been ingested. They consist of panels of drugs that usually contain the most commonly abused drugs. These tests may also be used to provide tentative identification of a drug that is believed to have been ingested. Screening tests fall into two general categories: chromatographic and immunoassay. Chromatographic tests are usually thin-layer chromatography or gas chromatography. More information on chromatographic tests is given in Chapter 6 "Separation Techniques" and Chapter 13 "Illicit Drugs."

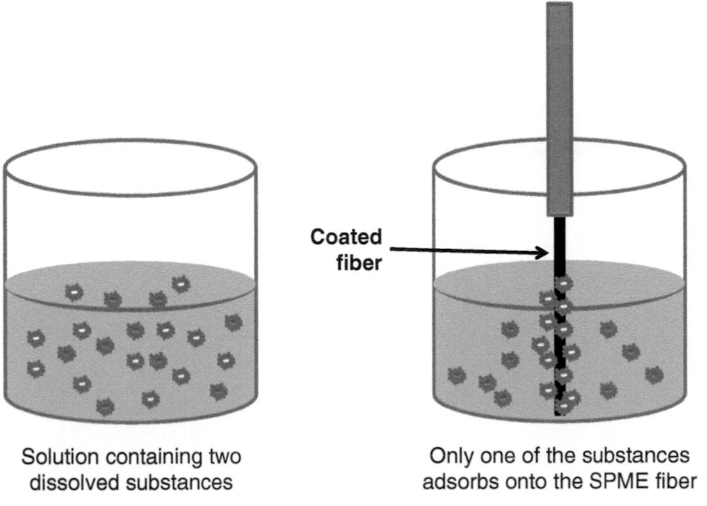

FIGURE 14.1

Solid phase microextraction (SPME). The coated wire on the end is immersed into the blood or urine sample that contains the drugs of interest. The drugs adsorb onto the surface of the wire. The wire can then be eluted with a solvent or introduced directly into the inlet of a gas chromatograph where the heat will remove the drugs and they will then be swept into the gas chromatograph.

Courtesy Meredith Haddon.

Immunoassay Techniques

Immunoassay techniques take advantage of the reaction that takes place between antigens and antibodies in human blood. This technique is described in more detail in Chapter 10 "Serology." An **antigen** is a substance that is resident on red blood cells and in the blood plasma itself. If a substance such as a virus or bacterium enters the body, it acts like a foreign antigen and causes the immune system to produce antibodies that can attack and immobilize the antigen before it can cause harm. The antibodies produced are specific for the type of antigen that is introduced. In forensic toxicology, this antigen/antibody reaction is exploited to detect very small quantities of drugs. A major advantage of immunoassay tests for drug screening is that they do not require prior extraction of the drugs from the urine.

One of the most popular immunoassay tests is called the **Enzyme Multiplied Immunoassay Test** (EMIT). A rabbit is injected with a form of the drug for which detection is sought, for example, methamphetamine. The rabbit's immune system produces an antibody to the methamphetamine. The rabbit's serum is removed. A known amount of the rabbit serum is added to the urine of the human subject being tested for drugs. If there is any methamphetamine in that person's urine, it will immediately bind to the antibodies. Next, a known amount of methamphetamine that has been labeled with an enzyme is added to the urine. If there are any antibodies from the rabbit that did not react with the methamphetamine in the subject's urine, they will now react with the enzyme-labeled methamphetamine, thus decreasing its concentration.

The amount of the remaining enzyme-labeled methamphetamine is now measured. This will correlate to the concentration of the antibodies that reacted and thus to the concentration of the antibodies that reacted with the methamphetamine that was in the urine. From this, the concentration of the methamphetamine can be determined.

Another related immunoassay technique is called **Radioimmunoassay** (RIA). RIA works in a similar manner to EMIT but the antigens are radioactively labeled. The major problem with RIA and EMIT is that the antibodies produced in the rabbit from injecting a drug are not generally specific for that drug. For example, antibodies produced as a result of the injection of methamphetamine into a rabbit may also bind to pseudoephedrine, a proprietary antihistamine sold in drug stores for allergy relief. Relying solely on an immunoassay test for identification of methamphetamine would mean that a false positive result would occur. Thus, all immunoassay tests as well as chromatographic screening tests must be confirmed with a suitable second test.

CONFIRMATION

Once a screening test has been completed, any drugs that appear to be present must be confirmed. The only accepted method for drug confirmation in forensic toxicology is mass spectrometry. This technique is explained in Chapter 5. Some laboratories take the position that performing two independent screening tests based on different chemical principles is an acceptable method for confirmation of a drug. An example of this would be to perform an EMIT test followed by thin-layer chromatography. In the practice of forensic toxicology this is not acceptable. No amount of presumptive, preliminary testing will add up to confirmation. Only mass spectrometry will provide acceptable confirmation of a drug in the body.

CUT-OFF LEVELS

Every analytical technique, be it mass spectrometry or a screening test, has a limit of detection, that is a level below which a reliable result cannot be obtained. This is because every instrument creates some electronic noise that shows up in the chart or graph of the analysis. If the signal that indicates the presence of a drug is too weak, it will not be seen above the noise. To avoid the possibility that noise will be mistaken for a signal, each laboratory sets a cut-off level for each drug. This is always used in cases where a living person is being tested for drugs in a pre-employment or incarceration situation. If a drug is found at a level at or below this cut-off, the result will be reported as "drug not detected." For example, the cut-off for cocaine using EMIT may be set at 50 ng/mL (nanograms of drug per milliliter of urine). This means that a result of "drug not detected" for cocaine in this test means only that the drug was either not present or was present at a level below 50 ng/mL. If a different, more sensitive test was used with a lower cut-off, this amount of cocaine may be reported. In postmortem cases or cases where it is necessary to determine if someone has taken any amount of a drug, then cut-offs are not used. The Department of Health and Human Services has established initial and confirmatory cut-off levels for common drugs. They are shown in Figure 14.2.

The following cut-off concentrations are used by certified laboratories to test urine specimens collected by Federal agencies and by employers regulated by the Department of Transportation:

Initial Test Cut-off Concentration (ng/ml)

Marijuana metabolites	50
Cocaine metabolites	300
Opiate metabolites	2,000
Phencyclidine	25
Amphetamines	1,000

Confirmatory Test Cut-off Concentration (ng/ml)

Marijuana metabolite (1)	15
Cocaine metabolite (2)	150
Opiates:	
Morphine	2,000
Codeine	2,000
6-Acetylmorphine (4)	10
Phencyclidine	25
Amphetamines:	
Amphetamine	500
Methamphetamine (3)	500

Footnotes:

(1) Delta-9-tetrahydrocannabinol-9-carboxylic acid
(2) Benzoylecgonine
(3) Specimen must also contain amphetamine at a concentration ≥ 200 ng/ml
(4) Test for 6-AM when morphine concentration exceeds 2,000 ng/ml

FIGURE 14.2

Cut-off levels for initial and confirmatory levels of common drugs. These numbers are derived empirically for each drug and each test.

Data supplied by the Department of Health and Human Services.

DRUG TESTING IN THE WORKPLACE

In recent years there has been increased emphasis on testing employees to make sure that they are not using drugs while on the job. This practice began with workers in sensitive situations or who worked in dangerous environments, such as police officers, locomotive engineers, pilots, etc. but has since spread to many other occupations. There have been a number of problems uncovered with workplace drug testing that are not found in other areas of forensic toxicology. Many drug testing programs have been run out of private clinics and laboratories where samples are taken and analyzed. These laboratories are not familiar with forensic science protocols and are not aware that any sample that they collect and analyze could end up in a legal situation and therefore, that a proper chain of custody must be maintained and analytical standards must be met. There are numerous examples of improper procedures and conclusions that have led to the termination of employees based on faulty drug testing. Below is a description of the various processes and procedures that are involved in workplace drug testing.

SAMPLING

The typical sample used for workplace drug testing is urine. The vast majority of commonly abused drugs will ultimately end up in urine with which they are excreted. Typically, the subject will go to a clinic or doctor's office to give a urine sample. Often, this is part of a general physical exam. In many clinics this is an unsupervised process that can lead to deliberate attempts to alter the sample. Sometimes a subject will dilute the urine with water from the commode or sink in the hopes that the drug will be so dilute that it will not be detected or will fall below the cut-off level for that drug. There have also been cases where subjects smuggle drug-free urine into the clinic and substitute it for their own. Some laboratories will try and prevent these activities by having a witness present when the sample is given. Others will put bluing agent in the commode and turn off the water in the sink. The laboratory will also have the collector immediately take the temperature of the urine. This will uncover attempts to dilute the sample with room temperature water. Some protocols call for determining the specific gravity of the urine sample. This is higher than that of water, so dilution of the urine will result in a decrease in the specific gravity. In some cases, workers have complained that they were not informed that their physical examination included a drug screening test.

Another problem that occurs in clinical laboratories is mixing up samples. Some laboratories generate a high volume of workplace drug samples and if proper labeling and chain of custody procedures are not followed, then it is possible for samples to get mixed up. Likewise, if the testing laboratory and/or the courier don't use proper chain of custody techniques, the samples could once again be mixed up. This problem can be exacerbated if multiple laboratories are used. For example, a subject may go to a medical laboratory to give a sample. This may then be screened at a different laboratory and then confirmed at a third laboratory. All of these transfers and handling increases the chances that an accidental mix up will occur.

IMPROPER ANALYSIS

Some clinical laboratories that are not familiar with the requirements of forensic chemistry may not employ mass spectrometry for confirmation of drug screens. They may use two or three screening tests and report the drug as being definitely present, when no mass spectrometry confirmation test had been done. As was mentioned above, this is not an acceptable forensic science procedure and runs the risk of false positive results. A testing protocol like this will surely be challenged if the case goes to court. An adverse ruling can result in an embarrassing and costly lawsuit. A related problem can occur if the laboratory doesn't properly explain the conclusions that can be reached from a workplace drug test. Screening tests are never confirmatory and an employer should never make decisions about a worker based on these tests. All drug tests must be confirmed by mass spectrometry and no actions should be taken unless and until the presence of the drug is confirmed.

FORENSIC TOXICOLOGY OF ETHYL ALCOHOL

The analysis of ethyl alcohol provides an excellent illustration of the basic principles of forensic toxicology. There are two independent measuring systems, blood alcohol concentration (BAC) and breath alcohol concentration (BrAC) for alcohol that correlate pretty well with each other. On top of the scientific issues with the measurement of alcohol, there are a number of social issues that provide another layer of concern for forensic scientists. Operating an automobile (or other conveyance) while under the influence of alcohol has been a serious problem in the United States for many years. An entire body of laws and regulations has been created by the Congress and the 50 state legislatures to deal with this problem. Central to all of these is the notion, unique to alcohol in forensic toxicology, that the degree of sanction or punishment for operating a motor vehicle under the influence of alcohol is tied directly to the concentration of alcohol in the body. This puts an extra burden on the forensic toxicologist who must determine the amount of alcohol in the body, estimate the alcohol concentration at a prior time when drinking was still occurring, determine the effects of the alcohol on that person, and sometimes determine the degree to which alcohol contributed to death. These considerations require a thorough knowledge of all stages of the pharmacokinetics of alcohol; ingestion, absorption, distribution, and elimination. Alcohol is very similar to water in its chemical structure and is soluble in water in all proportions. Because blood and body tissues are largely made up of water, alcohol is easily absorbed, distributes itself rapidly to all parts of the body, and is eliminated easily in urine.

For forensic purposes, blood is taken as the reference for alcohol concentrations and measurements of alcohol in other tissues or body fluids refer back to BAC. In blood, alcohol is measured in weight/volume units, specifically the number of grams of alcohol in 100 mL (1 dL) of blood. In breath, a different weight/volume measure is used. It is the number of grams of alcohol in 210 L of deep, alveolar (lung) air. There is an approximate correlation between BAC and BrAC of $2100{:}1 \pm 300$. Some breath testing instruments use 2100:1 conversion to blood alcohol, but some experts believe that the variation in this factor is so large that separate legal limits should be established for BAC and BrAC. In some states there are two parallel sets of regulations that govern drunk-driving behavior. One refers to BAC and the other to BrAC.

PHARMACOKINETICS OF ALCOHOL

Once alcohol is ingested, it is absorbed quite rapidly into the bloodstream. At this point, a dynamic equilibrium is reached which is affected by the rate of absorption, distribution, metabolism, and elimination. For a given person, the rates of distribution, metabolism, and elimination are fairly constant. This means that the ultimate level of alcohol in the blood is dependent upon the rate that it is absorbed from the gastrointestinal tract. The faster it is absorbed, the higher the ultimate BAC will be. An analogy would be a bucket with a hole at the bottom. If you pour water into the bucket it will leak out of the hole. If you pour the water in fast the bucket will start to fill up. You could adjust your rate of pouring water so that it empties as fast as it fills or you could pour it in slowly and it would all leak out even though you are still putting in water. In the case of alcohol, if you drink it rapidly or in strong drinks, the alcohol will be absorbed quickly and the BAC will increase rapidly. If you drink slowly and/or drink weak drinks such as beer, the absorption of the alcohol will proceed more slowly and the BAC will increase at a slower rate. At some point, absorption will cease and the BAC will decrease.

Absorption

Alcohol is absorbed mostly in the upper part of the small intestine. About a quarter of the alcohol is absorbed through the stomach lining and a few percent directly from the mouth into the bloodstream. There are a number of factors that determine the rate at which alcohol is absorbed from the gastrointestinal tract into the blood.

- The nature of the drink.
  More concentrated mixed drinks cause more rapid absorption of alcohol than do dilute drinks such as beer or wine. Alcohol from beer is absorbed more slowly than an equivalent amount of alcohol mixed with water. This is due to the carbohydrates and other additives in the beer.
- The rate and speed of drinking.
  The faster one consumes drinks, the more rapidly the alcohol is absorbed owing to the higher concentration in the stomach and intestine at a given time.
- The contents of the stomach at the time of drinking.
  This is a major factor in affecting the rate of alcohol absorption. The pyloric valve connects the stomach to the upper part of the small intestine. When the stomach is empty, the pyloric valve is open and the alcohol passes directly from the stomach to the small intestine where it is rapidly absorbed. If there is food in the stomach when the person drinks alcohol, the pyloric valve remains closed until digestion is complete. This means that alcohol cannot pass into the intestine. It must then be absorbed through the stomach lining. This process is slower than in the intestine and the alcohol must compete with the food for absorption into the blood. The alcohol is also diluted by the food. The result is slower absorption. It is also subject to metabolism in the stomach, thus reducing the amount of alcohol reaching the bloodstream and ultimately the maximum BAC. Figure 14.3 is a diagram of the human digestive system.

Distribution

Once alcohol gets into the blood it circulates rapidly through the body, and it will be distributed to all parts of the body in approximate proportion to the water content of each part. Hair and bones have little water content and will not keep much alcohol. The other parts of the body have fairly consistent water content and, since equilibration occurs rapidly, good estimates can be made of the relationship between BAC and alcohol content in other parts of the body. For example, brain tissue has about 85% of the amount of alcohol that would be in whole blood.

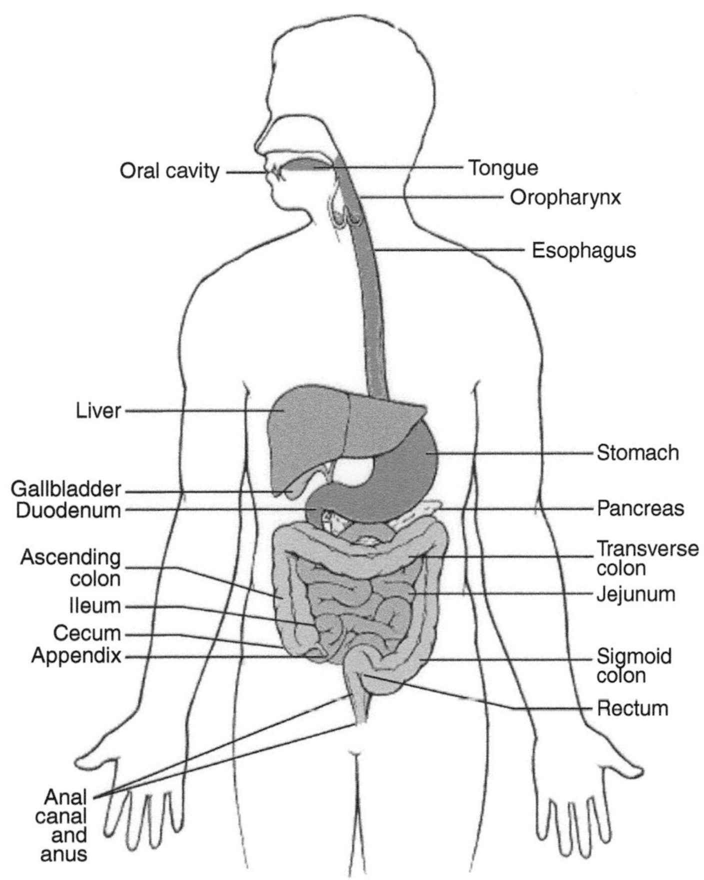

FIGURE 14.3

The human digestive system. Alcohol is absorbed into the bloodstream chiefly through the small intestine. When there is food in the stomach, alcohol will be absorbed through the stomach lining.

Elimination

There are two routes to the elimination of alcohol by the body. Metabolism accounts for more than 90% of elimination. It takes place mainly in the liver, which has an enzyme, **alcohol dehydrogenase** that first converts ethyl alcohol to acetaldehyde and then to acetic acid. The acetic acid is used by cells for energy and forms carbon dioxide and water. Metabolism takes place at somewhat different rates in different people. The average rate is about 0.015 ± 0.003%/h. This rate of elimination is approximately equivalent to less than one drink containing one ounce of 100 proof (50%) alcohol per hour. If an average man takes in enough alcohol to reach a maximum BAC of 0.23%, it would take more than 10h to reduce the level below

0.08%, which is the legal limit in some states to be charged with operating under the influence of alcohol (OUIL).

$$\frac{(0.23\% - 0.08\%)}{0.015\%/\text{h}} = 10\ \text{h}$$

The remaining few percent of alcohol is eliminated from the body as ethyl alcohol by excretion. This includes urine, breath, and perspiration. From this information, it can be easily seen that exertion, showering in cold water and other activities will have little or no effect on BAC. Removal of alcohol from the body is largely under the control of the liver, which doesn't react to contrition, anger, or pleading! It should also be noted that ingesting large amounts of caffeine in coffee, for instance, would not help much. Caffeine is a CNS stimulant and alcohol is a depressant, but they work on different brain receptors and do not cancel each other out. Taking caffeine while being drunk will leave you wide awake… and drunk! Some people believe that vigorous exercise will eliminate alcohol more rapidly. Since only a small percent of alcohol is removed through exhaling and/or perspiration, this will have little effect on the BAC. It should be obvious that taking a cold shower will also not affect the concentration of alcohol in the bloodstream.

BAC versus Time: The Widmark Curve

Assume that a 150 lb male imbibes the equivalent of 5 oz of 80 proof liquor all at once on an empty stomach. Absorption of alcohol would be quite rapid and he would reach a maximum of around 0.1% within about an hour. During that steep rise in the BAC, elimination would also start to take place after a while and the rate of increase in the BAC would start to slow. Then the BAC would start to drop, slowly at first, because absorption is still taking place to a lesser degree. Finally, after absorption is completed, the decrease in BAC would take place at a constant rate equal to the rate of metabolism in the liver until the BAC is zero. A plot of this BAC versus time is shown in the thinner line part of Figure 14.4.

If the same man has to drink the same amount of alcohol in the same amount of time, but this time after eating a meal, the rate of absorption of alcohol would be much lower owing to the competition for absorption into the blood with the food and the fact that most of the absorption would be from the stomach. The time it would take to reach the maximum BAC would be longer and the maximum BAC would be lower because metabolism would be able to better keep up with absorption. The latter part of the elimination curve in this case would have the same shape and slope as the curve generated by the drinking on an empty stomach because it also reflects metabolism by the liver. This can be seen by the thicker line plot in Figure 14.4.

Alcohol in the Breath

The blood circulatory system is closed. Oxygen gets into the blood and carbon dioxide and other volatile waste products are eliminated from the blood by diffusion from and to air that is inhaled into the lungs via the brachial tube which

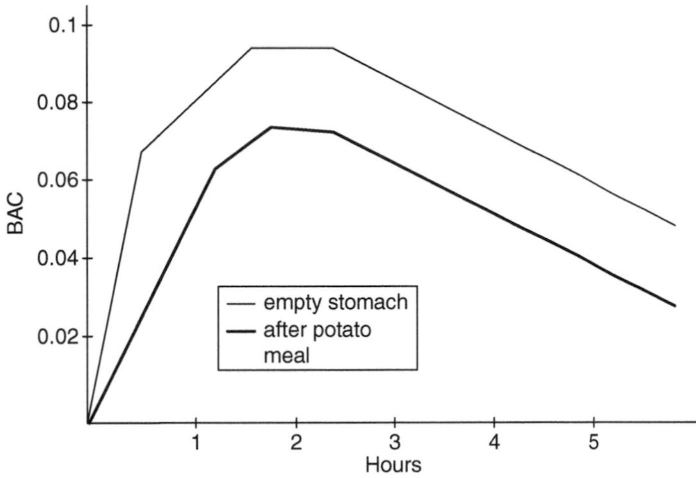

FIGURE 14.4

The Widmark curve. The thinner line graph represents the BAC level after drinking on an empty stomach whereas the thicker line represents the BAC level after a meal is eaten. You can see the effects of having food in the stomach before drinking. The same amount of alcohol is taken in each case. When food is already present, the maximum blood alcohol concentration is lower and takes longer to be reached than when drinking is done on an empty stomach.

is, in turn, connected to the mouth and nose. The pulmonary artery branches out into millions of capillaries that end in small sacs called **alveoli**. Diffusion of oxygen and carbon dioxide are exchanged between the blood and air through these alveoli. If there is alcohol in the blood, then that too is eliminated through the alveoli and is exhaled from the mouth and nose. Figure 14.5 shows the human respiratory system.

The amount of alcohol that gets into the breath from the alveoli is proportional to the amount of alcohol in the blood and is governed by **Henry's law**. This law states that when a volatile substance, such as alcohol, is dissolved in a liquid, such as blood, and then that liquid is brought in contact with a closed air space, such as alveolar breath, the ratio of the concentration of alcohol in the blood and breath is a constant at a given temperature. If the temperature is raised, the equilibrium shifts toward the concentration in the air. As the alcohol is removed from the lungs by respiration, more of it will move from the blood to the replaced air in the lungs in an effort to reestablish the equilibrium. Ultimately all of the alcohol will be removed from the blood as it passes through the lungs.

In the United States, most states have adopted 2100:1 (1 mL of blood contains as much alcohol as 2.1 L of air) at 34 °C for the ratio between blood alcohol and breath alcohol, although research indicates that the actual ratio at this temperature is closer to 2300:1. This ratio is somewhat person-dependent and the lower 2100:1 ratio favors the subject. There is a lot of variation among people.

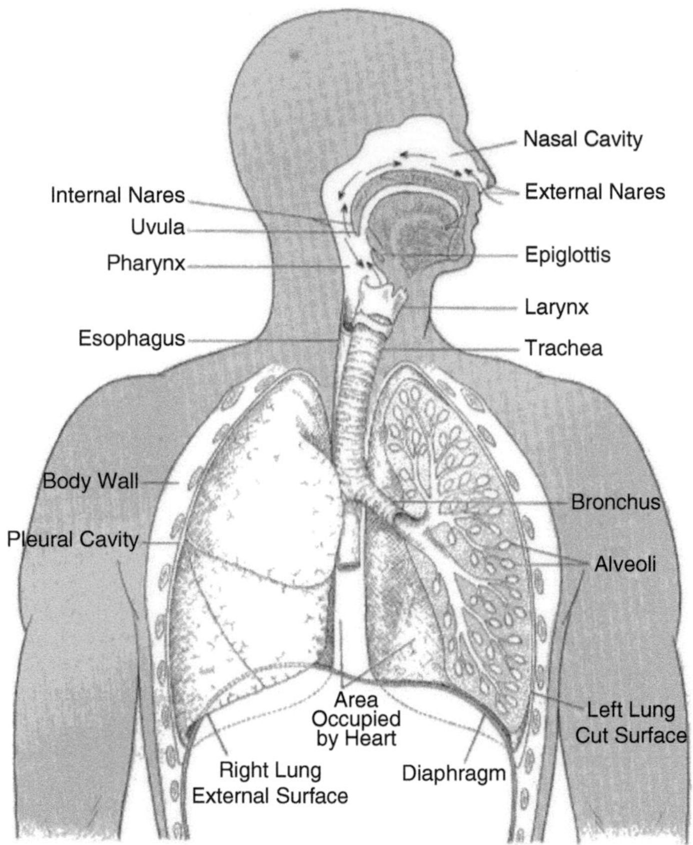

FIGURE 14.5

Diagram of human respiratory system. The lungs contain many branches called bronchi. These are further subdivided into alveoli. As the circulating blood reaches the alveoli, it releases carbon dioxide and picks up oxygen. If there are other dissolved volatile substances in the blood such as alcohol, they will also be released into the alveoli. These gases will be exhaled through the mouth. A breath alcohol testing instrument can measure the amount of alcohol in the exhaled breath.

IN MORE DEPTH: HOW MUCH DO YOU HAVE TO DRINK TO BE DRUNK?

In all states you are considered to be under the influence of alcohol when your BAC reaches 0.08%. How much do you have to drink to reach that level? You may be surprised to see how little alcohol you need to take to be drunk.

By way of an illustration, let's assume that you are drinking on an empty stomach. Further, let's assume that you are imbibing 100 proof (50%) alcohol. Some spirits such as bourbon or scotch may reach this concentration. The amount of alcohol of this type you would need to reach a given level of BAC depends upon your weight (in pounds) and your gender.

IN MORE DEPTH: HOW MUCH DO YOU HAVE TO DRINK TO BE DRUNK?—cont'd

The following formulas can be used to approximate the alcohol needed to reach a certain level of BAC:

For a male, use the following formula:

$$\text{Vol} = \frac{\text{wgt} \times \text{BAC}}{3.78}$$

For a female, use the following formula:

$$\text{Vol} = \frac{\text{wgt} \times \text{BAC}}{4.67}$$

where Vol = number of ounces of 100 proof alcohol, wgt is in pounds and BAC is in weight/volume percent. As an example, consider a 125 lb female. What volume of alcohol would be required for her to reach a level of 0.1% BAC?

$$\text{Vol} = \frac{125\ \text{lbs} \times 0.08\%}{4.67}\ \text{Vol} = 2.14\ \text{oz}$$

The average shot of a mixed drink is about 1.2 oz. This means that a woman could drink about two mixed drinks and her BAC would be over the limit. Wine is about 12% alcohol. This would mean that the same woman could drink about 9 oz of wine, or about 2, 5 oz glasses. Beer generally runs about 4% alcohol, so this woman could drink about 2.5, 12 oz beers. For a man of the same weight, the numbers would be about 2.6 oz of 100 proof alcohol, 11 oz of wine, or 38 oz of beer.

MEASUREMENT OF ALCOHOL IN THE BODY

Breath and blood are the most commonly used specimens for alcohol analysis. In the past, urine has been used but today it is seldom used, owing to the wide variation in measurements and lack of stable equilibrium between blood and urine concentrations. In postmortem cases, other body fluids such as vitreous humor or spinal fluid can be used although less is known about how they compare to blood or breath measurements than with other fluids.

BLOOD

Blood is the preferred medium for alcohol measurement because it provides the best surrogate for brain alcohol levels and because of this, most states have statutes that relate sanctions for drunk driving to blood alcohol levels. The ideal blood sample would be arterial blood because it most closely tracks brain alcohol content, whereas venous BAC tends to lag behind. Nonetheless, whole venous blood is most commonly used in drunk-driving cases. The most widely used method for the analysis of BAC for forensic purposes is gas chromatography. This has several advantages, including high specificity, accurate quantitative analysis, and ease of automation. Most forensic toxicology laboratories today use headspace alcohol that is injected into the GC.

In this technique, it is not necessary to separate the alcohol from the blood. A container of blood is put in a sealed vial with a top that can accept a syringe. An airtight syringe is then inserted into the vial and a known volume of the air space above the blood is withdrawn. At a given temperature, the amount of alcohol in the air space will be in equilibrium with the alcohol concentration in the blood. This air is injected into the gas chromatograph along with an internal standard. Most laboratories that do a significant amount of blood alcohol analysis use a gas chromatograph that has an auto sampler, which is essentially a robot that samples the air space above the blood and injects it into the GC. Many vials can be preloaded and analyzed without operator intervention. Typically, the auto sampler will be loaded at the end of the work day and then will run all night. As data are generated, the concentration of alcohol in each blood sample is calculated automatically and printed out, awaiting further review and reports the next morning. A typical chromatogram of alcohol is shown in Figure 14.6.

Besides GC there are also enzymatic methods for the analysis of alcohol. For example, the coenzyme nicotinamide adenine dinucleotide (NAD) will react with alcohol in the presence of alcohol dehydrogenase as a catalyst. The alcohol is converted to acetaldehyde and the NAD is reduced to NADH. The reaction is monitored by UV/visible spectrophotometry at 340 nm where NADH absorbs, in order to measure the concentration of alcohol.

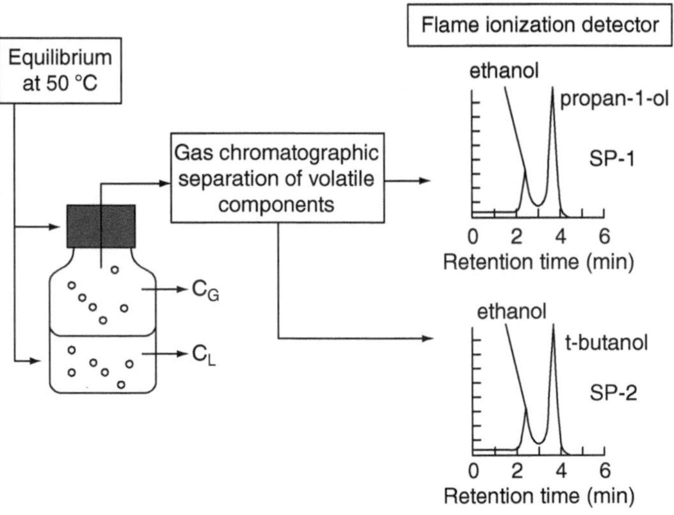

FIGURE 14.6

Gas chromatograms of ethyl alcohol. In the chromatograms, the propan-1-ol (isopropyl alcohol) and the t-butanol are internal standards. They are used to help determine the quantity of alcohol in the sample.

BREATH ALCOHOL TESTING

Breath testing of alcohol is by far, the most widely used method for alcohol testing in use today, especially given its near universal use in drunk-driving cases. Originally, breath testing instruments converted the BrAC to BAC using a constant ratio (usually 2100:1). As breath testing instruments evolved and research indicated that this ratio was imprecise, many states added laws that link violations directly to BrAC. Breath testing instruments can be divided into two general groups; those that are used primarily as preliminary breath testing instruments (PBTs) and those that are accepted for evidentiary purposes. There is some overlap, as some PBTs are useable as evidentiary instruments in some jurisdictions. Recent surveys indicate that the Alco-Sensors® (Intoximeter Company) are the most popular PBTs, and the Intoxilyzers (CMI, Inc.) are the most popular evidentiary instruments.

The first commercially popular and successful BrAC instrument was the Breathalyzer®. This instrument worked on the principle that acidified potassium dichromate will oxidize alcohol to acetic acid, while at the same time being reduced to chromium sulfate. The complete equation is given below:

$$\underset{\substack{\text{potassium dichromate} \\ \text{(yellow)}}}{2\,K_2Cr_2O_7} + \underset{\text{ethyl alcohol}}{3C_2H_5OH} + \underset{\text{sulfuric acid}}{8H_2SO_4} \longrightarrow \underset{\substack{\text{chromic sulfate} \\ \text{(green)}}}{2\,Cr_2(SO_4)_3} + \underset{\text{acetic acid}}{3CH_3COOH} + \underset{\text{water}}{11H_2O}$$

Preliminary Breath Testing Instruments

Most of the PBTs work by either of chemical oxidation or by fuel cell technology. Those that work by chemical oxidation operate using similar principles to the Breathalyzer although potassium permanganate may be employed in place of potassium dichromate.

Evidentiary Breath Testing Instruments

The Intoxilyzer uses infrared spectroscopy for the measurement of alcohol. The alcohol is trapped in a chamber and infrared light is passed through the sample to a detector. The more alcohol there is in the chamber, the less light gets through to the detector. The intensity of light that reaches the detector (or is absorbed by the analyte) is directly proportional to the amount of substance absorbing the light. Early instruments measured absorbance of alcohol at one wavelength of light only. There were concerns that other substances that may be present in the blood such as ketones or other alcohols could interfere with the measurement of the quantity of ethyl alcohol, so modern instruments measure the amount of alcohol at two wavelengths, with the added one chosen such that it is relatively insensitive to ketones and other alcohols. Figure 14.7 is a diagram of the intoxilyzer. Other breath testing instruments in current use include fuel cell-based instruments such as the "intoximeter" and dual IR-fuel cell instruments such as the Draeger 7110. The latter instrument has the advantage of giving two independent readings using two different technologies on the same sample.

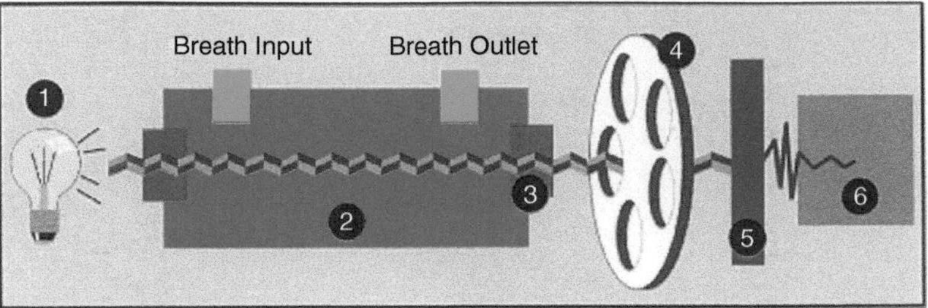

The Intoxilyzer 5000 measures the degree alcohol absorbs infrared energy...the more alcohol present, the greater the absorption. As shown, a quartz lamp (1) generates IR energy which travels through a sample chamber (2) containing the subject's breath. Upon leaving the chamber, a lens (3) focuses the energy onto the chopper wheel (4) containing three or five narrowband IR filters. The IR energy passed by the filters is focused on a highly sensitive photo detector (5) which converts the IR pulses into electrical pulses. The microprocessor (6) interprets the pulses and calculates the Blood Alcohol Concentration which is then displayed.

FIGURE 14.7

The Intoxilyzer. This instrument uses IR radiation to measure the amount of alcohol in breath. Only those wavelengths of IR light that are absorbed by alcohol reach the detector.

Courtesy of CMI, Inc.

FIELD SOBRIETY TESTING

When a driver is stopped by a police officer for driving under the influence of alcohol (DUIL), the subject is requested to perform some simple tests that might indicate his or her fitness to operate a motor vehicle. At one time, these tests were a necessary component of proof of OUIL or operating while impaired. Although these tests are no longer required as a component of proof in most states, they may still have an important function. In some states, specially trained police officers, called **drug recognition experts** can administer a battery of field sobriety tests to a driver. These tests, taken as a whole, can provide strong evidence that the driver is impaired or OUIL. They can provide probable cause to require further, quantitative alcohol testing. First developed in California, this battery of tests has spread widely across the United States. A typical protocol calls for three tests. The first is the **horizontal gaze nystagmus**. In this test, the subject is asked to follow with his or her eyes only, a pencil or other object as the officer moves it slowly back and forth across the subject's field of vision. If a person is sober, he will be able to follow the pencil easily and his eyes will move smoothly. If, however, the person is under the influence of alcohol (or certain drugs), the eyeballs will jerk as they move. The other two tests measure dexterity, which would be expected to deteriorate as BAC increases. Common ones are the "walk and turn" whereby a person must walk in a straight line putting one foot directly in front of the other and then turn around and come back. The other test is to close one's eyes and touch one's nose with the tip of a finger. When all three tests are used as a set, there is a high correlation between drunk or drugged behavior and the results of these tests.

OPERATING VERSUS DRIVING A MOTOR VEHICLE

If you examine the laws that control alcohol and driving an automobile in the United States, you will notice that some states frame their laws in terms of **operating** a motor vehicle whereas other states sanction **driving** a motor vehicle. In all states the alcohol level that is defined as being "under the influence" of alcohol is currently 0.08%. Some states have a secondary designation of "impaired" which is currently 0.05%. Is there a difference between operating a motor vehicle and driving it? The answer is "yes." Driving a car means that the subject is in the driver's seat with the engine turned on and the car in motion on a road or other surface. Operating a car means that the subject is in the driver's seat and the engine is turned on but the car can be in park—it doesn't have to be in motion. This means that someone who is sitting by the curb, with the car in idle, whose alcohol level exceeds 0.08% is guilty of OUIL but would not be guilty of DUIL.

DRUNK VERSUS DRUGGED DRIVING

You now know that each state sets a limit of 0.08% for a BAC in order to be OUIL or DUIL. What about someone who is driving erratically and found to have been smoking marihuana or ingesting cocaine or ecstasy? Are there lower limits to the concentration of such drugs above which someone is driving or operating under the influence of drugs? The answer is no. There are no definitions of impairment or influence of any drugs that are based upon its concentration in blood or breath or any other part of the body. There is insufficient data to accurately determine such levels and it is unlikely to do so since the effects of drugs vary so much from person to person for a given level. In all states, then, you can be charged with drugged driving if a laboratory is able to confirm the presence of a drug in your body without regard to the amount of the drug present. This approach is not difficult to understand in the case of such drugs as marihuana or cocaine. They are illegal to possess in any quantity. Remember, however, that you can be arrested for drugged driving even if you are under the influence of a prescribed drug for which you have a prescription. You can still be a danger to yourself or others if you are incapacitated by such drugs.

BACK TO THE CASE

The drunk-driving case presented at the beginning of the chapter has a number of interesting aspects that illustrate toxicology and drunk driving. There was sufficient alcohol taken to reach a breath level that was well above the legal limit and which would have explained the behavior of the subject during the field sobriety tests. The additional infrared breath test failed to confirm the presence of any of the solvents that were present in the sealant. The defense had claimed that these chemicals contaminated the breath test and that the subject was impaired by inhaling them during his job sealing driveways. This case involves the issue of what types of substances can interfere with a breath or blood alcohol tests. The pharmacology of commercial solvents is also at issue here with the conjecture that they impaired the subject and caused him to drive as if drunk and to fail the field sobriety tests.

SUMMARY

Forensic toxicology is a part of the science of pharmacology, which is concerned with the quantities and effects of various drugs and poisons on human beings. In forensic toxicology the main interest is the extent to which drugs and poisons may have contributed to impairment or death. More than half of the cases received by forensic toxicologists involve drinking alcohol and driving. Every state and the Federal Government has laws that prohibit drinking and driving and set levels above which a person is either impaired or OUIL. Forensic toxicologists are called upon to determine the level of alcohol present in the body and sometimes, the level at a previous time and the effects on the person. In cases involving drugs and poisons, forensic toxicologists usually only get involved when death has occurred. The toxicologist works with the medical examiner or coroner to help determine the cause and manner of death. The toxicologist will use data about what drugs are present and at what levels at the time of death, along with drug usage history and general health, to determine the role that drugs or poisons played in death.

TEST YOUR KNOWLEDGE

1. Define pharmacology. How does this differ from toxicology?
2. How do forensic toxicologists work as a team with forensic pathologists? What role does forensic toxicology have in determining the cause and manner of death?
3. In the typical forensic toxicology laboratory, what is the major type of case that is handled by the toxicologists? What makes this type of case unique?
4. What is metabolism as it applies to toxicology? What role does the liver play in metabolism?
5. What is the science that describes the fate of drugs in the body from the time they are taken until eliminated?
6. What factors can affect the rate at which alcohol is absorbed from the stomach into the bloodstream?
7. What are the major routes of elimination of drugs from the body?
8. For alcohol, what is the most important route of elimination from the body?
9. What is dependence? Tolerance? How do they differ?
10. When a pharmacologist has to determine the role that a given blood level of a drug may have had in the cause of death, why is it important that the drug history of the victim be known?
11. What test(s) is (are) commonly used for confirmation of a drug in the body?
12. What are immunoassay tests? When are they used? What are the two major types?
13. What is a cut-off level? Why does a toxicology laboratory use cut-off levels?
14. Why is blood generally the best sample for drugs for toxicology? Under what circumstances might blood not be the best source?
15. What is the Widmark curve? What does it measure?

16. The last portion of a typical Widmark curve has a straight-line slope? What does this measure?
17. What is the principle of operation of the Breathalyzer?
18. Most states use a conversion of blood to breath alcohol in the Breathalyzer of 2300:1? Why do other states reject this and have separate levels for blood and breath alcohol?
19. What types of instruments are used for measuring blood (not breath) alcohol?
20. Describe how the horizontal gaze nystagmus test works? When is it used?

CONSIDER THIS...

1. There is a lot of "urban folklore" surrounding the ingestion of alcohol and its effects and after effects. Some of the cautions and remedies include:
   a. Never mix your drinks. You won't get as drunk if you stick to one type of drink.
   b. You can sober up faster by drinking coffee.
   c. You can sober up faster by exercising heavily.
   d. You can counteract the effects of a hangover by having a drink the next day (hair of the dog that bit you).

   Explain why all of the above are not true or don't work in light of the principles of forensic toxicology.
2. In the case cited at the beginning of the chapter, what information would be useful to the forensic toxicologist in making a determination about the role of any drugs that the person might have been taking in the cause of death.
3. One of the long-term effects of chronic alcohol abuse is cirrhosis of the liver. This is a progressive disease that gradually reduces the ability of the liver to carry out its toxicological functions among others. If the man who died in the case cited above was found to have cirrhosis and was found to have ingested a drug, how would the pharmacologist take the liver condition into account when determining the cause of death? Would it be possible in such a case for a person to take a dose of a drug that would be sublethal for most other people, and still die from it? Why?

FURTHER READING

Baselt, R.H., Cravey, R.H., 1996. Disposition of Toxic Drugs and Chemicals in Man, fourth ed. Year Book, New York.

Garriott, J.C., 1996. Medicolegal Aspects of Alcohol. Lawyers and Judges, Tucson.

Jones, A.W., 1996. Measuring alcohol in blood and breath for forensic purposes – a historical review. Forensic Science Review 8, 13–14.

Moffat, A.C. (Ed.), 1986. Clarke's Isolation and Identification of Drugs. Pharmaceutical Press, London.

ON THE WEB

http://en.wikipedia.org/wiki/Forensic_toxicology good overview of forensic toxicology.

http://www.apsu.edu/oconnort/3210/3210lect05.htm another good overview of the field. Includes other web references and a good section on the qualifications of a forensic toxicologist.

http://www.abft.org/American Board of Forensic Toxicology homepage. Discusses certification and accreditation in toxicology.

http://www.soft-tox.org/Homepage of Society of Forensic Toxicologists. This is a group of practicing forensic toxicologists.

CHAPTER

Textile Fibers

15

CHAPTER OUTLINE

KEY TERMS

- Becke line
- Color

- Courses
- Crimp
- Cross-sectional shape
- Delustrants
- Denier
- Dye
- Fabric
- Filaments
- Interference colors
- Knit fabrics
- Lumen
- Manufactured fiber
- Metameric colors
- Microfibers
- Microspectrophotometer
- Natural fiber
- Nonwoven fabrics
- Plied yarn
- Polymers
- Refractive index
- S-twist
- Simultaneous contrast
- Spinneret
- Spinning
- Spinning dope
- Spiral elements
- Staple fiber
- Synthetic fibers
- Technical fiber
- Wales
- Warp yarns
- Weft yarns
- Woven fabric
- Yarn
- Z-twist

THE CASE: CROSS-TRANSFER

A woman comes home to find her house broken into and her daughter missing. As she frantically checks the house for signs of her 9-year-old child, she sees a neighbor fleeing the backyard through a fence. A variety of things are missing, including beer and food from the refrigerator, but the entire house is in disarray. When the police arrive, they search the house thoroughly and discover the battered body of the daughter under a pile of clothing, beaten and stabbed to death. The police question the neighbor, who had a history of criminal activity, including burglary and drug use. The neighbor allowed the police to search his home and told them he went to the front door of the house, asked for a glass of water, became dizzy, fell, and the girl caught him; he then went home. One of the officers found a beer can of the same brand that was stolen from the house: He touched it and it was very cold. He found that odd because the man's utilities had been shut off for some time, and he had no refrigeration. A further search turned up other items missing from the woman's house, including jewelery in the bathroom with bloodstains on it. The neighbor was taken into custody and his clothing collected as evidence.

INTRODUCTION

Textile fibers, as a class, are a ubiquitous type of evidence. They are "common" in the sense that textiles surround us in our homes, offices, and vehicles. We are in constant contact with textiles on a daily basis. We all move through a personal textile environment of clothing, cars, upholstery, things we touch, and people we encounter. Fibers from textiles are constantly being shed and transferred to people, places, and things; some are better "shedders," like fuzzy sweaters, than others—a tightly woven dress shirt, for example. Certain textiles also retain fibers better than others, depending on their construction, purpose, use, and other factors, such as how often they are cleaned.

Textile fibers are also among the most neglected and undervalued kinds of forensic evidence. Fibers provide many qualitative and quantitative traits for comparison. Textile fibers are often produced with specific end-use products in mind (underwear made from carpet fibers would be very uncomfortable), and these end uses lead to a variety of discrete traits designed into the fibers.

Color is another powerful discriminating characteristic. About 7000 commercial dyes and pigments are used to color textiles. No one dye is used to create any particular color, and millions of shades of colors are possible in textiles (Apsell, 1981). It is rare to find two fibers at random that exhibit the same microscopic characteristics and optical properties, especially color.

Applying statistical methods to trace evidence is difficult, however, because of a lack of frequency data. Very often, even the company that made a particular fiber will not know how many products those fibers went into. Attempts have been made to estimate the frequency of garments in populations; for example, based on databases from Germany and England, the chance of finding a woman's blouse made of turquoise acetate fibers among a random population of garments was calculated to be nearly 4 in 1,000,000 garments. Cases such as the Wayne Williams case in Atlanta, Georgia or the O.J. Simpson case in Los Angeles, California, also demonstrate the usefulness of forensic textile fiber analysis in demonstrating probative associations in criminal investigations.

TEXTILE FIBERS

A textile fiber is a unit of matter, either natural or manufactured, that forms the basic element of fabrics and other textiles and has a length at least 100 times its diameter. Fibers differ from each other in their chemical nature, cross-sectional shape, surface contour, color, as well as length and diameter.

Fibers are classified as either natural or manufactured. A **natural fiber** is any fiber that exists as a fiber in its natural state. A **manufactured fiber** is any fiber derived by a process of manufacture from any substance that, at any point in the manufacturing process, is not a fiber. Fibers can also be designated by their chemical make-up as either protein, cellulosic, mineral, or synthetic:

- Protein fibers are composed of polymers of amino acids.
- Cellulosic fibers are made of polymers formed from carbohydrates.
- Mineral (inorganic) fibers may be composed of silica obtained from rocks or sand.
- Synthetic fibers are made of polymers that originate from small organic molecules that combine with water and air.

The generic names for manufactured and synthetic fibers were established as part of the Textile Fiber Products Identification Act enacted by Congress in 1954 (see Table 15.1). In 1996, lyocell was named as a new sub-generic class of rayon.

The diameter of textile fibers is relatively small, generally 0.0004–0.002 in, or 11–50 μm. Their length can vary from about 7/8 in (2.2 cm) to, literally, miles. Based on length, fibers are classified as either filament or staple fiber. **Filaments** are a type of fiber having indefinite or extreme length, such as silk or a manufactured fiber. **Staple fibers** are natural fibers (except silk) or cut lengths of filament, typically being 7/8–8 in (2.2–28.5 cm) in length.

The size of natural fibers is usually given as a diameter measurement in micrometers. The size of silk and manufactured fibers is usually given in denier (in the United States) or tex (in other countries). Denier and tex are linear measurements based on weight per unit length. The **denier** is the weight in grams of 9000 m of the material fibrous. Denier is a direct numbering system in which the lower numbers represent the finer sizes and the higher numbers the larger sizes; glass fibers are the only manufactured fibers that are not measured by denier. A one-denier nylon fiber is not equal in size to a one-denier rayon fiber, however, because the fibers differ in density. Tex is equal to the weight in grams of 1000 m (1 km) of the material. To convert from tex to denier, divide the tex value by 0.1111; to convert from denier to tex, multiply the denier value by 0.1111.

YARNS

Yarn is a term for continuous strands of textile fibers, filaments, or material in a form suitable for weaving, knitting, or otherwise entangling to form a textile fabric; a yarn is diagramed in Figure 15.1. Yarns may be constructed to have an **S-twist** or **Z-twist** or no twist at all. A yarn may be constructed as a number of smaller single yarns twisted together to form a **plied yarn**; each ply will have its own twist as well

Table 15.1 Federal Trade Commission Textile Products Identification Act, 1954, Definitions

Acetate	A manufactured fiber in which the fiber-forming substance is cellulose acetate. Where not less than 92% of the hydroxyl groups are acetylated, the term "triacetate" may be used as a generic description of the fiber.
Acrylic	A manufactured fiber in which the fiber-forming substance is any long-chain synthetic polymer composed of at least 85% by weight of acrylonitrile units.
Anidex	A manufactured fiber in which the fiber-forming substance is any long-chain synthetic polymer composed of at least 50% by weight of one or more esters of a monohydric alcohol and acrylic acid.
Aramid	A manufactured fiber in which the fiber-forming substance is any long-chain synthetic polyamide in which at least 85% of the amide linkages are attached directly to two aromatic rings.
Glass	A manufactured fiber in which the fiber-forming substance is glass.
Lyocell	A manufactured fiber composed of precipitated cellulose and produced by a solvent extrusion process where no chemical intermediates are formed.
Metallic	A manufactured fiber composed of metal, plastic-coated metal, metal-coated plastic, or a core completely covered by metal.
Modacrylic	A manufactured fiber in which the fiber-forming substance is any long-chain synthetic polymer composed of less than 85% but at least 35% by weight of acrylonitrile units.
Novoloid	A manufactured fiber in which the fiber-forming substance is any long-chain synthetic polymer composed of at least 85% of a long-chain polymer of vinylidene dinitrile where the vinylidene dinitrile content is no less than every other unit in the polymer chain.
Nylon	A manufactured fiber in which the fiber-forming substance is any long-chain synthetic polyamide in which less than 85% of the amide linkages are attached directly to two aromatic rings.
Olefin	A manufactured fiber in which the fiber-forming substance is any long-chain synthetic polymer composed of at least 85% by weight of ethylene, propylene, or other olefin units.
Polyester	A manufactured fiber in which the fiber-forming substance is any long-chain synthetic polymer composed of at least 85% by weight of an ester or a substituted aromatic carboxylic acid, including but not restricted to substituted terephthalate units and parasubstituted hydroxybenzoate units.
Rayon	A manufactured fiber composed of regenerated cellulose, as well as manufactured fibers composed of regenerated cellulose in which substituents have replaced not more than 15% of the hydrogens of the hydroxyl groups.
Saran	A manufactured fiber in which the fiber-forming substance is any long-chain synthetic polymer composed of at least 80% by weight of vinylidene chloride units.
Spandex	A manufactured fiber in which the fiber-forming substance is any long-chain synthetic polymer composed of at least 85% of a segmented polyurethane.
Vinal	A manufactured fiber in which the fiber-forming substance is any long-chain synthetic polymer composed of at least 50% by weight of vinyl alcohol units and in which the total of the vinyl alcohol units and any one or more of the various acetal units is at least 85% by weight of the fiber.
Vinyon	A manufactured fiber in which the fiber-forming substance is any long-chain synthetic polymer composed of at least 85% by weight of vinyl chloride units.

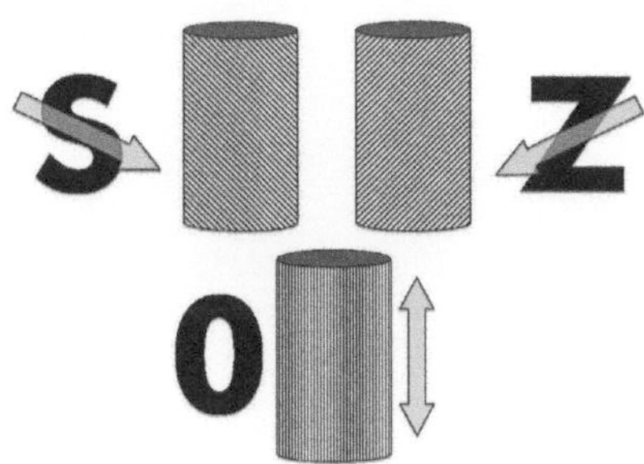

FIGURE 15.1

Yarns are continuous strands of textile fibers, filaments, or material in a form suitable for weaving, knitting, or otherwise entangling to form a textile fabric. Yarns can have an S-twist, Z-twist, or zero twist.

as the overall twist of the plied yarn. Do not confuse the words "yarn" and "thread": Thread refers to the product used to join pieces of fabric together, typically by sewing, whereas yarn is the product used to make fabric.

FABRIC CONSTRUCTION

Fabric is a textile structure produced by interlacing yarns, fibers, or filaments with a substantial surface area in relation to its thickness. Fabrics are defined by their method of assembly. The three major types of fabrics are woven, knitted, and nonwoven.

WOVEN FABRICS

Fabrics have been woven since the dawn of civilization. **Woven fabrics** are those fabrics composed of two sets of yarns, called warp and weft, and are formed by the interlacing of these sets of yarns. The way these sets of yarns are interlaced determines the weave. **Warp yarns** run lengthwise to the fabric, and **weft yarns** run crosswise; weft may also be referred to as filling, woof, or picks, as shown in Figure 15.2. An almost unlimited variety of constructions can be fashioned by weaving.

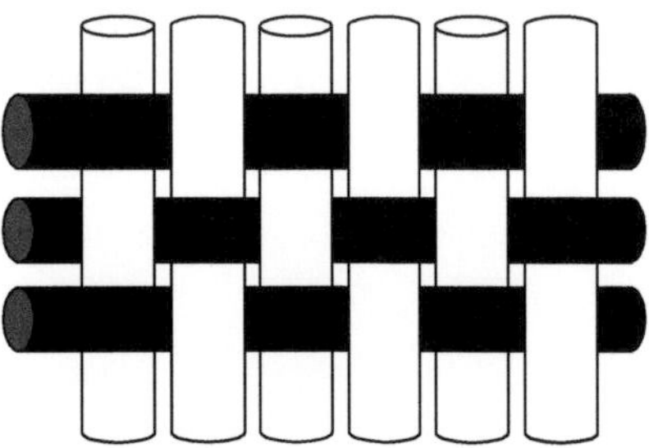

FIGURE 15.2

Woven fabrics are composed of two sets of yarns, called warp and weft, formed by the interlacing of these yarns. The way these sets of yarns are interlaced determines the weave. Warp yarns run lengthwise to the fabric and weft yarns run crosswise.

KNITTED FABRICS

Knitted fabrics are constructed of interlocking series of loops of one or more yarns and fall into two major categories: warp knitting and weft knitting. In warp knits the yarns generally run lengthwise in the fabric, whereas in weft knits the yarns generally run crosswise to the fabric. The basic components of a knit fabric are **courses**, which are rows of loops across the width of the fabric, and **wales**, which are rows of loops along the length of the fabric. Unlike woven fabrics, in which warp and weft are made up of different sets of yarns, courses and wales are formed by a single yarn.

NONWOVEN FABRICS

Nonwoven fabrics are an assembly of textile fibers held together by mechanical interlocking in a random web or mat, by fusing of the fibers or by bonding with a cementing medium. Felt is a good example, but a wide variety of nonwoven construction methods is currently in use and other examples are bandage pads, automotive textiles, and medical fabrics.

FIBER CHARACTERISTICS

The shapes of fibers relate to their identification. Natural fibers are used for certain products, such as cordage and rugs, more than others. Characteristics are imparted to manufactured fibers with particular end uses in mind. Beyond fiber size and type, many other traits serve to differentiate textile fibers.

Crimp is the waviness of a fiber expressed as crimps per unit length. Crimp may be two-dimensional or three-dimensional in nature. Some fibers are naturally crimped, like wool, whereas others are more linear, such as silk. Crimp must be imparted to manufactured fibers.

Color is introduced to manufactured fibers with dyes or pigments, while natural fibers may be originally white, off-white, or a shade of brown. Natural fibers may be bleached to remove any natural color, so they may be dyed more easily. The color may vary along a fiber due to differential dye uptake or because the color has been printed onto the fabric, rather than dyed. All these traits should be noted.

Cross-sectional shape, the shape of an individual filament when cut at a right angle to its long axis, is a critical characteristic of fiber analysis. Shapes for manufactured fibers vary by design; there are about 500 different cross-sections used for synthetic fibers. The cross-section of plant or animal fibers may assist the examiner in identifying the source.

A fiber's length may be an indication of its intended end use. All natural fibers are staple fibers except silk; manufactured fibers originate as filaments but may be cut to staple form. All fibers, natural and manufactured, are chain-like macromolecules called **polymers**, which are hundreds or thousands of repeating chemical units called monomers linked together.

NATURAL FIBERS

The first textiles were made of natural fibers. Currently, over half of the fibers produced each year are natural fibers, and the majority of these are cotton. In fact, about half of all fibers produced annually are cotton. Natural fibers come from animals, plants, or minerals. Used in many products, it is important for the forensic fiber examiner to have a thorough knowledge of natural fibers and their significance in casework.

Animal Fibers

Animal fibers come either from mammals (hairs) or from certain invertebrates, such as the silkworm. Animal fibers in textiles are most often from wool-bearing animals, such as sheep and goats or from fur-bearing animals, like rabbits, mink, and fox. A comprehensive reference collection is critical to animal hair identifications and comparisons. The microscopic anatomical structures of animal hairs are important to their identification.

Plant Fibers

The three major sources for fibers derived from plants are the seed, stem (bast fibers), and leaf, depending on which source works best for a particular plant. Plant fibers are found in two principal forms: the **technical fiber**, used in cordage, sacks, mats, etc. or individual cells, as in fabrics or paper. The examination of technical fibers should include a search for internal structures, such as the **lumen** (a central channel running through the middle of the fiber), spiral vessels (plant cells with helical walls), or crystals and the preparation of a cross-section. Technical fibers should be mashed, fabrics teased apart, and paper repulped for the examination of individual cells. The relative thickness of the cell walls and the size, shape, and thickness of the lumen; cell length and the presence, type, and distribution of dislocations should be noted. The most common plant fibers encountered in casework are cotton, flax, jute, hemp, ramie, sisal, abaca, coir, and kapok (see Table 15.2).

MANUFACTURED FIBERS

Manufactured fibers are the various families of fibers produced from fiber-forming substances, which may be synthesized polymers, modified or transformed natural polymers, or glass. **Synthetic fibers** are those manufactured fibers that are synthesized from chemical compounds (e.g., nylon, polyester). Therefore, all synthetic fibers are manufactured, but not all manufactured fibers are synthetic. The microscopic characteristics of manufactured fibers are the basic features used to distinguish them. Manufactured fibers differ physically in their shape, size, internal properties, and appearance.

Table 15.2 Various Natural Fibers and Their Microscopic Characteristics

Kind	Plant	Genus and Species	Characteristics
Bast (stem) fibers	Flax (linen)	*Linum usitatissimum*	The ultimates (individual fiber cells) are polygonal in cross-section, with thick walls and small lumina. Microscopically, the fibers have dark dislocations, which are roughly perpendicular to the long axis of the fiber.
	Jute	*Corchorus capsularis*	This fiber appears bundled microscopically and may have a yellowish cast. The ultimates are polygonal but angular with medium-sized lumina. It can be distinguished easily from flax by its counterclockwise twist. The dislocations appear as angular x' or v's and may be numerous.
	Ramie	*Boehmeria nivea*	Ramie has very long and very wide ultimates. The walls are thick and, in cross-section, appear flattened. Ramie has frequent, short dislocations, and longer transverse striations. In cross-section, radial cracks may be present.
	Hemp	*Cannabis sativa*	With the ultimates more bundled, a wider lumen, and fewer nodes, hemp is easy to distinguish from flax. Cross-sectioning hemp helps in distinguishing it from jute because hemp's lumina are rounder and more flattened than jute's. Hemp may also have a brownish cast to it.
Leaf fibers	Sisal	*Agave sisilana*	Sisal is relatively easy to identify due to its irregular lumen size, crystals, **spiral elements**, and annular vessels. In cross-section, sisal looks somewhat like cut celery.
	Abaca	*Musa textilis*	Although potentially difficult to distinguish from sisal, abaca's ultimates have a uniform diameter and a waxy appearance; often it is darker than sisal. Its ultimates are polygonal in cross-section and vary in size. Abaca may present spiral elements but often will have small crown-like structures.
Seed fibers	Cotton	Genus *Gossypium*	Mature cotton has a flat, twisted, ribbon-like appearance that is easy to identify. Cotton fibers are made up of several spiralling layers around a central lumen.
	Kapok	*Ceiba pentandra*	Kapok fiber is used primarily for life preservers and upholstery padding because the fibers are hollow, producing very buoyant products. But they are brittle, which prevents spinning or weaving.
	Coir	*Coco nucifera*	Coir comes from the husk of the coconut and, accordingly, is a very dense, stiff fiber easily identified microscopically. On a slide mount, coir appears very dark brown or opaque with very large, coarse ultimates.

FIBER MANUFACTURE

Synthetic fibers are formed by extruding a fiber-forming substance, called **spinning dope**, through a hole or holes in a shower head-like device called a **spinneret**, shown in Figure 15.3; this process is called **spinning**. The spinning dope is created by rendering solid monomeric material into a liquid or semiliquid form with a solvent or heat.

Optical properties, such as refractive index, birefringence, and color, are those traits that relate to a fiber's structure or treatment revealed through observation. Some of these characteristics aid in the identification of the generic polymer class of manufactured fibers. Others, such as color, are critical discriminators of fibers that have been dyed or chemically finished. A visual and analytical assessment of fiber color must be part of every fiber comparison.

The fluorescence of fibers and their dyes is another useful point of comparison. Thermal properties relate to the softening and melting temperatures for manufactured fibers and the changes the fiber exhibits when heated (see Table 15.3).

Based on a fiber's polymer composition, it will react differently to various instrumental methods, such as Fourier transform infrared spectroscopy (FTIR) or pyrolysis-gas chromatography (PGC), and chemicals, such as acids or bases. These reactions yield information about the fiber's molecular structure and composition.

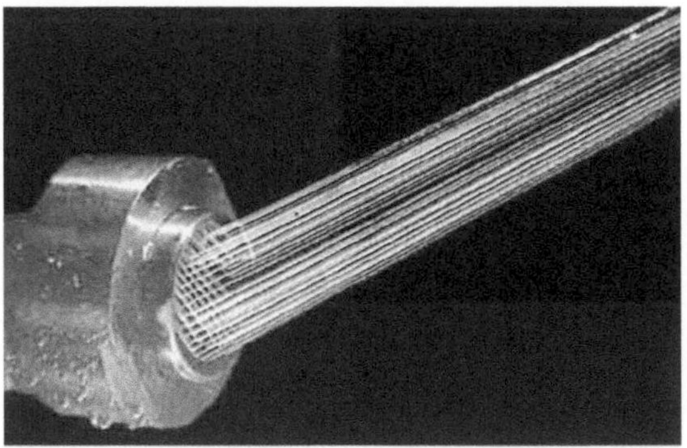

FIGURE 15.3

Synthetic fibers are formed by extruding a fiber-forming substance, called spinning dope, through a hole or holes in a shower head-like device called a spinneret.

This photograph appeared in the photographic essay, The Reign of Chemistry, *by Eugene Smith, W. in* Life Magazine, *January 5, 1954.*

MICROSCOPIC CHARACTERISTICS

A polarized light microscope is the primary tool for the identification and analysis of manufactured fibers. Many characteristics of manufactured fibers can be viewed in nonpolarized light, however, and these characteristics provide a fast, direct, and

Table 15.3 Melting Temperatures for Some Fiber Types

Fiber Type	Temperature (°C)
Acetate	224–280
Acrylic	Does not melt
Aramid	Does not melt
Modacrylic[1]	204–225
Nylon	
6	213
6,12	217–227
6,6	254–267
Olefin	
Polyethylene	122–135
Polypropylene	152–173
Polyester (PET)	256–268
Rayon	Does not melt
Saran	167–184
Spandex	231
Triacetate	260
Vinal	200–260

[1]Some members of this class do not melt.
From Carroll, G.R., 1992. Forensic fiber microscopy. In: Robertson, J. (Ed.), Forensic examination of fibers. Ellis Horwood, New York City, NY.

accurate method for the discrimination of similar fibers. A comparison light microscope is required to confirm whether the known and the questioned fibers truly present the same microscopic characteristics.

The cross-section is the shape of an individual fiber when cut at a right angle to its long axis. Shapes for manufactured fibers vary with the desired end result, such as the fiber's soil-hiding ability or a silky or coarse feel to the final fabric. Figure 15.4 shows some variations in fiber cross-sections. The particular cross-section also may be indicative of a fiber's intended end use: Many carpet fibers have a lobed shape to help hide dirt and create a specific visual texture to the carpet.

The way a fiber's diameter is measured depends on its cross-sectional shape; there is more than one way to measure the diameter of a nonround fiber. Manufactured fibers can be made in diameters from about 6 μm (so-called **microfibers**) up to a size limited only by the width of the spinneret holes. By comparison, natural fibers vary in diameter from cultivated silk (10–13 μm) to US sheep's wool (up to 40 μm or more) and human head hairs range from 50 to 100 μm.

Delustrants are finely ground particles of materials, such as titanium dioxide, that are introduced into the spinning dope. These particles help to diffract light passing through the fibers and reduce their luster, as illustrated in Figure 15.5. The size, shape, distribution, and concentration of delustrants should be noted.

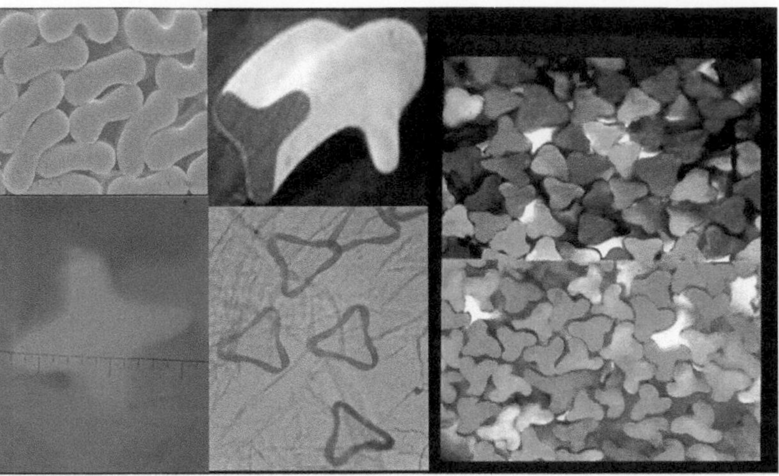

FIGURE 15.4

The cross-section of a fiber may relate to its end use. Carpet fibers, for example, often have cross-sections that are meant to keep the fiber upright (making the carpeting feel plush) and to hide dirt. About 500 cross-sectional shapes are used in the manufacture of fibers.

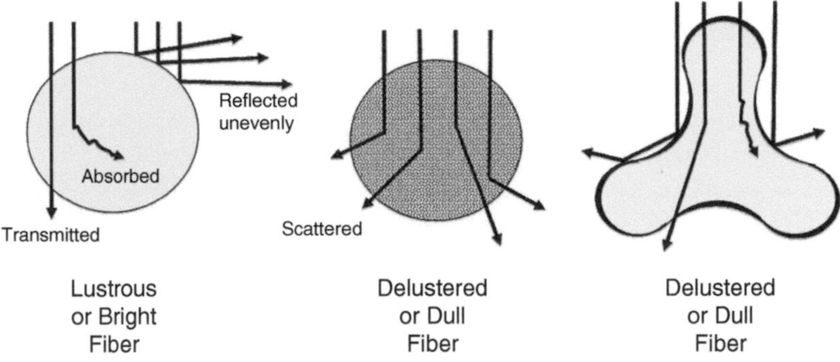

FIGURE 15.5

Tiny grains of material, usually titanium dioxide, are incorporated into a fiber as it is spun; these are called delustrants. Delustrants break up the light entering the fiber and make it appear dull or give a matte finish. A fiber with no delustrant is described as being "bright."

OPTICAL PROPERTIES OF MANUFACTURED FIBERS

The examination of the optical properties of manufactured fibers can yield a tremendous amount of information about their chemistry, production, end use, and environment. Careful measurements and analysis of these properties are crucial steps in the identification and later comparison of textile fibers.

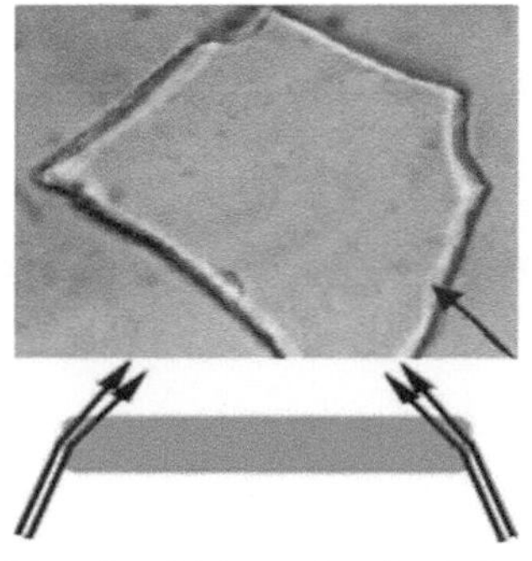

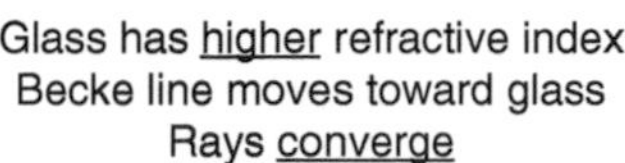

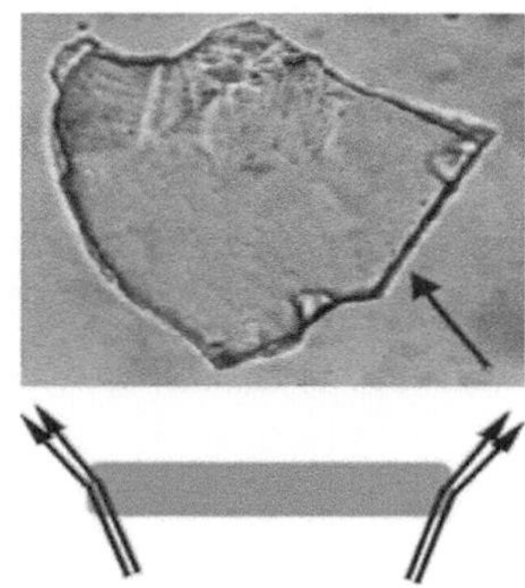

FIGURE 15.6

Fiber acts as a crude lens, either focusing light into or away from it. This has to do with the refractive index of the fiber, that is, the ratio of the speed of light in the fiber material over the speed of light in a vacuum. Appearing as a line of bright light, the Becke line can be used to determine the relative refractive index of a material, in this case, a fiber. When the distance between the microscope lens and the sample is increased, the Becke line moves toward the material with the higher refractive index.

Photographs courtesy Sarah Walbridge.

POLARIZED LIGHT MICROSCOPY

Polarized light microscopy is an easy, quick, and nondestructive way to determine the generic polymer class of manufactured and synthetic textile fibers. Beyond the immediate characteristics used to discriminate between polymer types, the examination of fibers in polarized light provides valuable information about the production and finishing of the fiber after spinning.

REFRACTIVE INDEX

Fibers vary in shape but are almost always thicker at the center than near the edges. Thus, they act as crude lenses, either concentrating or dispersing the light that passes through them. If a fiber has a higher **refractive index** than the medium in which it is mounted, it acts as a converging lens, concentrating light within the fiber. If the fiber has a lower refractive index than the mounting medium, it acts as a "diverging" lens and the light rays diverge from the fiber, as illustrated in Figure 15.6 with a fragment of glass. In most fibers, the light rays only slightly converge or diverge and thus appear as a thin bright line, called the **Becke line**, after the Austrian mineralogist Fredrich Becke who first described the phenomenon, at the interface between the fiber and the mounting medium (Good and Rothenberg, 1998). When an analyst is observing the fiber, the working distance on the microscope is increased (the stage is moved down); if the fiber has a higher refractive index, the Becke line moves toward the fiber as the working distance is increased. If the mounting medium has a higher index, the Becke line moves toward the medium

Fiber under polarized light (one filter)

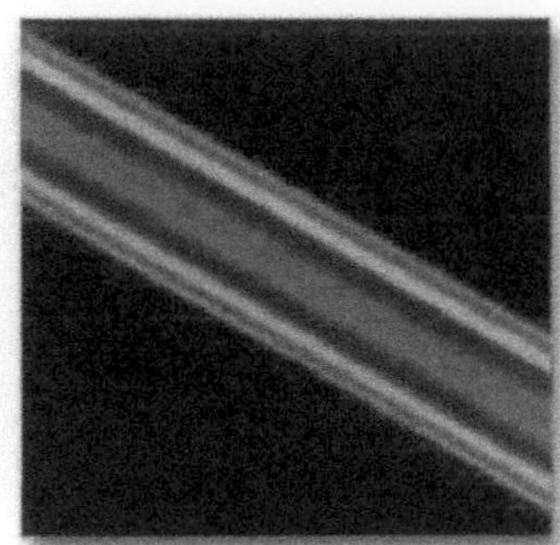

Fiber under cross-polar light (both filters) producing interference colors

FIGURE 15.7

Indicative of the fiber's polymer and molecular organization, **interference colors** can be used to help determine what kind of fiber is being examined.

Courtesy Sarah Walbridge.

(away from the fiber) as the working distance is increased (see Figure 15.6). If fibers are mounted in a medium that has a refractive index of 1.52, such as Permount®, then the fibers can be described as being greater than, equal to, or less than 1.52. The refractive indices of a fiber can be measured directly by placing the fiber in a series of liquids of specific refractive indices until the refractive indices of the fiber and liquid are the same. At this point, the fiber "disappears" because the fiber and the liquid are now isotropic, meaning that light is traveling at the same speed through both the fiber and the liquid.

BIREFRINGENCE

One of the more distinctive traits of a fiber is its birefringence. The interference colors seen after crossing the polarizing filters relate to a fiber's material nature, orientation, and crystallinity (see Figure 15.7). For the sake of comparison, most natural and synthetic fibers have birefringence from 0.001 to 1.8, but birefringence as high as 2.0 or more has been reported for specialty fibers (see Table 15.4). The refractive index is measured with the fiber parallel to the polarizing filter ($n\|$) and perpendicular to it ($n\perp$). The difference between the two is birefringence.

FLUORESCENCE MICROSCOPY

Many dyes used to color textiles have fluorescent components, and their response to certain wavelengths of light can be useful in comparing textile fibers. Not all textile dyes fluoresce, but fluorescence comparisons should be performed regardless: If the questioned and known fibers both fail to fluoresce, that is another point of meaningful comparison.

Fluorescence occurs when a substance is excited by specific wavelengths of light. A light of relatively short wavelength illuminates a substance, and the substance

Table 15.4 Table of Refractive Indices and Birefringences of Various Fiber Types

Fiber Type	n||	n⊥	n|| − n⊥
Acetate	**1.478**	1.473	0.005
Dicel	1.476	1.473	0.003
Triacetate			
Tricel	1.469	1.469	0
Arnel	1.469	1.468	0.001
Acrylic			
Acrilan 36	1.511	1.514	−0.003
Orlon	1.51	1.512	−0.002
Acrilan	1.52	1.525	−0.005
Modacrylic			
Dynel	1.535	1.533	0.002
Teklan	1.52	1.516	0.004
SEF	>1.52	>1.52	−(low)
Verel	1.535	1.539	−0.004
Vinyon			
Fibravyl	1.54	1.53	0.01
Rhovyl	1.541	1.536	0.005
Vinyon HH	1.528	1.524	0.004
Rayon			
Viscose (regular)	1.542	1.52	0.022
Viscose (regular)	1.545	1.525	0.02
Viscose (high tenacity)	1.544	1.505	0.039
Vincel (high wet modulus rayon)	1.551	1.513	0.038
Fortisan	1.547	1.523	0.024
Fortisan 36	1.551	1.52	0.031
Cuprammonium	1.553	1.519	0.034
Tencel	1.57	1.52	0.05
Olefin			
Courlene (PP)	1.53	1.496	0.034
Polypropylene	1.52	1.492	0.028
SWP (PE)	1.544	1.514	0.03
Courlene X3 (PE)	1.574	1.522	0.052
Polyethylene	1.556	1.512	0.044

Continued

Table 15.4 Table of Refractive Indices and Birefringences of Various Fiber Types—cont'd

Fiber Type	$n\parallel$	$n\perp$	$n\parallel - n\perp$
Nylon			
Enkalon (6)	1.575	1.526	0.049
ICI nylon (6,6)	1.578	1.522	0.056
Qiana	1.546	1.511	0.035
Rilsan (11)	1.553	1.507	0.046
Nylon 6	1.568	1.515	0.053
Nylon 6,6	1.582	1.519	0.063
Nylon 11	1.55	1.51	0.04
Silk (degummed)	1.57	1.52	0.05
Aramid			
Nomex	1.8	1.664	0.136
Kevlar	2.35	1.641	0.709
Polyester			
Vycron	1.713	1.53	0.183
Terylene	1.706	1.546	0.16
Fortrel/Dacron	1.72	1.535	0.185
Dacron	1.7	1.535	0.165
Kodel	1.632	1.534	0.098
Kodel II	1.642	1.54	0.102
Spandex			
Lycra/Vyrene	1.561	1.56	0.001
Others			
Vicara (Azlon)	1.538	1.536	0.002
Teflon	1.38	1.34	0.04
Calcium alginate	1.524	1.52	0.004
Saran	1.61	1.61	0
Novoloid	1.5–1.7	1.5–1.7	0
Kynol (drawn)	1.658	1.636	0.022
Kynol (undrawn)	1.649+	1.649	<0.001
Polyacrylostyrene	1.56	1.572	−0.012
Darvan (Nytril)	1.464	1.464+	0
Polycarbonate	1.626	1.566	0.06

Source: AATCC (1996), ASTM, D 276-87 (1996), McCrone et al. (1979), Rouen and Reeve (1970), and The Textile Institute (1985).

absorbs and/or converts (into heat, for example) a certain small part of the light. Most of the light that is not absorbed by the substance is re-emitted, which is called "fluorescence." The fluorescent light has lost some of its energy, and its wavelength will be longer than that of the source light.

Certain dye combinations may produce fluorescence of a particular intensity and color, both of which should be noted during the examination. Fibers dyed with similar dyes should exhibit the same fluorescence characteristics, unless the fibers and/or dye(s) have been degraded by UV exposure, bleaching, or some other similar means. It is important to consider these factors when collecting known samples.

COLOR IN TEXTILES

Color is one of the most critical characteristics in a fiber comparison. Almost all manufacturing industries are concerned with product appearance. Everything that is manufactured has a color to it, and often these colors are imparted to the end product. Particular colors are chosen for some products rather than others (it's difficult to find "safety orange" carpeting, for example), and these colors may indicate the end product. The number of producible colors is nearly infinite, and color is an easy discriminator.

COLOR PERCEPTION

The perception of color by a human observer is subject to a variety of factors, such as genetics, age, and environment. The human visual system is complex and adaptive. The phenomenon called **simultaneous contrast** is the perception of color based on context. As shown in Figure 15.8, the gray arrow on the left should look to be lighter or darker than the arrow on the right; the gray arrow on the right should look to be lighter or darker than the arrow on the left. In fact, they are the same gray. Humans' perception of the gray is affected by the background colors of yellow and blue. Another example of contextual color perception is known as the chameleon effect, illustrated in Figure 15.9. In this

FIGURE 15.8

The gray arrow on the left should look to be lighter or darker than the arrow on the right; the gray arrow on the right should look to be lighter or darker than the arrow on the left; in fact, they are the same gray. Humans' perception of the gray is affected by the background colors of yellow and blue. This phenomenon is called "simultaneous contrast."

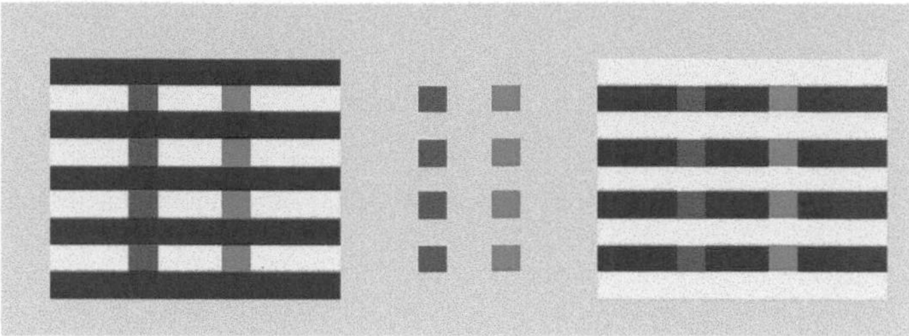

FIGURE 15.9

This phenomenon is called the "chameleon effect," where colors change based on the surrounding colors. The red and the green are the same colors in all the graphics.

effect, colors change based on the surrounding colors. Because of the factors influencing human color perception, any visual comparison, while effective as a first approximation of color, must be checked by an objective method of color measurement.

DYES AND PIGMENTS

Over 80 dyers worldwide are registered with the American Association of Textile Chemists and Colorists (AATCC), and almost 350 trademarked dyes are registered with this association. Some trademarked dyes have as many as 40 variants. Over 7000 dyes and pigments are currently produced worldwide. Natural dyes, such as indigo, have been known since before history, whereas synthetic dyes have gained prominence largely since World War I (Apsell, 1981).

A **dye** is an organic chemical that is able to absorb and reflect certain wavelengths of visible light. Pigments are microscopic, water-insoluble particles that are either incorporated into the fiber at the time of production or are bonded to the surface of the fiber by a resin. Some fiber types, such as olefins, are not easily dyed and therefore are often pigmented.

Based on the desired end product effects, the fiber substrate and the type of dye used, there are more than 12 different application categories for textile dyes. Very few textiles are colored with only one dye, and even a simple dye may be put through 8–10 processing steps to achieve a final dye form, shade, and strength. When all these factors are considered, it becomes apparent that it is virtually impossible to dye textiles in a continuous method; that is, dyeing separate batches of fibers or textiles is the rule rather than the exception. This color variability has the potential to be very significant in forensic fiber comparisons.

COLOR ASSESSMENT

The three main methods of analyzing the color in fibers are visual examination, chemical analysis, and instrumental analysis. Each of these methods has strengths and weaknesses that must be considered by the fiber examiner.

The most basic method is simple visual examination of single fibers with the aid of a comparison microscope. Visual examination is quick, and comparison is an excellent screening technique. However, this method is subjective and because of day-to-day and observer-to-observer variations, it is not always a repeatable method. Additionally, the dilemma of metameric colors exists. **Metameric colors** are those that appear to match in one set of lighting conditions but do not in another. By their nature, metamers are difficult to sort out visually. Visual examination must be used in conjunction with an objective method.

Chemical analysis involves extracting the dye and characterizing or identifying its chemistry. Typically, thin layer chromatography is the method of choice although others may be employed. Chemical analysis addresses the type of dye or dyes used to color the fiber and may help to sort out metameric colors. It can be difficult to extract the dye from the fiber, however, because forensic samples typically are small and textile dyers take great pains to ensure that the dye stays in the fiber. Dye analysis is also a destructive method, rendering the fiber useless for further color analysis. Because very light or very small fibers have little dye in them, weak or equivocal responses may result.

Instrumental analysis offers the best combinations of strengths and the fewest weaknesses of the three methods outlined. Instrumental readings are objective and repeatable, the results are quantitative, and the methods can be standardized. Importantly, it is not destructive to the fiber, and the analysis may be repeated. Again, very light fibers may present a problem with weak results, and natural fibers may exhibit high variations due to uneven dye uptake.

The **microspectrophotometer** (MSP) is an instrument that allows for the color measurement of individual fibers. The MSP is essentially a standard spectrophotometer with a microscope attached to focus on the sample. A spectrophotometer compares the amount of light passing through air with the amount of light transmitted through or reflected off a sample. The ratio of these measurements indicates the percentage of light reflected or transmitted. At each wavelength of the visible spectrum, this ratio is calculated, stored, and recorded. The light is broken into smaller regions of the visible spectrum by a monochrometer, which acts like a prism dividing the light into its spectral components (see Figure 15.10).

Color is a major factor in comparing textile fibers. If tape lifts are being searched, it is the predominant factor in selecting fibers for further comparison. Very fine gradations of color difference can be seen once fibers have been mounted; it is necessary, however, to train the observer's eye to make these distinctions in a uniform manner. The MSP is crucial to the comparison process because it can segregate colored fibers that appear visually the same but are subtly different. Objectively distinguishing between otherwise identical fibers is necessary to ensure a reliable comparison method.

CHEMICAL PROPERTIES

While microscopy offers an accurate method of fiber examination, it is often necessary to confirm these observations. Analyzing the fibers chemically offers not only a confirmation of the microscopic work, but also may provide additional information about the specific polymer type or types that make up the fiber. For most of the generic polymer classes, various subclasses exist that can assist in discriminating between optically

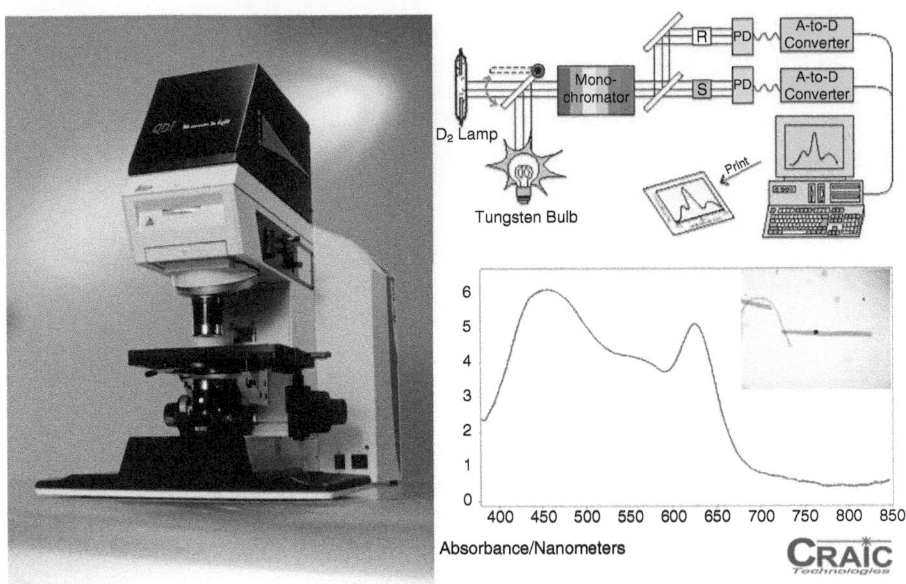

FIGURE 15.10

Schematic of a microspectrophotometer, what the instrument looks like, and an absorbance spectrum from a red fiber (fiber photo inset).

Courtesy of Paul Martin, CRAIC Technologies.

similar fibers. FTIR and PGC are both methods of assessing the chemical structure of polymers. FTIR is the preferred method because it is not destructive of the fibers.

Manufactured fibers also can be characterized by their reaction to certain chemicals; this method was popular prior to the introduction of instrumentation in crime laboratories. Solubility schemes tend to lack the specificity of instrumental methods and are destructive but can still be effective means to confirm a manufactured fiber's generic class.

Solubility tests should be performed on both the known and questioned fibers side by side either on a spot plate or on a microscope slide with a cover slip. A hot-stage microscope may be required for some methods. Numerous solubility schemes exist, and one should be chosen with available chemicals, equipment, and safety in mind. One scheme is shown in Figure 15.11.

INTERPRETATIONS

What does a positive fiber association mean? Numerous studies have shown that, other than white cotton, indigo-dyed cotton (denim), and certain types of black cotton, no fiber should be considered as being "common." These studies include looking for specific fibers on a wide variety of clothing, crosschecking fibers in particular locations (movie theater seats, for example) and performing frequency studies. One study crosschecked fibers from 20 unrelated cases, looking for incidental positive associations; in over two million comparisons, no incidental positive associations were found. This makes fiber evidence very powerful in demonstrating associations.

Table II—Solubilities of Fibers in Reagents Used in the Chemical Methods

Chemical Method

	NO. 1 100% CH_3COCH_3	NO. 2 20% HCl	NO. 3 59.5% H_2SO_4	NO. 4 70% H_2SO_4	NO. 5 NaOCl	NO. 6 90% HCOOH
ACETATE	S	I	S	S	I	S
ACRYLIC	I	I	I	I*	I	I
COTTON	I	I	SS	S	I	I
HAIR	I	I	I	I	S	I
HEMP	I	I	SS	S	I	I
LINEN	I	I	SS	S	I	I
MODACRYLIC	S or I*	I	I	I	I	I
NYLON	I	S	S	S	I	S
OLEFIN	I	I	I	I	I	I
POLYESTER	I	I	I	I	I	I
RAMIE	I	I	SS	S	I	I
RAYON	I	I	S	S	I	I
SILK	I	PS	S	S	S	PS
WOOL	I	I	I	I	S	I

*Depending on type

KEY TO SYMBOLS: S = SOLUBLE
PS = PARTIALLY SOLUBLE (Method not applicable)
SS = SLIGHTLY SOLUBLE (Useable but correction factor required)
I = INSOLUBLE

FIGURE 15.11

A solubility scheme for fibers.

From American Association of Textile Chemists and Colorists Technical Manual, 1997.

BACK TO THE CASE: CROSS-TRANSFER

Numerous hairs and fibers were found to have been cross-transferred between the girl and the suspect in the case described at the beginning of this Chapter Items from the suspect found on the victim that included:

- blue rayon fibers from his pants on the victim's hands, under her fingernails, and on her shoes;
- more of the blue rayon fibers on the body bag used to transport the victim;
- blue, gray, and beige polyester fibers from his poncho on her sweatshirt, hands, and under her fingernails;
- more of the blue and gray polyester fibers on the fence between the two houses where the mother had seen the neighbor running.

Items from the victim found on the suspect not only demonstrated his violent association with the girl but also contradicted the story he told the police:

- red cotton fibers from her sweatshirt were found on his poncho and shirt, as well as on bloody paper towels in the suspect's bathroom dustbin.
- brown head hairs exhibiting the same microscopic characteristics as the victim's were found on his poncho, shirt, and in the dustbin debris.

After a convincing prosecution, the jury deliberated for less than 3 h before finding the neighbor guilty.

From Houck (2009).

SUMMARY

Fibers make good evidence for a number of reasons: They vary greatly, are easy to analyze, and are everywhere present as textiles. Fibers have figured prominently in many high-profile cases and are researched extensively by forensic and textile scientists alike. Textile fibers are among the most frequently encountered types of physical evidence. Color is one of the most underutilized traits of a textile fiber; the color of fibers should be analyzed spectrally or chemically in any positive association. The combinations of characteristics make fibers very specific evidence: It is rare to find two fibers at random that exhibit the same characteristics.

TEST YOUR KNOWLEDGE

1. What is a fiber?
2. What is a yarn? How is it different from a thread?
3. How are woven and knitted fabrics different?
4. What is the difference between a manufactured fiber and a synthetic fiber?
5. What is the Becke line used for?
6. What is a spinneret?
7. What is the fiber-forming substance called before it is spun into fibers?
8. What is denier?
9. What is a microfiber?
10. What is refractive index?
11. Why are fibers birefringent?
12. What is a metameric pair?
13. Why is the cross-sectional shape of a fiber important?
14. What is a delustrant? How is it used in fibers?
15. How many cross-section shapes are used in making manufactured fibers?
16. How many commercial dyes are available?
17. How many colors can be produced in textiles?
18. What is a microspectrophotometer? What is it used for?

CONSIDER THIS...

1. Why is it important to use some other means of assessing a fiber's color than just visual examination? Why isn't comparison microscopy alone sufficient? If you compared two fibers' colors and they looked the same, what else could another method tell you?
2. Numerous transfer and target fiber studies have shown that, other than white cotton, indigo-dyed cotton, and some black-dyed cotton, it is exceedingly rare to

find two fibers at random that are analytically indistinguishable (e.g., see Roux and Margot (1997) or Houck (1999)). Why is this?

3. Inventory a portion of your closet by color and fiber type (look at the labels). How many different combinations are there? Do you think someone else's closet would be exactly the same?

BIBLIOGRAPHY AND FURTHER READING

AATCC, 1996. Technical Manual. American Association of Textile Chemists and Colorists, Research Triangle Park, NC.

Apsell, P., 1981. What Are Dyes? What Is Dyeing? Dyeing Primer. American Association of Textile Chemists and Colorists, Research Triangle Park, NC.

ASTM, 1996. D 276–87 Standard Test Methods for Identification of Fibers in Textiles. ASTM, Philadelphia, PA.

Carroll, G.R., 1992. Forensic fiber microscopy. In: Robertson, J. (Ed.), Forensic Examination of Fibers. Ellis Horwood, New York City.

Causin, V., 2010. Polymers on the crime scene: how can analytical chemistry help to exploit the information from these mute witnesses? Analytical Methods 2, 792–804.

Delly, J., July 2003. The Michel-Levy Interference Color Chart—Microscopy's Magical Color Key. Modern Microscopy McCrone Associates. Online at: www.modernmicroscopy.com.

Fenichell, S., 1996. Plastic: The Making of a Synthetic Century. HarperCollins, New York.

Gaudette, B., 1988. The forensic aspects of textile fiber examination. (Chapter X) In: Saferstein, R. (Ed.), Forensic Science Handbook, vol. II. Prentice Hall, Englewood Cliffs, NJ, pp. 209–272.

Good, G.A., Rothenberg, M., 1998. Sciences of the Earth: An Encyclopedia of Events, People, and Phenomena. Routledge, London.

Hatch, K., 1993. Textile Science. West Publishing, St Paul, MN.

Hemmings, J., 2013. Fiber microscopy. In: Siegel, J., Saukko, P. (Eds.), Encyclopedia of Forensic Sciences, second ed. Elsevier, Amsterdam, pp. 143–147.

Houck, M., 1999. Statistics and trace evidence: the tyranny of numbers. Forensic Science Communications 1 (3). Online at: www.fbi.gov.

Houck, M., 2009. A Case of Cross-transfer. Mute Witnesses. Academic Press, San Diego, CA, pp. 175–186.

Martin, P., 2013. Color analysis. In: Siegel, J., Saukko, P. (Eds.), Encyclopedia of Forensic Sciences, second ed. Elsevier, Amsterdam, pp. 148–154.

McCrone, W., Delly, J.G., Palenik, S.J., 1979. The Particle Atlas. McCrone Associates, Chicago, IL.

Robertson, J., Roux, C., Wiggins, K., 2015. Forensic fiber Examinations, third ed. Taylor and Francis, London.

Robertson, J., Roux, C., 2013. Fiber: protocols for examination. In: Siegel, J., Saukko, P. (Eds.), Encyclopedia of Forensic Sciences, second ed. Elsevier, Amsterdam, pp. 124–128.

Rouen, R.A., Reeve, V.C., 1970. A comparison and evaluation of techniques for identification of synthetic fibers. Journal of Forensic Sciences 15, 410–432.

Roux, C., Margot, P., 1997. An attempt to assess the relevance of textile fibers recovered from car seats. Science and Justice 37, 225–230.

Roux, C., Robertson, J., 2013. Interpretation of fiber evidence. In: Siegel, J., Saukko, P. (Eds.), Encyclopedia of Forensic Sciences, second ed. Elsevier, Amsterdam, pp. 155–160.

Rygula, A., Miskowiec, P., 2014. Chemometric analysis of Raman and IR spectra of natural dyes. In: Optical Spectroscopy and Computational Methods in Biology and Medicine. Springer, Netherlands, pp. 279–308.

Smith, W.E., January 5, 1954. The Reign of Chemistry. Life Magazine.

The Textile Institute, 1985. Identification of Textile Materials. The Textile Institute, Manchester, United Kingdom.

Was-Gubala, J., Machnowski, W., 2014. Application of Raman spectroscopy for differentiation among cotton and viscose fibers dyed with several dye classes. Spectroscopy Letters 47 (7), 527–535.

CHAPTER

Paint Analysis

16

CHAPTER OUTLINE

KEY TERMS

- Architectural paints
- Backscattered electrons
- Batch lot
- Binder
- Clearcoats
- Coatings
- Lacquer
- Latex
- Metamerism
- Microtome
- Paint
- Paint Data Query (PDQ)
- Pretreatment
- Primer
- Product coatings

- Secondary electrons
- Shellac
- Solvents
- Special-purpose coatings
- Stain
- Topcoat
- Varnish
- Vehicle

THE CASE: GARY RIDGWAY, THE GREEN RIVER KILLER

Gary Ridgway was convicted of 48 individual murders of women and girls, many alleged to be prostitutes, in the 1980s and 1990s in King County, WA; upwards of 100 victims have been attributed to him. Ridgway eluded detection for so long in part to his heightened awareness of forensic evidence, this despite his only having a high school diploma. Ridgway was considered several times as a Green River suspect admitting he "dated" prostitutes but had passed a polygraph test. Detectives seized numerous items from Ridgway's place of work, a truck manufacturing plant, including clothing, ropes, paint samples and tarps, as well as saliva sample from Ridgway.

Although DNA analysis was available during Ridgway's "career," a profile was not developed until 2001 but it only linked Ridgway to a few victims. It was enough, however, to create a task force to review all the evidence from all the known victims to determine if additional associations existed between them and Ridgway.

INTRODUCTION

The forensic analysis of paints, more properly called **coatings** to encompass any surface coating intended to protect, aesthetically improve, or provide some special quality, is one of the most complex areas of the forensic laboratory. The reason is that the manufacture and application of paints and coatings are among the most complex and complicated areas in all of industrial chemistry. Forensic paint examiners, even if they specialize in that one material, could never grasp the entire range of coatings, paints, and materials used throughout the world. As John Thornton, at Forensic Analytical Specialties, Inc. in Hayward, California, has noted,

> *The paint industry…[utilizes] more than a thousand kinds of raw materials and intermediates—more than virtually any other manufacturing enterprise. A thorough understanding of the use, properties, and identification of only the most commonly used materials may represent the entire professional career of a paint chemist. It is unrealistic to expect the same comprehension of the subject by the forensic scientist, but it is entirely reasonable to expect a basic familiarity with those aspects of paint chemistry that may affect either the analysis or the interpretation of paint evidence (2002, p. 430).*

This complexity is in the forensic scientist's favor, however, because variety and variation make for a more specific categorization of classes. More specificity presents the potential for a tighter interpretation and greater evidentiary significance in court.

WHAT IS PAINT?

A **paint** is a suspension of pigments and additives intended to color or protect a surface. A pigment is fine powder that is insoluble in the medium in which it is dispersed; that is, the granules do not dissolve and remain intact and are dispersed evenly across the surface, as shown in Figure 16.1. Pigments are intended to color and/or cover a surface; they may be organic, inorganic, or a mixture. The additives in paint come in a dizzying variety but have some constants. The **binder** is that portion of the coating, other than the pigment, that allows the pigment to be distributed across the surface. The term **vehicle** typically refers to the solvents, resins, and other additives that form a continuous film, binding the pigment to the surface. If "binder" and "vehicle" sound similar, they are sometimes used interchangeably in the coatings industry and the forensic laboratory. **Solvents** dissolve the binder and give the paint a suitable consistency for application (brushing, spraying, etc.). Once the paint has been applied, the solvent and many of the additives evaporate; a hard polymer film (the binder) containing the dispersed pigment remains to cover and seal the surface (see Table 16.1).

Paints can be divided into four major categories. The first is **architectural paints**, sometimes called household paints, and are those coatings most often found in residences and businesses. **Product coatings**, those applied in the process of manufacturing products including automobiles, are the second major category. Because automobiles play a central role in society and, therefore, in crime, much of this chapter will focus on the paints and coatings from the automotive manufacturing industry. The third kind, **special-purpose coatings**, fulfil some specific need beyond protection or aesthetic

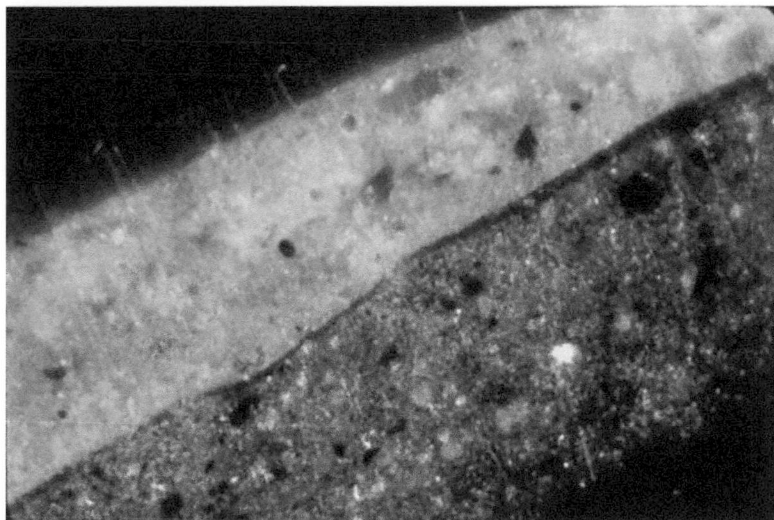

FIGURE 16.1

Paints contain pigments, fine powders that do not dissolve but are dispersed evenly across the surface. Pigments are intended to color and/or cover a surface; they may be organic, inorganic, or a mixture.

Courtesy: Paul Martin, CRAIC, Inc.

Table 16.1 The Components of a Hypothetical Gloss Enamel Architectural Paint

Ingredient	Function	Pounds/Gallon
Ultramarine blue	Pigment (coloring agent)	Trace
Thymol	Antimildew agent	0.01
Cobalt naphthenate	Drier	0.02
Soya oil	Oil	0.03
Calcium naphthenate	Drier	0.03
Zirconium naphthenate	Drier	0.06
Zinc oxide	Pigment	0.2
Calcium carbonate	Extender	0.5
Mineral spirits	Solvent	1.05
Titanium dioxide	Pigment	2.8
Soya alkyd resin	Binder	5.7
	Total	10.4

From Thornton (2002, p. 435).

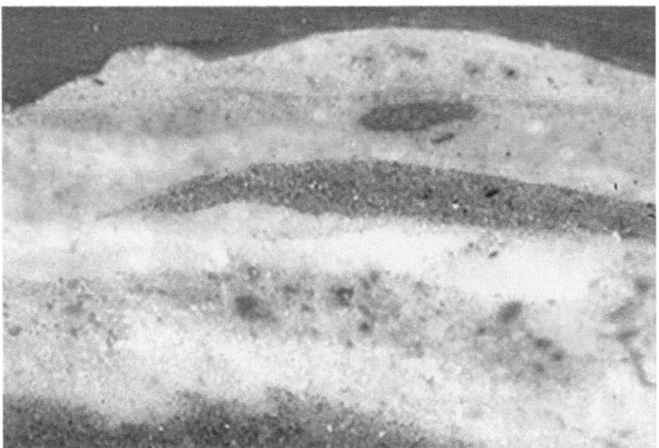

FIGURE 16.2

Modern art paints are mass-produced, but many artists formulate their own paints. The application process for art paints is obviously more varied and unstructured than for product coatings.

Courtesy: Paul Martin, CRAIC, Inc.

improvement, such as skid resistance, water proofing, or luminescence (as on the dials of wristwatches). Finally, art paints are occasionally encountered in forgery cases. Modern art paints are similar in many respects to architectural paints, but many artists formulate their own paints, leading to potentially unique sources (see Figure 16.2). See "In More Detail: Coating Definitions" for additional information regarding coatings.

IN MORE DETAIL: COATINGS DEFINITIONS

Many of the words used to describe coatings, such as "paint," "varnish," and "lacquer," in reality have very specific technical definitions used by the coatings industry. To avoid confusion between the casual and professional meanings, some of these definitions are listed here:

- **Architectural Paint**: Coatings encountered around a typical household.
- **Dye**: A coloring agent that is soluble in the medium in which it is dispersed.
- **Enamel**: A pigmented coating that has a high gloss (luminous reflectivity) when it dries.
- **Lacquer**: Clear or pigmented coatings that dry quickly through evaporation of the solvent.
- **Latex**: A suspension of a pigment in a water-based emulsion of any of several resins.
- **Paint**: A suspension of a pigment in a liquid vehicle; more broadly, any surface coating designed for protection and/or decoration of a surface.
- **Pigment**: A fine powder that is insoluble in the medium in which it is dispersed.
- **Shellac**: A solution of melted lac, a resinous excretion of the Lac insect (*Coccus* or *Carteria lacca*) dissolved in alcohol used as a sealant, adhesive, or insulating varnish.
- **Stain**: A solution of dye or a suspension of a pigment designed to color, but not protect, a wood surface. Technically speaking, a stain colors the wood but does not coat it.
- **Varnish**: A clear solution of oils and organic or synthetic resins in an organic solvent.

Source: *Thornton (2002) and Schweitzer (2005).*

PAINT MANUFACTURING

AUTOMOTIVE FINISHES

One of the most commonly encountered kinds of paint evidence is automotive paint. Cars, trucks, and similar vehicles are so deeply integrated into our daily lives; it's easy to see why this is so. Automotive paints are also a good example of how manufacturing styles and variation contribute to the significance of forensic evidence.

The automotive finishing process for vehicles consists of at least four separate coatings. The first is a **pretreatment**, typically zinc electroplating, applied to the steel body of the vehicle to inhibit rust. The steel is then washed with a detergent, rinsed, treated a second time, and then washed again. The significance of this coating is for the forensic paint analyst to be aware that any zinc found during elemental analysis may come from this coating and not necessarily the paint itself.

The second coating is a **primer**, usually an epoxy resin with corrosion-resistant pigments; the color of the primer is coordinated with the final vehicle color to minimize contrast and "bleed-through." The steel body of the vehicle is dipped in a large bath of the liquid primer and plated on by electrical conduction. The primer coating is finished with a powder "primer surfacer" that smooths the surface of the metal and provides better adhesion for the next coating.

The **topcoat** is the third coating applied to the vehicle and may be in the form of a single-color-layer coat, a multilayer coat, or a metallic color coat; this is the layer that most people think of when they think of a vehicle's color, shown in Figure 16.3. Topcoat chemistry is moving toward water-based chemistries to provide a healthier atmosphere for factory workers and the environment. For example, heavy metals, such as lead or chrome, are no longer used in the

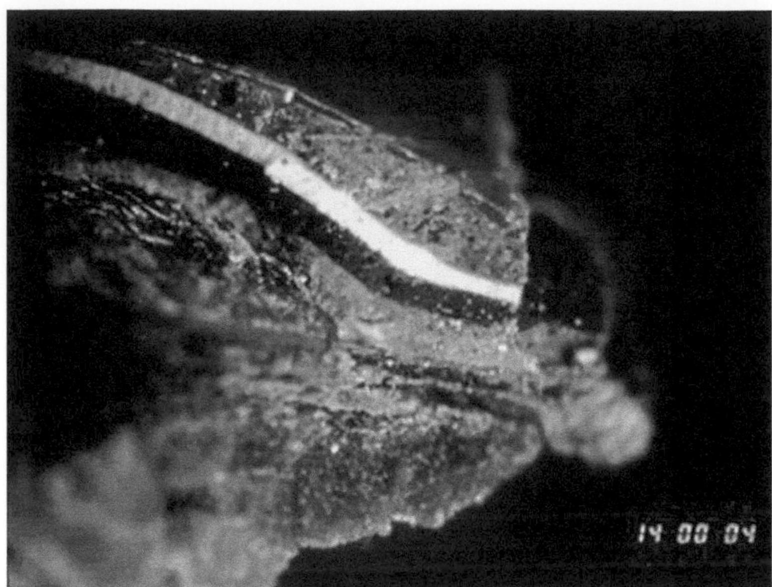

FIGURE 16.3

A green vehicle paint chip, showing the layer structure common to most automotive paints.

Courtesy: Mark Sandercock, Royal Canadian Mounted Police.

formulation of topcoats. Metallic or pearlescent coatings, growing in preference for new model vehicles, have small metal or mica flakes incorporated to provide a shimmering, changing color effect. Metallic pigments, including zinc, nickel, steel, and gold-bronze, give a glittering finish to a vehicle's color, while pearlescent pigments, mica chips coated with titanium dioxide and ferric oxide try to replicate the glowing luster of pearls. The topcoat is often applied and flashed, or partially cured, and then finished with the next and final coating, the clearcoat.

Clearcoats are unpigmented coatings applied to improve gloss and durability of a vehicle's coating. Historically, clearcoats were acrylic-based in their chemistry, but nearly half of the automotive manufacturers have moved to two-component urethanes.

It is important for forensic paint analysts to keep up-to-date with the latest trends and techniques in the paint industry. It is equally important, however, for them to be aware of the previously used formulations and manufacturing techniques because they constitute the bulk of vehicles currently on the road. A three- to five-year-old pickup truck is far more likely to be encountered in a forensic case than the newest model sports car, so forensic analysts must not be surprised by "history." Repaired and repainted vehicles are an additional consideration because they may have been coated with virtually anything, including spray paint!

A final note on vehicle coloration is that of the newer plastic substrates. Vehicle bodies are no longer made exclusively of steel; various plastics are now commonly used. For example, fenders may be nylon, polymer blends, or polyurethane resins;

door panels and hoods may be of thermosetting polymers; front grills and bumper strips have long been plastic or polymer but now may be colored to match the vehicle. Braking systems, chassis, and even entire cars (BASF unveiled an entirely plastic car in 1999, as an extreme example) are now constructed from plastics. It wouldn't be unusual for forensic paint examiners to encounter steel, aluminum, and polymer parts on the same vehicle, each colored by a very different coating system.

THE CASE: THE GREEN RIVER KILLER

Ridgway worked as a painter at a Kenworth truck manufacturing plant for over 30 years in Renton, WA. After the DNA profile linked Ridgway to a few of the crimes, the other evidence that had been seized in 1987 was sent to Microtrace, a private laboratory near Chicago, IL, run by Skip Palenik, a renowned trace evidence expert. Microtrace reported finding tiny spheres of sprayed paint on the clothing of two uncharged victims. The paint was analytically indistinguishable from the highly specialized DuPont Imron paint used at the Kenworth truck plant where Ridgway worked. Imron is a specialty paint and not generally available to the public. Its formulation was distinct from other paints produced during that time period (Figure 16.4(a) and (b)).

(a)

(b)

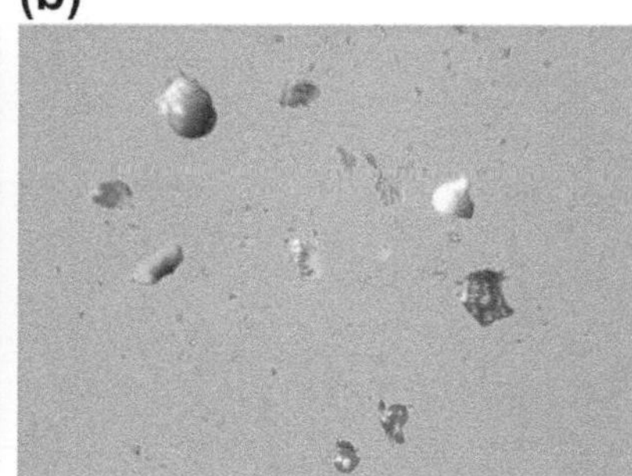

FIGURE 16.4

(a) Cans of Imron paint. (b) Spheres of Imron paint from the Green River case.

Courtesy Microtrace, Inc.

The paint was important trace evidence. It was a specific formulation of a brand of paint that was sold for particular applications. Moreover, the spheres indicated that the paint had been sprayed, in the same way that the paint was applied at the Kenworth plant, and not brushed on or spilt. More than just chemistry, microscopy aids paint analysis by demonstrating the *form* of the evidence, eliminating other potential hypotheses.

COLLECTION

Because it is possible a physical match exists between known and questioned paint samples, as demonstrated in Figure 16.5, the collection of paint samples should proceed with caution. This type of evidence carries great significance and care should be taken to preserve any potential physical matches.

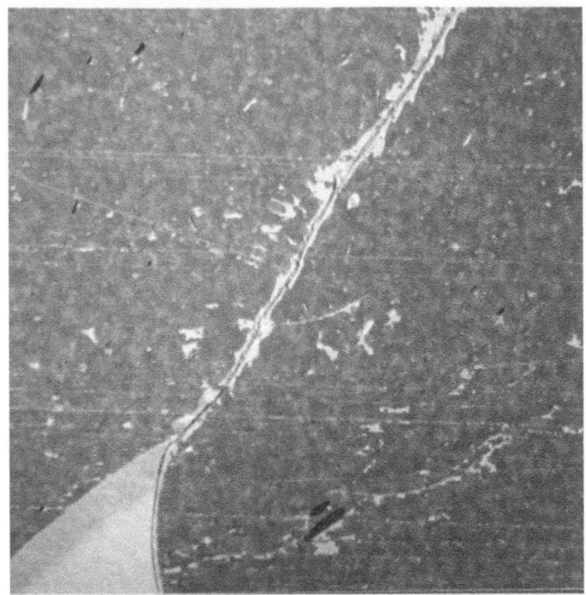

FIGURE 16.5

The strongest evidence of an association between a paint sample and a source is a physical match, considered unique and individualizing. These are somewhat uncommon and therefore carry strong probative value. Here, two paint chips are aligned to show the common border demonstrating that they were at one time one continuous coating.

Courtesy: Mark Sandercock, Royal Canadian Mounted Police.

Samples from the crime scene (questioned) should include all loose or transferred paint materials. Nearly any object or surface may retain a paint transfer and may include things as varied as tools, architectural structures and elements (floors, wainscoting), glass fragments, fabrics, hairs, fingernails, roadways and signs, and, of course, vehicles. Evidentiary items with paint transfers should be packaged and submitted to the laboratory in their entirety, if possible. Depending on the size of the object, packaging and submitting could prove problematic, so often sampling of paint transfers must take place in the field. It is also important to remember that cross-transfer could have occurred. Known and questioned samples should be collected from both surfaces.

Paint evidence should be first photographed and then removed manually with nonmetallic tools, such as small wooden sticks, toothpicks, or plastic forceps. If tape lifts are to be used, the paint evidence should be collected first. Because of their structure, fragility, and size, if paint samples are collected with tape lifts, it could be very difficult to impossible to easily manipulate paint samples that are sticky from the tape's adhesive. Additionally, the adhesive's components, or material stuck to the adhesive, could contaminate the paint sample and change its apparent chemistry (see Figure 16.6).

Flakes of paint can be removed from a surface in a variety of ways. Lifting or prying out loose flakes, cutting samples of the paint with a clean knife or blade, and

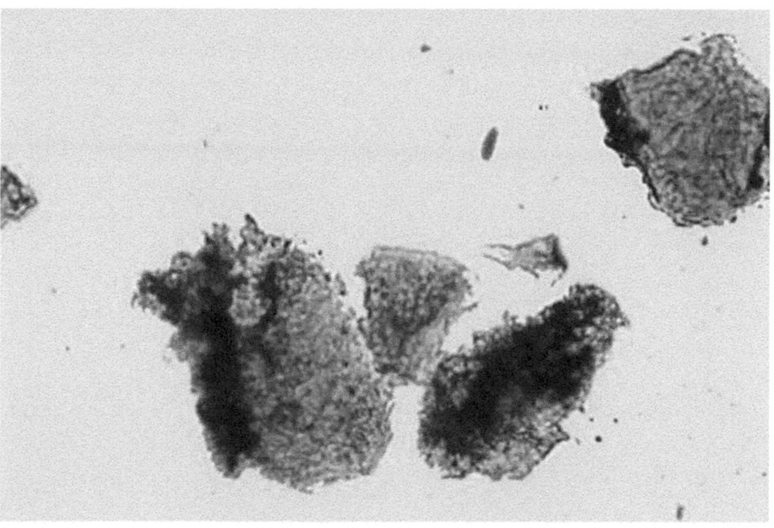

FIGURE 16.6

Paint fragments must be handled with care; being too aggressive in their collection can damage or contaminate them.

dislodging them by gently bumping the opposite side of the painted surface are all examples of appropriate collection methods. If the samples are cut, the blade should go all the way through the paint layers to the subcoating surface. The sampling method will vary considerably given the circumstances of the crime, the evidence items, their location, and environmental factors; no single method will work all of the time.

When a painted object strikes a glancing blow to another object, it can transfer paint in the form of a smear. A smeared transfer can be very confusing and difficult to work with because components from several layers of coatings can be commingled; this can reduce the forensic scientist's ability to accurately analyze the smeared paint. Even the best collection efforts can confuse the issue even more. When a forensic scientist is dealing with a smeared paint transfer, it is best to submit the entire object to the laboratory, if possible.

Paint, like any mass-produced material, varies. It is important when collecting known paint samples, therefore, that they be collected from areas as close as possible to, but not within, the point(s) of damage or transfer. This is important for two reasons. First, the damaged area itself is usually not suitable for providing a known sample: subcoating and other incidental materials may lie within the damage and confuse or confound analysis. Second, because of manufacturing variation, detectable differences may exist between parts of an object. On an automobile, for example, the paint on the right rear quarter panel may be analytically different from the hood. Or, as another example, the hood may have been repainted because of previous damage—it could even be a new hood! In the laboratory, the analyst may not be aware of the sampling that took place at the crime scene and, because of sample source variation, may find that the paint samples are analytically distinguishable when the proper samples would have been the same in all tested respects. All paint samples should be clearly labeled as per origin, with drawings or photographs as documentation.

Because paint is a multilayer composite material, the known samples should contain all layers of the undamaged paint. Differences in the thickness and sequence of layers can be significant over even short distances on a painted surface. This concept is very important with architectural paints, where substantial reworking of the surface (sanding, damage, overpainting) may have occurred. It could be important to collect known paint samples from several areas of an object if variation is noticeable or suspected; these samples from different areas should be packaged separately and labeled appropriately.

Depending on what it is made of, the subcoating surface under the suspected transfer area should be included for analysis when possible. This may extend to portions or objects near the evidentiary location, such as portions of walls, doors, window frames, handles, fenders, and decorations. These additional samples may be useful to assess any difference that may exist between the known and questioned samples.

ANALYSIS OF PAINT SAMPLES

As with any other examination, the initial step in forensic paint flake analysis is to simply look at the sample; a stereomicroscope is an invaluable aid in this process. Often, the first step may be the last: If significant differences are apparent in the known and questioned samples, the analysis is completed and the paints are excluded. The visual evaluation begins with the packaging and paperwork, looking for signs of potential cross-contamination between the submitted samples. If none is detected, then the paint samples are described, noting their condition, weathering characteristics, size, shape, exterior colors, and major layers present in each sample. The examiner's notes should include written descriptions, photographs, and drawings, as necessary. Because significant changes can be made to a portion of a sample in the process of preparation and examination, it is crucial to document how that sample was received.

PHYSICAL AND MICROSCOPIC EXAMINATIONS

A combination of microscopes (stereo, transmitted light and polarized light) at magnifications of 2× to 100× is used to examine the layers in a paint. Many layers will be visible without preparing the sample, but definitive paint layer identification often requires some sample preparation techniques. The paint layer structure can be seen by cutting through the sample with a scalpel blade at an angle; this technique increases the visible area of the sample. The structure of the layers and any irregularities and inhomogeneities are typically easier to see after this sectioning.

Very thin sections of the paint can be accomplished with a steady hand and a fresh scalpel blade; a device called a **microtome** can also be used. A microtome is a minivice that holds a sample in place while a heavy and very sharp glass- or diamond-edged knife slices off sections of a few tens of microns thick, as shown in Figure 16.7.

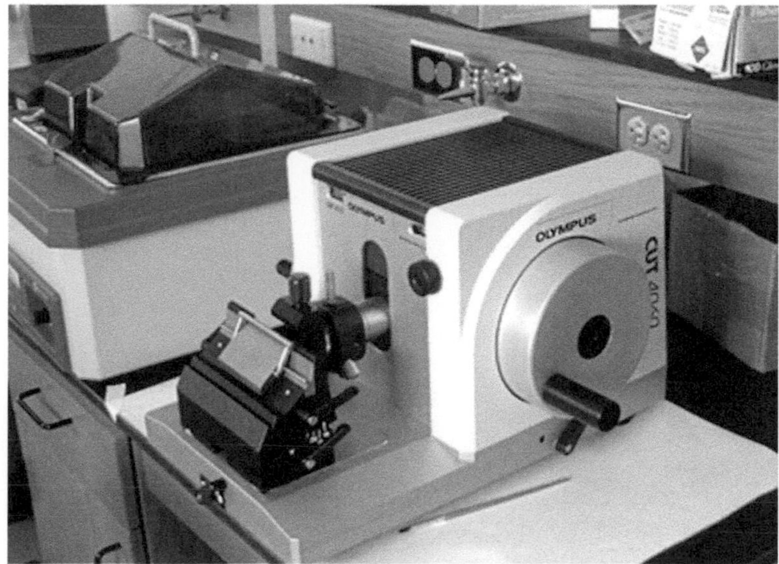

FIGURE 16.7

A microtome is a mini-vice that holds a sample in place while a heavy and very sharp glass- or diamond-edged knife slices off sections of a few tens of microns thick. Microtomes are useful for paint analysis by conserving sample consumption and preserving the samples for subsequent analyzes.

Courtesy: Olympus, Inc.

Cross-sections of the paint sample, either embedded in a material for support or thin-section preparations, provide information about the layers, their thicknesses, and colors, in addition to the size and distribution of pigments. Embedded preparations, as shown in Figure 16.8, work well because the sample is easily handled and can be subjected to many analytical techniques with a minimum of additional preparation.

Microscopic comparisons of paint layers can reveal slight variations between samples in color, pigment appearance, flake size and distribution, surface details, inclusions, and layer defects. Any visual comparisons must be done with the samples side by side in the same field of view (or with a comparison microscope), typically at the same magnification. Visual memory is quirky and samples must be seen next to each other at the same time so that subtle details are not overlooked.

Polarized light microscopy (PLM) is appropriate for the examination of layer structure as well as the comparison and/or identification of particles present in a paint film including, but not limited to, pigments, extenders, additives, and contaminants. The use of the PLM in the identification of pigments is detailed in a chapter titled "Application of Particle Study in Art and Archeology Conservation and Authentication," written by Dr Walter McCrone, in *The Particle Atlas* (1979). Other components of paint, including extenders, are large enough that they can be identified by PLM, although some pigment particles may be too small to be identified this way. The use of PLM for the identification of paint components requires a good deal of intensive training and

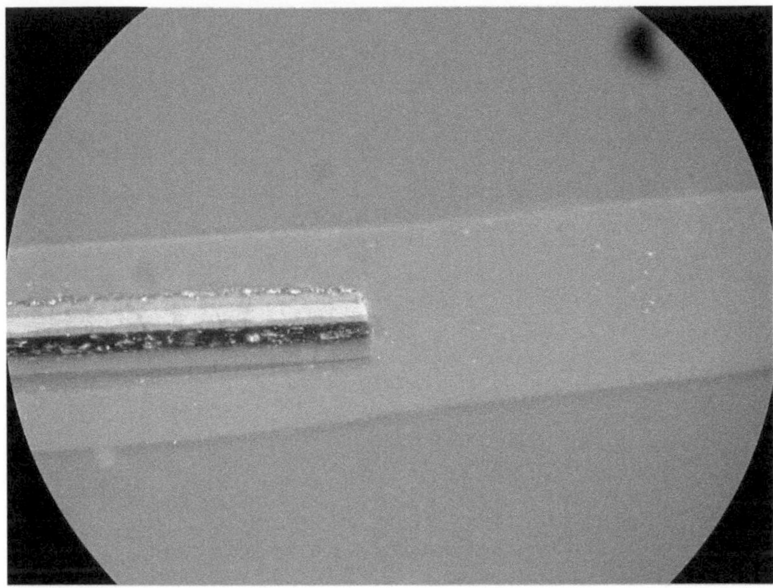

FIGURE 16.8

Embedding paint chips in an epoxy-resin support and preserve the sample, allow for thin-sectioning, and make a fragile specimen safer to handle and store.

Courtesy: Paul Martin, CRAIC, Inc.

experience; many training courses are available in PLM for a fee and similar analytical courses may be offered by materials science or geology departments at universities.

SOLVENT AND MICROCHEMICAL TESTS

Solvent and microchemical tests (hereafter referred to as "microchemical tests") have been used to discriminate between paint layers of different pigment and binder composition that are otherwise visually similar. The basis for these tests is that the different layers of paint have a different chemical composition and will, therefore, react differently with oxidizing, dehydrating, or reducing agents. Microchemical tests are destructive; therefore, they should be applied to known samples first to evaluate their utility to specific samples. They should also be used only when sufficient questioned samples are available to avoid consuming the entire sample.

Microchemical tests should be performed on the questioned and known materials at the same time and their effects recorded immediately; the effects may develop over time, so effects should also be recorded at intervals for the duration of each test. Additionally, microchemical tests can be applied to peeled individual layers of paint, to avoid interactivity with adjacent layers, as well as intact paint chips. Applying tests this way may make the specific reactions clearer than subjecting an intact chip to the tests.

When a chemical is applied, the paint chip or layers may soften or wrinkle, swell, or curl. Entire layers may dissolve or disaggregate. Pigment fillers may bubble or "fizz" or flake apart (called "flocculation"). Apparent color change may be seen in some layers. These traits are not clear-cut results that are easily quantified: They are mainly descriptive in nature but provide good discrimination at the early stages of an investigation and may help to initially classify a paint.

INSTRUMENTAL METHODS

Given the complex chemistry of paints and related coatings, it is not surprising that many instrumental methods are available for their analysis. Rarely will all of the instruments listed in this section appear in one laboratory—even if they did, the laboratory's analytical scheme would probably not include all of them—and the order of examination will be keyed to the instrumentation on hand.

Infrared (IR) spectroscopy can identify binders, pigments, and additives used in paints and coatings. Most IRs used in forensic science laboratories employ a microscope bench, as shown in Figure 16.9, to magnify the image of the sample and focus the beam on the sample. The bench is a microscope stage attached to the instrument chassis with optics to route the beam through the microscope and back to the detector. Most modern IRs will also be Fourier transform infrared spectroscopy (FT-IR) spectrometers, which employ a mathematical transformation (the fast Fourier transform) that translates the spectral frequency into wavelength. The analysis of paints by FT-IR can be done in transmittance (where the beam passes through a very thin sample and then

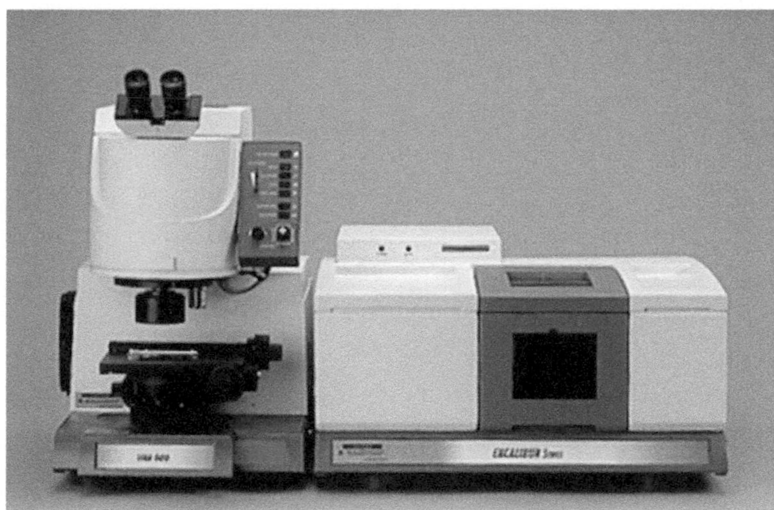

FIGURE 16.9

An IR spectrometer with a microscope attachment or "bench." Normal IRs require a sample to be pressed into a pellet or placed on a special specimen card to which the instrument is "blind." The microscope attachment allows for the handling and analysis of microscopic samples too small for either pellets or cards. This also provides for positional information about the sample to be analyzed; in the case of paints, individual layers or particles can be analyzed in place with no additional preparation.

onto the detector) and reflectance (where the beam is bounced off the sample and then to the detector), but transmittance is preferred because it equalizes the signal as well as the sample geometry; also, and probably more importantly, most of the reference information available from publications and instrument vendors is in transmittance.

IN MORE DETAIL: FOURIER TRANSFORM INFRARED SPECTROSCOPY

FT-IR is by far the most popular instrument for analyzing paint evidence today. An FT-IR instrument measures the absorption of IR energy, over a range of wavelengths, as different bonds in the molecule vibrate and move in characteristic fashions. This produces a "fingerprint" spectrum of a sample unique to that material. Coupling an FT-IR instrument to an IR microscope allows the IR light to be focused onto a small area, allowing these high-quality spectral "fingerprints" to be obtained from small samples or small areas of samples—as is often required in forensic analyzes.

After finding paint samples on the victim's clothing, Christopher Bommarito, a forensic scientist then with the Michigan State Police, visually compared them to samples from the assailant's car and determined they were visually similar. He then mounted the chips in wax and cut cross sections with a microtome (see Figure 16.10). He placed each cross section on a potassium bromide slide and mounted them on the FT-IR instrument stage. He then generated a visible image on the screen and specified an area for each of the five layers from which IR spectra were to be obtained. The instrument focused the IR radiation through the sample and measured the absorbed and transmitted light for each frequency, plotting a graph of wavelength versus percent transmittance. The sample was then moved over the linear MCT array to generate, in real time, an IR image of the layer comprising hundreds of spectra as a false-color visible image. Following this process for each layer in the two samples, Bommarito confirmed an association between each layer in both samples and testified to his conclusions in the assailant's trial in the jogger's murder (see Figure 16.11).

In addition to the paint evidence, prosecutors in the assailant's trial also introduced evidence from witnesses to the slaying and other forensic evidence, such as tissue found on the van. One of the victim's relatives also testified that she visited the assailant in jail and asked him, "Why the jogger?" and that the assailant told her, "I thought it was my ex-wife's boyfriend." A jury found him guilty of the murder and he was sentenced to a third term of life in prison.

Source: *"Case Study: Infrared Spectroscopy," PerkinElmer, copyright 2004–2009, by permission.*

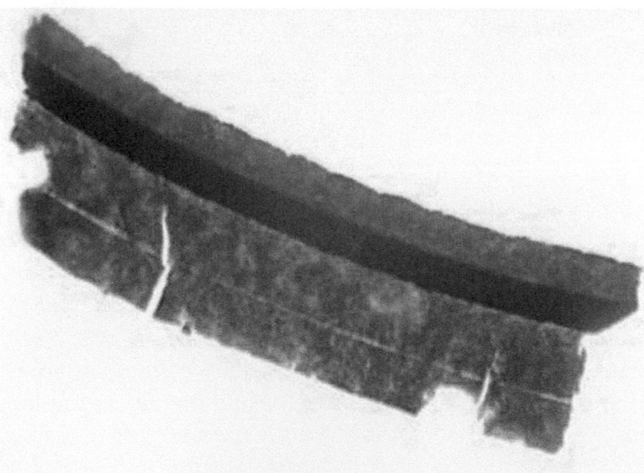

FIGURE 16.10

Cross-section of chips from hit-and-run case.

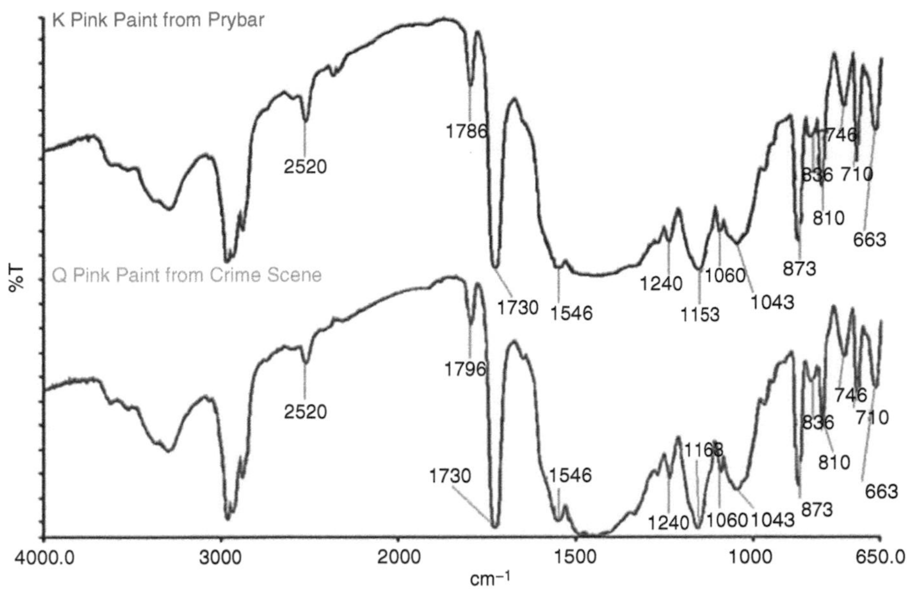

FIGURE 16.11

Spectrum of paint samples from hit-and-run case.

An IR-related technique that is gaining application in forensic science is Raman spectroscopy, which is based on light scattering rather than absorption. Because of this, Raman spectra provide complementary information to that obtained from IR spectroscopy. Raman spectroscopy shows great promise for a number of evidence types, but, for budget and training reasons, it will be some time before Raman spectroscopy becomes a standard method in forensic science laboratories.

Pyrolysis-gas chromatography (PGC) disassembles molecules through heat (pyrolysis). This destructive technique uses the breakdown products for comparison of paints and identification of the binder type. PGC is influenced by the size and shape of the samples and instrument parameters, such as rate of heating, the final temperature, the type of column, and gas flow rates. This can make PGC vary from day to day and sample to sample; this has several methodological implications. The conditions from one analysis to the next should be the same and should be run very close in time to each other. It is important to select the known samples as carefully as possible because of the influence of size and shape on the final chromatographic results. As little as 5–10 μg of sample are required for PGC. The patterns of peaks in the known and questioned sample chromatograms (also called "pyrograms") are compared and the peaks must coincide for the identification to be determined.

If the instrumentation is available, pyrolysis products may be identified by pyrolysis-gas chromatography-mass spectrometry (P-GC-MS). The resulting reconstructed total ion chromatogram may help to identify additives, organic pigments, and impurities in addition to binder components.

Because one of the major purposes of paints and coatings is to impart color to an object, the analysis of color has been integral to the coatings industry nearly since its inception. The gross visual color of paints can be categorized systematically by one of many color systems currently in use. Two of the main systems traditionally used are the Munsell system (developed in 1915 by Alfred Munsell, an artist) and the Commission Internationale de l'Eclairage (CIE) system, which is described in the ASTM International Standard Method D 1535 and Test Method E 308. Color systems are used to classify colors for description and communication of color information and for databases only; absorption spectra of any known and questioned paint samples are compared in forensic paint comparisons.

Absorption spectroscopy, using a microspectrophotometer (or MSP for short), has been used to categorize and discriminate between otherwise visually similar paints. MSP can also differentiate between metameric samples. **Metamerism** is the condition in which two colors appear similar under one set of conditions but different under others. One of the benefits of employing MSP is that it adds an objective method to the analysis of color. The instrumental parameters can be easily reproduced between instruments or laboratories and this provides a basis for interlaboratory testing and quality control. Careful reference sampling is essential to the success of color comparisons of such surfaces.

Comparison of paint layers by transmission MSP of paint thin sections is a more definite method of color analysis than reflectance techniques, but transmission MSP demands more careful preparation. The sample thickness and measurement location, for example, are critical for significant analytical comparisons, as illustrated by Figure 16.12.

One of the most generally useful instruments in forensic paint analysis is the scanning electron microscope outfitted with an energy dispersive X-ray spectrometer (SEM/EDS). SEM/EDS can be used to characterize the structure and elemental composition of paint layers. The SEM uses an electron beam rather than a light beam and changes the nature of the information received from the paint. The electron beam rasters over the area of interest; the electrons interact with the sample and generate a variety of signals, including surface information (**secondary electrons**), atomic number (**backscattered electrons**), and elemental information (X-rays). Secondary electrons impact the surface of the sample and are reflected to the detector, providing a visual representation of that surface, pictured in Figure 16.13. Backscattered electrons penetrate the surface of the sample and are kicked back out of the sample, with more being kicked out from the atomically denser regions. Therefore, backscattered electrons create an image where brightness is proportional to atomic number. These types of imaging can be of great assistance in distinguishing paint layers and structures within the layers.

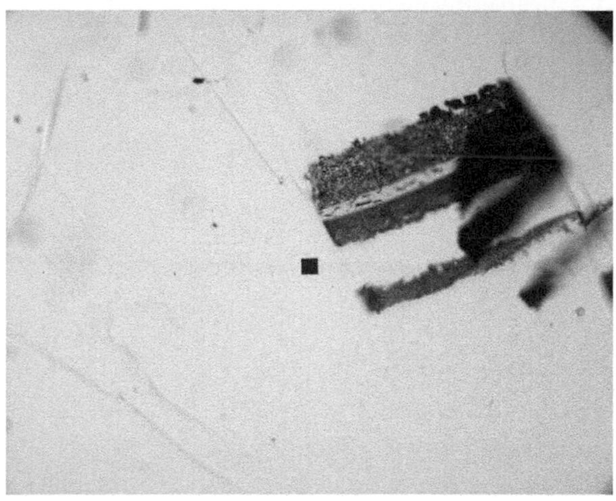

FIGURE 16.12

Microspectrophotometry (MSP) of paint layers by transmission of thin paint sections is an excellent method of discriminating between paint colors but demands more careful preparation. The sample thickness and measurement location, for example, are critical for significant analytical comparisons. In this figure, the small black square is the sampling area for the spectrum; it is located off the sample to collect a background spectrum.

Courtesy: Paul Martin, CRAIC, Inc.

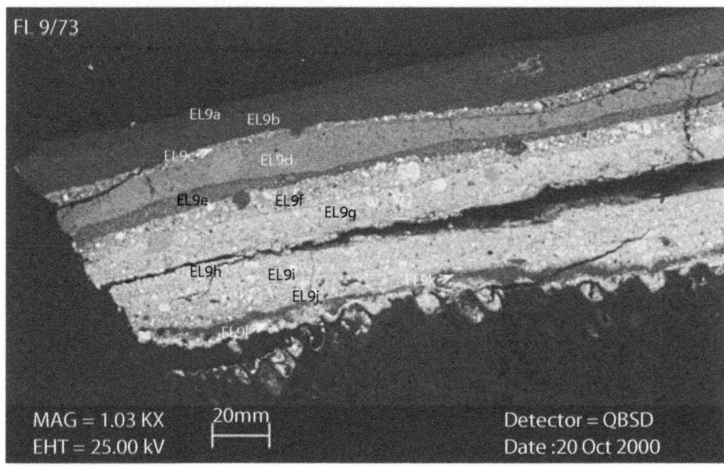

FIGURE 16.13

Secondary electrons impact the surface of a paint sample and are reflected to the detector, providing a visual representation of that surface. Electrons carry no color information; their resolution, however, is very good and can provide images magnified thousands of times. Samples can also be imaged by backscattered electrons (BSEs). Here, brightness is proportional to atomic number with larger numbered elements (iron, titanium) being brighter than smaller ones (silicon, oxygen). BSE images are useful for delineating paint layer structures and pigments. This SEM image shows a sample of paint taken from the entrance lobby of the Osborne House on the Isle of Wight, bought by Queen Victoria in 1845. The paint samples were mounted in resin and polished to show the successive layers of paint in cross-section. Since the raw materials used to produce paints have varied with time, the analytical information can be used to work out which paint schemes are contemporary. The image was taken in BSE mode.

Courtesy: English Heritage.

The primary reason for analyzing paint samples with an SEM/EDS system is to determine the elemental composition of the paint and its layers. When the electrons impact the surface, X-rays are produced as a result of high-energy electrons creating inner shell ionizations in sample atoms, with subsequent emission of X-rays unique to those atoms. The minimum detection limit under many conditions is 0.1%. Elements with atomic numbers ≥11 are customarily detectable. Detection of elements with atomic numbers ≥4 is possible using a detector with an organic film window or a windowless detector. Analysis can be performed in a rastered beam mode for bulk layer analysis or static beam (spot) mode for individual particle analysis. Goldstein et al. (2003) present a general treatment of all aspects of SEM and X-ray microanalysis.

Mapping of elements across the cross-section of a multilayer paint can be useful for explaining or demonstrating elemental distributions and elemental associations. Another technique that provides good visualization of elemental differences is atomic number contrast with backscattered electrons. These images can be used to characterize and compare the structure of paints, including layer number, layer thickness, distribution and size of pigment particles, and the presence of contaminants.

INTERPRETATIONS

Statistically evaluating trace evidence, including paint, is difficult. Most of the statements that can be made relate to samples tested in clinical or research trials although some are based on actual casework samples. A consensus of forensic paint examiners is that the following factors strengthen an association between two analytically indistinguishable paint samples:

- the number of layers;
- the sequence of layers;
- the color of each layer;
- cross-transfer of paint between items.

One of the best-known forensic paint examiners in the United States, Scott Ryland of the Florida Department of Law Enforcement forensic laboratory in Orlando and his colleagues have stated that an association between two paint samples with six or more correlating layers indicates that the chance the samples originated from two different sources is "extremely remote." In cases with evidence this strong, merely stating that the two samples "could have had a common origin" is not enough; that level of statement undermines the strength of a six-layer-plus association. Although an answer is not statistical or mathematical doesn't mean the statement isn't accurate, valid, and sound.

The significance of architectural paints varies and is in general not as well documented in the literature. This is most likely due to the enormous variability in colors, application styles, and the application of the paint itself (not all brushstrokes are equal, resulting in highly variable layers between samples). The situation is similar with spray paints, about which even less is known.

Instances of generating statistics to assess the evidentiary value of paint have been attempted in both the clinical literature and in casework. They are based, as are most manufacturing inquiries, on the concept of a **batch lot**, a unit of production and sampling that contains a set of analytically indistinguishable products. For example, a batch tank of automotive paint of a given color may hold 500 to 10,000 gallons, which would color between 170 and 1600 vehicles. This would then be the unit of comparison for the significance of an automotive paint comparison—the manufacturing batch lot. If analytically identifiable differences can be determined between batch lots, then the base population is set for any other analytically indistinguishable paint samples. The final significance will be determined by the number of vehicles in the area at the time of the crime and other characteristics that set that sample apart (very rare or very common makes or models). By comparison, a batch lot of architectural paint may be from 100 to 4500 gallons.

As with other forensic sciences, a reference collection is essential for training and casework, and paint is no exception. For paint, such collections take two forms: documented samples and data. From 1974 until 1989, the National Bureau of Standards (now the National Institute of Standards and Technology) published a reference collection of automotive paint colors derived from actual production samples. Later in the collection's history, chemically accurate samples were added to it. Although limited in time frame and representation (it contained only US-manufactured colors), this type of collection is invaluable for training and make and model searches. The FBI Laboratory Division maintains a color and chemical reference collection that is housed at the new laboratory in Quantico, Virginia; it is not a lending library, however, and the samples must remain at the laboratory.

A different approach overcomes these limitations. The **Paint Data Query** (PDQ) project is run by the Royal Canadian Mounted Police (RCMP) and is the largest international automotive paint database. It contains nearly 20,000 samples of paint systems, which represent over 74,000 individual paint layers used on most domestic and foreign vehicles being sold in North America, Australia, and Asia. To use the PDQ database, forensic scientists enter the color, chemical composition, and layer sequence information taken from unknown paint chip(s) recovered from a crime scene. Forensic laboratories can obtain the data by participating in PDQ by submitting 50 automotive paint samples per year, with some rare entries earning "double points." The database contains information on layer structures, primer colors, binders, pigment chemistry, and topcoat chemistry, in both visual and spectrometric formats.

ON THE WEB

Royal Canadian Mounted Police Paint Data Query: http://www.rcmp-grc.gc.ca/fsis-ssji/paint-peinture-eng.htm.

BACK TO THE CASE: THE GREEN RIVER KILLER

Over the next few years, working painstakingly on the microscopic evidence, Microtrace found paint evidence from the plant and other sources linking Ridgway to six victims, two of which he had been connected to through the DNA analysis. These findings led Ridgway to confess to 40 of the murders and the location of many other bodies he had dumped along the Green River. Because of his assistance to police in locating and identifying victims, he is serving a life sentence with no change of parole.

SUMMARY

The forensic analysis of coatings is an important part of many investigations. From art forgeries to hit-and-run accidents to kidnappings, coatings can be a powerful form of physical evidence. Coatings, especially paint, provide samples that are chemically complex yet relatively straightforward to analyze and yield distinctive results. The forensic analysis of automotive paints, in particular, in the modern forensic laboratory is important. The PDQ database provides important information about automotive manufacturers and styles that provides for accurate sourcing of known and questioned paint samples.

TEST YOUR KNOWLEDGE

1. What is the difference between a paint and a coating?
2. What is a binder?
3. What are the categories of coatings?
4. What is a varnish?
5. What is a primer?
6. What is a clearcoat?
7. How should paint be collected if it is fragile or fragmentary?
8. What does a microtome do?
9. What is a problem with solubility testing of paints?
10. What types of instrumentation are routinely used to analyze paints?
11. What is a color system? Name any two.
12. What is a metameric pair?
13. What factors strengthen an association between two indistinguishable paints?
14. What is PDQ?
15. What does a solvent do in regard to paint application?
16. Are physical matches possible with paint chips?
17. What is a batch lot?

CONSIDER THIS...

1. How does the size of a batch lot of paint relate to the significance of a paint "match?" How would you find out how large the batch lot was?
2. How does the age of a vehicle affect the significance of a paint "match?" Why?
3. How many 1987 cars do you think are registered to drivers? How would you go about finding out?

BIBLIOGRAPHY AND FURTHER READING

ASTM D16, 2014. Terminology for Paint, Related Coatings, Materials, and Applications, ASTM International, West Conshohocken, PA.

ASTM E-1610–14, 2014. Standard Guide for Forensic Paint Examination, ASTM International, West Conshohocken, PA.

Bender, L., 2013a. Overview (Paints). In: Siegel, J., Saukko, P. (Eds.), Encyclopedia of Forensic Sciences, second ed. Elsevier, Amsterdam, pp. 245–249.

Bender, L., 2013b. Architectural paints. In: Siegel, J., Saukko, P. (Eds.), Encyclopedia of Forensic Sciences, second ed. Elsevier, Amsterdam, pp. 250–256.

Bender, L., 2013c. Automotive paints. In: Siegel, J., Saukko, P. (Eds.), Encyclopedia of Forensic Sciences, second ed. Elsevier, Amsterdam, pp. 257–264.

Bender, L., 2013d. Interpretation of paint evidence. In: Siegel, J., Saukko, P. (Eds.), Encyclopedia of Forensic Sciences, second ed. Elsevier, Amsterdam, pp. 273–278.

Buckle, J., MacDougal, D., Grant, R., 1997. PDQ—Paint Data Queries: the history and technology behind the development of the Royal Canadian Mounted Police Laboratory. The Canadian Society of Forensic Science Journal 30, 199.

Goldstein, J., Newbury, D.E., Joy, D.C., Lyman, C.E., Echlin, P., Lifshin, E., Sawyer, L.C., Michael, J.R., 2003. Scanning Electron Microscopy and X-Ray Microanalysis. Plenum, New York.

Lavine, B.K., Fasasi, A., Sandercock, M., 2014. Improving PDQ database search strategies to enhance investigative lead information for automotive paints. Microchemical Journal 117, 133–137.

Maric, M., Van Bronswijk, W., Lewis, S.W., Pitts, K., 2014. Synchrotron FTIR characterisation of automotive primer surfacer paint coatings for forensic purposes. Talanta 118, 156–161.

McCrone, W.C., 1979. Application of particle study in art and archeology conservation and authentication. In: The Particle Atlas, vol. V, Ann Arbor Science, Ann Arbor, MI, pp. 1402–1413.

Muehlethaler, C., Gueissaz, L., Massonnet, G., 2013. Forensic paint analysis. In: Siegel, J., Saukko, P. (Eds.), Encyclopedia of Forensic Sciences, second ed. Elsevier, Amsterdam, pp. 265–272.

Muehlethaler, C., Massonnet, G., Esseiva, P., 2014. Discrimination and classification of FTIR spectra of red, blue and green spray paints using a multivariate statistical approach. Forensic Science International 244, 170–178.

Ryland, S.G., 1995. Infrared microspectroscopy of forensic paint evidence. In: Humecki, H.J. (Ed.), Practical Guide of Infrared Microspectroscopy. Marcel Dekker, New York.

Ryland, S., Kopec, J., 1979. The evidential value of automobile paint chips. Journal of Forensic Science 24, 140–147.

Ryland, S., Kopec, J., Somerville, P., 1981. The evidential value of automobile paint, Part II. Frequency of occurrence of topcoat colors. Journal of Forensic Sciences 26, 64–74.

Schweitzer, P., 2005. Paint and Coatings. CRC Press, Boca Raton, FL.

Thornton, J.I., 2002. Forensic paint examination. 2nd ed. In: Saferstein, R. (Ed.), Forensic Science Handbook. Vol. 1 Prentice Hall, Englewood Cliffs, NJ, pp. 429–478.

CHAPTER

Soil and Glass

17

CHAPTER OUTLINE

KEY TERMS

- Becke line
- Color and particle size
- Density
- Fracture match
- Glass
- Humus
- ICP-MS
- Liquid chromatography
- Refractive index
- Soil

INTRODUCTION

In this chapter, we present two types of trace evidence: soil and glass. They are in this chapter together because of commonalities in the way that their forensic analysis is approached. Soil and glass are primarily mineral in content and the methods used to analyze them relate to their composition. In addition, only under unusual circumstances it is feasible to individualize glass or soil to a specific object or an exact location. The people who know the most about soils and their analysis are mineralogists but very few crime laboratories employ them or contract with them to analyze soil samples. As a result, soil analysis is performed, if at all, by forensic chemists. The same is true of glass. It is not often analyzed in a crime laboratory and when it is done, forensic chemists do the analysis. Because soil and glass are usually class evidence and cannot be traced to a particular source, they are greatly undervalued in forensic science laboratories and by police and prosecutors and are often overlooked by crime scene investigators.

Soil represents one of the paradoxes in forensic science; it is very commonly encountered in the environment and is found at many crime scenes, but it is seldom recognized as valuable evidence. In fact, soil is most often used as evidence when a shoeprint or tire tread impression is found in it! The soil is thus the carrier of the evidence rather than the evidence itself. One of the problems with the interpretation of soil evidence is that it can travel over large distances carried by people or wind or water. This can make it difficult to draw meaningful conclusions about the composition of soil at a given place where a lot of soil movement has occurred. On the other hand, overlooking soil evidence can mean that a crucial part of the puzzle of reconstructing a crime is not being collected and analyzed. Soil can make important contributions to the reconstruction of a crime and sometimes is the only reliable way to associate a suspect with a crime. Several soil cases will illustrate how this can be done.

Glass is also very common in our environment. There are estimated to be more than 700 different types of glass used in commercial products in the United States alone. Glass has an unusual physical structure. We are taught in school that all matter is solid, liquid, or vapor, yet glass does not fall into any of these categories. It has properties of both solids and liquids. Glass is also an excellent example of trace evidence. Most often it occurs as tiny particles, although there are cases where large enough pieces are found that can be fit together like pieces of a jigsaw puzzle. In this chapter, the formation of glass and how it occurs in crimes and how it is analyzed in the laboratory will be covered.

SOIL

THE CASE: THE ADOLPH COORS KIDNAP MURDER

Adolph Coors owned a ranch in the foothills of the Rocky Mountains near Denver. While driving on his land, he was kidnapped by an employee of his company, who had been planning the crime for many months, with the intent of gaining a large ransom for Coors' return. During the kidnapping, a fight ensued and the would-be kidnapper killed Coors. He put the body in the trunk of his car and drove to a remote area of the mountains where he buried Coors in a shallow grave. He then took off across the country to New Jersey, where he abandoned the car in a dump and set it on fire to destroy any evidence that might link it to the crime.

THE CASE: THE ADOLPH COORS KIDNAP MURDER—cont'd

The FBI investigated the case. They located the area where the kidnap/murder took place when other inhabitants of the ranch reported having heard gunshots on the property. They then located the body in Colorado when witnesses reported the presence of a strange car and observed someone digging a large hole. A thorough search of personnel records of the Coors Company turned up a suspect and the FBI discovered that he had been using an alias. They determined his real name and were able to trace him to New Jersey, where they were able to locate the remains of the car used in the kidnapping. Even though the car was badly burned, the investigators were able to recover layers of soil that had been deposited in the wheel wells. They collected this soil as well as soil samples from the location of the kidnap/murder, the burial site, and other areas in the mountains where the suspect lived and had been known to travel. As one drives a vehicle, soil is deposited in the wheel wells in the order in which it is encountered. The layers of soil can thus tell a story of where the vehicle has been. Analysis of the soil samples in the Coors case showed that all were represented within the layers of soil taken from the suspect's car. Thus the investigators were able to show that the car had been in all of the locales that were relevant to the case. This was crucial evidence in the conviction of the suspect for kidnapping and murder.

WHAT IS SOIL?

The definition of soil depends upon who is working with it. Farmers are concerned with the topsoil in which they plant crops and they define soil in terms of the top few inches on the ground. Engineers, on the other hand, view soil as a component of construction material and are more concerned with its physical properties than its chemical make-up. Soil scientists study changes in soil chemistry and composition and are concerned with minute alterations and variations in soil. Forensic geologists look at soil a different way. Much of the soil that they study comes from areas that have been filled in such as garbage dumps, gardens, or soil patches around homes or businesses, gravesites, etc. They are concerned with the transfer of soil particles from such locations to objects such as cars or clothing, either accidentally or purposefully. The case described above is a good example. A forensic soil scientist might define **soil** as: earth material, either natural or manmade (concrete, gravel, other building materials), that is transferred from a crime scene to a person or object, or vice versa. This soil may then be recovered from that person or object or may have been shed and found at a different location. The objective of forensic soil analysis is thus to associate soil found at a crime scene to its source. This requires, of course, that a source has been identified and known soil samples have been collected.

Soil contains both organic and inorganic materials. The organic materials are essentially decayed and decaying vegetative and animal matter such as grass and other plants, and insects, animal droppings, animal parts, etc. Sometimes this collective organic fraction of soil is called **humus**. The inorganic part of soil is generally crushed rock and clay materials. These are made up of **minerals**. Minerals are generally combinations of metal and nonmetal ions. For example, iron and oxygen combine to form various minerals including ferric oxide (Fe_2O_3). Minerals are all crystalline solids with regular arrangements of atoms. Many have distinct colors that can be imparted to a soil sample. There are more than 2000 minerals but only about 50 occur commonly in US soils. Rocks are generally made up of several mineral types with definite percent compositions and the soil near the rocks will reflect this diversity. The emphasis on the analysis of soil from a forensic science standpoint is to compare soil from the original location to the person or object to which it was transferred, in order to show that the person or object was, at one time, in the location where the soil originated. In this comparative analysis, the forensic geologist seeks to measure those physical and chemical properties that are most effective in determining if two soil samples could have come from the same location, given the time, material, and instrumental constraints that are always a part of forensic science work.

COLLECTION OF SOIL EVIDENCE

As with all types of forensic evidence, the success of forensic soil analysis depends upon the proper collection of known and unknown evidence. In the Coors' kidnapping case described earlier, the unknown evidence consisted of the layers of soil found in the wheel wells of the suspect's car. The known evidence were samples of soil taken from the various areas of Colorado and New Jersey where the car would have been used to transport Coors' body to the burial site and then travel to New Jersey. The investigators wanted to establish that the kidnapper used that car to transport the body from the kidnapping site to the burial site and then to his "hideout" in New Jersey and finally to the dump. It was therefore necessary to collect soil samples from the car and determine their points of origin. In cases such as this, where several soil types are found, care must be taken to collect all of the layers of soil from the undercarriage intact, because the order of the layering can help establish the order in which the car came in contact with the soil present at the various important locations. This is because the layer of soil that adheres to the body of the car will be from the first place that the car came in contact with soil. Succeeding layers of soil will be deposited on top of the original in the order that the car came in contact with them. A problem with these questioned samples, and for that matter, in all cases, is that the forensic scientist has no control over the nature and amount of the unknown evidence. There can be problems with limited size and amount, contamination, fragility, and stability of the evidence. Thus, it is important to collect as much questioned evidence as possible and to preserve it so that it remains in substantially the same condition throughout. Soil evidence often occurs in layers as shown in Figure 17.1. These layers must be collected very carefully as their order can be important.

Control or known soil samples present different problems for the forensic geologist. If the scene covers a large area, care must be taken to get the known samples as close to the evidentiary soil location as possible. If there is some doubt, then samples should be collected from several areas to account for the natural variation of soil. In cases where the known sample is to be taken from a hole, such as a grave, the vertical layering is as important as the horizontal layers so that known samples should be taken from the same depth as the questioned samples came from. Time can also be an important consideration in soil analysis. If a long time has passed between the crime and the time that the knowns are collected, there may have been disruption to the area where the incident took place. For example, suppose a rape occurred on someone's back lawn and the victim got soil stains on her clothes. A few weeks later,

FIGURE 17.1

Layers of soil. These layers of soil taken from the side of a hill have been built up over many years. Sometimes layers of soil can be built up quickly, as with wheel wells of cars.

the backyard was resodded and then the known samples were obtained. The resodding may mean that the knowns really aren't proper controls because the type of soil in the new sod may be very different from the soil that was there previously. Dry soil samples can be put in plastic bags or film canisters or other airtight containers. Wet samples, however, should be put in paper or cloth sacks so the water can evaporate, otherwise, there can be irreversible chemical changes to some of the minerals.

IN DEPTH: SOIL ANALYSIS AND LOCATION

Thom Holpen, one of the country's leading trace evidence analysts, describes the value of soil evidence in the book "Trace Evidence Analysis: More Cases in Mute Witnesses," Max M. Houck, Ed., Elsevier, Amsterdam, 2004. One of the cases he describes shows that the location and circumstances surrounding the deposition of evidence such as soil can be very important. The summary of this case is reprinted below:

> *On a warm summer evening, a burglary was attempted on a business with the perpetrator trying to gain entrance through a foundation crawlspace having a dirt floor. A man meeting the description of the suspect was stopped a block from the business by police and taken in for questioning. The suspect wore no shirt and his jeans were soiled. When questioned as to how his jeans became soiled, he said he had been playing baseball at a local park several blocks away. His clothes were submitted to the laboratory along with soil samples from underneath and around the perimeter of the business as well as from the park. Examination of the jeans revealed several clumps of soil deposited on the inside of the front waistband. Analysis and comparison of the soil from the jeans with the reference samples revealed it to be consistent only with the soil from underneath the business. The suspect pled guilty when confronted with the evidence. How did the soil get inside the waistband? It is believed that when the suspect was crawling on his belly, and with no shirt to block it, the waistband of the jeans scooped the soil up. His perspiration moistened the soil and helped tack it to the inside material of the jeans.*

ANALYSIS OF SOILS

Soil possesses many physical and chemical properties that can be exploited in comparison of known and unknown samples. The properties that are chosen for measurement depend upon the nature of the case and the knowledge and skills of the forensic scientists in the laboratory. Most crime laboratories do not have personnel who possess the knowledge and skills to exploit soil comparisons fully. Instead, they rely on expertise that may reside at a local university, such as a mineralogist, geologist, or soil scientist. The majority of forensic soil cases consist of footwear where someone has left a shoe print in soil or automobile cases where a tire tread has been imprinted in soil. This usually doesn't involve analysis of the soil per se, although it probably should, but is limited to comparison of the shoe print or tire tread.

REPRESENTATIVE SAMPLES OF SOIL

Soil, like some other types of evidence, may occur in large quantities in a given case. When this happens, it may be necessary to make some decisions about how much of the exhibits will actually be analyzed. It is usually not necessary to examine all of the soil in an exhibit as long as the samples taken from the bulk exhibit are representative of the whole. There are a number of ways of determining how many samples to take, their size, etc., but the first consideration is to decide if and how an exhibit of soil is to be homogenized so that the samples taken will be representative. This presents some unique situations with soil evidence. One of the most important tests done on soils is to determine the particle size distribution. Some soils are coarse and contain large chunks of material, whereas others are finely divided. If a known and unknown sample of soil came from the same location, their particle size distributions are usually similar. This means that the determination of particle size distribution must be made before the soil is pulverized in an attempt to homogenize it. In this context, particle size distribution is an inventory of the various sizes of the particles present in a sample of soil. Once the particle size distribution is determined (see below for a discussion about how this is done), then the soil can be crushed and pulverized to make it consistent throughout so that samples taken for analysis represent the bulk exhibit and the physical and chemical analyses on the samples can be extrapolated to the bulk sample.

PHYSICAL PROPERTIES

In general, physical properties are fairly easy to measure and the tests are inexpensive and not too consumptive of material. Standard methods of analysis are available from the American Society of Testing and Materials and the US Geological Survey. The most common physical tests are color and particle size distribution. The color of soil is affected by moisture content, mineral distribution, and location. Dusty, dry soils tend to be light tan or white owing to lack of moisture. Agricultural or tropical soils tend to be dark brown owing to the high humic content. The naked eye

FIGURE 17.2

Different-color soils. This was taken from a case where several plants were uprooted and stolen from a plant nursery. Samples of soil taken from the plants were compared with samples taken from the pots the plants were in at the nursery.

is a very good discriminator of color when comparing soil samples and there are standard color charts to help with exact color characterization. Figure 17.2 shows a case involving several different soil colors. In this case, there was a theft of trees from a plant nursery. The tress was tracked to a rural location. Soil samples were taken from the earth balls at the base of the trees and compared to holes in the ground at the nursery. Although none of the soil samples could be traced to a particular tree, the comparisons showed that the soils from the trees all showed similarities to the holes in the ground at the nursery.

The first and most important tool in the forensic soil scientist's toolbox is the microscope. Soil samples should first be examined using a stereomicroscope. This will give the analyst a general idea of the organic and inorganic fractions of the soil and their relative percent. It will also provide information about the colors of the soil and the particle size distribution. The next step in the analysis is to use a polarizing microscope at 100–400× and identify the actual minerals present and their relative amounts. Particle analysis is key to understanding the nature of the samples under examination. The interested student should seek out the references and resources from the McCrone Institute on polarized light microscopy of particles and minerals. An easy method of ascertaining particle size in soil samples is by sieving. A weighed soil sample is dried and then put through a nest of sieves where each succeeding sieve has smaller holes than the one preceding it. Then each fraction is weighed and the percentage of each particle size range can be computed. Scanning electron microscopy (SEM) has become a useful tool for many crime laboratories and has been applied to the analysis of soils. Using an electron microscope, one can visualize very tiny particles that cannot be seen with a light microscope. In addition, the elemental composition of an individual particle can be determined at the same time using energy dispersive X-ray analysis.

CHEMICAL PROPERTIES

Chemical analysis of soil is performed less frequently than physical analysis. This is because there is no type of forensic classification for soils and because there is so much variation in chemical content of soils from similar locations. In spite of this, valuable information about the association of known and unknown soil samples can be gained by careful chemical analysis. One method receiving increased attention is high performance liquid chromatography (HPLC). A soil sample is extracted with an organic solvent such as acetonitrile and then analyzed by HPLC. The resulting chromatogram gives a profile of many of the organic substances found in the soil. This provides excellent comparative data for known and unknown samples. A liquid chromatogram of a soil sample is shown in Figure 17.3. The pseudo-three-dimensional appearance is due to simultaneous measurements of time, absorbance wavelengths, and intensity of absorption.

Infrared spectrophotometry of soils is also a useful technique. It is possible, for example, to obtain the infrared spectrum of a bulk soil sample, then extract the organic fraction and obtain its infrared spectrum, and then by spectral subtraction, obtain the infrared spectrum of the rest of the mostly inorganic fraction.

Other tests are sometimes done on organic fractions of soil. These include oxygen bioavailability and DNA analysis on bacteria or other microbes in the soil. The latter is a relatively new technique and is quite complex and expensive.

BACK TO THE CASE

The Adolph Coors kidnapping case illustrates a number of important concepts about the analysis of forensic evidence in general and soil evidence in particular. First, although the Locard exchange principle is very important in interpretation of trace evidence, it does not operate in all cases. In the Coors case, there was essentially a one-way transfer of evidence from the various road surfaces to the underside of the wheel wells of the suspect car. Second, this case illustrates the value of cumulative evidence in solving crimes. If only one type or one instance of physical evidence is present at a crime scene, especially class evidence, its probative value may be limited. If the wheel wells of the suspect's car contained only the soil from around the Coors ranch, it would have made only a very limited contribution to solving the case. The fact that investigators found layers of soil from several locations on the car, each of which resembled soil from an area which was important to the case, provided strong evidence that the suspect's car was the one where the body was transported and buried and linked the car to the suspect even though none of this was individual evidence. Finally, this case illustrates the value that an experienced soil scientist can bring to a criminal case. The scientist was able to accurately describe the type of soil in each layer found on the car and was able to describe the geographic areas where each soil was likely to be found, thus enabling investigators to track the car's movement and locate Coors' body.

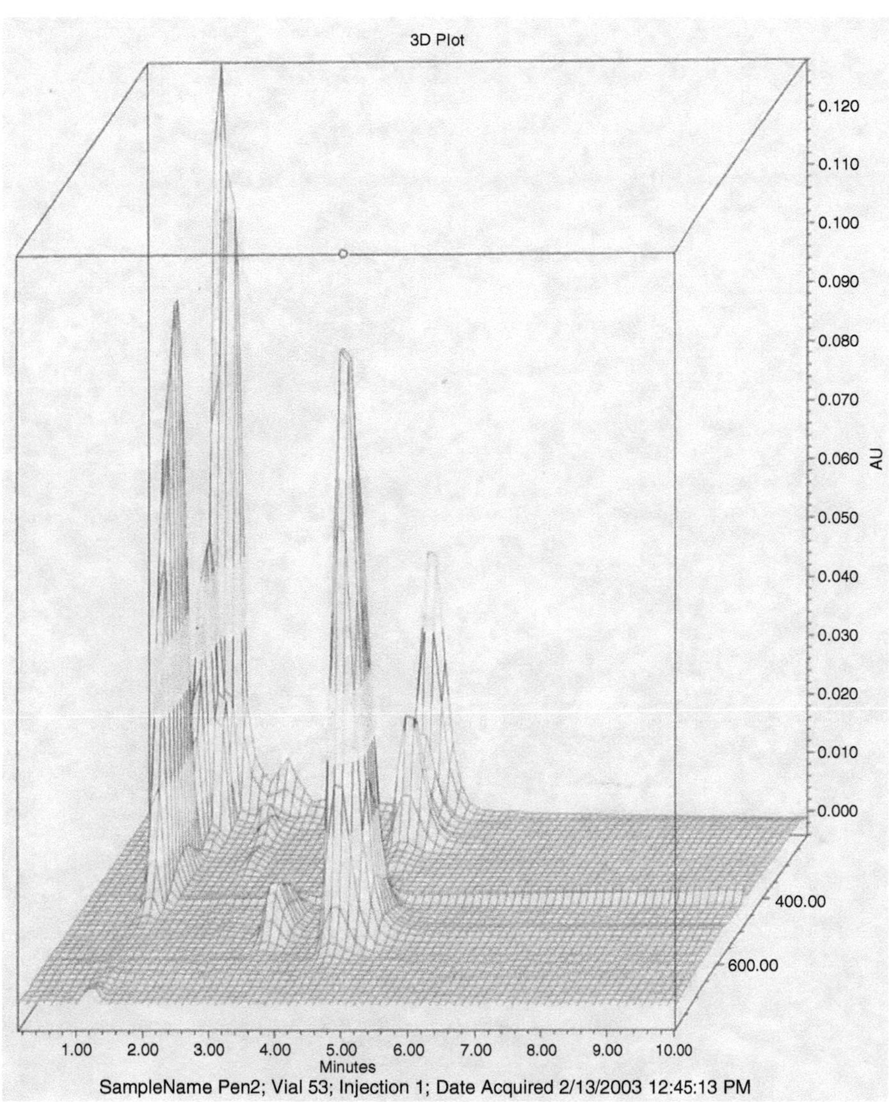

FIGURE 17.3

Liquid chromatogram of a soil sample extracted with acetonitrile. This is a pseudo three-dimensional plot. Many chromatograms are collected, each one at a different wavelength of the UV detector. The plot of wavelength versus time versus absorbance has a three-dimensional appearance. This presents much more data for comparison than can be gained from a single chromatogram.

There have been a number of other celebrated cases where soil analysis has had a major effect. In *South Dakota v. Eugene Moeller* in 1990, Becky O'Connell was kidnapped and murdered near a small town in South Dakota. The accused claimed that he had been elsewhere when the crime occurred. Soil taken from the wheel wells of his truck was similar chemically and physically to soil from the rural area where the victim was found. The soil from the area where the accused claimed to have been at the time of the crime had different chemical and physical characteristics. He was convicted of the crime in part because the soil analysis called his alibi into question.

Enrico Camerena was a United States Drug Enforcement Administration agent working in Mexico when he was kidnapped and murdered in February 1985 after leaving the United States Consulate in Guadalajara. His body was subsequently recovered from the grave where he had been buried. An FBI forensic geologist saw the body on television and noted that soil that was adhering to the body was different from soils in the location where authorities had indicated the body had been recovered. Subsequent investigation of the soil led investigators to the exact location where the body had been buried. This information indicated that a cover up of the murder was taking place.

GLASS

THE CASE: HIT AND RUN

In December 1979, a man was walking across a street in his North Chicago neighborhood. He was loaded down with packages from Christmas shopping. A car came down the street at a high rate of speed and hit the man, head on. He was thrown more than 10 ft and died instantly. The driver of the car didn't even slow down. A resident of the street, who was just coming out of his home, witnessed the crash and saw the car. He was able to describe the car in general terms and the letters "RTI" on the license plate. He called the police and then checked on the victim, who was dead. The police put out an all points bulletin (APB) for the car and then searched the crime scene. They found pieces of glass on the body and in the surrounding street. The body was sent to the morgue where the clothes containing glass fragments were sent to the forensic science laboratory. The pieces of glass found in the street were also sent to the laboratory. A car matching the description of the one involved in the incident was spotted later that day. It had one broken headlight. The driver was arrested and charged with hit and run. The remaining glass in the broken headlight would be compared to glass fragments from the victim's clothing. It was also interesting to note in this case that the right front fender of the car had a regular pattern imbedded in the paint along with some brown fibers. The victim was wearing brown, corduroy pants at the time of the incident. The fiber examiner at the forensic science laboratory was later able to determine that the imbedded pattern in the fender was similar to the "cords" in the corduroy pants and that the fibers in the fender were of the same type as those in the pants.

WHAT IS GLASS?

Glass can be defined as an **amorphous** solid. This is a hard, brittle material that is usually transparent, but which lacks the ordered arrangement of atoms (**a crystal lattice**) that is found in most solids. Instead, common glass is made

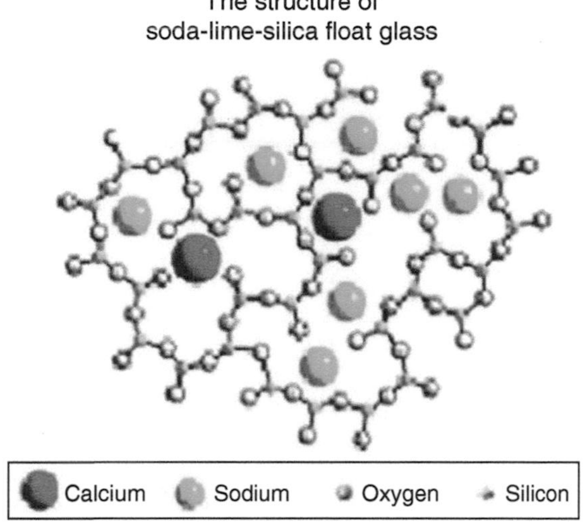

FIGURE 17.4

The chemical structure of basic glass—silicon dioxide. Note that there doesn't seem to be any ordered structure to the molecule. This type of bonding gives glass its dual properties of a solid and a liquid. http://www.pilkington.com/pilkington/corporate/english/education/chemistry/default.htm.

up largely of oxides of silicon that have been doped with other materials to give it its familiar properties. The silicon oxides come chiefly from sand. The silicon dioxide matrix and the methods used to produce glass impart properties of both solids and liquids. Such substances are sometimes called **fluids**. If you have ever bumped into a plate glass window or been hit with a glass bottle, you know that glass is hard like a solid, yet research has shown that glass flows under the influence of gravity, albeit very slowly. The amorphous structure of glass is shown in Figure 17.4.

GLASS MANUFACTURE

Glass is manufactured by melting sand and the other desired ingredients and then allowing them to cool without crystallizing. The cooling process may take place in a mold or it may be injected into a particular shape or it may be cooled in such a way that it is perfectly flat. For example, molten glass can be cooled on top of a bath of molten tin. This allows the glass to be very flat so it can be used in windows and other similar applications. This type of glass is called **float glass**. A diagram of how float glass is manufactured is shown in Figure 17.5.

Basic silicon glass is seldom used in a pure form. Instead, while it is in the melted state it is "doped" with measured amounts of various impurities that alter its properties in a predictable way. For example, when soda (sodium carbonate, Na_2CO_3) is

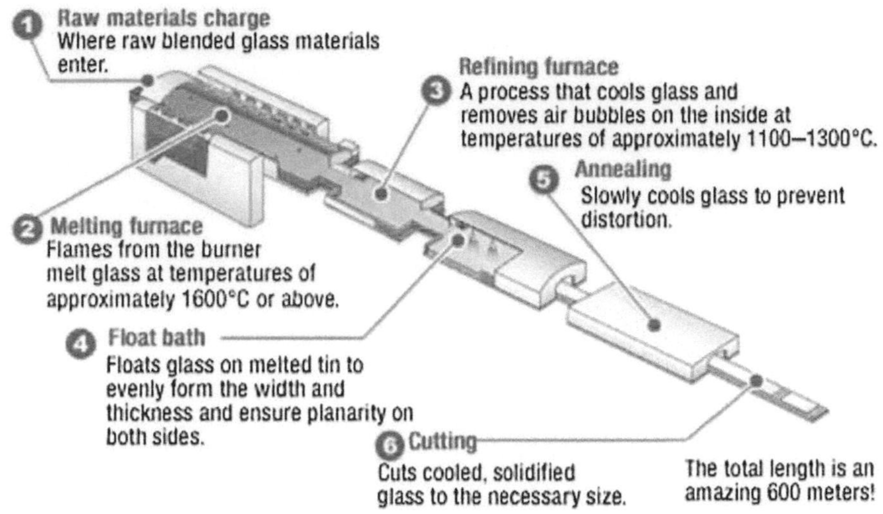

FIGURE 17.5

Method for manufacturing float glass. The molten glass is floated on a bed of liquid tin which has an extremely flat surface so that the glass surface in contact with the tin is very flat.

added, the glass will melt at a lower temperature and flow more easily, making it easier to work with. Other materials such as lime (calcium oxide, CaO) can be added to stabilize the glass and make it less soluble in solvents. When both calcium oxide and sodium carbonate are added, the product is called **soda lime** glass. If boron oxide (B_2O_3) is added to glass, it becomes more heat resistant. It is then called **borosilicate** glass (Pyrex©). This type of glass is used in cookware, thermometers, and automobile headlights because it can take fast, extreme changes in temperature without cracking or shattering. Glass may be strengthened by **tempering**. This is a process whereby the glass is heated and cooled rapidly producing deliberate stress in the surface. When this glass breaks, it shatters into small solid pieces rather than sharp shards. This type of glass is used in car windows. In the US, tempered glass is not used in front windshields. Instead, a laminate consisting of two layers of glass with a layer of plastic between is used. If the windshield is broken, the laminate helps keep shards of glass from flying around the car and injuring the passengers.

Three major types of glass are encountered as evidence in forensic cases: sheet or flat glass, container glass, and glass fibers. Flat glass is used to make windows and windshields and can also be shaped to form light bulbs, headlights, and other materials. Container glass is used to make bottles and drinking glasses. Glass fibers are used to make fiberglass and fiber optic cables as well as glass–plastic composite materials. Less frequently, optical glass used to make eyeglass lenses and similar materials may be encountered in forensic cases.

FORENSIC EXAMINATION OF GLASS

There are more than 700 types of glass in use today in the US. Obviously, some are more common than others. One would expect to find much more bottle and container glass as well as window glass in a given environment than optical or specialty glass. Because many types of glass are mass-produced, individual glass objects ordinarily do not possess any characteristics that are so unique that a piece of glass from this object could be individualized to it. As a result, small pieces of glass are considered to be class evidence.

THE MECHANICAL FIT (FRACTURE MATCH)

There is one set of circumstances where glass can be individualized to a particular object. This is called the **mechanical fit** or **fracture match**. This occurs where a piece of glass breaks into relatively large pieces that have at least one, good, intact edge that can be fitted to the edge of another piece from the same source. Since glass is hard and brittle, it doesn't deform when broken. Since it is amorphous, there are no lattice points along which the glass would fracture when subjected to force; so fractures would be random events and no two pieces of glass would be expected to break in the same manner. Thus, if there is a good mechanical fit between two pieces of broken glass, one can conclude with certainty that they were once joined. This fit is often aided by the presence of stress marks along the broken edge. These marks are also randomly generated and are caused by the application of force at the breaking point. They can be seen only with the aid of a microscope. Even if a broken edge is relatively featureless, the stress marks will align where the break occurs. In Figure 17.6(a), a glass fracture match can be seen along with stress marks. Figure 17.6(b) shows stress marks that appear in glass where it is broken.

EXAMINATION OF SMALL GLASS PARTICLES

The vast majority of cases involving glass consist of particles that are too small to be physically matched by a mechanical fit. Such particles generally do not contain any unique characteristics that would permit them to be individualized to a particular source. Thus, they are class evidence. There are a number of tests that can be performed on glass particles to characterize and compare them. The most important of these are identification of the material as glass, **density**, and **refractive index**. Other tests include color, thickness, flatness, surface features, and fluorescence. Some of these tests are discussed below.

Identification

Before testing of glass particles is undertaken, it must be shown that the particles actually are glass and not some other material. This can be done by measuring its hardness, structure, and behavior when exposed to polarized light. If a thin section of glass is examined under crossed polars, it will disappear because it is isotropic; it behaves

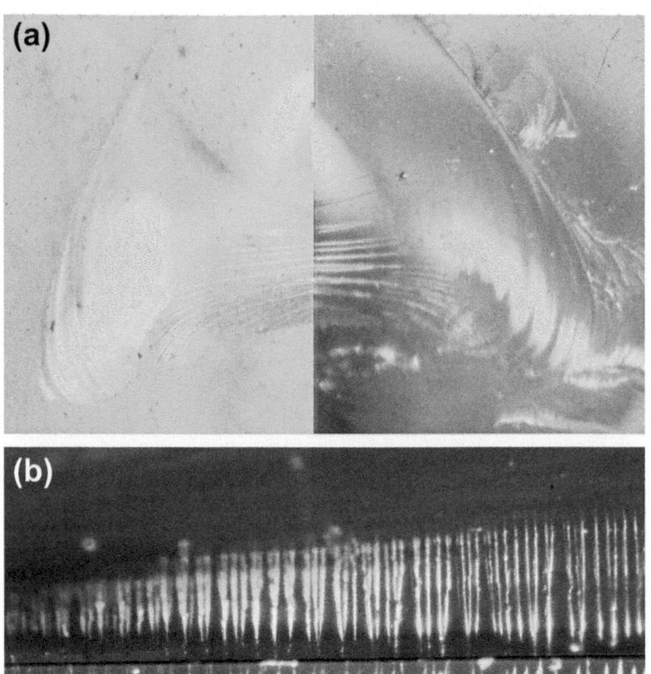

FIGURE 17.6

(a) A glass fracture match. The photomicrograph on the left is a piece of glass gouged out of a car windshield when the car struck a pedestrian. The photo on the right is the part of the windshield which showed the missing piece. (b) Stress marks produced when glass is broken. The piece at the top of the figure was found in a pair of glasses that were worn by the victim of a hit and run. The bottom piece was found at the scene. The detailed fracture match and stress mark match is strong evidence that the piece of glass at the scene came from the glasses.

the same at any orientation of a polarizer. Glass can be differentiated from plastic by pressing it with point of a needle. Most plastics will show an indentation from the needle whereas glass will not. Substances like table salt can be differentiated by their shape; they have a regular shape owing to an ordered chemical structure, whereas glass is amorphous. Table salt, for example, exhibits cubic crystals. Some minerals can be differentiated from glass using a polarizing microscope. Many minerals will show different colors and brightness than glass when exposed to polarized light.

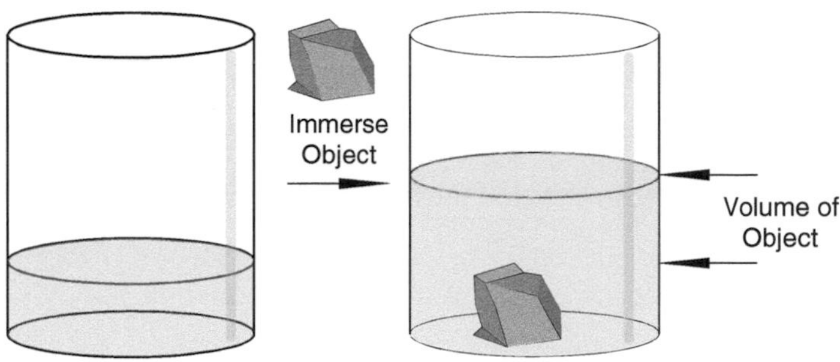

FIGURE 17.7

Measurement of volume by displacement of a liquid. A measured quantity of liquid is put into a container. Then an object is added. The object must be insoluble in the liquid and denser than the liquid. The object sinks to the bottom and displaces its own volume of liquid. The volume of the liquid is now measured again. The difference between the two volumes is the volume of the object.

Courtesy: Meredith Haddon.

Preliminary Tests

Prior to comparing glass fragments, it is advisable to do some preliminary testing to show that all of the pieces of glass in one exhibit could come from one single object. These preliminary tests include color, surface characteristics, flatness, thickness, and fluorescence. These tests are also valuable in comparing known and unknown samples.

Density

The density of an object is its mass divided by its volume.

$$D = M/V$$

For example, if a cubic block of wood weighs 250 g and is 10 cm on each side, its volume would be 1000 cm^3 (10 cm × 10 cm × 10 cm) and its density would be 250 g/1000 cm^3, or 0.25 g/cm^3. Note that the number obtained for the density is dependent on the units of mass and volume. Most objects can be easily weighed on a common balance. If an object has a regular shape such as a cube, whose volume can be easily measured, then its density is easily determined. If the object has an irregular shape, but is fairly large, its volume can be measured by displacement of a liquid. A liquid, such as water, is put into a container and its volume is determined and then the object is added. The volume of the liquid is then measured and then the volume of the liquid alone is subtracted, leaving the volume of the object. Recall the old tale about the thirsty bird who could not reach a small amount of water in a deep hole. It dropped pebbles into the hole, thus raising the level of the water until it could reach it. The rocks displaced the water and caused it to rise in the hole. This is shown graphically in Figure 17.7.

If an object is irregular in shape and too small to measure its volume by displacement, then indirect methods must be used. The easiest way to compare the densities of two small pieces of glass is by the sink/float method. In this method, two miscible liquids (liquids that can mix with each other) are chosen such that one is less dense than glass and the other is denser. Bromoform and bromobenzene are often used, although they are both toxic, so caution must be observed. A tube is filled with a mixture of the two liquids and then tiny pieces of the glass are inserted. The particles are allowed to settle in the liquid mixture and then a determination is made to see if they all settle at the same level. Then the liquids are heated slightly using a hair dryer. Heat decreases the density of liquids, so the glass particles should then move lower. If they all move to the same spot, then they have the same density. It should be noted that a glass object, such as a headlight will exhibit slight variations in density within the object. The sink/float method of density determination is very sensitive and it may sometimes occur that two pieces of glass may show slight differences in density but may actually arise from the same object. Using several particles from each source may minimize this problem.

Refractive Index

In Chapter 5, Spectroscopy, the property of **refraction** was discussed. Recall that refraction occurs when light passes through a transparent medium or object. The light bends away from its path and slows down. Refraction is much more pronounced in solids than liquids or gases. Glass is an excellent medium for exhibiting refraction. The amount of refraction caused by glass is an important physical property for the comparison of known and unknown exhibits. **Refractive index** (**n**) is the ratio of the velocity of light in a vacuum to the velocity as it passes through the medium. The refractive index of air is negligible and can be used in place of a vacuum.

$$\mathbf{n} = \frac{\text{Velocity of light in vacuum}}{\text{Velocity of light in medium}}$$

Refractive index is always greater than one because light travels fastest in a vacuum. For glass, the range of refractive indices is usually between 1.4 and 1.7. Different types of glass have different refractive indices, so this property can be valuable in determining what type of glass is present and for comparing glass fragments.

There are two other important properties of refractive index. One is its variation with temperature. Refractive index is inversely proportional to temperature.

$$N \propto 1/T$$

This means that, as the temperature is raised, the refractive index decreases. Over a range of perhaps 30° this effect is quite pronounced with liquids, but solids such as glass, exhibit almost no variation. The other important property of refractive index is its variation with wavelength of light. It is also inversely proportional to wavelength.

$$N \propto 1/\lambda$$

How is refractive index measured in a forensic science laboratory? Clearly it is not possible to measure the refractive index directly as it would be impractical to try to measure the speed of light as it passes through a piece of glass. Instead an indirect method must be used. There are a number of indirect methods used in forensic science laboratories. The most popular are **immersion** methods and the most commonly used of these is the **Becke line** method.

The Becke Line Immersion Method

The human eye can detect transparent objects in air such as glass fragments, because they refract light. If two objects have the same refractive index, then our eyes would not see any difference in the light that passed through them. The refraction of the light causes light beams that pass only through the air and beams that pass through the air and the object to reach our eyes at slightly different times and angles, thus enabling the eye to distinguish them. If a piece of glass is immersed in a liquid whose refractive index matches that of the glass, then the glass should be invisible because light that passes through the glass would have the same refractive index as the liquid and our eyes would not be able to detect any difference. In reality, if a piece of glass is immersed in a liquid with the same refractive index, the glass usually does not completely disappear. This is because there are other effects caused by light passing through glass. These are more pronounced when the glass is thick. The result is that we can still see faint borders of the glass even if they have the same refractive index. When a piece of glass is immersed in a liquid of different refractive index and observed under a microscope with transmitted light, a bright halo in the shape of the glass, will appear to surround the glass. This halo is called the Becke line and it is caused by the difference in refraction by the glass and the liquid. If the glass and liquid have the same refractive index, the Becke line will disappear even if the glass does not. The Becke line can be clearly seen in Figure 17.8.

FIGURE 17.8

A piece of glass immersed in a liquid of different refractive index. The Becke line can be seen as a bright halo around the glass. If the liquid and the glass had the same refractive index the halo would disappear. In theory the glass would also disappear; however, if it is relatively thick, then there are other factors such as diffraction that prevent the glass from disappearing completely.

In practice, the Becke line method takes advantage of several properties of refractive index. As an example, consider the case described at the beginning of this section of the chapter, of the hit and run where pieces of glass from the headlight of a car are found in the clothing of the victim. Samples would be collected from the headlight (knowns) and from the victim's clothes (unknowns). The glass chemist would need to have a set of liquids that are made to have an accurately determined refractive index. Each sample would be tested to determine its approximate refractive index using the standard liquids. This can be done by mounting a piece of glass that is immersed in a liquid under a microscope. The Becke line is found and then the focus of the microscope is changed so that the objective lens and the glass are moved away from each other. The Becke line will move in or out toward the medium (glass or liquid) that has the higher refractive index. Using this information, a liquid is chosen that has a slightly higher refractive index than the glass being examined. A microscope with a hot stage can be used to perform this analysis. This is shown in Figure 17.9. A commercial instrument known as a **Glass Refractive Index Measuring Instrument (GRIM)** is used in most forensic science laboratories to determine the refractive index of small glass particles. A particle of glass is immersed in a small amount of a liquid whose refractive index is slightly higher than that of the glass. The GRIM has a sensor that can determine when the Becke line disappears. It also has a thermocouple that measures changes

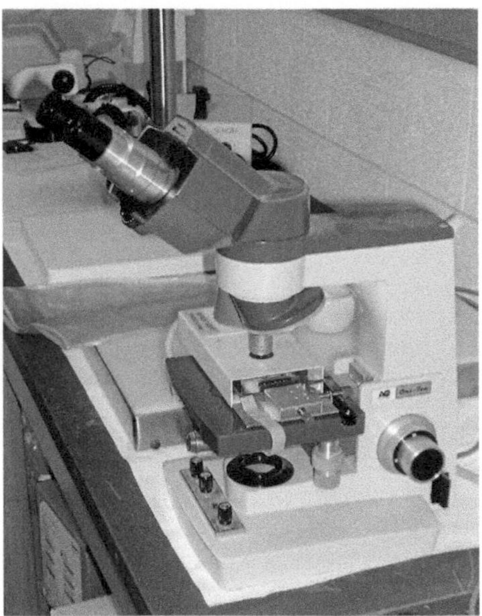

FIGURE 17.9

A compound microscope with micro hot stage that is used to determine the refractive index of a microscopic particle such as glass.

in temperature of the refractive index liquid. Under computer control, the GRIM raises the temperature of the liquid until the Becke line disappears and the refractive index of the glass can be determined.

REFRACTIVE INDEX CALCULATION: BECKE LINE METHOD

A piece of glass is immersed in a liquid whose refractive index at 25 °C is 1.520. The Becke line is plainly visible. This particular type of glass is known to have a refractive index of less than 1.520. The temperature is raised to 45° at which time the Becke line disappears, indicating that the glass and the liquid are now at the same refractive index. The bottle label indicates that the refractive index of the liquid drops 0.0003 units for every degree increase in temperature. What is the refractive index of this piece of glass?

Over this limited temperature range, we may consider the refractive index of the glass to remain constant. When the Becke line disappeared, the temperature had risen 20° (45–25). This corresponds to a decrease of 0.006 refractive index units (0.0003 × 20). This means that, at 45° the refractive index of the liquid and glass are 1.514 (1.520–0.006).

The Becke line method is very accurate and precise, but it is always advisable to get as much data as possible before rendering an opinion about the association of evidence. The Becke line experiment is usually performed using light at 589 nm (the sodium D line). If a different wavelength of light is used, the refractive index of the liquid and the glass will be different, so the experiment can be repeated at several different wavelengths. Then a plot of wavelength versus refractive index can be constructed for each glass particle. This is called a **dispersion** plot. See Figure 17.10. It is not uncommon for two pieces of glass to have the same refractive index at 589 nm (or another single wavelength) and yet have different refractive indices at other wavelengths. If two pieces of glass have the same dispersion curve, this is good evidence that they could have come from a common source.

Elemental Analysis of Glass

Glass may contain trace amounts of elements that arise either from contamination during the manufacturing process or on purpose when it is desirable to impart certain desirable properties to the glass. Measurement of the types and quantities of these trace elements can help in determining whether two pieces of glass were ever part of the same object. The problem here is to be able to digest the glass so as to free the trace elements. This is not easy to do. Inductively coupled mass spectrometry (ICP-MS) is one method that can enable the analysis of trace elements in glass. The plasma in the instrument vaporizes the glass and confirms the trace elements by mass spectrometry. The glass can also be dissolved by laser ablation or by using hydrogen fluoride. Electron microscopy can also be used to determine the presence and amounts of trace elements. Trace elemental analysis can provide an excellent profile of the impurities in the glass and help in formulating conclusions concerning associations of knowns and unknowns.

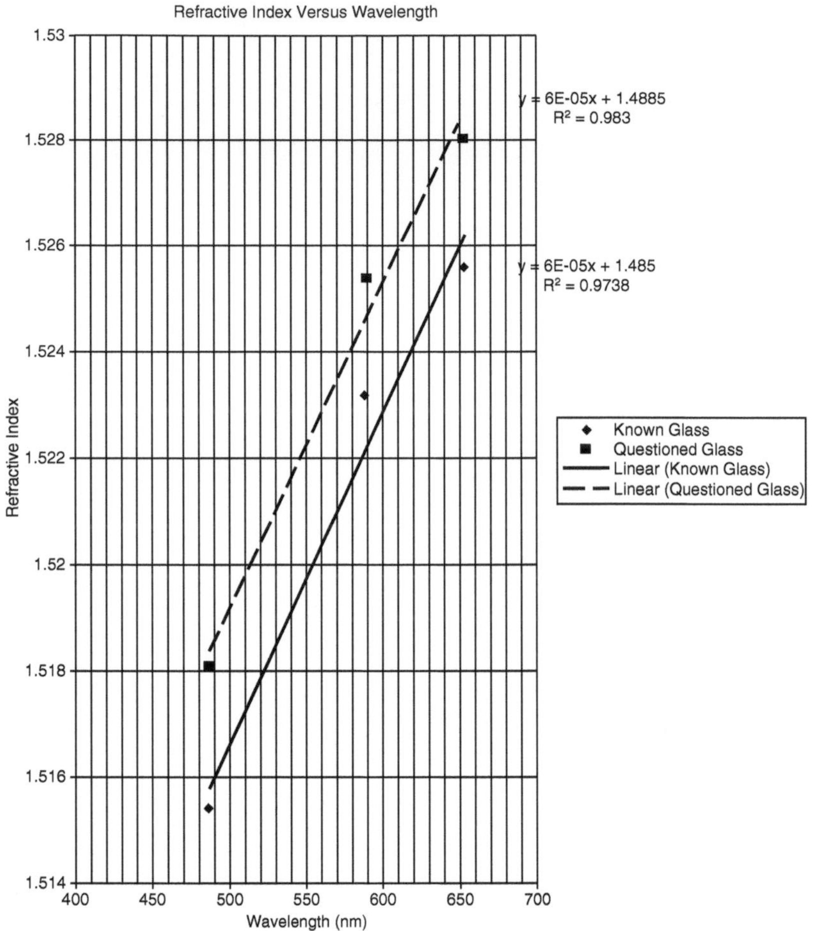

FIGURE 17.10

A dispersion curve. This curve measures the variation of refractive index of glass with the wavelength of light used to measure it. Shorter wavelengths produce higher refractive indices. These lines are constructed from three data points and the best fit line is constructed by regression analysis.

THE EFFECTS OF PROJECTILES ON GLASS

Besides the chemical and physical analysis of glass particles, there are other types of evidence where glass is the matrix rather than the analyte. For example, when a piece of glass such as a window is struck by a projectile, the resultant hole(s) in the glass can yield valuable information about the direction and angle of impact. The evidence that will be available depends upon the nature and thickness of the glass and the type of projectile. If the glass is very thin or the projectile is large

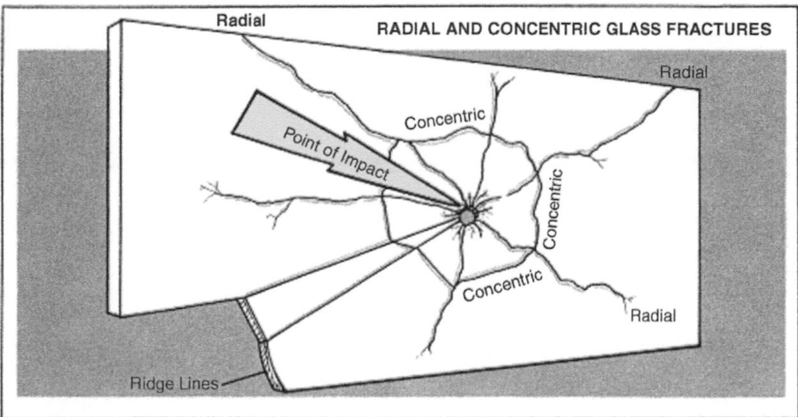

FIGURE 17.11

Radial and concentric cracks in glass and multiple penetrations in a piece of glass. Note that the radial cracks made by the second penetration stop at a crack made by the first penetration. This shows how it can be determined which penetration was made first. http://www.adtdl.army.mil/atdls.html.

or powerful, the glass will shatter. However, in the case of window glass and bullets, holes are left in the glass that can be examined. The observations that can be made include where the projectile ends up, the formation of a crater in the glass, the formation of a cone of glass, and the types and positions of cracks that appear in the glass.

When a high-speed projectile, such as a bullet, passes through a piece of glass, a crater will form in the glass that is larger on the exit side of the glass. This, by itself may reveal the direction of impact of the projectile. The crater may show some asymmetry that can yield information about the angle of impact. In addition, **radial cracks** will form on the side of the glass opposite to the side of the impact, as shown in Figure 17.11. These radiate out in all directions from the point of impact. In many cases, there will also be **concentric cracks** on the side of the direction of impact. In addition, the orientation of stress marks in the glass at the point of the break or penetration can help determine the direction of impact. Some of the marks will form a right angle at the point of impact. The direction of the angle will indicate the direction from which the projectile came.

LAMP ANALYSIS

Once again, consider the hit-and-run case described earlier in this chapter. Suppose the facts of the case are altered so that the incident took place at dusk and a question arose as to whether the headlights were on at the time. If a headlight breaks during the impact, it is usually possible to determine its status at the time of impact.

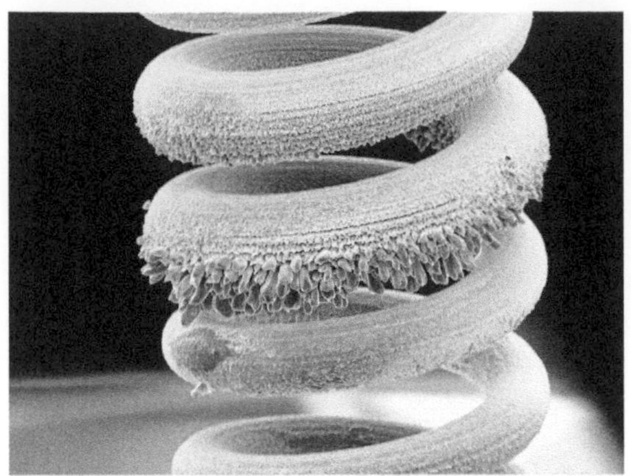

FIGURE 17.12

A headlight filament that was on when the lamp was broken.

Courtesy: Christopher Bommarito, Michigan State Police Forensic Science Division.

As shown in Figure 17.12, if a light filament is hot and then the vacuum in the light is broken, then oxygen in the air will react with the tungsten in the filament resulting in the formation of oxides on the surface of the filament. If the filament is not on at the time the lamp is breached, then no reaction will take place and no tungsten oxides will be seen. The filament in Figure 17.12 was photographed with an SEM.

SUMMARY

Glass and soil can be very important trace evidence in criminal cases. There are many types of glass present in our environment and they are often found at crimes, especially automobile accidents and home and business invasions. Glass is a material somewhat like a solid and a liquid. When glass fragments are large enough to be pieced together like pieces of a jigsaw puzzle, the evidence can be individualized to a particular source. In most cases, the glass fragments are too small to be fracture matched and class characteristics are emphasized. Most commonly this involves measuring the density and refractive index of the glass fragments. Electron microscopy or ICP-MS can also be used in the analysis of elemental composition of glass.

Soil is virtually always class evidence. They are easily transported from place to place and soil samples can differ significantly when they are only a few meters apart vertically or horizontally.

Soil consists of organic and inorganic fractions. The organic material consists chiefly of decaying and decayed animal and vegetable material. The inorganic part is mostly crushed minerals. Soil can range from nearly 100% organic to 100% inorganic. There are a variety of tests that can be performed on the organic and/or inorganic fractions. Mineral microscopy (petrography) is frequently carried out on known and unknown soils for comparison. Liquid chromatography can be used to separate organic fractions. Density and size gradients can also be determined on the soil sample as a whole. There have been many cases where the whereabouts of an automobile can be traced by the layers of soil that collect with time in protected areas such as the wheel wells.

TEST YOUR KNOWLEDGE

1. What is soil? What are its major components?
2. What is forensic geology? How does it differ from conventional geology?
3. Where does humus come from?
4. In the case that was presented at the beginning of the chapter, where was the soil collected that was used for comparison with various locations around the country?
5. How is glass defined?
6. What properties does glass have that are like those of a solid? A liquid?
7. What is density? What are its units?
8. What is refractive index? What are its units?
9. Glass is sometimes called an amorphous solid. What does this mean?
10. What is float glass? How is it made?
11. What is tempered glass?
12. What are radial cracks? How do they help determine the direction of impact of an object on glass?
13. What are concentric cracks? What is their role in determining the direction of impact of an object on glass?
14. What is dispersion? How are dispersion curves constructed?
15. What is a Becke line and how does it form?
16. If a piece of glass is immersed in a liquid and a Becke line is seen under a microscope, how can one tell which has the higher refractive index?
17. What is the relationship between refractive index and temperature?
18. What is the relationship between refractive index and incident light?
19. Under what conditions can a piece of glass be individualized to a particular source?
20. How can one tell if a headlight was on or off at the time it is broken?

CONSIDER THIS...

1. Soil cannot generally be individualized to a particular source. Explain why this is so? (Keep in mind the variations of soil horizontally and vertically within one location, the transportability of soil, and the forensic taxonomy of soil, if any.)
2. Suppose that, in the case given at the beginning of this section, there are only tiny fragments of glass found at the hit-and-run scene, instead of large pieces.

Since one could not accomplish a fracture match, what tests would you do on the glass fragments? What known samples would you obtain? Assuming that the results for the tests are the same for both knowns and unknowns, what would your conclusion be about the source of the tiny glass fragments?

3. When one does multiple tests on scientific evidence, they have the most value when they are entirely independent of one another; that is, they are based upon entirely different principles. If one does density and refractive index comparisons on known and unknown evidence, does this principle hold? Are density and refractive index completely independent of one another? (Hint: what happens when you try to walk under water compared to walking through air on land?)

FURTHER READING

Bonetti, J., Quarino, L., 2014. Comparative forensic soil analysis of New Jersey state Parks using a combination of simple techniques with multivariate statistics. Journal of Forensic Sciences 59 (3), 627–636.

Caddy, B. (Ed.), 2001. Forensic Examination of Glass and Paint: Analysis and Interpretation. Taylor and Francis, London.

Howes, L.M., Kirkbride, K.P., Kelty, S.F., Julian, R., Kemp, N., 2014. The readability of expert reports for non-scientist report-users: reports of forensic comparison of glass. Forensic Science International 236, 54–66.

Miller, E.T., 1982. Forensic glass comparisons. In: Saferstein, R. (Ed.), Forensic Science Handbook, vol. 1. Prentice-Hall, Englewood Cliffs, NJ.

Woods, B., Lennard, C., Kirkbride, K.P., Robertson, J., 2014a. Soil examination for a forensic trace evidence laboratory—part 1: spectroscopic techniques. Forensic Science International.

Woods, B., Kirkbride, K.P., Lennard, C., Robertson, J., 2014b. Soil examination for a forensic trace evidence laboratory–part 2: elemental analysis. Forensic Science International.

ON THE WEB

http://www.fbi.gov/hq/lab/fsc/current/review/2009_04_review01.htm FBI review article on analysis of glass.

http://www.fbi.gov/hq/lab/fsc/backissu/jan2005/standards/2005standards4.htm Introduction to glass analysis by FBI lab.

http://www.interpol.int/public/Forensic/IFSS/meeting13/Reviews/Soil.pdf excellent introduction to soil analysis.

CHAPTER

Fires and Explosions

18

CHAPTER OUTLINE

KEY TERMS

- Accelerant
- Activation energy
- Adsorption
- Adsorption elution
- Bomb seat
- Combustion reaction
- Detonation
- Endothermic reaction
- Exothermic reaction
- Explosive train
- Fire tetrahedron
- Flash point

- Griess reagents
- Headspace
- High explosive
- High-order explosion
- Ignition temperature
- Incendiary fire
- Incomplete combustion
- Low explosive
- Low-order explosion
- Nitroglycerine
- PETN
- RDX
- Solid phase microextraction
- TNT
- Spalling
- Vapor trace analyzer

CAMERON TODD WILLINGHAM: A CASE OF ARSON?

In 1991, Cameron Todd Willingham was convicted of murdering his own three children by deliberately setting fire to his home in Corsicana, Texas. He escaped the blaze with only minor injuries. He was tried and convicted of murder by arson and was executed in 2004 by lethal injection. Willingham proclaimed his innocence throughout the proceedings up until his execution. After the fire was suppressed the fire marshal and police department conducted an investigation of the cause. They concluded that the fire was started and promoted by the use of an accelerant. The physical evidence included charring on the floor, multiple places where the fire was started, and an observation that the fire was very hot. They concluded that these were all indicative of an arson fire. An area near the front door tested positive for an accelerant. Even though the investigators alleged that the fire was started in multiple locations, no accelerant was found anywhere else in the house. When Willingham was in jail awaiting trial, he was alleged to have confessed to the crime to another inmate. Willingham maintained that his home had been invaded by squirrels sometime before the fire and he alleged that they caused electrical problems in the home that caused the fire.

In 2004, a fire expert, Gerald Hurst, examined the evidence compiled by the fire marshal's office. He disputed the finding that evidence of extreme heat had to be caused by an accelerant in this case. Crazed glass was found in the home after the fire and this was attributed to the presence of an accelerant by the fire marshal but disputed by Hurst and subsequently other experts. Later, an experiment was carried out wherein a discarded house was set on fire under similar conditions to the Willingham fire and it was found that similar damage patterns occurred without the use of an accelerant. Ultimately, the fire marshal had indicated more than 20 observations that indicated the use of an accelerant. Hurst rebutted all of them.

After the execution, a number of experts reviewed the evidence of arson. Many indicated that there was no scientific proof of arson. One, Craig Beyler, who had been hired by the Texas

CAMERON TODD WILLINGHAM: A CASE OF ARSON?—cont'd

Forensic Science Commission, found that the finding of arson was not scientifically supportable. A subcommittee of the Commission, in 2010 found that flawed science was used in the determination of arson. The Washington Post reported in 2014 that the inmate who claimed that Willingham confessed to him in jail, recanted his story.

INTRODUCTION

Some of the most spectacular and horrific incidents of crime and terrorism in the United States involve fires and explosions. Perhaps, this is because they cause so much damage and destruction of property and of lives. Terrorist explosions have been on the increase for years in other parts of the world but have been brought home to the United States in the World Trade Center bombing and then later its destruction by aeroplane crashes and in the Oklahoma City bombing of the Murrah Federal Building. Fires and explosions are often linked. Seldom is there an explosion that is not accompanied by fire. Often fires result in explosions when energetic materials at the fire scene become involved.

Virtually all fires and explosions are the result of a chemical reaction known as **combustion**. Combustion is simply the reaction of a fuel with oxygen. The products of a complete combustion are carbon dioxide (and other oxides if present), water, and energy. An example of combustion is the reaction of natural gas (methane) with oxygen. The energy produced by this reaction is used everyday by millions of homes and businesses for heat and other purposes.

$$\underset{\text{methane}}{CH_4} + \underset{\text{oxygen}}{2O_2} \rightarrow \underset{\text{carbon dioxide}}{CO_2} + \underset{\text{water}}{2H_2O} + \underset{\Delta}{\text{energy}}$$

A chemical reaction that releases energy as one of its products is described as **exothermic**. All combustion reactions are exothermic. A reaction that requires the input of energy in order for the reaction to take place is called **endothermic**. In reality, all chemical reactions require an input of energy to get them started. This is the **activation energy**. So an exothermic reaction is one where energy is produced in excess of the energy put in as activation energy.

$$\underset{\text{activation energy}}{\Delta + CH_4 + 2O_2} \rightarrow \underset{\text{excess energy}}{CO_2 + 2H_2O + \Delta}$$

FIRE

The most familiar combustion reactions are fires or explosions. Whether a fuel burns or explodes has to do with the nature of the fuel and how close the oxygen and the fuel are to each other during the reaction. Everyone is familiar with fire, the various types of fires, and many ways that fires can start. From the forensic science standpoint, it is necessary to know the cause of a fire because, in many cases, fires are deliberately set with criminal intent. These fires are classified as **arson**. Deliberately setting fires constitutes criminal acts and the perpetrators must be punished. A chemical explosion results from the same type of chemical reaction as a fire. Fires take place by a slow or ordinary combustion wherein the fuel and the oxygen are physically and chemically separated; the oxygen being obtained from the air that surrounds the fuel. The oxygen in air is supplied in a molecular form, O_2.

$$\Delta + O_2 \rightarrow O + O$$

Part of activation energy

In order for the fire to take place, the oxygen molecules must be broken up into atoms and they must get close to the fuel molecules. This takes energy and time, so this type of combustion is relatively slow. The energy needed to sever the oxygen molecules is part of the activation energy for the fire. Other types of activation energy include that which is needed to vaporize the fuel or the source of oxygen.

The study of fires for forensic purposes involves determining the characteristics and damage caused by the fire as well as the point of origin and cause. In this chapter, we will deal with the following questions. The answers will provide a pretty complete picture of the investigation of fires, especially those of suspicious origin.

- What are the necessary conditions for a fire?
- What are the types of fires?
- How are fire scenes investigated?
- What are fire residues and how do they arise?
- What is the role of the forensic science laboratory in fire scene investigation?

CONDITIONS FOR A FIRE

A simple way of looking at the conditions necessary to have a fire is the **fire tetrahedron** as shown in Figure 18.1.

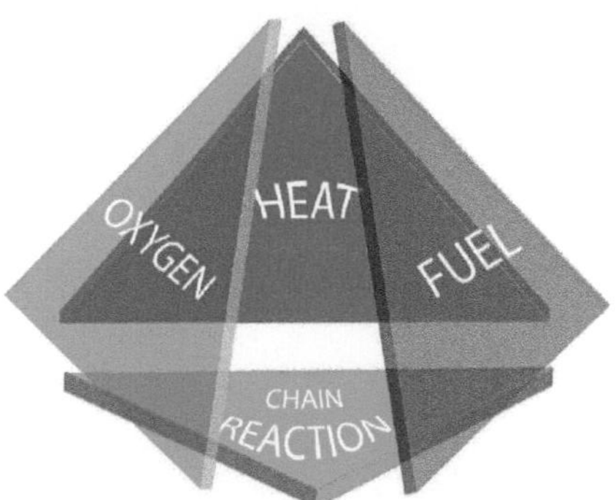

FIGURE 18.1

The fire tetrahedron. Each side of the figure is a factor that must be present in order to sustain a fire. Take any one of them away and the fire will go out.

The fire tetrahedron depicts the four elements that must be present in order to have a fire: a source of heat or energy, fuel, source of oxygen, and chain reaction between the fuel and oxygen. The source of energy is necessary to elevate the fuel and oxygen molecules into an excited state so that they can undergo chemical reactions. This is the aforementioned activation energy. The temperature necessary to do this varies with the fuel and is called the **ignition temperature**. Once this temperature is reached, a fire can continue on a self-sustaining basis. If any of these elements are eliminated the fire will not continue. This is the basis of fire extinguishers. Some merely use water to lower the temperature of the fire below the ignition temperature. Others smother the fire, depriving it of oxygen. Still others coat or disperse the fuel.

In most cases, the fuel must be a vapor in order for it to combust. Often it is necessary to supply energy to change a liquid or solid fuel to a vapor. This would be true, for example, in the case of gasoline. There must be sufficient energy present to convert enough of the liquid gasoline to a vapor to support combustion. This temperature varies with the nature of the fuel and is called the **flash point** of the fuel. Thus the flash point is the lowest temperature that will allow a liquid to produce a flammable vapor. Even if a fuel is heated to its flash point, it must still be ignited and so a source of ignition is still needed. In addition, the flash point of a fuel will allow combustion, but will not sustain it. This requires a higher temperature known as the **flame point**. Flash points of some common fuels are given below.

FLASH POINTS OF SOME COMMON LIQUID FUELS

Flammable and combustible liquids are divided into the following classes; based on flash points and boiling points. Flammable liquids are defined as those with flash points below 100 °F and combustible liquids have flash points at or above 100 °F. Flammable and combustible liquids are further subdivided into the following classes:

Class IA. Flash point below 73 °F (22.8 °C) and boiling point below 100 °F (37.8 °C). Examples include acetaldehyde, diethyl ether, pentane, ethyl chloride, ethyl mercaptan, hydrocyanic acid, and gasoline.

Class IB. Flash point below 73 °F (22.8 °C) and boiling point at or above 100 °F (37.8 °C). Examples include acetone, benzene, carbon disulfide, cyclohexane, ethyl alcohol, heptane, hexane, isopropyl alcohol, methyl alcohol, methyl ethyl ketone, toluene, petroleum ether, acetonitrile, and tetrahydrofuran.

Class IC. Flash point at or above 73 °F (22.8 °C) and below 100 °F (37.8 °C). Examples include glacial acetic acid, acetic anhydride, cyclohexanone, and dichloroethylether.

Class II. Flash point at or above 100 °F (37 °C) and below 140 °F (60 °C). Examples include kerosene, diesel fuel, hydrazine, and cyclohexanone.

Class IIIA. Flash point at or above 140 °F (60 °C) and below 200 °F (93.4 °C). Examples include aniline, cyclohexanol, phenol, *o*-cresol, naphthalene, nitrobenzene, and *p*-dichlorobenzene.

Class IIIB. Flash point at or above 200 °F (93.4 °C). Examples include diethyl sulfate, diethylene glycol, and *p*-cresol.

Besides flash point and flame point, there are other energy considerations if the fuel is a liquid or solid. Energy must be supplied to convert a solid to a vapor and a liquid to a vapor. All of this heat must be present before the fire will start and continue.

There is a well-known expression; "Where there is smoke there is fire." Observation of a fire also leads to the opposite observation; "Where there is fire there is smoke." What is smoke? **Smoke** occurs when there is **incomplete combustion** in a fire. The equation for the reaction of methane with oxygen operates when the conditions are right for complete combustion. Under ideal conditions, there would be little smoke from this reaction. The limiting factor here is usually the presence of oxygen. If there is not enough oxygen to completely combust the molecules of fuel, then some of the combustion will be incomplete. This will yield products such as carbon particles (soot), unburnt, and partially burnt gases. Together these comprise smoke. Sometimes a fire will occur in a building where the oxygen supply is limited and as the oxygen is used up, more smoke is formed. If this fire is then suddenly ventilated, the increased oxygen will cause an explosive fire. This phenomenon, familiar to all firefighters, is called **flashback**.

Accelerants

Because the fuel must normally be in the vapor phase in order to sustain a fire, many times it is surprisingly difficult to start a fire or to make one burn quickly. If one wanted to start a fire in a room where there is only wooden furnishings, it would be very difficult to do with just a match or lighter because there may not be enough heat available to provide the activation energy needed to start and sustain the fire. This is why kindling is used to start fires in fireplaces. The kindling requires lower activation energy to support combustion. The energy generated by the combustion of the kindling is sufficient to burn larger pieces of wood. In such cases, arsonists often turn to the use of **accelerants**; fuels that are easily vaporized and support combustion, and are highly exothermic. These liquids are poured around the area that is to be burnt and then ignited. They burn easily and the energy they emit provides the activation energy needed to get the large pieces of wood to combust. From the arsonist's standpoint, the problems with accelerants are that they often leave a residue behind even if burnt and procuring the accelerant may bring unwanted attention from citizens or law enforcement agents. This is probably why gasoline is by far the most common accelerant in the United States. People buy gasoline all of the time and it doesn't cause any unwanted attention. Other common accelerants are kerosene, charcoal lighters, and some paint thinners. These are common consumer products that many people keep in their homes. The National Fire Protection Association has developed a classification scheme for common ignitable liquids. All of the common accelerants used in fires today are found in this scheme. All of these accelerants will leave residues after they burn, which will enable the forensic examiner to determine what type of accelerant was used in the fire. Table 18.1 contains an abbreviated list of the common accelerants in this scheme.

TYPES OF FIRES

There are a number of ways of classifying fires depending upon the use of the classification system. From the forensic standpoint there are just three types of fires: **natural**, **accidental**, and **deliberate**. Of course, fire scene investigators

Table 18.1 National Fire Protection Association Classification Scheme for Ignitable Liquids

Class #	Class Name	Peak Spread	Examples
1	Light petroleum Distillates	C_4–C_{11}	Lighter fluids Camping fuels
2	Gasoline	C_4–C_{12}	Gasoline
3	Medium petroleum distillates	C_8–C_{12}	Some charcoal lighters and paint thinners, mineral spirits
4	Kerosene	C_8–C_{17}	#1 fuel oil, Jet-A Some charcoal lighters and paint thinners

are most interested in deliberate. A fire that is deliberately set is also called an **incendiary** fire. If an incendiary fire is set with the intent to illegally destroy a structure or evidence that may lie within it, or to cover up another crime, then the fire is classified as arson, as was stated earlier in the chapter. Not all incendiary fires are arson. It is possible for someone to set a fire on purpose but not have the intent to destroy something illegally. Brush fires may be set deliberately in a forest to minimize the danger of an uncontrolled accidental fire, but there would be no intent to illegally burn down the forest. Such a fire would be classified as incendiary but not arson. The same is true with homeowners who burn leaves under controlled conditions or light a charcoal grill.

Natural Fires

The vast majority of natural fires are caused by lightning strikes. There are thousands of fires started by lightning every year. In many places in the United States, there are more lightning fires than all other types combined. Lightning may also be the proximal cause of a fire even if it doesn't actually start the fire itself. For example, lightning can strike the electrical lines leading into a building, causing an overload that in turn may cause an electrical fire. See Figure 18.2 for damage from a lightning fire.

There are a few other types of naturally occurring fires. For example, flammable gases that escape from the ground around an oilfield and combust could be considered to be a natural fire, although these are often considered to be accidental, especially if there is an attempt to control the discharge of these gases and they ignite accidentally.

Accidental Fires

Accidental fires may arise from any of a number of different sources and may sometimes be difficult to distinguish from deliberate fires. For example, a furnace malfunction may cause a fire. This would ultimately be ruled an accidental fire. However, in the case where someone deliberately tampered with the furnace that led to a malfunction that in turn caused the fire, that would be arson. If the furnace is badly damaged in the fire, it may not be possible to tell if the malfunction was accidental

FIGURE 18.2

The gaping hole in this house was caused by lightning. When it struck the house, it caused a major fire and extensive damage. Such direct hits on buildings, especially those with lightning rods, are relatively rare.

Courtesy: John Lentini.

or deliberate. In many of these cases, the fire scene investigator would call in experts such as electricians, plumbers, or heating contractors to help determine if the appliances were tampered with. Even so, the investigator may not be able to determine if the fire was deliberate. Sometimes rags that have been used to clean up spills from kerosene or another fuel can heat up enough to cause what sometimes is termed "spontaneous combustion" if they are left in a closed area for a long time. This is a misnomer as the fire is caused by heat being released from chemical reactions of the fuel with the cloth.

Deliberate Fires

Determination of whether a fire has been deliberately started with malicious intent involves a number of steps. First, and the most important, is that all possible natural and accidental causes of the fire must be eliminated. If this is done, then the only other possibility is that the fire was deliberately set. Once this has been done, the investigator will seek to determine if the fire is arson. Remember that it is possible to have a fire that is started deliberately, but without malicious intent to destroy or damage. Determination of arson can be aided by finding residues from an accelerant or other evidence such as multiple points of origin, fire trails, etc. This will be discussed further in the section on fire scene investigation.

Other Ways of Classifying Fires

From the fire scene investigator's standpoint, it is important to not only be able to determine the type of fire as explained above, but also to determine the source of ignition or cause of the fire. Each of the more common causes of fire will be discussed below.

Direct ignition

This is the most basic of all of the causes of fire. It involves direct application of a spark or flame source to the fuel. It can be as simple as using a match or flint or lighter or as complicated as using a time delay mechanism. In the latter case, a mechanical or chemical or physical process is used to delay the application of the flame or spark so the fire setter is not around when the fire starts. Everything from candles to clocks to mousetraps to exothermic chemical reactions has been used in time delay mechanisms. This is one of the few types of fire where it is easy to determine intent. A time delay mechanism is almost never used unless the fire is arson. In Figure 18.3, a burning cigarette is used as a time delay fuse to set off a book of matches.

Electrical fires

Electric appliances, wires, components, and connections are all capable of giving off sparks or overheating given the proper set of conditions. Sometimes this may be due to a malfunction whereas other times it may be a natural part of the functioning of the object. If the proper mixture of fuel and oxygen is present under the right set of

FIGURE 18.3

A timing device used to set a fire. An open pack of matches was put on the floor of the car near an accelerant. A cigarette was lit and put next to the matches. Eventually, the burning part of the cigarette lit the matches which then set off the accelerant, causing the car fire.

Courtesy: Lawrence D. Rossini, CFPS, Fire Investigator, Orange County Fire Investigation Unit.

conditions, a spark that contains enough energy to raise the mixture beyond its flash point can cause a fire. An appliance may be rigged to fail and thus overheat or spark so that it can cause a fire. Other times, it may wear out or malfunction because of mistreatment or age. It may be difficult for the fire scene examiner to determine which happened in this case, thus making it problematic to reach a conclusion about the cause of the fire. An example of how electrical overloads may be deliberately created can be found in the movie "She-Devil," in which Roseanne Barr, having been jilted by her husband, exacts her revenge by overloading electrical circuits by plugging in many high current appliances into the same socket. This causes fires that eventually burn down the house.

Weather-related fires

As mentioned previously, lightning strikes are surprisingly common. They are responsible for hundreds of forest fires annually. Lightening striking a dead tree in a forest can provide more than enough energy to vaporize some of the wood or resin and raise it above its flash point, thus starting a fire. There are also many incidents of lightning striking homes and other buildings. Most tall buildings are protected by lightning rods, but others are not and a lightning strike can cause both structural damage and fire. Finally, it is possible for the sun to cause a fire although this is very rare. A magnifying glass can be used to focus the Sun's rays on a leaf or grass, causing it to smolder and even burn. Any object, such as a glass or vase, could conceivably act as such a lens and cause a fire, although actual incidents of this are very rare.

Mechanical fires

A machine can overheat either through misuse or incorrect placement. For example, a shaft or wheel that relies on bearings to reduce friction can overheat if the bearings become damaged or worn. The localized heating can cause lubricants to ignite and a fire to spread. This may be especially dangerous in cars where many parts operate at high temperatures and gasoline is present. Overheating of an engine or catalytic converter or muffler can cause a fire if fuel leaks in the wrong place. Even appliances such as toasters or clothes driers that give off heat and are not given proper ventilation could overheat and cause a fire. There have been many reported cases of clothes drier vents becoming clogged with lint. The hot air being vented from the drier when it is operating can ignite the lint and cause a fire.

RECOGNITION AND COLLECTION OF FIRE SCENE EVIDENCE

One of the critical steps in the determination of the cause of a fire is to determine the point of origin. This is the most likely place to discover physical evidence that can help in the determination of the cause of the fire. If an accelerant has been employed, it will most likely be found at or near the point of origin. Devices such as timers or trace evidence are most likely to be found near the point of origin. Many fire scene investigators concentrate on finding accelerants but the fact is that there are other types of evidence that can be quite helpful. This will be discussed in more detail later.

Investigation of Fire Scenes

Fire scenes are among the most difficult places to investigate. In many cases, a building may be completely destroyed by fire and upper floors may have collapsed onto the lower parts of the building. The fire department may have attended the fire and attempted to suppress it. This usually involves using many thousands of gallons of water to cool and douse the fire. The scene is usually dark, as the electricity would have been cut off. Fire scenes can be exceedingly dangerous. There may be smoldering embers buried in the debris. The structure of the building may be weakened so that walking in the building can be hazardous. There is the danger of parts of the building collapsing on the investigators. At the same time, it is necessary to avoid disturbing the scene as much as possible so as to not dislodge or contaminate potential evidence. Figure 18.4 shows the damage that can be caused by an indoor fire.

Fire scenes can be properly investigated only by highly trained fire scene investigators. They must be aware of the causes of fires, burning patterns, how different materials react to fire, the characteristics of points of fire origin, how fires normally proceed through a structure, unusual fire characteristics, and the effects of fire suppression on the scene. In addition, many experienced investigators are knowledgeable about appliances, especially furnaces and hot water heaters, and how they fail or can be tampered with. The main duty of the fire scene investigator is to determine the cause of the fire. The most important piece of evidence in this determination is the point of origin of the fire. Finding the point of origin is crucial to determination of the cause because it will permit the investigator to determine if a fire was accidental or incendiary.

Proper investigation of a fire scene involves many important processes. The investigator must proceed in an orderly, methodical way, and must make accurate, thorough records of the investigation through still or video photography and good

FIGURE 18.4

Indoor fire scene. The fire started in the couch and burnt up and out.

note taking. Like many criminal examinations, the investigation of a fire scene starts with a general examination of the scene and gradually focuses on the room or origin and then the point of origin. If the fire scene is a building, then the investigation would normally start with the exterior of the building and work toward the point of origin inside the building. If the fire is outside, such as forest, then the investigation proceeds from outside the damaged area into toward the area of origin.

IN MORE DEPTH: ARSON DOGS

One of the most effective tools for searching fire scenes for accelerants is the arson dog. These are specially trained dogs that can sniff out trace evidence of hydrocarbon accelerants. Dogs have an extremely refined and sensitive sense of smell that can be exploited at a fire scene where they can smell hydrocarbons even where there has been extensive burning. Arson dogs are used to locate possible sources of accelerants so that they can be collected by the fire scene investigator for laboratory analysis. They enable the search of a fire scene to proceed much faster and more efficiently. Research has shown that there is a higher level of positive findings for an accelerant by laboratory scientists in cases where arson dogs have located the accelerant first. The major disadvantage to the use of arson dogs is that they do not know what they have located. They cannot discriminate between a real accelerant and a hydrocarbon that is part of some object and was released by the fire. If the laboratory cannot confirm the presence of the accelerant, then the dog's reaction cannot be used as evidence that an accelerant was present.

Points of entry and exit

Conventional wisdom is that the most important piece of evidence about a fire is the point of origin or ignition of the fire. As will be shown later, this is crucial evidence, but in the case of a deliberate fire, the perpetrator may have started the fire from within the building, rather than remotely. In this case, there would be a point where this person entered the building—the point of entry. In order to leave the arsonist a route of escape, there may also be a remote point of exit. Of course, the points of entry and exit may be the same. These locations may be very important in determining who started the fire because there may be trace evidence left by the perpetrator upon entering or exiting the fire scene. Even if the fire is severe, these locations are often remote from the point of origin and the most severe damage from the fire. This is because the perpetrator would not want to be detected when starting the fire. In such cases, the trace evidence may be well preserved. Physical evidence that is found at points of origin and exit of fire scenes includes fingerprints, shoeprints, hairs and fibers, soil, and even blood. These items can provide circumstantial or direct evidence of the identity of the arsonist and they must not be overlooked.

Point of origin

Certainly, the points of entry and exit can provide important clues about **who** may have started an incendiary fire. The most important evidence about **how** a fire was started is the point of origin or ignition. This is the location where the initial ignition took place. If there are accelerants used in a fire, they are most likely to be here. As a general rule, the most intense burning and damage are found in the area around the point of origin. Deviations from this can occur for a number of reasons, including wind direction, efforts at fire suppression, locations of fuels and/or accelerants, drafts, etc. The point of origin of a fire can be seen in Figure 18.5.

Locating the point of origin

There are generally a number of characteristics present at the point of origin of a fire. They include the following:

- **Low burning**—Fires generally start in a low area of a building. Arson fires are seldom started at a high place because the perpetrator may not have a safe point of exit and the damage will generally not be as great since fires burn in an upward direction.
- **V patterns**—If the point of origin is near a wall or corner of a room, smoke damage on the wall(s) usually occurs in a "V" shape. This is not universally

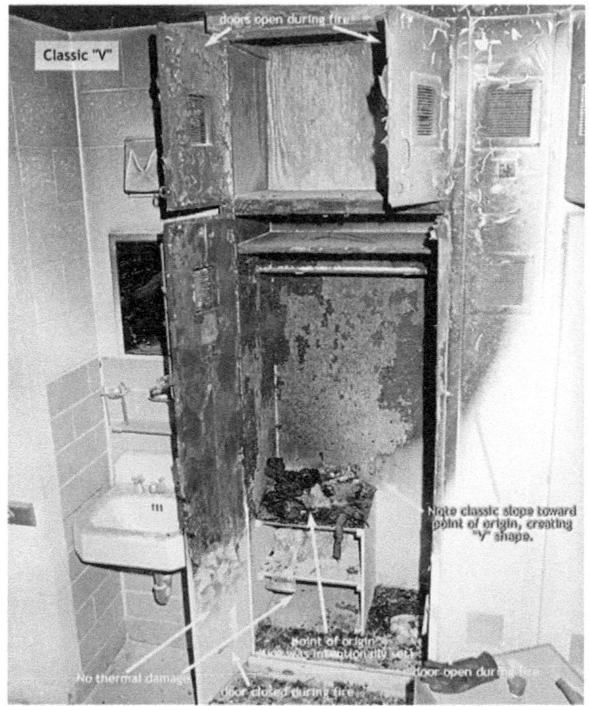

FIGURE 18.5

Point of origin of a fire showing the classic "V" burning pattern as fires burn up and out.

true and there may be other areas in the building where V patterns occur but this burn pattern can be good evidence of the point of origin. Figure 18.5 shows a classic "V" pattern in an interior fire.

- **Wood charring**—The depth of wood charring depends upon the intensity of the heat near the wood and the time of exposure. Often, wood near the point of origin of the fire will have charring to a greater depth than elsewhere in the building, although this is not always true, because there may be other points where the fire burns hotter or longer than at the point of origin.
- **Spalling of plaster or concrete**—Spalling is the destruction of a surface due to heat or other factors. In the case of concrete, the spalling may be explosive owing to trapped moisture and expansion of the concrete. Spalling usually occurs most where the heat is most intense. One of the pervasive myths about spalling is that it is only caused by the presence of an accelerant. This is not true. There can be enough localized heat from a fire in the absence of an accelerant to cause spalling.
- **Material distortion**—Metal and glass may melt or distort owing to high heat. Since melting points of many of these materials are well known, such destruction may indicate the approximate minimum temperature of the fire at that point. If the fuels that are supporting the fire are not capable of reaching that temperature during burning, an accelerant may be suspected.
- **Soot and smoke staining**—The amount of soot present in a fire may indicate the point of origin and the direction of travel of the fire. If there are indications that soot was first deposited on a surface and then burnt further, this may be good evidence of the point of origin.

Indications of an arson fire

In order to definitively determine the cause of a fire, the investigator must find the fuel that was first ignited to start the fire, the source of the heat that got the fire started, and how the two came together. Finding the point of origin of a fire is usually a necessary condition of determining if a fire was deliberately set for malicious purposes, but it may not be sufficient. There are a number of factors that **may** be present that would indicate that a fire was arson.

- **The presence of an accelerant**—If an accelerant is present at or near the point of origin of the fire, it usually, but not always means that the fire is arson. There may be some cases where a can of gasoline is stored in a building and the fire starts by some other means near the can and it subsequently becomes involved in the fire. The investigator would find the accelerant but in this case, a finding of arson on that basis alone, would not be correct.
- **Elimination of natural or accidental causes of a fire**—This is a necessary condition of determining that a fire is arson. If the point of origin is found and there is no evidence that the fire was started by natural or accidental causes, then the fire must have been incendiary. This may be difficult to determine at times. For example, a furnace may malfunction, leading to a fire. The furnace, being

at the point of origin, will be damaged or destroyed. It must be determined whether the furnace malfunctioned accidentally or it was due to deliberate tampering. This determination can be very difficult if there is extensive damage to the furnace.

- **Fire trails**—In order to enable a fire to travel rapidly in particular directions, a fire trail may be employed. This can be accomplished by pouring an accelerant along a floor in the desired direction. The result will be an uneven, intense burn along the fire trail. This would not be seen in an accidental or natural fire, thus fire trails of this nature are almost always arson. The investigator must be careful to not mistake a fire trail pattern caused by a burnt, plastic carpet runner or wear in a carpet or floor. Usually, such "fire trails" are much more regular in shape than those caused by pouring an accelerant. See Figure 18.6 for a fire trail.
- **Multiple points of origin**—Pouring some accelerant in each room of a building and then starting multiple fires, one in each room, is a tactic often used by arsonists to involve a building in a fire quickly. The investigation of this fire would show multiple points of origin and it would be easy to classify this fire as incendiary. This is usually, but not always the case with fires that have more than one apparent point of origin. There are exceptions. For example, suppose

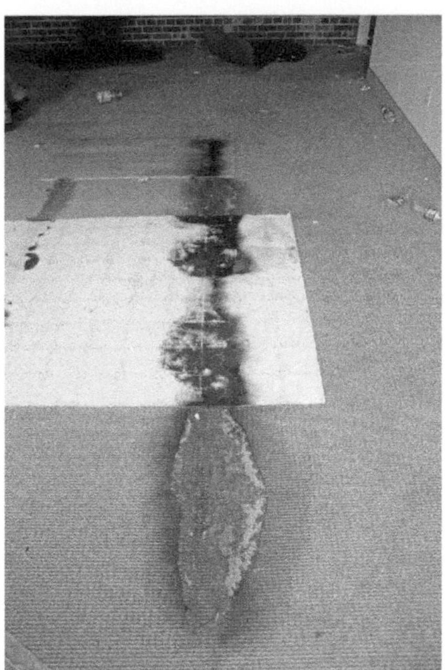

FIGURE 18.6

A fire trail made by pouring a flammable liquid on a floor. Note the irregular pattern of burning caused by pouring the liquid out of some container such as a bucket.

the electrical wiring inside a building was faulty and perhaps an overload occurred at an outlet. This might lead to overheating of the wiring and insulation at several points inside the walls of the house. Fires might start at some or all of these points of overheating. The investigation of the fire would show multiple points of origin, but the fire would not be arson (unless the original overload was made to happen deliberately). A good fire scene investigator can usually tell whether electrical wiring burned because it got overheated or it came into contact with fire that started elsewhere. Aside from such exceptions, multiple points of origin are generally indicative of incendiary fires.

Preservation of Fire Scene Evidence

Trace evidence such as hairs and fibers, fingerprints and shoeprints, soils, blood, documents, etc. can be found anywhere at a fire scene. Finding the evidence can be more difficult at a fire scene than other types of scenes because of fire suppression activities and the condition of the scene. As a result, fire scene investigators will usually concentrate their efforts to find trace evidence in the areas where a perpetrator would most likely have been at the start of or during the fire. These would be the points of entry, exit, and origin. As explained previously, points of entry and exit tend to be remote from the point of origin of the fire and thus more likely to contain trace evidence that has been relatively shielded from the fire. The same precautions need to be obeyed when collecting trace evidence from fire scenes as with any other scene. The additional problem is that contamination with combustion products, fuels, and water makes it more likely that evidence will be adulterated or destroyed at fire scenes. The presence of an accelerant such as gasoline, especially around the point of origin of a fire, is generally indicative of the fire being incendiary. This must be put into context, however. A fire scene investigator will determine the type of fire based on observation of all of the factors that have been listed above, including the presence of an accelerant. Merely finding gasoline at a fire does not mean that the fire was arson or even incendiary. The gasoline could have become involved in the fire incidentally rather than purposefully. On the other hand, the absence of an accelerant where the conditions of the fire scene would seem to indicate its presence, does not rule out arson as a possible cause. Depending upon the duration and intensity of the fire, suppression efforts, and the nature of the accelerant employed, there may not be enough accelerant residue available to detect. Also, owing to extensive damage from a fire and collapse of debris from higher to lower areas of the building, the fire scene investigator may not be able to collect residues that may be present. Thus, a fire scene investigator may have ample evidence that a fire was arson and yet there may not be a finding of an accelerant by the laboratory.

If an accelerant was present, it would be found most likely at the point(s) of origin or along fire trails. A number of methods are used to detect possible accelerants. The most sensitive method is the use of hydrocarbon-sniffing dogs. These dogs are specially trained to sniff out the smallest traces of hydrocarbons (the main constituents of fuels and accelerants) at fire scenes even after extensive burning and fire suppression. They are especially useful in finding traces of accelerant in large volumes of fire scene residue. There are also analytical devices that can detect small amounts of hydrocarbons in a large amount of debris. These are essentially stripped-down gas chromatographs with a gas sensor. They are also quite sensitive. In jurisdictions that do not have dogs or hydrocarbon sniffers, the investigator relies on experience and observation to determine which fire residues are most likely to have trapped accelerant residues. For example, cloth materials such as bedclothes, clothing, carpeting, and upholstery are usually good sources of evidence because accelerants will soak into these materials and, in some cases, may be recovered intact even though there has been considerable fire damage. Hard, nonporous items such as flooring or wallboards are generally poor sources of evidence because accelerants will not soak into them and are thus easily burned or evaporated away. On the other hand, if there are seams in wooden flooring, for example, some of the accelerant may seep inside and be protected from combustion. When a determination is made of what samples to collect, it is very important that sufficient sample quantity be taken and that **negative controls** are also collected. In general, one cannot collect too much sample, but there are, of course, practical considerations so the rule is to collect as much sample as is practical and likely to be fruitful. A negative control in this context is essentially the matrix where the accelerant residue is being collected. For example, if a partially burned carpet is suspected to contain accelerant residues, then some of the unburned carpet, far from the burned area to make sure that there is no unburned accelerant, should be collected. If possible, some of the burned carpet that is known to not contain any accelerant should also be collected. This is especially important when synthetic textiles are encountered because some of these may interfere with the chemical analysis of the accelerant residues. The analyst must have a control sample of this material to aid in the analysis of the evidence.

IN MORE DEPTH – FALSE POSITIVE EVIDENCE OF AN ACCELERANT

Many years ago, the author was involved in an arson case where a negative control was critical to figuring out what happened. This case involved a fire at a barracks at a military base in Virginia. Some of the bedding and furniture was piled up in a corner of the barracks and set on fire. There was extensive damage to the barracks. Evidence brought to the forensic science laboratory included charred remains of the fire at the probable point of origin. Chemical analysis by gas chromatography (GC) determined that there was a hydrocarbon based material present that resembled kerosene in the pattern of peaks but the positions (retention times) of the peaks were all displaced from where they should be if kerosene was present. The peaks were very strong so it was clear that there was something present. The criminal investigators were asked to go back to the barracks and retrieve some flooring and wall material that had not been involved in the fire (a negative control). Upon examination of the flooring, the cause of the peaks in the GC trace became clear. There was a large buildup of floor wax on the floor and this produced a similar peak pattern, albeit displaced to later retention times from that produced for kerosene. If there was kerosene or any other common accelerant present, it was swamped by the huge amounts of floor wax in the debris. This case illustrates the need to collect negative controls (sometimes called elimination samples) to make sure that there is nothing in the material that surrounds the physical evidence that could interfere with the analysis or interpretation of evidence.

Evidence packaging

If there is one rule about packaging of fire scene evidence that is to be tested for accelerant residues, it is that **airtight containers must be used**. Accelerants are generally volatile substances, that is, they evaporate easily. If airtight packaging is not used, then some or all of the accelerant may evaporate before the analysis is completed. Some crime laboratories will store all of their fire scene evidence in one cabinet or locker, usually an explosion-proof one. If some of the packages are leaking, then much of the other evidence may be contaminated with these vapors. If this takes place over a long enough period of time, false positive conclusions may be the result. In addition, the leaking evidence container may lose so much accelerant to evaporation, that, when it is finally examined, little or no accelerant may be found. Over the years, a number of containers have been used for storage of fire debris suspected to contain flammable residues. The most popular have been metal containers. Many fire scene investigators employ unused paint cans. These make excellent containers for fire residues because they are made to be airtight when sealed properly. They can be heated without danger of breaking and are generally rugged and easy to transport. Holes are easily punched in the top for access to the evidence without removing the top. They usually have a protective coating on the inside to retard rust. If this gets scratched, then the inside may rust quickly, especially when wet materials are stored there. Glass jars have also been used as containers for fire residues. Generally these are smaller than paint cans, which limit them to small samples. Either new Mason jars or used peanut butter or vegetable jars work. They are fragile and must be heated carefully to avoid breaking. Their metal tops are suitable for punching holes in to get access to the evidence.

Bags have also been used for packaging fire residue evidence. Paper bags are totally unsuitable because they can disintegrate if exposed to water and, more importantly, they "breathe," that is they will allow hydrocarbon or other flammable vapors to escape. Some plastic bags have also been used, albeit with mixed success. Polyethylene bags are very common, but not suitable. They can be sealed easily but may be reactive to some hydrocarbon vapors and some solvents. They are not impervious to hydrocarbons and thus, evidence will be lost. Contamination of the fire residues inside the bag may occur if the outside of the bag is exposed to hydrocarbons. On the other hand, polyvinylidine bags are quite suitable for storage, being impervious to solvents and flammable materials such as those found in fire residues. They come in various sizes and can accommodate many different types of evidence, however, they do not lend themselves well to hole punching for access to the evidence. Of course, as with all evidence, once the fire residues have been packaged, they must be sealed and properly labeled. They should be transported to the laboratory as soon as possible so that they can be analyzed with a minimum of sample loss due to evaporation of volatile materials.

Fire residues contained in soil present special packaging problems. It is well known among forensic chemists who analyze fire residues that microbes in soil can and do eat hydrocarbon residues. If this is not mitigated, soil microbes can consume so much accelerant over time that the result may be that the remainder cannot be identified. Recent research indicates that soil microbes can be quite picky about what types of hydrocarbons they eat. The laboratories that are concerned about this issue simply put such evidence in a refrigerator to slow down the action of microbes. This can be very expensive and of limited benefit. Recent research has shown that certain chemicals can retard microbial action without compromising the evidence. Chief among these is household bleach.

ANALYSIS OF FIRE SCENE RESIDUE EVIDENCE

The analysis of fire scene residues consists of two major steps. The first is to isolate the accelerant, which is usually an ignitable liquid or residue from the matrix of charred or unburned material. This usually involves an extraction but can, under certain conditions, be a direct capture. The second step is to determine the nature of the accelerant residue. This most often involves determining the type of ignitable liquid present, such as gasoline, a kerosene based material, etc. GC is universally employed to determine the type of hydrocarbon. An increasing number of laboratories are using mass spectrometry as a detector for the GC.

Isolation and Concentration of Accelerant Residues

A number of methods are commonly used for isolating and concentrating fire scene residues. The one(s) chosen will depend upon personal preference, available equipment, and the nature of the exhibits being processed. Below is a list of the typical types of exhibits that are encountered:

- **Neat ignitable liquid**—Occasionally, residues will contain some intact, unburned accelerant mixed with debris from the fire. Even if the exhibit is wet, hydrocarbons are not miscible with water so they would form a separate layer. It may be possible to pour off the liquid from the residue, filter it to remove solid particulates, separate the hydrocarbon from the water, and make a direct injection into the gas chromatograph.
- **Partially burned accelerants**—A much more common occurrence in fire scene residues is accelerants that have been partially burned. The major change that these substances undergo is evaporation of the most volatile components, leaving the higher boiling components behind. Usually, such exhibits must be extracted from the matrix in order to be concentrated.
- **Nearly completely burned accelerants**—If an accelerant has been subjected to extreme heat for a significant period, nearly all of the substances present will evaporate or burn. The best that can be hoped for, in such cases, is that there will be some nonvolatile residue left that can be extracted. Identification of these residues can be difficult owing to a lack of characteristic chromatographic information.

There are four methods and some variants that are used for isolation of accelerant residues. They are described below.

Headspace methods

Consider a fire residue containing some small amount of liquid accelerant. This residue is put in a sealed metal container at the scene by the fire scene investigator. Some of the accelerant will vaporize, while the rest will remain a liquid. The amount of liquid that becomes a vapor depends upon the **vapor pressure** of the substance and the temperature. The higher the temperature, the greater percentage of vapor there will be. Eventually, equilibrium will be established between the liquid accelerant in the residue and the vapor in the **headspace** above. Henry's Law describes this equilibrium. Once the equilibrium is established, then some of the vapor above the matrix, the headspace, can be sampled with a gastight syringe and injected into a gas chromatograph. The amount of heating that the container can be subjected to is limited. If there is too much heat applied then the ensuing increase in pressure in the container can cause the top to come off of a can or the glass to break in a jar. Typically, a container will be heated to no more than about 60 °C. A diagram of a can showing the headspace can be seen in Figure 18.7.

Adsorption methods

Although headspace methods are quite useful when there are volatile substances present in the accelerant residue, the equilibrium condition and the limitations on heating the container are drawbacks to the method. Another approach to isolating and concentrating accelerant residues is to employ adsorption methods. This group of methods utilizes the ability of charcoal (finely divided, pure carbon) or synthetic materials such as Tenax, to adsorb large quantities of hydrocarbons onto its surface. There are two variants of the adsorption method. The first is **passive adsorption**. A small container of charcoal or Tenax or a plastic strip coated with one of them is placed or suspended inside the container. It can either be left

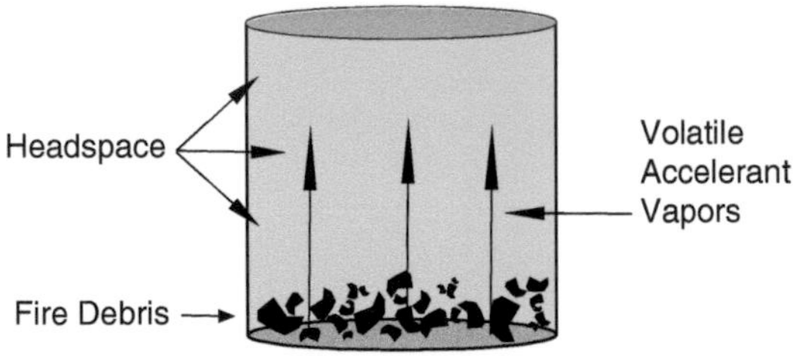

FIGURE 18.7

The headspace in a can. The fire debris is at the bottom. The headspace is the air layer on top of this that contains accelerant vapors.

Courtesy: Meredith Haddon.

overnight at room temperature or for a shorter time while being heated. Sometimes the fire scene investigator will put a charcoal strip into the container with the evidence at the crime scene. This means that the container won't have to be opened to insert the strip at the laboratory, thus minimizing the loss of accelerant vapors.

In **active adsorption**, sometimes called **adsorption-elution**, two tubes containing charcoal or Tenax are inserted partway into the container through holes in the top. Then air is pumped through one of the tubes into the container. This causes air to flow from inside the tube out through the other tube. As the container is heated, more accelerant evaporates into the headspace. It is swept through the outlet tube along with the air and is trapped or adsorbed onto the charcoal or Tenax. This upsets the vapor–liquid equilibrium in the container and the consequence is for more of the liquid accelerant residue to evaporate. This continues until there is no more accelerant in the container—it has all been trapped in the outlet tube. In some laboratories, a vacuum is applied to one of the tubes, drawing in air from the outside through the other one. The accelerant vapors are trapped in the tube where the vacuum is applied. The result is the same. See Figure 18.8 for a diagram showing absorption-elution using the vacuum method.

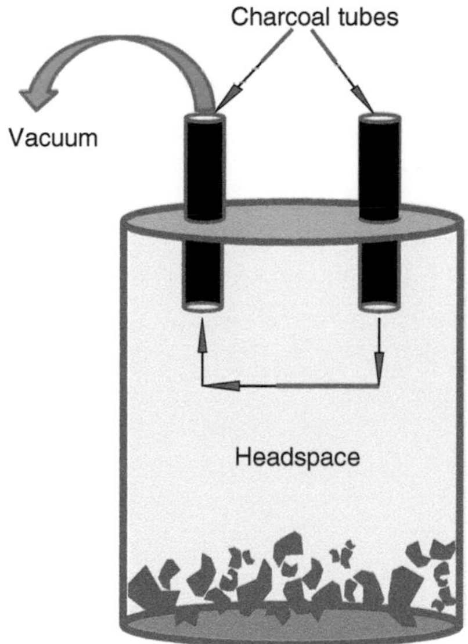

FIGURE 18.8

Absorption-elution. The paint can has two tubes that can trap accelerants. The vacuum pulls air through one tube into the can. Any contaminants in the air that might interfere with the analysis are trapped in the first tube. The headspace vapors are pulled out through the other tube and trapped in the charcoal in the tube.

Courtesy: Meredith Haddon.

Once the accelerant has been adsorbed onto the charcoal or Tenax, then it is eluted off using a suitable solvent. Carbon disulfide (CS_2) has been used for many years for this purpose, but it is toxic and highly flammable. Other solvents have been tried, including butane and pentane, but they are less satisfactory because they are also constituents of many accelerants.

Another variant of the adsorption methods is **solid phase microextraction**. In this method, a fiber made from fused silica is coated with an adsorbent such as charcoal or Tenax. This is inserted into the heated fire residue container. After adsorption is complete, the fiber can be inserted directly into the inlet of a gas chromatograph, where the high heat of the injector zone rapidly elutes the accelerant into the mobile phase stream for analysis. The advantages of this technique are extreme sensitivity and removing the necessity of a separate elution step.

Solvent extraction

Solvent extraction is a very simple and sensitive technique, useable with a wide range of accelerants. The evidence container is opened and a small quantity (depending on the amount of debris in the container) of a suitable solvent is added. Carbon disulfide is the most popular solvent for this process. The solvent is then poured off and filtered and then evaporated to a small volume leaving behind the accelerant residue. This solution can then be introduced into a gas chromatograph. Disadvantages of solvent extraction are, first, that the solvent will also dissolve unwanted pyrolysis products, matrix materials, and other substances, some of which may interfere with the subsequent analysis and second, that evaporation of the solvent may also cause evaporation of some of the volatile components of the accelerant residues.

Steam distillation

This is the oldest technique for isolation of accelerant residues. Some of the accelerant residue is put in a distillation apparatus with some water, which is then boiled and distilled. The steam will heat and carry over accelerant residues. Those that are immiscible with water will form a layer on top of the distilled water. If water-soluble residues suspected to be present, then the first aliquot of water must be collected and analyzed. Steam distillation is not very sensitive and relatively large quantities of matrix are needed. It is not as subject to contamination interferences as is solvent extraction, but it does favor high boiling fractions. It is also the most complicated to run.

ANALYSIS OF FIRE SCENE ACCELERANT RESIDUES BY GC

GC is almost universally employed in crime laboratories for the analysis of fire scene accelerant residues. Today, most laboratories use capillary GC columns for increased sensitivity and efficiency. Increasingly, mass spectrometry has been employed as the detector for the GC to identify certain components of the residues. All of the hydrocarbon accelerants, including gasoline, kerosene-based materials, fuel oils, and other consumer products have many components. Gasoline, for example, is made up of more than 300 substances. In basic GC analysis of accelerant residues, the resulting chromatogram will be a pattern of peaks that is characteristic of the accelerant type. Thus, one can identify an accelerant as gasoline or as a kerosene-based product, for example, but it is generally not possible to identify a specific product or manufacturer by this method.

The key to effective analysis of accelerants by GC is to have a comprehensive library of chromatograms that are obtained preferably on the same instrument as the analysis of unknowns, or at least taken under the same conditions. This library would include not only the various products, brands, and types of accelerants, but also their various forms. For instance, an accelerant may appear in its neat, unburnt form or partially burnt or almost totally consumed. The chromatograms of these materials will be quite different and it would be difficult to tell what is present unless there are good standards for comparison. Figure 18.9(a) and (b) shows chromatograms of pure gasoline and kerosene. Figure 18.10 shows the chromatogram of gasoline headspace.

Mass spectrometry has added flexibility and refinement to GC analysis of fire scene evidence. Individual components of residues can be unequivocally identified. In addition, mass spectrometry provides some features that make it especially valuable in identifying ignitable liquids in the presence of contaminants or in mixtures containing multiple ignitable liquids. The first of these is called **selective ion monitoring**, whereby the mass spectrometer looks for particular ions that are characteristic of particular types of flammables. The other enhancement is called **target compound** analysis. In this technique, a profile of compounds that are present in each type of accelerant, such as gasoline, are monitored by the mass spectrometer. These compounds can be easily identified even in complex mixtures. The mass spectra of individual components of a material such as gasoline can be easily displayed. The mass spectrum of one of the compounds found in gasoline is shown in Figure 18.11.

INTERPRETATION AND ASSOCIATION OF FIRE SCENE EVIDENCE

In a fire scene investigation, there are two major goals: determining the type of fire (e.g., accidental, natural, incendiary) and if the fire was deliberately started, who did it. In most cases, it is not particularly difficult to determine the type of fire. It is much more difficult to determine who committed the crime. Of course, the presence of evidence such as fingerprints, DNA, or trace evidence can be quite useful in determining the identity of the perpetrator. In the absence of such evidence, there is not much else that can provide identification.

When the forensic scientist extracts some of the accelerant residue from the matrix using the methods presented above, the resulting chromatogram seldom

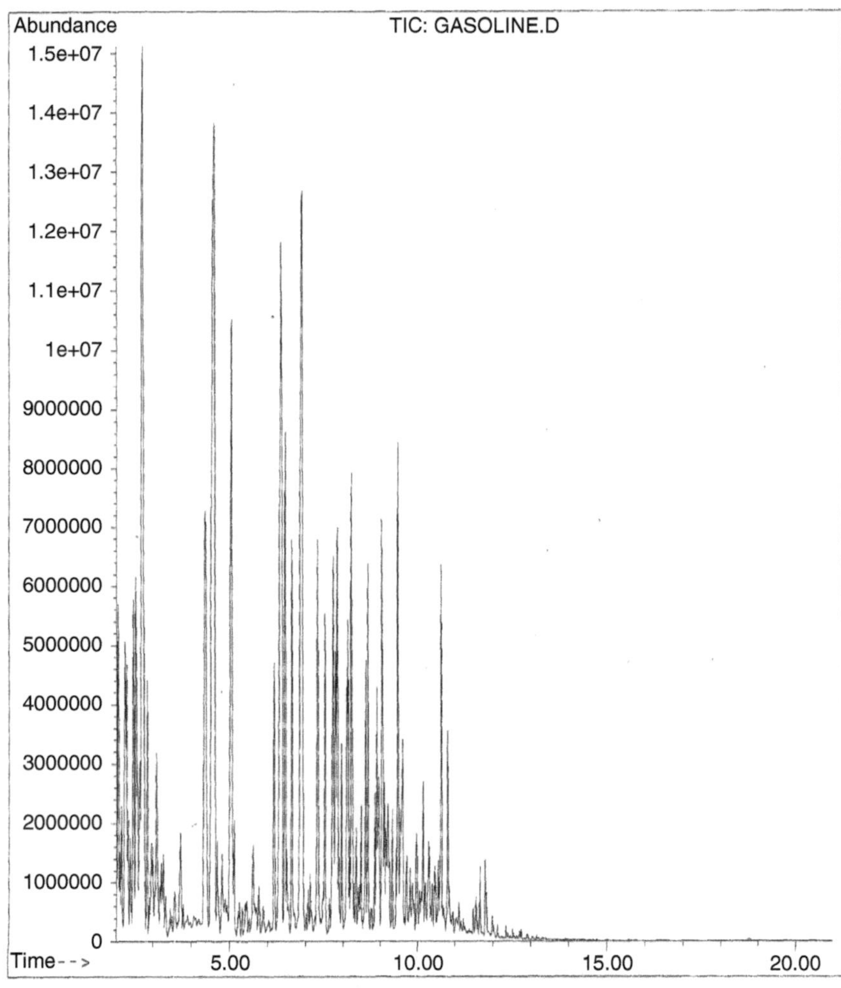

FIGURE 18.9

Chromatograms of neat (pure liquid) gasoline and kerosene. Note how different the patterns in the peaks of these chromatograms are. Gasoline is much more volatile as can be seen by the large number of peaks at the beginning of the run.

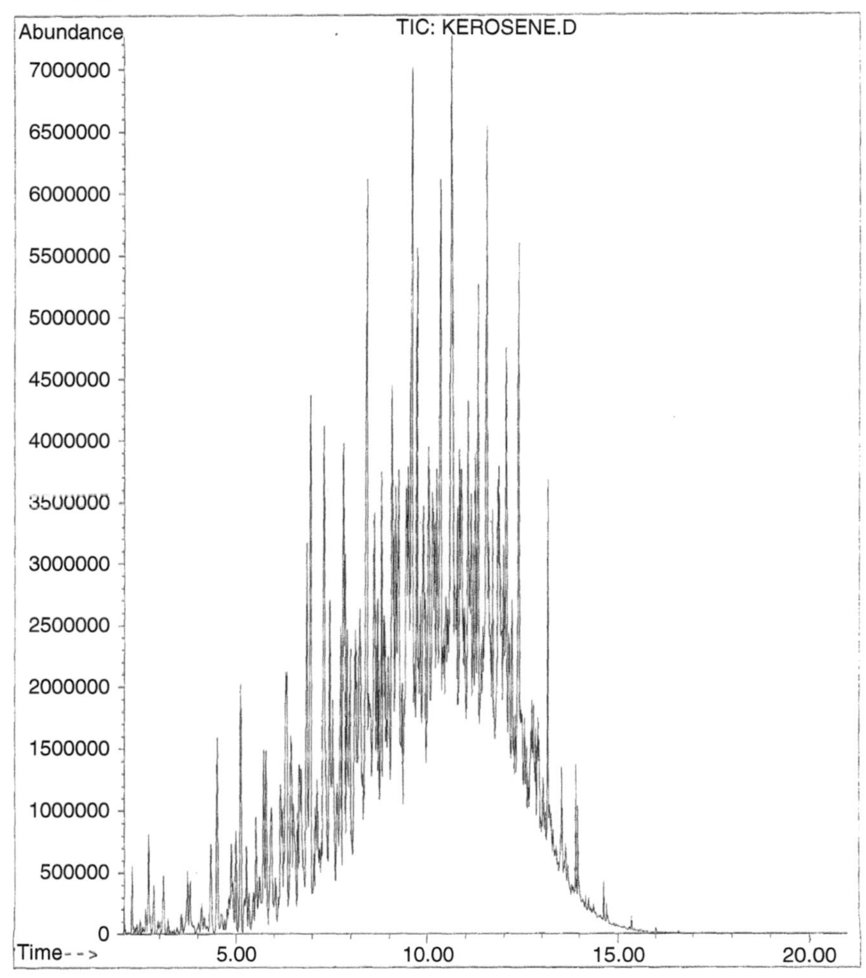

FIGURE 18.9 Cont'd

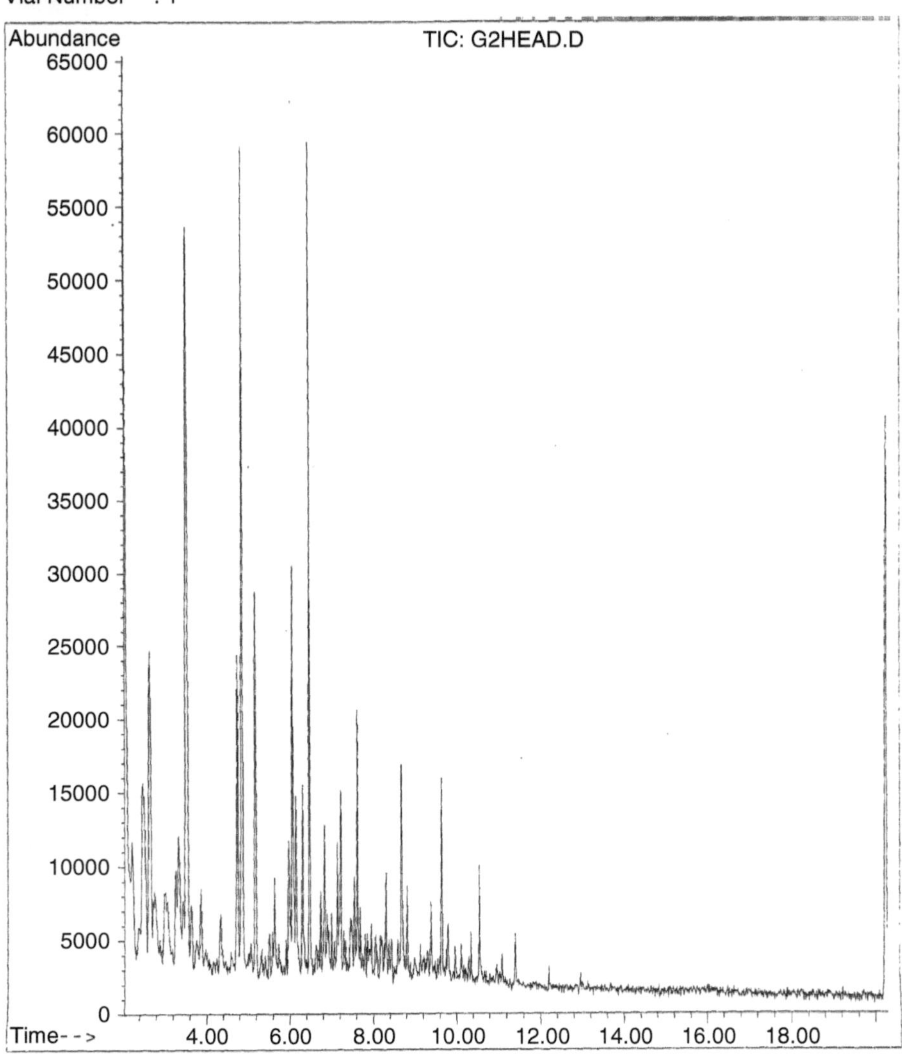

FIGURE 18.10

Chromatogram of gasoline headspace. In this chromatogram, most of the most-volatile peaks that come out early are missing, having been burned off by heat.

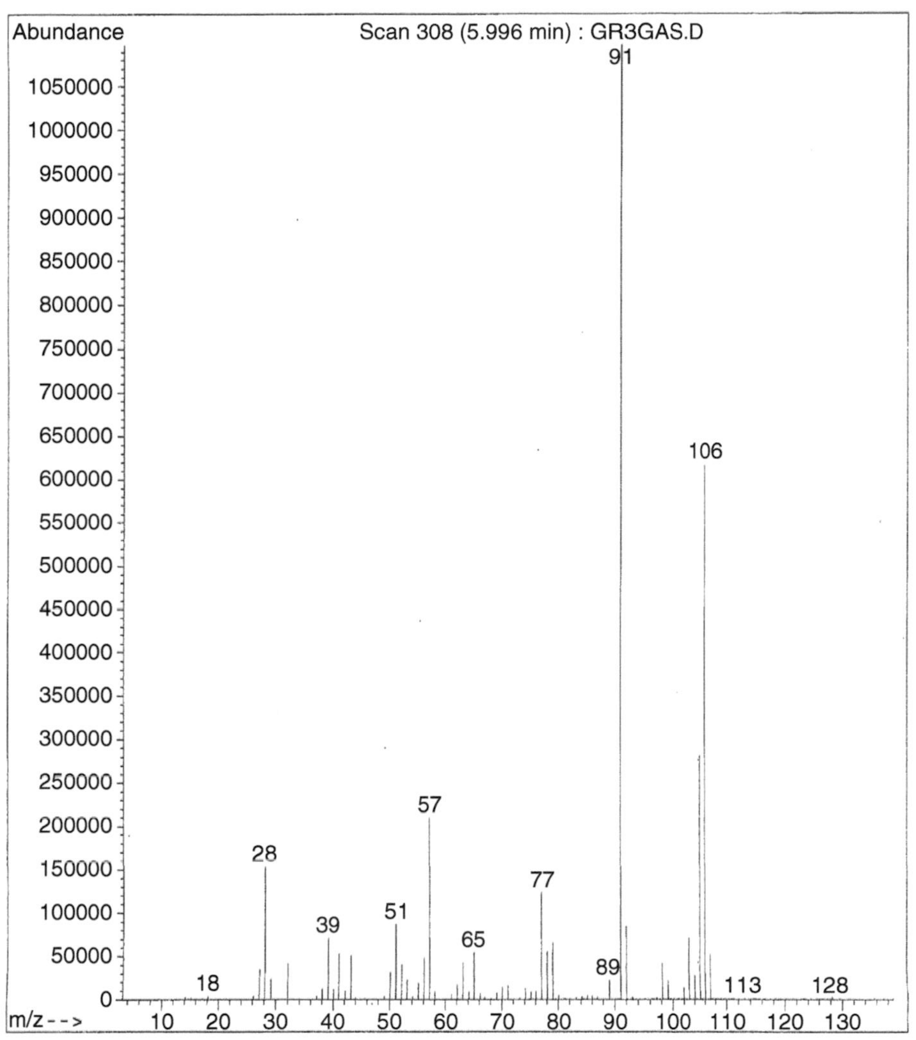

FIGURE 18.11

Mass spectrum of one of the components in a gasoline mixture. This peak pattern is characteristic of normal hydrocarbons.

looks exactly like the standards made from pure samples of various ignitable liquids. Remember that the accelerant has been in a fire and heat may have evaporated some of the more volatile substances away. There may be contamination by the matrix or other materials present. If the scientist is to report that a class or type of accelerant is present, then there must be a clear majority of characteristic peaks present with few if any unexplainable peaks. For example, examine the chromatogram of gasoline liquid in Figure 18.9(a). If a real fire residue sample had some of the early peaks missing, that would be explainable by evaporation caused by heat. But if all of the peaks were present at the beginning and end of the chromatogram but some were missing in the middle, then that would be a circumstance that might necessitate a finding of inconclusive or even negative in the report. A negative finding may also be reached even if there are some indications that an accelerant was used. This can occur when there is not enough material to give a good quality chromatogram or when there is too much contamination to identify the necessary peaks. The term **weathering** is used to describe the degradation of an accelerant due to heat or other environmental factors. It is also important to note that a negative finding in a report does not preclude the presence of an accelerant at a fire. As was pointed out previously, there are several reasons why an accelerant might not be found even it were actually used. It could have been burnt to such an extent that there is not enough left to detect or perhaps the evidence that contained the accelerant residues may have been overlooked. Fire scene investigators always try and take this into account when reaching conclusions about fire causation.

BACK TO THE CASE

This case illustrates a number of issues that have arisen about the investigation of fires in recent years. First, the limited role that the forensic science laboratory has in these types of cases needs to be emphasized. In the Willingham case, a number of samples of burnt materials were submitted for analysis. The laboratory found evidence of a substance that can be used as an accelerant in one location. That was the entire role of the laboratory in this case. The finding of arson was made solely by the fire marshal's office. That is nearly always the case.

In spite of research about fire behavior in the past few decades, there are a number of examples of folklore and myth about how accelerants affect a fire that continue to persist. Many fire scene examiners continue to believe that V-pattern burning, spalling in concrete, crazing in glass, and the appearance of burnt "puddles" on a floor are always indicative of the presence of an accelerant. These conclusions are not supported by science or research. Research approaches have become much more sophisticated and scientifically based. The Federal Bureau of Alcohol, Tobacco, Firearms, and Explosions has developed a fire research laboratory on its campus in Maryland. This laboratory is a self-contained facility for carrying out fires of various types under strictly controlled conditions, using modern computers and technology to monitor and record every aspect of a fire. Almost any type of structure can be used or fabricated at this laboratory to house a fire. Temperatures, the progress of the fires, and damage to various materials are all monitored and recorded. This laboratory and others like it are adding greatly to our knowledge of fires and the role of accelerants. If, in fact, the Willingham fire was misidentified as arson owing to flawed science and training and Cameron Willingham was improperly executed, perhaps accumulating data from more robust research will help prevent this in the future.

EXPLOSIONS AND EXPLOSIVES

If a fuel such as gasoline is confined to a closed space, such as a cylinder in an automobile engine, the fuel and oxygen are compressed, raising their temperature. The spark from the spark plug causes a very rapid combustion to take place. This is called a **conflagration**. The difference between an explosion and a fire in this case is the speed of the reaction. Explosions can also be made to occur without confining the fuel. For example, if the fuel and the oxygen are physically mixed and the oxygen is combined with another element instead of itself, it can be made to explode. An example of this is ANFO—ammonium nitrate (NH_4NO_3) and fuel oil. Pellets of ammonium nitrate are coated with fuel oil. The ammonium nitrate supplies the oxygen that is easily released and very close to the fuel. The resultant combustion is very rapid and is an explosion. ANFO is classified as a **low explosive** because the velocity of the explosion is not as powerful as in the case of more energetic explosives.

It is also possible to combine the oxygen and fuel into a single molecule. In this case, the oxygen and fuel are chemically combined. This is the most advantageous situation for combustion to take place. Such materials undergo **instantaneous combustion** or **detonation**. Of course, the combustion is not really instantaneous, there is always a time lag, but it is even more rapid than in a conflagration. The speed of a detonation is referred to as the **detonation velocity** and these can range from 9000 fps to over 25,000 fps, which works out to be almost 5 miles in 1 s. These are **high explosives**. Examples include trinitrotoluene (TNT) and nitroglycerine (NG).

THE CASE

On April 19, 1995, two men, Timothy McVeigh, with the help from Terry Nichols, detonated a bomb in a truck that was parked directly in front of the Alfred P. Murrah Federal Building in Oklahoma City. The resulting blast destroyed the building, killed 168 people, and left more than 800 people injured. At that time, it was the deadliest act of terrorism in American history. The principals had met during military training along with Michael Fortier, another accomplice in the bombing. The bombing was planned as a form of revenge against the Federal government for its role in the Branch Davidian incident of a few years earlier and the incident at Ruby Ridge, both of which resulted in deaths. The planning for the bombing took more than one year, during which time numerous locations were scouted out. The goal was to kill as many government employees as possible, preferably from law enforcement agencies such as the FBI, the DEA, and the ATF. They also professed to try to avoid killing nongovernmental personnel.

The bomb itself was made from nitromethane and ammonium nitrate fertilizer with associated fuses and blasting caps. Originally they wanted to use hydrazine as the fuel but rejected that because of the expense. Thirteen barrels were filled with the nitromethane/fertilizer mixture and placed in a rental truck in a configuration that would direct maximum force at the building. Ultimately, the truck contained more than three tons of explosive mixture. Before the truck was parked, two delay fuses were set so that McVeigh could escape the blast. The blast was very widespread and destructive; half of the Murrah Building was destroyed. More than 300 buildings were damaged, and some blocks were away from the site. Many cars were also destroyed or damaged. The detonation was estimated to be the equivalent of an earthquake of magnitude 3.0 (Richter scale), measured nearly 20 miles away.

EFFECTS OF EXPLOSIONS

The effects of an explosion can all be explained by understanding what happens when a conflagration or detonation takes place. Solid and/or liquid fuels combine with oxygen to form gaseous products such as carbon dioxide, and other products that are converted to gases from the heat of the combustion. These very hot gases expand rapidly away from the origin of the explosion (**the bomb seat**). These rapidly moving gases create three primary effects: **blast pressure**, **fragmentation, and thermal or heat effects**.

Blast Pressure

Escaping gases can travel as much as 8000 miles per hour and exert hundreds of tons per square inch of pressure. This compresses the gases and the surrounding air. The wave that is created by this blast will shatter anything that gets in its way. The damage decreases with distance as the wave loses energy. As the blast wave travels away from the bomb seat, it creates a partial vacuum because the air itself has been displaced. When the blast wave dissipates, the vacuum must be filled. The compressed air and gases now rush back toward the bomb seat. This causes another blast effect, the **negative pressure phase**. This is not as powerful as the positive pressure blast phase but it is capable of doing additional serious damage to objects that have already been damaged by the initial blast. The two phases of a blast can be seen in Figure 18.12(a)–(d).

Fragmentation Effects

Fragmentation damage from a bomb can occur in several ways. First, the bomb casing itself can shatter and the pieces can be propelled away from the bomb seat with great force. Second, the bomber may wrap nails or other pieces of metal around the bomb to create shrapnel that will cause fragmentation damage. Finally, the blast may break up objects in its way that may also fragment and be propelled.

Thermal Effects

Thermal or temperature effects are generally the least damaging of the effects of an explosion. At the instant of detonation a large ball of fire or flash is produced at the bomb seat. This will be very hot and very brief if a high explosive is used and will be longer in duration but not as hot in the case of low explosives. The flash usually dies very quickly and no further effects will be seen unless there is combustible material nearby the blast, in which case secondary fires may be ignited.

TYPES OF EXPLOSIVES

Explosives are commonly categorized by the velocity of the explosion or detonation. This gives rise to two types of explosives: low explosives and high explosives.

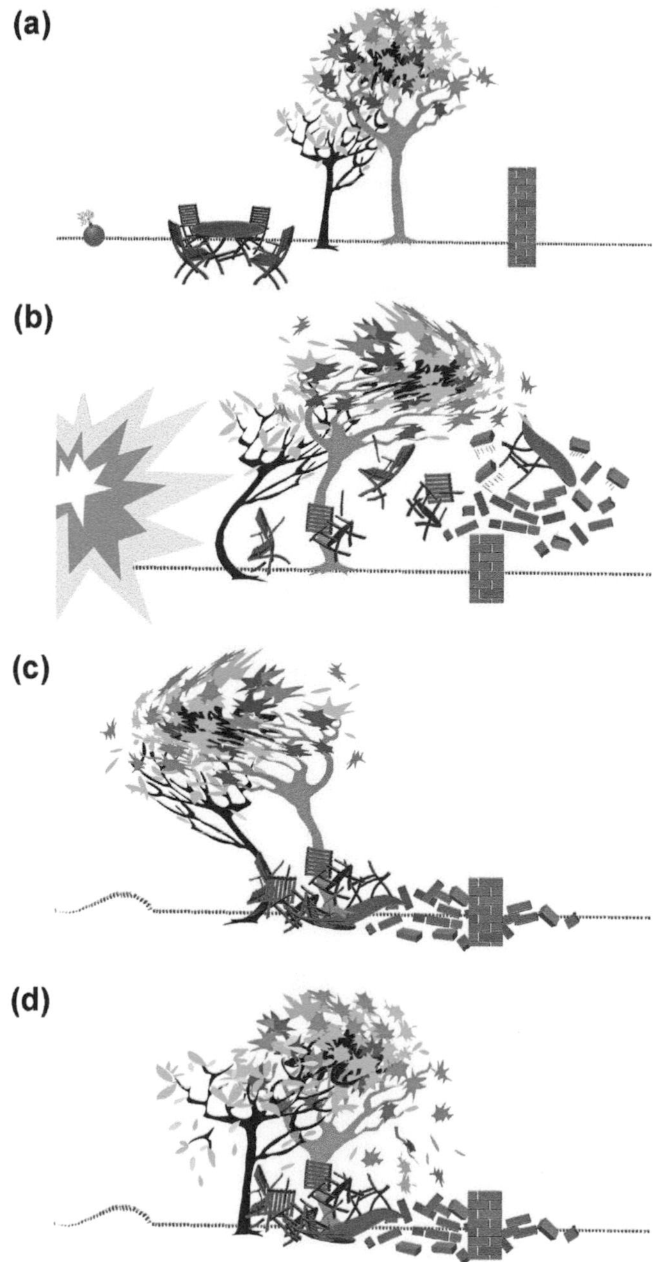

FIGURE 18.12

Positive and negative phases of blast pressure during an explosion. Note how the damage can be strewn around the site and cannot be explained by just the positive pressure phase. The negative pressure phase can cause considerable damage. (a) The scene before the blast; (b) the damage from the positive pressure phase; (c) the damage after the negative pressure phase; and (d) the scene after the explosion is over.

Courtesy: Meredith Haddon.

Low Explosives

By definition, **low explosives** have detonation velocities below 3280 fps. In low explosives, the oxygen is physically mixed with the fuel and the explosion takes place at a slower rate than would be the case if the fuel and oxygen were chemically combined. As a result, the main effect of low explosives is to push rather than to shatter. A common low explosive, smokeless powder, is used in weapons to propel a bullet away from the cartridge and out of the barrel of the gun without causing the weapon to blow apart. Low explosives are also often used in blasting operations when it is desired to push earth or other material out of the way. Smokeless powder consists of small particles containing nitrocellulose (single base) or nitrocellulose and NG (double base). Low explosives such as smokeless powder and black powder are used in pipe bombs. Black powder is a finely milled mixture of carbon, sulfur, and potassium nitrate. Here the explosive is confined inside a metal or plastic pipe. As the explosion takes place, pressure builds up inside the bomb until it shatters. Low explosives can be easily set off by using a flame, a spark, or chemicals such as acids.

High Explosives

High explosives have detonation rates above 3280 fps. Some dynamites, for example, have rates as low as 6000 fps, whereas some military explosives approach 28,000 fps. These explosives are designed to shatter objects and destroy them. The mechanism by which high explosives detonate is quite different than for low explosives. The latter are generally granular and at ignition, the burning travels from one particle to the next. Most high explosives, on the other hand, require a severe shock to get them to detonate. This can be accomplished using a blasting cap or a primary or **initiating** explosive. When these explode they create a strong shock wave that shatters the chemical bonds that hold molecules of fuel and oxygen together. Detonation takes place and this travels from molecule to molecule, picking up speed along the way so that the end result is practically instantaneous detonation.

There are two types of high explosives: **initiating (primary)** and **noninitiating (secondary)**.

Initiating high explosives

Initiating high explosives are usually very powerful and very sensitive. Even the slightest shock or spark can be enough to cause detonation. For this reason, they are used only in very small quantities, usually to detonate less sensitive explosives in **explosive trains**. Examples include pure NG and mercury fulminate. Figure 18.13 shows chemical structures of some common initiating high explosives.

Noninitiating high explosives

These are explosives that are not sensitive and it usually takes a good deal of effort to cause detonation. These explosives can be easily transported and used without fear of accidental detonation. They are generally so insensitive that it takes a major shock, such as that supplied by a nearby initiating explosive in an explosive train, to get them to detonate. Examples include many dynamites and the military explosive, C4.

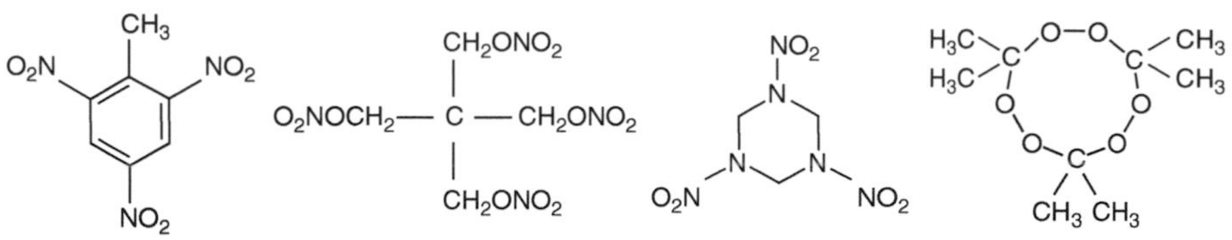

FIGURE 18.13

Structures of cyclotrimethylenetrinitramine (RDX), pentaerythritol tetranitrate (PETN), triacetone triperoxide (TATP) and trinitrotoluene (TNT). Note the large numbers of oxygen atoms that are part of the chemical structure of these materials. They react explosively and instantly with the carbon, hydrogen, and nitrogen atoms present, once the reaction is activated.

IN MORE DEPTH: THE WORLD TRADE CENTER BOMBING

On February 26, 1993, just afternoon a homemade explosive device was detonated on the second level of the parking garage in the World Trade Center in New York. The bomb was made from a commercial fertilizer known as urea nitrate. It weighed about 1400 lbs. The initiator for the explosive was lead azide. This was ignited using a burning fuse with a 20 min delay. Also incorporated into the bomb were three pressurized tanks of hydrogen gas, which is extremely flammable. This bomb had been placed in the cargo area of a Ford van, which was then left in a parking garage underneath Building One of the World Trade Center. The explosion produced a huge crater that extended five floors deep in the garage and was approximately 150 ft in diameter. The garage structure was mainly steel-reinforced concrete and was at least 1 ft thick in most places. Six people were killed by the blast and more than 1000 were injured. The entire World Trade Center complex was evacuated; more than 50,000 people. The crime scene was one of complete devastation. In addition to the thousands of tons of rubble, there was no light to see by and several water and sewer lines were ruptured, pouring millions of gallons of water and sewage into the crater. It took more than a week for 300 law enforcement agents from around the country to sift through the rubble and piece together the cause of the explosion. The damage done by the explosive was characteristic of a heaving or pushing rather than shattering. It was surmised that the escaping gases had a velocity of around 15,000 ft per second. There are a number of explosives that have these characteristics, and some fertilizer-based devices are among them. The FBI and ATF sent chemists to the scene and a makeshift laboratory was set up. Fragments were found that led to the identification of the van that carried the explosive and the explosive itself. Ultimately, four men were convicted of this terrorist bombing.

HIGH- AND LOW-ORDER EXPLOSIONS

There are two other terms that describe explosions that sometimes cause confusion. **Low- and High-Order Explosions** have nothing to do with a type of explosive, but instead, describe the efficiency of a particular explosion. A high-order explosion is one that occurs at or near its maximum theoretical detonation velocity. It is the explosion that you get if everything works out right. A low-order explosion, on the other hand, is one that takes place at less than optimal efficiency. This can be due to any of a number of factors. These include:

- Old, out-of-date explosive
- Explosive that is subject to excessive moisture or humidity
- Improperly constructed explosive device
- Improper placement of the device

EXPLOSIVE TRAINS

Sometimes it is necessary to use one explosion to set off another. Other times it may be desirable to have a series of explosions take place in a particular order. These situations may require the use of an **explosive train**. Explosive trains may contain as few as two steps or up to four or more. They are classified as low or high, depending upon whether the final explosive in the train is a high or low explosive. Examples of low- and high-explosive trains will be considered below.

Low-Explosive Trains

These are usually two-step trains. One example would be a pipe bomb wherein a fuse made of black powder is used to detonate smokeless powder inside the pipe. This would be classified as a low-explosive train because the final explosive, the smokeless powder, is a low explosive.

High-Explosive Trains

In high-explosive trains, the final explosive is usually a secondary explosive. The detonator may be a blasting cap or other suitable primary explosive. In between, there may be other secondary high explosives that act as boosters. See Figure 18.14 for an example of an explosive train.

ANALYSIS OF EXPLOSIVES

Two major types of explosive residues are encountered in bombs; undetonated explosive and exploded residues that are products or side products of the explosion.

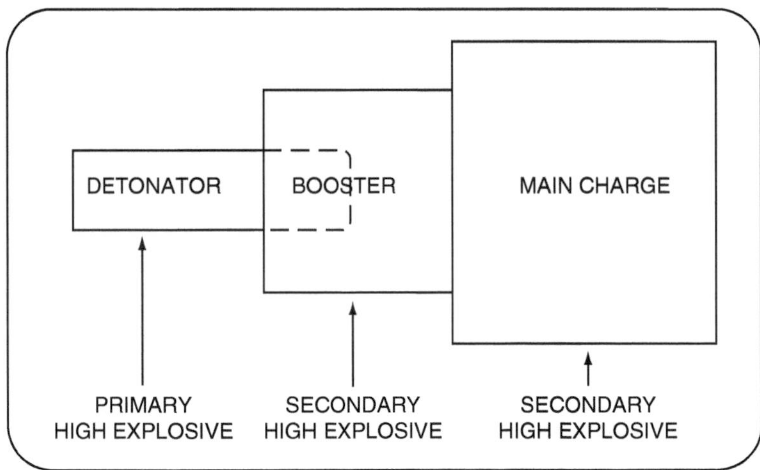

FIGURE 18.14

An explosive train made of high explosives. The detonator is made of an initiating explosive. The booster and main charge are noninitiating.

In addition, the bomb seat area may yield parts of the device that were used to hold the explosive and set it off. Those cases where undetonated explosive is found are the easiest to analyze because the exact explosive can be identified. In those cases where no exploded residue can be located, the analytical situation is more complex because it may be difficult to distinguish explosive residue from materials that are present in the normal environment. For example, in the case of black powder, various nitrate-containing compounds are the products of the explosion. Many of these are found naturally in soil and it may be difficult to determine their origin. This requires care in interpretation of a finding of explosive residues where no intact explosive is found. Finding bomb device parts can be a huge advantage in reconstructing the explosion. From surprisingly few pieces of device, an explosives examiner may be able to tell the type of device, how it was detonated, and perhaps what part of the world it came from and who made it. This has obvious advantages in terrorism situations.

The Vapor Trace Analyzer

To aid sifting through evidence to find explosive residues from the scene, a **vapor trace analyzer** or other, similar detector is often employed. The VTA is a specialized gas chromatograph that is optimized for explosives. The VTA utilizes a type of headspace analysis wherein vapors from the explosive residue are introduced into a collector and the polar explosive residues are isolated and chromatographed. A special detector, called an **electron capture detector** is used to detect the presence of explosive residues.

Visual Examination

In order to analyze explosive residues, they must be isolated from the matrix in which they are found at the crime scene. The best way to do this is by manually removing them under a low power microscope. This is often a tedious and time-consuming activity but can pay dividends later. Isolated residues can be more easily characterized without having to be concerned about the presence of impurities. More importantly, the forensic scientist can testify that actual particles of explosive were recovered from the debris and were chemically identified. If no large particles of undetonated explosive can be isolated, then it may be necessary to dissolve microscopic particles with a suitable solvent and remove them from the debris. This is a lot faster than manual sifting but suffers from several disadvantages. First, other substances may also dissolve so the explosive residue is not really being purified. Second, many explosives have components that are ionic, such as potassium nitrate; KNO_3. When this material is dissolved, it dissociates into potassium and nitrate ions. The resulting analysis indicates that the ions were present but not the actual compound. One could argue that these ions could have arisen from any of a number of sources and this doesn't prove that an explosive is present.

Instrumental and Other Methods of Analysis

Once an explosive residue has been isolated from bomb debris then it should be further characterized and ultimately, identified. A variety of techniques can be used depending upon the amount and type of explosive available. Various types of chromatography and infrared spectrophotometry are widely used for this purpose.

Thin-layer chromatography

Many explosives can be conveniently separated by thin-layer chromatography (TLC). These include many low and high explosives, including smokeless powder, dynamites, TNT, etc. Known explosives are normally spotted on the TLC plate (see Chapter 5) along with the unknowns so that the identifications can be more certain. A number of specific stationary and mobile phase combinations have been used for various classes of explosives. Several visualizing reagents have also been employed. For example, **Griess** reagent has been employed extensively because they will color most nitrate-containing species bright red. Most explosives have nitro groups making Griess reagent very versatile. Figure 18.15 shows three thin-layer chromatograms of some explosives sprayed with Griess reagent.

High performance liquid chromatography

High performance liquid chromatography (HPLC) is also useful for the analysis of explosive residues. It has advantages over TLC in that it can be used for quantitative analysis, should this be called for and it doesn't require the use of visualizing reagents. It is preferred of GC because high concentrations of explosives can cause problems with the high temperatures used in GC. Modern liquid chromatographs are outfitted with mass spectrometers as detectors, making the identification of explosives that have been separated from bomb debris much easier.

Capillary electrophoresis

Capillary electrophoresis (CE) is similar in some ways to HPLC but operates on somewhat different principles. It has some advantages over HPLC, the major one

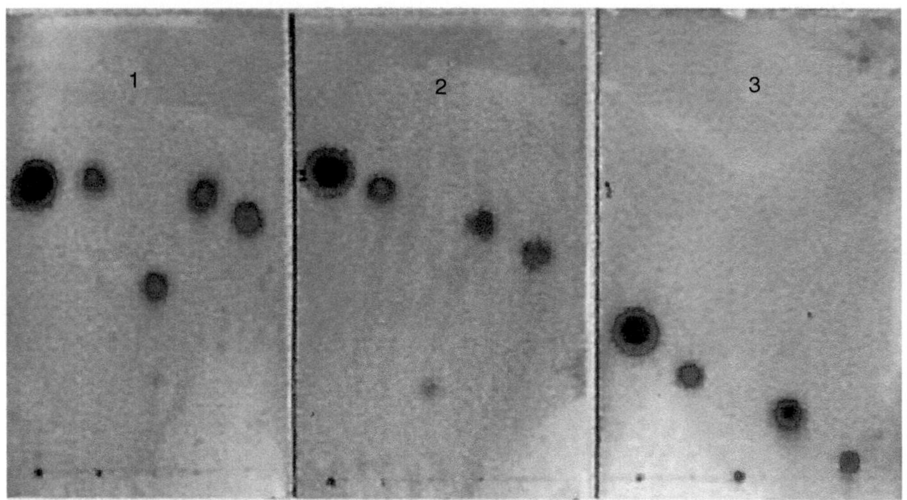

FIGURE 18.15

Three thin layer chromatograms of explosive mixtures. The red spots are where explosives are. The plates were treated with Griess reagents, which react with nitrate-containing compounds to produce the red color. PETN, pentaerythritol tetranitrate; RDX, cyclotrimethylenetrinitramine; TNT, trinitrotoluene; NG, nitroglycerine.

being the amount of sample required. CE is very sensitive and only tiny amounts of material are needed for analysis. This can be a real advantage when only trace amounts of explosive residue are present.

Infrared spectrophotometry

Because chromatographic methods provide only a tentative identification, a confirmatory test, IR, is often used. A variety of sample types can be used for IR including solids, liquids, mulls, and solutions. Similar compounds such as TNT and DNT (dinitrotoluene) can be differentiated by IR. See Figure 18.16 for the infrared spectrum of TNT.

> **BACK TO THE CASE**
>
> The Oklahoma City bombing illustrates the incredible power of confined explosions. 6000 pounds of explosive shaped toward the Murrah building blew out windows in buildings blocks away and was heard more than 50 miles away. Many bodies and survivors were buried in the rubble of the building. Cadaver dogs and even flies were used to locate bodies. Residues of the explosive were found in the rubble and in the crater left by the blast next to and underneath the truck. Even though the objective was the same, there are some interesting differences between the Oklahoma City bombing and the World Trade Center bombing. Both involved fertilizer based explosives in rental trucks. In the case of the World Trade Center, the truck was parked under the building in a parking garage. Much of the force of that blast was absorbed by the parking structure and all of the vehicles parked there. There was not nearly enough explosive to bring down the building, which was the goal of the terrorists who set off the explosion. In the Oklahoma City case, the truck was parked in the open, right outside the building, and there was nothing to soak up the energy of the explosion except the Murrah building. As a result, much more damage was done to that building.
>
> It is ironic that, during the trial of the men who engineered the World Trade Center bombing, there was testimony about the ability of the Center buildings to withstand a plane crash. This may have had a relationship to the destruction of the Center buildings a decade later.

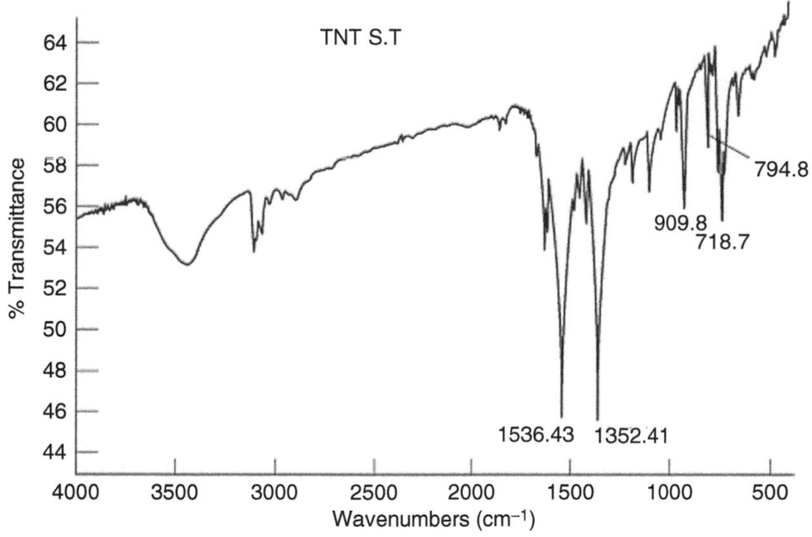

FIGURE 18.16

Infrared spectrum of trinitrotoluene (TNT).

SUMMARY

Fires and explosions are both the result of combustion reactions, where a fuel and oxygen react, sometimes violently and instantaneously to give off large amounts of energy. In fires, the combustion takes place relatively slowly because the fuel and the oxygen are separated, the oxygen being supplied by the air surrounding the fuel. The oxygen is in molecular form and these bonds must be broken before the oxygen can be used. Also, the fuel must be a vapor before it will burn. This also takes time and energy. A fire can be made to simulate an explosion by confining it to a closed space, as is the case with the combustion of gasoline in the cylinders of an internal combustion engine.

In explosions, the fuel and oxygen are more intimately mixed. In low explosions, the oxygen is present in molecules such as potassium nitrate. This oxygen is more readily available than in molecular oxygen form. In high explosions, the oxygen is actually chemically incorporated into the fuel and combustion is practically instantaneous.

In order to determine if a fire is arson (deliberately set), all accidental and natural causes of the fire must be eliminated. This is done by finding the point of origin of the fire and looking for particular characteristics. Many arson fires are set using an accelerant and hopefully, some of these residues will also be recovered. The nature of the accelerant is determined by GC after the accelerant is isolated by extraction.

In the investigation of an explosion, the point of origin, or bomb seat, must be located. This is where residues of the explosive are most likely to be found as well as parts of the device used to set off the bomb.

TEST YOUR KNOWLEDGE

1. What is the fire triangle? How is it important in explaining the elements necessary to have a fire?
2. What is an oxidation reaction? Give an example.
3. What is a combustion reaction? Give an example.
4. How do fire extinguishers work in general?
5. What does "exothermic" mean? Give an example of an exothermic reaction.
6. What is a flashpoint?
7. What is an accelerant? Give an example.
8. One of the possible types of fire is accidental. What are the others?
9. In order to determine that a fire is arson, what must a fire scene investigator be able to do?
10. Why is finding the point of origin of a fire so important in determining the cause of the fire?
11. What is the crucial difference between a fire and an explosion?

12. How is a detonation defined? Why do some explosives detonate while others do not?
13. What is an initiating explosive? A noninitiating explosive?
14. What is an explosive train? When are they used?
15. What is the difference between a high-explosive and a high-order explosion?
16. What characteristics of fuel and oxygen give rise to a high explosive?
17. What is smokeless powder? What type of explosive is this and where is it used?
18. How are explosive residues collected? Where is the most important place to look?
19. Why is it so important to be able to recover intact residues of unexploded material?
20. What is Griess reagent? What type of explosives is it used to help analyze?

CONSIDER THIS...

1. Both fires and explosions involve the same type of chemical reactions. They can be differentiated by the velocity of the gases that escape from the point of origin. Explain how the arrangements of the various reactants help dictate the power of the reactions and thus the velocity of escaping gases.
2. In the explosion that took place at the Murrah building, it was determined that ANFO was the explosive used. What are the reasons why someone would use this as an explosive? Why wouldn't the perpetrators have used dynamite or nitroglycerine? What could have been done to the truck containing the explosive to maximize the damage to the building?
3. The most popular methods of concentrating accelerant residues from a fire involve either active or passive adsorption onto charcoal. Explain why these methods are preferred over headspace, distillation, or solvent extraction methods.

FURTHER READING

DeHaan, J., 1991. Kirk's Fire Investigation, third ed. Prentice-Hall, Englewood Cliffs, NJ.

Redsiker, D., O'Connor, J., 1997. Practical Fire and Arson Investigation, second ed. CRC Press, New York.

Fire investigation. In: Siegel, J. (Ed.), 2000. Encyclopedia of Forensic Science. Academic Press, London.

Urbanski, T., 1964. Chemistry and Technology of Explosives, vols. 1–3. Pergamon Press, Oxford.

Yinon, J., Zitrin, S., 1991. The Analysis of Explosives. Pergamon Press, Oxford.

Yinon, J., Zitrin, S., 1993. Modern Methods and Applications in Analysis of Explosives. John Wiley, Chichester.

ON THE WEB

http://en.wikipedia.org/wiki/Arson. Good overview of fire and arson.

http://www.iii.org/media/hottopics/insurance/test1/. Lots of statistics on arson fires in United States.

http://www.interfire.org/. Excellent Website on fires and fire investigation.

http://www.youtube.com/watch?v=wcmmLvAYqkI. Video footage of major explosions.

http://www.chicagotribune.com/topic/disasters-accidents/emergency-incidents/explosions/03014001.topic. A collection of newspaper accounts of major explosions.

PART

Physical Sciences

5

CHAPTER

Friction Ridge Examination

19

CHAPTER OUTLINE

KEY TERMS

- Accidental
- Amido black
- Aqueous amido black
- Aqueous leucocrystal violet
- Arches
- Automated Fingerprint Identification Systems
- Bertillonage
- Central pocket loop
- Core
- Delta
- DFO

- Double loop
- Fingerprint powder
- Gentian crystal violet
- Glue fuming
- Iodine
- Latent prints
- Level 1 detail
- Level 2 detail
- Level 3 detail
- Loops
- Minutiae
- Ninhydrin
- Partial prints
- Patent prints
- Physical developer
- Plain arch
- Plain whorl
- Point-counting standard
- Primary classification
- Primary friction ridges
- Radial loop
- Secondary friction ridges
- Small particle reagent
- Sudan black
- Tented arch
- Type lines
- Ulnar loop
- Vacuum metal deposition
- Whorls

THE CASE: THE MADRID TRAIN BOMBING AND BRANDON MAYFIELD

A coordinated attack on a Spanish commuter train on March 11, 2004 killed 191 people and wounded 1800 in Madrid, Spain. Ten explosions occurred aboard four trains within 3 min of each other during the morning commute; three unexploded improvised explosive devices (IEDs) were found and detonated in a controlled fashion by police. In the course of the investigation, Brandon Mayfield, an American attorney living in Oregon, was linked to the Madrid bombings by a fingerprint found on a plastic bag at one of the scenes. Mayfield was held in jail for 2 weeks as a material witness. The fingerprint identification was later found to be erroneous. The Mayfield case is an excellent case study in laboratory process, confirmation bias, and quality assurance improvement.

INTRODUCTION

From the early days of complicated body measurements to today's sophisticated biometric devices, the identification of individuals by their bodies has been a mainstay of government and law enforcement. Fingerprints are the current leader in identification markers, especially in forensic science. Recent court challenges, however, have brought fingerprining into the spotlight again and may force some changes and questions regarding whether it is considered to be a science.

THE NATURAL-BORN CRIMINAL

Cesare Lombroso's theory of *l'umo delinquente*—the criminal man—influenced the entire history of criminal identification and criminology. Lombroso, an Italian physician in the late-1800s, espoused the idea that criminals "are evolutionary throwbacks in our midst...[and] these people are innately driven to act as a normal ape or savage would, but such behavior is considered criminal in our civilized society" (Gould, 1996, p. 153). He maintained that criminals could be identified because of the unattractive characteristics they had, their external features reflecting their internal aberrations. While normal "civilized" people may occasionally commit crimes, natural-born criminals could not escape their mark.

Lombroso's comparison of criminals to apes made those of the lower classes and "foreigners" most similar to criminals: The "nature" of criminals was reflected in the structure of Lombroso's society. His list of criminal "traits" sounds laughable to us today: Criminals were said to have large jaws, large faces, long arms, low and narrow foreheads, large ears, excess hair, darker skin, insensitivity to pain, and an inability to blush! It's easy to see the racial stereotypes of Lombroso's description, how society's "others" were automatically identified as criminal.

The idea of identifying "natural-born killers" caught the attention of many anthropologists and law enforcement officials in the late-1800s and, even though Lombroso's work was later repudiated (many of his assertions were not supported by objective data), it spawned a great deal of activity in the search for real, measurable traits that would assist the police in identifying criminals. One of them, a French police clerk named Alphonse Bertillon (Ber-TEE-yin), devised a complex system of anthropometric measurements, photographs, and a detailed description (which he called a *portrait parlé*) in 1883; it was later to be called **Bertillonage**, after its inventor. At that time, the body was considered to be constant and, as Lombroso's work then maintained, reflective of one's inner nature. Bertillon's system was devised to quantify the body; by his method, Bertillon hoped to identify criminals as they were arrested and booked for their transgressions. Repeat offenders, those whom we would today call career criminals or recidivists, were at that time considered a particular problem to European police agencies. The growing capitals and cities of Europe allowed for a certain anonymity, and criminals were free to travel from city to city or country to country, changing their names along the way as they plied their illegal trades. Bertillon hoped that his new system would allow the identification of criminals, no matter where they appeared and, thus, help authorities keep track of undesirables (Cole, 2001).

Bertillonage was considered the premier method of identification for at least two decades—despite its limitations. The entire Bertillonage of a person was a complicated and involved process requiring an almost obsessive attention to detail. This made it difficult to standardize and, therefore, replicate accurately. Bertillon often lamented the lack of skill he saw in operators he himself had not trained. If the way the measurements were taken varied, then the same person might not be identified as such by two different operators. The portrait parlé added distinctive descriptors to aid the identification process, but here, again, the adjectives lacked precise objective definitions. "Lips might be 'pouting,' 'thick or thin,' 'upper or lower prominent,' with 'nasolabial height great or little' with or without a 'border'" writes Simon Cole, quoting from Bertillon's own instruction manual (2001, p. 39). What was meant by pouting, prominent, or little was better defined in Bertillon's mind than in the manual.

Bertillonage was used across Britain and in its colonies, especially India. The officials in the Bengal office were concerned with its utility, however. They wondered if Bertillonage could distinguish individuals within the Indian population. Another concern the Bengali officials had with Bertillonage was the inconsistency between operators. There were variations in the way operators took the measurements: Some rounded the results up and some rounded them down, and some operators even decided which measurements were to be taken and which ones could be ignored. Staff in the Bengal office even attempted to solve the variance problem by mechanizing the system. All these variances made searches tedious, difficult, and ultimately prone to error, defeating the point of using the method. The problem became so extreme that the Bengal office dropped Bertillonage entirely except for one small component of the system: fingerprints.

Maintaining this component of the Bertillonage system begged for a way to classify fingerprints systematically and this was the limiting factor in the adoption of any identification system. Bertillonage was too cumbersome and finicky to systematize for quick sorting, as were photographs. Additionally, with the growing number of individuals who were being logged in to police records, any system of identification had to be able to handle hundreds, thousands, and eventually thousands of thousands of records quickly, correctly, and remotely.

FINGERPRINTING IN THE UNITED STATES

The first known systematic use of fingerprint identification in the United States occurred in 1902 in New York City. The New York Civil Service Commission faced a scandal in 1900 when several job applicants were discovered to have hired better-educated persons to take their civil service exams for them. The New York Civil Service Commission therefore began fingerprinting applicants to verify their identity for entrance exams and to prevent better-qualified persons taking tests for unscrupulous applicants. The first set of fingerprints was taken on December 19, 1902 and was the first use of fingerprints by a government agency in the United States (Cole, 2001).

Also in 1902, officials from the New York State Prison Department and the New York State Hospital traveled to England to study the British fingerprint system. The following year, the New York state prison system began to use fingerprints for the identification of criminals; the use of fingerprinting increased even more when the United States Penitentiary in Leavenworth, Kansas, established a fingerprint bureau. This was the first use of fingerprints for criminal identification in the United States. During the 1904 World's Fair in St Louis, John K. Ferrier of Scotland Yard taught the techniques and methods of fingerprinting to the public and law enforcement. Because of the notoriety of the fair and novelty of fingerprints as a "modern" method, the public and professional awareness of fingerprinting was greatly enhanced in the United States (Wilson and Wilson, 2003).

The first US criminal conviction using fingerprint evidence occurred in Chicago, in the case of Thomas Jennings. Charles Hiller had been murdered during a burglary, and Jennings was charged and tried for the crime and ultimately convicted in 1911. The International Association for Identification (IAI) was formed in 1915 initially as a professional association for "Bertillon clerks," but as fingerprinting grew and eventually replaced Bertillonage, the focus of the IAI also changed. *The Fingerprint Instructor* by Frederick Kuhne was published in 1916 and is considered the first authoritative textbook on fingerprinting in the United States.

The growing need for a national repository and clearinghouse for fingerprint records led to an Act of Congress on July 1, 1921, that established the Identification Division of the FBI in Washington, DC, in 1924. A boost to the noncriminal use of fingerprinting came in 1933 when the United States Civil Service Commission (now the Office of Personnel Management) submitted over 140,000 government employee and applicant fingerprints to the FBI's Identification Division; this prompted the FBI to establish a Civil Identification Section, whose fingerprint files would eventually expand well beyond the criminal files. In 1992, the Identification Division was renamed the Criminal Justice Information Services (CJIS) Division and is now housed in Clarksburg, West Virginia. The increasing use of biological identification methods, or biometrics, continues to expand the use of fingerprinting; see "In More Detail: Biometrics and Forensic Science" for more information.

IN MORE DETAIL: BIOMETRICS AND FORENSIC SCIENCE

The terms "biometrics" and "biometry" have been used since early in the twentieth century to refer to the field of development of statistical and mathematical methods applicable to data analysis problems in the biological sciences, such as the analysis of data from the yields of different varieties of wheat or data from human clinical trials evaluating the relative effectiveness of competing therapies for a disease. Recently, the term "biometrics" has also been used to refer to the emerging field of technology devoted to automated methods for authentication of individuals using physiological and behavioral traits, such as retinal or iris scans, fingerprints, hand geometry, face recognition, handwriting, and gait.

(Continued)

IN MORE DETAIL: BIOMETRICS AND FORENSIC SCIENCE—cont'd

Forensic science and biometrics both apply various identification sciences, some the same and some unique to the particular discipline, although they do so for very different reasons (see Figure 19.1). Biometrics uniformly applies to a *pre-event situation*, such as gaining access, surveillance, or

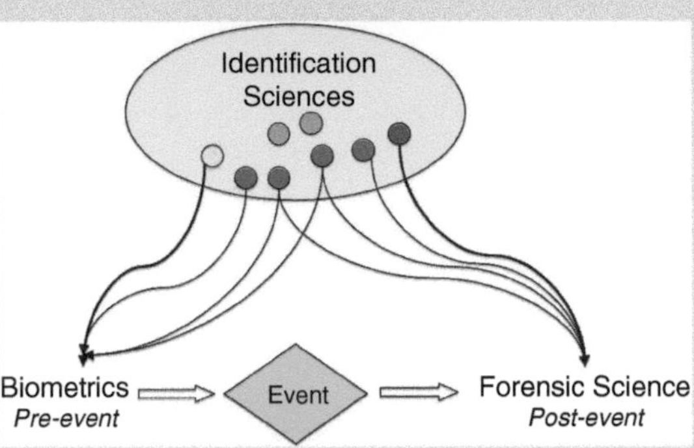

FIGURE 19.1

Biometrics versus forensic science.

verification. In this way, biometrics chooses which mode of identification will be used. Forensic science, however, applies to *post-event situations*; as a historical science, forensic science reconstructs past criminal events to assist adjudication. Some of the identification sciences may be used by both forensic science and biometrics (blue), some may be used by only one or the other (yellow and red) or await application (purple). Because forensic scientists never know which mode of identification will be used ahead of time (DNA, fingerprints, dentition, etc.), they must sort through all the information to discern significant clues. This highlights another important difference between the two disciplines: The results of a forensic science report may ultimately end up in court, whereas those of a biometric analysis rarely do.

For more about biometrics, see Woodward et al. (2003).

WHAT ARE FRICTION RIDGES?

Friction ridges appear on the palms, soles, and the ends of the fingers and toes (see Figure 19.2). These ridges are found on the palms and soles of all primates (humans, apes, monkeys, and prosimians); in primates with prehensile tails ("fingerlike" tails, such as spider monkeys), friction ridges also appear on the volar surface of the tails. All primates have an arboreal evolutionary heritage: Trees have been and continue to be the primary habitat for most apes and monkeys, and humans share this arboreal heritage. Primates' hands and feet show adaptations for locomotion and maneuvering in the branches of trees. The opposable thumb provides a flexible and sturdy means of grasping branches or the food that hangs from them. Primates, unlike other mammals such as squirrels or cats, have nails instead of claws at the distal end of their phalanges. Claws would get in the way of grasping a branch (imagine making

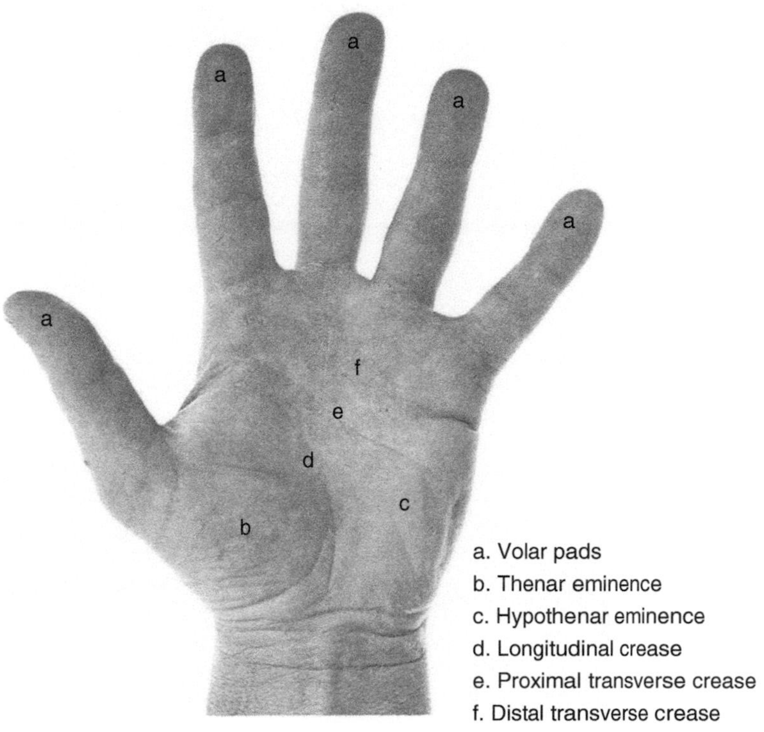

FIGURE 19.2

The terminology for the palms is important for the proper identification and description of friction ridges.

a fist with two-inch nails) and would provide insufficient structure to hold an animal with a high body weight (a one-pound squirrel is highly maneuverable in a tree, but a 150-pound jaguar is not). The fingerpads and friction ridges are part of a complex manipulation and sensory system that is still being explored and researched (e.g., see the work of Warman and Ennos, 2009).

Friction ridges begin forming in the ninth or tenth week of fetal development. These **primary friction ridges** develop deep in the dermal layer of the skin, as shown in Figure 19.3. At about 14 weeks of gestation, sweat glands and sweat ducts begin to form, proliferating from the primary friction ridges. They infiltrate into the dermis and develop into mature ducts and glands. The primary friction ridges proliferate until about the fifteenth or seventeenth week of gestation; at this point, the primary friction ridges stop proliferating and **secondary friction ridges** appear. Secondary friction ridges develop from week 17 and mature by week 24.

The interface or margin between the epidermis and the dermis provides a template of the configuration of the friction ridges on the surface. Numerous factors may affect the patterning and arrangement of friction ridges, including the fetus' genetics, environmental factors, drugs, disease, and perhaps even the shape of the volar pad itself.

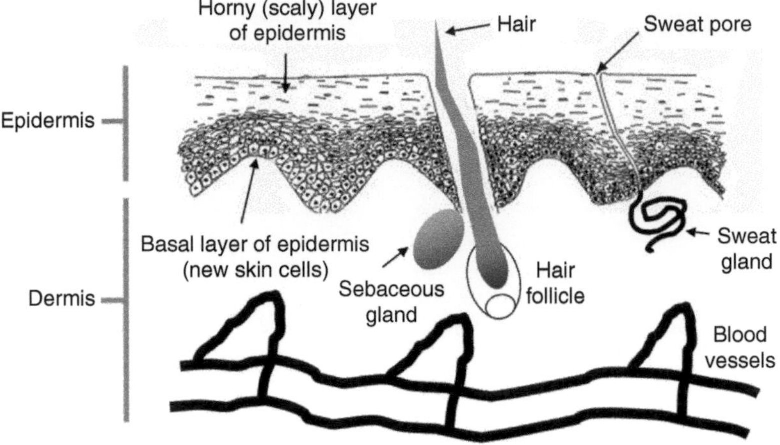

FIGURE 19.3

The primary friction ridges develop deep in the dermal layer of the skin.

Friction ridges develop in utero and remain the same throughout life, barring some sort of scarring or trauma to the epidermal–dermal margin of a friction ridge area. This interface between the epidermis and the dermis acts as a template for the configuration of the friction ridges seen on the surface of the skin. Although humans grow and increase in size, the friction ridge patterns on their bodies, which became permanent and fixed in their patterns from about 17 weeks of embryonic development, do not change like other parts of their bodies (Carlson, 2003).

WHAT'S A FRICTION RIDGE PRINT MADE OF?

A friction ridge print is a representation of a friction ridge pattern in some medium. Friction ridge prints can be classified as either patent, if they are visible with the unaided eye, or latent, if they require some sort of assistance to make them visible. **Patent prints** can appear because of some transferable material on the ridge pattern, such as liquid blood, liquid paint, or dust, or because the ridge pattern was transferred to a soft substrate that had "memory" and retained the impression, like clay, fresh paint, or putty.

Latent prints are composed of the sweat and oils of the body that are transferred from the ridge pattern to some substrate where they persist for some time until found by one of numerous visualizing techniques. The most familiar visualizing technique is the use of **fingerprint powder**, colored, fluorescent, or magnetic materials that are very finely ground, which is brushed lightly over a suspected print to produce contrast between the background and the now-visible print. More latent print visualization techniques are described later in this chapter.

COLLECTING PRINTS AT A CRIME SCENE

Friction ridge prints, especially fingerprints, can be left on a wide variety of surfaces and may persist for quite some time. Homes, cars, and offices can be littered with friction ridge prints, but only a very few directly relate to a specific incident. Friction ridge patterns suitable for comparison can be obtained from a variety of surfaces, including glass, painted surfaces, plastics, ceramics, paper, and books. Just because the culprit may have worn gloves doesn't mean that no prints were left. The glove could have slipped, allowing a partial palm print, or the criminal may have taken the gloves off for some reason and touched something. Even leather gloves can leave prints of the cowhide patterns; it is not safe to assume and forget to collect potentially important evidence!

FRICTION RIDGE PATTERN VISUALIZATION TECHNIQUES

Not all friction ridge patterns are patently obvious and some require physical, chemical, or optical enhancements to make them visible. The oldest and still most common method is to use one or more fingerprint powders to create contrast between the ridge pattern and the background. These powders typically are available in black, white, and other colors, including metallic. Black is the most popular color because it creates the most contrast on a white card, commonly used for filing and recording friction ridge prints. This provides a uniform medium for the comparison of black ridges of the questioned print to the black-inked ridges of the known print.

For photography, however, other colors are of considerable use, especially against the variety of colored backgrounds found in homes, offices, and cars. Once photographed, the prints can be lifted and placed on a black background card for further contrast. Some companies produce powders with two contrasting colors in them, like black and silver, to provide contrast regardless of the background. Magnetic powders, finely ground magnetic metals, work best on coated or shiny surfaces. Additionally, many fluorescent powders have been developed that fluoresce at specific wavelengths for easy visualization with tunable light sources and special film.

The powders are applied with a soft fiberglass brush that has long, very fine bristles, as shown in Figure 19.4; some examiners use brushes with natural bristles (usually squirrel or camel hair), but these are rare today. The brush is dipped into the powder and gently applied to the latent print with a light touch; it is very easy to stroke too hard and remove latent print evidence. Magnetic powders require a special magnetic applicator that picks up a "fuzzy ball" of magnetic powder that is then "brushed" over the print. The print is then photographed and/or lifted with frosted or clear tape for mounting on a contrasting background card. Information about the print—where, when, and how it was lifted and by whom—is also recorded on the card, along with an identifier for chain of custody and reference purposes.

Many other chemicals and processes have been developed for the visualization of latent prints, some of which are listed in Table 19.1.

Visual detection methods have the advantage of being nondestructive; therefore, these techniques do not prevent applying conventional fingerprint development

FIGURE 19.4

Fingerprint powders are applied with brushes that have very fine, long bristles.

methods afterward. Three main types of lasers have been used to detect fingerprints: the argon, the copper vapor, and the neodymium-yttrium/arsenide/gallium (Nd:YAG) lasers. These lasers have been shown to work well on metal surfaces, skin, and some plastics. The item of evidence should be illuminated with different wavelengths of light while observing the object through filtered goggles designed for the wavelengths used.

PRESERVING PRINTS FOR ANALYSIS

Friction ridge prints should be photographed as soon as they are found at the crime scene or in the laboratory. This emphasis on preserving latent print evidence has numerous advantages, including showing the object where the print was found and leaving the print untouched for further examination. Photographing friction ridge prints is not as easy as photographing other types of evidence at a crime scene. The friction ridge photographer must be skilled in various methods of lighting, exposure, filters, and latent print enhancement. The final image of the print should be 1:1—the real size of the print—to facilitate the eventual comparison.

If the item has a plastic print or is a difficult surface to process where it's found, like a knob or switch, it should be removed, packaged properly, and submitted to the laboratory.

Table 19.1 Various Methods of Visualizing Latent Prints and Precautions

Visualization Method	Use	Limitations
Amido black	Protein dye sensitive to blood, turning a blue-black color in its presence. Treatment with physical developer may be done after amido black to improve the developed print.	It will not stain the normal constituents in a latent print. Amido black should not be used as a presumptive test for blood because it reacts to more than only blood.
Aqueous amido black	Protein dye solution sensitive to blood, turning a blue-black color in its presence. Treatment with physical developer may be done after amido black to improve the developed print. Can be washed over any nonporous surface; the item may also be submerged in the solution.	It will not stain the normal constituents in a latent print. Amido black should not be used as a presumptive test for blood because it reacts to more than only blood. May permanently stain some surfaces. Presumptive tests for blood should be done *before* using aqueous amido black. It is corrosive and will damage metal surfaces if not washed off quickly.
Aqueous leucocrystal violet	Enhances and develops latent prints stained with blood on porous or nonporous surfaces. Best applied by washing or submersion.	It will not stain the normal constituents in a latent print. May permanently stain some surfaces.
Gentian crystal violet	A protein dye that stains the fatty portions of sebaceous sweat a deep purple color; it also works on bloody prints. GCV will visualize latent prints on the adhesive side of all tapes. Fluoresces at 525, 530, and 570 nm (use red goggles); also at 485 and 450 nm (use orange goggles).	May permanently stain some surfaces.
DFO (1,8-Diazafluoren-9-one)	A ninhydrin analog that reacts to the amino acids present in body proteins; especially good for paper evidence. Once DFO is applied, the evidence should be heated for 10 min at 100 °C (212 °F). Using orange goggles, best fluorescence is seen at 450, 485, 525, and 530 nm for most papers. For brown and yellow papers, DFO fluorescence occurs at 570–590 nm. When DFO, ninhydrin, and physical developer are each going to be used in the processing of a specimen, DFO must be used as the first process if there is to be any fluorescence.	*Not* recommended for spraying. Special conditions apply for photography.

Continued

Table 19.1 Various Methods of Visualizing Latent Prints and Precautions—cont'd

Visualization Method	Use	Limitations
Glue fuming	Fumes from cyanoacrylate ester adhesives (Super Glue® and similar products) will develop latent prints by binding the proteins in the prints. The cyanoacrylate ester adhesive is heated in the presence of water to create the fumes. The developed prints may then be dusted to enhance their details; fluorescent materials may be incorporated into this process.	The fumes from cyanoacrylate ester adhesives are irritating but nontoxic.
Iodine	Fumes from iodine crystals develop latent prints on surfaces that are impractical for traditional dusting or have residue such as grease. The FBI has developed a method for spraying iodine solutions on large surfaces, such as walls.	Latent prints developed with iodine are visible for only a few hours.
Ninhydrin	Develops latent prints on porous surfaces like paper by reacting with amino acids in latent print residue. In a fume hood, the specimens are submerged in the ninhydrin solution and then air dried. Ninhydrin may be applied after DFO and before physical developer.	Avoid contact with the powder and solution form of ninhydrin. Any source of heat or spark should be avoided.
Physical developer	A silver-based liquid reagent that reacts to lipids, fats, oils, and waxes present in the print residue. It is good for porous objects but should be the last process in the chemical sequence.	Numerous safety precautions are required for physical developer. Paper with a pH above 7 (like thermal fax paper) is not suitable for processing with physical developer.
Small particle reagent (Molybdenum disulfide, MoS_2)	A physical development technique in which small black particles adhere to the fatty substances left in print residue and is useful on many different surfaces. Well known for its ability to develop prints on wet surfaces and even under water.	Numerous safety precautions are required for small particle reagent. Developed prints should be photographed before lifting is attempted.
Sudan black	Working best on glass, metal, or plastic materials that are greasy or sticky, Sudan black is a dye that stains the fatty components of sebaceous secretions. Sudan black also works well on the inside of latex gloves. Specimens must be glue fumed prior to applying Sudan black.	Stains many surfaces. Should not be used on porous or absorbent surfaces.
Vacuum metal deposition	This is reported to be the most effective technique for most smooth, nonporous surfaces. The process evaporates gold or zinc in a vacuum chamber that coats the specimen surface with a microscopic layer of metal.	The equipment is expensive.

PRINCIPLES OF FRICTION RIDGE ANALYSIS

Although Francis Galton was not the first person to propose the use of fingerprints for identification, he was the first to study them scientifically, thereby laying the foundation for their use in criminal cases, biometrics, and anthropology. Galton, a dilettante who studied a wide variety of disciplines including anthropology, genetics, geology, and statistics, was influenced by his cousin Charles Darwin and collaborated with Karl Pearson. *Fingerprints*, the first scientific text on the subject, was published in 1892 by Macmillan; Galton went on to publish additional works on fingerprints in 1893 (*Decipherment of Blurred Fingerprints*) and *Fingerprint Directories* (1895). In his 1888 paper for the Royal Institution, Galton estimated the probability of two persons having the same fingerprint and studied the heritability and racial differences in fingerprints. Galton's work on fingerprints summarized common patterns in fingerprints and devised a classification system that is still used to this day. The method of identifying criminals by their fingerprints had been introduced in the 1860s by William Herschel in India, but their potential use in forensic work was first proposed by Dr Henry Faulds in 1880 (Cole, 2001).

The concept of uniqueness is typically associated with the philosopher Gottfried Wilhelm Leibniz, who stated, "For there are never in nature two beings that are perfectly alike and in which it is not possible to find a difference that is internal or is founded on an intrinsic denomination" (Rescher, 2001, p. 64). While it is one thing to understand all people and things are separate in space and time, it is quite another to prove this supposition. Galton was the first to attempt to calculate the likelihood of finding two friction ridge patterns that are the same. Numerous researchers have recalculated this probability over the years by various calculations based on differing assumptions (see Table 19.2). But they all indicate that the probability of any one particular fingerprint is somewhere between 0.000000954 and 1.2×10^{-80} (0.0 with 78 zeros and 12)—all very small numbers indeed. Technically, even infinitesimal probabilities such as these are still *probabilities* and do not represent true uniqueness (which would be a probability of 1 in ∞), but the values are such that latent fingerprints, with sufficient minutiae, can be considered practically unique in many cases. The values in Table 19.2 also demonstrate the importance of finding as many points of comparison as possible; more similarities—with no significant differences—lead to a lesser probability of a coincidental match (false positive). No standard model for random match probabilities has been adopted for forensic fingerprint casework, but that day is soon coming.

IN MORE DETAIL: JUST HOW ACCURATE ARE FINGERPRINTS?

Accuracy is of paramount concern in human identification. How often is the wrong person identified (false positive) or excluded (false negative)? The best study to date involved 169 latent print examiners each comparing 100 pairs of latent prints and exemplars from a sample of 744 pairs. Only five examiners made incorrectly identified individuals for an overall false positive rate of 0.1%; the rate of false excluding individuals was 7.5% (Ulery et al., 2011). Blind verifications detected all false positive errors and most of the false negatives; blind verification is when a second qualified examiner reviews the work of the original examiner without knowing their conclusions.

This landmark study indicates that latent fingerprint comparisons are very accurate with a low incidence of falsely identifying an individual, especially combined with a blind verification process.

Table 19.2 Comparison of Probability of a Particular Fingerprint Configuration Using Different Published Models for 36 Minutiae and 12 Minutiae (Matches Involve Full, Not Partial, Matches)

Author	Probability Value for a Latent Print with 36 Minutiae	Probability Value for a Latent Print with 12 Minutiae
Galton (1892)	1.45×10^{-11}	9.54×10^{-7}
Henry (1900)	1.32×10^{-23}	3.72×10^{-9}
Balthazard (1911)	2.12×10^{-22}	5.96×10^{-8}
Bose (1917)	2.12×10^{-22}	5.96×10^{-8}
Wentworth and Wilder (1918)	6.87×10^{-62}	4.10×10^{-22}
Pearson (1930, 1933)	1.09×10^{-41}	8.65×10^{-17}
Roxburgh (1933)	3.75×10^{-47}	3.35×10^{-18}
Cummins and Midlo (1943)	2.22×10^{-63}	1.32×10^{-22}
Trauring (1963)	2.47×10^{-26}	2.91×10^{-9}
Gupta (1968)	1.00×10^{-38}	1.00×10^{-14}
Osterburg et al. (1977)	1.33×10^{-27}	1.10×10^{-9}
Stoney (1985)	1.20×10^{-80}	3.5×10^{-26}

Data from Table 8.2 in Maltoni et al. (2003, p. 267).

Under low-power magnification, friction ridge patterns are studied for the kind, number, and location of various ridge characteristics, or **minutiae**. As with many other types of forensic evidence, it is not merely the presence or absence of minutiae that make a print unique: It is the *presence, kind, number*, and, especially, *arrangement* of those characteristics that create a one-of-a-kind pattern. When two or more prints are compared, a careful point-by-point study is needed to determine whether enough of the significant minutiae in the known print are present in the questioned print, with no relevant differences. This comparison process is demonstrated graphically in Figure 19.5.

Figure 19.5 shows the comparison of two fairly complete prints; in reality, the majority of prints that are identified, resolved, and compared are **partial prints**, representing only a portion of the complete print pattern. A friction ridge print scientist must then determine whether a partial print is suitable for comparison, that is, if the print has the necessary and sufficient information to allow a proper comparison. A partial print, or even a complete print for that matter, may be identifiable as such but be smudged, too grainy, or too small for the scientist to make an accurate and unbiased comparison. Often this is the crucial step in a friction ridge print examination that is dependent on the scientist's experience, visual acuity, and judgment.

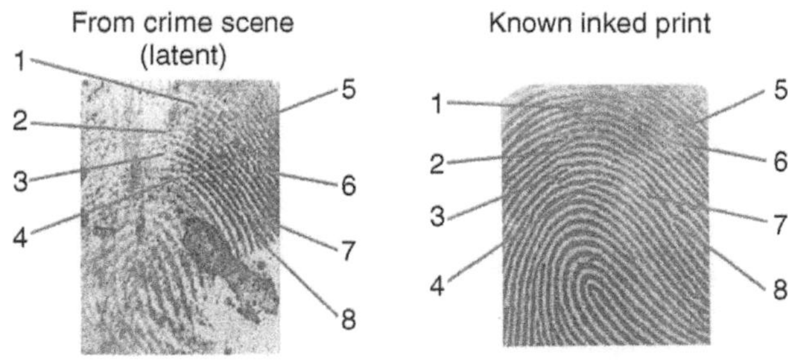

FIGURE 19.5

The presence, kind, number, and arrangement of minutiae create the pattern used in a fingerprint comparison. The points are studied side by side with a magnifying lens.

One of the ongoing debates among forensic scientists is how many points of comparison are necessary and sufficient to reach a conclusion of identification. For years, many agencies had a **point-counting standard** that dictated how many points of comparison were required before a positive conclusion could be reached. The number of points varied from 8 to 16 to even 20 in some agencies. A concern with point counting, however, is that no scientific or statistical basis has been established that would indicate that 8 is not enough, but 10 might be, or 16, or more. The frequency of individual kinds of minutiae (deltas, bifurcations, crossings, etc.) in any population is not known and so begs the question of a numerical standard's significance. Another concern is the question of the threshold limit: If an agency requires 10 points for an identification, what if 9 very clear points are found? Could a tenth point possibly be found or must an exclusion be made? What if it's a small partial print and nine very clear points are all that are found? At an agency with a threshold of eight, this would be a match, and the problem is obvious.

Many, if not most, agencies have now adopted a "no-point" standard, summarized in 1973 by the IAI, a professional association for forensic scientists involved in identification techniques, as "no valid basis exists for requiring a predetermined minimum number of friction ridge characteristics, which must be present in two impressions in order to establish positive identification" (1973, p. 1). The threshold then becomes one of a sufficient number of characteristics necessary to make a conclusion of identification, however many that might be. A scientist's experience and judgment become central to the process of a quality examination; this judgment, ultimately, is derived from proper and comprehensive training coupled with a mentoring process of practical experience. This does not absolve scientists of the obligation to be able to articulate the points of comparison, their significance, and why they lead them to a conclusion of identification. Two or more experts may disagree, but they need to be able to offer cogent arguments as to why and how they reached their different conclusions.

BACK TO THE CASE: THE MADRID TRAIN BOMBING

Interpol Washington requested the analysis of latent fingerprints that had been collected during the bombing investigation. An FBI Latent Print Unit Chief assigned the case to a supervisory fingerprint examiner. The Spanish National Police through Interpol Madrid sent electronic images of the latent prints to the supervisor. Eight latent images were of low resolution and without a scale. IAFIS searches were conducted without effecting an identification. Latent Print Unit personnel asked Interpol Washington to obtain higher resolution latent images with a scale so that the ridge detail would be more visible and the latent prints could be printed in their natural size to ensure the reliability of IAFIS searches.

Interpol Washington submitted additional e-mails with the latent prints and the known fingerprints of five individuals. The latent print images were of high resolution and displayed a scale. They were compared with the five suspects insofar as possible, but no conclusion could be made because the images of the known prints were of low resolution. The supervisory fingerprint examiner encoded seven minutiae points for the high-resolution image of latent fingerprint #17 and initiated an IAFIS search. The supervisory fingerprint examiner reviewed the candidate list. The misidentified subject was the number four candidate. The supervisory fingerprint examiner identified the subject on the basis of a comparison using the on-screen images and examination of the high-resolution digital printouts of the latent fingerprint and the known fingerprint record from IAFIS. The Unit Chief was notified and reviewed the on-screen images. The Unit Chief assigned the case to a verifier (a retired supervisory fingerprint examiner working as a contractor). The verifier requested original fingerprint cards from the FBI's Criminal Justice Information Services Division. The contractor verified the supervisory fingerprint examiner's identification on the basis of his examination of the same high-resolution digital copy of the latent fingerprint and the original fingerprint cards that were forwarded to the Latent Print Unit by the Criminal Justice Information Services Division.

The Latent Print Unit provided their initial report confirming that latent fingerprint #17 was the same as the known prints of the number four candidate. The Unit Chief provided this information by telephone to Interpol Washington. The Unit Chief did not complete a thorough examination of the identification prior to making the telephone call. The Spanish National Police confirmed that latent fingerprint #17 was collected from a plastic bag. An official FBI laboratory report was issued identifying latent fingerprint #17 with the number four candidate. Spanish National Police fingerprint examiners arrived at an inconclusive finding that the latent fingerprint discovered on a plastic bag belonged to the number four candidate. Consequently, the Spanish requested further clarification of the FBI laboratory's analysis.

The latent print was subsequently provided to the United States Attorney's Office for submission to the court. According to the court's order, the prints were to be independently compared to the number four candidate's known prints. The court's independent examiner reported in telephonic testimony that latent fingerprint #17 was that of the number four candidate. The Spanish National Police provided a letter to the FBI Legal Attache in Madrid advising that the Spanish laboratory had identified latent fingerprint #17 as belonging to another person. Personnel from the FBI Latent Print Unit traveled to Madrid to resolve the conflicting identifications. They were given access to all photographs and the original evidence that bore latent fingerprint #17. (Latent fingerprint #17 was no longer visible on the evidence because it had been destroyed during subsequent fingerprint processing techniques.) FBI Latent Print Unit personnel returned from Spain. An overnight review of the case was conducted and the error was recognized.

Source: *Stacey, R (2005). Text is quoted from original work for accuracy.*

CLASSIFYING FINGERPRINTS

The patterning and permanency of friction ridges allow for their classification. As discussed earlier, the fact that fingerprints could be systematically sorted and catalogued was a main reason for their widespread adoption among government agencies. The history of the classification of fingerprints is central to the understanding of the widespread adoption of the technique; see "History: Classifying Fingerprints" for more information. It is important to keep in mind that it is the general patterns, not the individualizing elements, that allow for this organization.

HISTORY: CLASSIFYING FINGERPRINTS

The first person to describe a taxonomy of fingerprints was Dr Jan Purkinje, a Czech physician and one of the historical giants in the field of physiology. In 1823, Dr Purkinje lectured on friction ridges in humans and primates and described a system of nine different basic ridge patterns. In 1880, Dr Henry Faulds, a Scott who worked in a Tokyo hospital, researched fingerprints after noticing some on ancient pottery; Faulds had even used "greasy fingermarks" to solve the theft of a bottle of liquor. He published his research on the use and classification of fingerprints in a letter to the scientific journal *Nature*. The publication of Faulds' letter drew a quick response from William Herschel, a chief administrator from the Bengali British government office in India, who claimed that he, Herschel, and not Faulds had prior claim to the technique of fingerprints. Herschel had been using finger- and palm prints to identify contractors in Bengal since the Indian Mutiny of 1857, employing a simplistic version of the system that was eventually instituted some 40 years later. In fact, it may not have been Herschel's own idea to use prints for identification: The Chinese and Assyrians used prints as "signatures" at least 9000 years before the present, and the Indians had probably borrowed this behavior. Sir Edward Henry had tried to institute fingerprinting as the primary means of identification across all of India, his supervisor thought otherwise, and Herschel's work languished until Faulds' letter was published. The argument between Faulds and Herschel about who was first would continue into the 1950s (Thorwald, 1965; Cole, 2001).

Today, all fingerprints are divided into three classes: loops, arches, and whorls. **Loops** have one or more ridges entering from one side of the print, curving back on themselves, and exiting the fingertip on the same side, as shown in Figure 19.6. If the

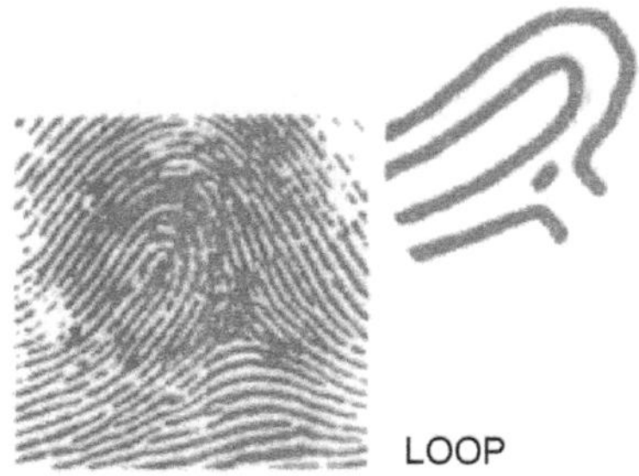

FIGURE 19.6

Loops have one or more ridges entering and exiting from the same side of the print, looping back on itself in the middle. Ulnar loops exit and enter the side of the finger toward the little finger, whereas radial loops are on the side toward the thumb.

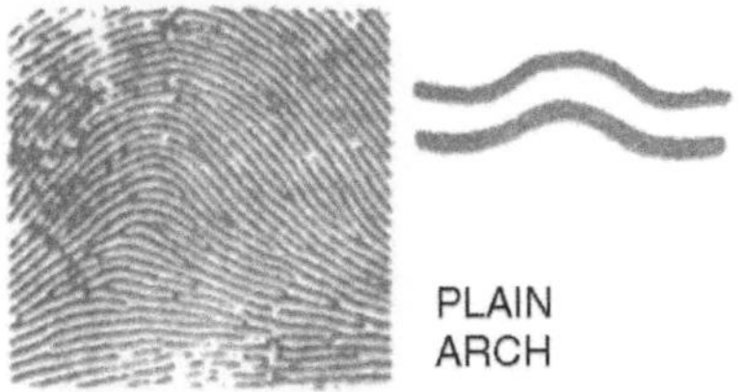

FIGURE 19.7

Arches enter one side of the fingertip, peak, and then exit the opposite side. Arches are either plain or tented.

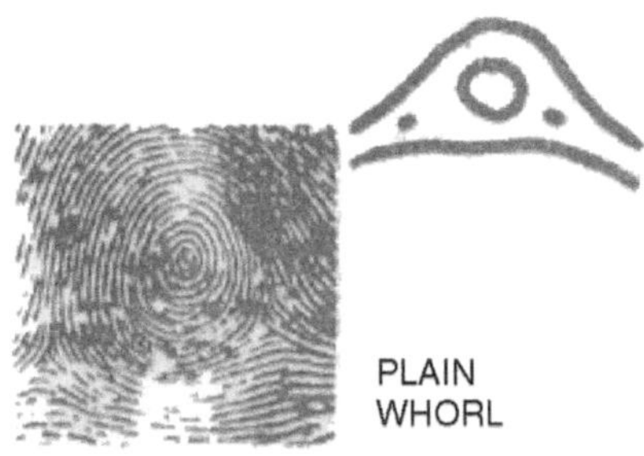

FIGURE 19.8

All whorls have type lines and at least two deltas. Whorls are classified as plain, central pocket loops, double loops, and accidentals.

loop enters and exits on the side of the finger toward the little finger, it is called an **ulnar loop**; if the loop enters and exits on the side toward the thumb, it is termed a **radial loop**. All loops are surrounded by two diverging ridges called **type lines**; the point of divergence is called a **delta** because of its resemblance to a river delta and the Greek letter Δ (*delta*). The central portion of the loop is called the **core**.

Arches are the rarest of the three main classes of patterns. Arches are either **plain arch** (see Figure 19.7), with ridges entering one side of the finger, gradually rising to a rounded peak, and exiting the other side, or **tented arch**, which are arches with a pronounced, sharp peak. A pattern that resembles a loop but lacks one of the required traits to be classified as a loop can also be designated as a tented arch. Arches do not have type lines, cores, or deltas.

Whorls are subdivided into **plain whorl** (see Figure 19.8), **central pocket loop, double loop**, and **accidental**. All whorls have type lines and at least two deltas. Central pocket loops and plain whorls have a minimum of one ridge that is continuous around the pattern, but this ridge does not necessarily have to be in the shape of a circle; it can be an oval, ellipse, or even a spiral. Plain whorls are located between the two deltas of the whorl pattern and central pocket loops are not. This difference can be easily determined by drawing a line equidistant between the two deltas: If the line touches the circular core, then the whorl is a plain whorl; if not, it is a central pocket loop (see Figure 19.9).

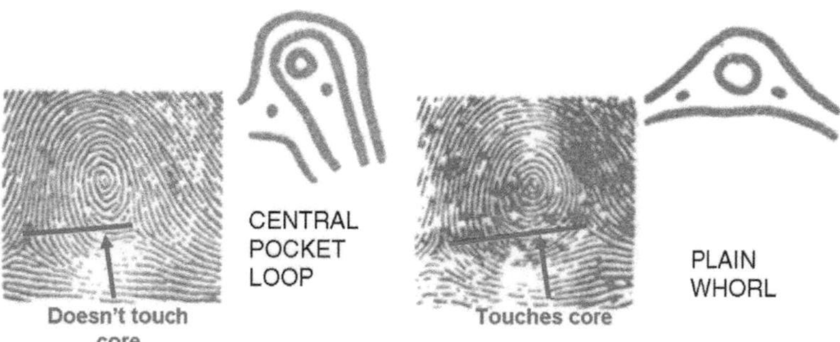

FIGURE 19.9

To determine whether a print is a plain whorl or a central pocket loop, draw a line between the two deltas. If the line touches the core, it's a plain whorl; if not, then the print is a central pocket loop.

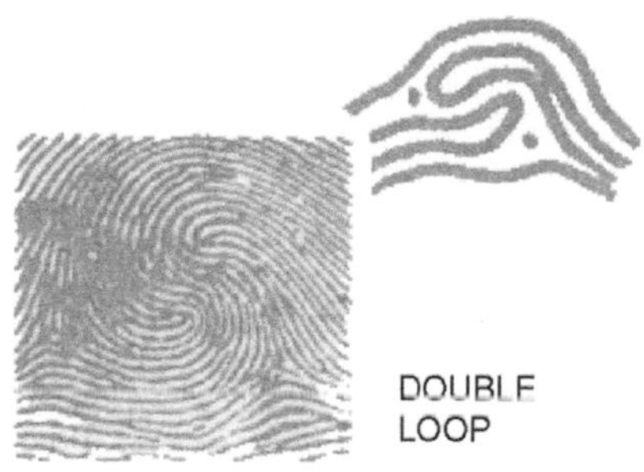

FIGURE 19.10

Double loops have two loops that swirl around each other; accidentals combine two or more patterns.

A double loop is made up of two loops that swirl around each other (see Figure 19.10). Finally, an accidental is a pattern that combines two or more patterns (excluding the plain arch) and/or does not clearly meet the criteria for any of the other patterns.

The relative appearance of loops overall is 60–65%; whorls, 30–35% and arches, 5%.

CLASSIFICATION

The modern system of fingerprint classification is based on Henry's original design, which could process a maximum of 100,000 sets of prints, with modifications by the FBI to allow for the huge number of entries that have accumulated over the years. The FBI Criminal Justice Information Services (CJIS) currently has over 80 million fingerprints stored in its files.

The modern fingerprint classification consists of a **primary classification** that encodes fingerprint pattern information into two numbers derived as follows. All arches

Table 19.3 Values for Fingers in the Henry Classification System

Right thumb, right index	16
Right middle, right ring	8
Right little, left thumb	4
Left index, left middle	2
Left ring, left little	1

and loops are considered "nonnumerical" patterns and are given a value of zero. Whorls are given the values depending on which finger they appear, as shown in Table 19.3.

The values are summed, with one added to both groups, and the resulting primary classification is displayed like a fraction:

$$\frac{\text{R index} + \text{R ring} + \text{L thumb} + \text{L middle} + \text{L little} + 1}{\text{R thumb} + \text{R middle} + \text{R little} + \text{L index} + \text{L ring} + 1}$$

If, for example, all of an individual's fingers had whorls, the formula would look like this:

$$16+8+4+2+1+1/16+8+4+2+1+1=32/32$$

If all of an individual's fingers had arches or loops instead, the formula would be as follows:

$$0+0+0+0+0+1/0+0+0+0+0+1=1/1$$

In and of itself, a primary classification is just that: class evidence. The primary classification was originally devised to sort individuals into smaller, more easily searched categories; this, of course, was when fingerprints were searched by hand. Additional subdivisions of the classification scheme may be used, but they still only serve as a sieve through which to organize and efficiently search through filed prints. Comparison of minutiae and higher level details is the only method for fingerprint identification.

The problem with storing and sorting fingerprints using only the Henry-FBI classification system is that while the system stores all 10 prints as a set, rarely are full sets of fingerprints found at a crime scene. To search through even a moderately sized database of 10 print sets for an individual print would take too long and be too prone to error. Many agencies used to keep single-print files that contained the separate fingerprints of only the most frequent locally repeating criminals.

HOW LONG DO FRICTION RIDGE PRINTS LAST?

Plastic prints will last as long as the impressed material remains structurally intact. Prints left in some medium, such as blood or dust, are quite fragile and do not last very long. Latent prints, however, if in the proper environments, can last for years. Currently, the age of a set of fingerprints is almost impossible to determine.

ELIMINATION PRINTS

As with any other type of evidence, obtaining known samples for elimination purposes can be of great assistance to the forensic scientist. These samples may not only eliminate individuals from an investigation's focus, but also demonstrate a proper scientific mind-set through a comprehensive series of comparisons. If these elimination knowns are incorporated into a trial presentation, they can create confidence in the mind of the trier-of-fact that not only do the defendant's known prints match, but also the other potential subjects' prints do *not* match. Displaying what is and is not a match can clarify the forensic scientist's process of identification and comparison to the lay person.

AUTOMATED FINGERPRINT IDENTIFICATION SYSTEMS

The advent of computers heralded a new age for many forensic sciences and among the first to utilize the technology was the science of fingerprints. Capturing, storing, searching, and retrieving fingerprints via computer are now standard occurrences among police agencies and forensic science laboratories. **Automated Fingerprint Identification Systems**, or AFIS (pronounced "AYE-fis"), are computerized databases of digitized fingerprints that are searchable through software—essentially, a computer and a scanner hooked to a network-type server computer. An AFIS can store millions of print images that can be searched in a matter of minutes by a single operator. The core of this electronic system is a standard format developed by the FBI and the National Institute of Standards and Technology (NIST), with the advice of the National Crime Information Center (NCIC), which provides for the conversion of fingerprints into electronic data and their subsequent exchange via telecommunications and computers. Although the data format was a standard, the software and computers that operate AFIS are not and several vendors offer products to law enforcement and forensic science agencies. The drawback was that these products were not compatible with each other, precluding the easy exchange of information between systems.

This situation began to change in 1999 when the FBI developed and implemented a new automated fingerprint system known as the Integrated Automated Fingerprint Identification System, or IAFIS (pronounced "EYE-aye-fis"). Although IAFIS is primarily a 10-print system for searching an individual's fingerprints like a standard AFIS, it can also digitally capture latent print and 10-print images and then

- enhance an image to improve its quality;
- compare crime scene fingerprints against known 10-print records retrieved from the database;
- search crime scene fingerprints against known fingerprints when no suspects have been developed; and
- automatically search the prints of an arrestee against a database of unsolved cases.

Other advances are being made to solve the problem of noncompatible AFIS computers. The Universal Latent Workstation is the first in a new generation of interoperable fingerprint workstations. Several state and local agencies, the FBI, NIST, and AFIS technology manufacturers are developing standards to provide for the interoperability and sharing of fingerprint identification services. The Workstation is part of that program and it assists agencies and manufacturers understand and develop the concept of "encode once and search anywhere." The Workstation allows agencies not only to enter data into the format of the system they purchased and use but also to share that data with other, previously incompatible systems. Agencies will eventually be able to use this type of workstation to search local, state, neighboring, and the FBI IAFIS system, all with a single entry.

IDENTIFICATION

The final identification decision in a fingerprint comparison is reached when sufficient quality and quantity of corresponding Levels 1, 2, and 3 friction ridge details are present. **Level 1 detail** includes the general ridge flow and pattern configuration. It is not sufficient for individualization but can exclude an individual. Level 1 detail may include information enabling orientation, core and delta location, and distinction of finger versus palm.

Level 2 detail includes formations, defined as a ridge endings, bifurcations, dots, or combinations of these features; Level 2 detail enables individualization. It is not the presence or absence of these features that can individualize a print, although they play a major role: It is the *relationship* of these features across the print that defines the uniqueness of the print. This is analogous to each of us having a nose, two eyes, a mouth, and ears, but our face being much more than a laundry list of those parts.

Finally, **Level 3 detail** includes all attributes of a *ridge*, such as ridge path deviation, width, shape, pores, edge contour, incipient ridges, breaks, creases, scars, and other permanent minutiae. Level 3 detail obviously can lead to individualization as well and, it has been argued, when fingerprint examiners look at a print, they automatically take Level 3 detail into account.

Some jurisdictions, both in the United States and abroad, require a number of points of comparison before an identification can be made and confirmed. Fingerprint examiners who argue against this approach maintain that friction ridge examination is much more holistic than just "counting points," and the entire print is considered and examined. Those who support point-counting standards claim that they *do* take the whole print into account, but some *objective* standard must be met for the good of the profession. The recent Llera Plaza case is a good example of the challenges that fingerprint examiners, and possibly other forensic sciences, face in the future (see "In More Detail: Is Forensic Fingerprint Examination a Science?").

IN MORE DETAIL: IS FORENSIC FINGERPRINT EXAMINATION A SCIENCE?

In a federal drug and murder prosecution case, *US v. Llera Plaza* (2002), the defendants moved the court to suppress the offered fingerprint evidence because, in their opinion, fingerprint evidence is not a science. The United States countered that the fingerprint evidence should be admitted at trial. The prosecutors also requested the judge to take official notice that "fingerprints offer an infallible means of personal identification" (www.fbi.gov).

Judge Pollak agreed with the defendants and ruled on January 7, 2002 that the FBI's experts would not testify at trial that the evidentiary fingerprints "matched" those of the defendants. After additional testimony, however, Judge Pollak changed his ruling. On March 13, 2002, he reversed his decision and ruled that the FBI's experts could testify to the fingerprint evidence.

Judge Pollak's initial ruling has been interpreted as "trashing" fingerprint evidence. This overstates his ruling—Judge Pollak ruled that FBI fingerprint examiners could testify to the processing of the latent fingerprints, give demonstrative evidence to the jury in the form of enlarged comparison prints, and indicate the points of comparison among them. What the judge disallowed was the experts' opinion that the fingerprints were the same. In Judge Pollak's view, that was the sole right of the jury.

In coming to this decision, Judge Pollak relied on two US Supreme Court opinions: *Daubert v. Merrell Dow Pharmaceuticals, Inc.* (113 S.Ct. 2786 [1993]) and *Kumho Tire Co. Ltd. V. Carmichael* (119 S.Ct. 1167 [1999]). The Supreme Court held that scientific evidence must meet four factors to be admitted under the *Daubert/Kumho* guidelines:

- the scientific technique must be testable;
- the technique must have been subjected to peer review and publication;
- the technique's known or potential error rate must be known, and standards for using the technique must exist and be followed; and
- the technique must be generally accepted.

Judge Pollak determined that fingerprint comparison, if it was a science, failed the first three points.

Thus the surprise when Judge Pollak reversed his decision. Part of the explanation for this was that the attorneys and the judge restricted their evidence in the first hearing to a two-year-old transcript of another case. Extensive evidence about the scientific reliability of fingerprints had been introduced by both the defendants and the prosecutors. Judge Pollak requested to hear additional evidence based on the prosecution's motion to reconsider his first ruling. Part of the evidence presented this second time was live testimony from one witness who had testified in the previous case; his "old" testimony had simply been read by Judge Pollak. The court also heard further testimony from additional experts that ultimately swayed his decision.

Does this mean fingerprints are now "off the hook?" Probably not, by anyone's guessing. Forensic scientists must be scientists in the laboratory *and* in the courtroom despite the change in basic rules between those venues. Any forensic scientists who step into a courtroom unprepared to provide supporting research, standards, and protocols for their methods are asking for trouble. More research is needed in all aspects of forensic science—no one study will solve a legal problem and make it "go away." Science is a search for understanding and knowledge and forensic scientists are as bound by this search as any other scientific discipline. In their recent book, Champod and his coauthors note that

> *When it comes to identification issues, it is clear that the criminal justice system is approaching fingerprint evidence with a much more critical eye than in the past. Certainly, the highly debated introduction of DNA evidence and its systematic comparison with fingerprint evidence has promoted such renewed critical interest. We welcome this regain of interest, as it will force the profession to analyze its foundations critically. (2004, p. 204)*

On the Web: www.onin.com.

BACK TO THE CASE: THE MADRID TRAIN BOMBING

If the FBI had insisted on more information (e.g., an image with scale for proper enlarging and an overall shot for orientation and proper finger determination), this error may have been avoided. The error was a "human" failure and not a methodology or technology failure.

The power of the IAFIS match, coupled with the inherent pressure of working an extremely high-profile case, was thought to have influenced the initial examiner's judgment and subsequent examination. This influence was recognized as confirmation bias (or context effect) and describes the mind-set in which the expectations with which people approach a task of observation will affect their perceptions and interpretations of what they observe. Once the mind-set occurred with the initial examiner, the subsequent examinations were tainted. Latent print examiners routinely conduct verifications in which they know the previous examiners' results without influencing their conclusions.

Confidence is a vital element of forensics, but humility is too. It was considered by the committee that when the individualization had been made by the examiner, it became increasingly difficult for others in the agency to disagree.

All of the committee members agree that the quality of the images that were used to make the erroneous identification was not a factor.

A new approach to quality assurance and quality control needs to be fostered. Personnel who are responsible for reviews of comparisons need to be considered as checkers and not verifiers. They must be trained to look for discrepancies as well as similarities. They also need to be extensively trained to do checking on-screen as well as with standard magnifiers.

Source: *Stacey, R (2005). Text is quoted from original work for accuracy.*

SUMMARY

Friction ridge examination is one of the bedrock disciplines in forensic science and has been employed for over 100 years. It is considered the pre-eminent method of individualization in forensic science. That status, however, has recently been upset by court challenges and high-profile misidentifications. Friction ridge examination will no doubt continue as a mainstay of forensic science, but changes in methodology and interpretation may be on the horizon. How the discipline weathers these changes depends on the willingness of the profession to critically examine their foundations, procedures, and methods.

TEST YOUR KNOWLEDGE

1. Who was Cesare Lombroso?
2. What was a *portrait parlé*?
3. What is Bertillonage?
4. When was the first systematic use of fingerprints in the United States?
5. When was the first US conviction using fingerprints?
6. What is CJIS?
7. Why are friction ridges important?
8. When do friction ridges begin to develop? When are they complete?
9. What is fingerprint powder?

10. List four methods of visualizing latent prints, how they are used and their limitations.
11. How are lasers used with latent prints?
12. What are minutiae?
13. What is a point-counting standard?
14. Name the types of fingerprint patterns and describe them.
15. What is AFIS? What's the difference between AFIS and IAFIS?
16. What are Level 1, Level 2, and Level 3 detail?
17. What are elimination prints?

CONSIDER THIS...

1. Is the discipline of forensic friction ridge analysis a science? What are the hallmarks of a science? Do they apply to fingerprints?
2. How would you present evidence in an admissibility hearing under the *Daubert* guidelines to support forensic friction ridge analysis as meeting those criteria? How would you counter those arguments if you were an opposing expert?
3. Why would you not want to use a point-counting standard in fingerprints? What's the positive aspect and what are the negatives?

BIBLIOGRAPHY AND FURTHER READING

Ashbaugh, D., Houck, M.M., 2005. Fingerprints and admissibility: friction, ridges, and science. The Canadian Journal of Police & Security Services Practice, Policy & Management.

Ashbaugh, D., 1999. Quantitative-qualitative Friction Ridge Analysis: An Introduction to Basic and Advanced Ridgeology. CRC Press, Boca Raton, FL.

Balthazard, V., 1911. De l'identification par les empreintes digitales. Comptes Redus des Seances de l'Academie des Sciences 152, 1862–1864.

Bose, H., 1917. Hints on Finger-Prints with a Telegraphic Code for Finger Impressions. Thacker Spink and Company, Calcutta/Simla.

Carlson, B., 2003. Human Embryology and Developmental Biology. Elsevier, Amsterdam (Updated Edition).

Champod, C., Lennard, C., Margot, P., Stoilovic, M., 2004. Fingerprints and Other Ridge Skin Impressions. CRC Press, Boca Raton, FL.

Champod, C., 2013. Friction ridge skin impression evidence—standards of proof. In: Siegel, J., Saukko, P. (Eds.), Encyclopedia of Forensic Sciences, second ed. Elsevier, Amsterdam, pp. 111–116.

Cole, S., 2001. Suspect Identities. Harvard University Press, Cambridge.

Cummins, H., Midlo, C., 1943. Fingerprints, Palms and Soles: An Introduction to Dermatoglyphics. Dover, New York.

Federal Bureau of Investigation, 1984. The Science of Fingerprints. Government Printing Office, Washington, DC.

Frick, A., Fritz, P., Lewis, S., 2013. Chemistry of print residue. In: Siegel, J., Saukko, P. (Eds.), Encyclopedia of Forensic Sciences, second ed. Elsevier, Amsterdam, pp. 92–97.

Galton, F., 1892. Finger Prints. Macmillan and Co., London.

Galton, F., 1893. Decipherment of Blurred Finger Prints. Macmillan and Co., London.

Galton, F., 1895. Fingerprint Directories. Macmillan and Co., London.

Gould, S., 1996. The Mismeasurement of Man. W.W. Norton, New York.

Gupta, S., 1968. Statistical survey of ridge characteristics. International Criminal Police Review 218, 130–134.

Henry, E., 1900. Classification and Uses of Fingerprints. George Routledge and Sons, Limited, London.

International Association for Identification Standardization Committee, 1973. Report of the Standardization Committee. International Association for Identification, Mendota Heights, MN.

Kuhne, F., 1916. The Finger Print Instructor. Munn & Company, New York.

Loll, A., 2013. Automated fingerprint identification systems (AFIS). In: Siegel, J., Saukko, P. (Eds.), Encyclopedia of Forensic Sciences, second ed. Elsevier, Amsterdam, pp. 86–91.

Maltoni, D., Maio, D., Jain, A., Prabhakar, S., 2009. Handbook of Fingerprint Recognition. Springer-Verlag, New York.

Osterburg, J., Parthasarathy, T., Raghaven, T., Sclove, S., 1977. Development of a mathematical formula for the calculation of fingerprint probabilities based on individual characteristic. Journal of the American Statistical Association 72, 772–778.

Pankanti, S., Prabhakar, S., Jain, A., December 11–13, 2001. On the individuality of fingerprint. In: Proceedings of Computer Vision and Pattern Recognition (CVPR), Hawaii.

Pearson, K., 1930. The Life and Letters of Francis Galton, vol. IIIACambridge University Press, Cambridge.

Pearson, K., 1933. Galton's work on evidential value of fingerprints. Sankhya: Indian Journal of Statistics 1 (50).

Rescher, N., 2001. Philosophical Reasoning. Blackwell Publishing, Malden, MA.

Roxburgh, T., 1933. On evidential value of fingerprints. Sankhya: Indian Journal of Statistics 1, 189–214.

Ruth, R., Reznicek, M., Schilens, D., 2013. Friction ridge print examination—interpretation and the comparative method. In: Siegel, J., Saukko, P. (Eds.), Encyclopedia of Forensic Sciences, second ed. Elsevier, Amsterdam, pp. 74–79.

Stacey, R., 2005. Report on the erroneous fingerprint individualization in the Madrid train bombing case. Forensic Science Communications 7 (1). online at www.fbi.gov.

Stoney, D., 1985. A Quantitative Assessment of Fingerprint Individuality (Ph.D. thesis). University of California..

Thomas, R., 1999. Detective Fiction and the Rise of Forensic Science. Cambridge University Press, Cambridge, UK.

Thorwald, J., 1965. The Century of the Detective. Harcourt, New York.

Trauring, M., 1963. Automatic comparison of finger-ridge patterns. Nature 197, 938–940.

Ulery, B., Hicklin, R., Buscaglia, J., Roberts, M., 2011. Accuracy and reliability of forensic latent fingerprint decisions. Proceedings of the National Academy of Sciences 108 (19), 7733–7738.

Warman, P., Ennos, R., 2009. Fingerprints are unlikely to increase the friction of primate fingerpads. The Journal of Experimental Biology 212, 2016–2022.

Wentworth, B., Wilder, H., 1918. Personal Identification. R.G. Badger, Boston.

Wilson, C., Wilson, D., 2003. Written in Blood: A History of Forensic Detection. Carroll and Graf Publishers, New York City.

Woodward, J.D., Orlans, N.M., Higgins, P.T., 2003. Biometrics. McGraw-Hill/Osborne, New York.

CHAPTER

Questioned Documents

20

CHAPTER OUTLINE

KEY TERMS

- Erasure
- Electrostatic detection apparatus (ESDA)
- Examplar
- Handwriting
- Nonrequested writing
- Questioned document
- Questioned document examiner
- Requested writing
- Signatures

THE CASE

Howard Hughes (1905–1976) was a self-made billionaire who made much of his money in designing and building military and civilian aircraft and at one time, owned TWA Airlines. He was an intensely private and reclusive man, especially later in life when he literally dropped out of society. At times, several writers attempted to write a biography of Hughes but were threatened or simply bought off. He refused to appear in court to answer various questions or to pursue lawsuits. Many people thought that he was terminally ill or was even dead and an impersonator was hired to replace him.

In 1970, a moderately successful author, Clifford Irving, conspired with a friend, Richard Susskind, to write an autobiography of Howard Hughes, which they would claim that Hughes wrote with Irving's help and which Hughes had given permission for Irving to sell. They felt that Hughes was so reclusive that he wouldn't challenge the book or charge them with any crimes. Susskind was to be the promoter and researcher and Irving was to "help" Hughes write the book. Irving began to forge letters in Hughes' handwriting as proof that the autobiography was authentic and that Hughes had given Irving permission to collaborate on the book. Irving subsequently convinced the publisher, McGraw-Hill, of the authenticity of the project by showing them several letters that were allegedly from Howard Hughes which indicated his willingness to have Irving write the autobiography based on exclusive interviews that Hughes was to give Irving about his life. One of the letters indicated Hughes' wish that the project remain under wraps. On the basis of discussions with Irving and the letters, McGraw-Hill agreed to publish the autobiography, ultimately paying Irving $100,000 and Hughes more than $600,000. Irving forged Hughes' signature to the publishing contract.

In order to achieve a ring of authenticity of the autobiography, Irving and Susskind did exhaustive research of everything that had been written about Hughes and Irving even concocted a series of interviews that were allegedly carried out all around the world with Hughes. Finally, Irving delivered the completed manuscript to the publisher along with a set of "notes" that were supposed to be in Hughes' handwriting but were again forged by Irving. Officials at "Time-Life," a book subsidiary of McGraw-Hill, had the notes examined by expert forensic document examiners who concurred that the manuscript was genuine and the handwritten notes were written by Hughes. TV interviews of Irving followed. Life Magazine, which was to publish excerpts of the biography, continued to support Irving. Even a famous document examination firm indicated that the writing was authentic. Soon, however, it all began to unravel. Several people who knew Hughes expressed skepticism about the autobiography.

THE CASE—cont'd

In early 1972, Howard Hughes finally made contact with the publisher, denouncing Irving and claiming that they had never met and he had never authorized Irving to write his autobiography. Hughes' lawyer filed suit against the Irvings and an investigation followed, including a Swiss bank account where Hughes' wife had allegedly deposited the Hughes' advance. Authorities finally determined that it was Edith Irving, Clifford's wife that had made the deposit. Irving confessed and served 18 months in prison. Susskind served 6 months.

INTRODUCTION

Most people think of a questioned document as a piece of paper containing handwriting whose author is unknown. It is true that historically, the majority of questioned document cases involved unknown handwriting and many still do today. The task of the forensic document examiner in these cases is to determine who wrote the document. This is done by comparing the characteristics of the handwriting on the document with known samples of the suspected author. Times have changed, however. Fewer documents are being handwritten. Many are now done on a computer. Much of our mail and other documents are now sent by smart phone and after delivery and reading, are deleted forever. Even in cases that still involve handwriting there is a lot more to analyze than simply handwriting on paper. Questioned documents have been written on mirrors, walls, large placards, and other objects. Document examiners are often called upon to compare typewritten or computer printer-generated documents, analyze inks and papers, determine the age of a document, uncover credit card forgeries and currency fraud, and reconstruct charred or obliterated writing. Questioned document examiners undergo years of painstaking training and apprenticeship before they can take their own cases. The field of questioned document examination is one of the "pattern evidence" areas of forensic science where examiners must reach conclusions based solely on their expertise, where no instrumental backup is available to confirm a conclusion.

WHAT IS A QUESTIONED DOCUMENT?

A questioned document need not be a piece of paper; it can be any object. To be a document, it must contain linguistic or numerical markings that are put there by handwriting, typewriting, copying, computer printing, or by other means. If there is doubt about whether the document is authentic (e.g., an authentic draft card or passport) or who the author is, such as the case of the documents alleged to have been written by Howard Hughes in the case cited at the beginning of the chapter, then it is a questioned document. For example, in a case in Virginia that occurred about 25 years ago, a man wrote a threatening note in large letters using spray paint, on the outside wall of a woman's house. By the broad definition given above, the wall is a questioned document. Usually, however, questioned documents are bills, wills, letters, checks, contracts, passports, lottery tickets, driver's licenses, etc. The important point here is that it contains markings, letter, or numbers, whose source or authenticity is in doubt. Although authorship is often the concern of the document examiner, there are many cases where the examiner is asked to determine if an "official" document such as a driver's license is authentic. In addition, there are cases where an authentic document has been altered by erasure, obliteration, destruction, or the addition of extra markings.

THE QUESTIONED DOCUMENT EXAMINER

The first questioned document examiners were photographers. Interestingly enough, photography is an area that questioned document examiners must be very familiar with, but being an expert photographer is by no means sufficient to qualify one as a questioned document examiner. One of the most notorious cases where a photographer acted as an expert in questioned document was the Dreyfus treason case. Alphonse Bertillion was a photographer and developer of the "science" of anthropometry, which purported to provide a set of body measurements of a person that is unique to that individual. Bertillion also billed himself as an expert in document examination and testified in court that Alfred Dreyfus authored the pivotal document in the case. Later, it was determined that Dreyfus was innocent, thus discrediting both Bertillion and the budding science of questioned document examination.

Until the twentieth century, questioned document analysis and testimony were not readily accepted in court. Under English Common law handwriting standards that were not already in evidence were not admissible if their sole purpose in the case was to be used for comparison with a questioned document. This prevented the comparison of questioned documents with known samples since they could not be introduced into court. Since much of early United States law was based on the Common law, this rule had the effect of delaying the use of forensic document examination in the United States until 1913, when through the efforts of the famous document examiner, Albert Osborne, the Congress passed a rule which allowed document standards into evidence in court. Prior to this time, the only way that a questioned document could be authenticated was if someone witnessed the writer actually writing the document and could testify in court that he saw the author write it. After 1913, the science of questioned document examination progressed rapidly. A set of guidelines were developed that governed the ways that known samples of handwriting should be obtained for comparison purposes.

TRAINING AND EDUCATION OF QUESTIONED DOCUMENT EXAMINERS

There are no formal college-based education programs in questioned document analysis in the United States and it is unlikely that there will be in the future. There are some college courses in questioned document analysis that can provide a theoretical foundation for the field, but questioned document analysis, like firearms and tool marks, and fingerprints, is essentially a classical apprenticeship field. The trainee may spend several years studying with an accomplished professional in the field. After passing a number of tests and exercises, the trainee may then become a journeyman questioned document examiner. There is a certification program in the United States for questioned document examiners administered by the American Society of Questioned Document Examiners (ASQDE). http://www.asqde.org/.

A typical training program for a questioned document examiner trainee would consist of formal coursework, if any is available, reading and studying the relevant basic and advanced books and journals that are concerned with all aspects of document examination, and study and examination of actual questioned documents under the supervision of the trainer. There are also quality assurance and control materials including blind tests and then mock trial exercises that must be successfully completed. The trainee would also be expected to learn the relevant statutes and legal considerations that govern the examination, reporting, and expert testimony of questioned documents. There is a significant shortage of trained questioned document examiners and the apprenticeship is very long. It might be possible for universities to develop programs whereby a prospective document examiner can do all of the "book learning" about history and practice that needs to be done as part of the learning process, and then join a journeyman examiner for the apprenticeship part. This could significantly reduce the cost and time of the apprenticeship.

HANDWRITING COMPARISONS

When children first learn to print or write, they are given exemplary samples of each letter and are told to copy them as neatly as possible. Then they are taught to put the letters together and make words. During this period, the handwriting of most children would be very similar. After learning how to form words, the children then put these skills to use in writing and teachers begin to focus on content. This means that the writers begin to focus more on what they are writing and less on how the letters are formed. Writing habits become internalized and the act of writing becomes subconscious and thus, individual characteristics develop, many of which the writer is unaware of. With time, handwriting becomes a sort of unconscious habit; however, this habit is not static. Handwriting changes with time. Over a period of years, one's handwriting undergoes gradual changes that result in different characteristics. This can have a profound influence on the collection of known handwriting samples. Handwriting can also change with changes in physical and emotional condition. Depression, drug abuse, physical illness can all have effects on handwriting. Handwriting also varies by the type of writing instrument and medium (e.g., paper) used. Many of these variables are accounted for when known handwriting samples are obtained.

The ability of a questioned document examiner to identify the author of a handwritten document by comparison of unknowns with **exemplars** (known, authentic writing samples) depends upon two factors; first, there must be sufficient individual characteristics present in the unknown sample and second, there must be sufficient samples of the purported writer's authentic handwriting. If both of these conditions are met, then questioned document examiners believe that it is possible to individualize an unknown handwriting exhibit to a particular person. If either of the above conditions is not met, then an equivocal conclusion may be necessary; that the suspect's writing could be the source for the unknown writing. Of course, it is also possible to use class or individual characteristics to eliminate a suspect as being the source of questioned handwriting. As with other types of comparative evidence such as shoeprints, bullets, fingerprints, etc., there are no standards as to the minimum number of characteristics of handwriting that must be present in known and unknown handwriting samples in order to reach a conclusion of individuality. The minimum number is dependent upon the size of the questioned and exemplar samples, the nature of the characteristics, and the experience of the examiner. If a handwriting sample contains many unusual characteristics, then a questioned document examiner may need to find fewer of them than would be the case with a more "normal" handwriting. In any case, the individual examiner must find enough points on the questioned document and exemplar to be convinced to a degree of reasonable, scientific certainty; that the questioned document was written by the same hand as the exemplar. Under no circumstances it is permissible to state a percent probability that the questioned document was written by the suspect. That is, it would not be permissible to state "I am 95% sure that the suspect wrote the will." This is an important concept that also applies to other types of evidence such as fingerprints and tool marks. In order for an examiner to be able to cite numerical probabilities about the likelihood that known and unknown evidence have a common source, there must be studies that yield information about how common a particular set of characteristics are in a given population. Although this works well for DNA, where there is a finite set of types of DNA, it is not possible to do this for handwriting, where characteristics do not fall into discrete groupings. This gives rise to two perceived weaknesses in the conclusions of individuality often reached by document examiners: there are no agreed-upon standards for determining when authorship has been determined, and there are no probabilistic conclusions that can be reached in a document comparison examination. The National Academy of Sciences Forensic Science Committee, in its 2009 report, highlighted these weaknesses in questioned document analysis as well as with fingerprints, firearms, tool marks, shoeprints and tire treads, and hair analysis.

HANDWRITING COMPARISON CHARACTERISTICS

There are a large number of handwriting characteristics, both class and individual, that can be used for comparisons of questioned and exemplar specimens. A few of the more common ones are listed below.

- Spacing between letters
- Spacing between words
- Relative proportions between letters and within letters
- Individual letter formations

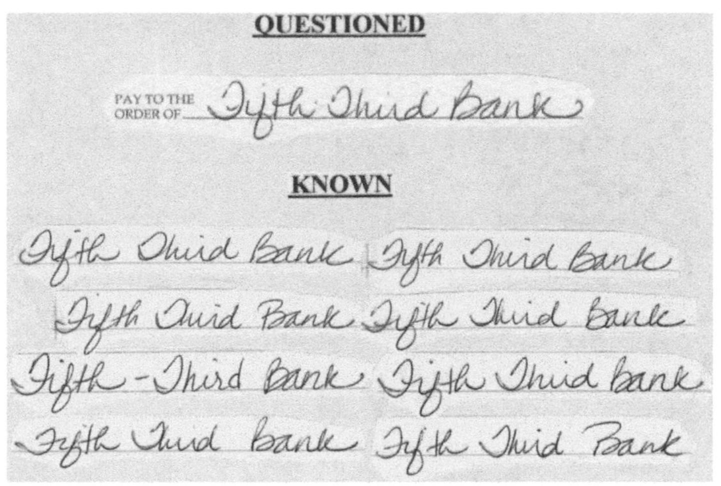

FIGURE 20.1

A handwriting comparison. The questioned document is a bank check.

Courtesy: Robert Kullman, Speckin Forensic labs.

- Formations of letter combinations
- The overall slant of the writing
- Connecting strokes
- Pen lifts
- Beginning and ending strokes
- Unusual flourishes
- Pen pressure

Unlike other pattern evidence such as fingerprints, handwriting changes throughout life. There may also be changes in a person's handwriting due to such factors as stress, physical and emotional condition, illness, influence of drugs, or alcohol and the conditions under which the writing is made including type of writing instrument and paper, level of comfort, and lighting. Figure 20.1 shows how handwriting characteristics can be used to compare known and unknown samples of handwriting.

COLLECTION OF HANDWRITING EXEMPLARS

Although questioned document examiners have little or no control over the quality and quantity of the questioned writing sample, they do have or should have control over the exemplars. Known writing samples are critical to a successful handwriting comparison. The quantity of exemplar material is also important and thus the full range of variation in the subject's writing should be obtained. Just as important, however, is the quality and type of exemplars. There must be some similarities between the known and unknown writings in order to make meaningful comparisons. There are two types of exemplars: requested and nonrequested writings.

Requested writings are writing samples taken from someone for the purpose of comparison with a questioned document. These writings are generally taken by multiple dictations of a passage that has words and phrases similar to the questioned document. This type of data collection minimizes the chance that the subject is deliberately trying to alter their handwriting style. The writing often consists of a few generic sentences or passages followed by all or part of the exact questioned document. Requested writings are often preferred because the questioned document examiner has a good deal of control about the content, paper, writing implement, etc. that is used in the writing and can request enough writing sample so as to minimize the chances that the writer will be able to disguise the writing and to account for natural variation in one's handwriting. The major disadvantage of requested writings is temporal; if a great deal of time has elapsed between the time the questioned document was written and the collection of the requested writing, there is a chance that the questioned document examiner may not be able to make a valid comparison because the handwriting could have changed dramatically during the period between the two samples.

Proper Collection of Requested Writings

Successful comparison of known and unknown handwritings depends in part on the quality and quantity of the exemplars. Listed below are some of the more important considerations that must be kept in mind when collecting known samples.

- The most important consideration is that there must be a sufficient amount of writing to ensure that the normal variations that are present in everyone's handwriting are represented. There is no standard amount of writing that would suffice, but some examiners believe that 10–20 samples of the comparable writing should be sufficient.
- Each writing sample should be on a separate sheet of paper and should be removed from the sight of the writer before collecting the next sample.
- Requested writings should be collected by dictation, not copying. Dictation minimizes the chance of deliberate alteration of handwriting because the subject must concentrate on listening to the dictation.
- Dictated passages should be long. This will also help uncover attempts to deliberately alter handwriting because the longer someone is forced to write, the harder it is to make deliberate alterations to what is essentially a subconscious process.
- The requested writing should contain some words and phrases that are present in the questioned document. If there are misspelled words in the questioned document, they should also be given in the exemplar. The same holds true with mistakes in punctuation.
- To the extent possible, the subject should be supplied with the same type of writing instrument and paper used in the questioned document. The subject should also be made as comfortable as is practical and there should be adequate lighting.

The temporal limitation of requested writings can sometimes be overcome by using **nonrequested writing** exemplars. These are examples of the subject's writing that are taken in the normal course of business or personal transactions. They might include checks, bills, a diary, deeds, etc. Every effort should be made to obtain nonrequest writings that were written around the same time as the questioned document. The major problem with nonrequested writings is establishing their authenticity. In order for such writings to be admissible in court, there must be proof that the subject wrote them. This may be accomplished in a number of ways including having a witness who saw the subject write the exemplar, having the subject available to testify that the subject wrote the exemplar, or getting an exception to the hearsay rule under the business records exception. Normally, evidence such as nonrequested handwriting would be inadmissible in court because it is hearsay: a statement (in this case the handwriting sample) that is made out of court by someone who was not under oath at the time the statement was uttered or written, and the statement is now being used to prove what it says. The hearsay rule protects defendants against the problem of having unsponsored evidence in court and no one to cross-examine about the truth of the evidence. An exception to the hearsay rule is the "business record." This is a document that is created in the normal course of a business and because it is important to the business, there would be little use in falsifying it. A nonrequested exemplar made in the normal course of business can sometimes be admitted as an authentic example of the writer's handwriting. There have also been situations where a questioned document examiner has compared nonrequested writings to admitted writings and shown them to be written by the same hand. In most questioned document examinations, it is preferable to have both request and nonrequest exemplars.

HISTORY OF QUESTIONED DOCUMENTS: ANOTHER HOWARD HUGHES CASE

The great wealth and mystery surrounding the later life of the billionaire Howard Hughes spawned a number of unusual events such as the attempt to forge his autobiography by Clifford Irving, as described at the beginning of this chapter. Another unusual occurrence was the so-called "Mormon Will", a will that was alleged to have been written by Howard Hughes, which left a large fortune to the Church of the Latter Day Saints (the Mormon Church). This case started in 1967, when Melvin Dummar (1944–present), owner of a filling station in Willard, Utah, claimed to have encountered Howard Hughes wandering alone in a Nevada desert and saved him. Dummar claimed to have picked up a disheveled man walking in the desert. The man asked Dummar to take him to the Sands Hotel in Las Vegas, about 150 miles away. During the trip, Dummar indicated that the man told him that he was Howard Hughes. After Hughes died in 1976, a handwritten will was discovered in Salt Lake City at the Headquarters of the Mormon Church. The will was dated in 1968. This will was later found to have a number of strange instructions and statements. For example, it appointed a former employee of Hughes, Noah Dietrich, as executor even though Dietrich had left Hughes' employ years before. Both of Hughes ex-wives were named in the will although they had both signed agreements that barred them from ever making any claims on the estate.

Hughes had never been a member of the LDS Church. Even names of Hughes' relatives were misspelled. Melvin Dummar was given a 16th part of the estate and his name was misspelled in the will. When the will went to probate in court, Dummar was questioned about the encounter in the desert and claimed he didn't know anything about the will. His fingerprints were later discovered on the envelope containing the will. He then said that someone had given him the will with instructions to deliver it to the headquarters of the LDS Church. In 1978, a Nevada jury ruled that the will was

(Continued)

HISTORY OF QUESTIONED DOCUMENTS: ANOTHER HOWARD HUGHES CASE—cont'd

a forgery and Dummar received nothing. No charges were filed against him. Interestingly enough, a re-examination of the evidence in this case by a retired FBI agent allegedly uncovered evidence by close associates of Hughes that seemed to confirm his story of being picked up in the desert by Dummar. He subsequently filed a suit to recover the inheritance he had claimed was his, but the suit was dismissed in 2007.

SIGNATURES

Signatures can present special problems for questioned document examiners. In many cases, a person's signature does not represent typical handwriting nor does it always contain the same individual characteristics as normal handwriting. A single signature may be the sole handwriting on the entire questioned document, giving rise to problems that the sample may be insufficient for a definite conclusion. Finally, signatures tend to be very sensitive to context. Consider the many situations where one is called upon to furnish a signature. Most people would sign an official document such as a will or property deed carefully, so there would be no doubt about the name. This would be a **formal signature**. An **informal signature** would be used in routine correspondence such as personal letters and other documents where you want the reader to recognize the signature but the exact spelling of the name isn't important. Finally, there is the **abbreviated or stylistic signature** that would be used in signing checks, credit card receipts, etc. This is also the famous "physician's signature" on a prescription. It is often highly stylistic and often looks like a scribble with little that would be recognizable as a signature. Because of the sensitivity to context of signatures, there are rules for the collection of exemplars of signatures. The circumstances under which the exemplar is collected should be as similar to the way that the questioned document was written as possible. Therefore, signatures are always collected in context. For example, if the questioned document is a forged check signature, the subject might be asked to fill out 10–20 blank checks for varying amounts and sign them.

Forged Signatures

Signatures are often the subjects of forgery attempts. Depending upon the circumstances, the forgery may be accomplished in a number of ways. If the signature were to be furnished on the spot as in a stolen check, forgers would attempt the forgery in one of two ways. Either they would practice it from a copy of the authentic signature beforehand and then try to duplicate the check-owner's signature on the check, or they would just write the check freehand, with no attempt to forge the signature. Hopefully for the forger, the merchant wouldn't pay much attention to the signature. Figure 20.2 shows how signatures are compared.

The forgery of a document that does not have to be signed in front of someone else may be accomplished in different ways. It may be traced, for example. This could be

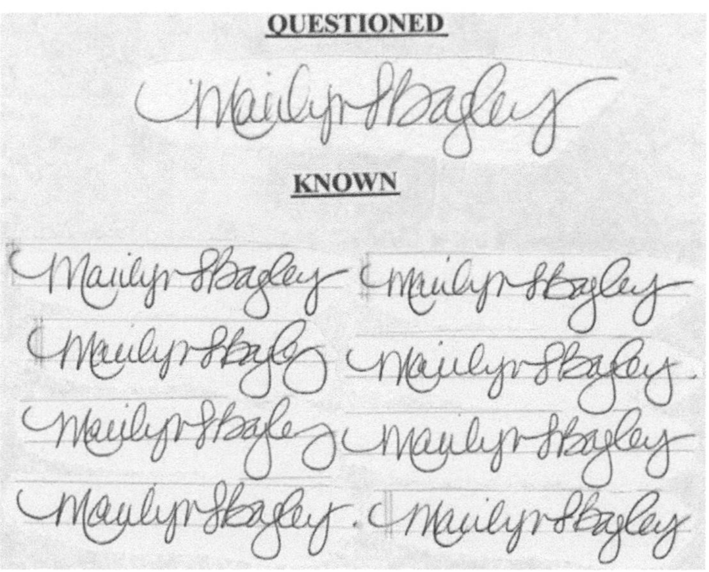

FIGURE 20.2

A signature comparison.

Courtesy: Robert Kullman, Speckin Forensic labs.

done using transmitted light or tracing making an indented writing of the signature in a piece of paper and then retracing it. Most tracings of either type have characteristics that make them look artificial and the tracing may be apparent to the trained questioned document examiner. As with all questioned documents, the key to discovering a forged signature is collecting sufficient numbers of exemplars.

PRINTED DOCUMENTS: TYPEWRITERS, COMPUTER PRINTERS, ELECTROSTATIC COPIERS

Printed documents are subject to different considerations than handwritten ones. Except under unusual circumstances, mass production of machines such as typewriters, printers, and copiers prevents individualization of a document to a particular machine. The only exception to this rule is in the case where there is a defect in the printing or copying mechanism that results in the repeated appearance of an unusual or unique characteristic, or preferably several such characteristics. Typewriters are more likely to show these defects than other types of printing instruments.

TYPEWRITERS

Although the use of typewriters has diminished greatly owing to the development of computer printers, they are still around and still in use. Forensic document examiners are normally asked two questions about typewritten documents: Can the document be traced to a particular machine, and can the make and model of the typewriter be determined? The answer to the first question requires some knowledge about how typewriters operate and how unique characteristics are likely to arise. Older style typewriters generally utilize a standard keyboard. When a key is struck the corresponding raised, metal character mounted on a long stem strikes a ribbon that then leaves an inked imprint of the letter on the paper. As time passes, the metal character may become worn, chipped, bent, or misaligned. This gives rise to reproducible defects that can serve to identify the particular typewriter. Newer model typewriters employ a metal sphere with all of the characters raised on its surface. When a character is struck on the keyboard, the sphere is aligned so that the portion containing that character is lined up with the ribbon. The sphere strikes the ribbon, leaving an inked impression on the paper. Because the characters are all on one sphere and are more rigidly held than if they are on individual stems, these typewriters are less prone to developing wear or misalignments in the typefaces, thus making individualization more difficult. This problem is compounded by the fact that the spheres are easily replaced, so that a comparison of a typewritten document with a particular machine requires the original sphere that typed the document. Determining the make and model of the typewriter that made a document requires that the examiner have a complete library of sample writings of every make and model of typewriter that is available. The font type and size is generally characteristic of particular manufacturer's models of typewriters, so a questioned, typewritten document can be compared with library entries to determine the make and model used. A typewriting comparison is shown in Figure 20.3.

Typewriter Exemplars

When a questioned document is written on a typewriter, the best policy is to get the actual, suspect machine into the hands of the questioned document examiner. There are a number of variables with typewriters that can affect the appearance of the type on paper and they need to be controlled by the document examiner. For example, many typewriters permit the typist to adjust the pressure of the keystrokes to make the typed image darker or lighter. In addition, having the typewriter gives the examiner the opportunity to examine all of the typefaces as well as the ribbon. In the case of IBM Selectric® models, the typeface ball that was alleged to have made the questioned document must also be submitted. If the typewriter cannot be submitted, then it will be necessary to get a complete set of all characters at all settings of pressure. It is also advisable to type the exact questioned document on the typewriter so the examiner can make direct comparisons. If possible, the ribbon should also be submitted for examination.

LASER PRINTERS AND COPIERS

Laser printers and copy machines that use Xerography© do not use ink to make characters on the paper. Instead, the characters are made using a toner made from finely

QUESTIONED

Do not call help
There is bomb in bank set
to go off at 5:45.
If we do not see or hear
police. Will call location of bomb
at 5:40.
Put all 100's, 50's, 20's, 10's & 5's
in contain & send out.
My partner is right behind me.
Act natural.

P.S. I now know your name.

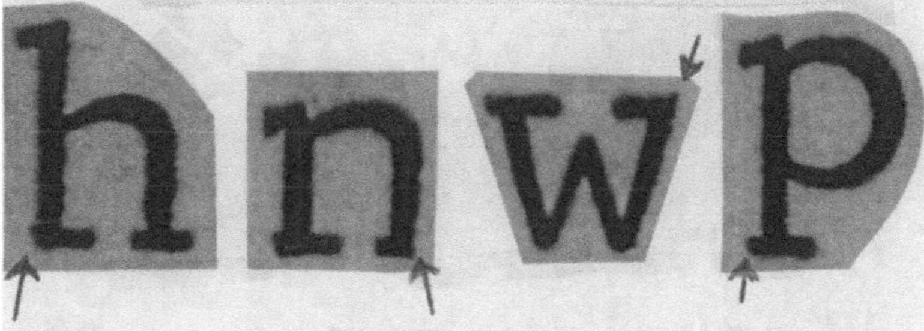

KNOWN

Do not call help
There is bomb in bank set
to go off at 5:45.
If we do not see or hear
police. Will call location of bomb
at 5:40.
Put all 100's, 50's, 20's, 10's & 5's
in contain & send out.
My partner is right behind me.
Act natural.

P.S. I now know your name.

FIGURE 20.3

A typewriter comparison. The arrows point to unusual features of certain letters made by the typewriter in question. The features show up in both the known and questioned typewritings.

Courtesy: Robert Kullman, Speckin Forensic labs.

divided carbon powder and binders and a laser. There is little chance that characters will become deformed over time. If the cartridge that contains the toner starts to run out, then the print quality may become irregular, but this will change with time and may not be of much help. There are situations, however, where extraneous marks or blotches of toner may show up repeatedly in the same location until the machine is cleaned or repaired. If the questioned document and exemplars both show these same markings in the same location on the copy, this may provide individual information about the source of the questioned document. It would not be necessary for the examiner to have the printer or copier. Instead, whoever investigates the incident should make sure that an adequate number of exemplars are taken to show the degree of consistency of the extraneous markings. If there are no reproducible, extraneous markings on the paper, and the source of the copy is not known, it may still be possible to determine the make of the copier or printer by chemical analysis and comparison of the toners with known samples. This evidence is not individual, however; it is normally not possible to determine with certainty that a particular machine was the source of a questioned document.

INKJET PRINTERS

Inkjet printers generally spray ink onto the paper for character and picture formation. As with laser printers and copiers, there is no issue of a user-defined pressure or darkness of the characters, and misalignment of particular characters is not normally an issue. In addition, as with laser printers or copiers, there is the chance that extraneous, reproducible markings may appear on the paper that may help in pinpointing the source of the copy. As the cartridge runs out of ink, the typescript may become uneven and fade. This is especially pronounced with color cartridges wherein the loss of one color ink will distort the colors that appear on the page. Again, however, this problem continues with time until there is no more ink or until the user changes cartridges. If there are no reproducible imperfections from the printer, it may still be possible to pinpoint the printer manufacturer from chemical analysis of the ink. Of course, there are other class characteristics such as font type that can be used to help associate a document with a computer and printer. As with laser printers and copiers, it is not normally possible to trace a document written on an inkjet printer back to a specific machine.

FAX MACHINES

Fax machines are similar to the machines that were discussed above with respect to ink or toner and the possible presence of extraneous, individual markings on the paper. In addition, however, facsimiles also possess a special header that describes some of the characteristics of the fax, such as originating and recipient fax numbers, date and time, etc. This header is called a transmitting terminal identifier or TTI. The TTI can be a very important characteristic in the comparison of known and unknown facsimiles. It will usually be in a special font that is different from the text font and attempts to forge TTIs and place them on a document is usually detectable by document examiners.

OTHER EXAMINATIONS PERFORMED BY DOCUMENT EXAMINERS

In addition to the comparison of handwritings and printed writings, questioned document examiners are sometimes called upon to perform a variety of other related examinations. One broad category is termed **document alterations**. These include obliterations, erasures, additional markings, indented writings, and charred documents. Another major category of analysis involves tools such as inks, papers, and pencil leads. Finally, there is the emerging issue of the age of documents, especially those that are handwritten using ink. This technology involves considerable skill and knowledge of chemistry and is presently being performed by only a handful of document examiners worldwide and research into new methods of ink dating is presently being carried out by a number of investigators.

DOCUMENT ALTERATIONS

Obliterations

Obliteration is the overwriting of a sample of writing or printing with another writing instrument. It may be accidental or deliberate. The document examiner may be called upon to discover what is contained in the writing beneath the obliteration. Obliterations can be made with pens or pencils or other types of writing instruments. The method used to discover what is written under an obliteration depends on the original writing and the means used. It may be possible to dissolve all or part of the obliteration or to use a light source that will be transmitted through the obliteration but not the original writing. This will permit the examiner to read the original writing underneath the obliteration. In some cases, it is possible to treat the paper with a special transparent liquid that changes its refractive index so that the original writing can be viewed from the back of the paper. In some cases, a strong backlit light source may penetrate the obliteration enough to read the underlying writing. A sample of obliterated handwriting is shown in Figure 20.4(a) and (b).

Over the past 10 years, one of the authors of this book encountered cases in which sections of printed documents were obliterated using a black marker. In one case, soaking the document in methyl alcohol removed enough of the marker to see through it without damaging the printing below. In another case, ethyl alcohol did the same thing. Such soaking techniques may not be successful if the original writing is made with ink as opposed to toner because the solvent used to dissolve the obliterating agent may also dissolve the ink. The use of infrared (IR) or ultraviolet light may visualize underlying handwriting that has been obliterated. The wavelength of light is chosen so that it is transmitted through the obliteration to the ink below. If the ink then absorbs the light, it will appear dark. Sometimes the light will cause the ink to fluoresce in the visible or IR region enabling it to be seen with the naked eye or a camera and special film or filters.

(a)

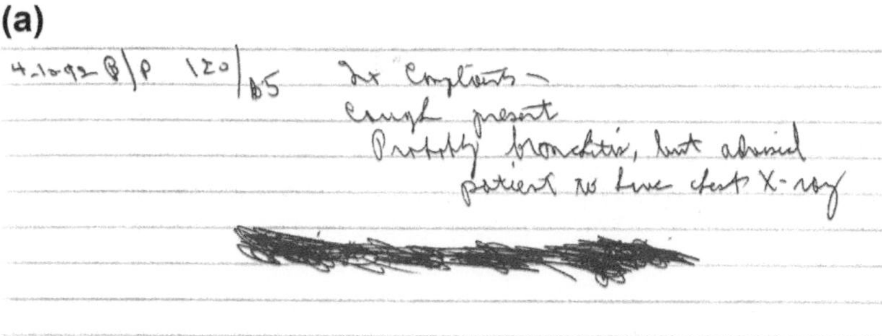

(b)

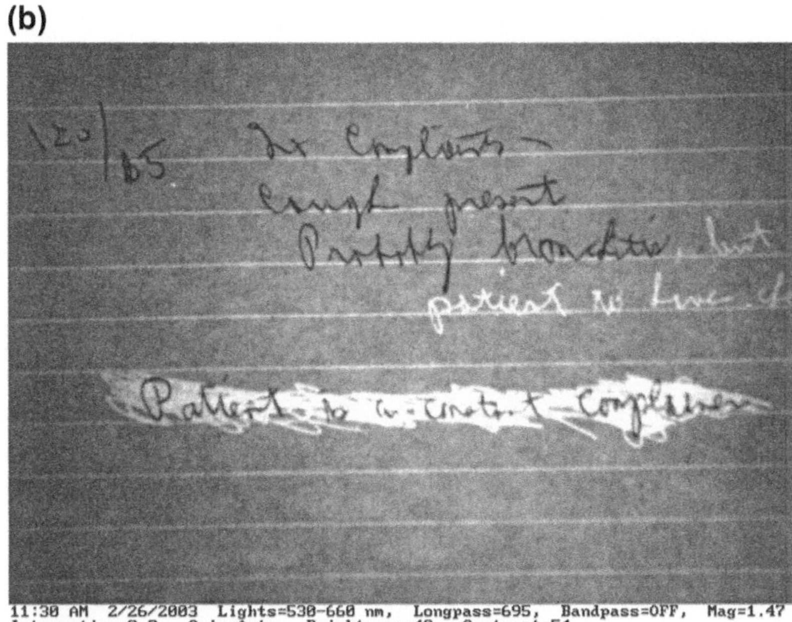

FIGURE 20.4

Obliteration. (a) A portion of a patient's medical record with an entry obliterated. (b) The same record photographed with infrared light.

Courtesy: Robert Kullman, Speckin Forensic labs.

Erasures

Erasures can occur in a number of ways. The familiar **abrasive erasure** involves removing writing (usually that made with a pencil) with an abrasive eraser material. **Chemical erasures** involve dissolving or bleaching ink so that it is no longer visible. Typewriter erasures involve the use of a ribbon that lifts typewritten images from the paper. All of these erasure types can, in principle, be detected. Abrasive erasures are the easiest to detect. They virtually always involve disturbance of paper coatings and fibers at the point of the erasure that can be seen with a low power microscope. Chemical erasures may be detected by differences in shades of color in the paper

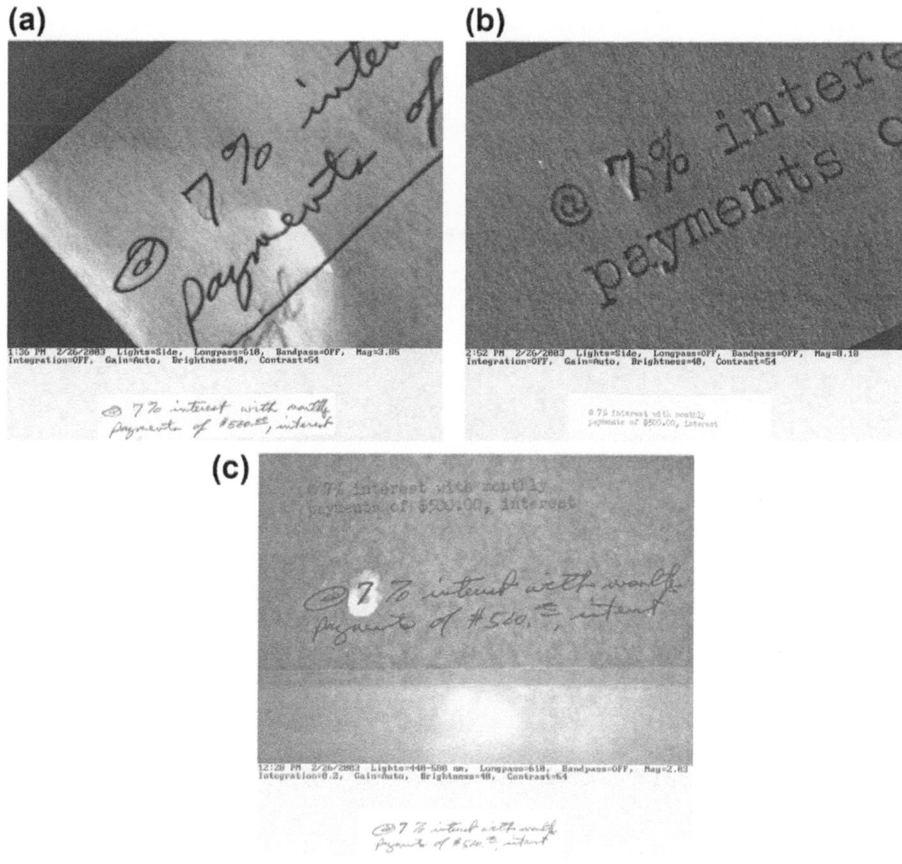

FIGURE 20.5

Erasures. Original documents read "6% interest…." (a) A pencil erasure. (b) A typewriter erasure (c) A chemical erasure.

Courtesy: Robert Kullman, Speckin Forensic labs.

from bleaching effects or by behavior of the chemicals in UV or IR light. Typewriter erasures can be detected by observing the indentations made by the typewriter in the paper. This can be done using oblique-angle photography and a low power microscope. Even though it may be relatively easy to detect that an erasure has taken place, it is usually more difficult to determine what was erased. An efficient erasure may be impossible to overcome and the writing may never be reconstructed. Partial erasures may enable the examiner to read some or all of what was erased as seen in Figure 20.5.

Indented Writings

There are many situations where a document is written on the top sheet of a pad of paper using a writing instrument, such as a ballpoint pen, that exerts pressure on the paper. This may result in an image of the writing being formed on one or more pages below.

I have been very sick and can't
leave my house. Please excuse me
from our meeting this month.
I will call you when I get
over this sickness.

Bob Nelson
#4731-624

FIGURE 20.6

The use of an electrostatic detection apparatus (ESDA). This is a note given to a bank teller during a robbery. ESDA reveals what was written on the piece of paper above the note in the pad of paper on which the note was written.

Courtesy: Robert Kullman, Speckin Forensic labs.

There are a number of ways of viewing this **indented writing**. The simplest and most popular method of viewing indented writings is with oblique lighting. If a light is directed across the surface of the page at an angle, the indentations may cast enough shadow on the paper to reveal the contents of the writing. This may work for several pages below the top sheet, especially if a high-resolution digital camera is used to capture the image. Sometimes TV or movies will show indented writing being visualized by rubbing the indented area with the side of a pencil. This will not only usually fail to visualize the indented part of the writing, but will destroy the evidence also so that workable methods cannot be used. There is also an instrumental method for capturing indented writings. It is called the **Electrostatic Detection Apparatus** (ESDA). This apparatus works a bit like an electrostatic copy machine, in that it uses a toner that is deposited preferentially in the indented writings so that they can be visualized. Figure 20.6 illustrates how ESDA is used.

Charred Documents

In many crimes and civil infractions, the perpetrator tries to destroy documentary evidence that would otherwise be incriminating. This can be conveniently accomplished by burning the documents. If the documents are recovered before being completely destroyed, there is a chance that some of the writing can be identified. This is because, although the paper may become charred, the ink or pencil may not char as easily. One of the problems with **charred documents** is that they are very fragile. Sometimes they can be strengthened by misting them with a lacquer or alcohol or

FIGURE 20.7

Charred writing. By using infrared light, the figures made with the ink fluoresce against the charred background.

water. This may provide enough strengthening to enable the examiner to preserve the document between sheets of glass or plastic. Analysis of charred documents is carried out somewhat like that for obliterations. The key is that the ink or toner is preserved and then the goal is to provide as much contrast as possible between the darkened, charred paper, and the ink. If the ink fluoresces with UV or IR light, then photography using specialized films may be used along with the proper lighting. Even intense incandescent light sources have sometimes provided the needed contrast to visualize the writing. See Figure 20.7 for an example of the analysis of charred writing.

INK ANALYSIS

In recent years forensic document examiners have become more comfortable performing chemical analyzes as part of their routine work. This has been aided by research into the composition of inks that has led to the development of easier methods of characterizing and comparing inks. Understanding the composition of an ink sample and the chemical changes that it undergoes as it dries can be very important in several types of document cases. For example, there are a number of questioned document cases where an examiner may be called upon to determine if two documents could have been written using the same writing instrument such as a particular ballpoint pen. In other cases, a question arises as to whether a document could have been altered by means of adding writings after the original document were written, as for example, a check that was altered by adding zeros to the amount of the check. Other cases involve a question of the possibility that a document could have been altered by adding additional writings and then backdating them to make it seem as if they were put in at an earlier date. The first two of these questions involves the chemical analysis of an ink sample and comparison of two or more writings. Although it is not possible to individualize an ink sample to a particular writing instrument, it is possible to show that a suspect pen, for example, could be included in the population of pens that could have written a document, or that it could not have possibly written a document. The last question involves determining the age of the ink sample either relative to other writings on the document or by estimating the actual age of the ink. This involves knowledge of what happens to the ink as it dries.

Analyzing and Comparing Ink Samples

There are many different types of inks as evidenced by the myriad types of pens available today. These range from the familiar ballpoint pens, roller ball pens, fiber or porous tip pens, gel pens, and the venerable India ink pens and fountain pens. There are also inkjet inks that are used in some computer printer cartridges. The inks for each of these pen and printer types are formulated especially for the ink delivery system. Inks can be quite complex materials. For example, modern ballpoint pen inks contain a solvent such as ethylene glycol and dyes. There may also be drying agents and other additives in an ink formulation. When the composition of an ink sample is determined, it can help determine what type of writing instrument it came from.

SAMPLING

Sampling ink on a questioned document presents unique problems because the legibility of the handwriting or printing must be maintained so that the handwriting characteristics are not destroyed. This means that the samples of ink taken for analysis must be very small. Sampling is typically accomplished by using a blunt-point syringe needle that takes tiny plugs from individual letters in the writing. Many plugs may be taken from a writing sample as long as there are sufficient writings available to maintain legibility. The number and size of the plugs will, of necessity, dictate the amount and types of testing that can be done.

THIN-LAYER CHROMATOGRAPHY

The most popular and one of the easiest methods of ink analysis and comparison is thin-layer chromatography (TLC). Normally about 10 plugs of ink are dissolved in a minimum amount of a solvent such as methanol and then spotted at the bottom of the TLC plate. When the plate is developed, there will usually be several spots from the dyes in the ink, since there may be a number of dyes used to formulate that particular color of ink. In addition to the dye peaks, there may be other peaks from some of the other materials present in the ink. These may not be colored so some sort of visualization would be necessary. Figure 20.8 shows a TLC of some ink samples.

OTHER TYPES OF CHROMATOGRAPHY

Both gas chromatography and liquid chromatography have been successfully employed in the analysis and comparison of inks. Their advantage over TLC is that

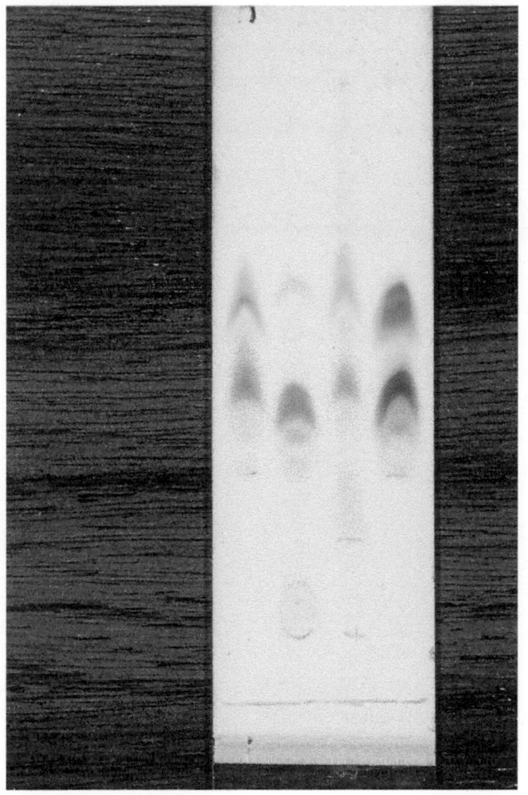

FIGURE 20.8

Thin-layer chromatography of inks. Lanes one and three are standard black, ballpoint pen inks. Lanes 2 and 4 are each different black inks.

Courtesy: Jamie Dunn, Michigan State University, Department of Chemistry.

they yield quantitative as well as qualitative data and they are both generally more sensitive than TLC, which means that they require fewer plugs of ink. In addition, GC-MS is often used, allowing identification of each of the components in the ink. Capillary electrophoresis has also been applied to ink analysis, although applications of ink analysis have been very limited thus far. Capillary electrophoresis is similar to HPLC but uses tiny columns for separation so that as little as one or two plugs may be used for analysis. This has great advantages in cases where the sample is very limited.

INFRARED SPECTROPHOTOMETRY

IR spectrophotometry has also been used for characterizing inks. This technique shows absorption peaks for all of the components of the ink at one time, including the solvent, dyes, and additives. Because of this, IR can be very helpful in comparing two ink samples to see if they could have originated from the same source.

One of the disadvantages of IR is that it requires more sample than do chromatographic methods in general. It is difficult to use micro plugs for sampling in IR. Various sampling methods have been tried including using IR microscopy.

MASS SPECTROMETRY

Mass spectrometry, with and without gas chromatography, has been used for the analysis of inks. Laser desorption mass spectrometry has been especially effective because the ink does not have to be removed from the paper first. A piece of paper with ink writing on it can be directly introduced into the instrument. It is also essentially nondestructive. Laser desorption can be used to track an ink dye as it ages. When dyes age, they undergo chemical degradation. One popular ballpoint pen ink dye, methyl violet, degrades by losing CH_3 groups, replacing them with hydrogen atoms. This results in the loss of 14 mass units from the molecule. Figures 20.9(a) and (b) show how methyl violet degrades and an aging study on a typical ballpoint pen.

MICROSPECTROPHOTOMETRY

One of the more difficult problems in ink analysis is to determine if a specimen of writing is the same color as the ink from a suspect pen. The human eye is an excellent discriminator of color but obviously cannot give objective data about the color of an ink sample. The exact color of an ink (or any other colored material) is defined by the wavelengths of visible light that are either absorbed or transmitted by the dyes in the ink. If one is working with very small samples of ink, a visible microspectrophotometer is the ideal instrument. It determines the absorption or transmission spectrum of the dyes. If two inks are the same color, their visible spectra will be the same.

Document Dating

In addition to analyzing and comparing inks, questioned document examiners are sometimes called upon to determine if the age of a document is consistent with what it is purported to be. An example involves a situation where some writing on a document is not written at the time it is dated. These cases involve determining the age of the document. The most common way of doing this is by determining the age of the ink on the document. For example, a few years ago there was a case in Michigan where a physician was accused of entering notes about a particular medical procedure in a patient's file after the patient died. A questioned document examiner was called upon to determine if the notes were written at the time that the date on them indicated.

There are a number of ways of estimating the age of an ink sample. The most common method is to examine chemical changes to the ink as it dries. When ink dries, a number of chemical processes are going on at the same time, for example, the solvent in the ink is constantly evaporating. As this happens, some of the components of the ink may form polymers (e.g., resins). In addition, the dyes in the ink will change in chemical composition over time. One way of tracking the drying of ink with time is to determine how easily it will redissolve in a suitable solvent as it dries.

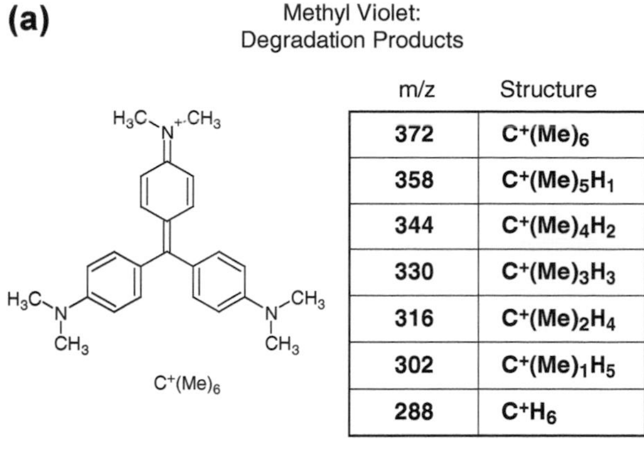

m/z	Structure
372	$C^+(Me)_6$
358	$C^+(Me)_5H_1$
344	$C^+(Me)_4H_2$
330	$C^+(Me)_3H_3$
316	$C^+(Me)_2H_4$
302	$C^+(Me)_1H_5$
288	C^+H_6

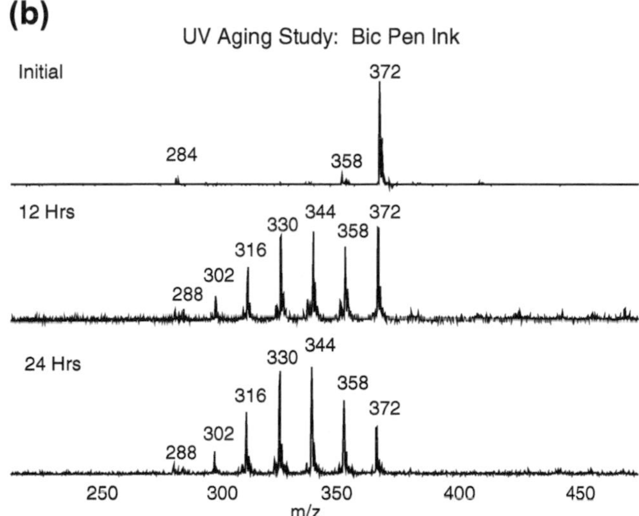

FIGURE 20.9

(a) The degradation of methyl violet. Each degradation causes the replacement of a methyl group with a hydrogen atom, resulting in the loss of 14 mass units. (b) An artificial aging study of methyl violet dye in a blue, ballpoint pen, by tracking with laser desorption mass spectrometry.

Inks become less soluble as they dry. This process can be tracked by TLC. IR spectrophotometry can also track this drying process. As the solvent evaporates, some of the IR peaks will decrease in intensity. As polymers form in the ink, some new peaks will appear. As the dyes in inks age, their chemical compositions change. Mass spectrometry or some types of chromatography can track this process. For example, as the composition of a dye changes, its molecular weight will change and this will be reflected in its mass spectrum. These techniques can be used to determine if one set of writings on a document is appreciably older or younger than others or if a document as a whole is as old as it is purported to be. It should be kept in mind that these processes that age documents take place over a long period of time and measuring these changes may not be entirely accurate. It may take several weeks or months before a change in the ink is reliably detectable.

ARTIFICIAL AGING OF INKS

Since inks age slowly over time, it is necessary to have a reliable method of speeding up the aging process so that drying processes may be conveniently studied. The only method that has been studied to any great extent is to heat the document in an oven. It has generally been shown that heating at 100°C for a few minutes or hours can age a document by several months. Since heating may cause unwanted interactions between ink and paper, other methods of artificial aging are also being studied. These include using UV light and using an oxygen-rich atmosphere. Whatever process is used, it must age the ink in the same way that natural aging takes place; that is, the same chemical processes must take place so that the artificial and natural aging processes can be correlated.

BACK TO THE CASE

The Clifford Irving hoax succeeded in part because experts were unable to determine that the various letters, signatures, and notes that Irving produced and attributed to Howard Hughes, were in fact, forgeries. This is somewhat surprising given that Irving had access to only a limited number of authentic examples of Hughes' writing. He was able to use some of Hughes' handwriting that was published in a news magazine. This same circumstance worked in Irving's favor, however, because expert questioned document examiners also had only limited access to exemplars of Hughes' writing. It is likely that Irving succeeded in this case because he was so confident in himself, was a really good salesman and an accomplished author, and was very convincing to the publishers and the document examiners. It is possible that they were biased in his favor and tended to give him the benefit of any doubt that they had about authenticity. This case illustrates the need for large, contemporaneous exemplars, especially requested samples. Hughes was unavailable to supply requested exemplars and it is unlikely that he would have if asked. The limited published samples of his handwriting were likely to be available to all of the parties.

This case also illustrates that the science of handwriting comparison is imperfect and today, 30 years after this case, there are many calls for more research to establish a rigorous scientific basis for the conclusions reached by document examiners. It may be that conclusions of individuality may not be sustained by the science and more equivocal conclusions may become the norm. Remember also that the issue of contextual bias may have played a role in this case. The expert questioned document examiners were presented only with Hughes' known writings and the unknowns and were asked if Hughes wrote the unknowns. Perhaps they were biased toward the conclusion of association.

SUMMARY

A questioned document is any piece of writing or printing whose source or authenticity is in doubt. Questioned document examiners undergo years of apprenticeship training before being certified to take their own cases. Questioned document examination involves many activities, including handwriting comparisons to determine the source of handwriting, typewriting or printing comparison, analysis of paper and inks, and restoration of altered documents. They also determine if a document has been forged or fraudulently produced. Handwriting comparisons are the most familiar of the tasks of the document examiner. Many characteristics of handwriting are characterized and it is necessary to have sufficient, timely, representative known samples of the subject's handwriting for comparison. There is no standard number of characteristics that must be found in the known and unknown sample, in order for the examiner to determine that a particular person wrote a document. There is a similar need for reliable known samples of typewriting, computer printing, or electrostatic copiers. Inks and papers are being given more attention in recent years. This especially applies to inks, where much research is being carried out to identify dyes in the inks. This analysis can also be used to determine the age of a writing sample by tracking the chemical aging of the dyes. Document examiners also examine charred and obliterated documents and documents where one line is written over top of another one.

TEST YOUR KNOWLEDGE

1. Why is it that it is more difficult to distinguish handwriting among a group of third graders than among adults?
2. Explain the precautions that should be taken when obtaining requested handwriting samples to check against a questioned document.
3. Why would it be easier over time, to individualize a sample of typewriting to a particular typewriter than it would be to do so with a computer printer page to a printer?
4. What are some of the major characteristics of forged handwriting?
5. Give an example of a handwritten questioned document that is not written on paper (or similar materials). What special procedures might have to be used in such a case?
6. What characteristics of ink are most useful for comparing known samples with unknowns?
7. How can chemical erasures be detected on a document?
8. How can mechanical erasures be detected on a document?
9. Suppose someone tries to alter a check written for $100 by adding a "0" so that it reads $1000. What are some of the ways this can be detected?
10. How should requested writings be taken if the entire questioned document is a check with an allegedly forged signature?
11. What is the definition of a questioned document in the broadest sense?
12. What is "ink dating?" What is its purpose?
13. How many points of identification are necessary for a questioned document examiner to be able to declare that a questioned document was written by a particular person?
14. What is the difference between requested writings and nonrequested writings?

15. What is ESDA? What is it used for?
16. What is the best way of deciphering indented writings? Why isn't rubbing the indented writing with the side of a pencil a good idea?
17. What are some ways that one could determine some pen handwriting that has been obliterated with another pen?
18. What is a charred document? How can the writing on a charred document be deciphered?
19. How does one become a questioned document examiner? Why is this considered to be an apprenticeship field?
20. What type of certification is there for questioned document examiners?

CONSIDER THIS...

1. How does handwriting vary over time? At what time of life is the change the greatest? How is this taken into account when comparing questioned documents to exemplars?
2. What is the basis for the conclusion that a handwritten questioned document can be matched to a particular writer? In what way is the status of handwriting comparison changing forensically?
3. What is "graphology" (or graphoanalysis)? What relationship does it bear to questioned document analysis? Many questioned document examiners do not trust or agree with the principles of graphoanalysis. What problems has this caused?

FURTHER READING

Ellen, D., August 1997. The Scientific Examination of Documents: Methods and Techniques, second ed. Taylor & Francis Forensic Science Series. Taylor & Francis.

Hilton, O., June 1992. Scientific Examination of Questioned Documents. CRC Press.

Hilton, O., March 1997. Detecting and Deciphering Erased Pencil Writing. Charles C Thomas Pub Ltd.

Robertson, E.W., July 1991. Fundamentals of Document Examination. Nelson-Hall Co.

ON THE WEB

http://www.asqde.org/. Homepage of American Society of Questioned Document Examiners.

http://www.bioforensics.com/kruglaw/f_questioned_docs.htm. A number of interesting links to questioned document home pages.

http://en.wikipedia.org/wiki/Questioned_document_examination. Good overview of questioned document examination.

http://www.interpol.int/public/Forensic/IFSS/meeting13/Reviews/QDHw.pdf. Excellent treatise on handwriting evidence by UK Forensic Science Service.

CHAPTER

Firearms and Tool Marks 21

CHAPTER OUTLINE

KEY TERMS

- Bore
- Breech block
- Broach
- Bullet wipe
- Caliber
- Choke
- Ejection marks
- Extraction marks
- Firing pin impression
- Gauge
- Grains

- Grooves
- Gunshot residues
- Lands
- Muzzle-to-target distance
- Rifled
- Rifling button
- Smokeless powder
- Sodium rhodizonate
- Striations/striae
- Trigger pull
- Twist

THE CASE: DC SNIPER ATTACKS

For 3 weeks in October 2002, 11 people were killed and 3 others were critically wounded in the Washington, DC, metropolitan area. Dubbed the DC sniper attacks because the victims were shot from a distance by a single bullet from a high-powered firearm, the timeline showed an unrelenting pattern of violence (see Figure 21.1).

- October 2: Man killed in Wheaton, Maryland
- October 3: Five killed, four in Maryland and one in DC
- October 4: Woman wounded in Spotsylvania, Virginia
- October 7: Teenager wounded in Bowie, Maryland
- October 9: Man killed near Manassas, Virginia
- October 11: Man killed near Fredericksburg, Virginia
- October 14: Woman killed near Falls Church, Virginia
- October 19: Man wounded in Ashland, Virginia
- October 22: Bus driver killed in Aspen Hill, Maryland

The sniper communicated with police through notes and even a phone call. In the phone call, the killer made a reference to a crime in Alabama, a liquor store holdup in the fall of the previous year. Federal officers worked with Alabama police, who linked the sniper to the liquor store crime through fingerprints.

INTRODUCTION

Firearms examination is one of the key services a forensic science laboratory provides; even smaller laboratories with cooperation or directly harm, and society has judged this implied or actual violence to be a severe crime. Firearms examination is complex, technical, detailed—and experiencing a renaissance with the development and growth of automated database searches. This computerization promises to revolutionize the nature of firearms examination and, perhaps, forensic science.

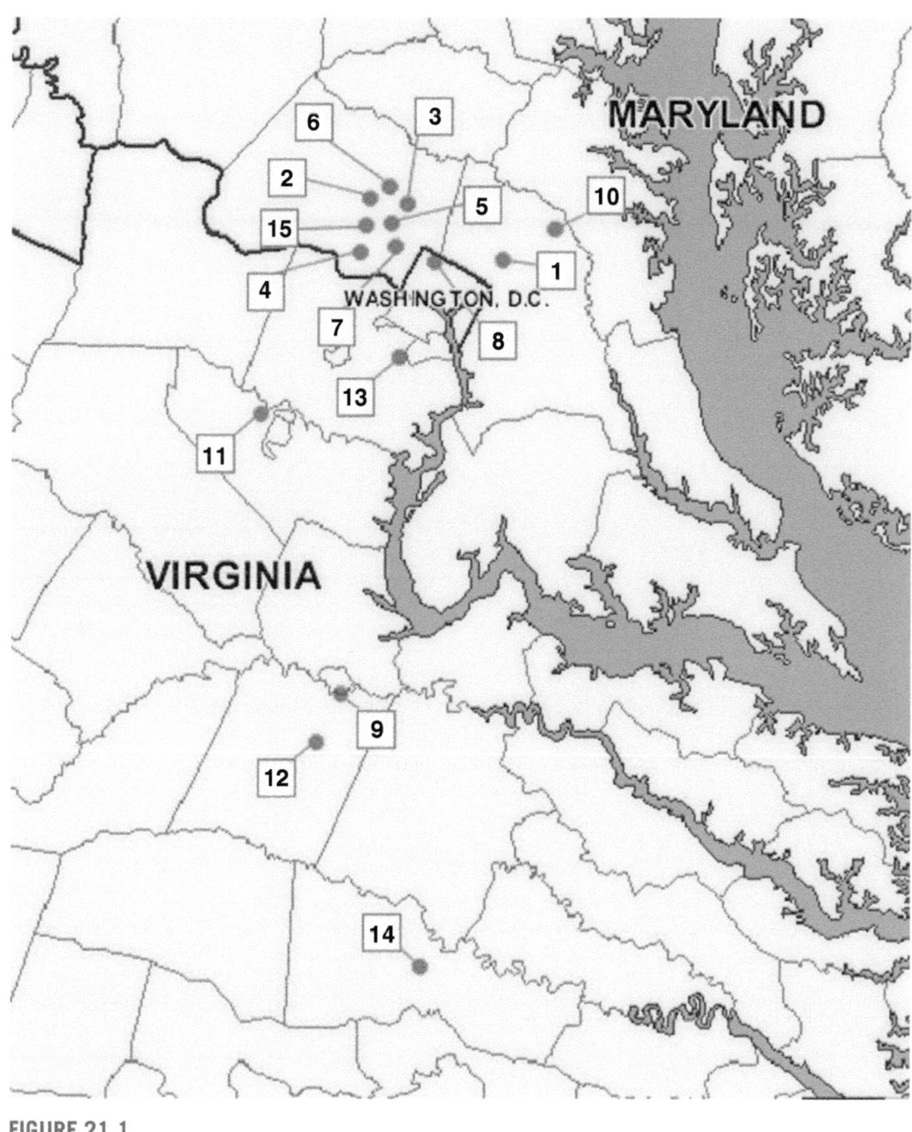

FIGURE 21.1

DC sniper map.

In 1863, Confederate General Stonewall Jackson was fatally wounded on the battlefield during the US Civil War. The deadly projectile was excised from his body and, through examination of its size and shape, determined to be 0.67-caliber ball ammunition. This was not the 0.58-caliber minie ball used by the Union army, but ammunition typical of the Confederate forces—Jackson had been shot by one of his own soldiers! In 1876, a Georgia state court allowed the testimony of an expert witness on the topic

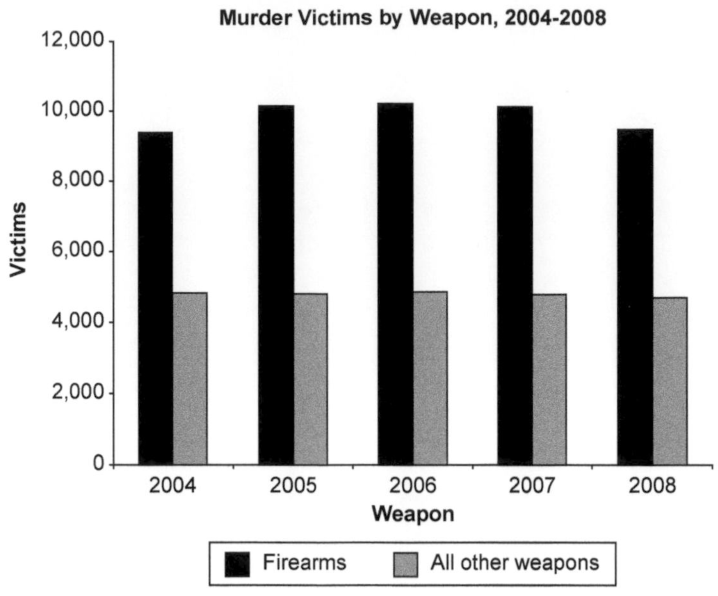

FIGURE 21.2

Murder victims by weapon, 2008–2012. Homicides committed with firearms occur more than twice as often as all other weapons combined. "Other" weapons include sharp objects, blunt objects, personal weapons (fists, e.g.), poison, explosives, fire, narcotics, drowning, strangulation, asphyxiation, and other weapon types not stated.

Source: FBI Uniform Crime Reports, 2014.

of firearms analysis. These are the first examples of firearms analysis and testimony in the United States (Thorwald, 1964; Wilson and Wilson, 2003).

In a report issued by the Bureau of Alcohol, Tobacco, and Firearms nearly 125 years after Jackson's death (ATF, 2000), over 84,000 guns were trafficked illegally in the United States and over 1700 defendants were charged with illegally trafficking guns. While the number of murders committed with firearms has stabilized in the past few years, it is still over 9000 (see Figure 21.2). About 66% of murders, 41% of all robberies, and 18% of all aggravated assaults that are reported to the police were committed with a firearm.

FIREARMS

The field of forensic firearms examination is sometimes referred to as "ballistics" or "forensic ballistics." This terminology is not wholly accurate: Ballistics is the study of an object in flight and is under the domain of physics. The term "forensic ballistics" may be somewhat more accurate but does not capture what forensic firearms examiners do in their job. They certainly are not analyzing the trajectories of bullets *while* they are in flight! Many of the principles, equations, and methodology of ballistics are used, for example, to reconstruct a shooting incident. But the discipline of forensic firearms

FIGURE 21.3

The largest sporting goods show of its kind, the Shooting, Hunting, and Outdoors Trade Show (SHOT Show), is a good source of information about firearms and their manufacturers.

From shotshow.org, with permission by the National Shooting Sports Foundation.

science is more than that and encompasses the study of firearms, their manufacture, operation, and performance; the analysis of ammunition and its byproducts (such as **muzzle-to-target distance** and gunshot residue (GSR)) and the individualizing characteristics that are transferred from firearms to bullets and cartridge cases.

The examination of tool marks is related to firearms in many ways but is also very different in others. It requires an understanding of the way in which tools are made and used; additionally, it includes the restoration of serial numbers that a criminal has attempted to obliterate.

TYPES OF FIREARMS

Very generally, firearms can be divided into two types: handguns and shoulder firearms. Handguns include revolvers and pistols, while shoulder firearms are more diverse, encompassing rifles, shotguns, machine guns, and submachine guns. A broad knowledge and familiarity with the various types, makes, models, and styles of firearms is crucial to being a successful forensic firearms scientist. This knowledge and familiarity should cover not only new products as they emerge on the market, but also older models and the history of manufacturers and their products. Each year, at the Shooting, Hunting and Outdoor Trade Show and Conference (SHOT Show), hundreds of exhibitors, many of them firearms related, display their new products and give out product information; in 2002, thousands of people attend the show (see Figure 21.3). The SHOT Show is an excellent source of information about firearms and related products.

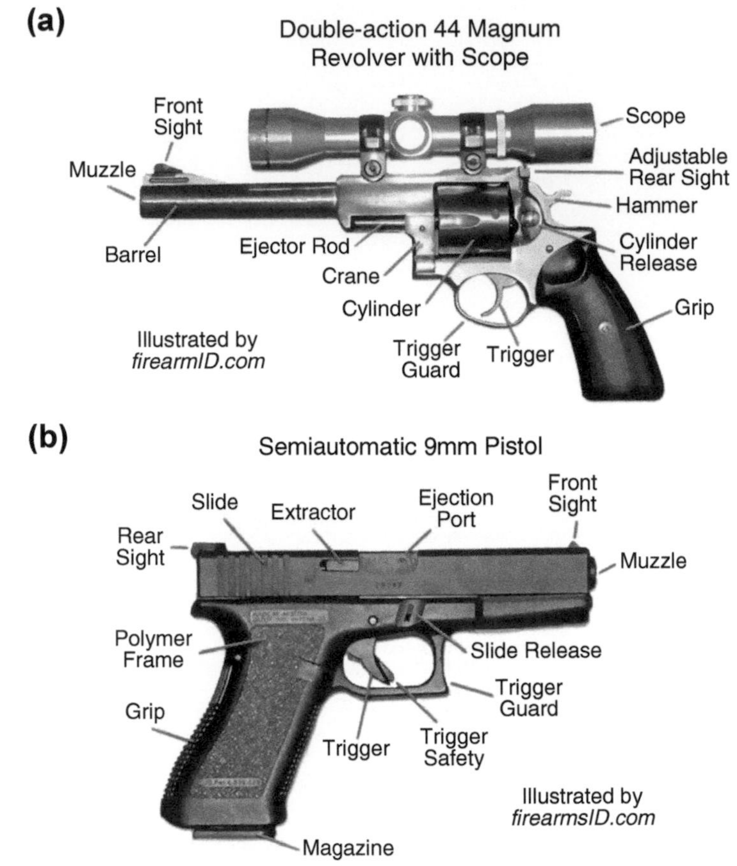

FIGURE 21.4

(a) A revolver is a handgun that feeds ammunition via a revolver cylinder (hence the name), while (b) a pistol feeds ammunition through a spring-loaded magazine.

Courtesy: www.FirearmsID.com, artwork by Erik Dahlberg.

Handguns are firearms designed to be fired with one hand. They appear in two major types: revolvers and (semi)automatic pistols (see Figure 21.4(a) and (b)). A revolver is a handgun that feeds ammunition into the firing chamber by means of a revolving cylinder. The cylinder can swing out to the side or be hinged to the frame and released by a latch or a pin for loading and unloading. A single-action revolver requires that the hammer be cocked each time it is fired; a double-action revolver can be cocked by hand or by the pulling of the trigger, which also rotates the cylinder.

A (semi)automatic pistol, on the other hand, feeds ammunition by means of a spring-loaded vertical magazine. Although the term "automatic" is often applied to pistols fed by magazines, they are not truly automatic in their firing. An automatic firearm is one that continues to fire ammunition while the trigger is pressed; a semiautomatic firearm fires one bullet for each pull of the trigger. When fired,

(a)

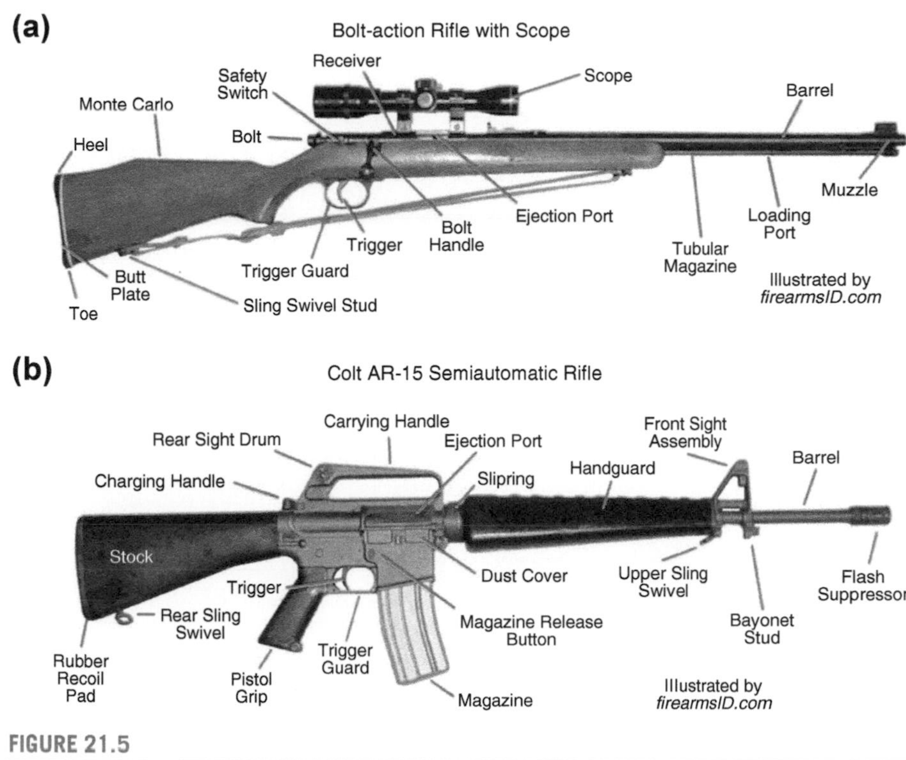

(b)

FIGURE 21.5

Rifles are firearms designed to be fired with two hands, one to pull the trigger, the other to stabilize the barrel for aiming. Rifles can be single-shot, repeating, or assault rifles (a, b).

Courtesy: www.FirearmsID.com, artwork by Erik Dahlberg.

semiautomatic pistols use the energy of the recoil and the sliding of the **breech block** (slide) or the recoil of the cartridge to expel the empty cartridge from the firearm and load a live round into the firing chamber. Springs are used to store the energy and expend it.

Shoulder arms consist of rifles, automatic rifles, machine guns, and shotguns. Rifles are designed to be fired from the shoulder with two hands (see Figure 21.5(a) and (b)). Rifles may be single-shot, repeating, semiautomatic, or automatic. A single-shot rifle must be loaded, fired, the cartridge extracted, and then reloaded; this type of rifle was common as a young boy's first firearm just after the turn of the century but is almost nonexistent now. Repeating rifles fire one bullet with each pull of the trigger, but the expended cartridge must be expelled, the firing mechanism cocked, and a live round reloaded from a magazine manually. Repeating rifles may be bolt-action (like the M1 from war movies or many hunting rifles) or lever-action (made popular by cowboy movies). Semiautomatic rifles use the energy of the fired ammunition to expel the empty cartridge, cock the firing mechanism, and reload a live round; thus, one pull of the trigger fires one round, and this may be done sequentially until the magazine is empty. Assault rifles, like the AK-47 or M-16, can be fired either like semiautomatic rifles or in automatic mode: Pull the trigger, and the firearm will fire ammunition continuously until all the ammunition is gone. A machine gun is a fully automatic firearm and therefore is fed ammunition from a high-capacity belt or box. Because of their size and the strength of the recoil, machine guns are meant to be fired from a tripod or other mounted/fixed position. A submachine gun is a machine gun meant to be fired while held in the hands.

FIREARM BARRELS

The interior surface of the barrels of the firearms discussed so far (handguns and rifles, but not shotguns) are **rifled** with a series of ridges and valleys, called **lands** and **grooves**, respectively, that spiral the length of barrel (see Figure 21.6). The lands dig into the bullet surface as it travels down the barrel, imparting spin to stabilize the bullet's flight once it leaves the barrel. This creates land and groove impressions on the bullet surface as well as impressions of the microscopic imperfections of the interior barrel surface called **striations** or **striae** (see Figure 21.7).

FIGURE 21.6

Spiral grooves are cut into the inner surface of a firearm barrel to impart spin to the bullet as it leaves the barrel, stabilizing its flight. The raised portions between the grooves are called lands.

Courtesy: Richard Ernest, Alliance Forensics, Inc.

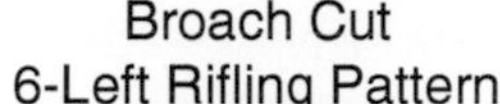

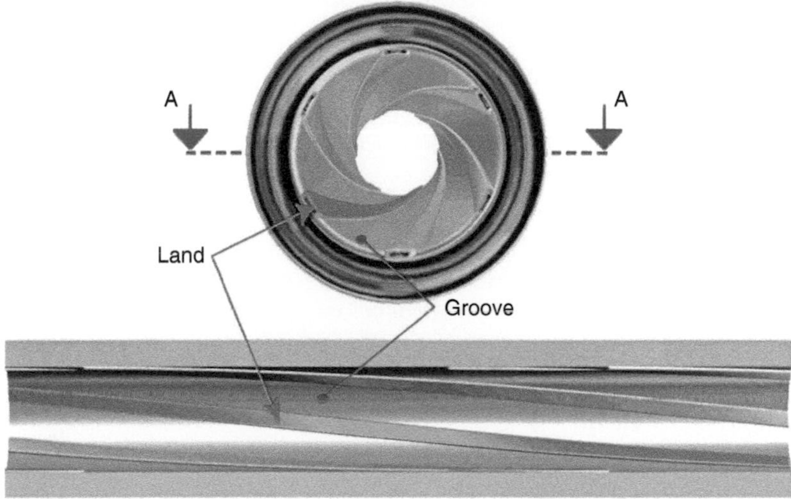

FIGURE 21.7

Imperfections in the surface of the tool that cuts the rifling grooves are transferred to the barrel's inner surface. These striations or striae are then transferred to a bullet's outer surface when it is fired. Striations are considered to be unique to a particular barrel, through manufacturing and use. These are on lead bullets fired from a revolver.

Courtesy: www.FirearmsID.com, artwork by Erik Dahlberg.

FIGURE 21.8

A shotgun is essentially a rifle that doesn't shoot bullets: instead, it fires many small, round pellets or a single large slug. Therefore, shotgun barrels do not have rifling and have a limited effective firing range.

Courtesy: www.FirearmsID.com, artwork by Erik Dahlberg.

During manufacture of a barrel, a hole is drilled down the length of a steel bar of the proper size for the intended firearm. The grooves are cut into the barrel by either a large segmented tool, called a **broach**, or a **rifling button**, a stiff metal rod with a flanged tip, which is run down the length of the hole. When the grooves are cut, they are cut in a spiral of a certain direction or **twist** (right-handed/clockwise or left-handed/counterclockwise); this is what spins the bullet and creates a stable flight path. Some manufacturers produce barrels with four grooves, some with five or six, depending on the design and desired performance of the firearm.

The interior or **bore** diameter of a rifled barrel is the diameter of a circle that touches the tops of the lands. The **caliber** of a firearm used to mean the same thing as bore diameter but now refers mostly to the size of a particular ammunition cartridge; firearms are still referred to in their nominal caliber, however. A barrel's internal diameter is an exact measurement, while caliber is an approximation; the barrel of a 0.38 firearm may actually measure between 0.345 and 0.365 in (also note that calibers do not use the zero before the decimal). The caliber of American and British ammunition is typically measured in inches, and all others are measured in millimeters (a Smith and Wesson 0.32 vs a Beretta 9 mm).

Shotguns can fire numerous projectiles, called pellets or "shot" of varying sizes (see Figure 21.8 and Table 21.1); they may also fire single projectiles called "slugs." A single-barrel shotgun can be either single-shot (manually loaded) or repeating-shot in design (with a spring-loaded auto-feeder or manual pump feeder with a reservoir of three to five shells). The interior of a shotgun barrel is smooth so that nothing deflects or slows down the pellets as they traverse its length. The muzzle of a shotgun barrel may be constricted by the manufacturer to produce a **choke**, which helps to keep the pellets grouped longer once they leave the barrel. The influence of choke on the shot pattern increases with the distance the pellets travel; the range of a shotgun is, compared to rifles, short, but the choke can improve the chance of hitting targets at near to mid-ranges (see Table 21.2). The choke may also be modified by barrel inserts.

Table 21.1 The Size of Pellets Is Organized Numerically, Except for the Two Largest, "BB" and "00" (or "Double Ought") Buckshot

Pellet Size	Diameter (inches)
9	0.08
8	0.09
7	0.10
6	0.11
5	0.12
4	0.13
2	0.15
4	0.16
BB	0.18
00 Buck	0.33

Table 21.2 Choke is the Measure of Constriction of a Shotgun Barrel, Intended to Group the Pellets, and Produce a Tighter Pattern at Impact. Some Shotgun Barrels May Have their Choke Modified by a Removable Insert

Choke	Pellets That Fall Within a 30-in Circle at 40 Yards (%)
Full choke	65–75
Modified choke	45–65
Improved cylinder	35–45
Cylinder bore	25–35

Table 21.3 The Size of a Shotgun Barrel is Measured in Gauge, Except for the Smallest, Which is Labeled as "410" ("Four-ten") Because the Barrel's Internal Diameter is 0.410-in Wide

Gauge	Inches	Millimeters
10	0.775	19.68
12	0.729	18.52
16	0.662	16.82
20	0.615	15.62
410	0.410	10.41

The diameter of the shotgun barrel is called **gauge** and is the number of lead balls with the same diameter as the barrel that would weigh 1 pound. For example, 12 lead balls, which together weigh 1 pound, have the same diameter as the interior of a 12-gauge shotgun (about 0.729 in). The exception to this system is the so-called 410-gauge shotgun, which has its bore diameter measured in inches (0.410 in) (see Table 21.3).

ANATOMY OF AMMUNITION

Ammunition is what a firearm fires; it is typically a self-contained cartridge that is composed of one or more projectiles, propellant (to act as fuel), and a primer (to ignite the propellant). As with firearms, ammunition comes in two major types: cartridges, for handguns and rifles, and shells, for shotguns (see Figure 21.9).

Bullets, the first type of projectile, can be classified as lead (or lead alloy), fully jacketed, and semi-jacketed. Lead (alloy) bullets are pieces of lead hardened with minute amounts of other metals (such as antimony) and formed into the desired shape. Although hardened, they are too soft to use in most modern firearms other than 0.22 rifles or pistols. A fully jacketed cartridge has a lead core that is encased in a harder material, usually copper–nickel alloys or steel. A semi-jacketed cartridge has a metal jacket that covers only a portion of the bullet with the nose often exposed. Because the nose of the bullet is softer than the surrounding jacket, the tip expands or "mushrooms" on impact, transferring its energy to the target. A hollow-point cartridge is a semi-jacketed bullet that has a hollowed-out tip to increase this effect. Some semi-jacketed cartridges leave the base exposed but cover the tip; these have a greater penetrating power due to the hardness of the tip material and tend to pass through the target.

Shotguns, as noted previously, can fire pellets or slugs. Dozens of varieties of projectiles, from explosive bullets to "safety" ammunition consisting of pellets in a small sack to disable airline hijackers, are currently available and may be encountered in casework.

The propellant is the fuel that propels the projectile down and out of the firearm's barrel. Black powder, the first propellant to be used in firearms, was invented across numerous cultures at various times. The most common formulation for black powder is 15 parts charcoal, 75 parts potassium nitrate, and 10 parts sulfur, but there are others also. Black powder is now pressed into cakes and broken up as needed (this prevents the separation of the mixed components); the size of the pieces, or **grains**, controls the rate of burning, with the smallest burning fastest. The grains are sorted by size, and small grains are used for handguns, medium grains for shotguns and small rifles, and large grains for larger rifles. Because it is still in use today, mostly with black-powder hunting enthusiasts and Civil War re-enactors, forensic firearms scientists must be familiar with this oldest of propellants.

The more common propellant by far is **smokeless powder**, which was developed in response to the huge plumes of smoke that black powder produces upon ignition. Smokeless powder is composed of nitrocellulose combined with various chemicals to stabilize the mix and modify it for safe manufacture and transport.

The primer is what ignites the propellant. It consists of a small metal cup containing a percussion-sensitive material (it explodes on impact) that, when struck, creates enough heat to ignite the propellant. The small cup is set in place at the rear of the cartridge, where it is struck by the firing pin. Modern primer materials consist of lead styphnate, antimony sulfide, barium nitrate, and tetracene. Because of the concerns of toxicity over long-term exposure to law enforcement officers, many primers are now made from organic primers that are lead-free.

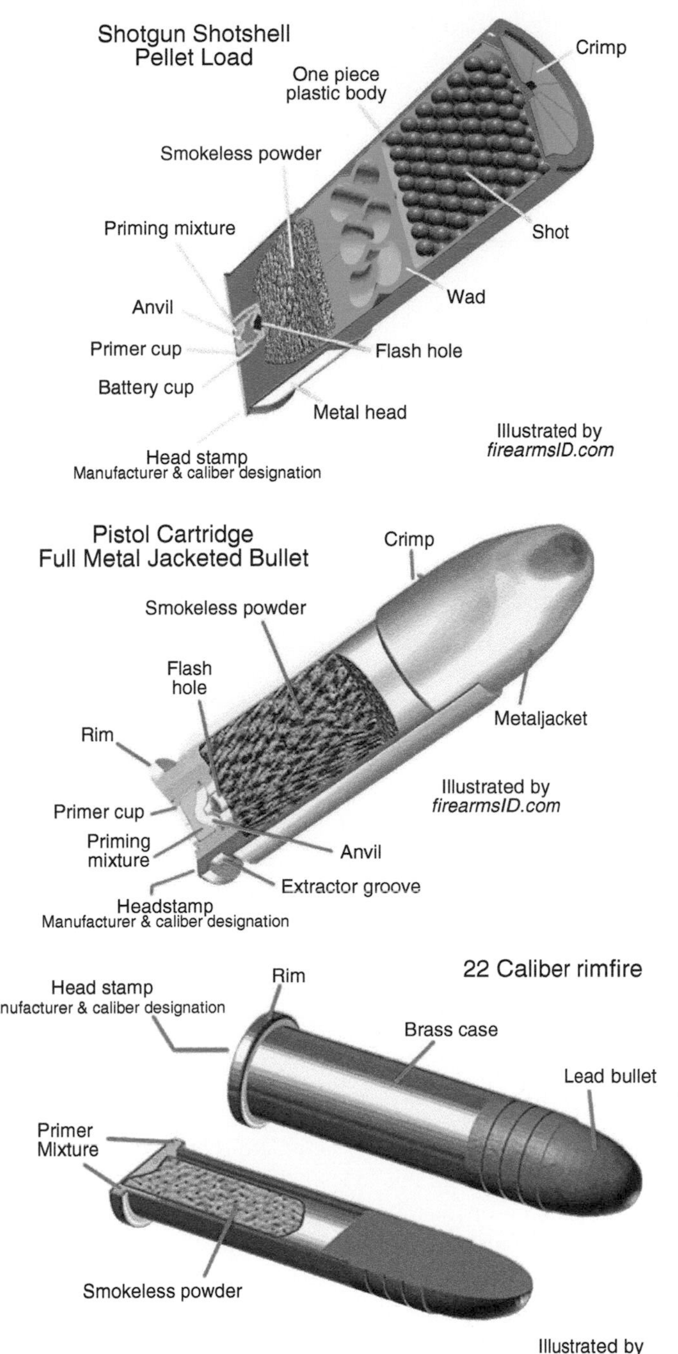

FIGURE 21.9

Ammunition comes in two basic types: bullets and shells. Bullets have a single solid projectile, propellant, a primer to ignite the propellant, and a casing to hold the components together until fired. Shells are similar to bullets, except that the pellets or shot must also be held together and wadding is inserted between them and the propellant. The wadding maintains an even pressure on the pellets, pushing them all out of the barrel at about the same time.

Courtesy: www.FirearmsID.com, artwork by Erik Dahlberg.

WHAT HAPPENS WHEN AMMUNITION IS DISCHARGED?

When the hammer strikes the primer cap on a live round chambered in a weapon, the primer explodes and ignites the propellant. The burning of the propellant generates hot gases, which expand and push the bullet from its cartridge case and down the barrel. The propellant is designed and the ammunition constructed so as to continue to burn—if the propellant stopped burning, the friction between the bullet and the rifling of the barrel would cause the bullet to stop. The friction between the bullet and the rifling also transfers the pattern of lands and grooves to the bullet's exterior. More importantly, it also transfers the microscopic striations—themselves transferred to the barrel's inner surface from the tool used to cut the lands and grooves—and these striations are used by the forensic firearms scientist in the microscopical comparison of known and questioned bullets.

If the firearm retains the spent cartridge, a revolver, for example, then the only marks to be found on the cartridge that could be used for comparison would be the **firing pin impression**, the mark made by the firing pin as it strikes the primer cap. Firearms that expel the spent cartridge, however, may produce a variety of marks indicative of the method of cartridge extraction (**extraction marks**) and ejection (**ejection marks**) from the chamber. Other common marks left on a cartridge case during discharge are breech marks. The discharge of a firearm creates recoil, forcing the cartridge case backward into the breech face of the firearm; the breech face holds the base of the cartridge case in the chamber. Recoil causes the cartridge base to smack against the breech face and receive an impression of any imperfections in the breech face (see Figure 21.10).

As the bullet leaves the muzzle of the barrel, it is followed by a plume of the hot gases that forced it down the barrel. This plume contains a variety of materials, such as partially burned gunpowder flakes, microscopic molten blobs of the primer chemicals, the bullet, and the cartridge. As these materials strike, or come to rest on, a surface, they transfer potential evidence of that surface's distance from the firearm's muzzle and other materials that may indicate that surface's association with the firing of a firearm or one that has been fired.

COLLECTION OF FIREARMS EVIDENCE

On popular crime-based TV programs, a detective finds a handgun at the crime scene, picks it up by sticking a pencil down the barrel (or with bare hands, or with gloved hands by the grip, or…), and says to her partner, "Hey, Charlie, I think this is what we're looking for…" There is hardly a more enduring, or inaccurate, image in the visual lexicon of police dramas. Although TV and movie dramas are hardly the place to learn the proper methods of evidence collection, they can provide a good way to learn what *not* to do.

Firearms are a durable piece of evidence, subject to analyzes beyond the standard forensic firearms examinations, such as latent prints, fibers, and hairs. Additionally, safety is a primary concern when collecting firearm evidence because any firearm could be loaded. After photography and documentation of the location of all

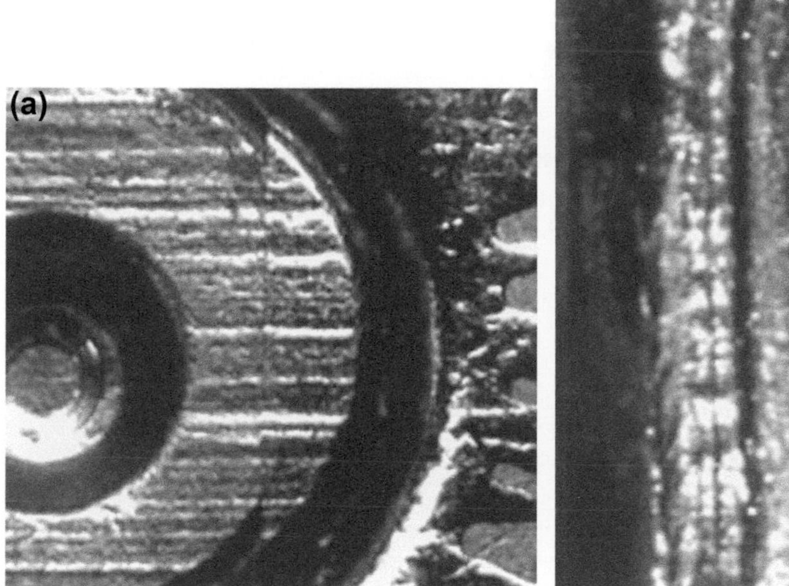

FIGURE 21.10

Various impressions can be left on the cartridge casing by the discharge of ammunition, such as firing pin impressions and breech marks (a), extraction marks (b) and ejection marks.

Courtesy: www.FirearmsID.com.

firearms, they should be secured in packaging that prevents shifting during transit and that locks the trigger into place (see Figure 21.11).

In shooting reconstructions, it is vital to locate, photograph, and measure the location of all bullets, bullet holes, and spent cartridges. This information will be used later to generate three-dimensional data about the shooting, possibly for court demonstrations (see Figure 21.12).

FIREARMS ANALYSIS

Safety and Operations Testing

Firearms, especially those collected as evidence, are inherently dangerous. It is of paramount importance that a firearm be checked prior to any testing or examination: A firearm should not be transferred or stored as evidence with a live round in the chamber unless there is an important reason to do so. A person trained in the safe handling of firearms should check any weapon to see if it's loaded, and if it is, the chamber should be cleared. Proper precautions should be taken to ensure the integrity of any evidence on, in or removed from a firearm.

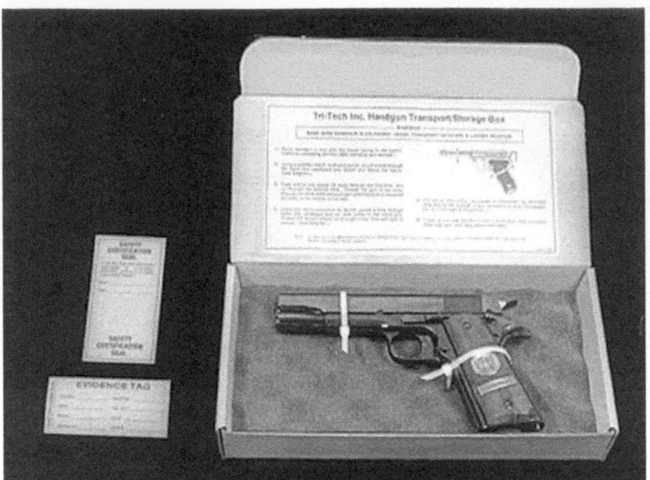

FIGURE 21.11

It is important to properly package firearms when submitting them to the laboratory. Companies that sell crime scene materials usually offer special packaging for firearms that prevent them from accidentally discharging during shipment or transport. This type of packaging is critical to preserve evidence and keep forensic professionals safe. Only unloaded firearms should be shipped.

Courtesy: TriTek, Inc.

Information that is important to note in a preliminary firearms examination is the manufacturer, caliber, type of firearm, model, ammunition capacity, barrel length, and serial number. Criminals will sometimes attempt to obliterate the serial numbers to avoid being traced through serial number registration; all firearms' serial numbers and their purchasers must be recorded by retailers.

Often the first step in a forensic firearms examination is to determine whether the firearm in question operates properly. The action, the safety, the **trigger pull**—the force required to pull the trigger to the firing position—and other typical functions of the firearm should be tested and recorded. The ability of a weapon to fire may be important in the investigation. These questions may sound mundane, but their answers could be the difference between an accidental death and a homicide.

IN MORE DETAIL: 3D PRINTED FIREARMS

Additive manufacturing, more popularly called "3D printing," is poised to revolutionize design and manufacturing around the world. The printers can build almost any object by adding material (typically polymers but metals, ceramics and even biological tissue have been used) in a design controlled by a computer; in essence, they print with solid materials instead of ink. The printers are relatively cheap (from a few hundred to a few thousand dollars) and readily available for purchase. One of the more controversial objects that can be built with these devices are firearms.

IN MORE DETAIL: 3D PRINTED FIREARMS—cont'd

Operational firearms have been built with 3D printers and are invisible to metal detectors; when disassembled, they look fairly harmless. These guns pose significant security and public safety risks. Additionally, with the barrels being printed and not cut, there are no striations to transfer to the bullet or cartridge casing; in most models, the "firing pin" is a simple hardware nail.

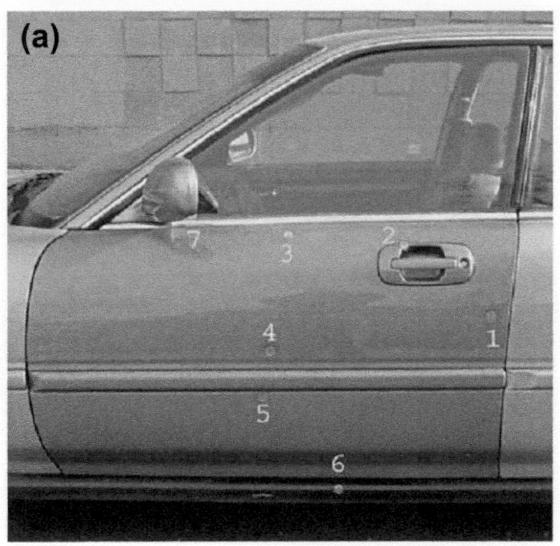

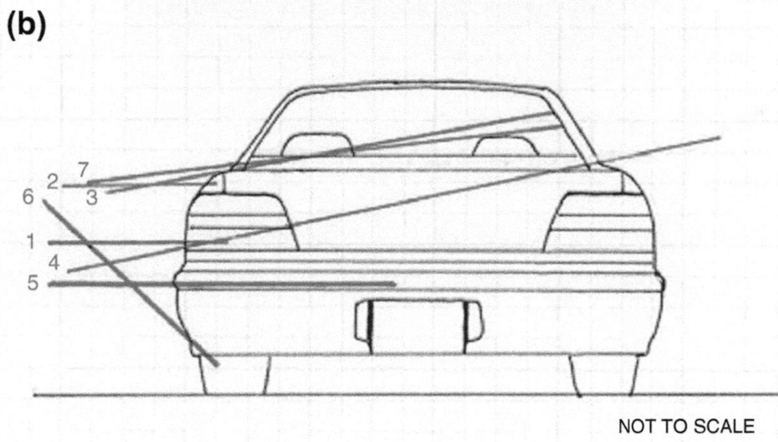

FIGURE 21.12

In shooting reconstructions, it is vital to locate, photograph, and measure the location of all bullets, bullet holes (a), and spent cartridges. This information provides the data for reconstructing the bullet pathways (b).

Courtesy: Alliance Forensic Science Consultants.

Bullet Comparisons

Many published studies have demonstrated that no two firearms produce the same unique marks on fired bullets and cartridge cases; this is even true with firearms of the same make and model. The machining of the manufacturing process combined with the use of the firearm leave surface marks on the metal parts of the firearm that are not reproducible in other firearms. These marks are transferred to the bullets and casings when discharged from the firearm.

Because there is no practical method of comparing the striations on the inner surface of a rifled weapon with the striations on a fired bullet, reference bullets of the same make, style, and caliber must be created by firing them from the questioned firearm. Not only would cutting the barrel open be impractical, but the comparison would then be between positive (the barrel) and negative (the questioned bullet) impressions. The known fired bullets must be captured and preserved, however, so that they are as "pristine" as possible and not deformed or damaged. Firearms are typically discharged into a water tank where the water slows and eventually stops the bullet without altering its striations; other bullet recovery systems are used from the simple (a bucket filled with rubber shavings) to the high tech (sandwiched layers of specialized materials); Figure 21.13 shows some examples. The known bullet is then recovered, labeled, and used as a reference in the comparison; multiple known bullets may be created, if necessary.

The questioned and known bullets are first examined with the naked eye and slight magnification. The number of lands, grooves, their twist, and the bullets' weights are recorded. Because these are higher-order class characteristics, any deviations from the known bullet indicate that the two bullets were fired from different barrels. If the lands, grooves, and direction of twist all concur, then the next step is microscopical comparison of the striations on the bullets.

The comparison is performed using a comparison stereomicroscope with special stages that facilitate positioning the bullets in the focal plane and allow for rotation of the bullets on their long axis (see Figure 21.14; see also Chapter 4 for more information). The bullets are positioned on the stages, one on each, both pointing in the same direction, and held in position with clay or putty; this allows for easy repositioning, and the soft material will not mark the bullets' surfaces. The known bullet is then positioned to visualize a land or groove with distinctive striations. The questioned bullet is then rotated until a land or groove, respectively, comes into view with the same striation markings (see Figure 21.15). The lands and grooves of the two bullets must have the same widths. More importantly, the two bullets must not be merely similar, but they must have the same striation patterns with no significant differences. This last point is critical: Not only must forensic firearms scientists see the positive correlation between the significant information on the bullets' surfaces, but they must also not see any unexplained differences. Each rifle barrel is unique: No two of them will have identical striation patterns. This is true even for barrels that have been rifled in succession, one after the other. It takes education, guidance, and mentoring to train a person's eye and judgment on the subtleties of bullet striation patterns.

FIGURE 21.13

Test-firing bullets into a water tank preserves the striae on the bullets but also slows down the bullet so it can be safely discharged and retrieved. Water tanks can be difficult to maintain, however, and other methods have been devised. Some are simple, like a 5-gallon bucket filled with rubber shavings (a), and some are technologically complex, like the bullet recovery system made by Ballistics Research Inc., Rome, Georgia (b). This system uses two specialized types of material sandwiched in a series of alternating layers inside a caster-mounted metal box. Projectiles come to rest within the series of layers, where they are easily recovered by hand.

(a) Courtesy of Richard Ernest, Alliance Forensics, Inc.; (b) courtesy of Ballistics Research, Inc.

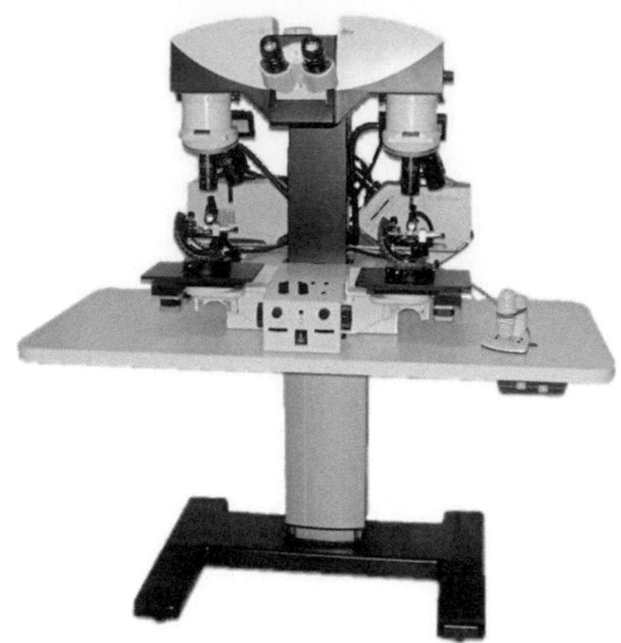

FIGURE 21.14

Much like the comparison microscope used for hairs and fibers work, the firearms comparison microscope optically joins two stereomicroscopes. This allows forensic scientists to view two objects simultaneously side by side.

Courtesy: www.FirearmsID.com.

FIGURE 21.15

A positive association between bullets must have the same land and groove patterns, widths, and striation patterning with no significant negative correlations. A negative association between bullets would demonstrate numerous significant misalignments of striations with no significant correlation of striae.

Courtesy: www.FirearmsID.com.

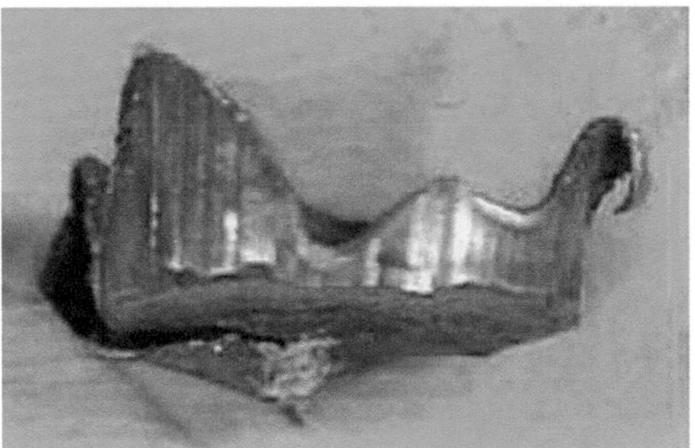

FIGURE 21.16

This lead bullet has deformed and separated from the copper jacket. It would be difficult, if not impossible, to find useful, suitable striations on a corresponding known bullet.

Courtesy: www.FirearmsID.com.

Recent research has indicated that bullet and cartridge case comparisons are accurate and very reliable. Studies show that the overall error rate for cartridge case comparisons is on the order of less than 0.1%; false positive rates are about 1.0% and false negative rates are around 0.36%. For bullets fired from consecutively manufactured barrels, the error rate is less than 0.1%. By comparison, a home pregnancy test conducted by a medical professional has an overall error rate of 2.6%.

Bullet striation comparisons are difficult enough with intact, clean bullets; in reality, most bullets recovered from crime scenes are mangled, deformed, and dirty. Often only a small portion of a bullet may have useful striations for comparison (see Figure 21.16). The barrel may not have been cleaned recently, and rust, grit, and built-up residues may have been transferred to the bullet when it was fired.

Firearm Databases and Automated Search Systems

Whether a firearm is used by the same criminal or shared between members of a criminal enterprise, firearm evidence can link a person or persons to multiple crimes. The problem in doing so is the difficulty in searching and comparing numerous bullets or casings. If the crimes were committed across multiple jurisdictions, then the task becomes even more involved.

The National Integration Ballistic Information Network (NIBIN) automates ballistics evaluations and provides investigative leads by revealing connections between crimes in which the same firearm is used. Before NIBIN, firearms examiners had to manually search and compare bullets and casings between crimes; this was extremely labor intensive. Firearms examiners scan cartridge cases and the images are compared against the database and correlations are reported.

More than 1000 NIBIN users have been certified to use the system and to date NIBIN partners have confirmed more than 50,000 NIBIN hits.

IN MORE DETAIL: 15 LEADS FOR THE BOSTON POLICE DEPARTMENT

The Boston, Massachusetts, Police Department is aggressive in the use of advanced technology to combat illegal firearms and firearms violence. Departmental regulations require that all recovered evidence relating to firearms be submitted to the laboratory for entry into its NIBIN unit. The power of ballistic imaging technology and Boston's thorough approach to its deployment have enabled the department to find links undetectable by other means. On September 9, 2000, in Boston, several subjects were apprehended and found to be in the possession of three handguns. (The public possession of firearms is in itself a criminal offence in Boston.) The subjects were arrested and charged with the possession offence; the three handguns—0.25 caliber, a 0.40 caliber, and a 9 mm—were all seized as evidence, test-fired, and entered into Integrated Ballistic Identification System (IBIS).

Correlation of the test-firings returned several promising similarities. Examiners from the department's firearms laboratory viewed the correlation results and then examined the recalled evidence. The following criminal offences were positively connected to the test-fired weapons:

- On June 2, 1999, in Boston, shots were fired, but no victim was identified; several 9-mm cartridge casings were recovered at the scene.
- On October 28, 1999, also in Boston, shots were fired, but no victim was identified; more 9-mm cartridge casings were recovered.
- On April 3, 2000, in Boston, one victim was wounded by gunfire; 9-mm cartridge casings were collected at the scene.
- Also on April 3, 2000, in Boston, shots were fired, but no victim was identified; 9-mm cartridge casings were recovered at the scene.
- On April 19, 2000, in Boston, one victim was wounded by gunfire; in the area, 9-mm cartridge casings were recovered.
- On April 23, 2000, in Boston, shots were fired, but no victim was identified; 9-mm cartridge casings were collected at the scene.
- On May 9, 2000, in Boston, shots were fired, but no victim was identified; 9-mm cartridge casings were recovered at the scene.
- On June 8, 2000, in Boston, four victims were shot; 9-mm cartridge casings were collected at the scene of this violent crime.
- On June 15, 2000, in Boston, a victim was assaulted with a firearm; 9-mm cartridge casings were recovered.
- Providence, Rhode Island, is located about 1 h south of Boston by car. On June 19, 2000, Providence police responded to the scene of a shooting and found a large amount of blood and several 9-mm cartridge casings, but no victim.
- On June 25, 2000, in the city of Brockton, about 25 min south of Boston, an assault with a firearm took place. The 9-mm casings recovered at this scene were transported to the Boston PD for entry into Boston's IBIS unit.
- On July 6, 2000, in the city of Randolph, just south of Boston, three victims were wounded in a shooting; 9-mm cartridge casings were recovered.
- On July 7, 2000, in Boston, shots were fired, but no victim was located; 9-mm cartridge evidence was collected at the scene.
- On July 20, 2000, in Boston, shots were fired, but no victim was located. Cartridge casings from a 0.40-caliber firearm were recovered.

A routine arrest for firearms possession charges resulted in the discovery of links among 15 shooting incidents spread over several police jurisdictions in two states. As a result, each agency involved now has a wealth of information to use in its investigation, including the identities of the possessors of the guns. Without Boston's participation in NIBIN, these crimes would likely not have been linked.

Source: *www.nibin.gov.*

TOOL MARK COMPARISONS

The potential sources for tool marks are many, and some are surprising. Metal tools are made by a variety of methods, but most are finished in a way that leaves microscopic striations on their working surfaces. A tool may leave class characteristics that may help to identify what kind of item it is: An ice pick will leave different markings than would a flat-head screwdriver, for example (see Figure 21.17). The types of markings left will depend not only on the type of tool, but also how it was used, the angle of contact, the force of contact, and what was contacted, among other factors. It is important for the tool mark examiner to have a foundational knowledge about how various tools are made and machined.

Bullets travel down the barrel of a firearm in nearly the same way each time; the same is not true of a tool mark. The forensic tool mark examiner must pay close attention to the potential orientations of the questioned tool; otherwise, the test marks may not be comparable with the questioned marks (see Figure 21.18). Like bullets, however, the questioned tool cannot be compared directly to the mark it may have left. Crime scene personnel or the tool mark examiner may take casts of the tool mark(s) for comparison purposes. These casts are lightweight, easy to handle, and easy to store; fine-grained polymer materials are sold by most forensic science supply companies. Dental stone is also a favored medium for making tool mark casts.

FIGURE 21.17

The machining of metals leaves microscopic striations that can be transferred to a softer surface, such as a screwdriver prying open a wooden window casing. The class characteristics can also be useful in identifying (but not individualizing) the tool used.

Courtesy: Wisconsin State Police.

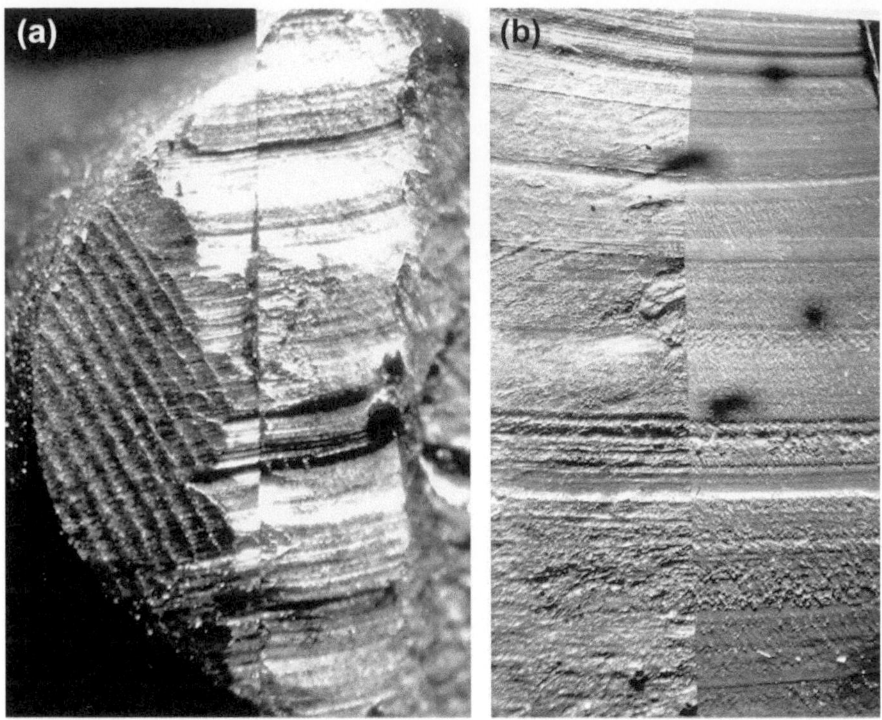

FIGURE 21.18

Examples of tool mark striations. (a) A pair of bolt cutters was used to cut a lock shackle. The comparison microphotograph shows the evidence lock shackle on the left side and the test cut produced by the bolt cutters in a piece of lead on the right. (b) An unusual example of a tool mark comparison is shown on the left where a knife edge from a suspect's knife was compared and matched to a piece of rib cartilage from a victim. On the left is a silicone rubber cast of the cut in the victim's rib cartilage compared with a cast of a test cut produced with the suspect's knife using a plastic material (Dip-Pak).

Courtesy: Alliance Forensic Science Consultants.

DISTANCE OF FIRING DETERMINATION

Gunpowder Residues

When a firearm is discharged, the bullet is not the only object expelled from the weapon (see Figure 21.19). The violent chemical reaction of the primer and accelerant results in a cloud of molten metals, partially burned gunpowder flakes, smoke, and other microscopic debris. This residue may be found on the person who discharged the firearm, on an entrance wound of a victim, or on other surfaces. The discharge of a firearm, particularly a revolver, can deposit residues 3 ft or more from the hand of the shooter, and interpretations about who fired the gun can be problematic. Some of these **GSR** may be used to make determinations about the location of the discharged firearm in relation to its surroundings and its target.

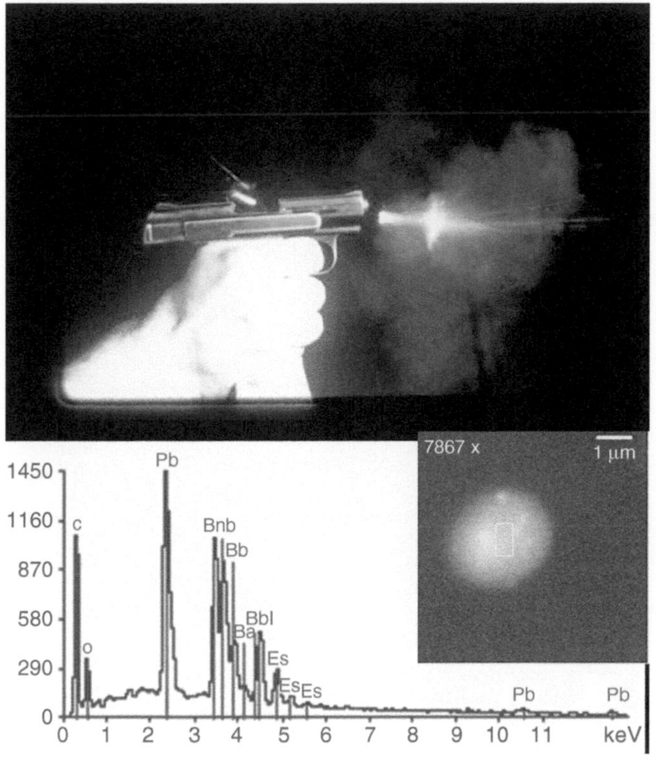

FIGURE 21.19

When a firearm is discharged, the projectile is not the only thing that leaves the barrel. The residues of completely or partially burnt propellant, volatilized metals from the projectile, and the casing (if any) and wadding (in the case of shotguns) are also ejected.

The patterning of GSRs on a target is indicative of the distance from the muzzle to the target (see Figure 21.20). The patterning and density of the GSRs will vary with the firearm and ammunition used. Therefore, the patterns must be empirically generated by discharging a questioned firearm to make a comparison with a questioned GSR pattern. The distances tested are typically contact (where the muzzle is against the target), 6, 12, 18, 24, 30, and 36 in; other distances may be tested based on the case circumstances.

Contact or near-contact bullet entrance holes demonstrate severe damage to a textile or garment. Bullets that strike an object before hitting their final target tend to have uneven edges. Typically, the greater the damage to the textile in a contact gunshot, the higher the velocity of the ammunition.

Firearms discharged more than about 3 ft from the target will not impart any residues other than a bullet wipe. A **bullet wipe** is a residue of lead, primer materials, carbon, and other materials from the barrel that are transferred ("wiped")

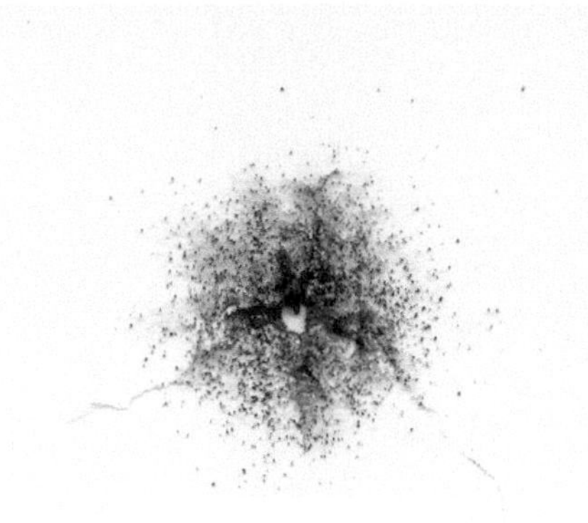

FIGURE 21.20

Gunshot residue materials expand over distance and can leave a transfer pattern on any objects between the barrel and the target. When a firearm with similar ammunition is test-fired, a range of patterns can be established and compared with the crime scene pattern. This leads to an estimate of the muzzle-to-target distance. This pattern was made by a 2-in muzzle-to-target distance, Federal Ammunition 0.357 Magnum, from a Smith & Wesson Magnum Revolver with a 6-in barrel.

Courtesy: Alliance Forensic Science Consultants.

onto the outermost surface of the target by the bullet as it passes through. For the sake of clarity and standardization, the questioned weapon is discharged onto a 1 ft by 1 ft piece of white cloth. If the firearm is not recovered as evidence, then the range of distance estimates will be greater (1–3 ft, e.g., instead of 1.5–2.5 ft) to reflect the uncertainty. Additionally, many circumstances may affect the distance estimate, including position of the shooter and target, weather, and intervening items.

To make the comparisons, the examiner often must visualize the GSR pattern on the target by some means. Infrared photography may reveal the residue pattern when the clothing is dark or heavily patterned (see Figure 21.21). The first test that should be used to reveal residues is the Modified Griess Test. In the Modified Griess Test, a piece of desensitized photographic paper is treated with a mixture of sulfanilic acid in distilled water and alpha-naphthol in methanol. Photographic paper is desensitized by exposing the paper to a hypo solution, desensitizing it to light but making it reactive to nitrite residues. The evidence is placed target-side down on the photographic paper and pressed with a steam iron filled with a dilute acetic acid solution. The resulting residues appear as orange dots on the photographic paper. This variant of the Modified Griess Test was developed and published by Scott Doyle of the Kentucky State Police Crime Laboratory, who has enjoyed great success with it.

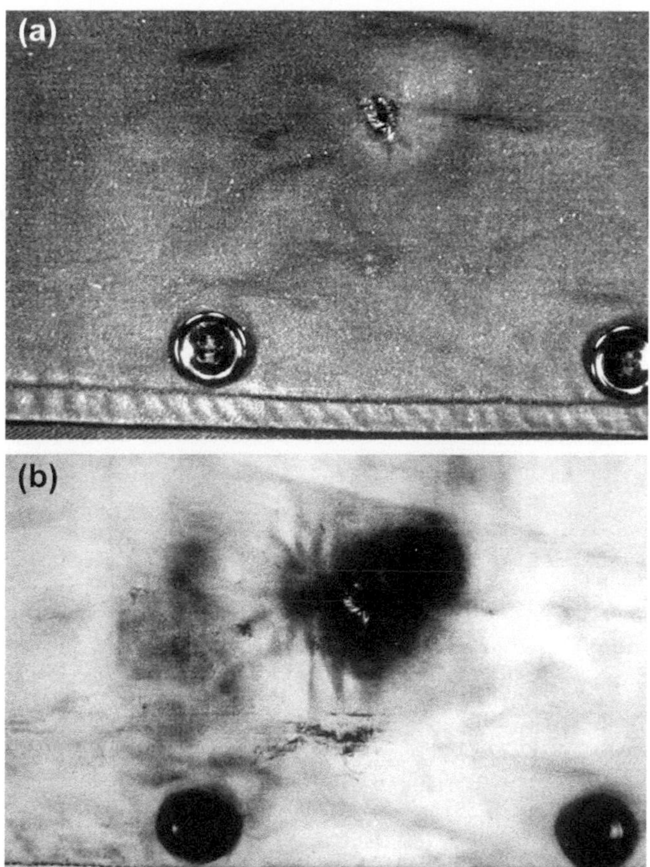

FIGURE 21.21

When a shooting victim's clothing is dark or heavily patterned, it may be difficult to see the pattern of gunshot residues (GSRs) (a). Infrared photography may reveal the GSR pattern (b).

Courtesy: Wisconsin State Police.

The last chemical treatment used to visualize GSR is to spray **sodium rhodizonate** on the surface and then treat that area with a series of acid sprays. The residues turn pink and then purplish-blue and are easily seen.

When a scene or body is examined for GSR, it is necessary to remember that lead residues may look like GSR. Lead residues may be found up to 30 ft from the muzzle and are present on the opposite side of a penetrated target.

Shotgun Distance Determination (Shot Patterns)

The determination of muzzle-to-target distance of a shotgun is similar to the method used for other firearms except it is the pattern of pellets that is measured. As the pellets leave the shotgun barrel, they begin to spread based on the distance they travel and the choke of the barrel. Their pattern of spreading is indicative of the distance between the end of the barrel and the target. Because of the variations in choke, gauge, and ammunition materials, it is important, just as it is with other firearms, to use the same weapon and ammunition as suspected in the crime.

Primer Residues

Primer residues may also land on the hands of a shooter. The residue is mostly microscopic blobs of the molten metals from the primer cap, the primer compound, the casing, and other metallic components (containing copper (Cu), zinc (Zn), nickel (Ni), aluminum (Al), among others). The major primer elements are lead (Pb), barium (Ba), and antimony (Sb); typically, all three are found in GSR. The minor elements include aluminum (Al), calcium (Ca), chlorine (Cl), potassium (K), silicon (Si), sulfur (S), and tin (Sn). As the blobs fly through the air, they condense into heterogeneous spheres of various sizes (submicron up to 50 or more microns, with most in the 2- to 10-μm range).

Several tests have been developed over the years, including the dermal nitrate test (which also tested positive for fertilizers) and atomic absorption (AA). Still used in some laboratories, AA suffers from a number of limitations, including collection problems (swabbing the suspect's hands with a mild acid solution), a lengthy analysis time, and, most importantly, lack of specificity. The result of an AA analysis yields quantities of the elements tested for but not their distribution. Because GSR particles are aggregates of compounds, no information about the form of the sample is known with AA. Fireworks, matches, and other common objects could yield a positive result by AA.

In 1976, Nesbitt, Wessell, and Jones published a method for detecting GSR particles using a scanning electron microscope (SEM) outfitted with an energy-dispersive spectrometer (EDS) and imaging system. The particles were collected from the hands of a suspected shooter and placed on a carbon-coated aluminum mount; then they were viewed in the SEM with a detection mode that relates brightness to atomic number. The bright particles on a dark background of carbon were those that were most likely GSR (Figure 21.22). The EDS detector would then analyze the individual spheres to detect the presence of antimony, barium, and lead—the three main components found to be in GSR but not other high-atomic number particulate matter. The shape and elemental content of the particles defined them as GSR. It is important to note that the primers in 0.22 ammunition differ from other primers and may not be detected by a system screening for PbSbBa particles.

This method gained greater acceptance when the technology allowed for the detection and analysis of the method to be automated for unattended operation. Multiple samples could be loaded into the SEM, the software calibrated, and then it could be left on its own to run samples overnight. The human operator still needed to verify any positive "hits" because other materials could produce elemental signatures that were overlapping with or confounded the signatures of true GSR particles, such as automotive brake pads.

FIGURE 21.22

Gunshot residue, more properly called "primer residue," forms as molten blobs of metals from the discharge of the ammunition. These spheres deposit on surfaces within about 3′ of the discharged firearm, depending on the design of the firearms and environmental conditions, such as wind.

Courtesy: Doug DeGaetano, Virginia Department of Forensic Services.

The only conclusion that can be drawn from a GSR test is that the subject discharged a firearm, was near a firearm when it discharged, or handled a recently discharged firearm. These factors, plus the potential for contamination during arrest from GSR-rich environments, like police officers' hands, patrol car seats, and handcuffs, make for a limited application of GSR analysis. Many laboratories continue to offer GSR analyzes, and some perform a high volume of casework (>500 cases) annually.

BACK TO THE CASE: DC SNIPER ATTACKS

The prints belonged to Lee Boyd Malvo (who called himself John Lee Malvo), an illegal teenage immigrant from Jamaica. He was closely associated with John Allen Muhammad (born John Allen Williams), a Gulf War veteran and expert army marksman. Muhammad spent time in Antigua, where he met Malvo.

This case became the largest manhunt in the history of the Washington, DC, area. On October 4, the previous shootings were linked to the same gun. Eyewitnesses reported a white box truck with dark lettering with two men inside speeding from one of the early scenes; this would push investigators down misleading and wasteful paths of inquiry. Information about the real

(Continued)

BACK TO THE CASE: DC SNIPER ATTACKS—cont'd

sniper vehicle, a former New Jersey State Police unmarked blue Chevrolet Caprice, was developed after investigation into Muhammad's background. The Caprice was spotted at a Maryland rest stop by a truck driver who blocked the exit until police arrived (see Figure 21.23).

FIGURE 21.23

DC sniper arrest photo.

The Caprice contained a stolen Bushmaster 0.223-caliber rifle, a scope, a tripod, and a trunk outfitted as a sniper's perch. Two holes had been drilled in the trunk so that the rifle and scope could be used from inside the vehicle. The backseat folded down so that a person could lie flat facing the rear of the vehicle, providing a perfect place to lie in wait for the next victim.

The Bureau of Alcohol, Tobacco, Firearms, and Explosives (ATF) laboratory in Maryland received and test-fired over 100 firearms during the first 2 weeks of the sniper case; a normal average month would be about 28 firearms examinations. Forensic examinations by the FBI and ATF linked the weapon to all but three of the sniper shootings.

Malvo and Muhammad were found guilty of the sniper attacks. On October 10, 2006, Malvo pleaded guilty to the six murders he was charged with in Maryland and, because he was a juvenile at the time of the crimes, was sentenced to six consecutive life sentences without the possibility of parole. Muhammad was executed by lethal injection on November 10, 2009.

Sources: Washington Post, CNN *and FBI Web sites; images public domain Wikipedia (map) and www.fbi.gov (photo).*

SUMMARY

Because of the ubiquity of firearms in the United States and their primary violent purpose, firearms examination is a central function of most forensic science laboratories. The exams performed, however, are more than just comparing bullets and cartridges. A wide range of knowledge is required to be a qualified firearms examiner, from chemistry to physics to computers and digital imaging. The field has advanced considerably since its battlefield beginnings and will continue to do so for some time to come.

TEST YOUR KNOWLEDGE

1. What's the difference between a revolver and a pistol?
2. List four differences between rifles and shotguns.
3. Why is a pistol not a rifle?
4. What is wadding?
5. What is gauge?
6. How is caliber determined?
7. Name the parts of a cartridge.
8. What does a primer do?
9. What are lands and grooves?
10. Why don't shotguns have lands and grooves?
11. What materials are used to estimate muzzle-to-target distance?
12. What is in gunshot residue?
13. Do striations appear only on bullets? Why or why not?
14. Are more firearms involved in homicides or suicides?
15. What determination can be made from a GSR analysis?
16. How are bullets compared?
17. How accurate is firearms comparison?
18. What is sodium rhodizonate used for?
19. What is "bullet wipe?"
20. How many firearms-related crimes occur in the United States each year?

CONSIDER THIS...

1. Firearms, like any other mechanism, are made up of parts; one of these parts is the barrel. The striations in each barrel are unique because of manufacturing and use. How could this information affect the comparison of questioned bullets with test-fired bullets from a suspected gun? Knowing this, what would you do differently, if anything, in your analysis?
2. One bullet is fired from a firearm in much the same way as the next bullet; this makes generating comparison of (known) bullets easy. Why is this not the case for tool marks? What implications does this have for a tool mark comparison?

BIBLIOGRAPHY AND FURTHER READING

Baldwin, D., May 6, 2014. Fired Cartridge Case Error Rate Study. Presentation to American Society of Crime Laboratory Directors Meeting.

Bastian, L., Nanda, K., Hasselblad, V., Simel, D., 1998. Diagnostic efficiency of home pregnancy test kits. A meta-analysis. Archives of Family Medicine 7, 465–469.

Biasotti, A., 1959. A statistical study of the individual characteristics of fired bullets. Journal of Forensic Sciences 4, 35–50.

Fadul, T., Hernandez, G., Stoiloff, S., Gulati, S., 2011. An Empirical Study to Improve the Scientific Foundation of Forensic Firearm and Tool Mark Identification Utilizing 10 Consecutively Manufactured Slides. Report 237960. National Institute of Justice, Washington, DC.

Di Maio, V., 1998. Gunshot Wounds, second ed. CRC Press, Boca Raton, FL.

Hamby, J., Brundage, D., Thorpe, J., 2009. The identification of bullets fired from 10 consecutively rifled 9 mm Ruger pistol barrels: a research project involving 507 participants from 20 countries. AFTE Journal 41, 99–110.

National Crime Victimization Survey, 2002. National Crime Victimization Survey 2002. United States Department of Justice, Office of Justice Programs, Bureau of Justice Statistics, Washington, DC.

Nesbitt, R.S., Wessel, J.E., Jones, P.F., 1976. Detection of gunshot residue by use of the scanning electron microscope. Journal of Forensic Sciences 21, 595–610.

Rowe, W., 1988. Firearms identification. In: Saferstein, R. (Ed.), Forensic Science Handbook, vol. II. Prentice Hall, Englewood Cliffs, NJ, pp. 393–449.

Thorwald, J., 1964. The Century of the Detective Harcourt. Brace & World, New York.

U.S. Bureau of Alcohol, Tobacco, Firearms, and Explosives, 2000. Following the Gun: Enforcing Federal Laws against Firearms Traffickers. U.S. Bureau of Alcohol, Tobacco, Firearms, and Explosives, Washington, DC.

Wilson, C., Wilson, D., 2003. Written in Blood: A History of Forensic Detection. Carroll and Graf Publishers, New York.

CHAPTER

Impression Evidence

22

CHAPTER OUTLINE

KEY TERMS

- Bite marks
- Fingerprint
- Footwear
- Imprints
- Shoeprint
- Tool marks
- Tire treads

THE CASE: FOOTWEAR EVIDENCE IN THE OJ SIMPSON CASE

In the summer of 1994, Orenthal James (OJ) Simpson was charged with the murders of Nicole Brown Simpson, his ex-wife, and Ronald Goldman, an acquaintance of Brown Simpson. Part of the evidence in the case included footwear impressions in blood that were found on a path near the home of Brown Simpson. The footwear impressions were photographed and sent to the FBI laboratory along with a request from the Los Angeles Police Department that the FBI laboratory determines the brand and size of the footwear. After examination of the impressions and checking their footwear database, an FBI examiner, William Bodziak, probably the United States' foremost expert in footwear, testified that the shoes were a brand known as Bruno Magli, Lorenzo style with a distinctive waffle-style sole and that they were of size 12. Bodziak was able to determine that approximately 40 retailers in the United States sold this type of shoe. Size 12 was relatively rare and only about 300 pairs of this size and style had ever been sold. When OJ Simpson was put on trial for the murders, there was no evidence that he owned such shoes and in fact he denied ever owning such shoes. Simpson was found "not guilty" of the crimes but was subsequently charged in civil court for the wrongful deaths of Nicole Simpson and Ronald Goldman. Between these trials, a photographer produced a photograph of OJ Simpson in which he was wearing the exact shoes described by Bodziak. This evidence was admitted in the civil trial along with Bodziak's testimony of his examination and conclusions. Simpson was subsequently found to be responsible for the wrongful deaths of Nicole Simpson and Ronald Goldman.

INTRODUCTION

Many objects have a texture or pattern on their outside surface. These include fingerprints, many shoe soles, motor-vehicle tire treads, and even markings imparted by tools onto objects. When one of these objects comes into contact with a recipient object or material and force is applied, an **impression** may be left on the surface. If, for example, someone touches a piece of putty with their finger, an impression of the fingerprint will be left in the putty. If a person walks on soft dirt with a tennis shoe, the sole will leave an impression in the dirt. If one person bites another, a bite mark impression may be left in the skin of the person bitten. Fingerprints and tool marks are discussed elsewhere in this book. In this chapter, we take up the subject of other types of impressions; principally shoeprints and tire treads. These occur fairly commonly in crimes. There are also less common types of impression evidence. For example, a somewhat rare type of impression evidence occurs when an automobile side swipes a pedestrian who is wearing clothing with a texture to it such as corduroy. If the blow is hard enough, an impression of the corduroy will be left in the paint of the vehicle. This case is described in more detail in Chapter 17—Soils and Glass.

Impression evidence can, under certain conditions, be quite powerful in its ability to associate the patterned or textured donor object with the impression left on the recipient. This depends a great deal on the age and condition of the pattern. Consider a brand new, left foot, size 10, men's tennis shoe of a particular brand and model. Suppose you went to a shoe store and obtained two of these left-footed tennis shoes. Careful examination of the soles of these shoes would indicate very little difference between them. If either one left an impression at a crime scene, it would be difficult or impossible to determine which one it was. Now, suppose that you bought two pairs (left and right feet) of these tennis shoes and these were worn by two different people for a period of months and the left soles were examined again, one would most likely see significant differences between them. Parts of the soles would become worn, pitted, cracked, or broken and these events would happen in a random way because each person would travel in shoes differently on different types of surfaces for different lengths of time. These random imperfections would soon accumulate to the point where each sole would be measurably different than the other sole—the evidence could reach a state where a forensic impressions examiner might conclude that the impression came from a particular shoe or tire or other object. Certain types of impressions lend themselves to this analysis. These include footwear, tire treads, and serial numbers as well as some less common types of impression evidence. There is an important distinction between fingerprint comparisons and shoeprint, tire tread, or other impressions. Fingerprints remain the same throughout life whereas the other impression evidence changes with time. Over several months, new impressions may appear in shoeprints or tire treads that are not on the exemplar and comparisons of these impressions must take that into account. A single, major disparity between a known and unknown fingerprint may eliminate the conclusion of a common source, whereas that would not necessarily be the case with other impressions.

TYPES OF IMPRESSION EVIDENCE

Remember that the definition of impression evidence involves a donor and a recipient. The donor contains some three-dimensional markings and the recipient is made of a material that can form and hold a negative image of the donor markings. Common donors that occur as evidence in crimes include shoe soles and heels, tire treads, fingerprints and other friction ridges such as footprints and lip prints (discussed in the chapter on Fingerprints), tools that leave markings on the objects on which they are used (discussed in the chapter on Firearms and tool marks), metal dies that are used to make serial numbers, ribbing and texture in fabrics, etc. Common recipients include soft plastics, soil, putty, paint, dust, metals, and some soft plastics. Bite marks are also a type of impression evidence and this will be discussed later in the chapter.

FOOTWEAR IMPRESSIONS

Footwear impressions are sometimes called shoeprints. The term "footwear" is preferred because there are types of footwear other than shoes such as sandals and boots. The impressions being discussed here are limited to those left by the soles and heels of the footwear. This does not include any impressions made by the foot on the inside of the shoe. At one time, a self-proclaimed footwear expert, Louise Robbins, performed many examinations where she concluded that a particular person wore the footwear by examining impressions of the foot on the inside of the footwear. No other experts including those from the FBI were ever able to reproduce her findings and she was generally discredited in the footwear analysis community at the time of her death.

FOOTWEAR AND CRIMINAL ACTIVITY

With rare exceptions, people usually wear some type of footwear when they are outside their home. Some exceptions might be when they are at the beach or in certain places of business. Certainly, most people have on footwear when they commit a crime. The potential is great that footwear impressions will be left at the scene, however, they are difficult to locate, especially if they are latent or invisible. In addition, suspect's footprints may be mixed with those of other people, including police investigators, paramedics, and crime scene technicians. Many crime scene technicians are not familiar with the best methods for visualizing and preserving footwear impressions and so they tend to overlook them or not bother to search for them.

INFORMATION THAT CAN BE DERIVED FROM FOOTWEAR IMPRESSIONS

Footwear impressions can indicate the type, manufacturer, model, and often, the exact size of the footwear. If there are enough unique characteristics present, footwear examiners believe that the impression can be matched to particular shoe, boot, or sandal. These impressions can indicate the route(s) taken into and away from the crime scene. They can also indicate some of the activities that took place during the crime. The number of people, and perhaps suspects, that were at the scene may be determined. Even if the footwear cannot be identified, characteristics of the walking (or running) gait of the wearer may be uncovered. Although this may not have much value in identifying the person, gait has been used successfully in tracking criminals, illegal aliens, missing persons, kidnap victims, and others.

WHEN FOOTWEAR TOUCHES THE GROUND...

A number of things can happen when footwear touches the ground. First, a static electricity charge can be applied to the impression if the shoe is clean and dry. This charge dissipates after a short time but is useful because it helps in the transfer of trace residues and dust to the impression. If the surface is soft or pliable, pressure exerted by the foot will cause the surface to deform and take on the contours of the surface of the footwear. If the surface is dirty or snow, the impression may be long lasting. If the surface is grass or carpet, the impression may be quite transitory. Even in cases where the impression is temporary, trace residues may be transferred to it. As mentioned previously, if the footwear surface contains unique characteristics, they may be transferred to a pliable surface of sufficient resolution to capture small features such as the wear and tear on shoe soles and heels that they accumulate with use. Figure 22.1 shows a shoeprint that was made in soil.

FIGURE 22.1

A shoeprint that was left in soil at a crime scene.

Courtesy: Cheryl Lozen, Michigan State Police, Forensic Science Division.

An **imprint** is where there is enough residue on the footwear to leave an impression on the recipient surface. This would be a positive impression because the residue is on the surface of the footwear that touches the surface. Positive impressions are the most common type of footwear imprints. If the shoe sole is clean and the recipient surface contains a lot of dust or residue, then a negative impression can form. Here the parts of the shoe that touch the floor remove the residue, leaving behind a negative impression. Imprints also result when someone tracks through blood, wet paint, or grease. Depending upon how much of this material is present, a negative impression may be left in the liquid and a positive impression may be deposited further away on a clean surface from the residue picked up by the shoe.

FOOTWEAR IMPRESSIONS AT THE CRIME SCENE

Detection

A major problem with footwear evidence is finding it. This may involve a systematic search that should include route of entry and exit as well as the scene itself. It must be remembered that impressions may be latent or invisible and the scene investigators must develop strategies based upon likely locations for impressions. Oblique lighting and physical methods of development, similar to those used for fingerprint residues, may be useful for discovering hard-to-see images. The search must encompass both two- and three-dimensional impressions. At this point, the purpose is just to locate impressions. Preserving them will come later.

General Treatment of Footwear Impressions at the Scene

Once footwear impressions have been detected at a crime scene, routine procedures are employed for processing. The most important consideration is to avoid altering an impression until examination-quality photographs have been taken. As with any crime scene, the first investigative activity is to make a complete visual record. Increasingly, digital still and video photography are replacing classical film and tape methods. No matter what method is used, photography will provide a permanent record of the position of all footwear impressions and their general conditions. As with all crime scenes, those containing impressions must be immortalized with careful, complete notes and sketches that further document exact locations and circumstances. These will also help associate photos, casts, and sketches with each other. For impression evidence of any type, it is important to take photographs that can be used for examination of the smallest characteristics. These must be close-up photos that have sufficient resolution and lighting to be used on their own for comparison, even if casts will also be made.

The next step is to make a decision about how to best preserve and/or enhance the impression. This will depend upon where the impression is, how easy it is to remove the recipient object and the impression from the scene, and whether the impression is two or three dimensional. If at all possible, the impression and the object on which it is found should be physically removed and transported to the laboratory where there are usually better facilities for additional photographic or other treatments. Even if carpeting or flooring has to be cut, it should be removed. If removal is not practical or possible, then a cast should be made if the impression is three dimensional or it should be lifted if two dimensional. If lifting isn't possible, then the impression should be enhanced to the maximum degree possible and more examination photographs taken.

Casting Three-Dimensional Footwear Impressions

The popularity of casting footwear impressions has varied greatly over the years and it has depended upon the quality of photography at a given time. Early on, photography was rather crude with uneven lighting and low-resolution film. This resulted in photographs that often did not show sufficient detail for comparison purposes. Thus, casting was heavily used. At that time, the major method for casting was to use plaster of Paris. This is a dense material and sometimes several pounds were required for each cast. In addition, plaster of Paris is relatively slow in drying and when dry, is not very hard. Thus, when impressions were taken in dirt, the cast was often damaged during the cleaning process to remove the dirt. Figure 22.2 is a plaster cast of a shoeprint.

In recent years, photography has improved greatly. New types of lights and lighting techniques have been developed. Higher resolution films have been introduced that show more impression detail. This has had the effect of decreasing the use of casting of impressions.

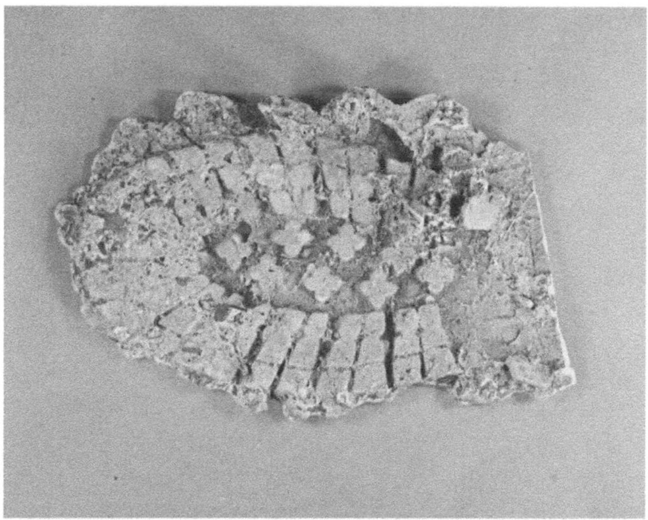

FIGURE 22.2

A plaster cast of a shoeprint.

Courtesy: Cheryl Lozen, Michigan State Police, Forensic Science Division.

At present, even with the development of digital photography and video, casting has made somewhat of a comeback. This is due to improved casting materials such as dental stone, which is less dense, dries faster, and shows more detail than plaster of Paris. Experts recognize several advantages of modern casts over photography. For example, even the best photography requires a level, two-dimensional subject to be most effective. If an impression is imbedded deeply into a substrate such as sand, it will be difficult to gain a proper perspective photographically. It will also be difficult to properly locate a measuring device and to even get a proper measurement of the size of the shoe that made the impression. In addition, if oblique lighting is used to photograph the impression, some of the most important details may be partially obscured in shadow. None of these are problems with a properly made cast.

Casting materials

Plaster of Paris has long been the most popular casting material for all types of impressions. Its major drawback is its softness even after drying. It is also made up of relatively large particles that may cause the loss of crucial detail. Today, dental plasters and stones are more often used. They are denser and have more uniform, smaller particle size than plaster of Paris. They dry quickly and show more detail. The softness of plaster of Paris necessitates that reinforcing materials such as pieces of wood be used within the cast. This requires that casts be at least two inches thick. In order to make a cast that thick, a form has to be used. With modern dental stones and plasters, the increased density and hardness of the dried casting material means that the cast doesn't have to be as thick and therefore, often doesn't require a form. Forms are still sometimes used if the impression is on a steep slope or is of different depths throughout.

Footwear impressions in snow

Many people are surprised that it is possible to make a cast of a footwear impression in snow. They visualize pouring plaster of Paris onto a snow print having the print melt or collapse under the weight of the plaster—and indeed it would. Today, the most popular and successful method for making casts of snow print impressions is by the use of snow print wax. This comes in a spray can and is sold in bright red and brown. It is sprayed on the snow print and dries in a few minutes. This thin cast shows excellent detail but is fragile. After the wax cast dries, it is filled with cold dental casting mixture. This adds strength and bulk to the stone. When using snow print wax, precautions must be taken to keep direct sunlight away from the cast because the dark colors of the wax absorb light and might cause the print to melt. Once the wax and stone cast is made, it should be covered with a box or other container to hasten drying. Other materials such as paint thinner, spray paints, paraffin, and sulfur can be used to make snow print castings. Figure 22.3 is a cast of a shoe print that was made in snow.

Lifting imprints

An imprint in a material like dust or one that has been visualized using a powder technique analogous to fingerprints can be lifted from a surface in a number of ways. One can use large pieces of tape just as would be done on a smaller scale with fingerprints or palm prints. There are also gelatine materials made especially for lifting prints. The most popular method used today, however, involves one of a number of electrostatic lifting devices. The principle behind these techniques is that a large, static electricity charge will strongly attract dust and other fine powders.

FIGURE 22.3

A cast of a shoeprint that had been left in snow.

Courtesy: Cheryl Lozen, Michigan State Police, Forensic Science Division.

A low-current, high-voltage charge is put across a film that attracts the particles from the impression, thus affecting a transfer. A contrasting color film can be used as the transfer surface. The transferred image can then be easily photographed. Figure 22.4 is an electrostatic lift of a shoeprint that was made in dust.

Some imprints are difficult or impossible to lift. These include those in grease or oil or in blood. There are also impressions made in materials that deform when impressed but then bounce back and lose the impression, such as cushions or carpeting materials. The three-dimensional image would be lost when the substrate regains its shape but there may be residues imbedded in the impression that form an imprint that may, in some cases, be lifted. Figure 22.5 is a picture of a shoeprint that was made in blood at a crime scene.

Comparison of Footwear Impressions

According to some examiners, footwear impressions can be individual evidence. There must be sufficient, unique characteristics present in the impression. The impression must be of good enough quality and the lifting or casting technique must be able to faithfully record the impression for comparison with the actual footwear. It is important to note that the impression will be a negative of the footwear; that is, raised areas on the footwear will be depressions in the impression. Figure 22.6 shows a comparison of a shoeprint and a cast made of the shoeprint at the crime scene.

There is no set number of unique characteristics that must be present on an impression in order for a forensic scientist to reach the conclusion that the impression was made by a particular shoe. Each case must be considered on its own merit and will have its own facts and circumstances. One must never be put into the position of making a conclusion that

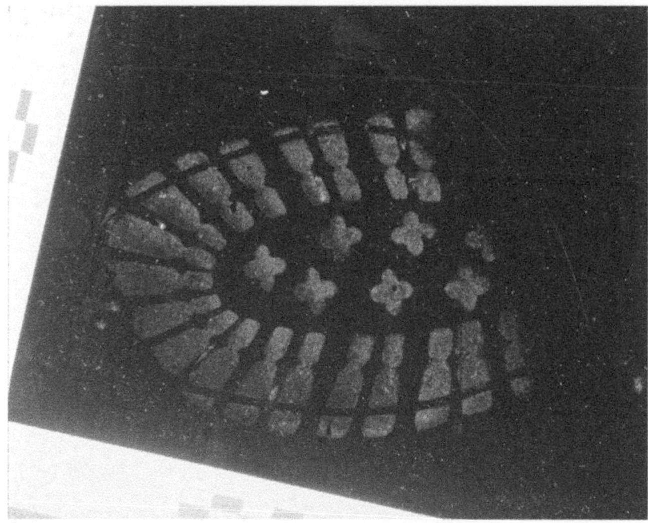

FIGURE 22.4

An electrostatic lift of a shoeprint left in dust.

Courtesy: Cheryl Lozen, Michigan State Police, Forensic Science Division.

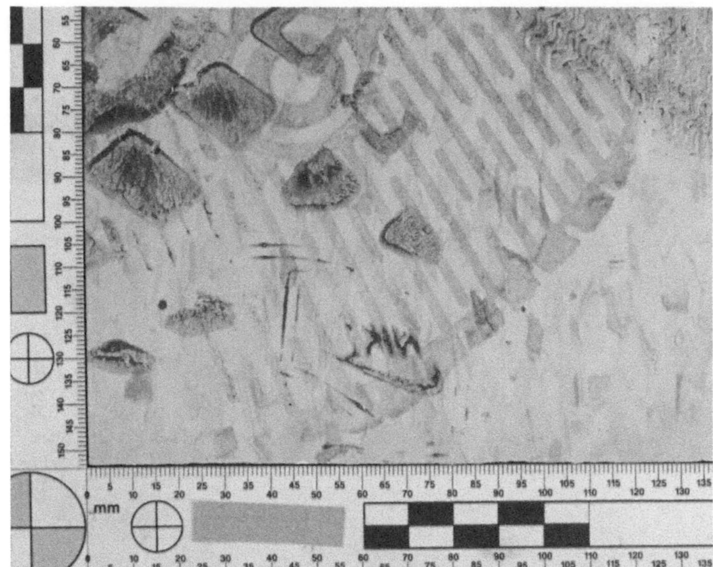

FIGURE 22.5

A shoeprint left on a floor after the wearer stepped in blood at a crime scene.

Courtesy: Cheryl Lozen, Michigan State Police, Forensic Science Division.

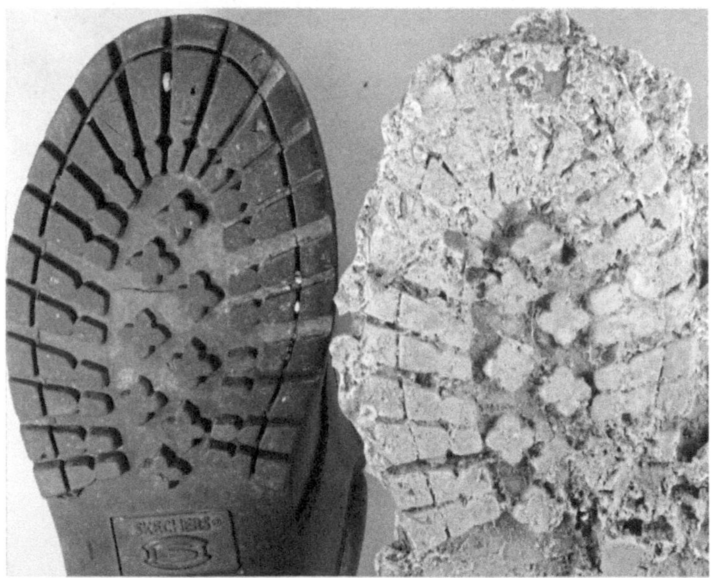

FIGURE 22.6

Comparison of a shoeprint with a plaster cast of the shoe.

Courtesy: Cheryl Lozen, Michigan State Police, Forensic Science Division.

it always takes a certain minimum number of characteristics to declare a match because there is no database that supports a single number. Generally, once a shoe has been worn to the point where it starts gaining unique characteristics, there will be plenty to choose from.

TIRE IMPRESSION EVIDENCE

Tire impressions are similar in some ways to footwear impressions. They both have the same purpose; to increase friction and minimize slippage. This can be more important in tires than in shoes because tires travel at much higher speeds under all sorts of weather conditions and must be able to start and stop more rapidly than shoes. The part of the modern tire that is in contact with the road is called the **tread**. Today, treads have many intricate designs that serve several functions. Like footwear and some other types of impressions, treads wear with time and pick up unique characteristics because of the random nature of the wearing. The two- or three-dimensional impressions that treads can transfer to a medium can be individualized in the same ways that footwear impressions can.

TIRE TREADS

The first recorded patent for something approaching the modern vehicle tire was granted in England in 1846 to Robert Thompson. His "aerial wheel" went unused and unappreciated until 1888, when the pneumatic (air-filled) tire was reinvented by John Dunlop (of Dunlop tires). There was no tread on these tires—they were bald. This caused problems that became evident when the first roads were built around the beginning of the twentieth century. It soon became clear that some sort of traction mechanism for tires would have to be developed because the roads were in such poor condition. In 1907, Harvey Firestone (of Firestone Tires) developed a traction design in the tread for the first time. He took the words "Firestone" and "Non-skid" and carved them into the tire, so that they were alternatively raised and lowered into the tread. An impression of the tire revealed these words. This was actually a crude but clever form of advertising. Today, tread design has become a science unto itself. Treads are designed not only for traction, but also for channeling away water to prevent hydroplaning, for noise reduction, and for comfortable driving. Many tread designs are quite intricate in order to be able to accomplish the goals of the tire.

IN DEPTH: WHAT DO ALL THOSE NUMBERS MEAN ON THE SIDEWALL OF A TIRE?

Take a look at the sidewall of a modern tire. There are lots of letters and numbers stamped or embossed on the tire. Some describe the company and model of the tire. These are pretty easy to figure out. But what about the mysterious combination of letters and numbers such as:

P235/75 R 15

The "P" means that the tire is built for a passenger car. If the vehicle were a pick-up truck, the tire would be designated "LT." The "235" is the cross-section width or diameter of the tire in millimeters measured from sidewall to sidewall. Since tires can be mounted on different size rims and

(Continued)

IN DEPTH: WHAT DO ALL THOSE NUMBERS MEAN ON THE SIDEWALL OF A TIRE?—cont'd

this would affect the diameter, the designated diameter is that when the tire is mounted on the rim that it was built for. The "75" is called the **aspect ratio**. This number is derived from the height of the tire, measured from the bead (where the tire seals to the rim) to the top of the tread. The actual number is the percentage of the tire width, so the number 75 means that the height of the tire is 75% of its width. In our example, the height would be 176 mm, which is 75% of 235 mm.

The "R" designates how the tire is manufactured. The most common method is radial. Other tires can be designated "D" for diagonal bias or "B" for bias belted. Finally, the "15" is the diameter in inches of the rim that the tire was designed for.

TIRE IMPRESSIONS AS EVIDENCE

It is surprising to learn that more than two-thirds of major crimes in the United States involve an automobile, if only as the "getaway car." It is also true that a tire impression is the most effective way of positively linking a motor vehicle that has been at a crime scene with some degree of certainty. Many crime scene investigators, however, do not look for or record tire impressions nearly as often as should be the case with such potentially important evidence. As with footwear impressions discussed previously, there are three methods for recording tire impressions at a crime scene. Tire impressions may be two or three dimensional and may be negative or positive depending upon how they are produced. As with any other crime scene, photography and drawings are the best methods of faithfully recording the overall scene and this should be done before examination-quality castings are made of tire impressions. As with footwear impressions, both recording the impression photographically and casting for three-dimensional impressions should be done. The main advantage of a cast is that all three dimensions can be easily seen. With tire impressions in particular, there is often a need to make a three-dimensional cast at the scene because, unlike footwear impressions, tire impressions often cannot be taken up and moved to the laboratory for further analysis. Figure 22.7 shows a portion of a tire tread cast in plaster.

There are disadvantages to casting tire impressions relative to photography. Some of these do not apply to footwear impressions. First, it can be difficult to make a cast on a steep incline because the casting material may tend to flow downhill and part of the cast made at the top of the hill may be too thin and fall apart. Second, unlike footwear impressions that are usually about a foot long, tire impressions may be many feet long and require very large casts that can be bulky and unwieldy. It is much easier to take a series of photographs of a long impression. Finally, there is the problem with three-dimensional impressions being negative; the raised areas of the tread become depressions in the cast. Negative impressions should never be compared to a positive image. To correct this problem, a photograph negative should be taken of the tire tread, which adds time and expense to the project. Not surprisingly, tire impressions are made from the same materials and are done in the same way as footwear impressions. Dental stone is the preferred medium for casts in soil, and snow-casting wax is best for impressions in snow. A suitable measuring instrument should be placed in all photographs.

FIGURE 22.7

A plaster cast of a portion of a tire tread.

Courtesy: Cheryl Lozen, Michigan State Police, Forensic Science Division.

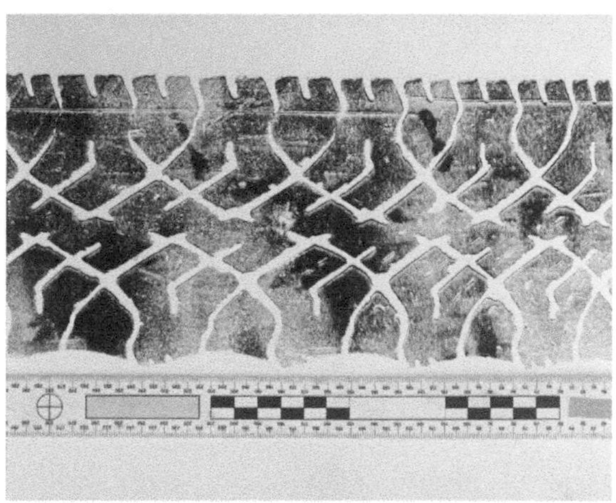

FIGURE 22.8

A portion of the tread of a known tire that has been inked and rolled out on paper to provide points of comparison with an unknown tire tread.

Courtesy: Cheryl Lozen, Michigan State Police, Forensic Science Division.

Lifts of two-dimensional tire impressions are made in the same way as with footwear impressions. Because of the great length of many tire impressions, several lifts of the same impression may have to be made in order to get the whole impression. In some cases, a roll of Mylar film, the full length of the impression, can be used to lift a long tire impression all at once. Figure 22.8 is a portion of a tire tread that was made in ink for comparison with an unknown tread.

In addition to the tread patterns, other data can be derived from tire impressions. For example, the Michigan State Police Forensic Science Laboratory collects data on **wheelbase** and tire tread **stance** measurements. The wheelbase of a motor vehicle is the distance from the center of the front hub to the center of the rear hub. The stance is the distance from the centerline of the right tire to the centerline of the left tire. The Michigan State Police Laboratory keeps a database of automobiles organized by these three measurements, and from these data and the tire tread design, one may be able to determine the make and model of a car or truck.

BITE MARK EVIDENCE

Ted Bundy was executed in an electric chair by the State of Florida on January 24, 1989. He had confessed to 30 homicides that he committed between 1974 and 1978 in seven states. His crime spree included two escapes from Colorado jails and three murders before he was captured in Florida in 1978. During his final crime spree, he attacked Lisa Levy in a sorority house at Florida State University. During the attack, he bit her deeply in her left buttock. At his trial for the murder of Lisa Levy and another student, bite mark evidence was introduced that matched the bite mark in Levy's body with impressions taken of Bundy's teeth. The match was made by forensic odontologists Richard Souviron and Lowell Levine. This was the first, and certainly the most famous case where bite marks played a major role in putting the defendant at the crime scene in such a graphic way.

Bite marks can be left in virtually any pliable material. There was a case in the 1970s where a home invader became hungry and took a large bit out of a piece of cheese that was in the refrigerator. He left the cheese behind and was later convicted, partially on the match made of the bite mark in the cheese. Human skin can be a good medium for accepting and holding bite marks although the healing process and the elasticity of human tissue means that the bite mark may only be visible for a period of time. Traditionally, bite mark evidence, especially bite marks in skin are analyzed in a two-dimensional fashion. Because the penetration into the surface may not be too deep and, until recently three-dimensional techniques had not been developed, it is the surface characteristics of the bite mark and the dental impression that are generally used for comparison. Figure 22.9 shows a well-formed bite mark in a small baby's arm.

Known bite marks are generally obtained by use of an impression of the teeth in dental stone or a similar medium. The material used for the impression must be fine-grained so that small details in the surface of the teeth will show up. Figure 22.10 is a dental impression of a set of teeth.

In recent years, as bite marks have been increasingly used as identification evidence in crimes of violence, questions have arisen concerning the underlying principle that bite marks in skin and other surfaces are unique and can be individualized to dental impressions. The NAS Forensic Science Report highlighted this in their

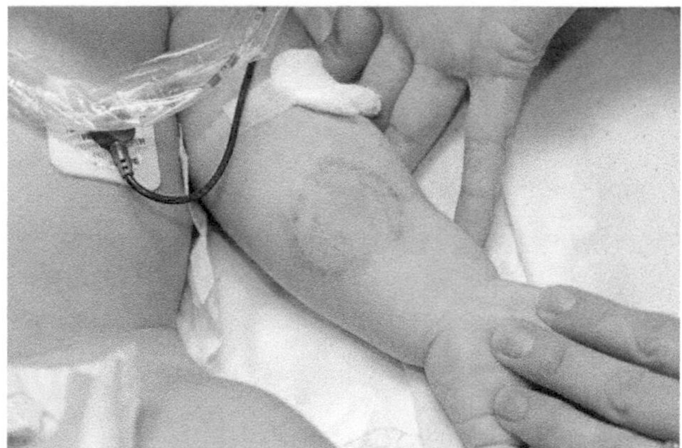

FIGURE 22.9

A bite mark in the arm of an infant child.

Courtesy of Edwin Parks, DDS.

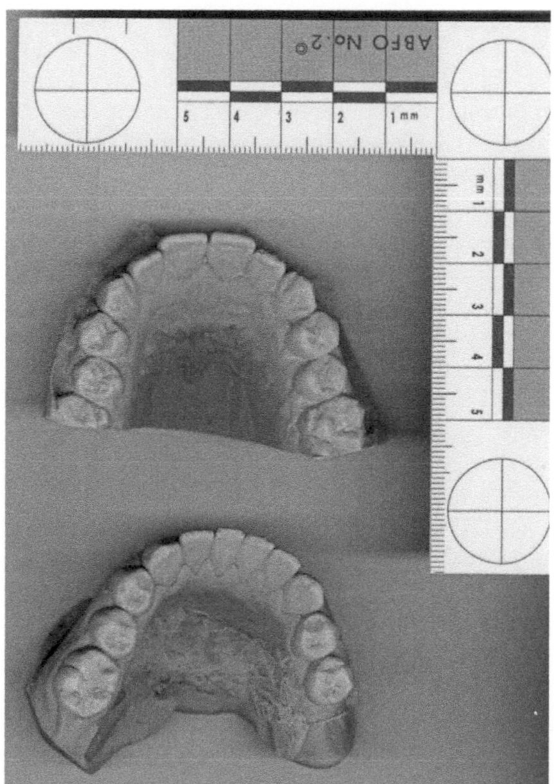

FIGURE 22.10

Bite mark castings in dental stone.

Courtesy of Edwin Parks, DDS.

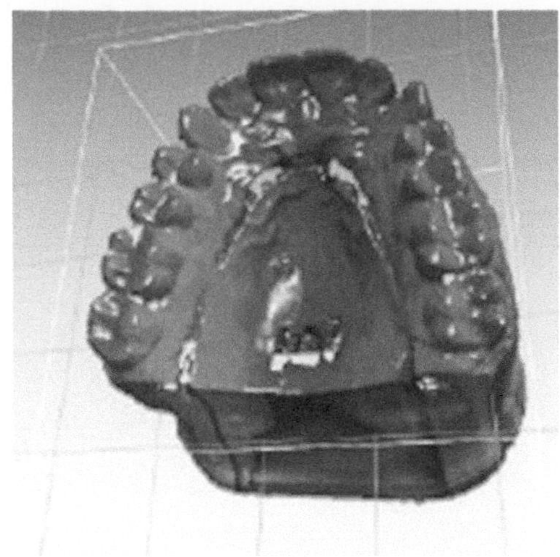

FIGURE 22.11

A three-dimensional bite mark casting.

Courtesy of Dr Mihran Tuceryan.

discussion of impression evidence in general. They expressed the concern that there was insufficient validation research that would support a claim of individuality in bite mark evidence as they did with other types of impression evidence.

One promising development in the analysis of bite mark evidence is the use of three-dimensional impressions and bite marks. In cases where there is sufficient depth to the bite mark, the comparison with dental impressions can include the three-dimensional structure of the teeth in addition to the biting surface. Figure 22.11 shows a three-dimensional bite mark impression. Figure 22.12 shows how three-dimensional bite marks are compared.

SERIAL NUMBERS RESTORATION

Many consumer products and commercial items are identified by a unique serial number. In some cases, this is required by law; firearms and certain auto parts are examples. If the object is metal, the serial number is often stamped into the surface of the metal using a set of alphanumeric dies. Like footwear and tire treads, serial numbers of this type are three-dimensional impressions. When serial numbers are at issue in a crime, it is often because someone attempted to obliterate them from the object, making it more difficult to identify its owner or source. The issue then is whether or not a forensic scientist can restore and read the serial number. Most people, when faced with the task of wiping out a stamped serial number on metal will use a file or grinder. They will consider the job to be a success if they can no longer read any of the numbers or letters. They fail to realize that, even though the serial number may not be visible or readable, it

FIGURE 22.12

A comparison of a three-dimensional bite mark impression with an impression taken from a suspect (in red).

Courtesy of Dr Mihran Tuceryan.

is not really destroyed. It is possible and quite common for a forensic chemist to restore an obliterated serial number impression. In order to understand how this is done, it is necessary to learn a bit about how the chemistry and physics of a piece of metal changes when subjected to the stress of having a serial number stamped into its surface.

Metals, like most solids, have a definite crystal structure and therefore an ordered arrangement of chemical bonds between atoms (called metal–metal bonds). When a serial number is stamped into a metal, two things happen to the metal under the number. First, it is compressed, making it denser than the surrounding metal. Second, the metal–metal bonds in the stamped area are disrupted and the metal structure becomes weakened. When someone tries to remove a serial number impression by abrasion with a file or grinder, the metal surrounding the stamped number is removed. Once the metal surface surrounding the numbers becomes level with the stamped numbers, then they cannot be seen anymore. However, the compressed, deformed metal *under* the numbers is still there unless the perpetrator continues the grinding process beyond where the numbers disappear. To restore the serial number, the metal surface that has been abraded is polished with a fine abrasive and then slowly treated with a corrosive acid. The acid slowly dissolves the metal. However, the metal that is under the serial numbers behaves differently toward the acid than the surrounding metal, which had not been disturbed by the stamping process. There are two possible ways that the stamped metal can behave differently. First, remember that it has become denser when compressed. Thus, this metal would be expected to dissolve more slowly than the less dense metal surrounding it. As the metal dissolves, the serial number would be seen to be raised above the faster dissolving, surrounding metal surface. Second, remember that the metal–metal bonds of the stamped metal have been disrupted by the stamping process, and thus weakened. This would be expected to cause the stamped metal to dissolve more quickly than the surrounding metal. The serial number would thus appear to be pressed into the metal once again. How do we know which mechanism dominates in the restoration of serial numbers? The best way is to observe the restoration process using a low-power stereomicroscope. It can be easily seen that the serial numbers are lower than the surrounding metal surface as the numbers are restored. This means that the weakened bond theory must be most responsible for the dissolving process of the acid.

The actual process of dissolving the metal to restore an obliterated serial number must be done carefully. Once a serial number is restored, it will eventually disappear and then will be gone forever. It is good practice to have a camera ready to take pictures of each number as it is restored so there will be a permanent, visual record of the restoration. The acid is generally applied with a cotton swab. When a number appears, the acid is washed off quickly to minimize further dissolving while the operator views the restored number and photographs it. There are a variety of metals that can have serial numbers stamped into them. Each type of metal requires different acids and conditions. Acidified, aqueous copper chloride solutions are used to restore serial numbers in iron and steel. The copper chloride acts to oxidize the iron so it will dissolve. The copper ions are reduced to metallic copper that will deposit on the metal surface. If the metal surface is stainless steel, a more powerful acidic solution is needed. Acids are too strong for aluminum surfaces, which would dissolve almost immediately. In such cases, mild alkaline solutions are used. Figure 22.13(a) and (b) shows a serial number that was stamped into the door of a farm tractor. The number had been ground off and then restored in the laboratory.

Today, serial numbers are stamped into many objects other than metals. Is it possible to restore obliterated numbers in other surfaces? Plastics present difficult problems. They are generally polymers. These are very stable substances that are generally insoluble in most solvents so it would be extremely difficult to restore serial numbers in most plastics. Not all serial numbers are stamped into surfaces. Some are applied with decals or etched. Others are embossed and are raised above the surface of the object. These types of serial numbers cannot be restored using the same methods as are used with stamped numbers.

IN THE LAB

Can one restore worn serial numbers from wood? This actually occurred in a case. An old wooden ladder was used to gain entry into a second-floor business that was then burgled. The prosecutor wanted to try and trace the origin of the ladder, which had been brought to and then left at the crime scene. There were some remnants of a serial number that had been stamped into the ladder when it was new, but then had worn away with time. The ladder was sent to the author's laboratory where a number of restorative methods were attempted; all ending in failure. Finally, a deceptively simple way was discovered that actually worked. Can you guess what the method is?

The area of the wood containing the serial number was wetted with water to increase its contrast with the surrounding wood. Then a strong light source was aimed at the serial number at a steep angle so that the light was almost parallel to the ladder surface. The indented serial numbers created faint shadows in the wood that were photographed and read.

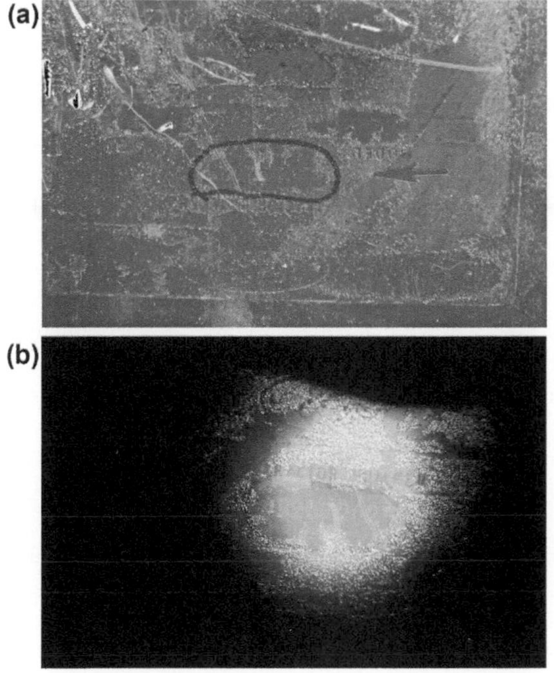

FIGURE 22.13

A restored serial number on the inside of the metal door of a tractor, where (a) shows the serial number has been obliterated by grinding and (b) shows how the number has been restored.

SIGNIFICANCE OF IMPRESSION EVIDENCE

As you are now aware, much of the time spent by forensic scientists in the laboratory is to try and associate evidence with its source. Sometimes this can be done with a great deal of certainty, whereas in other cases, the association is more equivocal. As you have also learned, the factor that determines whether one object can be associated with another is the presence of unique characteristics in the donor. This means that the three-dimensional pattern or markings must contain some characteristics that are unique to that object. For example, a footwear impression must contain some wearing characteristics such as pits or cracks that would make it unique. The same would hold true with a tire tread. These kinds of unique characteristics come about as the object is used. When a shoe or tire is brand new, it does not contain unique characteristics; one tire that comes off the assembly line looks pretty much like all of the others that come off the same line. It is only as the tire is used on a car that it picks up unique characteristics. This is because the processes that give rise to these characteristics are random in nature. No two tires or shoes will wear the same way, so each will change with time and become unique. When there are enough of these unique features present, then some examiners believe that this evidence can be individualized to a particular tire or shoe. Thus, these types of evidence can be very valuable in associating a particular shoe or vehicle with a crime scene. The problem with associating footwear and tire tread evidence to a particular source is not that these objects pick up unique markings with wear. Most people in and out of forensic science believe that this is a reasonable, if unproven hypothesis and research needs to be done to validate this. The problem is that the means of recording these imperfections are limited in resolution and it is often difficult or impossible to see these critical features using lifts or casts. Further, there is no agreement on what constitutes sufficient resolution or the number of features that must be present in order for a conclusion of individuality to be supported. Finally, there is the issue of the concept of individualization itself. Many people do not believe that this conclusion is justified under any forensic circumstances since it is not possible to test all shoes or tires to determine if in fact, they are unique. The National Academy of Sciences Forensic Science Committee concluded that impression evidence, like fingerprint evidence and questioned documents, lacked scientific validation of methods used for comparisons and lacked standards for reaching conclusions of associations. They also indicated that conclusions of individuality require that more validation research be conducted.

Serial numbers restorations present a different picture. Here the goal is to restore an obliterated serial number on an object so the number can be used for identification. The serial number itself is usually unique and makes the object unique by virtue of being the only object with that particular serial number. Some other types of impressions, such as the one made when a car strikes a pedestrian so hard that an imprint of the fabric pattern in the victim's clothes is impressed in the car's paint, do not lend themselves to individualization. It would not be possible to individualize an impression to a particular garment, but it wouldn't normally be necessary. There is almost always other evidence that can link a motor vehicle to a hit and run. The fabric pattern is class evidence that adds to the total picture.

BACK TO THE CASE

In the OJ Simpson case described above, there was no attempt to match the bloody shoeprints to the particular shoes that Simpson owned. During the criminal trial, there was no evidence that Simpson owned such a pair of shoes and no such shoes were ever found in his possession. He had also denied ever owning such shoes. But after the criminal trial, photographs were produced showing him wearing such shoes. In the civil trial, the evidence that he did in fact own such shoes, along with his statements denying that he owned them and the testimony of the FBI expert were all admitted. At that time, it was unnecessary to have had the actual shoes.

Suppose that the actual Bruno Magli shoes had been available during the criminal trial. Could they have been matched to the bloody footwear prints found at the crime scene near Nicole Brown Simpson's home? That would have depended upon the quality of the prints. Did they contain enough detail and were they smeared? It would also have depended upon the condition of the shoe soles. Had the shoes been worn enough to pick up wear and damage markings that are the natural consequence of wearing shoes? None of this was ever discussed in the trial because the shoes were never made available. One could speculate that such evidence would have been highly probative.

SUMMARY

Impressions can be two or three dimensional. The most common impression evidence types are footwear, tire treads, and serial numbers. Other types of evidence may also be in the form of impressions. An example of this would be a fingerprint left in putty. Impression evidence can be individualized to one particular object if there are sufficient unique characteristics present. These characteristics arise from the random wearing of the footwear or tire tread.

Preserving the impression is very important because they often cannot be transported to the forensic science laboratory intact. Proper, high-resolution photography is commonly done, with digital photography becoming more popular. A suitable measuring instrument must be in the picture to facilitate scale determination. The measuring instrument must be a ruler or other device that actually measures distance. Ordinary objects such as coins or a cigarette pack that could provide perspective, but not measurement, should not be used. Dental stone has become the casting material of choice in many impressions because of its ease of use and high definition.

Serial numbers that have been stamped into metal can be restored after scraping off if the scraping hasn't gone too deep into the metal. The fatiguing of the metal under the stamped numbers will dissolve faster than surrounding metal when subjected to oxidizing acids.

TEST YOUR KNOWLEDGE

1. What is "impression evidence"? What types of evidence are included?
2. What are the differences between two- and three-dimensional impressions?
3. Under what conditions can impression evidence be individualized?
4. How are imprints "lifted"?
5. How are three-dimensional impressions "lifted"?
6. How are casts made of impressions? What are the best casting materials?
7. How many characteristics are necessary in order to individualize a footwear or tire tread impression?
8. What are the major class characteristics present in footwear impressions?
9. What are the major individual characteristics in footwear impressions?
10. What are the major differences between footwear and tire tread impressions?
11. What is tire tread stance?
12. What is the wheelbase on a car? How is it measured?
13. What are the major reasons why tires have treads?
14. Write an equation that shows how copper chloride reacts with iron to dissolve it.
15. What is metal–metal bonding? What is its importance in serial number restoration?
16. Some serial numbers are "embossed" on a surface. Could an obliterated, embossed serial number be restored in the same way that stamped ones are?
17. Why cannot stamped serial numbers normally be restored in plastic?

18. What would happen if you used acid to restore a serial number set and just left the acid on the object and went away for a while?
19. Under what conditions would fingerprint evidence be considered to be impression evidence?
20. Why are firearms and tool marks considered to be impression evidence?

CONSIDER THIS...

1. Impression evidence can be either class or individual. Under what conditions does it change from class to individual? How do probabilities enter into the conclusion that such evidence is class or individual?
2. Describe how you would preserve and photograph a tire tread impression that was left in grease on a garage floor? How would you handle a tire tread impression left in dirt?
3. Besides the types of evidence described or mentioned in this chapter, are there other types of impression evidence? What are they?

FURTHER READING

Bodziak, W.J., 2000. Footwear Impression Evidence: Detection, Recovery, and Examination, second ed. CRC Press, Boca Raton, Florida.

McDonald, P., 1989. Tire Imprint Evidence. Elsevier, Amsterdam.

Bodziak, W.J., 1990. Footwear Impression Evidence. Elsevier, Amsterdam.

ON THE WEB

http://lucy.mrs.org/2006brazil/wedpix/j502.pdf. Good description of methods used to restore serial numbers on metals and polymers.

http://www.theiai.org/guidelines/swgtread/index.php. Homepage of the Scientific Working Group on Shoeprint and Tire Tread Evidence (SWGTREAD).

CHAPTER

Digital Evidence*

23

CHAPTER OUTLINE

KEY TERMS

- Bit
- Data carving
- Electronic control unit (ECU)
- Event data recorder (EDR)
- Hard drives
- Hashing
- Memory cards
- Metadata
- P2P
- Partition
- Phishing
- SIM card
- Spoofing

* With thanks to Paul Reedy and Simon Kert, DC Department of Forensic Sciences.

- Steganography
- Storage media
- System identification code
- Thumb drive/flash drive/USB drive
- Work copy

INTRODUCTION

Take a look around and count the number of digital devices in sight; now double that. This might be close to the actual number of objects holding digital information in the immediate area. Computers and digital devices are now ubiquitous in modern society. The number of cell phones, for example, has risen steadily worldwide (Figure 23.1). With computing power doubling every 2 years and the cost of memory plummeting (Figure 23.2(a) and (b)), the presence of digital devices will only increase and deepen in daily life.

Not only digital devices omnipresent, they are linked: Computers, networks, cell phone systems, satellites, security cameras, geographical positioning systems (GPS), the entirety of the Internet…the list goes on. The world is awash in data—fully 90% of all data were generated in the last 2 years, according to *Science Daily*:

> *An increasing amount of data is becoming available on the internet. Each and every one of us is constantly producing and releasing data about ourselves. We do this either by moving around passively – our behaviour being registered by cameras or card usage – or by logging onto our PCs and surfing the net.*[1]

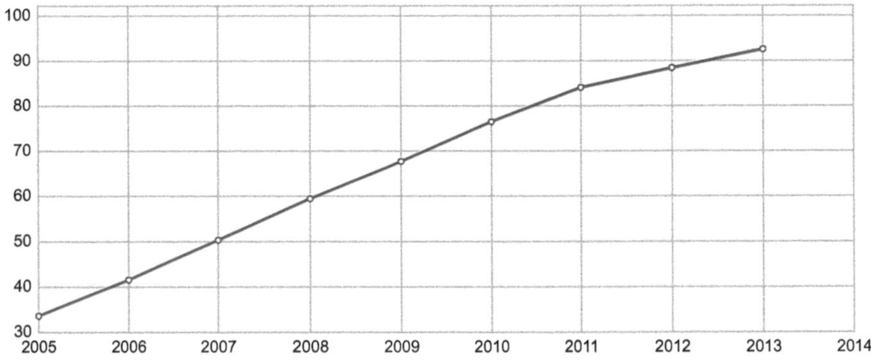

FIGURE 23.1

Mobile cellular subscriptions (per 100 people). Mobile cellular telephone subscriptions are subscriptions to a public mobile telephone service using cellular technology, which provide access to the public-switched telephone network. Postpaid and prepaid subscriptions are included. International Telecommunication Union, World Telecommunication/ICT Development Report and database, and World Bank estimates.

[1] SINTEF. Big Data, for better or worse: 90% of world's data generated over last two years. Science Daily, May 22, 2013.

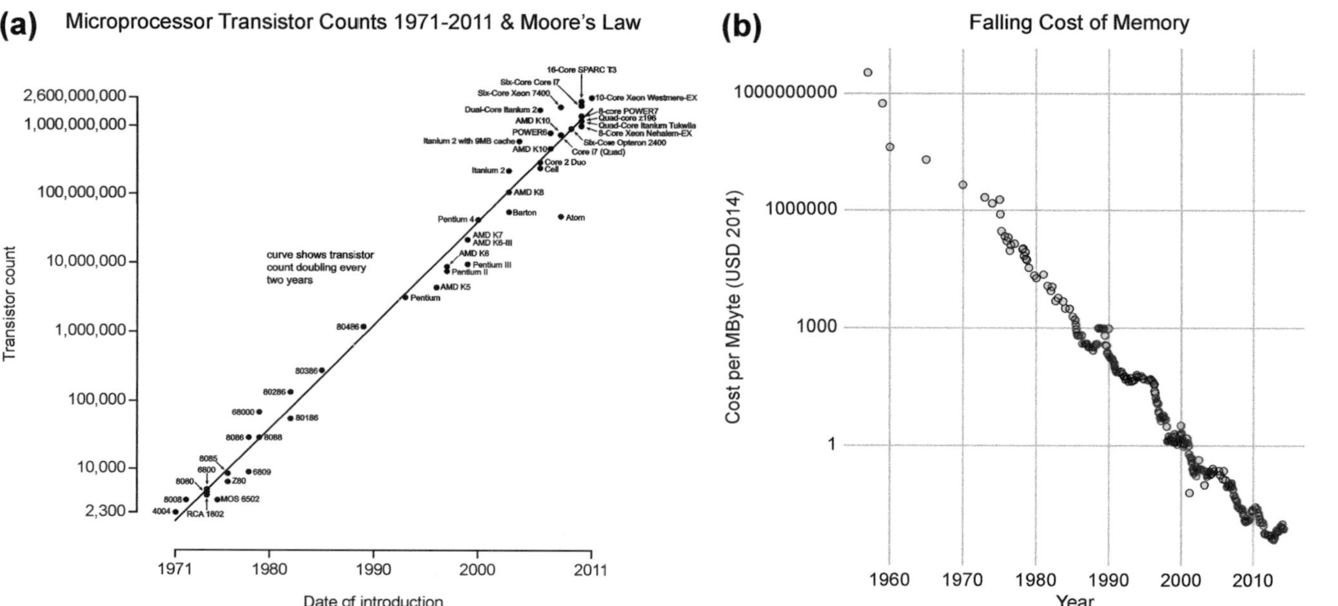

FIGURE 23.2

(a) Moore's Law states that the number of transistors on an integrated circuit doubles approximately every 2 years; this graphic shows the growth of computing power from 1971 onward. *(Wikimedia Commons.)* (b) While computing power has increased, the cost of memory has dropped significantly, and continues to do so (*http://letstalkdata.com/2014/04/falling-cost-of-memory-1957-to-present/*). This means that more digital devices will infiltrate daily life and, thus, more potential evidence for forensic investigations.

Increased connectivity means the world gets smaller; the original idea that each person is separated from any other person by no more than six connections has shrunk to only 3.4 connections, thanks to digital social media.[2] These factors mean that digital evidence is not only here to stay but it will also be a part of nearly every forensic investigation and analysis. More problematically, the amount of information, the diversity of formats it appears in, and the variety of consumer devices it is contained within will only increase and at an exponential rate. Take cell phones, for example. Thousands and thousands of models of cell phones—not phones but *types* of phones—are in existence worldwide; it is estimated that over 8000 different models of cell phones are sold in China alone. The answer to the question, "how many cell phone models are there?" is unknowable; it's that complex and changing. The design of cell phones has changed radically in just a few decades since their introduction (Figure 23.3). Keeping up to date with this rapid growth and diversity of technology, while keeping archival information about older models and features, makes digital evidence uniquely difficult for a forensic laboratory and its scientists.

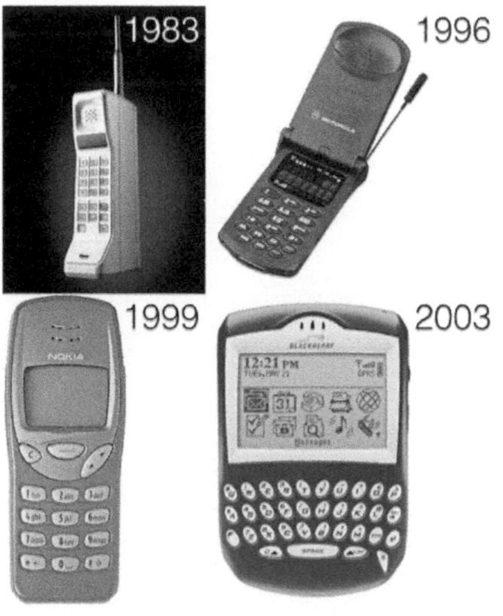

FIGURE 23.3

Cell phone design has changed radically in just a few short years. (a) Motorola Dynatac, 1983. (b) Motorola StarTac, 1996. (c) Nokia, 1999. (d) Blackberry, 2003. Images not to scale.

[2] Bakhshandeh, R., Samadi, M., Azimifar, Z., Schaeffer, J., 2011. Degrees of Separation in Social Networks. In: Association for the Advancement of Artificial Intelligence, Fourth Annual Symposium on Combinatorial Search. AAAI Press, Menlo Park, CA.

Because of the pervasive nature of digital devices and their varied uses, no one single case can capture the essence of this discipline. Different cases will be used to highlight different aspects of digital evidence in this chapter.

WHAT IS DIGITAL EVIDENCE?

Digital evidence is any stored or transmitted data in binary format that may be useful in a criminal or civil investigation. The binary format is how computers store information and is rendered in **bits** (either 0s and 1s); binary is used in almost all modern computers and digital devices. Digital evidence can take a very large number of forms and can be found on hard drives, cell phones, mobile storage media, networks, and many other sources. Digital evidence can be involved with any sort of crime, like suspects' e-mail or cell phone data indicating intent, their locations at the time of a crime, and relationships with the victim or other suspects. Some crimes are solely committed within the digital realm and involves information that is illegal or illegal through transmission or creation, such as:

- Child exploitation material
- Computer intrusion
- Counterfeiting
- Domestic violence, threats, and extortion
- E-mail threats, harassment, and stalking
- Gambling
- Identity and intellectual property theft
- Narcotics
- Online or economic fraud
- Prostitution
- Telecommunication fraud
- Terrorism

In what now seems a dated format, a 3.5″ floppy disk led investigators in 2005 to the "BTK" (for "bind, torture, kill") serial killer who had eluded police capture since 1974 and claimed the lives of at least 10 victims. Dennis Rader, the BTK killer, sent taunting letters describing details of his killings to police and news media. Despite over 1300 DNA samples being collected, Rader eluded detection for years. One of the communications was sent on a 1.44 MB floppy disk to a local TV station. Metadata (see "In more detail: Data about data") embedded in a deleted word processing file contained "Christ Lutheran Church" and that the document was last modified by "Dennis"; Rader was President of that church's council. Additional investigation led to the analysis of DNA evidence from Rader's daughter, which was a familial association to a DNA sample from under a victim's fingernails. Although "traditional" forensic science finally associated Rader with the killings, it was digital evidence that made that link possible.

IN MORE DETAIL: DATA ABOUT DATA

Saving a file to a storage medium does more than just save the content; it saves information about the file as well. This "data about data," or **metadata**, is critically important in digital forensic investigations. Metadata aids in the classification of the intended information, providing identification, location, time, author, archiving, and contextual information about the file. A good analogy would be a dictionary: Although the main purpose is to list the words and their meanings (original data), it does so alphabetically, with references to other words and page numbers, among other information, such as synonyms (all metadata). Some metadata is standardized, like with digital photographs, and some can be edited with appropriate software (again, images are a good example of this). If the file system metadata is lost or corrupted, the scientist may need to **data carve** the media to reconstruct the files, their structure, and content.

Using metadata in a forensic investigation can be a key method. Knowing that an image is child pornography is not as useful as knowing what kind of device was used to take it, when and where it was stored, and possibly where it was taken. Sometimes, the data about the data are more important than the data itself.

For more on metadata, see Guenther, R., Radebaugh, J., 2004. Understanding Metadata, NIST: Bethesda, MD, at http://www.niso.org/publications/press/UnderstandingMetadata.pdf.

COMPUTERIZED DEVICES

Digital evidence appears on computerized or digital devices. A computer consists of hardware (physical electronic components) and software (machine-readable instructions that tell a computer to perform specific operations) that process data. A computer typically includes:

- a case that contains circuit boards, storage media, and interface connections,
- a display device,
- a keyboard, and
- a pointing device, such as a mouse.

Other related, externally connected components (peripherals), such as printers, scanners, or storage media, may be plugged into the system. Computer systems can take many forms, such as tablets, laptops, desktops, and mainframe computers. A computer system and its components can be very valuable evidence in an investigation. Nearly every internal or external component of a computer system can hold some form of data or metadata that could be useful forensically. Some examples of forensically valuable data include (but certainly are not limited to):

- hardware,
- software and applications ("apps"),
- documents, photos and images, financial information,
- e-mail and attachments,
- databases,
- browsing history,
- social media data and activity,
- contact lists, and
- maintenance, error, or event logs.

Storage devices, a typical place to start looking for digital evidence, vary in the amount of data they can store and the manner in which they store that data. Regardless of the size or type of storage device, it is critical to remember that it may contain vital information; most document files tend to be fairly small but could carry probative evidence. **Hard drives** are data storage devices that have an external logic board, connections to external sources of information and power, and some form of storage media (magnetic, ceramic, or glass). Hard drives need not be connected to a computer to be possible evidence; like books on a shelf, they still contain information although they are not currently used. **Thumb drives** or **flash drives** are small removable data storage devices with USB (universal serial bus) connections; their size makes them easy to transport and, therefore, conceal. They come in a wide variety of shapes and sizes and can be customized for commercial purposes or branding; thumb drives can be incorporated into other objects, like pocket knives, pens, or watches (Figure 23.4). **Memory cards** are very small storage devices typically used in digital cameras, but can also be used with tablets, computers, cell phones, video game consoles, and other electronic devices. A type of memory card is the subscriber identification module, or **SIM card**. SIM cards are integrated circuits that store the international mobile subscriber identity (IMSI) and the identification and the network information required to authenticate with a mobile carrier network. It is typically found in a mobile device, such as a cell phone or tablet, and come in a variety of sizes (Figure 23.5). For their size, they can carry large amounts of data and are easily concealed (or overlooked!).

Increasingly, digital devices are mobile; the sales of cell phones have outstripped the sales of other digital devices and the sale of traditional computers is dropping steadily (Figure 23.6). Mobile devices are handheld, portable data storage that provide communications, digital photography, navigation systems,

FIGURE 23.4

Thumb or flash drives come in a wide variety of styles and sizes, even customized ones that look like toys or other objects, like keys.

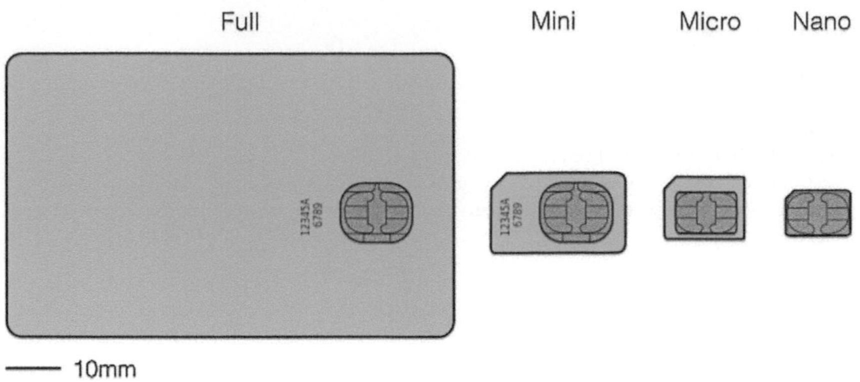

FIGURE 23.5

SIM cards carry device and user identification and authentication information for mobile communication devices, like cell phones and tablets. Their size depends on the device for which they are intended.

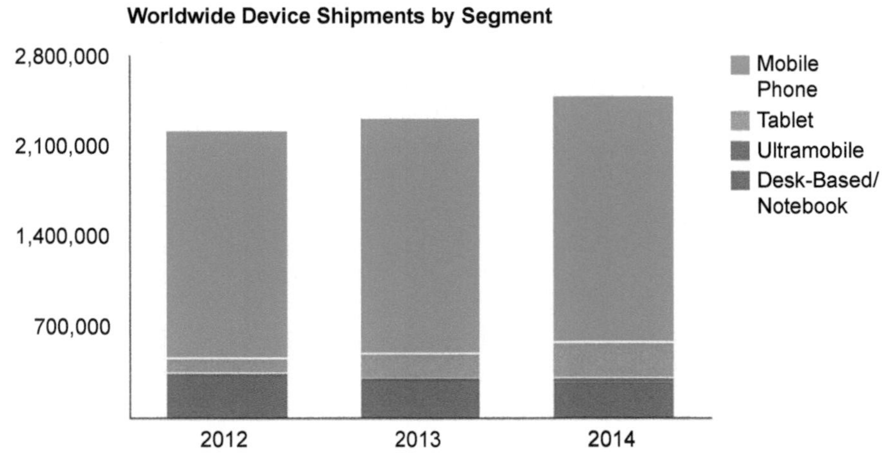

FIGURE 23.6

Shipments of digital devices by device type.

Redrawn from: Forecast: Devices by Operating System and User Type, Worldwide, 2010–2017, 3Q13 Update, http://www.gartner.com/resId=2596420.

IN MORE DETAIL: HOW CELL PHONES WORK

Cell phones are really just two-way radios with a transmitter and receiver, except they are point to point. Cell phones convert sounds into electrical signals that are transmitted to nearby receivers. The signals that cell phones send are transmitted in all directions but can only go a short distance. A network of receivers, called cell towers, relays a signal from tower to tower via nearby cells (areas of reception). A standard cell is hexagonal and about 10 square miles. This allows for cell phones to use less energy to find a nearby cell tower, consuming less energy.

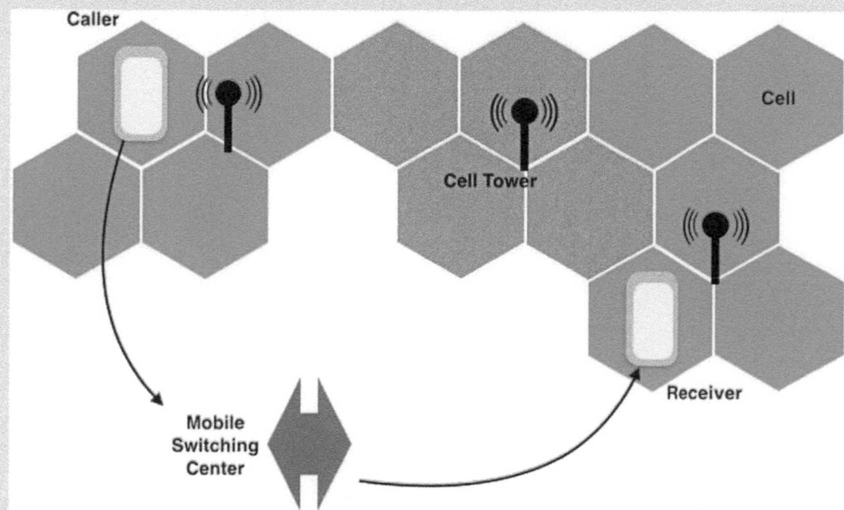

Each cell phone has a number of codes embedded into it identifying the user, the phone, and the telecommunications provider for the phone. The most important being the system identification code (SID), a five-digit code is assigned by the Federal Communications Commission to each different telecommunications company. When powered on, a cell phone finds the nearest cell tower and records the SID that is being transmitted from it; likewise, the phone identifies itself to the tower registering its location. As a cell phone moves between cells, the phone's signal strength changes, lowering as it moves away from one tower and increasing as it nears another; at some point, a signal is sent to the phone to change frequencies and it is shifted to the new cell. If the SIDs do not match, then the cell phone is considered to be "roaming" between cells.

A cell phone's location can be determined using cell tower data but it must use *multiple* towers to be accurate. A single-cell tower cannot provide all the necessary information to determine location and at least three towers are needed to triangulate a location; density of towers and interferences, like buildings, can have an effect on cell phone locations.

entertainment, data storage, and personal information management—increasingly all in the same device, like a smartphone. Smartphones can hold enormous amounts of data and metadata, including software applications (or apps), documents, e-mail, Internet browsing history, contacts, photographs, passwords, and location information that may be of value for investigations or alibis. The type of information and, most importantly, its format will be determined by the type

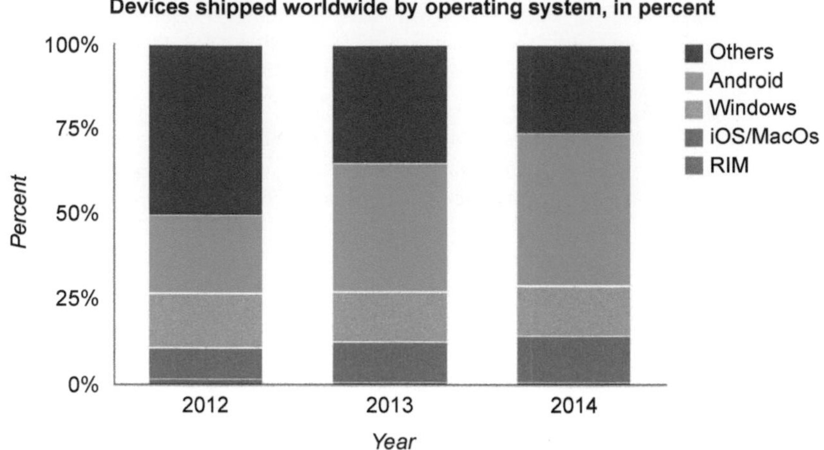

FIGURE 23.7

Shipments of digital devices by operating system, in percent.

Redrawn from: Forecast: Devices by Operating System and User Type, Worldwide, 2010–2017, 3Q13 Update, http://www.gartner.com/resId=2596420.

of device and its operating system, such as Android, Apple, Microsoft, or other (Figure 23.7).

Cell phones can be excellent evidence for a number of reasons. First, they are typically single-user devices and tend to have glass touch screens that make it easier to collect DNA. Second, their size relates to their mobility and is likely to be transported to, from, and during crimes. Finally, given the intensity of use, either for personal or professional purposes, cell phones tend to have more probative information per unit of storage than a typical computer.

As consumers shift to more mobile digital devices, the forensic scientist will have a difficult time keeping up with new products, new software, and updated versions and the interconnectivity of all these in an increasingly global networked communications system.

It is important to remember that any digital device can potentially function independently, in conjunction with, or be connected to other computer systems. Finding a cell phone or storage device alone does not necessarily mean it is not connected or networked.

NETWORKED DEVICES

Devices that are networked are linked by physical (cables) or wireless connections that potentially or actually share resources and data. Computer networks typically include a wide range of peripherals, like printers, and data routing devices such as hubs (connecting multiple devices, making them act as a single unit), switches (forward data to a destination device), and routers (connecting two or more data lines from different networks). Each device on a network should be identified and its functions listed along with other components of the computer system, connections (wired or wireless), Internet protocol (IP) settings, and local area network addresses associated with the computers and devices. Computers can also be connected directly to other computers without the need for servers or network hosts in a peer-to-peer (P2P) network; although P2P networks are not illegal, they are used for sharing illegal materials, like child pornography, pirated music or movies, and consumer fraud data. The existence of the network itself may be evidence! Remember, most devices are connected in some fashion and they need not be connected to devices that are present or immediately visible.

OTHER TYPES OF DEVICES

Nearly every electronic consumer good has a computer inside of it. Even refrigerators now come with the ability to watch television, listen to streaming music, make video phone calls, and track information about the food and where it is inside the appliance! Listing all the devices with potential digital evidence would be nearly impossible but there are several that may be of regular interest to the forensic scientist. Motor vehicles are now heavily computerized and **electronic control units** (ECUs) help to monitor and control systems and subsystems, like traction control and diagnostics for maintenance. ECUs store data for use in diagnostics (miles since last oil change, for example), status inputs (speed, telemetry, systems functions), and malfunctions (unscheduled maintenance). Other types of information stored or controlled by ECUs include:

- vehicle data, such as VIN, odometer reading, fuel levels,
- door and door lock status,
- passenger occupancy (weight in seats to activate air bags),
- data from the entertainment system, for example, muting the audio during telephone calls, etc.
- diagnostics trouble codes to inform the service garage about a nonscheduled problem with the vehicle,
- crash data during accident, ranging from noting that a crash has occurred, to location of the crash, where the vehicle has been damaged (front, rear, side, rollover, etc.), and even severity of the impact.

In vehicle accidents, an electronic control unit stores information about the crash that can be accessed for forensic investigation purposes, called an event data recorder which acts like the black box on aeroplanes (Figure 23.8). It records real-time data from the vehicle, including braking, acceleration, speed, and other data that can provide investigators with objective data about the vehicle and its status.

PROCESSING DIGITAL EVIDENCE

The overall process for digital evidence is similar to other types of evidence. However, some aspects of digital evidence require additional steps and precautions. The digital evidence process consists of five phases: identification, collection/acquisition, transportation, analysis/examination, and report.

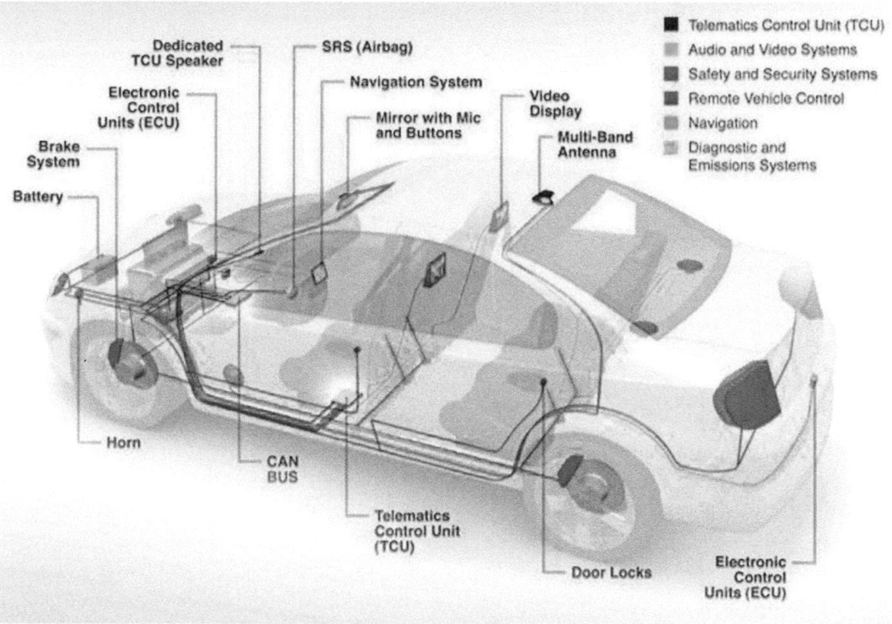

FIGURE 23.8

When collecting multiple computers, identify the first computer seized as "Computer A" or "Device #1" and then each cable and connection, including photographs. Subsequent computers can be labeled alphabetically or numerically.

IDENTIFICATION

Before collection, the potential digital evidence must be identified. This may pose significant difficulties because digital information is latent; the bits of data stored on the device or being transmitted through wires or the air cannot be immediately seen. Forensic scientists are dependent on other technologies to make these data readable and understood. Digital evidence identification needs to be done in a specific routine that checks every potential item of evidence. Obvious devices, like hard drives or thumb drives, are easy but many devices, like media players or Internet-enabled televisions, may also have storage capabilities. Even the obvious data sources can be very small, making them easy to conceal and, during a scene search, easy to dispose of.

The key concepts to identification would be that first to identify the types of devices visible/discoverable at the scene that contain digital evidence that may be of a probative nature.

The second part of identification is to be able identify the type of digital evidence that is stored on the physical evidence item and their relevance to the matter.

It may not be efficient or possible to examine each item at a scene.

COLLECTION/ACQUISITION

Unlike other types of evidence, digital evidence requires an electrical power source to operate. Having said that, digital evidence may be lost or corrupted if power is not maintained. For cell phones, this becomes complicated because digital evidence can be overwritten or deleted remotely if the cell phone remains active. Software is available, and some phones come with it, that allows for rendering the phone unusable (a so-called "kill switch" which "bricks" the phone, disabling it so it is as useful as a masonry brick). To secure cell phones from this type of tampering, crime scene responders should have shielding material to block incoming or outgoing signals. This can be done by placing the phone in "airplane mode" to cut off cellular and wireless (wifi) signals. The easiest and cheapest way to do this is to wrap the cell phone in at least three layers of aluminum foil, like the kind used in home kitchens.

Moving some digital devices while powered, like desktop computers, may damage the device or any mechanical storage media (hard drives, for example). If it is necessary to move a device during collection and documentation (to find and record a serial number, for example), the device should be hibernated or powered off first. Modern operating systems have the ability to hibernate to disk. It may be prudent to preserve volatile data by hibernating to disk instead of powering off the device. This may potentially overwrite deleted data, however; this is a critical decision that needs to weigh in the crime type and the types of evidence that hold the most probative value. Record any network and wireless access points that may be present and capable of linking computers and other devices to each other and the Internet. The existence of network and wireless access points may indicate that additional evidence exists beyond the initial scene. If multiple computers and devices are to be collected, all devices, cables, and connections should be labeled clearly and individually (Figure 23.9). For example, identify the first computer seized as "Computer A" or "Device #1" and then each cable and connection, including photographs. Subsequent computers can be labeled alphabetically or numerically.

Digital evidence is sensitive to extreme temperatures, humidity, physical shock, static electricity, and magnetic fields. Digital evidence should be packaged to prevent bending, scratching, damage, or other physical hazards. Leave cell phones in the power state (on or off) in which they were found. Importantly, remember to collect all power supplies and adapters for all digital devices seized; they will be needed eventually.

Peripherals or system components, like keyboards, mice, removable storage media, and printers may have other types of evidence on them, fingerprints or DNA, for example, and these objects must be handled in a way that does not contaminate or damage this nondigital evidence.

TRANSPORTATION

Digital evidence must be packaged for safe transportation back to the laboratory. Despite some impressive designs, digital devices are still fragile and, if broken, may be useless as evidence. As noted, digital evidence is also subject to damage or contamination from magnetic fields, radio frequencies, and temperature extremes. It is

Label computer, all cables, and corresponding connections.

FIGURE 23.9

Steganography is the practice of hiding one message inside of another; digital media make this particularly difficult to detect and analyze. The image of the cat is hidden in the image of the tree by removing all, but the two least significant bits of each color component and then normalizing the image.

good practice to place digital devices into antistatic bags and then place these into shock-resistant and water-resistant containers.

Storing digital devices in the laboratory poses certain problems. Digital evidence can decay like any other kind of evidence; magnetic storage, like hard drives, begins to degrade almost immediately and may lose integrity after 5 years or so. CDs and DVDs can also degrade, called "disk rot," due to the oxidation of the reflective layer or exposure to ultraviolet light (present in sunlight or indoor lighting), which damages and decomposes the adhesives holding the layers together. Digital devices should be stored in rooms insulated against stray radio and electrical fields; proper packaging that blocks light and water is necessary for longer term storage.

ANALYSIS AND EXAMINATION

Now that the digital devices are back at the laboratory, the evidence itself must now be collected from them, taking steps not to modify or alter the data. Analysis proceeds in three basic phases: Imaging the media, making a forensic archive, and exporting data related to the investigation.

Imaging the media depends on the device state and this determines the approach taken. The first approach is for a live system, where the device or system is powered on and will stay that way. The second, and preferable, is for a dead system, where the device is powered off or could be powered off safely. Powered-off devices are, for many reasons, the easiest to deal with: Communications are not possible, batteries last longer, and transportation is easier.

Collecting evidence from a live system is complicated. With other forensic evidence, one of the most basic principles is to not alter the evidence if at all possible. The same is true with digital forensics but with one important difference: The evidence is *active* and can change on its own or by remote activity. Therefore, with live systems, it is essential to make a copy—a snapshot—of all the volatile data (that which will be lost when the device the power supply is cut off) in play on a device before proceeding. Volatile data may include data stored in the random access memory (RAM), network connections, communications or print jobs in process, chat sessions, and other types. The forensic scientist would use an external device that is self-contained and does not need to access any of the programs on the evidentiary device other than what is in the RAM to operate. While this does replace a small portion of the volatile memory with the forensic software, and thus changes the data, it is currently the only way to image this highly changeable information. Once the RAM is imaged, it is safer to power down the live device.

Powered down devices are easier to work with. The storage device (typically a hard drive or memory card) is removed and a copy of the drive is made; this copy is called a forensic image and will be used from this point forward instead of the original device. The original storage device is then secured and is not used again, unless some problem arises with the forensic image. Two types of copies can be made, a physical copy, which contains all the data on the storage device, or a logical copy, which only captures the data in a defined portion of the drive (a volume or **partition**). A forensic archive of the forensic image is made and validated (called "hashing") against the first forensic image; if they are the same, then the forensic archive is considered to be an exact copy of the original. Multiple copies can thus be made from the forensic image without touching the original evidence or the archive.

Now the analysis of the data can begin. The first major problem at this phase is to determine what data is relevant to the case. Because of the large (and increasing) size of storage media, it is impractical, if not occasionally impossible, to review *all* of the data; this is called the "quantity problem." For example, if a 120-gigabyte evidence hard drive contained 30 gigabytes of pictures and movies with apparent child pornography and possibly related files (e-mails, spreadsheets, and documents), it would take seven DVDs to store it. Assuming each picture averaged about 100 kilobytes in size, 3 gigabytes of pictures could be stored on one of the DVDs. However, that would be *at least 30,000 pictures* that had to be reviewed, along with the thousands of other files on the remaining disks. A strategy for examination and a plan for analysis must be devised prior to getting down to work. Collaboration between investigators, attorneys, and scientists is necessary to sort through the mountains of files necessary to prosecute or exonerate a suspect.

The second major problem in the analysis phase is what is known as the "complexity problem." Informative data on digital devices occurs at the lowest and most raw formats, requiring skill and translation tools to find, translate, and comprehend it. A variety of software tools are available either through governmental access or commercial vendors for the analysis of forensic digital data. The analysis itself is highly technical and fills numerous books on the subject. Analysis can generally be broken down, however, into one or more of the following categories:

- Physical media: The analysis of the storage media itself through a standard interface; the recovery of overwritten or deleted data is an example.
- Media management: The analysis of the organization of the storage media; determining the file structure or subsections of a storage device.
- File system: The analysis of the infrastructure of files (folders, directories) and recovering deleted files.
- Application: The analysis of applications and their files, like documents, images, logs, configurations, and others.
- Network: The analysis of information systems, networks, connections, and traffic on them.
- Memory: The analysis of system memory media, like RAM, and system data.

The kinds of analysis will vary by the types of offences covered in the jurisdiction, the available types of digital evidence to be analyzed, and the capabilities of the laboratory.

ROUTINE TYPES OF DIGITAL EVIDENCE

Just as there are ever-expanding types of digital devices, the data they generate are varied and diverse. Some types of data are fairly routine for the forensic scientist, however, and these consistently show up in casework. E-mails are an excellent type of evidence given the volume sent daily for personal and professional purposes. E-mails also contain good metadata about the sender and recipient, such as the computer of the sent e-mail (the Internet protocol address, or IP address), the addresses of all systems the message passed through, and the type of software used to write the message.

Browsing the Internet using software like Safari, Internet Explorer, or Chrome, is a part of daily life at home and at work. Browsers keep a detailed history of the sites visited, downloads, search terms, and more. Search terms may be useful in indicating criminal intent or action ("Where can I buy guns without serial numbers?," "Does bleach remove all traces of blood?," "chloroform"). For example, Scott Peterson was convicted of murdering his pregnant wife, Laci, in 2002 and part of the evidence against Peterson was browser history for purchasing a boat, studying water currents, a map of an island, and the purchase of a gift for his mistress. Laci's body and that of the fetus were found on that island.

Social media, such as Facebook and Twitter, have dominated the popular culture in the last few years. The near-constant connections with others yield reams of texts, chats, and data about who knows whom, where they are, and what they are up to. Social media programs log these data and telecommunications providers store those information on their corporate servers. These links between people, places, and activities can be important evidence in an investigation, providing leads or alibis. People love to brag and many do not understand the depth of information available on the web (it is said that "the Internet never forgets"); criminals have been caught by posting their activities on social media, as incredible as that seems. Rodney Knight Jr stole a laptop, a coat, and cash from the house of a *Washington Post* reporter; he then posted about his criminal exploits on *the reporter's son's Facebook account*, using the stolen laptop. The son's friends alerted police and Knight was arrested for criminal larceny and possession of a handgun (Washington Post, 14 Dec 2010).

Select a file, click on "delete," and it's gone, right? Wrong. Deleted files still exist but the operating system has flagged their location on the storage media as being available for reuse. Deleted files whose location has not been overwritten are still recoverable. This is of particular use to the forensic scientist as deleted files are typically information that people want to get rid of.

Forensic science deals in the reconstruction of past events and digital evidence can greatly assist in the development of these investigative timelines. Timelines can help to prove innocence as well as guilt, for example, by providing location information based on cell phone data: Most cell phones log their geographical positions with cell towers and telecommunication companies store this information. Cell phone tracking has been used in a number of cases but is not without its critics; the use of single tower should be avoided and the system was never intended to be used like a GPS.

Most users store their documents and images in the default locations that come with their operating systems ("Documents"). These files come with metadata that can provide information about who authored the document, changes, comments, time stamps, and sometimes geographical locations. For example, with documents, all previous changes could be seen and might provide insight into intent or reveal a masked conversation conducted between versions of a shared file. Images have information about the kind of camera that was used to take them, location information, time stamp, and settings.

The types of digital crimes analyzed depend in part on the jurisdiction of the laboratory. Some crimes, like cyberbullying or cyberthreats, are local and others, like child pornography, may have a federal component. Some analyzes are very sophisticated and require highly skilled scientists and specialized tools. For example, messages that are hidden "inside" another message (**steganography**) can be extremely difficult to detect. The message could be hidden, for example, by starting with an innocent image file and changing the color of every 100th pixel to correspond with a letter of the alphabet, spelling out the hidden message. One image could be hidden inside another image (Figure 23.10). Originally thought to be too complex for "ordinary" criminals, steganography was being used by child pornographers by 2007. Steganography made news headlines in 2010 when the U.S. Department of Justice charged 11 suspected Russian Federation spies living as Americans in Boston, Seattle, and New Jersey. The alleged spies hid messages in over 100 images files on public websites using steganography.

Other types of analysis include sorting out attempts to gain sensitive information, like passwords or account numbers, or access to computer systems by masquerading as a trusted source (**phishing**), like a bank, or as another entity by falsifying information (**spoofing**) in electronic communications; header metadata identifying the sender and address may be stripped out and replaced, for example.

FIGURE 23.10

Electronic control units help to monitor, diagnose, and control the various electronic and computerized systems in modern automobiles. They also provide technical and geographic information to help reconstruct accidents, like the black box in an aeroplane.

http://wiki.hsc.com/Main/TelematicsControlUnit.

LEGAL ISSUES

All digital evidence is virtual and latent. Because of the physical nature of most other types of evidence and the immense complexity of modern digital technology, the legal system has approached digital evidence with a mixture of awe and skepticism. Some laypersons feel that technology is almost akin to magic and take whatever the digital evidence is as truth; others suspect it outright and think it all "junk science." As digital evidence continues to be involved in a wide variety of crimes and useful forensic evidence comes from it, the legal community will have to become more comfortable and realistic in dealing with this kind of information. Although it is a good bit different from other types of evidence, digital evidence must be held to the same scientific and legal standards as other forensic sciences.

SUMMARY

Although the technology that creates it is pervasive, digital evidence analysis still fit in with other scientific disciplines and for accreditation and standardization. Standards, methods, tools, and processes all need to be tested, validated, and properly applied, as with any other science. The trick with digital evidence is that the body of knowledge required to adequately work a case grows with every new model of cell phone, every new app, and every software update. Digital evidence analysis has an exciting future ahead of it. It combines the technical with the social, the physical with the virtual, and the licit with the illegal. Society will continue to depend on technology and this spills over into criminal activity. The need for digital evidence analysis will only grow as this dependence on digital devices broadens and deepens.

TEST YOUR KNOWLEDGE

1. How many different types of cell phones are there?
2. What is a key difficulty in keeping up with changing cell phone models?
3. What is digital evidence?
4. What is binary format? What is a bit?
5. List five types of crimes where digital evidence can play a key role?
6. What is metadata? How could it be used in a criminal case?
7. What is data carving?
8. What is a computer? What are the components?
9. List five types of forensically useful digital data.
10. What is a hard drive?
11. What is the difference between a thumb drive and a flash drive?
12. What is a SIM card?
13. How do cell phones work?

14. What is an SID?
15. Is it suitable to use only one cell tower to track a cell phone? Why or why not?
16. What are networked devices?
17. What is an ECU? What is an EDR?
18. Explain the difference between the live system and the dead system approaches.
19. List the categories of digital evidence analysis and give a brief explanation of each.
20. Are deleted files really deleted?

CONSIDER THIS...

1. What sells more—cell phones or computers? What about tablets? Why? What implications are there for digital evidence and its analysis?
2. Describe the "complexity problem" and the "quantity problem." How do these two issues affect digital evidence analysis? Can they be overcome? Why or why not?
3. Digital evidence is virtual and latent, unlike most other forensic evidence. How would you explain digital analysis to a jury of nontechnical people? What are the difficulties involved?

PART

Law and Forensic Science

6

CHAPTER

Legal Aspects of Forensic Science

24

CHAPTER OUTLINE

KEY TERMS

- Admissibility of evidence
- Chain of custody
- Competence
- Criminal investigation
- Demonstrative evidence
- Deposition
- Discovery
- Due process
- Due process clause
- Expert witness

Fundamentals of Forensic Science

- General acceptance
- Material
- Materiality
- Probative
- Probativeness
- Real evidence
- Relevance
- Rules of evidence
- Subpoena
- Subpoena duces tecum
- Unreasonable search and seizure

INTRODUCTION

What makes forensic science unique among the other areas of science? The main thing is that forensic science is practiced within a legal context. The results of forensic scientific examinations often end up in a courtroom. Even if the case doesn't get into court, prosecutors, defense attorneys, and judges use forensic laboratory reports to help them decide if the accused should be charged and, if so, with what crimes. Most often, a criminal case will lead to a plea bargain and conclusions reached by forensic scientists help inform the discussions. Forensic scientists must be familiar not only with the scientific and legal principles that guide their analyzes, but also the proper framing of conclusions from the analysis of evidence, the rules and regulations that govern their conduct in a civil or criminal court, and the rules that guide expert testimony.

In the United States legal system, the admissibility of all evidence is guided by **rules of evidence**. These rules determine what evidence may be admitted, for what uses, and under what conditions. This is especially true of scientific evidence, which must not only obey the general rules of evidence but also a set of rules and guidelines that were designed especially for scientific and technical evidence. In practice, forensic scientists examine evidence and then write a report on the examinations performed and then, if needed, testify to those results in a court of law. The very word forensic means "applied to public or legal concerns" and is as important as the word "science." If someone were the greatest scientist on earth but could not effectively testify to what they did in the laboratory, that person would be a failure as a forensic scientist. Professional forensic scientists must be able to explain the theories, methods, procedures, analyzes, results, and interpretations of the scientific examinations he or she performed. And the scientist must do this without being an advocate for either side in a case: Impartiality is the hallmark of science and this is especially true of forensic science. Often they must impart this information to a jury made up of people who do not have a sophisticated knowledge of scientific principles.

There are many ways that forensic science and the law intersect. First, where and how and at what points forensic science comes into play will be described. Then the rules that govern the admissibility of evidence, particularly scientific evidence will be covered. The ways that forensic science laboratory reports are used in court is very important and can be complex. Finally, the nature of expert testimony and how it is presented in court will be covered.

FORENSIC SCIENCE IN THE CRIMINAL JUSTICE SYSTEM

As our world has become more complex and increasingly driven by science and technology, the nature of crime and the evidence that helps convict the guilty and exonerate the innocent have also become more technical. This, in turn, has increased the responsibility and importance of forensic science and the scientists who practice it. Forensic science is widely considered to be part of the investigation process. From the moment that a crime or civil infraction is discovered, the investigation process begins. This process includes such important processes as developing and interviewing witness, interrogating suspects, and collecting and processing evidence. This chapter covers the role that forensic scientists play in the investigation process with emphasis on the criminal investigation process. For the most part, the same considerations hold if there is a civil infraction.

THE CRIMINAL INVESTIGATION PROCESS

When a criminal action begins as a result of activity by the police, prosecutor, or grand jury, the **criminal investigation** process also begins. This involves discovering who committed a crime or, if someone is arrested for the crime, searching for evidence that helps convict or exonerate that suspect. Criminal investigation is a continuous process. It begins when the crime is first discovered and may continue up to the time of a preliminary hearing, a grand jury hearing, or a trial and beyond. Forensic scientists become involved in this process in a number of ways:

- **Response to the crime scene**—It is the policy of many law enforcement agencies to have a forensic scientist, or perhaps several, attend crime scenes whenever there is a homicide suspected or in cases where there may be a high profile or otherwise notorious crime committed. No one knows better than forensic scientists how to recognize, collect, and preserve evidence within their area of responsibility. Because of time constraints and the need to preserve human resources, forensic scientists are usually sent only to the most important or high-profile crime scenes.
- **Analysis of evidence**—This of course is the primary task that forensic scientists perform. This is an on-going job during a criminal investigation process. Investigators may bring in evidence to the crime laboratory at many points during the investigation and the results of the analyzes can have profound effects upon the

course of the investigation and the outcome of the case. Forensic scientists will issue reports on their analyzes which are then evaluated by the prosecutor and criminal investigators.

- **Depositions**—At one time, **depositions** were used almost exclusively in the civil justice system but recently more states have begun to use them in criminal cases. A deposition is a proceeding in which testimony is given under oath but not in court or before a judge. A reporter or recorder authorized to administer oaths is present to take down the testimony. The main purpose of the deposition is to preserve testimony for trial, but it may also be used as a discovery tool to gain information about what the opposition knows and what witnesses are prepared to say at trial. A witness giving a deposition is usually questioned in the same manner as at a trial; the proponent asks questions first, followed by cross-examination by the opponent counsel. One major difference is that there is no one present to rule on objections to questions. In such cases, the objection is lodged and the witness will usually answer the question, but the challenged testimony may not be used at trial until the court has ruled on the objection.
- **Court testimony**—Along with the analysis of evidence, court testimony is the heart of the job of a forensic scientist. It is the most effective way to impart highly technical and complicated facts and opinions to the judge or jury. Forensic scientists may also testify at preliminary hearings. They do not ordinarily offer testimony in a grand jury proceeding. Forensic scientists are designated as expert witnesses when testifying within the areas of their expertise. This may confer extra privileges as a witness but may also carry extra duties and burdens. This will be discussed later in the chapter.

Legal Constraints on the Criminal Investigation Process

The United States Constitution, The United States Congress, and state legislatures have created rules that govern the criminal justice system, including the criminal investigation process. Some of these rules apply only to federal courts, some to all of the states, and some represent law that is valid only in the state where it was legislated. A few of the more important rules that sometimes have bearing on forensic scientists will be discussed below.

Discovery

Discovery is a process whereby one side in litigation seeks to gather information about testimony and evidence that is in the hands of the other side. Historically, the rule in the United States has been that the defendant in a criminal case is not entitled to inspection or disclosure of evidence that is in possession of the prosecution. The modern trend is to broaden discovery in criminal cases, both in favor of the defendant and the prosecution. This is known as **reciprocal discovery**. In practice, each party makes a discovery motion to the judge asking for particular items that they wish to inspect or get copies of. These can include witness lists and laboratory reports from forensic analysis.

In the Federal Code, Federal Rule of Evidence (FRE) Rule 16 governs pretrial discovery in the federal courts and many states have similar rules. Rule 16(F) of the Federal Rules of Criminal Procedure states that: "(t)he government must permit a defendant to inspect and to copy or photograph the results or reports of any physical or mental examination and of any scientific test or experiment" subject to certain conditions. Rule 16(G) states that the government is obliged to "give to the defendant a written summary of any testimony that the government intends to use that could constitute expert testimony as defined by the Federal Rules of Evidence." The Jencks Act permits the defense in a criminal case to obtain any written and oral statements made by a prosecution witness, but only after the witness has testified at trial. A reasonable recess is allowed for inspection of the written statement. It may then be used by the defense to challenge or even impeach a witness. Finally, the Supreme Court ruled, in *Brady v. Maryland*, that the government has a continuing burden in a criminal case, to turn over to the defense, any evidence that can reasonably be construed as favorable to the defense. The evidence must be disclosed at a time when it would be valuable to the defense. Exculpatory laboratory reports fall within the purview of the Brady doctrine. Failure to comply with this doctrine can result in a mistrial or even dismissal of the charges against the defendant.

Search and Seizure

The Fourth Amendment of the United States Constitution states:

> *The right of the people to be secure in their persons, houses, papers, and effects against unreasonable searches and seizures shall not be violated and no warrants shall issue, but upon probable cause, supported by oath or affirmation, and particularly describing the place to be searched and the person or things to be seized.*

This Amendment to the United States Constitution prohibits **unreasonable searches and seizures**. What actually constitutes an unreasonable search or seizure has been the subject of numerous court decisions during the past 200 years. The Supreme Court has held that the Constitution expresses a clear preference for searches conducted only after judicial authorization, that is, after a search warrant has been obtained. It is also true, however, that the courts have carved out many exceptions to the Fourth Amendment and there are many times when warrantless searches are permitted. The authority to search for and seize also may be limited by other laws enacted by Congress and state legislatures. There may be times when forensic scientists are called upon to attend crime scenes and help in the collection of physical evidence. They should understand the legal limitations on this collection process so as to avoid improper seizure of important evidence. There are numerous instances where evidence has been collected and analyzed and shown to be highly important in the prosecution of the defendant, only to be stricken because the evidence collector ran afoul of the prohibition against unreasonable searches. If there is any question about the reasonableness of a search or seizure, a search warrant should be obtained. This is the responsibility of the criminal investigators and the prosecutor.

Self-incrimination

A portion of the Fifth Amendment of the United States Constitution reads in part:

> *Nor shall any person be compelled in any criminal case to be a witness against himself.*

Statements made by a suspect confessing to all or part of a crime, and later used against that suspect to prove guilt, constitute self-incrimination. Self-incrimination is not prohibited. Only *compelled* self-incrimination falls within the scope of the Fifth Amendment. Self-incrimination is allowed subject to certain limitations. It applies to both the verbal and written statements of a suspect. The protection of objects, property, personal papers and effect, and so forth is the subject of the Fourth Amendment. The Fifth Amendment also contains the so-called **Due Process Clause**. This protects people against outrageous government behavior, such as the case where a person's stomach is pumped to get to illicit drugs. Obtaining exemplars of hair, blood, etc., can constitute a seizure requiring a warrant under the Fourth Amendment, however, evidence of this nature does not constitute "incrimination" that falls within the scope of the Fifth Amendment. The Supreme Court has also ruled that, when a person is lawfully arrested, they may be photographed and their fingerprints taken without a warrant and this would not be a violation according to the Fourth or Fifth Amendments.

PRODUCTION OF EVIDENCE: THE SUBPOENA

The United States Constitution guarantees accused persons in a criminal case the right to confront all witnesses against them. A forensic scientist who examines physical evidence and reaches relevant conclusions is included within the definition of a witness. In order to summon a witness to offer testimony in a criminal or civil case, a **subpoena** is issued. The term "subpoena" comes from the Latin and means "under penalty." A subpoena is an order issued under the direction of a court commanding the presence of a witness at a specific time and place to give testimony or other evidence. If a witness ignores a subpoena, he or she may be charged with being in contempt of court. In most cases, a subpoena must be delivered to the subject in person, although sometimes a subpoena for a forensic scientist is mailed or delivered to the laboratory where the scientist retrieves it. Usually a forensic scientist will receive a certain type of subpoena called a **Subpoena Duces Tecum**. This type of subpoena commands not only the presence of the witness in court but also any documentation or evidence in his or her possession that is material to the case. Thus the forensic scientist must bring in all laboratory reports as well as other related charts and graphs. This type of command carries with it the same potential penalties for disobeying as do other types of subpoenas.

IN DEPTH: THE ADVERSARY SYSTEM VERSUS THE INQUISITORIAL SYSTEM

The United States criminal justice system, along with those in Canada, England, and Wales, uses the adversary system to manage the investigative and adjudicative processes. Under this system, a trial is essentially a contest between the prosecution and defense in a criminal case, or the plaintiff and defendant in a civil case. Each side marshals its evidence and resources and presents their case in a court. The prosecutor and police conduct criminal investigations. The role of the judge is normally to referee the trial unless the judge also acts as the trier of fact in place of the jury (a bench trial). The judge makes sure that each side in the case operates within the rules. Each side (or party) is pretty much free to conduct the case as he or she sees fit. There is always a presumption of innocence in criminal cases. The government must prove all of the elements of the crime beyond a reasonable doubt. There is no requirement that the defendant mounts any kind of affirmative defense. In practice, a defendant will usually call witnesses on his behalf or to rebut the testimony of prosecution witnesses. In civil cases, the standard of proof is the preponderance of evidence, which means that the party having the burden of proof, usually the plaintiff, must prove that its facts are more likely than not true. In civil cases, both parties always put on a case including evidence and witnesses.

In the inquisitorial system, practiced in many countries in Europe and the Americas outside the U.S., the judge has a much more central role in the case. The judge takes an active role in the investigation of the case and often directs the police and prosecutor in what evidence to collect and how to proceed. In France and other civil law countries, the investigating judge conducts investigations, questions witnesses, orders searches, and issues warrants. Both parties to the case may make requests to the judge and can appeal his or her decisions to an appeals court. Once the investigating judge has determined that a particular person should stand trial for a crime or answer a civil charge, that person is turned over to a trial court. Here the trial takes place before a different judge and possibly a jury and the process is more adversarial but not nearly as much as in the adversarial system. In civil law countries where the inquisitorial process is used, the presumption of innocence is still the norm.

THE RULES OF EVIDENCE

Evidence is defined as anything that will help prove or disprove a material fact. It helps the judge or jury reach conclusions about the guilt or innocence of the defendant. There are two major types of evidence: real and testimonial. **Real evidence** is physical; it consists of things that help link a suspect to a crime or explain the circumstances of the incident. It may be physical evidence such as fingerprints, fibers, blood, weapons or it may be **demonstrative evidence**, which consists of supporting materials such as crime scene photos or sketches. Demonstrative evidence does not arise directly from the commission of the crime, but is generated by observation and documentation of the crime scene.

Testimonial evidence is the oral recitation of facts and sometimes impressions or opinions by a witness under oath. Lay (nonexpert) witnesses' testimony is usually limited to first-hand observations and impressions. Lay witnesses are not normally permitted to offer opinions; they may only state facts. **Expert witnesses**, on the other hand, are often called upon to state conclusions and opinions based upon their examination of evidence or observation of the crime scene or parties to the crime. These conclusions and opinions must be within the purview of their expertise.

AUTHENTICATION OF EVIDENCE: THE CHAIN OF CUSTODY

Virtually all real evidence is subject to authentication. There must be a showing that the evidence is in the same condition from the moment it has been seized at the crime scene until it is used in court. It must have "sponsors" who can identify it and follow its trail. The only exception to rigorous authentication of real evidence is when it has some unique characteristic that makes it differentiable from all other objects. This might include a weapon with a unique serial number that has been noted by a police officer when the weapon was first seized. Even in this case, the evidence must have a sponsor. The most commonly accepted method for authentication of evidence is the **chain of custody**. The chain of custody is both a process and a document that memorializes the transfer of evidence from the custody of one person to another. The process of authentication starts at the crime scene or anywhere where evidence is seized. Each item of evidence is given a unique identifier. Each piece of evidence is packaged separately in a tamper-evident container and sealed. The official who packages the evidence affixes a signature or initials and the date to the evidence container. Every time someone, such as a forensic scientist, opens the container to examine the evidence, it must be done so as to not disturb the already affixed seals. The evidence must be resealed and labeled with unique identifiers so it can be easily seen who opened it. The evidence is also accompanied by a chain of custody form as shown in Figure 24.1. This is a document that contains a description of the evidence and a place for the signatures of everyone who handles the evidence. That person signs for the evidence when it is received and then signs it over to the next person. Each signature is accompanied by the date and time. This way, one can tell who had custody of the evidence at any time and that person can be called to testify what condition the evidence was in, what was done to it, and how it was stored. The chain of custody in Figure 24.1 is imprinted on a tamper-evident evidence bag.

A substantial break in the chain of custody, either the process or the documentation, can result in the evidence being excluded from admission to court. In such cases, the opponent must show that the break in the chain could have reasonably resulted in the evidence being adulterated or otherwise tampered with. This used to be a problem in hospitals and clinics where sexual assault victims were taken after the incident. The main concern of health care professionals is, of course, the health and welfare of the patient. As a result, important physical evidence was often left unattended and not properly packaged. Often, it was not admissible in court owing to the faulty chain of custody. In recent years, forensic science laboratories have developed and implemented a system of "rape kits" that contain proper packaging and chain of custody forms for this evidence. The result has been far fewer incidents of exclusion of evidence owing to chain of custody problems.

THE ADMISSIBILITY OF EVIDENCE

The major question that must be answered about evidence in a courtroom setting is: What types of evidence may properly be brought to the attention of the trier of fact (the judge or the jury) and what uses may the trier of fact make of the evidence that it is

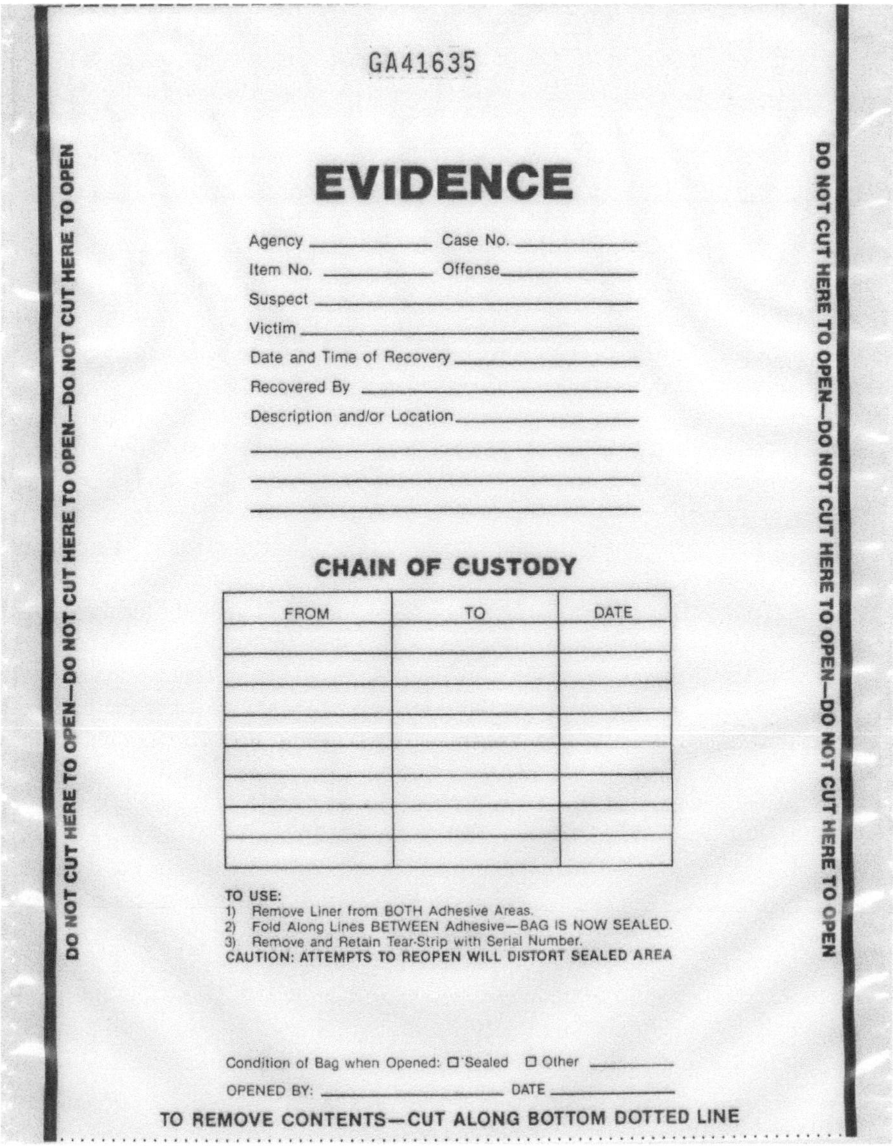

GA41635

DO NOT CUT HERE TO OPEN—DO NOT CUT HERE TO OPEN—DO NOT CUT HERE TO OPEN—DO NOT CUT HERE TO OPEN

EVIDENCE

Agency ________ Case No. ________

Item No. ________ Offense________

Suspect ________

Victim ________

Date and Time of Recovery ________

Recovered By ________

Description and/or Location ________

CHAIN OF CUSTODY

FROM	TO	DATE

TO USE:

1) Remove Liner from BOTH Adhesive Areas.
2) Fold Along Lines BETWEEN Adhesive—BAG IS NOW SEALED.
3) Remove and Retain Tear-Strip with Serial Number.

CAUTION: ATTEMPTS TO REOPEN WILL DISTORT SEALED AREA

Condition of Bag when Opened: ☐ Sealed ☐ Other ________

OPENED BY: ________ DATE ________

TO REMOVE CONTENTS—CUT ALONG BOTTOM DOTTED LINE

FIGURE 24.1

Chain of custody form. The form is on the front of a secure evidence package. As the evidence moves through the law enforcement, forensic science, and judicial system, anyone who has custody of the evidence must sign for it. This package is convenient because it provides a secure environment for the evidence as well as the chain of custody form.

permitted to consider? This is the essence of the **admissibility of evidence**. There are a number of rules that determine what evidence may be admitted and under what conditions. Most of the rules of evidence govern admissibility. There are fewer rules that govern how a judge or jury may use evidence that is admitted properly. The consideration of what uses a jury can make of admitted evidence is beyond the scope of this book. We will consider only the question of admissibility here. The rules of admissibility of evidence provide a framework to help preserve the integrity of the evidence.

The Rules of Admissibility

In general, any evidence is admissible if it is both **relevant** and **competent**. It cannot be admitted if only one of these two conditions is satisfied. Both relevance and competence are defined in the rules of evidence.

Relevance

Relevance has two components: **materiality** and **probativeness**.

RELEVANCE = MATERIALITY + PROBATIVENESS

If evidence is material, it means that it applies to a matter dealing with the case at hand, and not some other case. As an example of materiality, assume that a man is on trial for injuring another person with a knife during a street robbery. Evidence that the accused had a stash of stolen guns at his home at the time might indicate that he was violent or that he liked to sell guns, but it would not be material to the robbery charge. The other component of relevance is probativeness. Evidence is probative if it tends to make a fact or issue more or less probable than if the evidence were not present. Another way of expressing this is, does the evidence tend to prove something about a fact at issue in this case? Let's take the example of a man who is arrested on suspicion of distribution of methamphetamine. A search warrant is issued to search his home. No methamphetamine is found, but the police uncover a large number of plastic bags, a postal scale, a large bag of a material that is commonly used as a diluent for drugs, and a book that describes in detail how methamphetamine is made. Is this evidence probative? Most certainly it is. Although it doesn't prove by itself that the accused is a drug dealer, it tends to make this assertion more probable. So we can see that the test for relevance is two-pronged. The evidence at issue must be both material and probative in order for it to be considered relevant. But this is only half the story. Even if evidence is highly relevant, it may still be inadmissible because it lacks competence.

Competence

Competence doesn't mean the same thing in the law as it does in everyday life. It doesn't have anything to do with the ability to do something. It is a collection of rules and constraints that evidence must pass muster with in order to be admissible.

- **Prejudice**—Prejudicial evidence may be highly relevant but also has the effect of being viewed negatively by the jury. It can impugn the reputation or the accused or turn the jury against him. Consider some examples. In many jurisdictions, color photographs of an autopsy of the victim of a violent homicide may not be admissible because their graphic nature may cause the jury to focus on the gore and blood they depict, at the expense of their value as evidence. They may view the defendant as being guilty because of the photographs of the victim. Unless the sponsoring pathologist can make a case that these color photographs are necessary to illustrate certain probative facts about the killing, these photos may not be admissible. In many cases, black and white photographs are used instead because they do not have the same negative impact of color photos. Prejudice is also one of the major reasons why a defendant's prior criminal record is not admissible evidence of guilt in a trial on a similar charge because the jury may feel that, because he or she committed similar crimes before, means that he or she did it again. Thus, the jury may convict the defendant because of the previous crimes and not because of the facts of the case at issue.

- **Time wasting**—Although attorneys are generally given wide latitude to prosecute and defend in criminal cases, judges will generally not tolerate evidence that wastes time because it is unnecessarily cumulative or repetitive or lacks relevance. This has the effect of distracting and perhaps even confusing the jury. An example of this is illustrated by a situation where a large number of people witness the same event and the prosecutor wants to bring all of them in to testify as to what they saw. In such cases, the judge may limit the testimony to one or two representative witnesses.
- **Unreliable**—This is one of the criteria that govern the admissibility of certain scientific (and perhaps pseudoscientific) evidence. Evidence must be reliable if the jury is to be able to weigh it properly in reaching a decision about guilt or innocence. This is also the reason that much eyewitness testimony is discredited in court. Research has shown that, when witnesses experience a startling or surprise event, their recollections can differ widely from one person to the next. Each person reacts to such events differently and their reactions will bias their perceptions about what they experienced. Another form of unreliable evidence is **hearsay**. Hearsay is defined as a statement, made by someone outside of a courtroom and not under oath, and which is now being used inside court to prove what it asserts. An example of hearsay would be if John Smith witnessed a crime committed by Joe Smash and Smith tells George Ruth what he saw and then Ruth offers to testify in court what Smith told him about the crime. If the testimony by Ruth is being used to prove that Smash committed the crime, this would be hearsay. Some types of hearsay may be considered unreliable because they are difficult or impossible to effectively cross-examine someone who did not witness something but is only repeating something that he heard. There are numerous exceptions to the hearsay rule. For example, suppose that a forensic scientist analyzed some plant material and concluded that it was marihuana and wrote a report that communicated these findings. At trial, the prosecutor wishes to introduce the report as evidence to prove that the plant material was marihuana. The report may be admissible under certain circumstances even if the scientist is not present, even though it would be technically considered to be hearsay. The difficulty of cross-examining a laboratory report can be appreciated, but it may

be admissible if properly attested and agreed to by both sides. The laboratory report may also be important when a long period of time has elapsed between the time the scientist analyzed the evidence and wrote the report, and the time of the trial. The scientist may not remember doing the analysis in this specific case and the laboratory report then stands as the most reliable evidence of what was done to the evidence. This will be discussed in the section below on laboratory reports.

- **Improper procedures**—Courts generally do not allow surprise witnesses to testify without giving notice to the other side. Evidence is also generally inadmissible if it is offered out of turn or after the proponent has already rested his case. Attorneys are not allowed to present testimony during an opening or closing argument. These prohibitions against improper evidence are all in place to protect the jury as well as the rights of the accused.
- **Existence of privileges**—In the legal context, a privilege is a protection given to someone to protect that person from having to offer testimony against another person. There are certain privileges that exist in many locales that have been created by legislation. These include the **attorney–client, doctor–patient, cleric–penitent, and marital** privileges. All of these in some way are designed to protect sensitive or intimate or otherwise special communications. The attorney–client privilege, for example, protects communications between an attorney and the client by allowing an attorney to refuse to testify to such communications. Likewise a priest is protected from testifying about the contents of confessions made by a member of the congregation. There are two marital privileges: one that protects one partner in a marriage from testifying against the other, and a privilege that permits one partner to silence the other partner who wishes to testify. There are, of course, many exceptions to the privileges mentioned here. In many states, privileges do not exist in the absence of legislation that explicitly permits them. Even in these cases, however, it would be impractical to prosecute someone for exercising a privilege such as a minister who refuses to testify about what he heard in a confession.
- **Constitutional constraints**—Certain provisions of the Constitution, discussed earlier provide for the exclusion of evidence and/or testimony where violations have occurred. These include evidence seized in violation of the Fourth Amendment and testimony of self-incrimination covered by the Fifth Amendment.

In summary, evidence will be admissible in court only if it is both relevant and competent. This applies to all evidence in a criminal case. Next we will turn to the question specifically of the admissibility of scientific or expert evidence. We will see that because of its technical nature, it is treated somewhat differently than nonscientific evidence.

Admissibility of Novel Scientific and Technical Evidence

Scientific and technical evidence differ from ordinary evidence in a number of significant ways. First, such evidence is given by people who have been qualified as experts by the court. This permits them to offer opinions and conclusions about such evidence that would be beyond the knowledge of the average person. Experts are, in effect, interpreters of technical evidence for the jury. Second, because technical evidence is given by scientists and experts, it sometimes has an aura of truth and infallibility about it, which necessitates insuring that the evidence is valid and reliable when it is presented to the jury. Most jurors and judges do not have the knowledge to determine if the testimony about technical evidence they are receiving is correct or reliable or valid, so there must be legal protections in place to ensure or at least promote reliability. These considerations are most important for evidence involving new or novel scientific techniques or instruments. There must be some assurance that the new technique has been sufficiently tested and validated so that the jury or judge may rely on its conclusions. The history of the admissibility of scientific evidence involves two very instructive and interesting cases that illustrate the difficulties that courts have had in determining the standards for admissibility of **novel** scientific evidence.

The Frye Case

Prior to 1923 in the United States, most courts treated scientific evidence the same as any other type. The rules governing the admissibility of evidence were derived from the Common Law. There was no codification of specific rules. In 1923, the landscape changed for novel scientific evidence, owing to a case in Washington, D.C. where James Frye was on trial for murder. As part of his defense, he sought to have the results of a test that utilized a machine that could be considered the forerunner of today's polygraph, introduced as evidence of his innocence. The prosecution objected to the admission of this novel evidence and the judge agreed. On appeal, the court upheld the trial judge's decision. In effect the appeals court stated that, with respect to novel scientific evidence, not only must it meet the relevancy standard, but an additional hurdle must be overcome, as revealed in its ruling:

> *Just when a scientific principle or discovery crosses the line between the experimental and demonstrable stages is difficult to define. Somewhere in this twilight zone the evidence force of the principle must be recognized, and, while courts will go a long way in admitting expert testimony deduced from a well-recognized scientific principle or discovery, the thing from which the deduction is made must be sufficiently established to have gained general acceptance in the particular field to which it belongs (emphasis added). (Frye v. United States, 293F. 1013, 1014 (D.C. Cir. 1923))*

The standard for novel scientific or technical evidence that came out of this decision was, that before a *new scientific technique* could be introduced in court, the underlying principle that governed it must have achieved general acceptance within the particular scientific field to which it belongs. One important issue that was not decided by the court is what constitutes general acceptance. In fact, this issue has never been clearly decided. It has come to mean, more or less by default, that the technique and principles have been published in a peer-reviewed journal or other equivalent exposure to the field. This implies that peer review for a journal and publication means that a technique will be generally accepted. There are numerous examples in all scientific endeavors where this has not been borne out. Many valid and reliable scientific principles have never been published and there are numerous examples of techniques that have been published and were later shown to be unreliable. Nonetheless, the doctrine of general acceptance became known as the *Frye Rule*.

Over the next 70 years, the federal courts and about half of the states used this as the yardstick to evaluate the admissibility of new scientific techniques. During that time a number of novel scientific techniques have been subject to "Frye challenges" in various courts. These include voiceprint spectrography, blood spatter pattern analysis, polygraph analysis, and even DNA typing techniques. On January 2, 1975, the Congress completely overhauled its rules of evidence. This had been proposed by the United States Supreme Court in a preliminary draft form in 1969. Its effective date was July 1, 1975. The initial set of rules of evidence contained a specific article dealing with expert and opinion testimony (Article VII) that contained individual rules that have since been amended. Under those rules, specifically Rule 702, the proponent of expert testimony has the burden of demonstrating that the expert is qualified and that the opinion evidence would be helpful to the fact finder (the judge or jury). After the new evidence code was adopted by Congress, federal and many state courts became divided as to whether *Frye* or the new Federal Rules should be used to determine the admissibility of novel scientific evidence. The question was addressed and settled by the United States Supreme Court in *Daubert v. Merrell-Dow*.

Daubert v. Merrell-Dow

The plaintiff in this case, heard in Federal District Court in San Diego, California, was a pregnant woman who took Bendectin, a Merrell-Dow Pharmaceutical Company product that had been prescribed for many years to relieve nausea that occurred during pregnancy. Mrs Daubert had given birth twice to children both of whom were born with birth defects. After the second child was born, she sued Merrell-Dow, claiming that Bendectin caused the birth defects. This type of civil case is called a **tort**, specifically a toxic tort. In a civil suit for toxic tort, the plaintiff alleges that a substance, such as a pharmaceutical, is the cause of a harm that is suffered by someone who ingests the substance. Since the biochemical causes of birth defects are not fully understood, there was no direct way for Daubert to establish directly that Bendectin was the cause of the defects. Instead, the plaintiff resorted to epidemiology, the study of the cause and effects of disease on large populations. The plaintiff and defendant both retained statisticians to determine whether the instances of birth defects among women who took Bendectin during pregnancy were statistically significantly greater than birth defects in the general population. The plaintiff's experts concluded that there was a significant increase in birth defects among Bendectin users' babies, whereas the defendant's experts concluded that any increase was not statistically significant. The defendant also argued that the plaintiff's experts did not use methods that were *generally accepted by the scientific community* in reaching their conclusions; that is they argued that the plaintiff had failed to meet the Frye standard for the admissibility of their statistical evidence. The court agreed with

Merrell-Dow and, upon a motion for summary judgment, found for Merrell-Dow. Daubert appealed and eventually the United States Supreme Court heard the case. The Court ruled that the trial judge had used the wrong standard of admissibility in reaching his ruling. The Supreme Court concluded that the Federal Courts could not use the *Frye* rule anymore in deciding questions about the admissibility of scientific or technical evidence, and that the doctrine of general acceptance espoused in *Frye* was not the proper yardstick. Instead, the Supreme Court ruled that courts must use the Federal Rules of Evidence in determining the standard for the evaluation of the admissibility of scientific or technical evidence. The Court drew particular attention to FRE 702, reproduced below:

> *If scientific, technical, or other specialized knowledge will assist the trier-of-fact to understand the evidence or to determine a fact in issue, a witness qualified as an expert by knowledge, skill, experience, training or education, may testify thereto in the form of an opinion or otherwise.*

In interpreting the Federal Rule 702 as well as other relevant rules, the Court indicated that the judge must be the "gatekeeper" who decides when scientific evidence is admissible. In doing so, the court must use rational criteria for determining whether evidence is reliable and valid. The Court went so far as to suggest several criteria that a judge could use in the gatekeeper role. These were not meant to be exhaustive, but only suggestions.

- **Falsifiability**—If the underlying theory or principle behind a novel technique has been repeatedly tested to see if it is false and in all cases the theory is verified, this can be a good measure of validity. This is not amenable to all principles and proper research designs must be implemented for this to be a valid criterion.
- **Knowledge of error rates**—If the error rates of the results of a technique are known or can be estimated, then a judge could presumably make some determination as to the reliability and validity of a technique. For some techniques, there is little or no quantifiable data available to determine an error rate.
- **Peer review**—Certainly a technique or method or principle that has survived the peer review process and has been found worthy of publication, has demonstrated some level of scientific validity. This is tempered, however, by the issue of the quality and scholarliness of the journals in the applicable field.
- **General acceptance**—The Supreme Court never meant to discard general acceptance as an acceptable criterion for determining scientific validity. The Court concluded that this should not be the only criterion and that there exist other, perhaps better ones. The Court did not however, seek to define what it meant by general acceptance.

In addition, the Court's decision mandated that scientific techniques must be based on scientific principles, not speculation, and that the scientific basis for the principles had to be demonstrated. It should be noted that the Supreme Court sent the case back to the trial court for retrial and instructed the court that they must use the Federal Rules of Evidence in evaluating if Daubert's statistical evidence should be admitted. At the second trial the judge ruled on a motion for directed verdict by Merrell-Dow, that the statistical evidence proffered by Daubert didn't meet the requirements of the Federal Rules and he once again, directed the jury to find for Merrell-Dow. Even though they won the case, Merrell-Dow shortly thereafter removed Bendectin from the marketplace.

Admissibility of Scientific and Technical Evidence Today: Fallout from Daubert

Since the Daubert decision in 1993, most states in the United States have adopted the principles of the decision in whole or in part. The rest still use the Frye rule. There has also been interesting fallout from the Daubert decision. The mandate for having a demonstrable scientific basis for introducing novel scientific or technical techniques in court has caused the legal and forensic scientific communities to take a fresh look at forensic scientific disciplines that were heretofore assumed to be proper and correct from a scientific basis. For example, there have been some recent challenges to the admissibility of testimony by expert questioned document examiners where there is a definite conclusion of authorship of a handwritten document. The basis for the challenges is that there has been little or no demonstrated scientific research that proves that handwriting comparisons are valid techniques for establishing definite authorship. At least one case has had a challenge to morphological human hair comparisons. In this case, the forensic scientist was going to testify that the defendant was one of an indeterminate population of people that could have been the source of the hairs found at the crime (rape) scene. The judge excluded the evidence as being too speculative and not scientific enough for the jury to consider. There have also been some recent challenges to the validity of "matching" partial latent fingerprints with known prints of a suspect. As in the cases with handwriting comparisons, the issue is the scientific basis (or lack of it) for concluding that fingerprints are unique and can be matched reliably. There is little doubt that the courts will be dealing with additional issues of the sufficiency of the science that underlies scientific and technical methods, processes, and techniques. Recently, as a result of the findings in *Daubert*, the Congress changed some of the rules regarding the admissibility of novel scientific evidence. For example, language was added to FRE 702 at the end. The rule now reads:

> *If scientific, technical, or other specialized knowledge will assist the trier-of-fact to understand the evidence or to determine a fact in issue, a witness qualified as an expert by knowledge, skill, experience, training or education, may testify thereto in the form of an opinion or otherwise, if (1) the testimony is based upon sufficient facts or data, (2) the testimony is the product of reliable principles and methods, and (3) the witness has applied the principles and methods reliably to the facts of the case.*

Since Daubert was adjudicated, two other important cases were heard and went to the Supreme Court that refined Daubert. *Kumho Tire*, a case involving defective tires, put forth the principle that the admissibility requirements of Daubert extend beyond scientific evidence into the realm of technical and engineering cases.

The other case, *General Electric v. Joiner*, was concerned with fluids that keep electrical transformers from overheating and the possible harm of these fluids. The judge was asked to determine the admissibility of testimony involving these fluids. The judge exercised his discretion as a "gatekeeper" under Daubert, to exclude the testimony. The Supreme Court ruled that this discretion fell within the judge's discretion. These three cases (Daubert, Kumho Tire, and Joiner) have become known as the "Daubert Trilogy."

The National Academy of Sciences Forensic Science Committee also weighed in on these issues in its 2009 report. They stated that more research was needed to establish the validity of many types of scientific evidence in order to bolster conclusions of association reached by experts. The conclusions reached by the Committee were based, in part, on the outcome of the *Daubert* case.

LABORATORY REPORTS

The laboratory report is the public face of forensic science. All of the evidence analysis, interpretation, and conclusions that take place in a forensic science laboratory culminate in a laboratory report. The report goes directly to the official who submitted the evidence to the laboratory for analysis. In public forensic science laboratories, the submitting official is the police officer or criminal investigator who is investigating the crime. In addition, a copy of the report goes to the prosecuting attorney who is responsible for the case. Depending upon the jurisdiction, the report will also go automatically to the defense attorney or will be furnished upon request. Once the laboratory report has been submitted, it can be used by the prosecutor to help determine what charges, if any, will be filed against the suspect. It can also be used by the defense attorney to help advise the accused of what charges are being filed and to help estimate the strength of the government's case. If the case goes to trial, then the report may be used as evidence under certain conditions.

In 2009, the United States Supreme Court, in the *Melendez Diaz v. Massachusetts* case ruled that the submission of a forensic science laboratory report into evidence without the testimony of the scientist who performed the tests on the evidence, was a violation of the Sixth Amendment right of confrontation. The Court did allow the continual practice of "notice-and-demand," whereby the prosecutor would put the defendant on notice of the intention to submit the report without the scientist's testimony and also giving the defendant time to file an objection. In 2011, the Supreme Court extended the provisions of the confrontation clause of the Sixth Amendment, by forbidding a supervisor of the scientist who performed testing to testify on behalf of the scientist. These two cases, along with previous ones, mean that, in most cases, a scientist must testify on the contents of a laboratory report, except under defined circumstances. Most states have a "notice-and-demand" rule and thus, many laboratory reports are still admitted as evidence without the scientist's testimony.

One of the major issues concerning forensic science laboratory reports is what they should like and how complete they should be. The National Academy of Sciences Forensic Science Committee, in its 2009 report, indicated that model laboratory formats should be created and the information given in the reports should be

Certificate of Analysis
State Police

State Police Laboratory | Telephone: Fax:

May 30, 2005

TO: INVESTIGATING OFFICER
POLICE AGENCY
123 NORTH STREET
ANYTOWN, IN 46219

Lab File #:

Agency Case #:

Evidence Submitted by: Officer John Smith

Received by Laboratory: 05/10/05 at 9:00

Item 1 Sealed plastic bag containing a ziploc plastic bag containing a white powder.

Results:

Item 1 was found to contain Cocaine, a controlled substance.
The net weight was 2.54 grams.

DKR

Reviewed by 5656

Page 1 of 1

FIGURE 24.2

An example of a "certificate of analysis" type of laboratory report. Although this type of report is easily understood by judges and attorneys, it is not a scientific laboratory report because it lacks methods, detailed procedures, data, the underlying reasoning that lead to the conclusions, and the limitations of the analysis.

specified. Current practice in many scientific laboratories is to issue brief laboratory reports that are little more than "Certificates of Analysis," and indeed, some are titled that way. Figure 24.2 is an example of a Certificate of Analysis type report.

If forensic science is truly science and its laboratory reports are the public face of forensic science, then it stands to reason that these reports should be outstanding examples of scientific reports. They should be complete with all data, results, conclusions, limitations, and reasoning. In 2012, one of the authors of this book embarked upon a research project that would gather data from which recommendations could be made concerning the proper content of a scientific forensic science laboratory report. To that end, 421 redacted forensic science reports were obtained from more than 40 laboratories. These were subjected to content analysis to determine what information they contained. This was measured against recommendations made by some 30 organizations inside and outside forensic science as to what laboratory reports should look like. The results indicated that many reports were brief certificates of analysis that lacked detailed methods and procedures, results and conclusions, and the reasoning behind the conclusions, the data that were gathered and relied upon to establish the conclusions and the limitations (e.g., error rates) of the methods used.

Although the reactions of many in forensic science to the call for more scientific reports implied in this research, were generally positive, several issues were raised. First, complete scientific reports are long, scientific, and may be complicated. Since prosecutors, defense attorneys, judges, and juries are not sophisticated in the sciences, they would not understand the reports. The response to this concern could be to put an "executive summary" at the beginning of the report that sets out the main conclusions. This is the information that the attorneys indicated that they need from the report and thus, they could find it easily.

Another concern is that many types of analysis rely on standard operating procedures and thus, laboratory reports would be repetitive and unduly consumptive of time. There is nothing wrong with using "boilerplate" in reports if the procedures and results are the same from report to report. This information could also be put on a website for access by those with a need to know.

Finally, the concern was raised that the laboratory report would be exceedingly long if all of the data and accompanying charts, graphs, spectra, chromatographs, databases, etc., were included in the report. In cases where the defendant hires a defense expert to review the scientific evidence, that expert will want to see all of the data that were gathered during the analysis and that were relied upon in crafting the report. Currently, this information can only be obtained by the use of discovery or by voluntary cooperation by the laboratory. In many cases, discovery is laborious and time-consuming and voluntary cooperation of some laboratories is found wanting. It would be scientifically proper and responsible for all of the data to be in the report or easily obtained either in printed form or on a protected website.

It remains to be seen if a consensus scientific laboratory report format arises from the forensic science system. Doubtless it would improve the delivery of forensic science services and the outside image of forensic science as a scientific discipline.

ANOTHER ISSUE WITH LABORATORY REPORTS: RECORDING THE ANALYSIS

There are many situations where a scientist is called to the stand to testify about the methods, procedures, results, and conclusions concerning a particular case. If the trial occurs shortly after the evidence was analyzed, then the scientist should remember analyzing the evidence and should be able to testify directly from memory. The laboratory report then serves to memorialize the analysis. Suppose, however, that the trial occurs months or even years after the evidence was analyzed. Unless that particular case was very unusual and stood out for some reason, then it is unlikely that the scientist will remember the particulars of the case or even having analyzed it! In such cases, there are two legal precepts that can come into play: the first is **past recollection refreshed**. In these cases, the scientist is testifying in court and is asked by the prosecutor if he or she remembers doing the analysis on the evidence. If the answer is "no" then the prosecutor will show the report to the scientist and will ask if the report refreshes his or her memory about doing the analysis. If so, then the scientist can testify from memory about the analysis. What happens, however, if the scientist can still not remember the case? Then the second precept comes into play: **past recollection recorded**. In this case, the laboratory report becomes the crucial evidence. Presumably it contains all of the information needed to explain what was done, how it was done, and the results and conclusions of the analysis. In this case, the scientist will be asked if the laboratory report represents standard operating procedures in cases such as this. For example, if the case involves the routine analysis of a white powder and the conclusion is that cocaine is present, are the methods and procedures used the ones that are used every time this type of evidence is analyzed? Are the data the same? Are the results and conclusions consistent with other cases of this type? There is nothing inherently wrong with this type of testimony. It is quite common. It illustrates the importance of having a complete laboratory report available since it is the only "memory" of the case.

IN MORE DETAIL: WHAT'S THE DIFFERENCE BETWEEN CIVIL AND CRIMINAL CASES?

Civil cases usually involve private disputes between persons or organizations. Criminal cases involve an action that is considered to be harmful to society as a whole.

Civil Case

A civil case begins when a person or entity (such as a corporation or the government), called the plaintiff, claims that another person or entity, called the defendant, has failed to carry out a legal duty owed to the plaintiff. Both the plaintiff and the defendant are also referred to as parties or litigants. The plaintiff may ask the court to tell the defendant to fulfil the duty, or make compensation for the harm done, or both. Legal duties include respecting rights established under the Constitution, under federal or state law, or by prior agreement of the parties. Civil suits are brought in both state and federal courts. An example of a civil case in a state court would be if a citizen (including a corporation) sued another citizen for not living up to a contract. For example, if a lumberyard enters a contract to sell a specific amount of wood to a carpenter for an agreed-upon price and then fails to deliver the wood, forcing the carpenter to buy it elsewhere at a higher price, the carpenter might sue the lumberyard to pay the extra costs incurred because of the lumberyard's failure to deliver. These costs are called damages. If these parties were from different states, however, then that suit could be brought in federal court under diversity jurisdiction if the amount in question exceeded the minimum required by statute ($75,000). Individuals, corporations, and the federal government can also bring civil suits in federal court claiming violations of federal statutes or constitutional rights. For example, the federal government can sue a hospital for over-billing Medicare and Medicaid, a violation of a federal statute. An individual could sue a local police department for violation of his or her constitutional rights—for example, the right to assemble peacefully.

> **IN MORE DETAIL: WHAT'S THE DIFFERENCE BETWEEN CIVIL AND CRIMINAL CASES?—cont'd**
>
> **Criminal Case**
>
> A person accused of a crime is generally charged in a formal accusation called an indictment or information. The government, on behalf of the people of the United States, prosecutes the case through the United States Attorney's Office if the person is charged with a federal crime. A state's attorney's office prosecutes state crimes. It is not the victim's responsibility to bring a criminal case. In a kidnapping case, for instance, the government would prosecute the kidnapper, the victim would not be a party to the action. In some criminal cases, there may not be a specific victim. For example, state governments arrest and prosecute people accused of violating laws against driving while intoxicated because society regards that as a serious offence that can result in harm to others. When a court determines that an individual committed a crime, that person will receive a sentence. The sentence may be an order to pay a monetary penalty (a fine and/or restitution to the victim), imprisonment, or supervision in the community (by a court employee called a United States probation officer if a federal crime), or some combination of these three things.
>
> *From: The Federal Judicial Center, Washington, D.C., online at: www.fjc.gov.*

EXPERT TESTIMONY

Besides the analysis of evidence, the most important duty of a forensic scientist is to testify in court as an expert witness. This activity separates forensic science from all of the other sciences. Some excellent scientists cannot function in the pressurized atmosphere of a courtroom and would not be effective as an expert witness. Some proficient orators do not make good scientists and would be equally ineffective. A successful forensic scientist will be proficient at both the science and the testimony. What follows are some guidelines and tips that help make an effective expert witness.

WHEN DOES AN EXPERT TESTIFY?

Not every case that a forensic scientist works will go to trial. In fact, opportunities for testifying may be infrequent and irregular. They may not be summoned to testify for a number of reasons, such as the defendant may plead guilty, a plea arrangement made be made for a lesser sentence, the attorney may decide that particular scientific evidence isn't needed for trial, or the charges may be dropped. If the case does go to trial, the laboratory report issued by the scientist may be admitted with the scientist's testimony under certain conditions, as explained in the previous section. If a scientist is going to be called as a witness at trial, a subpoena will be issued. This will usually contain the defendant's name, the jurisdiction, the date and time that the subject is requested to appear, and contact information for the requesting attorney. There are many types of subpoenas that can be issued in a criminal or civil case. The type most often issued to a forensic scientist is a **subpoena duces** tecum. This is a request for production of evidence. This means that, not only must the scientist appear at the place, date and time specified, but all evidence pertaining to the case must also be

STATE OF ______________________) IN THE ______________________ COURT
COUNTY OF ______________________) SS:
) CAUSE NO:

____
Plaintiff/Petitioner

vs.

____
Respondent/Defendant

SUBPOENA DUCES TECUM

TO: NAME
ADDRESS
ADDRESS

You are hereby commanded to produce for inspection and/or copying on or before **DATE at TIME** at the offices/home of **NAME and ADDRESS**, any and all documents, records, or other tangible things which are in your possession or under your control relating to

____
____
____

Fail not under penalty of law.

____
Clerk

FIGURE 24.3

A subpoena duces tecum. This is a request for the production of evidence. As such, it requires that the scientist appears and brings all evidence that pertains to the case including laboratory reports and supporting materials.

produced. This includes all laboratory reports and any supporting documentation. Figure 24.3 is an example of a subpoena duces tecum.

When a subpoena is received, the scientist should call the requesting attorney as soon as possible to establish what is being requested. Even though the scientist will usually receive the subpoena from the prosecutor's office, the defense attorney may have requested it. Coordination with the requesting attorney is crucial to success as a witness on the stand. Most attorneys know very little about science and will need to discuss the intricacies of the scientist's expertise in order to be prepared for court. In this respect, the forensic scientist is a teacher for the attorney and it is up to him or her to help the attorney understand what was done in this case, and what can be said and what cannot be said. Insisting on a pretrial conference, coming prepared and being helpful is the best way to make a testimony experience proceed as smoothly as possible.

TESTIFYING

When a forensic scientist steps into a courtroom to testify, he or she is, in essence, entering a foreign realm where only some of the rules of science apply. As Lee Goff, a noted forensic entomologist, has described it in his book, "A Fly for the Prosecution,"

> *Academics and the legal system do not usually coexist in comfort. The laws of science and the rules of evidence have little in common. In theory, Academia functions on the principle of collegiality. In theory and reality, the American legal system is adversarial. The average academic entering the legal system is in for a tremendous culture shock.*

The legal arena has its own rules and most, but not all, apply to the scientist as expert and they must abide by the rules; experts, however, have leeway in the courtroom that no other witnesses have. It is a strange intersection between science and the law where even words have different meanings. Take, for example, the word "error." To a scientist, error is something that occurs naturally in all measurements and is accounted for in the statistics that are generated, such as "standard error of the mean." Errors in science cannot be avoided and are reported in due process. An attorney, on the other hand, hears the word "error" and thinks: Mistake! The scientist has just admitted to doing something wrong, in the lawyer's view, and has opened the door for further questioning. This "clash of cultures" does not always serve either side very well and may obscure what both parties seek. Another example, mentioned earlier in this chapter, is competence. To a scientist this connotes the ability to accomplish a task at a level of high quality. To an attorney, competence refers to a characteristic of evidence. It must be competent if it is to be admissible.

BEING A WITNESS AND AN EXPERT

Ordinary witnesses may only testify to what they have directly experienced through their five senses. This testimony must be factual in nature and the witness, in nearly all cases, is barred from offering opinions, conjectures, or hypothetical information. Unlike other types of witnesses, however, expert witnesses are allowed to offer their opinions about evidence or situations that fall within their area of expertise. These opinions are allowed because the scientist is an expert in that area and knows more than anyone else in the courtroom about that topic; their opinion and expertise will assist the trier of fact in deciding the case. Scientific evidence can be powerful. It can also be suspect. Judges and juries may ignore an expert's opinion evidence because it is just that: the expert's view on that issue. Often, however, those opinions and views are based upon solid scientific data generated through valid analyzes and therefore have a firm basis, in fact. Expert witnesses must always remember that they are speaking for the evidence. They must be an advocate for the evidence and not for one of the parties in the case.

When a forensic scientist testifies, he or she does so as an **expert witness**, that is, someone who knows more about a topic or subject than the average person. The scientist is brought to court by either the prosecution or defense and offered as an expert in some area of study that will aid the judge or jury (generically referred to as "**the trier of fact**") in reaching their verdict. The scientist then undergoes a process of establishing his or her education, training, experience, and expertise in that discipline. The scientist will often need to cite his or her educational degrees, work history, previous testimony experience, publications, professional associations, and other relevant information that will justify their expertise to the court. The attorney offering the scientist as an expert asks questions that will lay a foundation for the scientist's credentials; the opposing attorney may then ask questions in an attempt to weaken that foundation. This process is called **voir dire**, which is French for "speaking true." It is important for the scientist to provide *relevant* qualifications to the court: being coach of the local high school soccer team has no bearing on whether someone should be considered an expert in drug analysis, for example. If the court rules that the scientist does possess sufficient credentials, then he or she may testify on that subject in the case at hand. The scientist must be careful to remain within the bounds of their expertise. It may be tempting to answer questions at the margin of your experience and offer speculative answers to be helpful or sound authoritative—*but don't do it!* Few things will reduce your expertise in the jurors' minds faster. The following fictitious example of over-extended testimony may clarify this idea.

> Attorney: Dr Medical Examiner, what type of wound was found on the victim's head?
> Dr ME: It was a contact gunshot wound.
> Attorney: Would the perpetrator have had gunshot residue on his or her hands?
> Dr ME: Undoubtedly. Gunshot residue would have been on their hands.
> Attorney: What is gunshot residue, Dr?
> Dr ME: Small particles of material expelled from the weapon when it is discharged.
> Attorney: What are those small particles composed of? What elements?
> Dr ME: Uhm …
> Attorney: What's the best method to analyze gunshot residue?
> Dr ME: Scanning electron microscopy. We have one in our lab.
> Attorney: How does it work?
> Dr ME: Well …

The medical examiner obviously has overstepped his bounds of knowledge and is now in danger of looking foolish or arrogant to the jury. Although he knows something about gunshot residue, he is clearly not an expert in this area and should have answered the attorney's second question with something like, "I'm a forensic pathologist and do not have specific expertise in the analysis of gunshot residue." It is better to answer truthfully with "I don't know" than to exceed your limits of knowledge, training, or experience.

CONSIDERATIONS FOR TESTIMONY

Proper expert testimony takes a good deal of practice and there are many considerations that must be kept in mind when testifying. Preparation is the most important aspect of testimony. This cannot be overemphasized. There are also important considerations when a witness is asked a question and when answering it. Some of the more important points are given below.

Preparation

- *Prepare Yourself*

Review your paperwork and reports. Be familiar with the circumstances, times, dates, and names involved in the case. If possible, visit the courtroom in advance to get a feel of the room.

- *Always Tell the Truth*

As a witness, you have sworn to tell the truth to the best of your ability. Whatever the effects the facts may have on the case is solely the concern of the judge or jury. When you finish testifying, your part in the court proceedings is over.

- *Prior Statements*

Anytime a person tells the same story twice, no matter how carefully, there are likely to be at least some differences. If there is an inconsistency with a prior statement you made, simply tell what you known to the best recollection you have. If there is an explanation for the inconsistency, give it ("If I said the evidence was returned on April 7th, I misspoke. It was returned on April 17th"). Your paperwork and notes should support your statements, be aware of this as you work.

- *Don't Discuss the Case with Anyone*

It is possible that the defendant, his attorney, or someone on his or her behalf may try to talk with you about the case. You may if you wish, but you don't have to discuss the case with anyone. It is not up to the prosecution or the defense to tell you whom to talk with. The only time you must answer questions is on the witness stand—that is the only time you are required to talk. If you do discuss the case prior to taking the stand, you may be asked about any alleged inconsistencies between your testimony and what you told whomever you spoke with. You will not have a court reporter's transcript to confirm or refute your claims. If the opposing attorney pulls you aside or wants to talk privately in the hallway, simply tell him or her that you'd be glad to do so with the other attorney also present. Otherwise you may make a statement ex parte (away from one party in the case) that will then become part of the attorney's questioning in the courtroom ("Didn't you just tell me in the hallway…").

The Importance of a Pretrial Conference

Arguably, the single most important part of your testimony experience is the pretrial conference that you have with the attorney. Both you and the attorney should be prepared to review all the significant aspects of the case and your testimony. The pretrial conference is like a dress rehearsal—it is critical that you thoroughly familiarize yourself with all the evidence, charts, and your paperwork. The pretrial conference is as important for the attorney as it is for the witness and you should prepare a list of qualifying questions to aid the attorney in questioning you.

ABOUT QUESTIONS

- *Listen To the Question Carefully*

One rule about questions: Answer as completely yet simply as possible. If you don't understand a question, ask for clarification; this is especially important if the question seems vague, value-laden ("Don't you feel that laboratory accreditation is important?"), or complicated.

- *Don't Volunteer Information*

Confine your answers to what you are asked. Any information you volunteer may be inadmissible, irrelevant to the case, or may even open up a line of questioning that leads to confusion and trouble.

- *You Cannot Be Asked Leading Questions on Direct Examinations*

You cannot be asked leading questions, that is, questions that suggest an answer, on direct examination. For example, "Didn't you find marijuana in the sample submitted to you?" is leading question; the question should be worded as, "What did find in the sample submitted to you?" Take your time and answer the question completely. If you are asked, "Did anything else happen at that time?" or "Did you find anything else?," you may have omitted something you previously mentioned to the attorney.

- *Beware of Compound Questions*

If you are asked several questions rolled into one, it will be difficult to answer them all accurately unless you do so one at a time. You could say, "I will answer your questions one by one," or you could ask, "Can you ask me those questions one at a time?"

ABOUT ANSWERS

- *Avoid Hearsay Testimony*

Unless you are specifically asked to testify about a conversation you had or to give your expert opinion, assume that every question calls solely for what you actually saw, heard, or did. Be careful of hearsay: Don't volunteer hearsay, such as, "Well, all the other examiners in my Unit say…"

- *Objections*

Lawyers have an absolute right and sometimes a duty to object and you must give them that opportunity—it can be to your advantage. Don't answer too quickly; pause a second before every answer. If an attorney objects, *stop*! Don't answer! Wait until the Judge rules and then either answer the question or stay silent.

- *Reference to Documents*

It is more effective if you can testify from memory without referring to your notes but if you must refresh your recollection, you are allowed to. Request permission from the judge: "If I had an opportunity to look at my notes, that would refresh my recollection as to the date."

- *Don't Guess*

If you don't know the answer to a question, just say so. If you know most of the answer but not all of the details, just say so. No one remembers everything.

- *Don't Argue With the Questioner*

The cross-examiner is at a distinct advantage in being able to ask the questions. Argument or gamesmanship by a witness is not appreciated by a Judge or Jury. Good witnesses respond fairly and honestly and thereby retain their creditability and believability. Answer questions from the prosecutor and the defense attorney with the same tone, demeanor, and attitude.

- *Never Get Angry*

When you are angry, you are least likely to do your duty as a witness, which is to give truthful answers. Your best reply is to remain calm, even-tempered, and answer the questions. The more an attorney attempts to aggravate you, the more courteous and professional you should remain.

- *Beware of Yes or No*

Some witnesses have the notion that all questions should be answered "Yes" or "No." Many questions cannot be answered accurately with only "Yes" or "No" because they are complicated, or require additional qualification to not sound misleading. If the lawyer asks you to answer "Yes or No," you are entitled to tell him or her that it can't be answered "Yes or No" without the answer being misleading. If he or she insists, you may respond "I cannot answer 'Yes' or 'No' without misleading the Court." The Judge normally will not direct you to answer "Yes" or "No;" if he or she does, do so but expect additional questioning by the opposing attorney about your explanation.

- *Remain Professional on the Stand at All Times*

As a witness called on behalf of a party in a criminal case, it is your duty to remain professional on the stand at all times, from the moment you enter the courtroom and take the oath to when you leave the courtroom. Do not chew gum. Do not have things which you may have brought with you, other than necessary records, in your hands while testifying. Wear appropriate business clothing. Look at the jury when you answer questions. Follow the instructions of the judge. You represent forensic science, your laboratory, and yourself—do so with honesty, integrity, and pride.

SUMMARY

Forensic science must operate in a legal context. The ultimate result of many scientific analyzes is in a court room and the admissibility of this evidence is controlled by rules of evidence. Forensic science is part of the criminal investigation process which starts with the discovery of a crime. It is crucial that crime scene technicians properly recognize, collect, and preserve evidence in order to be effectively analyzed by forensic scientists. There are Constitutional and other legal constraints on how a criminal investigation can be carried out. These include discovery, search and seizure, protections against self-incrimination, and due process. The production of evidence at a trial is compelled by a subpoena, and order to appear in court. The admissibility of evidence is controlled by a set of rules that govern security of the evidence, authenticity, relevance, and other issues. Scientific evidence is subject to all of these constraints as well as some that apply only to this type of evidence. These constraints arose in part from the decisions in *US v. Frye* and *Daubert v. Merrell-Dow*. These cases set out validity and reliability rules for the admission of scientific evidence.

When forensic scientists examine evidence, they issue a scientific report. This report must be written to particular standards of accuracy and completeness. In some states, the report is admissible by itself as proof of the facts it contains. Although the same courts handle both civil and criminal cases in the United States, they are different in their scope, rules, and penalties. Discovery is much more liberal in civil cases. The only penalty for violation of civil laws is payment of money to the aggrieved party, whereas in criminal cases, life and liberty are at stake. In both cases, scientists act as expert witnesses, a status that enables them to offer expert opinions in matters within their expertise. Each time a scientist appears in court he or she must be qualified as an expert by the judge.

TEST YOUR KNOWLEDGE

1. Should you answer questions with only "yes" or "no?"
2. What is an expert witness?
3. Do you have to respond to a subpoena?
4. What is a pretrial conference?
5. What should be included in a report?
6. How do forensic science laboratory casework reports differ from scientific papers?
7. List three things you should do when you testify.
8. List four things you should *not* do when you testify.
9. Why do some people describe all expert testimony as being opinion testimony?
10. Who is the trier of fact?
11. What parts of the Fifth Amendment of the United States Constitution affect evidence? How?
12. Who was James Frye? What was he accused of? What did he try and do in his defense?

13. The judge in *United States v. Frye* issued an opinion that affected the admissibility of scientific evidence for many years. What was the substance of his opinion?
14. Why is the practice of forensic science in crime labs considered to be part of the criminal investigation process?
15. What is an expert? Who decides if a witness is an expert? How is this done?
16. What privileges and responsibilities does an expert witness have that make him or her different from a non-expert (lay) witness?
17. How is evidence defined?
18. What is the difference between indirect and direct evidence?
19. What does voir dire mean? When is it used? What purpose does it fulfil?
20. What parts of the Fourth Amendment of the US Constitution affect evidence? How?

CONSIDER THIS...

1. You are on the stand testifying in a case and the attorney asks you a complicated question, one with several questions entangled in it, and then demands that you answer it with either a "Yes" or a "No." What are your options as an expert witness?
2. Part of the way through your testimony, you realize you misstated some statistics about the significance of your results (for example, you stated a frequency of 1 in 200,000 and you meant to say 1 in 200). What should you do?
3. What is the chain of custody? Explain the process that gives rise to the chain of custody and the document called the chain of custody. Why do expert witnesses often get more questions about the chain of custody in court than about the scientific testing they did? Give an example when a chain of custody may be broken. Why is evidence that is part of a broken chain of custody, sometimes rendered inadmissible?

FURTHER READING

Coulson, S.A., Buckleton, J.S., Gummer, A.B., Triggs, C.M., 2001. Glass on clothing and shoes of members of the general population and people suspected of breaking crimes. Science and Justice 41 (1), 39–48.

Gianelli, P.C., 1996. Giannelli Snyder Rules of Evidence Handbook: Ohio Practice 1996. West Information Pub Group.

Houck, M.M, 1995. The Tyranny of numbers: statistics and trace evidence. Forensic Science Communications 1 (1). Available at: www.fbi.gov.

Kiely, T.F., 2001. Forensic Evidence: Science and the Criminal Law. CRC Press.

Moenssens, A.A., Starrs, J.E., Henderson, C.E., Inbau, F.E., 1995. Scientific Evidence in Civil and Criminal Cases, fourth ed. Foundation Press.

ON THE WEB

http://www.daubertontheweb.com/. A collection of resources about the *Daubert v. Merrell-Dow* case.

http://www.law.cornell.edu/supct/html/92-102.ZS.html. The Supreme Court ruling in *Daubert v. Merrell-Dow*.

http://www.daubertontheweb.com/frye_opinion.htm. The opinion of the Appeals Court in *Frye v. United States*.

http://www.bioforensics.com/kruglaw/. Collection of resources on law and forensic science.

CHAPTER

Ethical and Professional Issues 25

CHAPTER OUTLINE

KEY TERMS

- Attribution bias
- Cognitive bias
- Confirmation bias
- Continuing education
- Dry-labbing
- Ethics
- Hired gun
- Proficiency testing

INTRODUCTION

The work of a forensic scientist has a significant result to society: It may influence the life and liberty of citizens, whether they are victims or suspects of crimes. Other professions, like medicine, policing, or the military, bear similar ethical burdens. Forensic science therefore requires a high degree of personal and professional integrity. Without this integrity at the individual and organizational level, damage can be done to lives and institutions. This chapter discusses some of the ethical and professional issues in forensic science and how individuals and organizations should behave as responsible representatives of science in the criminal justice system.

Ethics is a branch of philosophy that is concerned with right and wrong actions and their outcomes. People often confuse morals with ethics. Morals are a person's ideals about right versus wrong and what is considered appropriate behavior. Ethics, on the other hand, are applied morals, either individually, within a group, or between groups. What is "right" and what is "wrong" can vary between cultures and professions. It can be difficult to find universally accepted ethics (although the Golden Rule—treat others as you want to be treated—comes close), especially in a diverse workplace and among globally connected societies. Finding universal examples of shared values and beliefs has become increasingly difficult. Ethics is rarely taught as a separate subject and has largely been absent from education since the early 1980s. Practitioners learn applied ethics daily in the literature they read, the media they follow, the methods they use, the behaviors of friends and colleagues that are modeled and/or avoided, and the virtues promoted by their organizations and agencies. Ethics must be taught and continuing professional training in ethics is crucial to a successful organization and profession; simply assuming that people will absorb acceptable or desired behavior and that into practice is not a useful strategy.

PROFESSIONAL EXPECTATIONS

An introduction to professional ethics provides a foundation for acceptable behaviors, starting at university, through to employment, and on to management and beyond. Organizations must have some way of letting its members know what is expected of them. In science, for example, scientists are expected to be unbiased but if this has not been taught to them or reinforced at work, they may not be aware of sources or types of bias and drift into unacceptable behaviors. People also bring their own morals and beliefs to a group that can effect the group and the person's role in it.

No matter what the professional culture, ethics are important in the workforce. Every profession experiences unethical behaviors that arise due to human nature, self-justification, pressures, and greed or desire. While issues, responsibilities, and scenarios differ, the underlying causes remain similar and any professional culture that employs people faces the possibility for misconduct. Very simply, ethical issues can be divided into "sins of commission" (doing the wrong thing) and "sins of omission" (not doing the right thing). Blame tends to fall on an individual rather than on a group; people tend to like simple answers to complex problems. The reality, however, is more complicated and the sources of ethical failures can be remembered through A-B-C:

- Bad **A**pple (individual),
- Bad **B**ushel (group),
- Bad **C**rop (system).

A fourth option should also be considered, that of a bad farmer, a supervisor, or manager that allows inappropriate behavior to continue by supporting or turning a blind eye to it.

BASIC GUIDING PRINCIPLES

To be successful in their career, forensic scientists must follow the guiding principles for their profession and meet the ethical obligations of the field. These include but are not limited to being:

- Technically competent and employ reliable (accurate and precise) and validated methods of analysis.
- Honest about their qualifications and staying within their area(s) of expertise.
- Intellectually honest about their data, conclusions, and opinions.
- Objective when reviewing evidence and testifying as an expert.

These guiding principles are the *minimum* of ethics in forensic science. Although there is no single code of ethics for forensic science, many individual professional organizations, agencies, and department codes contain similar provisions. Ethical behavior helps to ensure consistency and reliability of behavior within the forensic science profession.

COMMON MISTAKES IN THINKING ABOUT ETHICS

Starting with an "Ethics 101" approach. Not every ethics issues needs to begin with Aristotle.

Ethics is the responsibility of management. Ethical behavior is every employee's responsibility.

Not everything is "an ethical issue." Paralysis over fear of committing an ethical mistake can be just as damaging (remember "sins of omission?"). This is where awareness of potential issues can be as important as avoiding them.

Expecting managers to be experts on ethics just because they are "in charge." Ethics are learned, not inherent to a person or position.

Treating ethics like an event. Ethics is a process, a way of working, not a rigid process or an annual training event.

Thinking there is always a right answer. Multiple right—or wrong—answers may exist for the same issue, or there may be no knowable answer at all.

Those who commit unethical behavior are bad people. Do not judge a person by their worst day; ethical misconduct may be as simple as one bad decision.

Scientists are inherently ethical. Anyone in any profession can make a mistake or succumb to pressures or biases.

People in the same profession share the same views. People are individuals and may look at things through a different ethical lens because their background and experiences.

FORENSIC-SPECIFIC ETHICAL ISSUES

Forensic scientists face two major types of ethical dilemmas: those that occur because they are scientists and those that occur because they interact with the justice system. Most forensic scientists see themselves as scientists first and they concentrate most heavily on scientific ethical questions and may not appreciate the complexity and seriousness of the ones that arise from justice system interactions. One way that forensic science is unique, especially in relation to ethics, is the close professional relationship the field has with some other professional cultures. Forensic scientists, law enforcement officers, lawyers, judges, and other scientists work very closely together, but may have very different objectives, rules, and philosophies. Despite the differences, forensic scientists must find a way to get along to support the justice system without succumbing to being unduly influenced or biased by differing ethical behaviors. A good way to do this is to recognize that differences do exist, learn about the rules and customs of the other professions, and then educate others regarding what professional expectations forensic scientists must meet and how they relate to the other profession's behaviors ("I know you want me to say that the evidence 'matches' but what I can say is…"). This sort of open and regular discussion works through issues early before they become unmanageable. Awareness of where the pitfalls and problems may be is key to avoiding them. Examining and exploring common pressures between professions enables individuals to realize common "red flags" to potential ethical misconduct. Looking at the outcome of case studies or examples, and especially events and circumstances leading up to those events, is an invaluable teaching tool for students and professionals.

Some ethical issues arise in the forensic science field more than others, including those that involve the use of best practices, validated methods of analysis, instances of bias, seeking notoriety of a personal nature, and becoming advocates for one side or the other.

BIAS

Bias is a preference for or against a person, thing, group, idea, or behavior. Being biased means being "one-sided" and being less willing to consider alternatives. Prejudice and bigotry against certain social or ethnic groups is a form of bias, for example. Although most people like to think of themselves as being unbiased, fair, and impartial, it is nearly impossible to be able to take a completely neutral position. All of our opinions and feelings are based upon our own experiences and we tend to think and act in ways that we were taught as we grew up and which tend to make us more comfortable. Being biased is, in a way, hard-wired into human beings but that does not mean biases cannot be overcome or controlled for. In many cases, people do not even have a conscious realization that they are being biased. Bias is not something that can be turned on or off like a switch and cannot be wished away.

The scientific method is designed to prevent or reduce bias; many other methods take similar precautions. Bias in science can have serious consequences and there are many ways that scientists seek to minimize bias. For example, the United States Food and Drug Administration (FDA) has the responsibility of approving new therapeutic drugs for use in treating disease and other medical indications. When a pharmaceutical company wishes to submit a new drug for FDA approval, a lengthy process is required to ensure that the drug will be safe, will have the effects for which it was designed, and will have identifiable side effects. This process includes extensive testing, first on animals and then on humans. In both of these phases, there are significant points where bias can affect the process of approval. The efficacy of a drug is evaluated in two ways during the testing phases of the drug. There are objective measurements of the biochemical and physiological effects of the drug, such as blood pressure, heart rate, tissue damage, etc. Then there are more subjective observations that are made by the examiners/observers and by the subjects of the testing. This is where bias can cause problems. One of the most common methods used for the evaluation of the effects of new drugs is so-called "double blind" testing. In this process, a population of people who are suffering from the disease or condition for which the new drug is being proposed, is gathered together and divided into two groups. One of the groups will receive the drug and the other will receive a placebo, a formulation that looks exactly like the drug does and contains everything that the drug contains except the active ingredient. Then the effects of the drug and placebo will be observed by the examiners and reported by the subjects. To mitigate the bias that can occur among the patients who think they are getting a drug that will help them, none of the patients know whether they are getting the drug or the placebo. Likewise the people who are administering the drug and placebo do not know which one they are giving to which patient. This blinding reduces the chances that biases will affect observations about the efficacy of the drug.

Forensic science is not immune to bias. In fact, forensic science has *more* opportunities for potential bias because of the close relationship it has with professions that are *required* to have a particular viewpoint; like police officers, prosecutors, and defense attorneys. Remember that most public laboratories are administered and funded by a unit of government, which has the responsibility to prosecute people for committing crimes. The fact that a forensic scientist is employed by a public laboratory may imply that he or she is biased toward the prosecution and is a "member" of the prosecution "team." Many forensic scientists who are employed by police agencies are themselves enlisted police officers or civilians sworn as officers who may wear uniforms and carry weapons. These associations may not only give the *appearance* of bias, but may also actually lead the scientist to become biased toward the prosecution.

The topic of bias is diverse, complex, and, at times, contentious. **Cognitive bias**, poor or bad judgment based on perceptual distortion, illogical interpretations, or irrationality, has been recognized for many years by scientists but its implications for forensic science practice have come to light in recent years, thanks to the research

(a) ABC

(b) 12 13 14

FIGURE 25.1

(a) and (b). When asked to read out the letters in (a), people naturally read out "A, B, C;" when asked to do the same for the numbers in (b), they read "12, 13, 14." They do not realize that asking for letters or numbers biases them toward an interpretation of the middle item ("B/13").

performed by Dr Itiel Dror, a cognitive psychologist, and other researchers. Only two of the many types of bias will be discussed in this chapter. The first is termed **contextual bias**, where a person is influenced by clues surrounding the topic but not the content itself. For example, when asked to read the letters in Figure 25.1(a), people routinely answer "A, B, C." When asked to read the numbers in Figure 25.1(b), people normally read out, "12, 13, 14." The interpretation of the middle item depends on whether the viewer has been primed to think of it as a letter or a number. They do this naturally without considering their interpretation has been biased by being asked about letters or numbers.

In a typical investigation, the police focus on a particular suspect. Evidence is collected from that individual, along with items from the victim and the scene. All of the focus is on that suspect and may be very difficult for the forensic scientist to not be biased toward associating that individual to the items in the case. In addition, the scientist may be furnished with information pertaining to how the crime occurred ("It was a really vicious crime"), how the suspect became the focus of the investigation ("He's the victim's boyfriend, so naturally…"), what other evidence exists that implicates the suspect ("We found a gun in his bedroom"), and other influencing information, little if any that matters to the scientist's analysis.

This situation gives rise to two questions: How much information should an examiner have about the circumstances of the case and how can the focus on the suspect be lessened during the evidence examination process? A number of suggestions have come forth recently to answer both questions. As to the amount of information that the examiner should have when examining the evidence, it has been suggested that only the information needed to perform the examinations should be given out. There have also been suggestions for taking the focus off the suspect. These include giving the examiner several known samples from different but similar sources and not telling the examiner which of these belong to the suspect. Another suggestion involves giving the examiner the unknown evidence first for examination and then only after this is done, are the knowns supplied; in

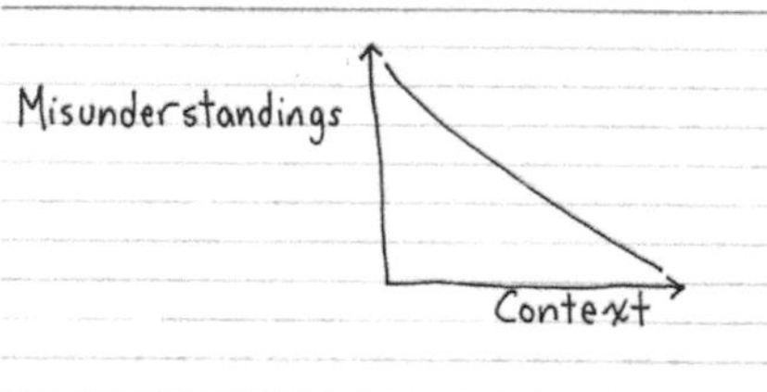

FIGURE 25.2

Rather than being thought of as binary—one is biased or one is not biased—the reality is that context and bias are on a continuum and the amount of information depends on the crime, its circumstances, and what the scientist is being asked to do.

Courtesy Jessica Hagy, www.thisisindexed.com.

many laboratories, this is currently the process. Without context, no investigation could be conducted nor any forensic examinations be completed—where would one start? However, too much information in favor of one view or another could lead the investigator or scientist astray. Too many view bias as binary, one is or one is not biased. In reality, the situation is more complicated and how much and what information is necessary and sufficient depends on the crime, its context, and what is being asked of the scientist (Figure 25.2).

The other type of bias is **confirmation bias**. Confirmation bias is the tendency to search for and use *only* information that *supports* a belief or hypothesis; any information that conflicts with the belief or hypothesis is discounted or ignored. The most notorious case of confirmation bias in forensic science occurred in the *Madrid Bombing* case of 2004. In this case, the Madrid police sent a partial fingerprint recovered from a terrorist bombing to the FBI Laboratory and requested that the FBI run the print through their AFIS system to help develop leads. In doing so, the FBI examiner focused upon one of the prints that was returned by the AFIS system. The print belonged to Brandon Mayfield, an Oregon attorney. An FBI fingerprint expert associated the crime scene print to Mayfield. This association was then confirmed by two other FBI examiners, both of whom had access to the report from the first examiner. Even an independent examiner (although a former FBI Laboratory fingerprint examiner) hired by Mayfield's attorney confirmed the results from the FBI. Every examiner *knew* that the previous examiner(s) had associated the print to Mayfield and this led them to be biased in favor of also associating it to Mayfield. As it turned out, the Madrid police found the correct suspect and his print was an excellent comparison for the one from the bombing scene; Mayfield was exonerated. Confirmation bias had led to the misidentifications. A subsequent internal investigation by the FBI pointed out the problems of systematic confirmation bias and took steps to mitigate them in their verification protocols. Confirmation bias is especially dangerous at the verification stage of examinations if another qualified scientist is conducting the same type of subjective exam.

SCIENCE-RELATED ETHICAL ISSUES

PROFESSIONAL CREDENTIALS

A scientist may be called upon to demonstrate personal credentials or qualifications when applying for a job, a promotion, or attracting clients to a business. For forensic scientists, however, additional situations exist where professional credentials are needed. The most important example is when a forensic scientist is being qualified as an expert witness in court. A judge must declare someone to be an expert before they can testify in trial. When an expert witness is challenged or at least questioned about their qualifications as an expert, specific questions may be asked about education, training, number of expert testimonies, for whom they testified, payment, and other relevant questions. The witness is under oath and lying about or misrepresenting one's qualifications or credentials is perjury. Misrepresenting credentials on the stand does not mean the liar will be caught, but it is a precursor to being caught: Testimony is a public record and transcripts can be reviewed and their accuracy checked. "The internet never forgets" and a few simple clicks on a search engine can reveal much. Misrepresentations of credentials include getting an educational degree (claiming a PhD without having one or claiming a degree was earned from a particular institution when, in fact, it was not), professional licensures, or certifications (falsely claiming certification as a specialist from a certifying body or the improper action of equating having attained actual certification with being "eligible" to be certified), employment history, and data about previous testimonies such as number of testimonies, locations, and areas in which the expert was qualified.

Training and continuing education also play a role in professional ethics. Some areas of forensic science, such as fingerprints, firearms, and questioned documents, require long periods of training in order to become an expert. In other areas, such as illicit drug analysis, the training period may be shorter because the formal scientific education is paramount. It can be difficult in some cases to ascertain how long and how rigorous the training is in a particular agency or discipline. There are issues such as how relevant is the training to actual casework, how much learning is there compared to hands on training, who in the laboratory is actually carrying out the training, and how is it determined that the scientist is fully trained and is now competent. It can be difficult to answer these questions. In these cases, the more documentation that the scientist can produce about what was covered and completed in a training program helps establish their credibility.

The other component to professional credentials in establishing the expertise of a witness is continuing education. All scientists, forensic, and others have the duty of maintaining currency in their field. They must be aware of the latest techniques and methods, research on limitations and errors in areas of their expertise, new instruments, and other current issues. The importance of staying current in one's field cannot be overemphasized and it must be a continual process. There are a number of ways that this can be accomplished. One, of course, is to regularly read the literature in one's field, such as journals, textbooks, and reference books. One of the best ways to keep up with what is going on in a scientific field is regular participation in activities that create and enhance awareness of current trends in the discipline, such as trainings, workshops, conferences, webinars, online courses, and others. These types of activities are available in virtually all areas of forensic science.

LABORATORY ANALYTICAL PROCEDURES

Most forensic science laboratories commit their analytical procedures to writing (standard operating procedures, or SOPs), validate all methods, and develop schemes for the analysis of various types of scientific evidence. All laboratories should have rigorous protocols for administrative and technical reviews of their analyzes and reports, but there are no consensus standards or uniformity across agencies for when and how to accomplish this. Potential ethical violations can occur when forensic scientists do not follow established procedures for the analysis of evidence or use unvalidated methods. This can happen in a number of ways.

One issue is the determination of when sufficient testing has been done in a given case that will scientifically support the examiner's conclusions. Mostly it is up to the individual laboratory or even each examiner as to the sufficiency of analysis. Certainly the courtroom is no place to determine this; the judge, jury, and attorneys do not know enough about the science to determine that the chosen analytical scheme was dispositive. Related to the issue of sufficiency is another problem, indiscriminate analysis of evidence. In these cases, the examiner doesn't have a plan or scheme in mind, they use every possible test for which the laboratory has the resources, in an effort to impress the court, find the desired or expected answer, or to increase their payment (in the case of private experts). Without objective measures about sufficiency of analysis and what constitutes a proper analytical scheme, indiscriminate analysis will continue to confound judges, juries, and attorneys. A scientist may even perform insufficient testing to support the conclusions about the evidence. An analyst may do a set of preliminary examinations on evidence and then fail to perform the final, confirmatory test which provides the clinching data to support the conclusion. The opposite can also occur. An analyst, in order to save time, skips all of the preliminary tests and goes right to the confirmatory test even though this may give misleading results because the preliminary tests may have yielded data that the confirmation misses. Confidence is enhanced if two or more different methodologies yield the same result. An example of this is in drug cases, where doing only a GC/MS test without more general screening and separation tests may miss the presence of additional drugs or with textile fibers where only FTIR is conducted and not microscopy (cotton and rayon are both cellulosic, giving the same spectrum, but are easily distinguished by microscopy). The "why" becomes important in such cases, as it leads to the cause and the solution; it may be insufficient training, laziness, or poorly maintained equipment.

Sometimes forensic scientists are guilty of analyzing their evidence to meet the conditions of the law. This means that the potential data outcome is preselected—chosen or manipulated—to conform to one or more conditions of the applicable law(s) controlling that evidence, so that the results cause the evidence to fall into a specific category that might carry a higher penalty. There are a number of examples of this in the analysis of drugs, wherein the penalties for possession or distribution may depend upon the quantity present. If the quantity is very close to the amount that triggers a higher penalty, some drug chemists may shade the weight to get over the trigger point in order to permit charging the higher penalty offence. This can also cut the other way, where the chemist deliberately shades the weight down to prevent a higher charge from being filed. Both practices might be considered unethical—but if there is a rounding issue or a truncation of a result, for example, in a DUI case, the blood alcohol might be reported as 0.07 gm/dL, truncating the value, or as 0.08 g/dL, rounding up, based on the analytical result of 0.079 g/dL, when the legal threshold is 0.08 g/dL. If such reporting modifications are employed, the best practice would be to provide all the data, the actual result, and what the manipulation was. When in doubt, always err on the side of caution and transparency.

Perhaps the most extreme form of unethical practice in a forensic science laboratory is the practice of "dry-labbing." This occurs when an analyst reports results without performing the analysis; that is, he or she makes up the answers. In some cases, dry-labbing is done when the results appear to be obvious, such as when the evidence is a clear, plastic bag containing suspected marihuana. The look and smell is a good indication of the presence of marihuana, but dry-labbing could miss the presence of other drugs coating it or mixed in with it. This practice can never be accidental except in the instance of a gross mix up of cases and is never a training issue: The analyst simply does not do some or all of the work. Examples of dry-labbing almost always end with an inculpatory result, favoring the prosecution. There are some indications that Fred Zain, the West Virginia criminalist who was alleged to have nearly always achieved inculpatory results, may have engaged in this practice and it would take more than an administrative review of cases to uncover it.[1] Dry-labbing need not be all or nothing. Jacqueline Blake, a scientist with the FBI Laboratory from 1988 to 2002 resigned after it was found that she had not processed negative controls for DNA analyzes, resulting in genetic profiles being pulled from databases, evidence being consumed with none remaining, and delay of results. She did this through lying to her supervisors and a weak agency policy on reviewing certain data.[2] Reanalysis of evidence would be most effective but this is very time-consuming and difficult. In any case, regardless of the "how" or "why," dry-labbing is *always* a serious ethical violation and it is inconceivable to construct a valid defense for willfully saying a test was performed that was never done.

Another ethical issue in regards to the analysis of evidence can be termed "analyzing to the law." An example can be found in the laws that many states and the Congress have written over the years that set out graduated penalties for possession and/or distribution of certain illicit drugs. These statutes proscribe higher penalties for dealing in larger quantities of drugs. For example, possession of more than one pound (453 g) of cocaine will trigger a longer prison sentence than a lesser amount of the drug. In a case where the weight of the exhibit is very close to a pound, the

---

[1] http://www.innocenceproject.org/Content/Gerald_Davis.php.
[2] http://www.justice.gov/oig/special/0405/chapter4.htm.

analyst might report that the weight is over the limit, thus triggering the higher penalty. If reanalysis of the evidence is absent, a rare occurrence, then there would be no way of discovering that the weight had been incorrectly recorded.

ETHICS OF REPORTING AND INTERPRETATION

The major duties of a forensic scientist are to perform scientific analysis of evidence, report on the conclusions reached on the basis of that analysis, and—possibly—testify about that work and those results in court. A formal laboratory report is written for every case that is analyzed in a public forensic science laboratory in a criminal case. Formal reports may not be written for work done by independent experts in some criminal cases or by experts in civil matters. Only a small percentage of criminal or civil cases ever make it into a courtroom; nearly all are settled out of court. Most of these are the result of a plea bargain in criminal cases or an agreement between the parties in a civil case. The rules of evidence favor a court trial. Discovery is limited in criminal cases in most jurisdictions, which encourages the accused to seek information via the trial. Laboratory reports tend to be brief; in many cases they are little more than certificates of analysis (see Chapter 24). Just the opposite is true in civil cases: Since only money (and not life or liberty) is at stake in a civil case, discovery is more liberal and the parties are strongly encouraged to settle out of court. Laboratory reports tend to be comprehensive and should lay out all of the details of the analysis and present all of the data. The brevity of many laboratory reports in criminal cases raises ethical questions on the ground that important information that could be used by the defense in a case is not forthcoming by the laboratory unless discovery is exercised or there is a trial. Because very few cases get to court, the forensic science laboratory report becomes the public face of the laboratory. The report is, in many cases, the only product that the public sees from the laboratory. If it is not a comprehensive scientific report, this practice can reflect poorly on the field as not being scientific enough.

Clearly, the most important component of a forensic science laboratory report consists of the conclusions reached by the examiner about each piece of evidence examined. In the course of analysis, all evidence is identified and characterized to one extent or another. In some cases, efforts are made to provide a degree of association between evidence whose source is known with evidence from the crime scene and whose source is unknown and needs to be determined. The association of crime scene evidence with a source can be critical information in the determination of guilt or innocence. For example, it may be important to determine if fingerprints on a murder weapon came from the accused, or whether a bank robber wrote a note demanding money, or if fibers found at the scene of a kidnapping came from a sweater worn by the victim. The need to explain these relationships gives rise to terms of association that express the degree of certainty that the unknown evidence came from a particular source. Only in a fraction of criminal cases it is possible to individualize evidence to a particular source and even many of these situations were called into question by the NAS Report and other sources. Only in the case of DNA typing it is currently possible to provide reliable probabilities that evidence arose from a particular person. This means that more relative, less certain descriptors must be used in associating other types of evidence. A possible ethical problem with the use of the terms of association is that their meanings are not well understood or agreed upon even by the forensic scientific community that uses them. Some examples follow that will illustrate the problem. A prime example is the term **match**. This is often used to describe the association of fingerprints, bullets, handwriting, etc., with a known source. This term is often used to connote that the known and unknown have a common source (individualization), as in, "The fingerprints on the gun matched those of the defendant." The implication is that there are no other fingerprints in the world that could have the same characteristics exhibited in the same way. In other instances, the term is used to impart a strong association but not individualization. "The fibers from the car seat matched the fibers in the victim's sweater." Without a standard, agreed-upon meaning for this and related terms, such as "similar to," juries, judges, and attorneys can be confused, and rightly so.

There is another ethical issue with courtroom testimony that is related to imprecise use of associative terminology. Not only it is important for the forensic scientist to use proper terminology and define it clearly for the trier of fact, but also they must give the evidence its due and they should not overstate or understate their results or the meaning of them. For example, take the case where someone is abducted and taken away in the perpetrator's automobile. After the victim is rescued, a search is performed in the interior of the vehicle. Loose fibers are found. These are compared with fibers from a sweater that the victim was wearing at the time of the kidnapping. The known samples from the sweater are blue acrylic fibers with a round cross-section; the same is true for the fibers recovered from the car seat. At trial, the forensic scientist testifies that the fibers found on the car seat *came from* the sweater. This is a conclusion of single source—the sweater was the only possible source of the fibers! As a mass-produced garment, the sweater cannot be the only source of those fibers. On the other hand, if a scientist identifies a white powder as containing cocaine but testifies in court that the powder could be cocaine, then that is just as bad because the molecular structure of cocaine is unique to that class of material. In either case, the science is not being well used and the trier of fact is being misled.

THE ETHICS OF EMPLOYMENT STATUS

Most practicing forensic scientists in the United States work for a laboratory that is under the administrative control of a unit of government, federal, state, regional, or local. Most of these laboratories are within a law enforcement agency such as a police department, sheriff's department, or prosecutor's office. Public forensic science laboratories are supported by the taxpayers of that governmental unit and the scientists are paid a salary for their work. Forensic scientists who work in public laboratories are often viewed by workers in the justice system and in the general public as being part of the police department, for example, and they are viewed as being part of the police team even though the forensic scientists view themselves as unbiased, neutral scientists. This is a form of attribution bias, discussed earlier: The assumption is that because the scientists work for the police, they hold the same views.

Other forensic scientists make their living working for nongovernmental laboratories in the private sector. A few of these private laboratories perform services for governmental agencies. The Northern Illinois Forensic Science Laboratory does work for police agencies in Northeast Illinois, for example. Most private laboratories get most of their work from criminal defendants or in civil cases where they may work for either party. The scientists who work for these private laboratories may also receive a salary for their services. Still other forensic scientists have one-person laboratories and they receive a fee for service. They also do most of their work for criminal defense or in civil cases. They also face issues of attribution bias. It is a common tactic for a prosecutor to question a defense expert forensic scientist about the fees that they are collecting for appearing in court, implying that the expert is saying what he or she is being paid to say and is thus biased and unethical. This leads to the issue of the **hired gun**. This is an expert witness who gains a reputation for, in effect, offering testimony that is suited to the client for a fee. Hired guns are viewed to be unethical because they tailor their testimony to the needs of the client without regard to what the science says. They will do tests and select the results that fit their testimony. In addition, many expert witnesses will build their practice by working only as plaintiff's expert or defense expert. Thus, they are not only hired guns, but they will only work for the same side of a case in all cases, regardless of the merit. Sometimes charges of prosecution bias will be leveled at forensic scientists who work for a governmental agency such as a police department. The fact is that this is the nature of their employment. Most public forensic science laboratories are required by statute to accept cases only from law enforcement agencies and may not be permitted to work for a defense attorney. Calling these scientists hired guns is misleading.

PROFESSIONAL ETHICS

The profession of being a scientist carries with it a number of possible ethical issues. This is also true for forensic scientists, who are first and foremost, scientists. The first of these considerations is the need to stay current scientific knowledge and research. The hallmark of science is that it is always changing. What was true 10 years ago may not be true today; new methods and instrumentation appear constantly. It is incumbent upon laboratory forensic scientists to keep up with changes in their field of expertise and to make sure that the methods they use for the analysis of evidence represent best practices. Using outmoded practices runs the risks of results that can be refuted or proven to be the detriment of the justice system. In drug analysis, for example, there is a continuous stream of new illicit drugs showing up such as synthetic cannabinoids and steroids. In DNA typing, new methods for determination of mixtures, next-generation sequencing, familial relations, and myriad other new practices are altering the landscape of identification.

How do forensic scientists prove that they are competent to perform evidence analysis within their expertise? This is, after all, an important way to demonstrate to a court that they are worthy of consideration as expert witnesses. In the United States, there is no universal mandatory requirement for either certification or accreditation. Although about 90% of the public forensic science laboratories are accredited, the process is voluntary. Likewise, no mandatory requirement exists for forensic scientists to be certified, although there are voluntary programs set up for various forensic science disciplines. The issue of mandatory certification raises many questions, such as acceptance of certifying bodies, who pays for the certifications (which travel with the employee), and what to do about disciplines with no certifications.

A NATIONAL CODE OF ETHICS IN FORENSIC SCIENCE

Many professional fields have developed a consensus code of ethics with robust enforcement provisions. These are often tied to a licensure process that can be used to enforce adherence to the ethics code. Two familiar examples are in medicine and law. Forensic science has no licensure requirement and no agreed-upon code of ethics. To be sure, there are a large number of forensic science organizations that have a code of ethics, including national and regional associations, as well as discipline specific groups. Although there is obviously some overlap between these organizations with respect to the types of behaviors that constitute ethical violations, there are also significant differences. The major problem with this patchwork system is the lack of consequences for violators. The only serious consequence for violating the ethical code of the American Academy of Forensic Sciences, for example, is expulsion; this does not prevent the scientist from continuing to practice in the forensic science field, nor does it necessarily stop the unethical behavior. Unethical forensic scientists can cause significant damage to the whole justice system and there are few practical ways to stop it. The 11th recommendation of the NAS Committee report on forensic science is that there be a national code of ethics that is tied to certification. In order for this to have any real effect on the bad actors, however, there must be real consequences for serious ethical violations, up to and including loss of the right to practice forensic science, and offer expert testimony in court.

Since the NAS report came out in 2009, there has been much discussion about creating a national code of ethics and a few small attempts to do so. The major problem is that there is no national organization that speaks for all forensic scientists with one voice, analogous to the American Bar Association for attorneys or the American Medical Association for doctors. The recently formed National Commission on Forensic Science will attempt to forge a consensus for a national code of ethics and hopefully the United States Congress will provide some funding and perhaps legislation to move this effort along. A national code of ethics with strong enforcement will go a long way to help reduce the number of ethical violators and advance the forensic sciences to the level of other professional fields.

SUMMARY

Ethics and professional responsibilities are central to the success of and respect for a profession. Everyone is subject to bias in virtually all of their activities and interactions with others. All scientists face biasing issues by nature of their involvement in scientific activities. Forensic scientists face all of these bias issues and, in addition, they face biasing situations by virtue of their interactions with the justice system. Awareness of sources of bias is a necessary step in becoming a good professional but it is not sufficient. Forensic scientists must practice ethical behavior daily and act as role models for their peers and colleagues so that their scientific expertise aids the criminal justice system and does not damage it.

TEST YOUR KNOWLEDGE

1. How is ethics defined?
2. What is the difference between ethics and morals?
3. What is bias? Why is it so difficult to control?
4. Define and give examples of cognitive bias.
5. Define and give examples of contextual bias.
6. Define and give examples of confirmation bias.
7. What types of ethical situations relate to professional credentials?
8. How are forensic scientists more exposed to ethical issues than other scientists?
9. Define "hired gun." What is derogatory about this label? What are the ethical issues associated with this term?
10. What is dry-labbing? Why would someone do this?
11. What are the ethical related to continuing education?
12. What steps are taken to minimize bias in the approval of new drugs by the FDA?
13. Give an example of biasing that can occur when a forensic scientist is being offered as an expert in a trial.
14. What are some of the considerations in making certification mandatory?
15. Witnesses are often admonished to answer only the questions asked and not elaborate. How could this practice result in an ethical violation if it were strictly carried out by a forensic scientist testifying in court?

CONSIDER THIS...

1. What type of bias was encountered most prominently in the Madrid Bombing Case? Why did this occur? How could it have been minimized?
2. Cognitive bias can be difficult to control because an examiner has to know some details about a case in order to analyze the evidence. Several ways have been

proposed to minimize cognitive bias without withholding all information about a case. These include having a "case agent" distribute the evidence and give the examiner just the information needed to analyze it; the practice of "sequential unmasking," whereby an examiner is given information about the case incrementally as he or she proceeds to analyze it; and having evidence "line-ups" where multiple knowns are given to the examiner along with the unknowns, so that he or she cannot focus on just one person. Describe how each of these would work with a fingerprint case where the examiner is asked to compare unknown prints from a crime scene and known prints from a suspect.

3. If there was a national code of ethics in forensic science, should it be very detailed in its descriptions of ethical violations or should they be broadly described? What types of enforcement could there be when violations occur from the very serious to the minor ones?

FURTHER READING

Downs, J.U., Swienton, A.R. (Eds.), 2012. Ethics in Forensic Science. Academic Press.

Bowen, R.T., 2009. Ethics and the Practice of Forensic Science. CRC Press.

Barnett, P.D., 2001. Ethics in Forensic Science: Professional Standards for the Practice of Criminalistics. CRC Press.

Dror, I.E., Hampikian, G., 2011. Subjectivity and bias in forensic DNA mixture interpretation. Science and Justice 51 (4), 204–208.

Dror, I.E., Charlton, D., Péron, A.E., 2006. Contextual information renders experts vulnerable to making erroneous identifications. Forensic Science International 156 (1), 74–78.

Dror, I.E., Champod, C., Langenburg, G., Charlton, D., Hunt, H., Rosenthal, R., 2011. Cognitive issues in fingerprint analysis: inter- and intra-expert consistency and the effect of a 'target' comparison. Forensic Science International 208 (1), 10–17.

Dror, I.E., Cole, S.A., 2010. The vision in "blind" justice: expert perception, judgment, and visual cognition in forensic pattern recognition. Psychonomic Bulletin and Review 17 (2), 161–167.

Glossary

Abrasive erasure Removes writing with an abrasive erasure material.
Absorption Introduction of drugs into the body and movement into the bloodstream.
Absorption spectrum A spectrum of the intensity of light absorbed by a substance plotted against wavelength or frequency.
Accelerant A flammable liquid used to speed up a combustion or permit one to take place that wouldn't in the absence of the accelerant.
Activation energy The energy needed to get a chemical reaction started. Part of it may be used to break chemical bonds. Part may be used to vaporize liquids and solids.
Addiction A condition of physical dependence on a drug that is manifested by symptoms of withdrawal if the drug is not taken.
Admissibility of evidence The issue of what evidence will be admitted to a trial Amendment of the United States Constitution.
Adsorption The attraction by a solid surface for analyte components. The process whereby vapors of flammable liquids adhere to the surface of a specially prepared solid such as charcoal.
Adsorption elution A process for concentrating flammable liquids on a solid substrate and then eluting it off with a solvent.
Agonist A drug that binds to a receptor and causes it to exert its function on the cell.
Allele Different forms of the same gene or other DNA fragment at the same locus.
Amelogenin Sex-determining locus on X and Y chromosomes.
Analyte The substance or substances being identified or analyzed.
Anneal A process whereby two complementary strands of DNA come together to form double-stranded DNA.
Antagonist A drug that binds to a receptor but not causes it to exert the action of the cell to which the receptor is attached.
Atomic absorption spectroscopy A type of atomic spectroscopy whereby a known element is vaporized and then visible light of known wavelengths is passed through the vapor to determine, by absorption, how much of the element is present.
Atomic emission spectroscopy A type of atomic spectroscopy whereby an element is heated and then the wavelengths of light emitted by the sample are measured and the elements identified.
Attenuated total reflectance A type of reflectance spectroscopy whereby a sample is pressed by a special reflecting crystal that causes the incident infrared light to bounce one or more times off the sample.
Attribution bias A cognitive bias that attributes qualities to a person or group of people based on insufficient or inappropriate evidence. For example, determining that all forensic laboratories are biased toward law enforcement because most are administratively under a police department.
Autorad A piece of X-ray or photographic film that has been exposed by radioactive- or chemiluminescence-labeled DNA strand.
BAC Blood alcohol concentration. Measured in grams per deciliter (100 ml) of blood.
Barbiturate A group of chemical substances based on the compounds barbituric acid and thiobarbituric acid.
Becke line A halo that forms around a solid, transparent object that is immersed in a liquid of different refractive index.

Beer's Law The rule that relates the concentration of a light-absorbing substance to the amount of light it absorbs.

Bit Short for binary digit. Fundamental unit in computing. It has two possible values: 1 or 0.

Bomb seat The point of origin of an explosion.

Borosilicate glass Glass doped with boron oxide. This glass is very resistant to rapid heating and cooling.

BrAC Breath alcohol concentration. Measured in grams per 2101 of alveolar air.

Chain of custody A document and process that is used to identify, authenticate, and trace evidence from the crime scene to the court room. It contains the signatures of everyone who comes into possession of the evidence.

Chemical erasure Removes writing using a chemical reaction that dissolves or bleaches the ink.

Chemical ionization A type of fragmentation of molecules in a mass spectrometer where the energy is imparted to the molecule by a beam of small molecules like butane.

Chromatogram A plot of the response of the detector versus time.

Chromatograph The instrument that separates analytes using a stationary and mobile phase.

Chromatography A family of techniques that separate complex mixtures into individual components by competition for analyte components by a mobile phase and a stationary phase.

Chromosome A structure that contains the nuclear DNA. There are the same 46 chromosomes in each cell (except sperm and egg) of a human being. They are arranged in 23 pairs. One of each pair is inherited from the mother and the other, the father.

Clinical Pharmacology Study of ingestion and distribution and effects of drugs on humans.

Cognitive bias Poor or bad judgment based on perceptual distortion, illogical interpretations, or irrationality. A range of cognitive biases have been detailed and studied, although the definitions and categories may vary.

Combined DNA Indexing System (CODIS) A set of local, state, and national DNA databases that use 13 specific loci to type DNA.

Combustion reaction A reaction between a fuel and oxygen to produce energy.

Competence A collection of rules that evidence must obey if it is to be admitted in court. These include constitutional constraints, privileges, hearsay, prejudice, etc.

Comprehensive Controlled Substances Act of 1970 Repealed or updated all previous laws that controlled both narcotics and dangerous drugs. This law put all controlled substances in the Federal realm. This meant that the Federal Government could prosecute anyone for a drug offence regardless of whether interstate trafficking was involved and irrespective of state laws.

Concentric cracks Cracks formed on the same side of a piece of glass by a projectile such as a bullet. They form roughly circular cracks with the hole at the center.

Confirmation bias The tendency to look for, interpret, and use only information that confirms a preconceived idea or perspective.

Conjugated double bond Alternating double and single bonds.

Continuing education Short courses, readings, lectures, workshops, and other activities that provide additional or specialized information to professionals.

Controlled substance Illicit and licit drugs that are controlled by federal and state statutes by putting them in one of five (or more) schedules.

Crack A form of cocaine-free base that is smoked.

Criminal investigation The process of discovering who committed a crime and the search for evidence to prove it.

Cut-off level An amount of a drug present in a body below which the laboratory will report out a negative result.

Data carving The reconstruction of files, structures, and content necessary when file system metadata is lost or corrupted.

Demonstrative evidence Illustrative supporting materials that are not produced by the crime but which are used to help explain evidence or the circumstances of the crime.

Denature To separate double-stranded DNA into single strands using heat or sometimes chemicals.

Density Mass divided by volume.

Deoxyribonucleic acid (DNA) A polymeric, double helix molecule made up of four bases that are connected in pairs to each other and to a chemical backbone. DNA contains a genetic code that directs a cell to produce specific proteins that are the building blocks of life.

Dependence A strong psychological craving for a drug that does not lead to withdrawal symptoms if the drug is removed.

Deposition Taking of a statement from a witness under oath but not in a court room and no judge is present.

Detonation An instantaneous combustion.

Diamond cell A device in an infrared spectrophotometer that is used for the analysis of small particles. A chip of diamond is put in tight contact with the sample and light is transmitted through the diamond and the material.

Diffuse reflectance A type of reflectance spectroscopy whereby a series of mirrors directs infrared light at a sample from an oblique angle.

Diluent Chemicals that are used to dilute an illicit drug and to give it more bulk.

Diode array detector A detector for HPLC that is essentially a UV/visible spectrophotometer that performs essentially instantaneous scans.

Discovery A legal process whereby one party in a litigation seeks information in the possession of the other party.

Distribution Movement of drugs throughout the body as they are carried to all cells by the bloodstream.

DNA ladder A mixture of many or all of the alleles of a DNA fragment that is used for calibration.

Document alterations An obliteration, erasure, additional markings, indented writings, and charred documents.

Drug A natural or synthetic substance that is designed to produce a specific set of psychological or physiological effects on the human body or, in some cases, other animals.

Drug abuse When people take drugs for purposes other than for which they are intended, usually for their psychoactive effects.

Drug screen A test or tests that give presumptive indication that a drug is present in the body.

Dry labbing Making up data in a scientific experiment or process, as opposed to actually conducting the experiment or method and yielding real data.

Due process clause A clause in the Fifth Amendment of the United States Constitution which requires that a defendant be accorded minimal standards of conduct in the prosecution of a case.

Electromagnetic radiation Various types of energy in the form of waves.

Electron impact A type of fragmentation of molecules in a mass spectrometer where the energy is imparted to the molecule by a beam of energetic electrons.

Electronic control unit (ECU) Computerized devices that help to monitor and control vehicle systems and subsystems, like traction control, diagnostics, and crash data.

Electrophoresis A chromatography technique whereby the stationary phase is a solid or viscous liquid and the mobile phase is an electric current.

Electrostatic detection apparatus (ESDA) An instrument that works in a similar fashion to an electrostatic copier to visualize indented writing.

Elimination Removal of drugs from the body by excretion, respiration, etc.

Endothermic reaction A chemical reaction that uses more heat than it releases.

Enzyme Multiplied Immunoassay Test (EMIT) An immunological test used as a screening test for abused drugs. It uses specific antibodies to a drug being screened for to detect and quantify the drug.

Ethics A branch of philosophy that is concerned with concepts of right and wrong conduct; a system of moral principles.

Event data recorder (EDR) The "black box" of a vehicle; an ECU that records data about a crash event.

Excipient Substances that may mimic the activity of the main illicit drug present in order to make it more difficult for the user to know just how much of the drug there really is in the exhibit.

Exemplar A known or authentic writing or printing sample.

Exothermic reaction A chemical reaction that produces heat as a product.

Expert witness A witness who possesses knowledge, skills, and aptitudes that enable his or her to offer opinions on matters beyond the knowledge of the average person.

Explosive train A series of explosives whereby the first is used to detonate the second, etc.

Extension A process in PCR whereby base pairs are added sequentially to a new strand of DNA under the influence of a polymerase enzyme.

Fire tetrahedron The four conditions necessary for a fire: a source of heat or energy, a fuel, a source of oxygen, and a chain reaction between the fuel and oxygen.

Flame ionization detector A gas chromatography detector that uses a flame to ionize analyte components, creating an electric current that is amplified and displayed on a computer.

Flash point The minimum temperature needed to convert a liquid fuel to a vapor and begin combustion.

Flashback Episodes of hallucinations months or years after a dose of the drug was taken. Happens mainly with LSD.

Float glass A type of glass that is made by pouring molten glass onto a bed of molten tin so that the surface is very flat.

Fluorescence The interaction of light and matter whereby a substance absorbs light and then emits light of a lower frequency.

Footwear A shoe, boot, or sandal.

Forensic toxicology Effects of drugs and poisons on people who die or are injured under suspicious circumstances.

Formal signature A signature on an official document such as a will.

Fracture match (mechanical fit) A process whereby two pieces of broken glass can be fit back together using the irregular edge and stress markings.

Frequency The number of waves that pass a given point in 1 s.

Gamma rays A form of electromagnetic radiation with very high frequencies.

Gas chromatography (GC or GLC) A chromatography technique whereby the stationary phase is a solid or viscous liquid and the mobile phase is an inert gas.

Gene A section of DNA that provides for the formation of specific proteins that form all physical and other characteristics in a person (or other organism).

General acceptance A criterion for the admissibility of scientific or technical evidence that requires the evidence generally agreed upon by the particular scientific community to which it belongs.

Genotype Genetic description of an allele (e.g., XY for a male).

Glass An amorphous solid with properties of both a solid and a liquid.

Griess reagents A set of two reagents that turn red in the presence of nitrate or nitrite-containing chemicals such as many explosives.

Half life The time it takes for the concentration of a drug to be reduced by half in the body.

Hard drives Storage devices with external power requirements that have logic boards and some medium to store data.

Harrison Act An Act to provide for the registration of, with collectors of internal revenue, and to impose a special tax upon all persons who produce, import, manufacture, compound, deal in, dispense or give away opium or coca leaves, their salts, derivatives, or preparations, and for other purposes.

Hashing A mathematical calculation that generates a numerical value based on input data from a storage device or a forensic image that provides a mechanism for ensuring data integrity; called the hash or hash value.

Headspace The airspace above fire debris in a sealed container.

Henry's Law A law of chemistry that governs the equilibrium between a volatile substance in solution and in the gas phase.

Hertz One cycle per second. A measure of frequency of a wave.

Heterozygous A condition whereby the two forms of an allele received from each parent are different.

High explosive An explosive that produces a pressure wave with velocities greater than 3280 ft/s.

High order explosion An explosion that occurs at or near its maximum theoretical force.

High-performance liquid chromatography (HPLC) A chromatography technique whereby the stationary phase is a solid or viscous liquid and the mobile phase is a liquid or liquid solution.

Hired gun A pejorative term given to an expert witness with a bias who adjusts analyzes, results, and testimony to the benefit of the party that hired him or her.

Homozygous A condition whereby the two forms of an allele received from each parent are the same.

Ignition temperature The minimum temperature needed for fuels to ignite without an exterior source of ignition.

Impression Many objects have a texture or pattern on their outside surface. These include fingerprints, many shoe soles, motor-vehicle tire treads, and even markings imparted by tools onto objects. When one of these objects comes into contact with a recipient object or material and force is applied, an impression may be left on the recipient.

Imprint A residue on footwear that leaves a two-dimensional impression on a recipient surface.

Incendiary fire A fire that is set deliberately.

Incomplete combustion A combustion reaction that does not have sufficient oxygen present to complete the reaction, giving rise to products such as carbon monoxide and soot.

Indented writing Writing on a top sheet of a pad of paper that leaves an indented image of the writing on sheets underneath.

Informal signature A signature written on routine correspondence such as a personal letter.

Infrared (IR) The region of electromagnetic radiation just lower in frequency than the UV/visible region.

Injector The part of a chromatograph where the analyte and mobile phases are mixed.

Ion trap A type of ion separator in a mass spectrometer whereby the ions are accelerated through a magnetic field created by four magnets arranged at the corners of a square. The separated ions are then trapped in a chamber for analysis.

Laser desorption A type of fragmentation of molecules in a mass spectrometer where the energy is imparted to the molecule by a laser beam.

Length polymorphism Two or more strands of DNA at the same locus that differ in the number of base pairs as in the number of repeating units in a tandem repeat.

Light Electromagnetic radiation that is visible to the human eye.

Low explosive An explosive that produces a pressure wave with velocities less than 3280 ft/s.

Low-order explosion An explosion that occurs below its maximum theoretical force due to factor such as old, deteriorated explosive material, or improper construction of the explosive.

Magnetic sector A type of ion separator in a mass spectrometer whereby the ions are accelerated through a curved magnetic field.

Mass spectrometry The fragmenting of molecules by bombarding with energy in a vacuum.

Materiality Part of relevance. The concept that evidence pertain to the case at hand and not some other unrelated case.

Matrix-assisted laser desorption ionization (MALDI) A type of fragmentation of molecules in a mass spectrometer where the energy is imparted to the molecule by a laser beam. The sample is embedded in a matrix that helps transfer the laser's energy.

Memory cards Small storage devices, typically used in digital cameras and some mobile phone devices.

Metabolite Secondary substance created by action of liver on drugs or poisons.

Metadata "Data about data". Information either embedded within a file, or part of a file system, that describes a file, like where the content is stored, dates and times, authorship, and other file type specific information.

Microsatellite A piece of polymorphic DNA with repeating units of 2–6 base pairs in length.

Microspectrophotometry The measurement of light by a spectrophotometer connected to a microscope.

Microwave The region of electromagnetic radiation just lower in frequency than the infrared.

Minisatellite A piece of polymorphic DNA with repeating units of 10–100 base pairs in length.

Mitochondria Bodies in a cell that have a role in respiration. They contain DNA that is inherited from the mother.

Mobile phase The moving phase in chromatography. It carries the analyte through the stationary phase.

Monochromator A device in a spectrophotometer that selects one wavelength of light to reach a sample or detector.

Narcotic Drugs with the ability to relieve pain and cause sleep; opium and its derivatives became known as **narcotics**. This is derived from the Greek word *narkotikos*, which means "sleep."

Narcotic Drug Control Act 1956 law that called for the increased penalties for illicit use of these drugs. Stiff jail sentences went to all but first-time offenders and anyone who sold drugs to a minor faced the death penalty. This law also had another important feature. If a new drug came into the marketplace that had a potential for abuse, a recommendation to control it could be made by the Food and Drug Administration to the Secretary of Health, Education and Welfare.

Nonrequested writing A sample of known handwriting that existed before the case. It is usually a business or personal document that is known to have been written by the subject.

Normal phase A type of chromatography where the stationary phase is more polar than the mobile phase.

Nucleotide Also known as a base. There are four of these: adenine, guanine, cytosine, and thymine. They pair up to form double-stranded DNA according to the rules of genetics. The order of the billions of base pairs determines their genetic instructions.

Obliteration Overwriting of handwriting with another writing instrument.

Orbital An area around the nucleus of an atom where an electron resides.

P2P Peer-to-peer networks (P2P) are made up of computers that are directly connected to each other with no intermediaries, like servers or network hosts.

Partition A collection of consecutive sectors in a volume or electronic media.

Partitioning Competition of two solvents for an analyte. The distribution of an analyte between two solvents.

pH The negative logarithm of the molar concentration of hydrogen ions in an aqueous solution.

Pharmacodynamics Study of how drugs act in the body.

Pharmacokinetics Study of movement of drugs in and out of the body.

Phenotype The physical expression of a genotype (e.g., a person who is XY would be a male).

Phishing Masquerading as a trusted source, like a vendor or a bank, to gain sensitive information.

Photocell A device that converts UV/visible light to an electric current. Used as a detector in a UV/visible spectrophotometer.

Photon A discreet package of electromagnetic radiation.

Pi bonds The type of chemical bonds that hold electrons in carbon–carbon double bonds.

Polarity The tendency of a compound to behave like a magnet with a positive and negative end.

Polymerase chain reaction (PCR) A method for replicating DNA by denaturing double-stranded DNA and then adding primers to one end of each strand and then adding individual nucleotides until a complete complementary strand is built.

Population genetics Determination of the frequencies with which particular genetic markers occur in a given population.

Probativeness The part of relevance that requires that an item of evidence actually proves something about the case.

Probe hybridization The addition of a complementary fragment of DNA to a single strand which has been analyzed by RFLP.

Proficiency testing A written and/or practical test that determines an individual's performance at one or more tasks.

Pure Food and Drugs Act 1906 law that prohibited interstate commerce in mislabeled or adulterated food or drugs. Among the substances targeted by the law were marihuana, cocaine, heroin, and opium. This act was administered by the Department of Agriculture.

Pyrolysis A process of heating a solid sample to high temperatures in the absence of air so that it decomposes rather than burns.

Quadrupole A type of ion separator in a mass spectrometer whereby the ions are accelerated through a magnetic field created by four magnets arranged at the corners of a square.

Quantized The concept of the interaction of electromagnetic radiation and matter, whereby only discrete photons whose energy is exactly equal to the difference in energy between two molecular energy levels, can be absorbed by the molecule.

Questioned document Any document whose source or authenticity is in doubt.

Radial cracks Cracks formed on the side of a piece of glass opposite the side of impact by a projectile such as a bullet. They radiate out from the hole in the glass.

Radio waves The region of electromagnetic radiation just lower in frequency than the microwave region.

Radioimmunoassay test An immunological test used as a screening test for drugs. It uses radioactively labeled antigens to determine the presence and quantity of a drug.

Raman spectroscopy A type of spectroscopy whereby UV/visible light is scattered by molecules. It is complementary to infrared spectrophotometry.

Real evidence Physical evidence that helps link a suspect to a crime.

Reflectance spectrum A type of spectroscopy whereby light is bounced off a sample and the amount of this light absorbed is measured.

Refraction Bending and slowing of a light beam as it passes through a transparent medium.

Refractive index The ratio between the velocity of light through a vacuum and the velocity through a transparent object.

Relevance The concept that requires that evidence be material to a case and that it actually proves something.

Requested writing A sample of known handwriting that has been requested and specified by the document examiner.

Restriction fragment length polymorphism (RFLP) A DNA typing method that isolates and measures VNTRs.

Retention factor In thin-layer chromatography, the ratio of the distance that the mobile phase travels to the distance that a given analyte component travels.

Retention time In gas chromatography, the time interval between the introduction of the analyte into the injector and when a component of the analyte reaches the detector.

Reverse phase A type of chromatography where the stationary phase is less polar than the mobile phase.

Rules of evidence A set of rules made by a legislature that guide the admissibility and use of evidence in court.

Sequence polymorphism Two or more strands of DNA at the same locus that differ by only one or a few base pairs within a sequence.

Short tandem repeats (STRs) Repeating DNA sequences of 2–6 base pairs. They can be highly polymorphic. Thirteen STR loci with repeating units of four base pairs are used in STR DNA typing.

SIM card Subscriber Identity Module. A type of memory card that stores the international mobile subscriber identity (IMSI) and network information required to authenticate with a mobile carrier network.

Soda lime glass Glass doped with calcium oxide and sodium carbonate.

Soil Earth material, either natural or man-made (concrete, gravel, other building materials), that is transferred from a crime scene to a person or object, or vice versa.

Solid-phase microextraction A process whereby flammable liquid vapors are adsorbed onto the surface of a coated needle which is then inserted directly into the inlet of a gas chromatograph where the heat in the inlet causes the vapors to elute into the instrument.

Solute A substance that is dissolved in a solvent.

Solvent A liquid or liquid solution used to dissolve an analyte.

Spalling Burning and cracking of concrete caused by high temperatures.

Spectrum A plot of wavelength or frequency versus amount of light absorbed or transmitted.

Split injector A type of injector where some of the analyte/mobile phase is vented away so that the column doesn't get saturated.

Splitless injector A type of injector where all of the analyte/mobile phase is introduced into the column.

Spoofing Masquerading as another entity by falsifying information to gain sensitive information.

Stationary phase The fixed phase in chromatography. It adsorbs the analyte components onto its surface and separates them.

Steganography The practice of hiding a message, file or image inside of another.

Stimulant Drugs that elevate one's mood. They help people feel better who are sad or depressed. They give people extra energy.

Storage media An object on which data is stored.

Stylistic signature A signature used in signing checks, credit card receipts. It is very individual and may bear little resemblance to a formal or informal signature.

Subpoena A document served on a witness in a crime or civil matter that compels the presence of the witness to offer testimony.

Subpoena duces tecum A subpoena that compels the appearance of a witness along with all documents in his possession that pertain to the case.

Synergism A condition whereby the effects of two or more drugs are magnified beyond their singular effects.

System identification code A five digit code is assigned by the Federal Communications Commission (FCC) to each different telecommunications company used by cellphones to communicate with cell towers.

Tempered glass Glass made by rapid heating and cooling to induce tiny cracks on its surface so it will form round balls if it breaks.

Thermal cycler An instrument that is used in the amplification of DNA by carefully manipulating the temperature of the reaction mixture.

Thermocouple A device that converts heat into electricity. This is used as a detector in IR spectrophotometry.

Thin-layer chromatography (TLC) A chromatography technique whereby the stationary phase is a thin coating of a solid on a substrate such as a microscope slide and the mobile phase is a liquid or liquid solution.

Thumb drive/flash drive/USB drive Small removable data storage devices with USB (universal serial bus) connections.

Time of flight A type of ion separator in a mass spectrometer whereby the ions are accelerated through a magnetic field of known strength and then separated by the time it takes for them to traverse the field.

Tolerance A phenomenon whereby a person needs increasing amounts of a drug in order to continue deriving the same effects from the drug.

Toxicology Study of the effects of a nonfood substance ingested by living organism.

Transmission spectrum A spectrum of the intensity of light transmitted through a substance plotted against wavelength or frequency.

Ultraviolet The region of the electromagnetic spectrum below X-rays in frequency. Also includes the visible region.

Uniform Controlled Substances Act 1976 law that developed and recommends a model state law entitled the *Uniform Controlled Substances Act*. Most states have adopted this as a framework to replace their existing drug laws. Under this Act, states use the same scheduling system for controlling illicit drugs. Some states have added schedules, changed the specific drugs within a schedule, or have changed penalties for possession or distribution of drugs, but the basic framework remains the same as for the Federal laws.

Unreasonable search and seizure A search and seizure process that is prohibited by the Fourth Amendment of the United States Constitution.

Useable quantity An amount of a drug that is likely to have a demonstrable psychoactive effect on an average person.

Vapor-trace analyzer A device that uses head space analysis for the detection of explosives. It is essentially a specialized gas chromatograph.

Variable number of tandem repeats (VNTR) A strand of DNA of medium length, 10–100 base pairs that exhibits length polymorphism.

Wavelength The distance between two corresponding points on a wave.

Wave number A measure of frequency. 1/wavelength in centimeters.

Widmark Curve A plot of time versus blood or breath alcohol concentration.

Withdrawal A set of symptoms brought on by withholding a drug to which a user has become addicted.

Work copy A copy of a recording or forensic image sets that can be used for subsequent processing and/or analysis.

X-rays A form of electromagnetic radiation with frequencies just lower than gamma rays.

Index

Note: Page numbers followed by "b", "f" and "t" indicate boxes, figures and tables respectively.

B

E

H

M

O

P

T